Implementing Sustainable Development

Strategies and Initiatives in High Consumption Societies

Edited by

WILLIAM M. LAFFERTY
and
JAMES MEADOWCROFT

OXFORD
UNIVERSITY PRESS

*This book has been printed digitally and produced in a standard specification
in order to ensure its continuing availability*

OXFORD
UNIVERSITY PRESS

Great Clarendon Street, Oxford OX2 6DP

Oxford University Press is a department of the University of Oxford.
It furthers the University's objective of excellence in research, scholarship,
and education by publishing worldwide in

Oxford New York

Auckland Bangkok Buenos Aires Cape Town Chennai
Dar es Salaam Delhi Hong Kong Istanbul Karachi Kolkata
Kuala Lumpur Madrid Melbourne Mexico City Mumbai Nairobi
São Paulo Shanghai Taipei Tokyo Toronto

Oxford is a registered trade mark of Oxford University Press
in the UK and in certain other countries

Published in the United States
by Oxford University Press Inc., New York

© William M. Lafferty, and James Meadowcroft 2000

The moral rights of the author have been asserted

Database right Oxford University Press (maker)

Reprinted 2003

ISBN 0-19-924201-1

Acknowledgements

The research on which this volume is based was supported by the Research Council of Norway through its Programme for Research and Documentation for a Sustainable Society (ProSus) and by the United Kingdom Economic and Social Research Council (R000221956). The editors would like to thank the staff of ProSus, and particularly Gørild Mathisen for her efforts as research assistant to the project, and for the attention she devoted to preparing the manuscript for submission to the publisher. We gratefully acknowledge the assistance of all those who took the time to comment on earlier drafts of sections of the manuscript including Joe Baker, Helene Bank, Manus van Brakel, Elizabeth Bomberg, Hans Bressers, Richard Forrest, Sukehiro Gotoh, Mike Harcourt, Monty Hempel, Tony Hodge, Paul Hofseth, Michael Howlett, Hidefumi Imura, Andrew Jordan, Helge Jörgens, Yasuko Kawashima, Annika Kronsell, Rudi Kurz, Keith E. Laughlin, Lennart Lundqvist, Daniel Mazmanian, Pat Mullins, Per Kristen Mydske, James Nickum, Hiroshi Ohta, Anna Reynolds, E. Roller, Yvonne Rydin, Rob Swart, Kazuhiro Ueta, and Angelika Zahrnt. The project co-ordinators would like to thank the individual members of the COMPSUS research team for their commitment to the project throughout, and for their vital input to the comparative and concluding chapters.

W.M.L.
J.M.

Contents

List of Contributors

Susan Baker is Senior Lecturer in European Social Research at the Cardiff School of the Social Sciences, Cardiff University. Her main research interest is European Union environmental policy. Recent publications include *Dilemmas of Transition: The Environment, Democracy and Economic Reform in East Central Europe*, ed. with P. Jehlička (London: Frank Cass, 1998) and *Sustainable Development: Theory, Policy and Practice within the European Union*, ed. with M. Kousis, D. Richardson, and S. Young (London: Routledge, 1997).

Christiane Beuermann is a project manager in the Climate Policy Division of the Wuppertal Institute for Climate, Environment and Energy in Wuppertal, Germany. Trained as an economist, her main areas of research are international and German climate policy, particularly the flexibility mechanisms under the Kyoto Protocol. Other interests include institutional adjustment and social learning in response to climate change and sustainable development, and the implementation of Local Agenda 21.

Gary C. Bryner is Director of the Natural Resources Law Centre and Research Professor at the University of Colorado School of Law. His research interests are in public policy and policy analysis. Publications include: *Bureaucratic Discretion: Law and Policy in Federal Regulatory Agencies* (New York; Pergammon Press, 1987); *Blue Skies, Green Politics: The Clean Air Act Amendments of 1990 and its Implementation* (Washington, DC: CQ Press, 2nd edn. 1995); and *From Promises to Performance: Achieving Global Environmental Goals* (New York: W.W. Norton, 1997).

Katarina Eckerberg is Associate Professor at the Department of Political Science, Umeå University, Sweden. Her research and lecturing concern environmental policy and its implementation. She is the author of *Environmental Protection in Swedish Forestry* (Aldershot: Avebury, 1990), *From the Earth Summit to Local Agenda 21: Working Towards Sustainable Development*, ed. with William M. Lafferty (London: Earthscan, 1998), and numerous articles ranging from sectoral studies (particularly of forestry and agriculture) to more general comparative international studies within the Nordic and Baltic countries.

William M. Lafferty is Director of the Norwegian Centre for Research and Documentation for a Sustainable Society (ProSus) and Professor in the

Department of Political Science at the University of Oslo. His publications include *Participation and Democracy in Norway* (1981); *Demokrati og demokratisering* (1984, with Bernt Hagtvet); *Democracy and the Environment: Problems and Prospects*, ed. with James Meadowcroft (Cheltenham: Edward Elgar, 1996); and *Towards Sustainable Development: On the Goals of Development and the Conditions of Sustainability*, ed. with Oluf Langhelle (London: Macmillan, 1999).

Oluf Langhelle is currently a Senior Researcher at Rogaland Research-RF. For three years he worked as a Research Associate at ProSus. His major field of interest is normative political theory with special emphasis on issues of social justice, democracy, and sustainable development. He has published articles in both English and Norwegian, and is co-editor of *Rio + 5* (1997), and with William Lafferty, *Towards Sustainable Development: On the Goals of Development and the Conditions of Sustainability* (London: Macmillan, 1999).

James Meadowcroft is a Senior Lecturer in the Department of Politics at the University of Sheffield. His interests include contemporary political thought and ideologies, and the politics of the environment and sustainable development. Recent publications include: *Democracy and the Environment: Problems and Prospects*, ed. with William Lafferty (Cheltenham: Edward Elgar, 1996), and *Planning Sustainability*, ed. with Michael Kenny (London: Routledge, 1999).

Marie-Louise van Muijen is project co-ordinator at the Dutch Ministry of the Interior. She is a political scientist by training. Her dissertation, a policy science study on governance and policy learning on security and defence issues, was published in 1993. As an assistant professor at the Erasmus University in Rotterdam her research focused on environmental policy implementation.

Elim Papadakis is Professor of Modern European Studies at the Australian National University. His most recent books include *Environmental Politics and Institutional Change* (Cambridge: Cambridge University Press, 1996) and *An Historical Dictionary of the Green Movement* (Scarecrow Press, 1998). He has published widely on environmental politics and policy, public opinion and the welfare state.

Miranda Schreurs is an Assistant Professor in the Department of Government and Politics at the University of Maryland, College Park. Her primary areas of research are in Japanese and German global environmental and energy policy formation. Schreurs is co-editor (with Elizabeth Economy) of *The Internationalization of Environmental Protection* (Cambridge: Cambridge

University Press, 1997) and co-editor (with Dennis Pirages) of *Ecological Security in Northeast Asia* (Seoul: Yonsei University Press, 1998).

Glen Toner is the author of numerous articles on energy, environment and sustainable development policy. He is Professor of Environment and Sustainable Development Policy in the Carleton Research Unit in Innovation, Science and Environment (CRUISE), School of Public Administration, Carleton University, Ottawa, Canada.

Stephen C. Young is a Senior Lecturer in Government at Manchester University, UK; and joint editor of *Environmental Politics*. Publications include *Cities in the 1990s: Local Choice for Balanced Strategy*, with Gerry Stoker (Harlow: Longman, 1993); *The Politics of the Environment* (1993); and chapters and articles on privatization, government/industry relations, local governance, participation, biodiversity, Local Agenda 21, and other environmental issues.

List of Tables

List of Figures

List of Abbreviations

A21	Agenda 21
ABARE	Australian Bureau of Agricultural and Resource Economics
ABS	Australian Bureau of Statistics
ACBE	Advisory Committee on Business and the Environment (UK)
AER	Algemene Energieraad (Advisory Council for Energy Affairs—the Netherlands)
ALA	Asian and Latin American States
ANZECC	Australian and New Zealand Environment and Conservation Council
APEC	Asia-Pacific Economic Co-operation
BfN	Bundesamt für Naturschutz (Federal Agency for Nature Conservation—Germany)
BGPSD	British Government Panel on Sustainable Development
BMBau	Bundesministerium für Raumordnung, Bauwesen und Städtebau (Federal Ministry for Regional Planning, Building and Urban Development—Germany)
BML	Bundesministerium für Landwirtschaft, Ernährung und Forsten (Federal Ministry for Agriculture, Nutrition and Forestry—Germany)
BMU	Bundesministerium für Umwelt Naturschutz und Reaktorsicherheit (Federal Ministry for the Environment, Nature Conservation, and Reactor Safety—Germany)
BMZ	Bundesministerium für wirtschaftliche Zusammenarbeit und Entwicklung (Federal Ministry for Economic Co-operation and Development—Germany)
BTO	British Trust for Ornithology
BUND	Bund für Umwelt und Naturschutz Deutschland (Friends of the Earth—Germany)
Buza	Ministerie van Buitenlandse Zaken (Ministry of Foreign Affairs—the Netherlands)
CASA	Citizens Alliance for Saving the Atmosphere and the Earth (Japan)
CBD	Convention on Biological Diversity
CBS	Centraal Bureau voor de Statistiek (Central Bureau for Statistics—the Netherlands)

CCME	Canadian Council of Ministers of the Environment
CCREM	Canadian Council of Resource and Environment Ministers
CEC	Commission of the European Communities
CESD	Commissioner of Environment and Sustainable Development (Canada)
CESPA	Canadian Endangered Species Protection Act
CEAA	Canadian Environmental Assessment Act
CIDA	Canadian International Development Agency
CIM	Co-ordination Commission for International Environmental Affairs (the Netherlands)
CITES	Convention on International Trade in Endangered Species
CO_2	Carbon dioxide
COAG	Council of Australian Governments
CONCOM	Council of Nature Conservation Ministers (Australia)
COP	Conference of the Parties
CPRE	Council for the Protection of Rural England
CRMH	Centrale Raad voor de Milieu Hygiene (National Council for Environmental Health—the Netherlands)
CSD	Commission on Sustainable Development
DETR	Department for the Environment, Transport and the Regions (UK)
DG	Directorate Generals (in CEC)
DGXI	Directorate-General for the Environment (EU)
DoE	Department of the Environment (UK)
DTI	Department of Trade and Industry (UK)
DTp	Department of Transport (UK)
DVO	Sustainable Development Treaties (the Netherlands)
EA	Environment Agency (UK)
EAC	Environmental Audit Committee (UK)
EAC	Environmental Advisory Council (Sweden)
EAGLE	Effects on Aboriginals from the Great Lakes Environment (Canada)
EAP	Environmental Action Programme (of EU)
EC	European Council
ECJ	European Court of Justice
EE	Electric and Electronic
EEA	European Environment Agency
EEB	European Environmental Bureau
EKU	Ekologisk hållbar upphandling (Commission for Ecologically Sustainable Procurement—Sweden)
ENGO	Environmental Non-Governmental Organization

EP	European Parliament
EPM	Environmental Protection in the Municipalities (Norway)
EPR	Extended Product Responsibility
EPRG	Environment Policy Review Group (of EU)
ESA	Endangered Species Act
ESD	Ecologically Sustainable Development
ESDSC	Ecologically Sustainable Development Steering Committee (Australia)
EU	European Union
EZ	Ministerie van Economische Zaken (Ministry of Economic Affairs—the Netherlands)
FCCC	Framework Convention on Climate Change
FNCA	Federal Nature Conservation Act (Germany)
FRG	Federal Republic of Germany
FRN	Forskningsrådsnämnden (Council for Planning and Co-ordination of Research—Sweden)
FSC	Forest Stewardship Council
FY	Fiscal Year
GDP	Gross Domestic Product
GDR	German Democratic Republic
GEF	Global Environment Facility
GfG	Going for Green (UK)
GLOBE	Global Legislators' Organization for a Balanced Environment
GMOs	Genetically Modified Organisms
GNP	Gross National Product
HEAL	Health and Environment of Aboriginal Life (Canada)
HELCOM	Helsinki Commisssion
HRDC	Human Resources Development Canada
ICESD	Intergovernmental Committee on Ecologically Sustainable Development (Australia)
ICLEI	International Council for Local Environmental Initiatives
IGAE	Intergovernmental Agreement on the Environment (Australia)
IISD	International Institute for Sustainable Development
IMF	International Monetary Fund
INC	International Negotiating Committee
IPO	Interprovinciaal Overleg (Association of Provinces—the Netherlands)
IPPC	Integrated Pollution Prevention and Control

ISD	Initiatives for Sustainable Development
JBIC	Japan Bank for International Co-operation
JCSD	Japan Council for Sustainable Development
JI	Joint Implementation
JICA	Japan International Co-operation Agency
KP	Kyoto Protocol
LA21	Local Agenda 21
LDP	Jiyûminshuto (Liberal Democratic Party—Japan)
LGMB	Local Government Management Board (UK)
LNV	Ministerie voor Landbouw, Natuurbeheer en Visserij (Ministry of Agriculture, Nature Management and Fisheries—the Netherlands)
MAFF	Ministry of Agriculture, Fisheries and Food (UK)
MAI	Multilateral Agreement on Investment
MISTRA	(Strategic Fund for Environmental Research—Sweden)
MITI	Tsûshû Sangyôshô (Ministry of International Trade and Industry—Japan)
MoA	Ministry of Agriculture (Sweden)
MoE	Ministry of Environment (Sweden)
MoF	Ôkurashô (Ministry of Finance—Japan)
MoFA	Gaimushô (Ministry of Foreign Affairs—Japan)
MoHW	Koseishô (Ministry of Health and Welfare—Japan)
MP	Member of Parliament
MW	Megawatts
NACEC	North American Commission for Environmental Co-operation
NAR	Nationale Adviesraad voor Ontwikkelingssamenwerking (National Advisory Council for Development Co-operation—the Netherlands)
NCDO	Nationale Commissie voor internationale samenwerking en duurzame ontwikkeling (National Commission for International Co-operation on Sustainable Development—the Netherlands)
NCPISA	National Collaborative Project on Indicators of Sustainable Agriculture (Australia)
NEPP	National Environmental Policy Plan (the Netherlands)
NFR	Naturvetenskapliga Forskningsrådet (Natural Science Research Council—Sweden)
NGO	Non-Governmental Organization
NGRS	National Greenhouse Response Strategy (Australia)

NIM	Nasjonalkomiteen for internasjonale miljøspørsmål (National Committee for International Environmental Matters—Norway)
NINA	Norsk Institutt for Naturforskning (Norwegian Institute of Nature Research)
NMP	Nationaal MilieubeleidsPlan (National Environmental Policy Planning—the Netherlands)
NOK	Norwegian kroner
NOU	Norges Offentlige Utredninger (Official Norwegian Report)
NRCan	Natural Resources Canada
NRTEE	National Round Table on the Environment and Economy (Canada)
NSDS	National Sustainable Development Strategy (Canada)
NSESD	National Strategy for Ecologically Sustainable Development (Australia)
NTFEE	National Task Force on Environment and Economy (Canada)
ODA	Official Development Assistance
OECD	Organization for Economic Co-operation and Development
OECF	Overseas Economic Co-operation Fund (Japan)
OS	Ministerie voor Ontwikkelingssamenwerking (Ministry of Development Co-operation—the Netherlands)
PCSD	The President's Council on Sustainable Development (USA)
PJ	petajoule
PPG	Planning Policy Guidance Note (UK)
Prop	Government Bill (Sweden)
q2000	Youth Network for Sustainable Development (Sweden)
RCEP	Royal Commission on Environmental Pollution (UK)
RITE	Research Institute of Innovative Technology for the Environment (Japan)
RIVM	Rijksinstituut voor Volksgezondheid en Milieuhygiene (National Institute for Public Health and the Environment—the Netherlands)
RRV	Riksrevisionsverket (National Audit Office—Sweden)
Rskr	Regeringsskrivelse (Government Report to the Riksdag—Sweden)
RSPB	Royal Society for the Protection of Birds (UK)
SALA	Swedish Association of Local Authorities
SAP	Strategic Action Plan for Biodiversity (the Netherlands)
SCB	Statistiska centralbyrån (Statistics Sweden)

SDC	Sustainable Development Commission (UK)
SDS	Sustainable Development Strategy
SDU	Sustainable Development Unit within DETR or EA (UK)
SEK	Swedish Kronors
SEM	Single European Market
SEPA	Swedish Environmental Protection Agency
SER	Sociaal-economische Raad (National Social Economic Council—the Netherlands)
SIDA	Swedish International Development Agency
SJFR	Skogs- och Jordbrukets Forskningsråd (Council for Forestry and Agriculture Research—Sweden)
SMEs	Small and Medium Enterprises
SoE	State of the Environment
SOU	Statens Offentliga Utredningar (Government Official Reports—Sweden)
SRU	Rat von Sachverständigen für Umweltfragen (Council of Environmental Experts—Germany)
SSCN	Swedish Society for Conservation of Nature
SSSI	Site of Special Scientific Interest (UK)
UBA	Umweltbundesamt (Federal Environmental Agency—Germany)
UKRTSD	UK Round Table on Sustainable Development
UN	United Nations
UNCED	United Nations Conference on Environment and Development
UNCSD	United Nations Commission on Sustainable Development
UNDP	United Nations Development Programme
UNEP	United Nations Environment Programme
UNGASS	United Nations General Assembly Special Session
US AID	United States Agency for International Development
US EPA	United States Environmental Protection Agency
US	United States
UvW	Unie van Waterschappen (Association of Water Boards—the Netherlands)
VCR	Voluntary Challenge and Registry (Canada)
VNG	Vereniging Nederlandse Gemeenten (Association of Municipalities—the Netherlands)
VOGM	Vervolg-bijdrage regeling ontwikkeling gemeentelijk milieubeleid (Follow up grants scheme for the development of municipal environmental policy—the Netherlands)
VROM	Ministerie van Volksgezondheid, Ruimtelijke Ordening en

	Milieu (Ministry of Housing, Physical Planning and the Environment—the Netherlands)
V&W	Ministerie van Verkeer en Waterstaat (Ministry of Transport, Public Works and Water Management—the Netherlands)
WBGU	Wissenschaftlicher Beirat der Bundesregierung für Globale Umweltfragen (Scientific Advisory Council of the Federal Government for Global Environmental Change—Germany)
WCED	World Commission on Environment and Development
WTO	World Trade Organization
WWF	World Wide Fund for Nature
WWII	World War II

1

Introduction

WILLIAM M. LAFFERTY AND JAMES MEADOWCROFT

Over the past decade the idiom of sustainable development increasingly has come to frame international debates about environment and development policy-making. Catapulted to prominence by the report of the Brundtland Commission[1] in 1987, sustainable development was formally endorsed as a policy objective by world leaders at the Rio Earth Summit[2] five years later. It has been absorbed into the conceptual lexicon of international organizations such as the World Bank and the OECD; been accorded its own global secretariat in the form of the UN Commission on Sustainable Development (CSD); and achieved near-constitutional status in the European Union through its incorporation in the Maastricht and Amsterdam treaties. Around the globe political leaders and public administrators now routinely justify policies, projects, and initiatives in terms of the contribution they make to realizing sustainable development.

Yet, while the idea has come to assume a central place in contemporary discussions of environment and development issues, there has been little

[1] 'The Brundtland Commission' is the conventional name for the World Commission on Environment and Development (WCED). The Commission was appointed as an independent body by the UN General Assembly in 1983, with the former Prime Minister (1981) and Minister of the Environment (1974-9) of Norway, Gro Harlem Brundtland, as Chairperson. The Commission was composed of 21 'commissioners', with representation equally divided between developed and developing countries, and with two Canadians as chief administrative officers (Maurice Strong as President, and Jim MacNeill as Secretary General). In the enabling resolution the general Assembly called on the Commission to 'to propose long-term environmental strategies for achieving sustainable development to the year 2000 and beyond' (UNGA 1983).

[2] The official name of the Rio Earth Summit was 'The United Nations Conference on Environment and Development' (UNCED). The conference took place in Rio de Janeiro from 3 to 14 June 1992, and has been generally profiled as the largest conference yet assembled by the United Nations. Although the exact number of participants is somewhat unclear, more than 160 governments were represented and more than 100 heads of state attended the proceedings. Representatives from NGOs, business organizations, and expert groups attending the official sessions or the array of parallel meeting and exhibitions, as well as the international press corps, brought the total influx to about 30,000 people (Grubb et al. 1993).

serious comparative research on the practical political ramifications of the 'turn' towards sustainable development. Among academics we have seen a great deal of discursive 'smoke'—but little in the way of empirical 'fire'. But what has actually happened with the concept in terms of policy implementation? Where and how has it been taken seriously as a prioritized goal for change; and what differences can be detected in the ways the idea has been interpreted and applied in different national, regional, and cultural contexts?

These are the issues to be addressed in the present volume. More particularly, we aim to explore how the governments of nine highly developed countries—Australia, Canada, Germany, Japan, the Netherlands, Norway, Sweden, the United Kingdom, and the United States—along with the central institutions of the European Union, have engaged with the idea of sustainable development over the past decade, particularly during the first five years after the 1992 Rio Earth Summit.

The study deals, therefore, with the political ideas, policy orientations, and programmes designed to clarify and operationalize the concept, as well as the practical measures adopted to move the idea from goal to reality. It examines how a specifically normative concept, articulated largely through debate in international forums, has been integrated into the policy discussions and political programmes of national political arenas. It tracks the scale and character of the distinctive responses of the various governments, bringing into comparative perspective patterns of convergence and divergence across the jurisdictions under investigation.

Sustainable Development in High Consumption Societies

Recognizing the particular responsibility which both the Brundtland Commission and the Rio Earth Summit have placed on the most highly developed countries for achieving sustainable development, we have defined the objects of this study as 'high-consumption societies'. The selected units for analysis include some of the most highly developed and wealthiest countries in the world. In so far as leading levels of aggregate production and consumption contribute to environmental degradation on a global scale, the units here selected are clearly candidates for scrutiny.[3]

Moreover, given their productive, technological, and financial capacity,

---

[3] At the time of the Earth Summit (1992) the countries in question were ranked as follows in terms of per-capita income (USD): Japan, 3 (29,915); Norway, 4 (28,470); Sweden, 5 (28,360); Germany, 8 (24,490); United States, 9 (23,600); Netherlands, 14 (21,205); Canada, 16 (19,494); Australia, 17 (18,715); United Kingdom, 18 (18,064).

these nations are well placed to undertake remedial efforts. It is important to recognize that the international consensus around sustainable development is based upon a principle of 'differentiated responsibility', with the rich countries having publicly acknowledged an obligation to take action—particularly with respect to climate change, sustainable production and consumption, and the provision of development assistance and environmental technology transfer. To put this differently: if the affluent societies of the North do not demonstrably take sustainable development seriously, it is unlikely that developing countries will do so either. Thus the attitude of developed counties becomes crucial to the viability of the entire international process of engagement with sustainable development.

With respect to the selection of specific countries for comparison, assuming OECD membership as a rough criterion for 'high-consumption', there were some twenty-five countries from which to choose. The aim was a sample including states with different population and geographic sizes, covering European and non-European settings, and reflecting variation in a range of political system characteristics and socio-economic traits that might conceivably influence responses to sustainable development.

The resulting selection includes populous countries (USA, Germany, the United Kingdom, and Japan) and small-scale units (Norway, Netherlands); geographically extensive states (Canada, USA, Australia) and more compact countries (Netherlands, the UK). There are sustainability innovators (Norway, Canada, the Netherlands) and apparent laggards (USA). Different forms of interaction with the global political economy are represented. Four countries are members of the European Union; one is a non-Union European state; two are members of the North American Free Trade Association (NAFTA). There are five unitary states and four federal states. Different legislative / executive linkages are represented, as are quite different ('state') traditions of public administration and regulatory culture. The world's three largest economies and five of the G7 countries are included. Thus the sample allows for comparison along a number of different dimensions, at the same time that it establishes a baseline for subsequent comparisons with other types of unit.

Finally, we have also included the European Union as a unit in its own right. The evolution of the European Union represents a serious complicating factor for comparative research based around national polities affected by the Union. Today European central institutions play a significant role in environmental policy-making within the European Union (Lévêque 1996, Andersen and Liefferink 1997). On the other hand, the continued vitality of national political structures and processes, and the still limited powers of the overall Union framework, mean that the EU cannot simply be treated as a (new) single country (within which constituent states are subsumed as subordinate entities). To reflect this emerging reality, we have supplemented the country studies with a separate analysis of the response of central EU institutions to sustainable development.

Implementing Sustainable Development

The implementation of sustainable development could in principle be related to an immense array of governmental activities; to policy formation and subsidiary implementation in distinct sectors (transport, health care, regional regeneration, and so on); and to initiatives undertaken by all tiers of government (national, regional, local). Such complexity is rooted in the synthetic ambitions of sustainable development as an orienting concept for governance, and is reflected in the wide-ranging character of the issues and recommendations included in Agenda 21. Several important choices were, therefore, necessary at the outset.

Perhaps most important, was the decision to concentrate on *central* government, rather than to try also to monitor local and regional administrations. One reason for this was the obvious problem of scope, i.e. that it would have been impossible to cover implementation activities across the entire spectrum of relevant domains and levels of government. Another key reason, however, was the issue of political responsibility. While it is obvious that activities related to sustainable development are being undertaken by local and regional governments (particularly in countries with federal regimes), we none the less made the decision to concentrate on national responsibility, since it is the state (and the European Union) which are signatories to the Rio accords. Local and regional initiatives will, therefore, only be considered insofar as they are part of the strategies of national governments, or contribute to characterizing and possibly explaining actions at the national level.

A second vital choice involved selecting particular dimensions of central government activity for detailed analysis. This has been addressed by, on the one hand, marking out what we understand to be the essential 'core' of the governmental response to sustainable development, while, on the other hand, identifying two specific policy domains for closer attention: climate change and biodiversity. Governments may (or may not) be doing many different things in relation to sustainable development, but our primary interest is with the main 'story' characterizing governmental reaction. Examination of the parameters of the debate around sustainable development, and knowledge of broader political and administrative processes gained in early phases of the project, led us to focus on six components of the core response. These components were formulated as a baseline 'protocol' for initial reporting for the country studies:

1. *Basic governmental understanding.* How sustainable development has been conceptualized in the national context, what it is believed to entail, and the main contours of the government's overall reaction. Of importance here is the vision of how sustainable development is to be achieved given the country's particular ecological, economic, social, political, and cultural circumstances.

2. *The pattern of institutional engagement.* Whether sustainable development has been accorded a constitutional or legal base. Whether new organizations have been established to undertake sustainable development related initiatives, and the levels of commitment displayed by existing ministries and agencies. The underlying assumption is that structures and resources matter.

3. *Measurement and monitoring.* This concerns the difficulty of 'fixing' the meaning of sustainable development and establishing benchmarks to assess implementation. Has progress been made in defining indicators to evaluate existing practices and to monitor policy innovation? How are measures of environmental condition, economic activity, and life quality to be interrelated?

4. *Involvement of other domestic actors.* How seriously have governments taken the participatory/collaborative dimension of sustainable development; in particular, how have central governments understood their initiatives in relation to other layers of government and non-governmental actors. What approach has been adopted toward the mobilization of 'major stakeholders'?

5. *Internationally oriented initiatives.* Sustainable development is both a domestic and an international policy objective, and the UNCED agreements call upon national actors to co-operate in unprecedented ways to achieve its realization. Thus the integration of national and international action is an essential dimension of sustainable development implementation. Of particular significance is the attitude adopted towards the specific responsibilities of the developed states spelled out at Rio.

6. *Sustainable production and consumption.* This relates to one of the more innovative themes to emerge from the UNCED process—the challenge of modifying existing patterns of production and consumption so that they become compatible with environmentally sustainable development.

While all sorts of environmental initiatives (from energy conservation to product labelling) can be included under this item, we were particularly concerned with issues and programmes taken up explicitly under this heading.

Together these six elements provide a well-grounded impression of the main lines of governmental interaction with the notion of sustainable development. In addition, we have focused on the policy domains of climate change and biodiversity. These areas relate to the major treaty regimes initiated at Rio, and both issues are treated by chapters in Agenda 21: chapters 9, 'Protecting the Atmosphere', and 15, 'Conservation of Biological Diversity'.

Climate change was one of the key themes which first motivated international concern with sustainable development (WCED 1987). It is an issue which indirectly raises complex problems of production–consumption and life-style change in the developed countries, at the same time that it has increasingly come to focus North/South tensions. Biodiversity is perhaps a less obvious choice, although it links into many established conservation and habitat-protection issues, and can also be interpreted as posing complex questions about the proportion of global 'ecological space' to be appropriated for human ends. But precisely because it is so often thought about in terms of what the less developed countries should be doing to protect their ecosystems and resources, it forms an attractive counterpoint for a study focusing on governmental behaviour in the developed states.

Activity in these two policy domains has expanded rapidly over the past few years. Climate change in particular has been the subject of widespread debate and media attention (particularly up to and immediately after the signing of the Kyoto Protocol), with both national positions and the implications for North/South relations evolving rapidly. Despite the increasing sophistication of the specialist literature on climate change and biodiversity (reflecting the inherent complexity of the two policy domains), their integration into the UNCED process and goals, as well as their intrinsic importance for sustainable development, justify the emphasis accorded to them here.

The research on which this volume is based was for most part conducted over a two-year period between September 1996 and September 1998. The decision to base the analysis on case-studies prepared by specialists in each of the target jurisdictions was dictated by the complex and inchoate nature of the subject matter, as well as the detailed contextual knowledge required to interpret the results. Although each contributor assumed primary responsibility for preparing the chapters which bear their name, the project was a collaborative endeavour in which team members learned from each other's insights and developed a common approach.

The work has been organized as an iterative process, with researchers conducting successive forays into the material and progressively assembling more elaborate drafts of their contributions. The entire research team met at regular intervals to discuss findings and to adjust the orientation of the next phase of the enquiry. To assure comparability of the analysis across cases, the protocol mentioned above was applied during the initial phase of jurisdictional reporting. In the preparation of the final reports, however, authors were encouraged to take as much latitude as necessary to tell the distinctive 'story' of each government's response to sustainable development. These jurisdictional case studies have been prepared so that they may stand on their own; but they also provide the principal foundation for the comparative analysis presented in later chapters. The precise configuration of sources consulted varies somewhat from study to study, but includes official publications and academic assessments, supplemented by interviews with key officials and other participants. A full list of printed sources is included in the consolidated bibliography. We also circulated draft reports to independent assessors drawn from government, academia, and the non-governmental sector.

Given the exploratory nature of the project, we have not attempted to structure the presentation within any one theoretical orientation. We have conducted a running dialogue within the project on the relevance of different possible approaches (discourse analysis, implementation research, comparative politics, public-policy perspectives, eco-modernization theory, and so on), yet we have chosen not to use any one of these as a single analytical framework. A major reason for this is the very particular nature of the empirical focus: a global 'programme' which has largely emerged external to normal national political processes, and which has, particularly since the Earth Summit, been pursued through a unique combination of, on the one hand, international incentives and obligations, and, on the other, highly diverse national interpretations and strategic initiatives. We are not, in other words, just talking about 'traditional politics'—either in a policy-implementation or comparative-politics frame.

Another major consideration, however, has been the applied nature of the knowledge task. The volume is intended for practitioners as well as for academic political scientists and sociologists. We hope to engage the attention of those, whether in governmental or international bodies, business or non-governmental organizations, who have responsibility for making decisions on crucial environment-and-development issues. Indeed, we hope that the study will interest broader publics and diverse collective actors in both the developed and developing countries, who are concerned with understanding and debating just what the governments of high-consumption societies actually have done over the past decade to engage with the challenge of sustainable development.

In terms of political science literatures, the work which relates most obviously to this study is that on comparative environmental politics and policy. Recent years have witnessed what might be described as a 'third wave' of comparative studies[4] as researchers have attempted to provide more synthetic perspectives on approaches to environmental governance (Christiansen 1996; Jänicke and Weidner 1997; Hanf and Jansen 1998); to assess the overall parameters of national environmental performance (Jänicke 1992; Jahn 1998); to explore the political impacts of emergent policy domains such as climate change (O'Riordan and Jager 1996; Collier and Löfstedt 1997); and to review national experience with innovative policy 'instruments' (Dente 1995) such as environmental taxation (Andersen 1994), 'green plans' (Dalal-Clayton 1996; Jänicke et al. 1997; Jänicke and Jörgens 1999) and environmental agreements (Glasbergen 1998).

Despite contrasting historical and cultural traditions, varied legal and constitutional structures, and alternative constellations of political actors, there are remarkable similarities in institutional forms, policy outputs, and environmental–quality indicators across the developed world (Knoepfel et al. 1987). In part this can be explained by parallels of underlying economic and political structure, by a shared social trajectory, and pressures of productive dynamism, technological change, and competitive interaction. But there has also been conscious cross-national imitation and learning in the environmental policy domain, and practices initiated in one jurisdiction have spread to other states (Jänicke and Weidner 1997b). The increasing activity of transnational actors—whether corporate, non-governmental, or official—has maintained momentum towards convergence in environmental governance. Yet a fine-grained analysis reveals profound differences in the environmental priorities of publics in different countries, contrasting forms

---

[4] Early comparative work which explored the emergence of environmental issues onto the political agenda (Lundqvist 1973; Enloe 1975; Solesbury 1976), which compared the institutions and practices of pollution control (Mangun 1979; Sabatier and Mazmanian 1980; Downing and Hanf 1983) and assessed the activity of environmental groups (O'Riordan 1979) gradually gave way to a second wave of more detailed and comprehensive studies (Vogel and Kun 1987). These tended to focus on specific policy fields or arenas of interaction, offering in-depth analysis of paired jurisdictions (Lundqvist 1980; Vogel 1986; Boehmer-Christiansen and Skea 1991), or making broader cross national comparisons (Haigh and Irwin 1990, Knoepful and Weidner 1990). The range of environmental themes which preoccupied scholars grew (reflecting the greater political salience and diversity of environmental debate in the 1980s), giving rise to significant comparative work on green parties (Muller Rommel 1982; Kitschelt 1988; Hoffmann-Martinot 1991), environmental public opinion (Gillroy and Shapiro 1986; Rohrschneider 1988) and regulatory processes (Badaracco 1985).

of political articulation of environmental issues (consider the fortunes of Green parties in various systems), and differing regulatory styles, policy mixes, and sets of preferred instruments. Perhaps the clearest observation is the ceaseless change and dynamism in the environmental policy field over the past thirty years—as issues and approaches have continued to evolve, and a more substantial proportion of social resources have been devoted to the environmental domain (Glasbergen 1996; Weale 1992).

The subject matter of the current volume extends beyond 'environmental policy'—at least in so far as this has been traditionally conceived. And yet existing environmental politics and policy provide the basis from which any attempt to implement sustainable development must proceed. Since sustainable development was formulated to bridge divisions among economic, social and environmental decision-making, and to soften the fire-wall erected between domestic and international obligations, it is hardly surprising that it not only provides an alternative frame for issues that already had been included in the 'environmental policy' portfolio, but has implications in areas more traditionally associated with economic, social, and foreign policy decision-making. What is clear is that sustainable development policy and politics are not necessarily coterminous with environmental policy and politics—although the extent of overlap will vary with perspective and context.

Given the centrality of the concept of sustainable development to the study, we feel a need to provide a brief introductory overview of our understanding of the idea. We fully appreciate both the complexity of the concept, and the fact that there is considerable disagreement as to what the idea *should* imply. As will become clear below, we are not interested in promulgating a particular normative position on the issue. The purpose of our project is not to 'sell' sustainable development, but to document and analyse how high-consumption societies have interpreted and pursued the idea through their respective political systems. To achieve this, however, it was necessary to establish a baseline understanding of the idea within the research project itself. Only by working from a common understanding of what it was we were jointly monitoring, could we lay the foundation for a consistent research dialogue and cross-national empirical effort.

The Emergence of Sustainable Development in International Political Discourse

The intellectual history of the idea of sustainable development has yet to be written in full, but the publication of *Our Common Future* by the World

Commission on Environment and Development (WCED 1987) marked a decisive phase in its emergence as a privileged category for conceptualizing environment-and-development interaction in international debate.

The authors of *Our Common Future* were not the first to invoke 'sustainability' or 'sustainable development' (Redclift 1987; Lélé 1991; Pezzy 1992*a*). The concept of 'sustainable yield' (a yield that can in principle be harvested indefinitely because it does not exceed a natural system's capacity for regeneration) emerged from the resource management literature, but by the early 1970s notions of 'sustainability' were being employed more broadly in environmental debate (Adams 1990; Kidd 1992). 'Sustainable utilization' of natural resource systems (and later of environmental amenities in general) was used in international conservationist circles, while the image of a 'sustainable society' was deployed by environmental activists to denote an ecologically enlightened community—one that repudiated profligate consumerism and lived within the limits of the Earth's carrying capacity (Pirages 1977; Brown 1981).

'Sustainable development' assumed a prominent place in the 1980 *World Conservation Strategy*, issued by the World Conservation Union (IUCN), the World-Wide Fund for Nature (WWF) and the United Nations Environment Programme (UNEP), where it served to link traditional conservationist preoccupations with nature preservation to a basic-needs-oriented strand in development thinking (IUCN/WWF/UNEP 1980). In the early 1980s activities to prepare national conservation strategies and active sponsorship by UNEP further spread awareness of sustainable development, and by the second half of the decade it was appearing in a growing volume of official publications and beginning to attract the attention of academic commentators (Clark and Munn 1986; Redclift 1987).

What the report of the WCED accomplished was to 'relaunch' sustainable development by casting it in a form which could appeal to a wide range of political actors, and which derived legitimacy from the consultative and UN-sponsored process through which it had been formulated. Established in 1983 by the United Nations General Assembly in response to growing concerns about the scale of environmental destruction and the apparent stagnation of economic growth in many of the poorest counties, the WCED was active for nearly four years, soliciting opinions from groups and individuals, analysing submissions from expert bodies, and holding public sessions in a number of countries. Its final report called for urgent action to revive and to reorient growth, while conserving natural resources and protecting the global environment. What was required was 'a new approach in which all nations aim at a type of development that integrates production with resource conservation and enhancement, and that links both to the provision for all of an adequate livelihood base and equitable access to resources' (WCED 1987: 39–40).[5]

In a now famous passage *Our Common Future* defined 'sustainable development' as 'development that meets the needs of the present without compromising the ability of future generations to meet their own needs' (WCED 1987: 43). The explanation continued: sustainable development 'contains within it two key concepts: the concept of "needs", in particular the essential needs of the world's poor, to which overriding priority should be given; and the idea of limitations imposed by the state of technology and social organization on the environment's ability to meet present and future needs'. Thus sustainable development represented a continuing process of societal improvement; a process which should prioritize the requirements of the most disadvantaged, while protecting the environmental support systems and amenities on which the welfare of present and future generations depended.

The conception of sustainable development presented by *Our Common Future* neatly drew together diverse strands of the international discourses of environment and development. The 'environment' *versus* 'growth' controversy that so polarized debate in the 1970s was partially side-stepped by emphasizing the reorientation of growth to meet the urgent needs of the world's poor and to reduce the impacts of economic activity on the environment. The notion of 'development' which until then had been applied mainly to the poor countries was extended to cover the industrialized regions: thus sustainable development could be understood as a common challenge faced by all nations. And yet it was also a challenge which would

[5] The Commission's approach was summarized by Gro Harlem Brundtland's foreword to the final report: 'When the terms of reference of our Commission were originally being discussed in 1982, there were those who wanted its considerations to be limited to "environmental" issues only. This would have been a grave mistake. The environment does not exist as a sphere separate from human actions, ambitions, and needs, and attempts to defend it in isolation from human concerns have given the very word "environment" a connotation of naiveté in some political circles. The word "development" has also been narrowed by some into a very limited focus, along the lines of "what poor nations should do to become richer", and thus again is automatically dismissed by many in the international arena as being a concern of specialists, of those involved in questions of "development assistance".

But the "environment" is where we all live; and "development" is what we all do in attempting to improve our lot within that abode. The two are inseparable. Further, development issues must be seen as crucial by the political leaders who feel that their countries have reached a plateau towards which other nations must strive. Many of the development paths of the industrialised nations are clearly unsustainable. And the development decisions of these countries, because of their great economic and political power, will have a profound effect upon the ability of all peoples to sustain human progress for generations to come' (WCED 1987: xii).

imply very *different* policies and priorities according to the developmental stage already attained.

Sustainable development engaged directly, therefore, with problems of great international import. It appealed to established notions of progress, equity, prudence, and stewardship, but combined and extended these in novel ways. The basic idea that human societies should continue their quest for a better life, but do so in a manner that gave precedence to the needs of the poor while protecting the basic sustenance capabilities of natural systems on which the livelihoods of future generations depended, was intuitively appealing. So too were the principles of common responsibility, mutual solidarity, and differentiated obligation which emerged as integral parts of the idea. In short, sustainable development was about dynamic balance; about providing a framework within which to reconcile different sorts of interest and consideration: economy and environment, conservation and progress, efficiency and equity, the pre-occupations of North and South (Adams 1990; Meadowcroft 1997; Lafferty and Langhelle 1999).

The political sensitivity with which the WCED report had been prepared was reflected in the generally positive response to its publication. As various national and international bodies reacted to its recommendations, the notion of sustainable development became familiar to a wider range of actors (Reid 1995). Although many of the specific reforms suggested in the report were not carried through, others met with more success. Indeed, proposals to prepare a detailed 'UN Programme of Action on Sustainable Development', and to organize a major conference on the problems of environment and development, helped set in train the process which provided sustainable development with its next major international platform.

The decision to convene the United Nations Conference on Environment and Development (UNCED) was formally taken by the General Assembly in December 1989. According to the enabling resolution its purpose was to 'elaborate strategies and measures to halt and reverse the effects of environmental degradation in the context of increased national and international efforts to promote sustainable and environmentally sound development in all countries' (UNGA 1989). Preparations for the meeting lasted two and a half years and involved a complex array of interactions. In addition to four official 'PrepComs' (month-long organizing and negotiating sessions), separate discussions were underway to secure agreement on the draft conventions on climate change and on biodiversity, and UNCED agenda items were also examined by an array of international organizations including the OECD and the G7 summits (Grubb *et al.* 1993). Not only states and international organizations, but also technical and scientific bodies, business associations, local governments, and voluntary groups took part in the preparatory work.

As previously pointed out, the UNCED meeting itself attracted enormous international attention, and resulted in five major documents (the 'Rio Accords'): the Rio Declaration on Environment and Development (a brief statement of principles orienting international action on environment and development issues); the Framework Convention on Climate Change; the Convention on Biodiversity; a Statement of Forest Principles; and Agenda 21 (an elaborate 'Programme of Action for Sustainable Development' which detailed initiatives required to manage environment and development problems into the next century). While the two conventions had the status of legally binding treaties, the three other documents fell into the class of non-legally-binding international agreements (so-called 'soft law'). These were significant in moral and political terms (and over time may acquire weight in judicial determinations), but did not directly give rise to binding legal obligations.

The idea of sustainable development was central to the whole UNCED enterprise. It appears in twelve of the twenty-seven articles of the Rio Declaration, and is explicitly mentioned in the texts of the Climate Change and Biodiversity Conventions,[6] as well as in the Statement of Forest Principles. And of course Agenda 21 itself was designed as 'a blueprint for action for global sustainable development into the 21st century' (UNCED 1992: 13).

Nevertheless, sustainable development was never formally defined in any of the UNCED outputs. Instead its meaning was taken as essentially given (deriving from the Brundtland Report); and the emphasis was placed upon reaffirming its importance, and detailing what sorts of action were required to bring it about. Still the UNCED process can be understood to have further refined the accepted notion of sustainable development, particularly by emphasizing the importance of participation (by local communities and social sectors) in environment-and-development related decision-making— a theme which had been present, though not strongly developed, in the report of the WCED.

The UNCED process clearly imparted further momentum to international engagement with the idea of sustainable development. Its culmination in a highly public global forum where international leaders pledged renewed efforts to deal with acute problems of environment and development focused attention on the master concept that was intended to shape the international response. Moreover in the wake of UNCED the UN system

---

[6] In fact sustainable development is treated somewhat differently in the various UNCED outputs—no doubt reflecting the different forums in which the texts were negotiated.

moved relatively rapidly to institutionalize the follow-up, with the General Assembly voting in December 1992 to establish a high-level Commission on Sustainable Development under the Economic and Social Council to monitor international progress in managing environmental and development issues and in implementing Agenda 21.

Since its creation, the CSD has pursued an active agenda, exploring thematic issues related to environment and development, reviewing progress on a variety of international negotiating processes, and collating reports on national implementation activities. It also played a key role in preparing the five-year review of Agenda 21 conducted by a Special Session of the UN General Assembly in June of 1997 (UNGASS). This Special Session published a six point 'Statement of Commitment' reaffirming international support for Agenda 21, along with a much longer document assessing the international effort to come to terms with problems of environment and development since Rio, which also fixed priorities for the work of the CSD for the five-year period running up to the next major review of Agenda 21 implementation scheduled for 2002.

Thus by the close of the 1990s, the idea of sustainable development had not only become deeply embedded in the international discourse on environment-and-development issues, but had achieved a status of paramount norm with respect to discourses on 'development' in general. Just what has been the response of national governments to the coming of sustainable development—to the normative principles and programmatic intent of the UNCED process—is the issue to be considered here.

Sustainable Development as a Political Science Research Theme

The emergence of sustainable development as a research theme in the social sciences has broadly shadowed its emergence in international political discourse. The occasional references of the 1970s gave way to the pioneering studies of the 1980s, and then to a steady stream of material by the early 1990s. Concern has been uneven across the disciplines, however, with economists (in the development and/or environment sub-fields) showing substantial interest, followed by geographers and sociologists, and latterly by students of politics. Each group has tended to adapt the concept to its favoured categories and preoccupations. Debate among economists, for example, has often focused on understanding sustainability in terms of welfare functions, income flows and capital accounts (Daly 1994; Pezzy

1992*b*; Costanza 1991); on determining how the concept might be measured and/or reconciled with techniques of environmental valuation (Pearce, Markandya and Barbier 1989; Pearce and Warford 1993); and on deciding whether it adds something substantive to the structure of economic theory (Bergh and Straaten 1994; Beckerman 1994). Geographers have been particularly intrigued with issues of scale and spatial disposition, and with the implications of sustainable development for land-use planning, and for urban and transport policies (Naess 1995; Owens 1994 and 1997; Reed and Slaymaker 1993; Rees 1995).

Until recently political scientists have paid comparatively little attention to sustainable development. Not that there has been a shortage of literature on the conflicts, especially the North/South tensions, associated with debates about sustainable development and the UNCED process; but for the most part such commentary has come from sources outside institutional political science. Some work has been produced by analysts concerned with environment and development issues (Redclift 1987), and by students of 'green' politics or 'green' political movements. Yet much of the politics literature has focused on conceptual, definitional, or programmatic themes— engaging with disputes over different interpretations of sustainability (Dobson 1996; McManus 1996) and about the scale and character of the social transformations sustainable development might be understood to entail (O'Riordan 1996; Dryzek 1997). Only in the last few years has research concerned with the more practical issue of what governments and other actors are already *doing* in the name of sustainable development begun to appear (Meadowcroft 1999). Such work now includes studies of particular jurisdictions and contexts (Collier 1997) as well as attempts to set such perspectives into wider comparative frameworks (Bäckstrand, Kronsell and Söderholm 1996; O'Mahony 1996; Baker *et al.* 1997; O'Riordan and Voisey 1997). There is also a burgeoning literature on local attempts to engage with Agenda 21 (LA 21) (Lafferty and Eckerberg 1997; Lafferty 1999; Voisey *et al.* 1996; Young 1996).

Why it has taken political science (particularly American political science) so long to engage with the concept of sustainable development is difficult to determine. No doubt there is a lingering perception that the idea has more to do with the politics of developing countries than the problems of highly industrialized states. Possibly some of those most closely involved with the analysis of environment or development policy-making suspect that sustainable development represents little more than a fashionable rhetorical flourish—the latest twist to the story that will do little to alter long-established patterns of domestic and international interaction with environment-and-development issues, a fact that may be greeted with dismay or enthusiasm according to personal proclivities. Certainly analysts in the international relations field seem more drawn to study negotiations surrounding the 'hard' law of treaties and conventions, rather than the more diffuse ideas associated with sustainable development or Agenda 21. And among students of domestic politics, it would often appear to be the case that only when an issue becomes of immediate electoral, legislative or judicial relevance does it begin to attract substantial research attention.

Be this as it may, we clearly believe that there are several reasons why sustainable development should interest political scientists. First, it is obviously an idea with considerable 'staying power'. It has already served in international political interchange for more than a decade and a half, and there is no current indication that its rhetorical relevance is declining. Second, it is also an increasingly cosmopolitan idea. It is not bound to a particular institution, profession, or narrow discursive context, but has been taken up in many forms of argument (diplomatic, political, academic, popular); at different political 'levels' (international, national, regional, local); and by an array of actors within politics, business, and civil society.

Furthermore, sustainable development is not only confined to grand declarations of intent, but is increasingly associated with concrete policy initiatives and programmes. As a concept which weaves together normative ideas of equity, participation, prudence, welfare, and environmental concern in novel ways, sustainable development potentially signals a shift in the manner in which problems are defined. It has, for example, encouraged reframing the relationship between environment-and-development policy-making; sparked cross-sectoral linkages among previously distinct policy domains; favoured policy inputs from new groups and coalitions; and encouraged adjustments in relationships between governments and other social actors.

Sustainable development can thus be understood to engage with many long-standing themes of political enquiry, particularly with respect to conceptual innovation and change, and the way shifts in patterns of ideas are related to modifications of behaviour, process, and outcome. It is relevant to discussion about new forms of state/civil-society interaction, reform of regulatory processes and instruments, decentralized versus centralized decision-making, and the genesis of international regimes. The emergence of sustainable development raises questions about the nature of linkages among local, regional, national and international political processes, and is highly pertinent to the topical issue of 'globalization'. In its widest context, sustainable development can be understood as one of a series of responses to the perception that new sorts of political problems are emerging, related to the expanding scale of human impacts on the natural environment, along with the increased interdependence of global economic, social, cultural, and political circumstances.

Bringing Rio Home: The Task of Implementation

If one is to study the comparative implementation of sustainable development, it is important to specify just what this process is understood to entail. Sustainable development is a complex and contested idea, and the varied ways in which the term has been invoked and the contrasting policy proscriptions with which it has been associated have caused some consternation within the research community. Some investigators have attempted to deal with the proliferation of usages by stipulating their own preferred definitions, and rejecting other interpretations as incomplete, misleading, or deliberate deception. Some analysts have arrayed varieties of sustainability in a hierarchy, with successive steps (or stages) being held to represent a more profound and essential engagement with the underlying logic. Others have suggested that sustainable development is so vague as to be virtually meaningless, pointing out that almost any policy might be justified under its rubric.

These approaches are not helpful for comparative research into national engagement with sustainable development. Here the starting point must be the observed discursive and practical behaviour of political leaders and officials. These decision-makers have agreed publicly to undertake something called 'sustainable development', and the interest is in seeing what this actually implies. Thus this study does not start from an autonomously derived (either logical or philosophical) interpretation of what sustainable development 'really' means; nor do we propose to write-off sustainable development as mere rhetorical trope. Instead, we take sustainable development to be an expression whose sense is given by relevant usage: in this case, *the international discussions and accords through which it has become an accepted goal of international and national policy*. This could be described as the 'official' or 'authorized' usage. As we have seen, it is the product of 'the UNCED process'—that is to say the process of international dialogue and agreement that led from the initial report of the Brundtland Commission, through the UNCED Prepcoms, into the documents and commitments of the Rio Earth Summit.

The essential elements of this understanding have been outlined in the brief description of the historical uptake of sustainable development presented above. But it is worth pausing to consider core dimensions of the idea a little more closely. One approach is to conceptualize sustainable development as operating on three planes: the economic, the social, and the environmental. Thus achieving sustainable development involves the pursuit of economic, social, and environmental goods to enhance the welfare of current and future generations. In particular this implies reconciling economic advance, social equity, and environmental protection—and neglect of any one of these strands means a drift away from the line of sustainable development (World Bank 1994). This perspective was emphasized in the 'Programme for the Further Implementation of Agenda 21' adopted at UNGASS in 1997 which described 'economic development, social development and environmental protection' as 'interdependent and mutually reinforcing components of sustainable development'.[7]

Alternatively, one can emphasize two sorts of 'constraints' on developmental activity embedded within the notion of sustainable development. First, there are physical environmental constraints: beyond a certain point, the erosion of environmental assets will threaten development progress. Thus the maintenance of an adequate environmental base becomes a precondition for making continuing development possible. In other words, there are ultimate limits to the burdens the environment can bear—although the Brundtland Commission emphasized that these limits are mediated through patterns of human social organization and levels of technological development. Second, there are ethical constraints rooted in the imperatives of social justice. It is morally right to have regard for the needs of future persons (inter-generational justice), and to address the pressing needs of the world's poor (intra-generational justice). These requirements in turn establish limits to the forms of development activity which legitimately can be pursued today (Langhelle 1998; Lafferty and Langhelle 1999).

Another approach to elucidating sustainable development is to focus on the range of component ideas included within the concept. Lafferty (1996), for example, has referred to four normative principles embodied in the UNCED usage of sustainable development. Change which is to be considered sustainable *development* aims: (1) 'to satisfy basic human needs and reasonable standards of welfare for all living beings', and (2) 'to achieve more equitable standards of living both within and among global populations'. To be *sustainable*, such change should: (3) 'be pursued with great caution' so as to avoid 'disruption of biodiversity and the regenerative capacity of nature,

[7] The report on progress since UNCED submitted in January 1997 by the UN Secretary General to the 5th Session of CSD in preparation for UNGASS suggested that: 'sustainable development may be regarded as the progressive and balanced achievement of sustained economic development, improved social equity and environmental sustainability' (UNSG 1997).

both locally and globally', and (4) 'be achieved without undermining the possibility for future generations to attain similar standards of living and similar
or improved standards of equity'.

Jacobs (1996) has offered a slightly different formulation of the key principles embedded in sustainable development, referring more generally to
commitments to: (1) 'environment–economy integration'; (2) the welfare of
future generations; (3) 'environmental protection' (resource and amenity
conservation, and the acceptance of biospheric limits); (4) equity (meeting
the basic needs of the poor and equity across generations); (5) 'quality of
life' issues; and (6) 'participation'.

Neither of these lists are presented as formal 'definitions' of sustainable
development. Rather they are specifications of the normative dimensions
included in the concept, as it has developed in international usage—dimensions around which specific interpretations can be formulated and applied.
A recognition that: (1) it is possible to arrive at slightly different formulations
of the normative principles embodied in the official understanding of sustainable development; (2) there can be great variation in interpreting what
such principles actually imply; or (3) there are those who ignore or reject the
received international usage altogether and invoke entirely different meanings of the word 'sustainable development'—has not deterred the aim of our
project. It is the fate of all successful and indicative concepts invoked in political life to be subject to contrasting interpretations and to be loaded with
different meanings—a feature which has sometimes been described as the
'essential contestability' of widely supported political and social concepts
(Gallie 1956; Connolly 1983). Divergence of understanding and usage is especially likely with highly charged normative concepts, such as 'democracy',
'freedom' or 'equality'. The range of understandings hardly prevents,
however, the application of such contestable concepts in specific policies and
programmes for social and economic change.

For the purpose of the present study, it is not necessary to adjudicate
among slightly different presentations of the core principles of sustainable development. In our view, it is sufficient to note that, within the
conceptual–political range adopted here, sustainable development indicates
an interdependent concern with: promoting human welfare; satisfying basic
needs; protecting the environment; considering the fate of future generations; achieving equity between rich and poor; and participating on a broad
basis in development decision-making. While these points may appear
vague, they are not without content: indeed, they are sufficient to mark out
many usages of 'development' which do *not* correspond to the Brundtland–UNCED usage. Approaches to development and economic growth
which do not consider environmental protection and/or environmental

limits; or which give no place to equity issues; or which ignore popular inputs to environment and development related decision-making—would not be in accord with the broadly accepted understanding applied here.[8]

In addition to (and supporting) this conceptual understanding, is the more specific textual and political context inherent in the UNCED process and its international agreements: particularly the Rio Declaration, the Climate Change and Biodiversity Conventions, and Agenda 21. These reflect a very general political consensus within the international community—at a particular moment in time, at least—as to how the sustainable development agenda should be consolidated as to principle, and moved forward in practice. We do not infer that every state or government endorsed every particular policy recommendation in Agenda 21, or that the Rio Accords are to be etched in stone for all time as the quintessence of sustainable development, but rather that they represent the mainstream view of what sustainable development could reasonably be held to imply at the moment when it was officially endorsed by the world's nation-states as a crucial objective of policy.

These two benchmarks—the normative themes validated through the WCED/UNCED process, and the practical consensus represented by the Rio Accords—provide an anchor for the understanding of sustainable development employed in this study. Our general goal has been to determine empirically the extent to which the normative themes and practical proscriptions have actually been taken up in the sustainable development related initiatives undertaken in the jurisdictions under investigation.

As for the idea of 'implementation', we have understood this in a general sense to denote the process whereby national governments engage explicitly with the idea of sustainable development; integrate it as a norm in public decision-making processes; and ensure the adoption of policies congruent with its orientation.[9] These aspects are clearly reflected in the research 'pro-

[8] There is now a huge profusion of usages of 'sustainable' in adjectival and adverbial contexts ('sustainable growth', 'sustainable sales', 'sustainable agriculture', 'sustainable communities', and so on) as well as of 'sustainability' *tout court*. Throughout this study we take sustainable development to be the internationally legitimated master concept, and we will approach other 'sustainabilities' from the perspective of the extent to which they are (or are not) compatible with sustainable development.

[9] The 'implementation' considered here is somewhat different from that which has typically preoccupied political researchers, which concerns a particular programme located within a determinate policy sector, 'authoritatively formulated' by government, and applied within a national or sub-national matrix (Mazmanian and Sabatier 1983; Goggin 1990; Palumbo and Calista 1990). As we have seen, sustainable development is not an individual 'programme', but a normative frame associated with a wide set of policy proscriptions, which requires 'translation' into national priorities and measures, and which cuts across established sectoral domains. Although legitimised by international agreement, most commitments are not in the form of legally binding accords. Furthermore, analysis of national engagement

tocol' listed above. There are, however, two additional features of the approach which warrant further comment: (1) the emphasis on *political processes* rather than ultimate developmental outcomes, and (2) the primary focus on the actions of *government* rather than on the behaviour of the full spectrum of social actors.

Since sustainable development refers to a particular pattern of social change, 'implementing' sustainable development might in the broadest sense be thought to refer to the actual achievement of substantive results—that is, specific outcomes of sustainable development initiatives. Making comprehensive judgements about developmental trajectories presents fundamental conceptual and practical difficulties, and at a point when even the most enthusiastic states have only recently accepted sustainable development as a macro policy objective—and when international discussions over indicator sets to assess progress are far from resolved—such judgements are beyond the comparative intentions of the study. We are, in short, more interested in political *process* rather than developmental *substance*.

With respect to actors, one could also argue that 'implementation' in a broad sense denotes not just action by governments, but also that undertaken by other societal groups. Here again we adopt the more restrictive connotation, defining implementation in terms of government initiatives, rather than with respect to the autonomous sustainable development related activities of non-governmental actors. This accords with the formal delimitation of responsibilities for ensuring national implementation established in the Earth Summit agreements, and confines the enquiry to manageable proportions.

In sum, our position is that the concept of sustainable development was given a *relatively* distinct formulation as a particular type, or path, of development by the Brundtland Commission; that the essence of this formulation created a common implicit 'platform' for the Rio Earth Summit; and that the concept's greatest strength as a focus for implementation analysis, is the combination of relative conceptual distinctness and relative political consensus attaching to the UNCED process. In the following, we first present the individual country reports and analyses, allowing each 'story-line' to emerge as the individual authors have deemed most appropriate. We then provide (in Chapter 12) a comprehensive comparative overview of the ten cases, focusing on a number of key dimensions derived from the research protocol—dimensions which we believe provide an initial empirical basis for more theoretical explanatory approaches. We conclude the comparative

with sustainable development necessitates reference to both domestic and extra-national dimensions of the countries' responses—for the UNCED process anticipates that compliance will entail national initiatives in both domestic and international policy.

analysis with a general comparative evaluation, where we group the different cases with respect to the degree of political 'enthusiasm' indicated for sustainable development within each jurisdiction, but where we also try to grasp the distinctness and particular nature of the different national responses. Finally, in Chapter 13, we draw out some of the conclusions of the analysis in terms we believe to be of central importance for further developments and practical applications.

2

Australia: Ecological Sustainable Development in the National Interest

ELIM PAPADAKIS

There are several important considerations for understanding the Australian approach to sustainable development policy, including the geography, political economy, and political system of the country. The land that comprises Australia covers a vast 7,682,000 square kilometres. There is also another one-and-a-half times that area of sea to which ecologically sustainable development could be applied. Though Australia has a low population density, with most people concentrated in a few cities and largely on the eastern coast, the current population of 18.4 million is likely to continue to grow rapidly compared to most OECD countries. The distinctive geography of an island continent with a sparse population is particularly relevant to efforts to protect biodiversity.

The idiosyncratic character of Australia's political economy (Bell and Head 1994) is another important consideration, and it has sparked controversy over greenhouse-gas emissions. The strong reliance on exporting agricultural products (4 per cent of GDP and accounting, in 1996–7, for 30 per cent of merchandise exports) is one factor. Another is that Australia exports more wool than any other country, ranks second in the export of meat and sugar, and third in the export of cotton. Australia leads all other nations in the export of coal, bauxite, alumina, lead, and titanium. These resource-processing industries accounted, in 1996–7, for 44 per cent of merchandise exports, created about 8.5 per cent of national GDP and about 5 per cent of

I am grateful to senior officers and executives in the Department of the Environment and the Department of Foreign Affairs and Trade, Dr Joe Baker, Commissioner for the Environment in the Australian Capital Territory, Ms Anna Reynolds, National Liaison Officer of the Australian Conservation Foundation, and Dr Clive Hamilton, Executive Director of The Australia Institute for providing information, answering questions and offering insights into sustainable development in Australia. Participants in the Academy of Social Sciences in Australia Workshop on 'The Ecologically Sustainable Development Process: Evaluating a Policy Experiment' also broadened my understanding of the issues.

all jobs. These factors as well as Australia's location in the Asia-Pacific region are pivotal in understanding controversies over how Australia can meet international obligations, and citizen aspirations for secure employment and environmental protection.

The structure of the political system can play an important part in fulfilling aspirations. The Australian system of government includes three tiers (federal, states and territories, and local government). States and territories have their own parliaments and have been invested with most of the powers to legislate, manage, and regulate the environment. Local government has responsibilities for many services, and land-use planning. However, the federal government has become an increasingly important actor, making use of powers to enact laws on the environment and sustainable development.

Environmental Policy and Sustainable Development

In Australia the focus by political and other elites on integrating consideration for the environment with traditional concerns about economic growth can be traced to the early 1970s and the emergent practice, particularly in New South Wales, of the Environmental Impact Statement. This was widely welcomed as a way of identifying the consequences of development and achieving a balance between economic and ecological imperatives, though many have questioned the effectiveness of this process (Woodhead 1990).

Moreover, until the 1970s, the environment was not prominent on the national political agenda. Measures of a shift in policy included the 1974 endorsement of the UN World Heritage Convention, which contributed to reshaping relations between state and federal governments, and a *de facto* redefinition of powers of the states to legislate, manage, and regulate the environment. Australia also participated in the UN Environment Program (1972), and pressure by environmentalists prompted reforms like the creation of the Australian National Parks and Wildlife Service and the Australian Heritage Commission. The 1974 Environment Protection (Impact of Proposals) Act improved the capacity for gathering data and provided the public with opportunities for more involvement in decision-making processes. Other milestones include the enactment of the Great Barrier Reef Marine Park Act (1975), and the 1981 inclusion of the Great Barrier Reef and Kakadu National Park on the World Heritage List.

Although most of the legislation on environmental policy is still enacted by the states, action by the federal government has increased considerably (see Commonwealth of Australia 1994). In the 1980s this led to confrontations between federal and state authorities, some of which ended up in the High Court. Only in the 1990s did federal governments begin to focus on a more co-operative approach with the states, and on 1 May 1992 both parties signed the Intergovernmental Agreement on the Environment (IGAE). This agreement and the events that preceded it have shaped the official response to the UNCED process.

The engagement with sustainable development from the submission of the Brundtland Report to the conclusion of the Earth Summit is interesting because of the effort by the government to develop a distinctive approach known as 'ecologically sustainable development'. There were some precedents for this which built on the *World Conservation Strategy: Living Resource for Sustainable Development* (1980) issued by the International Union for the Conservation of Nature and Natural Resources, the United Nations Environment Program and the World Wildlife Fund. The report recommended the development of national strategies to integrate conservation and development. Like the previous Liberal government, the 1983 Labor government took this report seriously, hosting a conference to develop a *National Conservation Strategy for Australia* (Commonwealth of Australia 1984). The strategy espoused principles like the integration and interdependence of conservation and development, retention of options for future use, accumulation of knowledge for the future, and the integration of sustainable development and conservation.

For several years this report was largely forgotten, and the resurrection of the idea of sustainable development occurred following competing pressures on the government to address the protection of native forests and defend the mining and logging industries. Initially, the government had shown little interest in the process of preparing the Brundtland Report. Widespread discussion of the report in Australia occurred only after the Minister for Primary Industries and Energy, John Kerin, latched onto the component of the document that focused on economic growth. The government then used the notion of sustainable development in its efforts to arbitrate between competing interests and defuse sharp divisions within its own ranks over development and environment. In August 1989 it brought together industry, labour, and environmental groups in order to forge a consensus on the meaning of sustainable development. That was the first stage in the process of developing strategies for ecologically sustainable development.

The inclusion of the word 'ecologically' was in response to concerns by environmental groups about a process that had been largely initiated by pro-development rather than pro-environment ministers. Environmentalists would probably have refused to participate in an extensive dialogue if the term had not been included. The inclusion of the word 'ecologically' reflected the awareness among environmentalists and policy-makers that, relative to many other OECD countries, Australia still perceived itself as being mainly concerned about the development of resources (rather than a balanced approach which included environmental considerations). There followed an innovative process of consultation centred on the formation, in 1990, of ecologically sustainable development (ESD) working-groups that involved business and industry, labour, environmental organizations, and government departments and agencies at all levels.

The groups contributed to a comprehensive effort to engage with the UNCED process and sustainable development. They also represented a response to problems of governance within Australia, changing perceptions about the importance of environmental protection and conflicts between competing interests. The aim of the dialogue was to prompt different groups to consider alternative ways of viewing problems. Though the government recognized that economic and environmental goals could not always be pursued simultaneously, it hoped that sustainable development would optimize economic growth and environmental protection (Commonwealth of Australia 1990: 4). The notion of ESD was also used to refocus the traditional emphasis on economic objectives: 'Ecologically sustainable development provides a conceptual framework for integrating these economic and environmental objectives, so that products, production processes and services can be developed that are both internationally competitive and more environmentally compatible' (Commonwealth of Australia 1990: 1).

The ESD groups adopted the Brundtland definition of sustainable development (as meeting 'the needs of the present without compromising the ability of future generations to meet their own needs'). In November 1991, following extensive consultations, the groups presented reports on agriculture, energy use, energy production, forest use, fisheries, manufacturing, mining, tourism, and transport. Reports were also submitted on intersectoral issues and the greenhouse effect. Over 500 policy recommendations were made for achieving ecologically sustainable development. Though there was consensus among interest groups over many topics, there was concern about the lack of detail on how to deal with some controversial issues, and environmental groups criticized the lack of a timetable for implementing the recommendations.

The approach by governments to ESD presents a paradox. Before the Rio conference the ESD process represented one of the most comprehensive attempts to address issues raised in the Brundtland Report. However, changes in leadership (the 1992 replacement of Bob Hawke by Paul Keating as Prime Minister) and changes in government (the 1996 victory of the Liberal–National Coalition) have meant that since Rio there has been an apparent decline in commitment to ESD. Yet, the legacy of that period (from around 1989 to 1992) has not disappeared.

Another landmark in environmental policy, linked to growing interest in sustainable development, was a 1989 government statement which recognized, among other things, the seriousness of the problem of soil degradation (Commonwealth of Australia 1989). There followed a National Soil Conservation Strategy whereby the government encouraged co-operation between the National Farmers Federation and the Australian Conservation Foundation. The government adopted a proposal by farmers and conservationists to declare the 1990s the decade of Landcare. It committed A$320 million to planting one billion trees over the decade, and thereby achieve 'sustainable farming'. Apart from meeting these targets, the Landcare movement included, by July 1990, over 500 Community Landcare Groups, and the number has since risen to over 4,000.

Though governments made explicit use of the Brundtland concept of sustainable development before and after the endorsement of the Rio process, they have been primarily concerned about adapting the concept to suit the imperatives of national politics.

The political system, and its inherent inertia, shape the style and content of policy. For instance, the government was keen to avoid previous conflicts between itself and the states. This was an important stimulus to framing the 1992 Intergovernmental Agreement on the Environment (IGAE). The government referred to this agreement as a 'new approach to intergovernmental dealings on the environment' (Commonwealth of Australia 1996d) which specified the roles of various layers of government and the 'ground rules' (including principles and schedules for co-operation). Work on this agreement had begun in 1990, long before the UNCED meeting. The IGAE attempted to define more clearly the roles of tiers of government, reduce disputes and achieve greater certainty in decision-making. The IGAE presupposed the recognition of ecologically sustainable development principles by all layers of government.

In an effort to reduce disputes the agreement specified the 'accreditation' of any process or system introduced by federal or state governments in order 'to avoid the arbitrary revisiting of environmental issues by the parties' (Commonwealth of Australia 1996d). On the question of international conventions it attempted to improve consultation between the parties. The agreement also espoused a precautionary approach to environmental issues and 'the effective integration of environmental and economic considerations in decision-making'. Other initiatives included: data gathering; collaboration between governments when consulting those affected by decisions on land-use; eliminating duplication in procedures for environmental impact assessment; national environmental standards, guidelines and goals; developing a National Greenhouse Response Strategy (NGRS); implementing the Convention on Biological Diversity; and a co-operative approach to nominations for World Heritage listing.

Australian Responses to the Rio Challenge

The initial engagement with the UNCED process was influenced by tensions between competing interests both within and outside the Labor government. Paradoxically, following the Rio conference, the character of the response was modified by a leadership change in the ruling Labor party, and the 1996 election of a Liberal–National government. While the latter acknowledged the importance of UNCED objectives, its stand on international agreements and its relationship with environmental groups represent important shifts.

The new government took at least one initiative that illustrated continuities and discontinuities in approaches to sustainable development, and the distinctiveness of a national response. Reflecting popular interest in environmental protection the government for the first time competed seriously with the Labor party on environmental issues by creating a A$1.15 billion Natural Heritage Trust following the partial privatization of the Telstra national telephone company. The funds are being directed towards a national vegetation plan, rehabilitating the Murray–Darling River Basin, conducting a national land and water resources audit, establishing a national reserve system and tackling pollution of the coast and seas. The principles of sustainable development apply to the Natural Heritage Trust.

The Concept of Sustainable Development: Australian Interpretations

Understanding of sustainable development was shaped by a previous regime which launched the 1992 National Strategy for Ecologically Sustainable Development (NSESD) (Commonwealth of Australia 1992a). The NSESD posits the need to 'develop ways of using those environmental resources which form the basis of our economy in a way which maintains and, where possible, improves their range, variety and quality' and to 'utilize those resources to develop industry and generate employment' (Commonwealth of Australia 1992c). The core aims are to improve individual and community well-being by focusing on economic development that secures 'the welfare of future generations', 'equity within and between generations', biological diversity and 'essential ecological processes and life-support systems'.

The government has been circumspect about how to evaluate the implementation of ESD: 'there is no identifiable point where we can say we have achieved ESD'. However, it distinguishes between development and an ecologically sustainable approach to development. The latter involves consideration 'in an integrated way' of 'the wider economic, social and environmental implications of our decisions and actions for Australia, the international community and the biosphere'; and of 'a long-term rather than short-term view when taking those decisions and actions' (Commonwealth of Australia 1992c).

The NSESD anticipates a role for all tiers of government, and for business, labour, and the wider community. The role of federal and state governments is to establish a framework for greater co-operation between them. Again, reflecting the distinctive development of Australia, the federal structure of government and the potential for conflict between various levels, the NSESD has supposed the possibility of differences in the implementation of policies between the states.

In outlining the guiding principles and core objectives of the NSESD the government focused on the integration of concerns about the economy, the environment, and social equity; recognition of the 'global dimension' of impacts on the environment; need for 'a strong, growing and diversified economy which can enhance the capacity for environmental protection' and promoting 'international competitiveness in an environmentally sound manner'; improvements in policy instruments for valuation, pricing, and incentives; a precautionary approach; and community participation.

After 1992 government departments were expected to incorporate these principles into their mission statements. In addition, the principle of ecologically sustainable development was included in the Cabinet Handbook from February 1994. Still, there is considerable scepticism about the capacity of various government agencies to implement these principles. Crucially, there has so far been little indication of specific timetables for achieving stated goals and clear definition of responsibilities.

The government has adopted a 'whole-of-government' approach to the implementation of sustainable development. The Office of the Prime Minister and Cabinet provided the secretariat for the Intergovernmental Committee on Ecologically Sustainable Development (ICESD), though this was wound down in 1997.

The 1996 change in government also shifted perceptions about the realization of a sustainable development trajectory. One of the most publicized changes was the concerted diplomatic effort to persuade other countries to adopt the principle of individual or more flexible greenhouse-gas targets rather than uniform targets among members of the OECD. The government maintained that the costs to Australia of adopting an approach that was uniform, because of the structure of its economy, would be considerably greater than the costs to other member countries (Commonwealth of Australia 1997a).

Environmental organizations have questioned the commitment by successive governments to implement sustainable development, especially when Paul Keating became Prime Minister in 1992, and following the 1996 election of John Howard (Australian Conservation Foundation 1997a; 1997b). The reluctance by government to adopt legally binding targets on greenhouse-gas emissions may reflect this lack of commitment. However, the official position is that mechanisms have been established to ensure better co-ordination between all layers of government, NGOs can contribute to reviews of policies like those pertaining to biodiversity and climate change, and local communities are encouraged to develop their own methods for monitoring the state of the environment.

The period between 1990 and 1992 is seen by many people as an exciting and constructive era in relations between governmental and non-governmental organizations. The Howard government (1996) may have shifted the emphasis through significant reductions in public expenditure and an ideology that stresses privatization rather than state involvement. This complements government efforts to devolve responsibility for the implementation of sustainable development to different stakeholders including business, industry, and local communities. It is unlikely that additional resources will be allocated to these processes without significant political pressure by the mass public.

Still, the bases for a NSESD were laid by a previous regime, which endorsed the reports of the ESD working groups, and the federal government is still apparently committed to this process. The formulation of a national strategy was facilitated by a November 1991 Heads of Government agreement to form an Ecologically Sustainable Development Steering Committee (ESDSC). Its role was to liase between tiers of government in their evaluation of the recommendations of the ESD working groups and report to Heads of Government on outcomes. In December 1992 the Council of Australian Governments (COAG) endorsed the NSESD subject to adequate funds and specific circumstances prevailing in particular states. Despite these potentially colossal restraints, the recommendations of the working groups and the IGAE formed the basis for developing policy. COAG, comprising leaders of federal, state and territory governments, and the President of the Local Government Association is the most authoritative association for inter-governmental co-operation. A new COAG agreement was signed in November 1997 and changes made to the IGAE. The parties agreed on the need for a more effective framework for intergovernmental relations on the environment, particularly on matters of national environmental significance; environmental assessment and approval processes; listing, protection and management of heritage places; compliance with state environmental and planning legislation; and better delivery of national environmental programmes. This process reflects enduring efforts to co-ordinate, better define roles and responsibilities, and achieve agreement between federal government and the states on a wide range of environmental issues.

Institutionalizing Environmentally Sustainable Development

The commitment to sustainable development has been institutionalized through the NSESD. There are also connections between the NSESD and other initiatives, including the IGAE, the NGRS, the National Strategy for the Conservation of Australia's Biological Diversity, the National Waste Minimization and Recycling Strategy, the Commonwealth Major Projects Facilitation Initiative, and National Forest Policy Statement. Further work is being undertaken on developing the framework for dealing with questions arising from international agreements like Agenda 21, the Framework Convention on Climate Change and the Convention on Biological Diversity.

Other important aspects of institutional engagement include developing policies which reflect the precautionary principle and the axiom of inter-generational equity. However, the stipulation remains that they are subject to the availability of funds. Governments have also focused on the limits to enforcing compliance, how local government authorities cannot be bound to adhere to the NSESD (Commonwealth of Australia 1992a). Furthermore, under the Liberal–National government, there are signs of challenges to the precautionary principle.

On a more positive note, the federal government has produced a compendium of ESD recommendations, showing the connection between the NSESD (as well as the NGRS) and the 500 recommendations arising from the ESD working groups. The compendium specifies the response by governments to each recommendation, and refers to some policies and time-frames for action.

Although there have been no formal changes to the Constitution as a result of initiatives like the NSESD, the 'whole-of-government' approach and processes established to ensure greater co-operation between layers of government reflect a fundamental change in mechanisms for implementing sustainable development. In so far as these arrangements lead the states to accept that environmental issues also fall within the purview of the federal government there has been a *de facto* amendment to the Constitution. There are several explanations for this shift in the distribution of power within a given territory. They include pressure by environmentalists, the international obligations on governments, and the response by some political organizations to these forces. Moreover, initiatives like the Natural Heritage Trust will be largely controlled by central government agencies like the Department of Primary Industry and Energy and the Department of the Environment.

Prior to its abolition the Intergovernmental Committee on Ecologically Sustainable Development (ICESD) had a pivotal responsibility in overseeing the enactment of legislation as regards sustainable development. It was responsible for the supervision of the IGAE, the NSESD, and the NGRS. The committee included representatives from the federal, state, and territory governments and was responsible for monitoring how federal government departments incorporated the principles of ESD into their charters and corporate plans. The ICESD also reported to COAG. The 'whole-of-government' approach to sustainable development is now co-ordinated by COAG. The Department of the Environment also plays a pivotal role in the process of co-ordination.

It is difficult to evaluate the impact of legislative enactments on actual practices. However, the conflict that prevailed in the 1980s between developers and environmentalists has diminished considerably. This may reflect shifts in perception and a new ethos for co-operation. It may mirror a waning of interest in reform at the highest levels, and the absence of a powerful political champion. There is also evidence that conflicts persist at the local and regional level.

How far have existing institutions actively taken up the theme of sustainable development? Among the mechanisms identified by the government in its response to chapter 8 of Agenda 21 are those of institutional co-operation between different levels of government as well as the integration of specific instruments which focus on the economy, on national accounts, on data gathering and information. Apart from the 'whole-of-government' approach to ecologically sustainable development and to the mechanisms for ensuring co-ordination and supervision of policy, the portfolios for Primary Industry and Energy as well as the Environment play a pivotal role in the implementation of sustainable development, particularly through their joint supervision of the Natural Heritage Trust. The apparent commitment by the Liberal–National government to the implementation of Agenda 21 seems to reflect continuity in governmental responses.

In the 1995 report to the UNCSD on implementing chapter 8 of Agenda 21 the government focused on market mechanisms for pricing resources based on the environmental and social costs. This was seen as complementing legislative and regulatory mechanisms. Still, the government acknowledged potential hindrances to the introduction of these instruments like the questions of international competitiveness and intra-generational equity. Among the initial measures explored by the government were the pricing and allocation of water; ensuring cost recovery for solid waste disposal; and the pricing of leaded petrol.

As regards national accounts the Australian Bureau of Statistics (ABS) has worked on measures of the valuation of forests, minerals, and land, though the estimates were based on 'resource-use values' and did not encompass 'non-monetary environmental values'. About A$5.5 million has been allocated for the period 1996 to 2001 in order to enable the ABS to develop 'environmental accounts'. These 'national balance sheets' should provide information on assets and liabilities, particularly with respect to land, subsoil, and forests. The ABS will also gather information that can be used in creating indicators of sustainable development (Commonwealth of Australia 1997b: 28). The government has also attempted to refine the methods and techniques for gathering data (the National Wilderness Inventory, the National Forest Inventory, and the Environmental Resources Information Network). Work is underway on the compilation of a National Greenhouse Gases Inventory, a National Environment Information Database, and a National Pollutant Inventory.

Governments at all levels have issued state-of-the-environment reports and in New South Wales there is a statutory obligation to produce them. The first independent and extensive review of the state of the environment in Australia highlighted the importance of Agenda 21 and used the same definition of sustainable development as the Brundtland Report (State of the Environment Advisory Council 1996a). Though recording how aspects of environmental management in Australia had won 'international recognition', the report called for more data and research and significant policy changes. Concern was expressed about the dangers of adopting piecemeal approaches that tended to treat 'symptoms rather than underlying causes'. Though recognizing some changes to institutional structures, the report criticized the absence of co-ordinated responses: 'Overall, economic planning appears to take little account of environmental impacts. It is assumed that the first priority should be a healthy economy, and that problems can always be solved using the wealth created' (State of the Environment Advisory Council 1996b: 15).

Assessing Progress

Overall responsibility for measuring and monitoring progress towards sustainable development rested with the ICESD. The NSESD also has a role in this process, including the development of 'appropriate performance measures' (Commonwealth of Australia 1996a: 200). The government has stressed 'the primary responsibilities of line agencies in requiring programme managers to implement, monitor and review the performance of policies and programmes' mentioned in the NSESD (Commonwealth of Australia 1996e). The NSESD stipulates a biennial report to the heads of government and a broader consultation with the wider community on the effectiveness of the strategy.

A review is underway of concepts and methods used in the development of performance indicators. The NSESD wants state of the environment reporting to become a regular feature. The 1996 State of the Environment Advisory Council report provides an important benchmark and the aim is to produce an updated report by the year 2000. Other initiatives include a proposed research paper on Subsidies on the Use of Natural Resources, further work on environmental indicators, the ABS environmental accounts and a proposed National Land and Water Audit. The Department of the Environment is developing environmental indicators to support national state of the environment reporting. The Australian and New Zealand Environment and Conservation Council State of the Environment Reporting Task Force aims to produce environmental indicators that can be used for consistent reporting across jurisdictions. In some sectors, like forestry and fisheries, efforts are underway to develop indicators for 'sustainability'. The most advanced is the National Collaborative Project on Indicators of Sustainable Agriculture (NCPISA), under the supervision of the Standing Committee on Agriculture and Resource Management.

Established in 1992, this expert group identified four crucial indicators relating to long term real net farm income, land and water quality, managerial skills, and off-site environmental effects. Participation in this scheme included all the states and the Northern Territory, and the outcomes of the NCPISA may have a powerful impact on approaches to managing natural resources in a sustainable manner (Commonwealth of Australia 1996a: 201). According to one government source: 'a lot of conceptual work has gone into projects such as NCPISA and environmental indicators for state of the environment reporting. Although synergies are possible, different purposes demand different indicators and different concepts' (personal communication). The government also appears committed to these developments: 'fundamental to building an ecologically sustainable economy is the ability to benchmark our actions, so that we have some measure as to whether we are heading in the right direction' (Hill 1996b).

However, Australia presents unique challenges (Commonwealth of Australia 1995a; State of the Environment Advisory Council 1996b), and the task of gathering information on over a million species (including invertebrate animals and micro-organisms) is daunting. The existing knowledge base has been described as 'inadequate', making it 'impossible to assess the impact of human activity on biodiversity—a critical aspect of ecosystem health and resilience', which in turn makes it difficult to answer the question as to whether the pattern of development is 'genuinely sustainable' (State of the Environment Advisory Council 1996b: 9). Some of these concerns are echoed by external examiners (OECD 1998a).

In their reports to the UNCSD governments have painted a rosy picture, identifying the numerous agencies and organizations involved in the collection and analysis of information on sustainable development (Commonwealth of Australia 1996b:80–1, Table 1). At the international level, Australia has rendered assistance to other countries, 'to strengthen developing countries' capacities to collect and use multi-sectoral data for environmental, natural resources and land-use planning' (Commonwealth of Australia 1996b: 81). Both of these claims are supported in certain respects by external examiners (OECD 1998a).

Despite initiatives to measure and monitor policies for sustainable development, government officials have indicated that it is premature to specify the connections between measures of the environment, economy and quality of life. The focus is on disaggregated indicators since they are easier to communicate and interpret. The scientific basis for aggregated procedures is inadequately developed and aggregate figures are either extremely subjective or hard to interpret. Most aggregated indicators are expressed in physical terms. Although consideration has been given to placing monetary values on environmental attributes, there is uncertainty about the validity of such measures. The ABS environmental accounting project has used mainly physical measures. According to one informant, in the future a limited number of financial measures may be introduced 'as indicators of societal response to perceived environmental problems' (personal communication). Such measures may be inadequate and inappropriate by themselves when one considers the time-frame of ecological processes.

International Engagement

Federal governments have perceived a direct connection between national action and international sustainable development objectives, notably through the creation of ESD working groups and initiatives like the NSESD. Agenda 21 (ch. 2) focuses on how governments of developed nations should contribute technical assistance, if requested, to capacity building in developing countries to design and implement economic policies, efficient tax systems, accounting systems, and the promotion of entrepreneurship. The primary responsibility for addressing the topics under chapter 2 rests with the Department of Foreign Affairs and Trade, especially the Environment and Antarctic Branch, and with Environment Australia. The Australian government responded to chapter 2 (and the related questions of financial resources and mechanisms (ch. 33) and the transfer of environmentally sound technology, co-operation and capacity-building (ch. 34)) in various ways.

On the connection between international trade and environmental protection, the government argued that microeconomic reforms (which strengthen the competitive position of Australia and raise living standards) improve efficiencies in the allocation of resources and thereby contribute to sustainable patterns of development. Unilateral reductions in tariffs over recent years have entailed a reduction in assistance to manufacturing and commodities sectors. Trade liberalization (through the GATT/WTO) is regarded as central to achieving the objectives of chapter 2, though this has drawn mixed responses from environmental groups. Some argue this will undermine efforts to protect the environment while others draw attention to beneficial aspects of trade liberalization (the eradication of poverty, and a sustainable pattern of development).

At any rate, the major political parties have made concessions to opponents of trade liberalization (notably in the car, clothing, and footwear industries). In its submissions to UNCSD the government has supported restrictions on those forms of trade that contribute to the exploitation and degradation of the environment and to the reduction in export income for developing countries that produce commodities. Finally, previous emphasis on multilateral agreements has been significantly modified by the present regime (see Commonwealth of Australia 1997b). Until recently, Australia argued that it followed guidelines issued by the OECD on integrating trade and environment policies. Similarly, the government saw itself as promoting the incorporation of environmental considerations and sustainable development in APEC.

As regards chapter 33 of Agenda 21 (financial resources and mechanisms), the Australian Agency for International Development has guidelines for assessing the impact on the environment of all activities, and established projects focusing specifically on environmental concerns. Since 1991 these projects have been subject to audits.[1] With respect to chapter 34 (the transfer of environmentally sound technology, co-operation, and capacity-building) the Commonwealth Scientific and Industrial Research Organization has formal accords with research agencies in Asia-Pacific countries, including projects on coastal zone management, marine ecosystems and measuring ocean currents.[2] Another initiative, the development of a National Environment Industries Database, provides information on technologies and skills for tackling environmental problems nationally, and to trading partners in other countries. The government has also committed itself to an Environmental Co-operation with Asia Program to promote awareness of Australian expertise in environmental management.

Participation in the Process of Sustainable Development

On the question of participation by NGOs, the NSESD relies on the experience and expertise of business, industry, labour, and the wider community to solve practical problems and to create a 'partnership' between all groups (Commonwealth of Australia 1992c). The ESD process was the best example of participation by all these groups. The NSESD recognizes their importance in public education and influencing behaviour (as in purchasing consumer goods), policies on the pricing of water, energy, waste disposal, packaging of products, and recycling.

In reports to the UNCSD the Keeting government argued that it has supported the leading role played by women in working on farms, initiatives like Landcare and rural industry boards, and their participation through the UN Development Fund for Women and the UN Fourth World Conference on Women (Beijing, September 1995). As regards young people, the previous government endorsed the UN Convention on the Rights of the Child

---

[1] The aid programme has also included support for the Montreal Protocol Fund ($A10.18 million, between 1994 and 1996); the Global Environment Facility ($A72.76 million, from 1991 to 1997); United Nations Environment Program ($A5.25million, from 1991 to 1996); and the South Pacific Environment Program ($A1.2 million annually).

[2] In the framework of a Regional Co-operative Agreement of the International Atomic Energy Commission, the Australian Nuclear Science and Technology Organization has provided training in the application of techniques based on nuclear science to environmental issues (like the measurement of water quality).

(1990), the World Declaration on the Survival, Protection, and Development of Children (1991), and supported the World Plan of Action for Children (designed, partly, to combat exploitation of child labour).[3]

Government policies on the role of indigenous people have aroused considerable controversy. About 1.6 per cent of the Australian population are of Aboriginal and Torres Strait Islander origin. They own about 15 per cent of the land, and though most of it is unsuitable for agriculture, it contains valuable mineral resources. This has led to serious conflicts over how to manage the land in a sustainable manner.

The 1989 creation of the Aboriginal and Torres Strait Islander Commission was designed to foster the independence and meet the needs of indigenous people. 'Land councils' representing indigenous people were also created. The most significant event, however, was the High Court Mabo decision of June 1992 on native title. This led to the enactment by the Labor government of the Native Title Act (1993) which sought to accommodate two considerations: recognition and protection of rights of native title holders and the interests of the whole population in land development. Both initiatives have aroused controversy and the Liberal–National Coalition government has partly shared the views of many non-indigenous people, particularly farmers, that too many concessions have been made to indigenous people.

Another contentious domain is the relationship between federal government and environmental NGOs. Since the 1980s there has been an ongoing dialogue between green groups and the Ministry for the Environment. There have also been consultations focusing on Agenda 21 topics, and discussions on the implementation of the NSESD. One of the foundations for contacts with NGOs is a programme that originated in the 1960s for government grants to voluntary conservation organizations. The aim of these programmes is to increase community awareness and understanding of environmental issues.[4] However, environmental organizations have questioned the government's commitment to implementing sustainable development, and an indication of their dissatisfaction was the unprecedented

---

[3] A more controversial initiative was the establishment, in January 1997, of a Green Corps programme to assist young people in obtaining full-time training for up to a year on environmental projects like land care, eco-tourism, restoring the environment and gathering data. The objectives include improving career prospects of participants in environmental management, science and conservation. Criticism of these initiatives by opposition parties and the labour movement has occurred against a backdrop of drastic reduction by the government in commitments to broader job creation and training programmes.

[4] The willingness by governments to embrace the Brundtland Report and UNCED process means that promoting awareness of ecologically sustainable development principles has become a criterion in determining distribution of these funds.

decision in July 1997 by organizations like the Australian Conservation Foundation, Greenpeace, and the World Wide Fund for Nature not to accompany the official Australian delegation to the meeting of the Parties to the Framework Convention on Climate Change in Bonn, Germany.

As regards the involvement by local government authorities in Agenda 21, although the federal government cannot force them to implement the NSESD, mechanisms like COAG ensure their involvement in the process. Most of the 680 or so local government authorities are represented nationally by the Australian Local Government Association. The association is mainly concerned with intergovernmental relations, and, as a member of COAG, played an important role on the ICESD. Another important initiative is the effort by the Municipal Conservation Association to promote the implementation of Agenda 21 by local government authorities. The federal government provides financial support to a programme entitled 'Local Agenda 21, Managing for the Future' which offers guidance on implementing Local Agenda 21, and there are many examples of local government authorities developing strategies in this area.

A pivotal issue in implementing sustainable development on this vast continent is the involvement by farmers and the rural community. Though there has been some collaboration between government, farmers, and environmentalists, significant conflicts remain, for instance, over policies proposed by federal and state agencies like the Murray–Darling Basin Commission on the pricing of water resources. Farmer organizations have strongly opposed such initiatives.

Changing Patterns of Production and Consumption

In the areas of sustainable production and consumption, governments have implemented policies on energy conservation, waste management, cleaner production, product redesign and technology, and reforms in the management of water supplies, transportation, and forestry.

Concern about energy conservation arose in the 1970s following the rise in oil prices and studies like 'The Limits to Growth' (Meadows et al. 1972) that predicted a catastrophe by 2000 if prevailing patterns of exponential economic growth were left unchecked. Micro-economic reforms like the introduction of a National Electricity Market (beginning in 1997) and proposals for a new gas-market are seen as addressing the consumption of energy and reducing greenhouse-gas emissions by moving from coal to gas. Greater competition between energy providers may lead, on the demand side, to improvements in energy efficiency. The establishment of technologies like co-generation and remote area power systems may, on the supply side, also serve to reduce greenhouse-gas emissions. The government is working on a Sustainable Energy Policy White Paper with a 25-year perspective.

As regards waste management, the Labor government had, in 1994, set as a national target the reduction by 50 per cent of wastes (measured in per capita waste) to landfill by the year 2000 through recycling and other measures.[5] Publicity materials issued by the government have attempted to increase awareness of possibilities for cleaner production. In Victoria and South Australia governments provided financial assistance to industry to facilitate this process. In the Australian Capital Territory the government has published a strategy for 'zero waste' by 2010.

The federal government has funded the Centre for Design at the Royal Melbourne Institute of Technology in order to assist firms in product redesign and technology that will reduce environmental damage and create products for an internationally competitive market. The outcome has included the production of goods like recyclable kettles, dishwashers that use less resources, systems for collecting and recycling packaging, and devices for saving water.

Technological innovation creates possibilities for promoting sustainable development in sectors like transport. Some initiatives predate the Rio conference: reductions in pollution following the 1986 enactment of regulations on carbon-monoxide, nitrogen-oxides, and hydrocarbon emissions from new cars. The enforcement of new rules on unleaded petrol, including higher taxes on leaded petrol and smaller amounts of lead in fuel, have also improved the situation. There are also plans for introducing stricter standards on vehicle emissions.

Some of the most controversial and pivotal proposals for reform relate to water-use policy. This topic was broached in 1994 by COAG, when it promoted a strategy of pricing the consumption of water and removing or rendering transparent the use of subsidies. COAG wanted to clarify property rights, adopt trading arrangements in water, and achieve institutional reform. Despite strong opposition from farmer groups, this process is well underway and will influence pricing, allocation, and management of water supplies.

The management of forests has also been highly controversial. Recent initiatives include a National Forest Policy for developing a broad and representative forest reserve system and creating a sustainable and internationally

---

[5] Similarly, the previous government supported initiatives like the Cleaner Production Program, the Best Practice Environmental Management Program and the Energy Audit Program and 'EcoReDesign'.

competitive forest products industry. Among the measures adopted are 'regional assessments' of environmental, heritage, economic, and social values of forests prior to negotiation of Regional Forest Agreements about long-term management and use of forests. The aim is to create a system of reserves based on criteria agreed to across the country. The outcomes have been mixed, with some success in New South Wales but problems in states like Victoria and Tasmania.

Finally, on the question of sustainable consumption, Environment Australia completed a study in 1996 which gauged the effectiveness of measures to change patterns of consumption (in sectors like transport, energy, food, clothing, chemicals and cleaning supplies, and water) with a view to identifying other possibilities for reducing their impact on the environment.

Climate Change: Australia's Cautious Approach

The question of climate change is a vexed one in Australia. In 1996 the government launched a major diplomatic effort to persuade other OECD countries to adopt the principle of differentiated, rather than uniform greenhouse-gas targets. According to the government the costs to Australia of adopting a uniform approach would be much greater than those borne by other countries. The disadvantages for Australia are seen in terms, for instance relative to the European Union, of a more rapid population increase and greater reliance on export industries requiring high levels of energy. The government also pointed out that the European Union itself adopted a differentiated approach enabling countries like Portugal to increase their emissions by 40 per cent.

The Minister for the Environment argued that the Ministerial Declaration from the Second Conference of Parties to the Framework Convention on Climate Change in Geneva (July 1996) was supported in all but this respect by the government: 'The challenge that now confronts us is to produce an outcome which will accommodate our particular economic and trade circumstances, while contributing effectively to the stabilization of greenhouse-gas concentrations in a global sense' (Hill 1996a).

A government 'issues paper' highlighted the related themes of population, agriculture, and the structure of a 'resource-based' economy, comparing Australia to other OECD countries (Commonwealth of Australia 1997a). Between 1990 and 2020 Australia is likely to experience higher rates of population growth than these countries. Though the differences between Australia and countries like Canada and the United States are modest, the anticipated population growth in Australia (29.6 per cent) is huge in comparison with nations belonging to the European Union (1.7 per cent). The enduring reliance by Australia on agriculture may constitute an added hurdle when it comes to reducing emissions. Activities associated with agriculture account for 17 per cent of carbon-dioxide emissions. Land clearing also accounts for a significant proportion of emissions.

The Australian economy has long relied on fossil fuels, more so than other OECD countries. The abundance of fossil fuels means that the energy-supply industry relies almost exclusively on this source. Australia also exports more coal than any other country, and increasing amounts of natural gas and oil. The reliance on fossil fuels also means the development of industries like the production of aluminium at a faster rate than elsewhere. Finally, Australia's pattern of trade, apart from depending heavily on exporting 'resource-based' products manufactured by using large volumes of energy, is shaped by the focus on exports to the Asia-Pacific region which has experienced high rates of economic growth. The outcome of the 1997 Kyoto Conference, when Australia secured an agreement allowing it to raise levels of greenhouse-gas emissions by 8 per cent (in 2010 from 1990 levels) therefore represented, from the government's point of view, a significant success. Iceland was the only other wealthy nation granted this concession. Australia won a further concession: inclusion of a clause in the agreement which covered emissions from land-clearing. The advantage to Australia is that land-clearing emissions have fallen since 1990 (the base line year for calculating changes in emissions). Critics of the government regarded these as hollow victories since Australia may be ill-prepared to face tougher targets in the future (see Hamilton 1998). They may also have damaged Australia's reputation among some groups as a responsible member of the international community. For the government the agreement may none the less provide vital room for manoeuvre to consider more effective strategies for tackling the greenhouse issue.

In its formal response to chapter 9 (Agenda 21) the government developed a National Greenhouse Response Strategy (endorsed by COAG in 1992). In December 1992 Australia signed the UN Framework Convention on Climate Change. This followed the 1990 agreement by the government to aim for a 20 per cent reduction in greenhouse-gas emissions (from 1988 levels) by 2005. Although this agreement has been discarded by the Liberal–National government, some measures were adopted to reduce the rate of emissions, including co-operation with industry through initiatives like Greenhouse Challenge, a programme of co-operative agreements with companies across various industry sectors and the promotion of sustainable agricultural practices. By November 1997 a hundred companies and industry associations (including some large mining corporations) had signed agreements under this plan to reduce emissions by about 22 million tonnes of CO_2 by 2000, and these companies accounted for over 45 per cent of industrial emissions in Australia.

Other government initiatives include research, as in the National Greenhouse Gas Inventories covering the period 1988–94 (which showed that CO_2 emissions increased by 3.9 per cent, from 394 million tons in 1990 to 410 tons in 1994). The government has issued a discussion paper on a national greenhouse strategy with detailed proposals about how to achieve reductions in emissions, including the wide range of measures associated with the Natural Heritage Trust (Commonwealth of Australia 1997c). This follows previous statements on a national greenhouse strategy (Commonwealth of Australia 1992b; 1995b), and the creation of Co-operative Research Centres (for Southern Hemisphere Meteorology, and Renewable Energy) to investigate the greenhouse question. In 1998 the government created an Australian Greenhouse Office to co-ordinate and implement the NGRS and manage partnership programmes like the Greenhouse Challenge.

Critics have focused on a number of problems including the reluctance by both Labor and Liberal–National governments to meet legally binding targets. In response to another reproach, that they reduced expenditure on energy-efficiency programmes in the 1997 budget, the Liberal–National government argued that this measure was offset by greater competition in energy markets and state and local government as well as private sector initiatives (Commonwealth of Australia 1997b: 7).

None the less many economists, among others, argue that the approach by the Liberal–Nationalist government is flawed in a number of crucial respects. First, there is inadequate focus on measures for energy efficiency like the introduction of mandatory standards for fuel-efficiency of vehicles, restructuring the taxation system (Hamilton, Hundloe, and Quiggin 1997), and reducing land clearing (Hamilton 1994). The Australian Conservation Foundation has also highlighted several strategies that could be devised to achieve energy efficiencies (Australia Conservation Foundation 1997b). Second, the use of economic modelling to project the costs to Australia of agreeing to reduce greenhouse-gas emissions, in research carried out by the Australian Bureau of Agricultural and Resource Economics (ABARE), is open to dispute (Hamilton and Quiggin 1997). There is a further consideration, namely, the financing of this research largely by the private sector, notably the coal and oil companies that sell and use fossil fuel. The arrangement by ABARE, a government agency, to offer seats on its research steering committee to any organization that contributed A\$50,000 per annum, meant that major corporations that could afford the fee were heavily represented on the committee. Environmentalists were not. In 1998 the Australian Conservation Foundation lodged a complaint against ABARE with the Ombudsman, who found in its favour and recommended that ABARE restructure any steering committee to ensure 'an appropriate balance of views' and involvement of all relevant stakeholders.

Even some industry groups are critical of government efforts to encourage innovation in environmental protection technologies. The Environment Management Industry Association estimated that Australian business made huge financial gains in East and South East Asia by providing environmental technologies and education. Green political organizations like the Australian Conservation Foundation want to form alliances with business and industry in a bid to mobilize opinion on issues like greenhouse-gas emissions. Critics of government policies like the New South Wales Sustainable Energy Development Authority point out that Australia has the capacity to do much more in reducing greenhouse-gas emissions by adopting new technologies (*The Australian*, 23 October 1997: 14).

Though the government evokes a struggle between employment and meeting stringent greenhouse-gas emission targets, critics have shown that the models for making predictions about employment underestimate possibilities for reducing emissions. The Australian Democrats' Senator Meg Lees argued that agencies like the Department of Primary Industry and Energy have identified potential energy efficiencies of around A\$2 billion to A\$3 billion in Australian industry without any net economic cost, and a proposal by the Centre for Policy Studies (which combines a tax on greenhouse-gas emissions with the abolition of payroll tax) could reduce emissions and increase employment (by 55,000) (*The Australian*, 1 October 1997). Though the present government has not changed its fundamental position on these issues, it has foreshadowed further measures for reducing greenhouse-gas emissions, and including perhaps direct costs to taxpayers.

Biodiversity: Protecting Australia's Unique Heritage

According to the 1996 State of the Environment Advisory Council, 'Australia is one of 12 nations in the world that contain major repositories of biological diversity. It is the only one that is industrially developed, has a relatively small human population, and occupies an entire continent. Thus we have a good opportunity, as well as the responsibility, to balance conservation, human population growth and demands, and economic development' (1996b: 24).

The preservation of biodiversity represents a greater challenge to Australia than to most other countries. Scientists and policy-makers regard this issue as one of the most pivotal to any strategy for sustainable development. The 1996 State of the Environment Report defines biodiversity as 'the variety of all life forms', comprising 'different plants, animals and micro-organisms, their genes and the ecosystems of which they are a part'. There is concern about the rapid rate of destruction of habitats, the primary cause of the loss of biodiversity on this vast continent: 'Some 5 per cent of higher plants, 23 per cent of mammals, 9 per cent of birds, 7 per cent of reptiles, 16 per cent of amphibians and 9 per cent of fresh-water fish are extinct, endangered or vulnerable. Australia has the world's worst record of mammal extinction. In the past 200 years, we have lost 10 of 144 species of marsupials and 8 of 53 species of native rodents' (State of the Environment Advisory Council 1996b: 24).

Due to its relative isolation for around 50 million years, Australia contains numerous species that are endemic to this continent, including 82 per cent of its mammals, 45 per cent of land birds, 85 per cent of flowering plants, 89 per cent of reptiles and about 93 per cent of frogs (Commonwealth of Australia 1996c: 1). A crucial domain for the preservation of biodiversity is 'the vast and less visible world of invertebrate animals and micro-organisms', which comprises more than one million species in Australia, most of which (about 85 per cent) have not been described or investigated adequately (State of the Environment Advisory Council 1996b: 22).

The conservation of biological diversity is a primary objective of the NSESD, and a National Strategy for the Conservation of Australia's Biological Diversity has been ratified by all tiers of government in response to the Convention on Biological Diversity (Commonwealth of Australia 1996c). The rationale presented for preserving biological diversity includes the provision of food, medicines, and industrial products (as in fishing, forestry, and wildflower industries); maintenance of hydrological cycles (replenishing groundwater and protecting watersheds); climate regulation; soil production and fertility; preserving ecological systems; enhancing cultural diversity (the attachment of Aboriginal and Torres Strait Islander peoples to the environment); aesthetic values and spiritual benefits; recreation; and ethical considerations like preserving the earth for future generations and avoiding the tendency for humans to lay exclusive claims to the earth (Commonwealth of Australia 1996c: 1–2).

Moreover, the National Reserve System aims to maintain a national representative system of protected areas, and has contributed to the development of methods for identifying protected areas. The scheme is based on co-operation between levels of government to achieve consistent standards for managing protected areas. Other important initiatives which preceded the response to the UNCED process and serve to achieve some government objectives include the Endangered Species Program, the Wetlands Program and the National Landcare Program.

In its report to the UNCSD the government indicated that protected areas covered about 7.8 per cent of the land, there were 4,187 terrestrial and about 306 marine protected areas, and 11 World Heritage Areas, 12 Biosphere Reserves, and 42 Wetlands of International Importance under the Ramsar Convention. The report noted that 1,031 species were under threat. Of these, 312 were classed as endangered and 719 as vulnerable. There were 264 recovery plans in preparation and 148 were being implemented. The National Strategy for the Conservation of Australia's Biological Diversity is linked to initiatives on forests (National Forest Policy Statement), controlling feral animals (Feral Pests Program), and several national strategies which are in draft form (National Strategy for Rangeland Management, and National Weeds Strategy).[6]

The government has acknowledged the issue of a lack of information about biological diversity, and one aim of the Natural Heritage Trust is to address this problem. However, the State of the Environment Advisory Council (1996b) criticized the failure to provide adequate resources and reform the structure of governmental institutions which hinder 'co-ordinated responses' to such problems.

The National Strategy for the Conservation of Australia's Biological Diversity recognizes that effective implementation will require identification of priorities and time frames for their achievement.[7] While the

[6] The focus on gathering information on biodiversity occurs through agencies like the Australian National Botanic Gardens and the Environmental Resources Information Network. Key databases supported by these agencies include the Integrated Botanical Information System and the Census of Australian Plants and the Australian Plant Name Index. Another initiative is the National Wilderness Inventory project which gathers data on the quality of the wilderness.

[7] By 2000 the strategy aims to identify bio-geographical regions and develop priorities for conservation; implement 'co-operative ethno-biological programs' with Aboriginal and Torres Strait Islander peoples; create a national system of protected areas (representing major ecosystems); realize plans for protected areas which have conservation significance; reverse the decline of native vegetation; avoid or limit 'broad-scale clearance of native vegetation, consistent with ecologically sustainable management and bio-regional planning'; and implement fully international agreements on conservation and sustainable use of biological diversity signed by Australia (Commonwealth of Australia 1996c: 43–4). By 2005 the strategy aims to create a system of voluntary reserves on private lands, and networks of community groups to manage and monitor biological diversity; rehabilitate at least ten endangered or vulnerable species; and control 'three introduced mammals, ten introduced plants and one pathogen that pose major threats to biological diversity' (Commonwealth of Australia 1996c: 42).

measures reflect possibilities for tackling threats to biodiversity, there remain some enormous problems. They include land clearing, loss of native forests, impact of introduced species, absence of some representative ecosystems in national parks and other reserves, lack of knowledge, and failure to enact effective legislation to tackle the fragmented institutional approach: 'Australia lacks major, co-ordinated programmes for the discovery, monitoring, management and sustainable use of biodiversity. New strategies, particularly ecologically sustainable development, give us the opportunity to provide world leadership in the wise use of natural resources, including their conservation for future generations. Without this comprehensive approach, the future is bleak for much of Australia's unique flora and fauna' (State of the Environment Advisory Council 1996b: 24).

The government has taken or promised to enact measures to tackle the problem of co-ordination. For instance, the Australian and New Zealand Environment and Conservation Council (ANZECC), a non-statutory Commonwealth, State, Territory and New Zealand Ministerial Council, was formed in 1991 by amalgamating the former ANZEC (established in 1972) and the Council of Nature Conservation Ministers (CONCOM) (established in 1974). Its function is to provide a forum for member Governments to exchange information and experience, and co-ordinate policies on national and international environmental and conservation issues. The ANZECC, in consultation with other ministerial councils, will co-ordinate the implementation of the National Strategy, monitor outcomes and conduct reviews of the implementation process every five years. The strategy aims to integrate conservation of biological diversity into decision-making at all tiers of government, in alignment with the principles of the NSESD. The government has also presented new legislation, the Environment Protection and Biodiversity Conservation Bill (1998) which combines several pieces of existing legislation and several new stipulations. Though recognizing some of the positive aspects of the proposed legislation, for instance greater influence by the Minister for the Environment in decision-making, the initial response among environmental groups was critical of the lack of mention of the integration of ESD principles into all aspects of legislation, and the tendency of the federal government to propose a 'far too limited role for itself in environmental matters' (Environmental Defender's Office 1998: 7). When the legislation was presented and read to the Senate it enshrined in legislation for the first time the promotion of ESD (Section 1), outlined the principles of ESD (Section 136), and required their consideration by the Minister when dealing, for instance, with enforcement of conservation orders (Section 465).

Australian Implementation of Sustainable Development: Some Central Observations

The annual reports submitted to the UNCSD have highlighted the government's response to Agenda 21, and new initiatives in climate change and bio-diversity. Overall, there has been a concerted effort to elaborate on and introduce principles underpinning sustainable development both in government agencies and across different tiers of government. Although, in their response to Agenda 21, governments have often included initiatives that existed prior to the UNCED process, this is hardly surprising. It reflects the growing interest, over two decades, in the relationship between development and environmental protection, and in integrating concerns about the environment in areas that previously focused primarily on development and vice-versa. The recent OECD report also noted 'considerable progress in developing a framework for the integration of environmental and economic policies' (1998: 28).

At the national level, sustainable development has been used by governments and business and environmental groups to forge close links between economic and environmental concerns; and political parties have played a pivotal role in this process (Papadakis 1996). Recalling the 1983 National Conservation Strategy, the 1991 platform of the Labor party appealed for 'the maintenance of ecological processes and genetic diversity' and 'the integration of environmental and economic goals across all areas of decision-making' (Australian Labor Party 1991: 88). In the 1993 election campaign the National party proposed the creation of a new Department of Sustainable Development. The 1994 Labor party platform emphasized the importance of international co-operation, including participation in the UNCSD, contributions to the Global Environment Facility and implementation of resolutions by UNCED. Finally, initiatives like the Natural Heritage Trust represented an attempt by the Liberal Party to win voters' confidence on sustainable development.

None the less, reports commissioned by the government and from other sources point to enduring obstacles to reform, problems in implementing policies on climate change, institutional barriers to effective integration of policy across all tiers of government and inadequate knowledge of the state of the environment (State of the Environment Advisory Council 1996a; Papadakis 1996; Christoff 1995; OECD 1998a). The commitment by government agencies to environmental protection also remains uneven (Productivity Commission 1999).

On the question of sustainable production and consumption, modest tax incentives (subsidies, deductions, and credits) have been introduced at the national level for developing clean technologies and capital expenditure on soil and water conservation. State and local governments have introduced user-charges for industrial waste and sewerage treatment. Local governments have introduced charges for municipal waste; and state governments have instituted tradable resource-entitlements and emission-rights in industries like fishing, timber-harvesting and water-use by farmers (Christoff 1995: 175). Still, an OECD (1994b) study found that Australia trailed countries like the Netherlands, Sweden, and the United States with respect to the introduction of charges for carbon-dioxide emissions and aircraft noise; product charges (on items like petrol, electricity, coal, fertilizer and vehicles); and schemes for deposit-refunds on bottles and cans (see Christoff 1995: 182–4). Much of the policy debate on greenhouse-gas emissions hinges on evaluations of government enacting measures that stimulate energy efficiency, and innovation in environmental protection technologies. A recent performance review found that there was 'significant potential' for improvement in areas like setting environmental standards, greater use of economic instruments (like product charges, deposit-refund systems, and emission trading), and application of the 'user pays' principle in waste management and waste water treatment (OECD 1998a: 2). The report recognized achievements like environmental auditing of development assistance proposals, promotion of sustainable forest management in the South Pacific and Asia-Pacific regions, and the 'special circumstances' of Australia as a 'large exporter of fossil fuels and energy-intensive products' (1998a: 10–11). It also pointed to the inadequacy of existing measures and funding 'to halt or reverse the degradation' of land and water resources (1998a: 4).

The commitment by political elites has been crucial in explaining support for sustainable development. Efforts by Labor governments to address internal conflicts, and struggles between interest groups, were pivotal in bringing sustainable development onto the political agenda. The formation of the ESD working groups also represented a new form of corporatism by promoting constructive dialogue between competing groups (Papadakis 1996).

These efforts to place sustainable development high on the political agenda were also reflected in media accounts and in public awareness about these issues. Analysis of some media demonstrates how sustainable development was subject to the phenomenon of 'cycles of attention' posited by Downs (1972). These cycles occurred from 1987 to 1989 and 1991 to 1994 (Papadakis 1996). Survey research also shows that many people had become aware of the significance of 'ecologically sustainable development'. In 1991 20 per cent were aware of ESD and able to define it, 5 per cent were aware but unable to define it and the remainder were either not aware of ESD or unsure (ANOP 1991). The question was framed in terms of whether respondents had heard or read anything about ecologically sustainable development and, if so, what they understood it to mean. Respondents defined ESD as development without harming the environment, a balance between development and environment, preservation and regeneration of resources, saving the environment and preserving forests and reforestation. The 1993 figures were almost identical (ANOP 1993). The understanding of ESD was high among people with tertiary education (53 per cent), white-collar workers (33 per cent) and members of environmental groups (45 per cent). Public opinion had begun to reflect changes in government policy and in social values (Papadakis 1996). However, the attention of public opinion to environmental issues has waned, and the government appears reluctant to stimulate interest in them other than in terms of defending national economic concerns.

At one level possibilities have emerged for implementing sustainable development, as policy-makers attempt to clarify objectives for biodiversity and sustainable-production policies. The commitment has been institutionalized (through the IGAE and NSESD), significant financial commitments have been made to initiatives like the Natural Heritage Trust, there is some co-operation between agencies and progress on developing measures for and monitoring sustainable development. On the other hand political elites are less committed to multilateral agreements (particularly on greenhouse-gas emissions). This has weakened the engagement in constructive dialogue between environmental NGOs and government compared to the early 1990s. The Liberal–National government has sharpened the focus on defining the national interest largely in economic terms, thereby threatening a revival of adversarial debates over environment and development. In a climate of insecurity about employment prospects and Australia's capacity to compete in a global economy, the focus on the environment has declined. The explanation for all this may lie in the fact that 'most decision makers' believe 'that the wealth created by economic activities will overcome environmental effects' (OECD 1998a: 8). It may also relate to the argument that decision makers still have some room for manœuvre in setting national agendas irrespective of forces of globalization and internationalization (see Weiss 1998).

The scope for national agenda-setting does not mean that policy co-ordination will be achieved across tiers of government. In Australia much remains to be done in ensuring coherence in the implementation of sustainable development. Interest has declined in adopting long-range perspectives. The tendency is to delegate responsibilities for sustainable development from central to state or local government. Again, apart from factors associated with an ideological stance that queries the role of 'big government', this may reflect the focus on balancing the budget. Many policies for implementing sustainable development and the NSESD itself are subject to adequate funds being available. The abiding institutional arrangements continue to play a potentially obstructive role. Policies in one area can still easily contradict those in another. Implementation of the NSESD is also subject to circumstances prevailing in particular states. More could be done within the existing framework to refine economic and regulatory instruments for implementing sustainable development (see OECD 1998a). While some agencies, notably those responsible for natural resource management and environmental protection, treated ESD as 'a core policy concern', the majority were not performing well because they were unclear about what constitutes ESD, lacked relevant information, fell short of 'good practice' guidelines for policy-making, did not have committed decision-makers, failed to co-ordinate activities across areas of government, and neglected long-term horizons on sustainable development (Productivity Commission 1999).

There is scope for longer-term perspectives, and creating a policy-culture that encourages innovation. At any rate, the original adoption of strategies for sustainable development signalled a willingness to consider options and alternatives to the traditional conflict between environment and development. There was certainly evidence of a move in this direction during the early 1990s.

The conflict over greenhouse-gas emissions has threatened advances in co-operation between environmental NGOs and the federal government. It remains to be seen whether disagreements over greenhouse-gas emission policies and alternative ways of tackling this problem will have a lasting impact on the implementation of sustainable development. In many non-controversial areas, there is still engagement between environmental groups and government agencies.

Conclusions

The promotion of sustainable development by the Brundtland Commission was timely. The Labor government used it to reduce conflicts among interest groups (and its own supporters and representatives) and reconsider policy directions, particularly through the consultative process of ESD working groups.

Though governments have responded to obligations under international treaties, serious problems have emerged because of perceived short-term costs associated with signing conventions, particularly legally binding ones on climate change. Other problems include discharging responsibilities in the preservation of biological diversity in a vast but sparsely populated continent, and the structure of an economy heavily reliant on exports of minerals and fossil fuels.

Apart from questions of geography, demography, and economic structure, there is the enduring issue of defining the national interest. The European Union has long struggled with perceptions of national and supra-national interests. In Australia, defining the national interest is partly conditioned by electoral considerations (including a relatively short electoral cycle), and an ideology privileging economic measures of success and interests. Economic standards of success are themselves open to challenge and involve assumptions about the practicality of time-frames for gauging such measures, and beliefs about how best to achieve goals, notably best possible outcomes for wealth creation and environmental protection. Economic interests, like those articulated by resource industries, play a pivotal role in discouraging implementation of certain aspects of sustainable development.

Australian responses to the UNCED process reflect both an effort to meet international obligations and assertion of a distinct national agenda. The prevalent focus on the national interest (in Australia and elsewhere) may be an important part of a process which clears the way for the implementation of sustainable development. The paradox is that some of the most progressive measures and processes were introduced prior to 1992 in Australia. Since then advances have been slow, and in some areas there may be some retreat from the realization of sustainable development.

3

Canada: From Early Frontrunner to Plodding Anchorman

GLEN TONER

Introduction

When it comes to implementing sustainable development, Canada often compares favourably with other countries (Johnson 1995; Dalal-Clayton 1996). Perhaps this is not surprising. Canada has a strong internationalist tradition and has been an enthusiastic joiner when it comes to international organizations and agreements. This was true of the processes surrounding the World Commission on Environment and Development (Brundtland Commission) which popularized the concept of sustainable development. One Commissioner (Maurice Strong) and the Secretary General (Jim MacNeill) were Canadians. Strong was later named Secretary General for UNCED and had been Secretary General of the UN Conference on the Human Environment in Stockholm in 1972. Canada was one of four countries the Commission visited on fact-finding missions and many individual Canadians and numerous Canadian organizations presented briefs to the Commission (WCED 1987: 366–87). Canada took its participation in UNCED seriously and was an important player at Rio. While Agenda 21 is seldom mentioned in Canadian discourse, 'sustainable development' is now in common use in both the public and private sectors (OECD 1995: 201).

This chapter reviews the government of Canada's engagement with sustainable development. Environmental policy comprises a fundamental component of the sustainable development equation. In the Canadian federal system, jurisdiction over environmental policy is shared. Moreover, provincial and municipal governments also have important powers related to the economic and social policy dimensions of sustainable development. While there has been policy activity in support of sustainable development at the sub-national level in Canada, developments across the provinces and municipalities are very uneven and impossible to generalize about. Since the sub-national level is not the subject of this volume, the focus here is the federal government and its initiatives.[1]

December 1997 marked a potentially historic date in the Canadian government's engagement with sustainable development. At that point, each government department had to have tabled in Parliament its first-ever sustainable development strategy (SDS). An independent officer of Parliament, the Commissioner of Environment and Sustainable Development, then assessed the departmental SDSs. The office of Commissioner is itself an institutional innovation.[2] While the first SDSs varied in quality, depending on the degree to which departmental officials had integrated sustainable development values into their mandate planning, they are potentially important cultural-change instruments within the department and across the government. Since ministers are responsible for tabling departmental strategies in Parliament, and because the strategies will be independently assessed and publicly reported on by the Commissioner, departments have an incentive to take them seriously.[3] If the sustainable development paradigm is to become entrenched in public policy, such strategic planning functions will have to become institutionalized in all organizations—and become as routine as annual budgets and business plans.[4]

The Liberal government of Prime Minister Jean Chretien won re-election in May 1997. Since releasing their electoral manifesto for the fall 1993 general election, in which they defeated a two term Conservative government, the Liberals have experienced a 'crisis of rising expectations'. The 1993 electoral manifesto laid out a series of policy goals in this area that raised expectations that the Liberals would surpass the record of the Conservative government that had led Canada during the Brundtland-Rio era. Yet,

[1] Nor is the focus on federal environmental policy *per se*. It will only be addressed if it is relevant to the analysis of federal engagement with sustainable development.

[2] The government allocated CAN$3.5 million annually in new funds to support the Commissioner, who is located in the Office of the Auditor General. The AG agreed to continue to allocate CAN$1 million annually to value-for-money audit work in support of the Commissioner. The first Commissioner was appointed in June 1996 and has developed a staff of thirty, consisting of seventeen new appointments and thirteen internal transfers from within the OAG.

[3] The release of the Commissioner's first comprehensive report in May 1998 attracted wide coverage in the national media. The second comprehensive report, and third overall, also received broad media coverage when it was released in May 1999.

[4] The paradox in Canada in the late 1990s is that this important institutional innovation in support of sustainable development is emerging in the midst of a highly conflictual period of environmental politics. Policy conflicts in a number of areas—environmental assessment, toxics management, the protection of endangered species, climate change, and resource development—reflect the ongoing reality that the main actors in Canadian environment politics continue to contest the entrenchment of environmental policies. Current and future efforts to institutionalize sustainable development have to contend with this reality.

commentators as diverse as the Sierra Club of Canada and the Commissioner have identified major problems with the Liberals' record. In its 1996 Rio Report Card, the Sierra Club argued that 'the Liberal government record, thus far in its mandate, is significantly worse than their Conservative predecessors. In fact, in terms of environmental performance, this Government is arguably the worst since the creation of Environment Canada twenty-five years ago' (Sierra Club of Canada 1996: 22). The Sierra Club's 1997, 1998, and 1999 Reports were just as critical. In his first Report to Parliament in March 1997, the Commissioner argued that the government exhibited an 'implementation gap in which performance falls short of its stated objectives. This gap reflects the failure to translate policy direction into effective action' (CESD 1997: 11). In his Second Report the Commissioner stated that the government had to pay more attention to the management side of the sustainable development equation (CESD 1998: 7). The implementation-gap critique applies equally to the Liberals' Conservative predecessors. That is, where the Conservatives raised 'great expectations and then ecobacktracked' the Liberals promised 'great leaps forward but took only baby steps' (Toner 1994; Juillet and Toner 1997).

While the post-Brundtland Conservative and Liberal governments had slightly different ideological orientations, both parties faced the reality of a set of structural, institutional, and political-ideological variables which constrained their adoption of sustainable development practices and contributed to the conflictual nature of environmental politics. Structurally, Canada's economic history was shaped by the exploitation of natural resources and the Canadian economy maintains a greater reliance on natural-resource extraction and export than most industrialized economies. Canada remains a trading nation, with over a quarter of its GDP coming from exports. Canada has a huge landmass of nearly ten million square kilometres, borders on three oceans and encompasses fifteen ecozones and six time zones. Forest covers almost half of Canada and represents 10 per cent of the world's total forest cover. Twenty-one per cent of the world trade in forest products originates in Canada. Canada accounts for over half the world's exports of softwood lumber and newsprint. Forestry and products alone account for 3.5 per cent of the nation's GDP. One in fifteen workers rely on forestry for their livelihood. Commercial production from the Atlantic, Pacific, and freshwater fisheries totalled CAN$3.1 billion in 1990. However, the collapse of the Atlantic cod fishery in 1993 and the decline of the Pacific salmon fishery, dramatically reduced both employment and the economic value of the fish harvest. Agriculture and food processing contribute 4 per cent to the country's GDP. Canada possesses nine billion barrels of proven oil reserves and ninety five trillion cubic feet of natural gas reserves. Sixty per cent of Canada's electricity is hydro generated, and the energy sector accounts for 7.1 per cent of Canada's GDP. Over 30 per cent of the worlds nickel, 8 per cent of its iron ore, and 20 per cent of its zinc is produced in Canada. The minerals industry is responsible for 4.3 per cent of GDP and 2.1 per cent of national employment. Given this reality, it is not surprising that many of the toughest sustainable development battles, those which highlight tensions between environmental protection and job creation and economic growth and social stability, take place in these pivotally important sectors (OECD 1995; Canada 1997b).

The environment is not mentioned directly in the Canadian constitution and authority over it flows from a complicated distribution of powers. Jurisdiction over both the environment and the economy is shared between the federal and provincial governments, with the provinces having very significant powers over natural resources. Consequently, intergovernmental co-ordination is a major and time-consuming preoccupation and the politics of the intergovernmental arena is often extremely conflictual. Several of the most controversial environmental protection and sustainable development issues fall under provincial jurisdiction in the resource and land-use management areas. The municipal level of government is also an important player for sustainable development. Over three-quarters of Canada's thirty million citizens live in urban areas, and a number of cities have larger populations than several of the provinces. For example, Toronto is the fifth most populous jurisdiction in Canada. Municipal governments have to deal with waste management, urban sprawl/land-use planning, water and sewage, urban transportation, and local air quality. However, because the municipal governments are constitutionally under provincial jurisdiction they have little formal, ongoing interaction with the federal government.

Institutionally, Canada is a constitutional monarchy and the cabinet–parliamentary system organizes government vertically around sectoral ministries. Some of the prominent departments with sustainable development responsibilities are Environment, Transport, Industry, Natural Resources, Fisheries and Oceans, Agriculture and Agri-food, Public Works and Government Services, Health, and Finance. While sustainable development has not been formalized in the Constitution, it is increasingly cited as a policy goal in major pieces of legislation such as the Canadian Environmental Protection Act and the Canadian Environmental Assessment Act, and in legislation, regulations, and programmes of departments such as Agriculture and Agri-Food, Natural Resources, and Industry. This vertical division of authority, at both the federal and provincial levels, between those departments charged with protecting the environment and those responsible for resource and economic development means that relationships among departments of the same government are often as problematic as relationships between different governments and among governments, industry, and environmental non-governmental organizations (ENGOs). Because of this vertical division of authority, the federal government is often at war with itself interdepartmentally on major sustainable development issues. Indeed, the Commissioner identified the lack of horizontal co-ordination and integration across federal departments as one of the major constraints hobbling the federal government's performance in this area (CESD 1997: 11). In his 1999 Report, the Commissioner cited interdepartmental division and conflict as a major problem in the management of toxic substances (CESD 1999a).

Overlaying these structural/institutional variables, is a recent shift in ideological mood that has seen the emergence of a broad-based social consensus on the need to eliminate government deficits and reduce government debt. While this shift has been promoted by the political right, industry and the business press, the consensus has been bought-into by governing parties of all political stripes. The result has been major cuts to governmental budgets at all levels, which has reduced the overall size and capacity of the Canadian state.[5] Reinforcing and coinciding with this ideological shift, there has been a campaign, led by the private sector, to limit the use of regulation in economic and environmental policy. As regulation has been the traditional instrument of choice in the environmental policy field, this has had major impacts, when combined with the reductions in scientific and enforcement capacity at both the federal and provincial levels (Harrison 1999; Hessing and Howlett 1997). This has triggered growth in the popularity, once again championed by business, of voluntary and non-regulatory initiatives to address environment-economy issues. Yet, many questions remain about the efficacy of voluntary and non-regulatory initiatives (Gibson 1999; New Directions Group 1997).

Given this economic, institutional and political-ideological backdrop, it is hardly surprising that sustainable development initiatives have emerged into a conflictual context. To cope, Canadians have developed elaborate

[5] For example, in the environmental portfolio alone between 1994-5 and 1997-8, provincial and territorial governments as a whole reduced the size of their environment departments by 25 per cent, cutting CAN$425 million from a combined budget of CAN$1.6 billion. The major provinces have cut even more deeply: Quebec (65 per cent), Ontario (44 per cent), and Alberta (37 per cent). During this same time frame the federal government will have reduced the size of Environment Canada by 32 per cent, lopping off 1,400 staff and CAN$234 million in spending. There are additional plans to cut 200 more staff and another CAN$25 million between 1998 and 2000. Other departments relevant to sustainable development have also undergone similarly drastic cuts (Toner 1996; Harrison 1998).

processes, both within the state sector and between government and non-governmental actors, to mediate and resolve conflicts.[6] By its very nature, sustainable development requires cross-sectoral dialogue amongst the various social and economic actors and Canadians have developed considerable expertise at creating processes to facilitate such exchange. Indeed, Canadians have become rather good at articulating sustainable development policy-goals and at creating inter-sectoral dialogue, even if there are often serious problems implementing agreements. Still, in a comparative context, Canadians have been amongst the most engaged with the post-Brundtland international effort to implement sustainable development.

The Road to Rio

The May 1986 Brundtland Commission visit to Canada had an institutional impact, when the Canadian Council of Resource and Environment Ministers (CCREM) created the National Task Force on Environment and Economy (NTFEE) in October.[7] The NTFEE brought together federal, provincial, and territorial ministers and senior members of the corporate, environmental, and academic communities. One of its most far-reaching recommendations was its proposal to institutionalize its method of multisectoral collaboration by having each government establish a Round Table on Environment and Economy. The idea was to have a body of influential sectoral leaders reporting directly to the Prime Minister and premiers. And, indeed, governments did adopt this NTFEE recommendation in the heady

---

[6] George Hoberg (1993) has argued that Canadians have engaged in a much higher degree of multisectoral bargaining than have Americans, whose environmental politics is characterized by a higher level of court-based legalism. However, over the past decade there has been both an increase in the use of the courts by Canadian environmental groups and a significant increase in multi-stakeholder forums. In the late 1990s American firms launched lawsuits against Canadian environmental laws under the North American Free Trade Agreement. The Commissioner's 1999 Report had a chapter dedicated to assessing the strengths and weaknesses of the public consultation processes associated with producing the first departmental sustainable development strategies. Based on a survey of consultation participants the Report laid out the 'building blocks of a consultative culture'.

[7] CCREM was later subdivided into the Canadian Council of Ministers of the Environment (CCME) and the Canadian Council of Energy Ministers. These are intergovernmental councils comprised of the federal, provincial and territorial ministers, which meet regularly to discuss issues of joint interest. The CCME, for instance, is supported by a separate secretariat and manages some joint initiatives. In the climate change area, where both sets of ministers have responsibilities, the two councils meet in Joint Ministerial Meetings.

days of the early 1990s and Round Tables were created at the national, provincial, and municipal levels.[8]

In December 1990 the Conservative government introduced a five-year, CAN$3 billion Green Plan. It was an early effort by an OECD government to deal with environment-economy issues in a comprehensive manner. Indeed, one analyst has called it 'arguably the "mother" of green planning' (Dalal-Clayton 1996: 21). It was a combination environmental cleanup/ protection and a sustainable development plan. The Green Plan was the sustainable development strategy the Canadian government took to UNCED in 1992. The Green Plan began with a broad commitment to sustainable development, calling it no less than an effort at 'planning for life'. This commitment was then linked through the ecosystem approach to the natural environment and the human decisions and actions which impact on it. While much of the spending had to do with cleaning up past mistakes, there was also an emphasis on introducing industrial technologies and practices to promote pollution prevention and sustainable development. The second focus was directed at programmes that would contribute to sustainable development by addressing normative principles that shape decision-making systems in government and society.

The early bureaucratic drafts of the Green Plan were actually much closer to a sustainable development strategy than the version that ultimately emerged from the cabinet process. Indeed, the drafts written in the autumn of 1989 identified the societal and economic decision-making systems as the 'root cause' of environmental degradation. Those early drafts envisioned the Green Plan as representing a turning point in the Canadian discourse by moving the conceptual basis of environmental policy away from resource management and environmental clean-up to pollution prevention and sustainable development. When the politicians on the Cabinet Committee on the Environment undertook their detailed review of the draft Green Plan in the autumn of 1990, they imposed a traditional 'distributive politics' template on the document by moving the expensive environmental clean-up programmes to the front and burying the chapter on the need to change societal decision-making in the back (Toner 1994). As a result, the Green Plan looked less like a novel sustainable development strategy and more like just another environmental protection programme. Even then, it eschewed greater reliance on the traditional regulatory approach (Hoberg and Harrison 1994).

In accordance with the UNCED Secretary General's Guidelines for the Preparation of National Reports, Canada created a multi-stakeholder

---

[8] By 1998 the idea had lost much of its lustre and only the national, a few provincial, and some municipal Round Tables were still in existence. Those that survived were working far from the limelight, compared to the early years of the decade.

participatory process around the writing of Canada's Report for Rio. Specifically, a National Report Steering Committee was created to assist the government in the preparation of the Report. Business and labour organizations, the provincial governments, the Round Tables, aboriginal organizations, and the NGO community participated in the Steering Committee under the general co-ordination of Environment Canada (Canada 1991a). Interestingly, the official twenty-four-member Canadian delegation to Rio included representatives from all of the Steering Committee organizations. Each morning during the Earth Summit, the Canadian delegation along with all other Canadians participating in the other Rio meetings were invited to a briefing with Environment Minister Jean Charest. These sessions could have as many as 200 attendees and became dubbed the 'Team Canada' briefings. The previous day's activities would be reviewed and Canada's response would be discussed. The current day's agenda would also be discussed. This provided Canadian NGO and industry representatives participating in the other events with a special insight into developments at the official conference.

This was an extraordinarily inclusive and open process for an international, intergovernmental meeting.[9] Indeed, the exhilaration of the 'Team Canada' experience led the government to coin the term the 'Rio Way' to characterize the government's new-found 'commitment to improving the way we conduct our business and the increasing recognition of the need for transparency, accountability and inclusion in the way we make decisions relating to the environment' (Canada 1992: 22). However, the 'Rio Way' label had little staying power and quickly disappeared from usage. Frankly, several departments never shared Environment Canada's enthusiasm for transparency and inclusion in the decision-making processes.

The initial plan was to use the Green Plan as a follow-up to Rio, signalling the development of a Green Plan II as the Rio results were folded into the existing Green Plan. This never happened, however, as the Conservatives lost interest in the environment and sustainable development policy file in their last year in government, which coincided with the year following Rio. While the Conservatives found the political will to launch the Green Plan, they had difficulty sustaining their commitment because it was not based on any

---

[9] Looking back in 1997, the Sierra Club lamented the passing of the spirit of the Rio period when it stated that 'Canada's efforts in assisting the involvement of NGOs in the UNCED process was outstanding and has yet to be duplicated . . . But more than money was involved. Canada quite simply puts its very best people together in an extremely effective, innovative and dedicated team. Interdepartmental communication and co-operation were superb. Relationships with the NGO community were at an all time high' (Sierra Club of Canada 1997: 8).

strong ideological or emotional foundation in their party. Their commitment was simply poll driven. As the economic recession deepened in the
1992–3 post-Rio period, environmental issues declined in the 'top-of-mind'
public opinion surveys and the Conservatives backtracked from their commitment to the Green Plan without ever explicitly or publicly renouncing it.
It would be left to the victorious Liberals who were elected in October 1993,
fifteen months after the Earth Summit, to determine the manner in which
Canada's Rio commitments would be met.

The Road from Rio

At Rio, the Canadian government outlined a six-part 'quick-start agenda' and
challenged other countries to take immediate action. One of these agenda
items included the development of a national report on plans and policies
related to the Conference's objectives. Agenda 21 encouraged countries to
adopt national sustainable development strategies (NSDSs) as a central
mechanism for implementing the actions and accords agreed to at the Earth
Summit. For its part, the federal government stated that 'in keeping with the
government's commitment to Canadians to review the Green Plan on the
basis of changing conditions, the government will bring the Green Plan into
line with the standards set by UNCED' (Canada 1992: 3).

There was pressure, however, to go beyond updating the Green Plan to
try and maintain the momentum generated by the 'Team Canada' multi-
stakeholder approach developed around the Rio process. In the July–October
1992 period discussions were held about how Canada might develop a multi-
stakeholder process to develop the NSDS called for in Agenda 21. In a speech
to Parliament in November 1992, Charest proposed a national response to
the commitments of Rio and to the challenge of sustainable development.
Later that month, a national stakeholder meeting with representatives of
over forty sectors of Canadian society agreed to launch a 'Projet de société'.
The Projet was to analyse Canadian responses to Rio and to draft a concept
paper on sustainability planning. It was not intended to be a representative
assembly, though by its conclusion in 1995 representatives of over 100 sectors
of society had participated in its work (Projet de société 1995). The Projet
was more of a coalition of networks working together to generate a national
strategy. As might be expected of such a broad-based initiative, the Projet
had both organizational and conceptual difficulties. Over time, the National
Round Table became increasingly involved in managing the process. Tensions arose between participants who were attracted to developing strategic

plans and those inclined to do more specific projects. The Projet also lost political momentum very quickly. Within a year, Jean Charest, the Conservative minister who had a stake in making the Projet work, was gone. The new Liberal minister, despite claims of support, never fully embraced the Projet. As government support slowly bled away, and as the difficulties of writing a document through an open-ended, volunteer-driven process became obvious, the Round Table became increasingly involved in actually writing the document. The final draft of the document was published in May 1995 and by then there was no longer even an illusion of government support or involvement.

The Projet strove to meet Agenda 21's standard for NSDSs by integrating economic, environmental, and social objectives; by involving the widest possible participation; and by providing a thorough assessment of the current situation. While the broad and inclusive nature of the process was its great attraction, it's unofficial, that is non-governmental, status proved, over time, to be its greatest weakness. As Dalal-Clayton has concluded:

Because the process was based on inclusiveness—anyone who represented a sector could become involved—every time a new stakeholder joined, past discussions and decisions, had to be revisited, which slowed down the process. On many 'big issues' (such as acid rain) there was (and is) no national consensus.

The traditional, institutionalized response of stakeholders was to 'protect their own community' or 'fight their own corner' and, even though they were willing to cooperate, they tended to defend their own interest first. Much effort was needed to maintain the business sector's interest and willingness to attend. Decisions made by companies tend to have a greater impact on sustainable development than many of those made by government. Numerous companies became involved in the Projet de société because they were concerned about what government might do as a regulator, but when they realized that it was 'only' an independent, multi-stakeholder forum and not an agency of government, they became less keen to participate. (Dalal-Clayton 1996: 106)

The National Round Table withdrew is support for the Projet in early 1996 and it expired. Canada, thus, has no NSDS, official or unofficial (Sadler 1996).

Sustainable Development and the Liberals

The Conservative government was defeated in October 1993 half way through the Green Plan's intended life span. The new Liberal government dedicated a chapter of its 1993 electoral manifesto to sustainable development and initially claimed it would not dump the Green Plan simply because it was introduced by its partisan rival. However, it soon began to ignore the title 'Green Plan' when discussing initiatives that had been developed under the Green Plan's authority or budget, and within a year or so after taking power the Liberals killed all reference to it in official government documents. On the face of it, both the Conservative's Green Plan and the Liberal's electoral manifesto—titled 'Creating Opportunity: The Liberal Plan for Canada'—articulated a version of sustainable development, and committed to institutionalize it in the practices and operations of the Government of Canada. Both went some way toward this, but both fell far short of what was required.

In opposition the Liberals had been highly critical of the Conservatives' Green Plan, arguing that it did not go far enough in changing the decision-making system to institutionalize a sustainable development framework. 'Creating Opportunity' called for a 'fundamental shift in values and public policy,' arguing that 'sustainable development—integrating economic with environmental goals—fits the Liberal tradition of social investment as sound economic policy' (Liberal Party of Canada 1993: 63). Several dimensions of the Liberals' sustainable development programme surpassed Conservative promises in the Green Plan and challenged the bureaucratic forces within the federal departments which, often successfully, had resisted the institutionalization of new administrative practices and policy priorities under the Conservatives. After coming to power, the Liberals created, for the first time, a Parliamentary Standing Committee with Sustainable Development in its title. Despite the fine sentiments of 'Creating Opportunity' and the first Throne Speech, the transition from the campaign trail to the cabinet room has been disappointing. The Liberals' vision of aggressive activism has been blunted by the contact with the hard realities of Canadian politics in the 1990s.

The first Liberal budget in February 1994 announced that a multi-stakeholder task force would be established to undertake a major campaign commitment to review federal taxes, grants, and subsidies, in order to identify barriers and disincentives to sound environmental practices. The forty-member multi-stakeholder Task Force was established in July 1994 with a membership consisting of industry representatives, environmentalists, academics, and government officials. The Task Force reported in November 1994, proposing a series of immediate options for the 1995 budget and recommending market-based instruments that could be developed and implemented over a longer time-frame. Further work in this area has not materialized, however, as the Department of Finance believes that the most egregious environmental barriers and disincentives have already been removed by extensive cuts to business subsidies that were undertaken as part of a broader deficit-fighting programme introduced with the 1995 budget.

As a result, a systematic review of the use and impact of fiscal instruments for sustainable development would not take place in Canada in the twentieth century (Canada 1995b). Consequently, Canada has made very little progress in the use of economic instruments for sustainable development. This is most unfortunate if one accepts the argument that the tax system is one of the most important sustainable development policy instruments (MacNeill, Winsemius, and Yakushiji 1991).

In June 1995, the Liberals released a vision document called 'A Guide to Green Government'. It was signed by the Prime Minister and all cabinet members, and represented a government-wide commitment to sustainable development. It argued that 'achieving sustainable development requires an approach to public policy that is comprehensive, integrated, open and accountable. It should also embody a commitment to continuous improvement' (Canada 1995a: 1). It went on to provide a framework to guide the preparation of departmental strategies. To legally institutionalize this approach, the Liberal government established a requirement that departments develop and implement SDSs and created the Commissioner's Office to monitor departments' performance. The Commissioner's first Report was released in May 1997 and identified three key weaknesses in the federal government's management of sustainable development issues:

• the gap between commitments and concrete action;
• a lack of co-ordination among departments and across jurisdictions; and
• inadequate review of performance and provision of information to Parliament.

The Commissioner's second Report in May 1998 had chapters on environmental assessment, performance measurement for SDSs, advances in environmental accounting, developing a strategic approach to sustainable development, meeting Canada's international environmental commitments, climate change implementation, and biodiversity strategy implementation.

The Second Report also assessed the first generation SDSs. As the Brundtland Commission indicated, sustainable development is not a fixed state but rather a process of change (WCED 1987: 9). The SDSs were intended to encourage this process of change, challenging departments' entrenched normative assumptions about their roles and mandates by encouraging them to think about the sustainable development impacts of their policies and administrative practices. To ensure openness and accountability, the departments were required to seek stakeholders' views on departmental priorities for sustainable development and plans for achieving them. In his assessment, the Commissioner noted that 'for the first time, we have a picture of how each department views sustainable development and the actions each department plans to take to promote it. Preparing their strategies has also raised awareness of sustainable development issues within departments' (CESD 1998: 15). However, he also identified two fundamental weaknesses in the strategies. First, almost all departments failed to set clear targets that could be used to judge whether or not the strategy is being successfully implemented. Second, many of the strategies were more a restatement of the status quo than a commitment to change. The Commissioner put departments on notice that he expected them to correct this second weakness and to explain what they would do differently in the future when they updated their SDSs in 2000.

The Third Report assessed the first annual progress reports to Parliament on sustainable development submitted by departments. It concluded that 'the links between the large number of actions that departments reported and the objectives set out in their strategies are frequently too abstract to provide insights about progress. As a result, beyond tallying the activities reported accomplished by departments, we are unable to conclude whether the strategies are on track or whether corrective action is required' (CESD 1999: 5). The Commissioner once again underscored the importance of departments putting in place management systems and training programmes to build departmental capacity to get the implementation job done. As part of the Commissioner's commitment to help departments build sustainable development capacity, the Report included chapters on how seventeen North American and European organizations are building sustainable development considerations into the way they do business, government departments can measure progress in greening their day-to-day operations, and, departments can support sustainable development decision-making by greening their policies and programmes.

The issue of information, monitoring, and performance measurement has haunted the sustainable development implementation project in Canada throughout the 1990s. All successful policy initiatives require concrete measurement and monitoring systems to determine if policy-goals are being achieved (Pal 1997). In the case of sustainable development, the novelty of the policy goals meant that new indicators had to be developed in the first place, before measuring and monitoring of progress could commence. Between 1990 and 1995 both the Conservatives and the Liberals committed resources to determine how better to measure and report sustainable development indicators. Some progress was made. The period since 1995 has been spent trying to figure out how to cope with the cuts to monitoring and reporting dished out in the February 1995 deficit-slashing budget. The Green Plan spoke of the importance of 'authoritative, easy-to-use indicators to measure national, regional and local progress in achieving sustainable development' (Canada 1990: 141). While the emphasis was on environmental reporting and on creating new physical indicators, there was also a commitment to extend the traditional national accounts to incorporate environmental components. The Green Plan committed millions of dollars to strengthen the State of the Environment Reporting Directorate in Environment Canada. This group produced the high quality 1991 and 1996 State of the Environment Reports, which include richly detailed, well-documented, peer-reviewed chapters on every aspect of Canada's environment (Canada 1991*b*; 1996*a*). These Reports are recognized worldwide as some of the best work done in this area.

In December 1993 the National Round Table submitted a Report to the Prime Minister, titled 'Toward Reporting Progress on Sustainable Development in Canada' (NRTEE 1993). It asked the seemingly simple question 'is Canada making progress toward sustainable development?'. The report concluded that Canada did not have in place a system to monitor such progress and therefore the question could not yet be answered. There had been discussion during the early days of the Green Plan of establishing an independent organization, separate from any one department, with a capability for annually assessing and reporting on progress toward sustainable development within the federal government as a corporate entity. The Round Table reiterated the need for an independent organization and recommended that discussions be initiated with the provincial and territorial governments, and other stakeholders, to establish a mechanism for assessing and reporting, at five year intervals, on progress toward sustainable development for the nation as a whole (NRTEE 1993).[10] Such an organization never materialized, and under the Liberals the departmental SDSs have become the instrument for self-monitoring departmental progress.

Not surprisingly, the Commissioner cited performance review as a serious problem both within departments and horizontally across departments. As part of the continuous learning approach, he has launched a research programme to assist departments with the development of key indicators. In the ongoing process of monitoring the implementation of the SDSs, the Commissioner will report on whether departments are doing what they said they would do and will provide criteria outlining his expectations for the SDS updates in 2000.

Internationally, Canadians continue to contribute to the debate. The International Institute for Sustainable Development helped sponsor the development of the ten Bellagio Principles for the 'Practical Assessment of Progress

[10] To its credit the Round Table continued to address the measurement and evaluation issue itself releasing in 1995 its study 'Pathways to Sustainability: Assessing Our Progress' (Hodge *et al.* 1995).

Toward Sustainable Development' (IISD 1996). The North American Commission for Environmental Cooperation (NACEC) is launching its own State of the Environment reporting activities. It recognized that while the governments of Mexico, Canada, and the United States have published reports in the past, budget cuts in all three countries have reduced the resources available for SoE reporting. The NACEC report will provide important information on the North American region by analysing the interactions among economic, social, and institutional change in the region and the environment. Naturally, it will pay particular attention to transboundary issues, and the relationship between environmental issues and socio-economic trends such as economic restructuring and regional co-operation.

After a series of controversial court decisions in the late 1980s, the Conservatives passed a new Canadian Environmental Assessment Act (CEAA) in 1992, but because of internal bureaucratic opposition did not proclaim it before being defeated. In 'Creating Opportunity' the Liberals criticized the Conservatives' effort stating that 'the gap between rhetoric and action under Conservative rule has been most visible in the area of environmental assessment' (Liberal Party of Canada 1993: 64). The Liberals promised to revise the still unproclaimed legislation to shift decision-making power to a new independent Canadian Environment Assessment Agency, subject to appeal to Cabinet, and to legally recognize intervenor funding as an integral component of the assessment process (Hazell 1999).

Environmental assessment, or the prior examination of the potential environmental impacts of industrial projects, is a fundamental tool of sustainable development. Despite proclaiming the Act in January 1995, the Liberal record reflects the implementation gap identified by the Commissioner in his first Report. For example, the Agency was never granted independent status. In a 1994 amendment to the Act, the Liberals shifted the final authorization of projects examined by review panels from the responsible minister to the Cabinet as a whole. In other words, rather than simply considering appeals of decisions taken by an independent agency, Cabinet will make the decisions in the first place. When CEAA was drafted in the early 1990s, resource departments and industry associations strongly opposed the centralization of the assessment process in the hands of an independent agency. They never relented in this opposition and under the Liberals vocal criticism from resource ministers about bureaucratic delays created by the new assessment process made the allocation of more independence and decision-making powers to the Agency politically impossible.

In his second Report, the Commissioner undertook a detailed review of the government's implementation of the new CEAA. Numerous shortcomings were identified, though none were 'universal or catastrophic' (CESD

1998: 6–28). Of the nearly 13,000 environmental assessments (EA) under-taken between January 1995 and December 1997, 99.7 per cent were screen-ings, or the most limited form of EA. These are self-directed assessments undertaken directly by departments. Only 0.1 per cent or ten assessments reached the most demanding stage of being subjected to independent panel reviews.

A 1990 cabinet directive under the Conservatives established a non-legislative process for environmental assessment of policy and programme initiatives submitted for Cabinet consideration and for programme decisions made by ministers without reference to Cabinet. This form of EA is known as 'strategic environmental assessment' and is an essential tool for dealing with the broad sustainable development implications of programmes and policies that are not easily addressed at the project level. The Commissioner found that overall the implementation effort was woeful. This reflected a lack of effort by senior management who control departmental initiatives connected to the Cabinet process. The Commissioner is concerned that without proper environmental assessment of programmes and policies, federal departments will be unable to implement the government's sustain-able development objectives.

Human Resources Development Canada is one of the key social-policy departments of the federal government. It is responsible for programmes and legislation on unemployment insurance, pensions, old age security, student loans, labour standards, occupational health and safety, and indus-trial relations. It has sponsored major studies on the human-resource needs of the Canadian environmental industry, and on the links between environ-mental issues, jobs, and competitiveness. It has committed to undertake future research on the environmental implications of income-support pro-grammes such as employment insurance and other income-support pro-grammes in areas of seasonal and high unemployment. Such programmes, it is suspected, maintain an over-capacity of labour in various resource sectors, which contributes to pressures to over-harvest (Canada 1997h).

While Canadians are among the healthiest people in the world by all standards, Canada's aboriginal population experiences overall lower levels of health than the general population. Health Canada has a special respons-ibility for the health-care of aboriginal communities. Aboriginal people are more frequently exposed to environmental contaminants than most Cana-dians because they eat larger amounts of traditional country foods. Some of these foods, especially marine mammals and fish, can contain high levels of environmental contaminants which bioaccumulate up the food chain. Levels of several contaminants are five to ten times higher in aboriginal people in the North, than in the non-aboriginal population. Health Canada is working with aboriginal organizations in programmes such as the Northern Contaminants Program to identify and address these health risks. In the South, Health Canada is working in formal partnerships with aboriginal organizations in programmes like the EAGLE (Effects on Aboriginals from the Great Lakes Environment) Project and the HEAL (Health and Environment of Aboriginal Life) Project. The goal is to understand and document the effects of environmental contamination on health and well-being by blending the traditional knowledge of aboriginal people with scientific information and methods. These programmes also encourage aboriginal students to pursue careers in environmental health (Canada 1997g: 21–4).

International Dimensions

The Liberal government undertook a major foreign policy review during 1994. The review placed considerable importance on international sustainable development issues. Indeed, Canada committed itself to making sustainable development a pillar of Canadian foreign policy. Hence, most government literature tries explicitly to link national and international obligations and responsibilities (Canada 1995c). The review acknowledges that Canada's international image has been tarnished by bad publicity regarding the treatment of its own environment. For example, both federal and provincial policy regarding forestry practices, fisheries management, and environmental assessment, have had an influence on international trade and foreign policy. The chapters of the review on shared security argue that domestic policies on environment, trade, and development assistance have an effect on international security by influencing international developments. Building shared security, it argued, involves creating a long-term international trade and investment agenda that focuses the Word Trade Organization's attention on issues such as agricultural export subsidies, labour standards, anti-dumping actions, and other domestic practices that harm the environment.

Indeed, the trade-and-environment linkage became increasingly important throughout the Liberal era. Meetings of environment ministers of organizations like the Asia-Pacific Economic Co-operation (APEC) forum have had a major focus on trade in environmental technology and services. This is viewed as important for Canada because an increasing percentage of the CAN$14 billion in revenues of the environmental industries sector is earned from exports. Cleaning up the polluted air, water, and soil around the Pacific Rim could mean big business for Canadian companies. The environmental industry is now a significant sector of the Canadian economy (larger than aerospace) encompassing 4,500 companies with 200,000 employees and growing at a rate of 5–6 per cent per year (Canada 1997a: 11). Unfortunately, in mid-1998 the Liberal Cabinet cut financial support for the Canadian Environmental Industry Strategy, the federal programme that has assisted the growth of this sector and helped position it as part of the new knowledge economy. As more and more decisions about what and how we produce and trade are governed by international rules, business interests are pushing Canada to promote the development of common rules on trade and the environment. For these reasons and others, Canada has participated actively in the work of the OECD and the WTO on trade and the environment (Toner and Conway 1996).

While Canada has a broad range of bilateral agreements with the USA, and is a signatory to numerous multilateral and bilateral arrangements with other industrialized countries, it also participates in a number of bilateral and multilateral arrangements with developing countries. Some of these precede UNCED and some flow from it. For example, Canada has helped the process and worked with developing countries on the Desertification Convention, and the UN Conference on Straddling Fish Stocks and Highly Migratory Fish Stocks. Since 1995, the Canadian International Development Agency (CIDA) has administered the Central and Eastern Europe programme to assist these countries with environmental enhancement projects and other supports in their transition to market economies and democratic political systems. Over CAN$500 million has been committed to twenty-six countries (Canada 1997e: 31).

Canada has developed a domestic Arctic Protection Strategy which focuses on scientific research on contaminants, the clean-up of hazardous wastes in the North, the monitoring of water quality, and the use of 'traditional knowledge' concerning marine resources. This domestic strategy has been linked to the international Arctic Environmental Protection Strategy, which attempts to develop an integrated approach to the shared concerns of circumpolar countries (OECD 1995: 179–80). Aboriginal organizations are important actors in northern Canada and their role in ocean and coastal-zone management is significant both within and beyond their land claim settlement areas (Canada 1996b: 60). Twenty-three per cent of Canadians live in coastal communities. A new Canada Oceans Act came into effect in December 1996, supported by an Oceans Management Strategy, which is intended to ensure the integrated management of activities in estuaries and coastal and marine waters. Provincial jurisdiction over shorelines and land-based activities will be a major influence on the success of these federal sustainable development initiatives. In another oceans-related issue, Canada has made efforts to reach out to small island states that share a common concern about the sustainable use of the ocean's resources. The Caribbean and the South Pacific regions are the site of several CIDA projects aimed at building the domestic capacity of developing countries to address sustainable development issues.

In the post-UNCED era, virtually all of the Canadian literature highlights the relationship between poverty in developing countries and sustainable development. CIDA has a poverty reduction policy, which commits the agency to a number of specific activities designed to improve Canada's response to poverty in the developing world. A key objective is to ensure that CIDA's strategies are complimentary to those of recipient countries. CIDA is active in Africa, Asia, and Latin America. The percentage of poverty reduction projects in these regions rose from 7.4 per cent in 1983 to 34.4 per cent in 1993 (Canada 1996b: 31).

The relationship between poverty, population growth, and sustainable development emphasized in chapter 5 of Agenda 21, is a central theme of Canada's ODA. In 1994, CIDA developed a Statement on Population and Sustainable Development and Canada participated actively in both the International Conference on Population and Development in Cairo and the Fourth World Conference on Women in Beijing. Within overall Canadian official development assistance (ODA) support for population activities is increasing. While Canada is nowhere near reaching the 0.7 per cent of GNP target for ODA confirmed at UNCED (it is closer to 0.3 per cent), Canada at least pays its bills to international multilateral organizations and mechanisms. Canada has pushed for reform of international financial institutions such as the multilateral development banks and was a proponent of the Global Environmental Facility.

One of the main obstacles to implementing Agenda 21 is the lack of mobilization of adequate financial resources internationally. Canada has been a champion of debt relief and trade liberalization as a means of getting more financial capacity for sustainable development initiatives in the treasuries of developing countries. Going into Rio Canada pledged to eliminate CAN$145 million ODA debt to Latin American countries in exchange for sustainable development projects. Since then, Canada has continued to encourage other members of the 'Paris Club' of major international lender governments to consider mechanisms to ease the debt burden of developing countries (Canada 1996b: 25). While the Sierra Club is generally critical of the government's performance on ODA, it acknowledges its efforts in multilateral and bilateral debt relief (Sierra Club of Canada 1997; 1999).

Canada officially recognizes the urgent need to accelerate the transfer of cost-effective and innovative environmental technologies to developing countries. It also stresses the need to preserve intellectual property rights and establish fair trading practices. Canada has several technology-transfer relationships with countries such as Chile, Mexico, and China. Canada's International Development Research Centre has an ongoing Sustainable Technologies Program based in Asia that facilitates the development, diffusion, and adoption of cleaner production technologies.

So while Canada has often been a leader in the past when it came to environmental issues, it is probably safe to say that the overall reduction in federal government spending has weakened Canada's capacity to take leadership positions, especially where additional resource commitments are required. Equally constraining on the federal government is pressure from industry and some provincial governments to step back into the pack of nations and 'wait for a consensus' before committing Canada to various international initiatives. This attitude bothers Canadians who liked the idea of Canada being an international leader. The study 'Connecting With the World: Priorities for Canadian Internationalism in the Twenty-first Century', by a group of eminent Canadians argued that Canada's place in the world will have to be earned 'through intellectual and policy leadership and through its strategic advantage as a multidimensional "knowledge-broker"' (International Development Research and Policy Task Force 1996: v). To be a knowledge-broker a country needs moral authority, and moral authority does not flow from walking away from international agreements like the Climate Change Convention, as was suggested by the Canadian oil-producing province of Alberta.

The UNCED Conventions

The Framework Convention on Climate Change

Climate change epitomizes the challenge of sustainable development. It is not just an environmental issue. It has important dimensions related to the economy, including trade and competitiveness considerations, as well as social aspects. It also raises concerns about equity between generations and among Canadian provinces and economic sectors, as well as nations and regions of the world. These considerations have to be taken into account in deciding the policy response (CESD 1998: 3–15). At Rio, the Conservatives committed Canada to stabilize CO_2 emissions at 1990 levels by the year 2000 in accordance with the terms of the Framework Convention. In their electoral Red Book, the Liberals 'raised' the Conservatives by stating that they would work with provincial and urban governments to improve energy efficiency and increase the use of renewable energies, with the goal of cutting CO_2 emissions by 20 per cent from 1988 levels by 2005.

In 1998 Canada's average temperature was about one degree warmer than in 1895, and there has been a discernible increase in the frequency of winter storms throughout the twentieth century. Because of its size and location, Canada is projected to experience greater temperature changes than most regions of the world. As a coastal and northern country, and as a renewable-resource producer in the forestry, agriculture and fisheries sectors, Canada is vulnerable to damage from climate change (Canada 1997c).

'In 1995, approximately 89 per cent of total greenhouse-gas emissions in Canada were attributable to transportation and fossil-fuel production and consumption. Reducing fossil-fuel use in Canada is a challenge, due in part to our large landmass, cold climate, an increasing population, and a growing economy' (Canada 1997a: 5). Despite the increasing certainty of the science, the climate change debate in Canada has been divisive along sectoral, regional, ideological, and policy lines. Canada has major oil, gas, and coal-producing industries in western Canada, centred in the province of Alberta, and they have resisted action by challenging both the science and the economics of climate change.

The climate change issue has bedevilled the Liberals throughout their tenure. An extensive multi-stakeholder consultative process during 1993 and 1994 was unable to come to agreement on a national strategy. As a result, Canada attended the first Conference of the Parties in Berlin in May 1995 noting that it was on course to be 13 per cent above the target 1990 emissions level by 2000, but still committed to meeting the stabilization goal by 2000. By the Second Conference in Geneva in July 1996, Canadian ministers admitted that Canada's emissions had increased by over 9 per cent since 1990 and that Canada would not meet the target.

The first Liberal environment minister adopted an aggressive stance on climate change which placed her in a confrontation with the oil and gas industry, the Conservative government of Alberta, and her Cabinet colleague the Minister of Natural Resources Canada (NRCan), who was the Alberta representative in the federal Cabinet. The Minister of Natural Resources rode her cabinet colleagues' anxiety about jobs and growth to gain acceptance of a cautious go-slow approach to climate change. As a result of these dynamics, open conflict between the federal environment and natural-resource ministers and departments was a prominent feature of climate change politics under the Liberals. This open warfare within cabinet reflected the total lack of leadership or even engagement by Prime Minister Chretien between 1993 and late 1997.

Despite efforts by some industry groups and their allies in the business press and the right-wing Reform party to cast doubt on the science, there is really no longer any serious dispute on that front. The real conflict has already moved to the debate over the policy instruments required to reduce emissions. Alberta and industry groups advocate voluntary emission-reduction initiatives. Alberta is strongly opposed to the use of regulatory or fiscal instruments, such as a carbon tax, that could reduce consumption of its oil, gas, and coal resources, while environmentalists have taken increasingly strong positions in favour of both. Up to time of writing, the fossil-fuel sector, the government of Alberta, and NRCan have formed a formidable juggernaut against regulating economic activities to achieve reductions in greenhouse gases. They have been successful in promoting a National Action Plan on Climate Change that consists primarily of a voluntary challenge and registry (VCR) initiative. The VCR involves individual companies from the major greenhouse-gas emitting industrial sectors (electrical utilities, manufacturing, energy, transportation and commercial, forestry, pulp and paper, agriculture, mining) submitting action plans detailing the measures they will take to reduce greenhouse-gas emissions. Over 700 companies responsible for more than 50 per cent of Canada's total greenhouse-gas emissions have signed on to the registry, but with little impact to date (Russell 1997; Hornung 1999).

Environment Canada, the scientific community and environmentalists share a much greater sense of urgency and question the effectiveness of voluntary initiatives to fully meet the targets. The Climate Action Network in Canada, made up of more than eighty environmental and other non-governmental organizations, argued for a portfolio of measures that combine voluntary, regulatory, and economic instruments. Economic instruments would include higher excise taxes on gasoline and a carbon charge (called an atmospheric user charge) which would be compensated for in part by a reduction in the federal Goods and Services (value-added) Tax. Existing regulatory and incentive initiatives would be strengthened to enhance fuel economy standards for vehicles, encourage commercial and residential building retrofit measures, and increase industrial energy use efficiency. Recognizing the importance of the 'jobs agenda', environmentalists have emphasized the job creation potential of a major energy-efficiency initiative. Indeed, they argue that climate change provides Canada with an employment-generating and technology-advancing opportunity (Climate Action Network 1997). As part of its response, the federal government launched a multi-volume scientific research project called the 'Canada Country Study', which was released in 1997. This study undertook the first nationally integrated assessment of the social, biological, and economic impacts of climate change in Canada (Dotto 1999).

Chretien was a late entrant into the build-up to the third Conference of the Parties in Kyoto in December 1997. He finally engaged with the issue after discussions with European leaders during a trip to Europe in October 1997. He only entered the domestic debate, which had been tearing his cabinet apart, after President Bill Clinton released the US position in the third week in October. Chretien called from Europe ordering his officials to develop a position that would 'beat the Americans.' His first formal statement was only four weeks before Kyoto on 3 November. Canada was the last G-7 country to state its position going into Kyoto.

The business coalition exerted extensive pressure in October–November, including intensive backroom lobbying of government officials and full-page newspaper advertisements. For instance, the Canadian coal industry employed a highly emotional, fear-based campaign characterizing action on Rio as 'Ritual Suicide by Honour—Economic Suicide by Ignorance.' Business research organizations released reports supporting the go-slow approach. Environmentalists countered with their own full-page ads, research studies, and opinion polls showing Canadians supported a serious effort on climate change and lamented the loss of international leadership by Canada. Just as Clinton had renounced energy taxes under pressure from the Senate and industrialists, Chretien had rejected a carbon tax under pressure from Alberta. Yet, in his 3 November speech, he skewered those sceptical of climate change science, comparing them to the tobacco industry and their allies who for decades denied that smoking causes lung cancer. He went on to argue that Canada should get international credit when Canadian natural gas exported to the United States reduces the use of coal and oil there, and when Candu nuclear reactors exported to China reduce coal consumption there. He also dismissed the horror stories being spread by the fossil-fuel industry and its allies, including the right-wing Reform party in Parliament, that climate change action would cause massive reductions in GNP and jobs, arguing that Canadian exports of environmental and energy technologies would benefit from a global consensus for action (Chretien 1997).

In the Kyoto Protocol Canada agreed to reduce emissions of greenhouse gases to 6 per cent below 1990 levels by the commitment period 2008–12. In his second Report, the Commissioner audited the federal implementation effort for the period between Rio and Kyoto. The audit found a totally inadequate implementation effort, characterized by a lack of co-ordination amongst federal departments, a lack of federal–provincial co-operation, and an overall management structure that lacked accountability (CESD 1998). In a meeting immediately following Kyoto, federal, provincial, and territorial leaders agreed to renew the implementation effort. To that end, the federal government has clarified the respective roles of Environment Canada and NRCan, created a Federal Climate Change Secretariat and committed CAN$150 million over three years for further research and public education. The Secretariat will oversee another multi-stakeholder consultation effort to examine the impacts, costs, and benefits of the Protocol and to determine both immediate and longer-term actions to provide sustained reductions in emissions. The new goal is to have a step-by-step national implementation strategy that will apportion emission-reduction targets to the various sectors and jurisdictions.

Just as the industry coalition opposed to Kyoto is crumbling internationally, industry in Canada has split on the issue. On one side, Exxon subsidiary Imperial Oil has continued to deny the science and to charge that action to reduce emissions will destroy the economy. Petro-Canada, on the other hand, has entered into agreements with ethanol fuel manufacturers and hydrogen fuel-cell producers to ensure that the alternative fuels have access to the marketplace when alternatively powered automobiles emerge early in the new century.

Biodiversity

The United Nations Convention on the Conservation of Biological Diversity came into effect in December 1993. Canada was active in its negotiation and was the first industrialized country to ratify the Convention. 'Creating Opportunity' included a general commitment to the protection of biodiversity and the goal of maintaining the Green Plan commitment to complete the national parks system by 2000. It also stated that the federal government would work with the provinces to protect, in its natural state, a representative sample of each of the country's natural regions, amounting to twelve per cent of Canada. To this end, Chretien announced the creation of two new national parks in October 1996.

Wildlife resources are very important to sustainable development in Canada:

nearly 19 million Canadians spent CAN$8.3 billion in 1991 on . . . wildlife-related activities in Canada, such as wildlife photography, bird-watching, hunting and fishing, leading to the creation of 200,000 jobs and contributing CAN$5 billion in government tax revenues and CAN$11 billion to Canada's Gross National Product. Wildlife resources also provided additional direct benefits to Canadians of over CAN$700 million. This shows a 33% increase in expenditure since 1981. In addition, about 1.8 million tourists from the United States travelled to Canada to take part in these activities. They spent an estimated CAN$800 million.   (Canada 1998: 2)

In 1995 the government introduced the Canadian Endangered Species Protection Act (CESPA) as a legislative proposal. A multi-stakeholder task force was established to provide advice on the drafting of the bill. CESPA would enshrine into law the existing administrative process used to list endangered species, with some modifications, and would make it illegal to harm or capture a member of a listed species or to damage its residence. Subsequent to its listing as endangered, the government would have one year to submit a plan stating how it intends to protect a species and assist in its recovery. Notwithstanding the consensus previously achieved by the multi-stakeholder task force, the government's bill quickly became the object of harsh criticism from virtually all sides (Juillet and Toner 1997). A main point of contention was the limited scope of the legislation. While over-harvesting remains a threat to some species, the vast majority of endangered species are threatened by the destruction or contamination of their natural habitat through commercial activity (industrial pollution, forest clear-cutting, mining, and farming practices) or urban sprawl. The protection of habitat involves the regulation and voluntary modification of a wide array of activities on federal, provincial, and private lands. As such, it is a formidable challenge that requires extensive inter-jurisdictional co-operation.

While recognizing the requirement for such co-operation and acknowledging that Canada has a strong tradition of co-operation on wildlife management issues, many environmental groups have accused the federal government of refusing to fully occupy its jurisdiction regarding endangered species. They believe that the federal government possesses much more extensive jurisdiction than that proposed under CESPA, which only protects species found on federal lands (while they remain on federal lands) and only applies to 'federally managed' species (those covered by the Migratory Birds Convention or the Fisheries Act). The legislation also contains provisions enabling, but not requiring, the Environment Minister to make regulations for species crossing international borders. In total, CESPA would cover only about 40 per cent of the species currently found on the national endangered species list.

The federal government must count on provincial co-operation to assure adequate protection across the country. In October 1996, the national government and the provinces signed an agreement, the National Accord for the Protection of Species at Risk, committing the signatories to adopt complementary legislation. While five provinces have developed legislation to protect endangered species, others are reluctant to do so. For example, even after the Accord was signed, British Columbia's Environment Minister warned that he would not propose such legislation in the near future in order to avoid alienating the provincial resource industries.

Despite polls that consistently show strong public support for federal legislation for the protection of endangered species, the Liberals have been unwilling to confront industry and landowners by establishing stringent habitat protection regulations. This federal reluctance to be confrontational reflects, in part, the tradition of multisectoral co-operation that has characterized the wildlife policy area (OECD 1995). Industrial associations and resource departments have opposed more stringent habitat provisions. Indeed, they are already unhappy with the current limited provisions and have argued that the Act should not apply to private lands, and that producers should participate directly in the drafting of recovery plans. They maintain that the Act does not rely sufficiently on voluntary measures and that the regulations against the destruction of species' residences should not apply to habitat. Federal departments like Agriculture and Agri-Food, Transport, and Fisheries and Oceans also argued for limited regulatory measures, so that habitat protection would not hold up commercial activity. All this opposition from the provinces, the private sector, and federal departments slowed progress through the parliamentary process and consequently CESPA died when Parliament was dissolved for the June 1997 general election. Thus, the Liberals have not yet secured the major legislative basis for fulfilling the UNCED commitments, though they are expected to reintroduce the legislation as the Species at Risk Act in 2000.

On the non-legislative front, the government released the 'Canadian Biodiversity Strategy: Canada's Response to the Convention on Biological Diversity' in 1995, after a lengthy consultation process. The Strategy is a voluntary agreement among Canadian governments to improve citizens' understanding of the value of biological resources and to develop incentives and legislation to support their conservation and sustainable use. Internationally, one stated goal was to put in place a regime to share equitably the benefits that derive from the utilization of genetic resources between the developing countries that husband them and the industrial sectors that utilize them (Canada 1995d). At the Second Conference to the Parties in 1995 Canada competed with Switzerland, Kenya, and Spain for the right to be the seat of the Convention Office. Canada won and the office was opened in Montreal in 1996. The federal government also created a Biodiversity Convention Office in Environment Canada.

An important amendment to the Income Tax Act in June 1996 encourages Canadian landowners to participate in the preservation of biodiversity and wildlife habitats by donating ecologically sensitive land for conservation purposes. Fifteen additional national parks have been added to the national system since 1970, to bring the total number of parks in the system to thirty-eight. Provincial governments have also been adding additional protected areas. The problem with this positive news is that most of the newly protected spaces are in the north, while the ecosystems in the more heavily populated south continue to be stressed by growth pressures and inefficient models of urban development. In total, protected areas in Canada account for about 8 per cent of the country, while the goal is 12 per cent. Only twenty-four of Canada's thirty-one natural regions are currently represented by national parks or park reserves (Canada 1997f: 7). Drastic budget cuts to Parks Canada means the government will not reach its goal of completing the terrestrial park system by 2000.

In his 1998 Report, the Commissioner audited the federal government's effort at implementing the Biodiversity Strategy and gave the effort poor marks. Only two of eight federal departmental biodiversity implementation plans had been completed by early 1998. Even these lacked time-frames, resource allocations, expected results, or performance indicators. The strategy requires an overall implementation plan that has targets and time-frames, both to achieve national goals and to measure Canada's performance against its international commitments. The Commissioner concluded that even though the Convention has been in place for six years, progress in Canada has been slower than projected and deadlines have been missed. A growing hostility to the legislative protection of lands or species by the provinces in the face of industrial pressures (Sierra Club 1997 and 1998), combined with significant budgetary cuts by both levels of government, led the Commissioner to conclude that the 'present level of resources dedicated to biodiversity is inadequate for the magnitude of the task at hand' (CESD 1998: 4–11). Even the federal government's own Report to the Biodiversity Convention acknowledged that the eroding national scientific and monitoring capacity will slow Canada's implementation effort (Canada 1998).

Conclusions

The above discussion has identified a sampling of federal actions in support of sustainable development. As the Brundtland Report argued 'sustainable development is a process of change in which the exploitation of resources, the direction of investments, the orientation of technological development and institutional change' move in harmony over the long term (WCED 1987: 46). The pace of change at the federal level in Canada over the 1990s was constrained by three factors related to the structural, institutional, and political-ideological variables outlined in the introduction. All three factors contributed to the conflictual nature of environmental policy, which impacts directly on efforts to further sustainable development.

First, the economic recession in the early-to-mid 1990s allowed for the re-emergence of the traditional economic growth agenda. In the late 1980s and early 1990s, a wave of public concern about the environment combined with economic prosperity and the emergence of sustainable development as a public policy paradigm to soften the confrontational nature of environmental politics (Doern and Conway 1994). The focus on employment, productivity, and competitiveness during and after the early-to-mid 1990s' recession allowed industry and resource departments to slip back into the mode of portraying environmental protection as a job killer. Despite its articulation of sustainable development as the convergence of environmental and economic agendas, the Liberal government has been slow to force this convergence. Moreover, its determination to eliminate its deficit has dramatically reduced programme spending and shaved the size of the public service. The provinces have followed suit in a generalized attack on public-sector deficits. Because of the increased dependence upon the private sector to create badly needed jobs, governments have been reluctant to force environmental measures upon industry, or to compel departments to converge environment and economy goals. As a consequence, environmental policy goals are often secondary to economic concerns.

Often the dispute is less about the goals than the instruments, with environmentalists calling for stronger formal controls and industrialists seeking greater use of voluntary and non-regulatory initiatives. Complicating this discord is the government's diminishing capacity to develop effective regulations as a result of cuts to its scientific, policy analysis, and information collection capability. Despite the growth of its knowledge-based economy, Canada's continued reliance on natural-resource exploitation has meant that domestic sustainable development debates have sometimes taken on the character of international conflicts. For example, in the climate change case, the domestic fossil-fuel industry and the governments of the oil, coal, and gas-producing provinces have mirrored the role played internationally by the global fossil-fuel industry and the OPEC governments in leading the attack on the Rio commitments (Dotto 1999). There are signs in 1999, however, that this parallel is eroding as firms begin to take the challenge of climate change seriously (*Calgary Sun* 1999).

Second, there has been a palpable lack of political leadership by Prime Minister Chretien and a paucity of political will by the cabinet in the face of apparent declining public interest and hostility from the right-wing media. Chretien was essentially 'missing in action' on the sustainable development file from 1993 until his eleventh hour entry into the climate change debate in October 1997, just before Kyoto. Paul Martin, the Minister of Finance, who was Liberal environment critic during the Green Plan era, and author of the 'Creating Opportunity' chapter on the environment and sustainable development, has essentially been hijacked by the deficit fight and his 'progressive' credentials on this issue have been left in tatters. The conservative wing of cabinet has dominated during the Liberals' years in power and has been reluctant to allow the environmental and social dimensions of the sustainable development equation to rise to a level equal to the economic side, despite the rhetorical commitment of many of their government's documents. The enervating impact of the conflicts over sustainable development issues within cabinet and between departments has sapped the political will to lead, particularly if it means challenging the major provinces or powerful industrial sectors.

Economic interests and some provincial governments have been upset by the federal government's alleged penchant for taking leadership positions on international issues and have pressured the federal government to slide back into the pack of nations and only agree to move when there is an international consensus. This position bothers many in the Liberal party, and many Canadians in general, who were proud of the reputation Canada has built up over the years for leadership on sustainable development issues. Generating policy consensus amongst Canadian governments is extremely difficult on most issues, and this is particularly true for sustainable development issues that intersect economic, social and environmental policy. Waiting for consensus is often equivalent to giving a veto to the lowest common denominator.

The rightward shift in the Canadian ideological mood has had an effect on the Liberals' willingness to use the state to catalyse social change. The election of a right-wing official opposition party in Parliament in 1997, the emergence of two of the most right-wing provincial governments in Canadian political history in Alberta and Ontario, and the purchase of a major newspaper chain by right-wing financier Conrad Black, has contributed to an anti-regulation, anti-tax, anti-state intervention ideological mood which has constrained state action at both levels. These attitudinal shifts combined with the overall downsizing of government as a result of the deficit fight, has resulted in a diminution in federal capacity to initiate and implement sustainable development.

A third factor constraining the implementation of sustainable development has been the shift in the balance of power toward the provinces since the narrow federalist victory in the October 1995 Quebec referendum. Since then, the federal government has shifted powers to the provinces in an attempt to prove to Quebecois that 'federalism is flexible.' Quebec's tactics have not gone unnoticed by other regional politicians, and senior politicians from British Columbia and Alberta have muttered darkly about their provinces separating over sustainable development disputes in the salmon fishery and climate change areas. These bizarre antics aside, the reality of significant provincial powers over the economy and the environment has made it increasingly difficult for the federal government to speak for the country in international fora or even to develop policies. With some rare exceptions, provincial governments have shown little leadership in implementing sustainable development initiatives.[11] Indeed, provincial opposition has blocked further action on endangered species and acid rain and Alberta has threatened to unilaterally block collective action on climate change. The federal government's reluctance to use its fiscal and tax-policy tools to support sustainable development, combined with its diminished scientific capacity and aversion to further regulation has meant that it is increasingly incapable of leading.

Environmentalists fear that the January 1998 'Canada-Wide Accord on Environmental Harmonization' signed by the provinces, territories, and the federal government, marks the beginning of a new period of decline in national standards of environmental protection. They see the Accord as an attempt by the federal government to cope with its own diminished capacity by transferring environmental responsibilities to the provinces. The Parliamentary Standing Committee on Environment and Sustainable Development shares these concerns, given that the provinces have also massively reduced their administrative capacity, often even more so than the federal government (Canada 1997d). The Commissioner's 1999 Report included a chapter that assessed a number of bilateral federal–provincial environmental protection agreements that were in effect prior to the Accord. The chapter outlined a litany of design and implementation problems associated with the management of the early agreements and outlined a series of recommendations for improvement (CESD 1999).

The federal government defends the Accord by arguing that it is simply a framework under which governments can better co-ordinate their efforts to address environmental problems. The vehemence of the environmental groups' reactions indicates the level to which they distrust both the motivations and the capabilities of most provincial governments. Ironically, the

---

[11] For a veritable catalogue of actions taken since 1995 to roll back environmental protection and reduce government capacity by the right-wing Conservative government of Canada's largest province of Ontario, see Canadian Institute for Environmental Law and Policy (1998). These cuts and reductions are directed at the traditional range of environmental protection regulations as well as sustainable development related activities in the municipal planning and natural resource development areas.

separatist government of Quebec refused to sign the Accord, arguing that it did not go far enough in the process of decentralization.

This chapter has focused on the broad steering strategies and policies developed by the federal government to address Canada's UNCED commitments. Canada cannot yet claim to be effectively implementing either the climate change or biodiversity conventions, and the record is mixed on the remainder of the Agenda 21 ledger. Canadian formulations of sustainable development have focused on the environment–economy relationship with scant attention paid to the social dimension or equity. The best that can be said is that Canada continues to lurch along—with some advances and some setbacks—far from an ideal state, but with some renewed momentum due to the mandated requirement that federal departments develop and implement sustainable development strategies. The creation of a new Parliamentary official, independent of the executive branch, to oversee this process is an important development. Still, it will take several years to determine the degree to which this institutionalized process has changed politics and policy-making within the federal government. It is important to remember that the effort to implement sustainable development is a long-term project. The process to date has been a struggle.

There are, however, signs that the Liberal government is moving early in the new Century to re-engage the sustainable development challenge. The last half of the 1990s have seen strong economic growth, healthy job creation, economic surpluses in both federal and provincial budgets and the escalation of environmental issues up public opinion polls. In the last half of 1999, a strong and experienced Minister was appointed to the Environment portfolio, a co-ordinating committee of Deputy Ministers created a document outlining a sustainable development agenda for Canada, and the October Speech From the Throne included several positive references to sustainable development. In December 1999, the Commissioner of Environment and Sustainable Development released an 'expectations' document titled 'Moving Up the Learning Curve: The Second Generation of Sustainable Development Strategies' (CESD 1999b) which outlined the improvements in process and substance that the Commissioner expected to see in the 2000 departmental Sustainable Development Strategies. In early 2000, 29 departments and agencies are preparing their second Strategies for tabling in Parliament by Ministers by December.

However, the February 2000 budget was the most palpable sign that the Liberal government was willing to recommit resources to support sustainable development initiatives now that fiscal problems have been addressed. The Budget proposed to invest CAN$700 million over three years. Included were initiatives such as, CAN$210 million for green energy development and the Climate Change Action Fund, CAN$100 million for a new Sustainable Development Technology Fund, CAN$100 for a new Green Municipal Investment Fund, CAN$90 million for a National Strategy on Species at Risk, CAN$60 million for a new Canadian Foundation for Climate and Atmospheric Sciences, CAN$25 million for a new Green Municipal Enabling Fund, CAN$22 million for improved pollution enforcement, and CAN$9 million for work on sustainable development indicators (Canada 2000). The federal government also will change its procurement policy to purchase, where possible, renewable energy. It will also reduce the capital gains tax on donations of Ecologically Sensitive Lands. Several other budget initiatives related to children, innovation and international assistance, for example, will also contribute directly to sustainable development both in Canada and abroad.

4

Germany: Regulation and the Precautionary Principle

CHRISTIANE BEUERMANN

Reunification on 3 October 1990 was the most momentous political event of post-war German history. With the adoption of the accession treaty, the German Democratic Republic (GDR) joined the political and economic system of the Federal Republic of Germany (FRG). Looking back on the first decade of a unified Germany, it is apparent that the domestic policy challenges were significantly underestimated in the initial period of enthusiasm following the 'silent revolution' which swept the GDR during 1989. Ten years on, the economic problems have still not been resolved, with unemployment rates averaging 19.5 per cent in the Eastern areas. Nor has social integration been achieved. Behind the defeat of the Christian Democrat/Free Democrat coalition government at the general elections in September 1998, after sixteen years of rule, lay a widespread belief that Germany required significant political and social reform across a range of policy areas.

Germany is a federal republic with sixteen federal states ('*Bundesländer*', eleven West German and five East German), and more than 14,000 municipalities. Federal elections to parliament every four years are complemented by elections to the parliaments of the *Bundesländer* and to municipal councils. After the 1998 election the Social Democrats, in coalition with Bündnis 90/the Greens formed the national government. The economic system is described as a 'social market economy' which emerged in 1947 to fight the devastation of World War II by combining the market mechanism with social elements. The concept was successfully implemented, resulting in the German post-war economic boom (*Wirtschaftswunder*).

A number of basic elements provide the background to German engagement with sustainable development, including high population density, a high degree of industrialization, a large proportion of environmentally problematic industries, intensely industrialized agriculture, a dense transport network, and high and increasing traffic volumes (Jänicke and Weidner 1997*a*: 133). For example, average population density is 228 persons per square kilometre—one of the highest in Europe. Fifty-eight per cent of the population live in municipalities with more than 20,000 inhabitants (data for 1994, Statistisches Bundesamt 1996). With respect to land usage, 55 per cent is devoted to agriculture and 29 per cent is covered by forests. Buildings/open space and transport account for less than 6 per cent each, water resources for less than 3 per cent, and industrial space and recreation each for less than 1 per cent. The typical German landscape is a centuries' old man-made landscape. Due to the high population density, competition for land use is increasing. For example, between 70 and 120 hectares of countryside per day (depending on source, e.g. BMU 1998*a*) is being paved over for commercial, residential, and transport purposes. This puts a particular burden on biodiversity, as a considerable number of species are endangered or already extinct. Germany is a 'high production and consumption country': GDP is the third highest in the world (behind the US and Japan). Foreign trade is of particular relevance: in 1994, 28 per cent of the German value added resulted from exports. At the same time, imports of resources and goods are significant. Furthermore, Germans are 'world champions' in tourism abroad, and every second German owns a car. In 1995 total primary energy consumption was 14,191 PJ, resulting in 895 million tons of CO_2 emissions. Per capita CO_2 emissions in 1995 were 10.9 tons. At the point of reunification (1990) per capita emissions amounted to 12.8 tons of CO_2 in the former FRG and 18.6 tons of CO_2 in the former GDR, reflecting the outdated capital stock in the East.

German Environmental Policy

There is a comparatively long tradition of environmental policy in Germany. Initially the focus was on air and water pollution and related health impacts (Wallace 1995: 63).[1] Political interest in environmental issues has grown considerably since the 1960s. In the FRG during the 1980s there was a relative decoupling of economic development from energy consumption and pollutant emissions (BMU 1994*a*). In contrast, the GDR was increasingly faced with acute environmental problems. Article 34 of the accession treaty obliged the federal government to undertake significant efforts to increase environmental standards in the former GDR. Compared with many other

---

[1] A historical review of German environmental policy since 1900 is provided, e.g. in Wey 1982.

developed countries German environmental policy has achieved considerable success (OECD 1993*b*).

Environmental policy was initially introduced as an 'insider initiative' by
the Social Democratic government, without significant pressure from forces
outside parliament.[2] It was largely stimulated by political developments
abroad, particularly preparations for the 1972 Stockholm Conference on the
Human Environment. By 1974 the basic organizational, political, and legal
framework for environmental policy had been established. Institutions such
as the Federal Environmental Agency (*Umweltbundesamt*, UBA) and the
German Council of Environmental Experts (*Rat von Sachverständigen für
Umweltfragen*, SRU) had been modelled on US experience. But the worldwide
recession which followed the oil crisis of 1974/5 led to a revision of political priorities and to a relative stagnation in environmental policy. Some significant pieces of environmental legislation were passed but implementation
was inadequate. In response, the ecological grass roots and the green movement became better organized. As public environmental awareness rose
steadily in the second half of the 1970s, the environment re-emerged as a
significant political issue. The Green Party was founded at the end of the
1970s. Gaining representatives first in *Bundesländer* elections, it entered the
federal parliament in 1983. Fifteen years later, the Greens have become
junior coalition partners in the federal government.

In response to the early successes of the Greens the established political
parties initiated a greening of their own party programmes. Following the
Chernobyl nuclear catastrophe, criticism of the government's reactions and
of the structure of German environmental policy generally sharpened. In
1986 the Federal Ministry for the Environment, Nature Conservation, and
Reactor Safety (*Bundesministerium für Umwelt, Naturschutz und Reaktorsicher-
heit*, BMU) was established in order to increase the attention devoted to
environmental issues in governmental decision-making processes and to
further cross-sectoral policy approaches. Yet the BMU remains one of the
smaller ministries in terms of staff and budget (Beuermann and Jäger 1996),
and critics are worried that it has been unable to defend environmental interests against stronger ministries such Finance, Economics, Transport, and
Agriculture.

In terms of policy style and principles, until the 1960s the German
approach was largely characterized by regulation and hierarchy (Dyson
1982). A rather inflexible perspective and a conventional attitude towards
regulation are still prevalent (Jänicke and Weidner 1997*b*: 140), although
a trend towards consensus building is now evident. Another important

---

[2] When not otherwise mentioned, the description of German environmental policy
follows Müller (1986), Simonis (1991), Weidner (1995), and Jänicke and Weidner (1997).

characteristic of German policy-making is the predominance of 'incremental change' (Katzenstein 1987). Aspects of Germany's institutional arrangements and political culture (such as coalition governments, co-operative federalism, and the wide range of parapublic institutions) have encouraged a dense network of interdependencies which inhibit all actors—including the federal government—from taking bold steps in new directions. In response to environmental risks, however, discrete jumps in policy development have been forthcoming (Cavender Bares 1993). Particularly important was the adoption of the precautionary, polluter-pays, and co-operation principles as the basic elements of German environmental policy in the first environment programme in 1971. Implementation of these principles focused on law-based command-and-control policy (Jänicke and Weidner 1997a: 139). However, a general implementation gap (*Vollzugsdefizit*) soon emerged (Wey 1982: 214 ff.). The regulatory approach is also reflected in the dominance of lawyers throughout the environmental administration. A good example of this approach is to be found in the *Bundesimmissionsschutzgesetz*, a complex law that regulates standards for several sources of air pollution and prescribes adoption of the best available technologies. Yet such an approach is often criticized for having delayed the diffusion of technological innovation.

The German Road to Rio

In contrast to the situation in many other countries, the 1987 report of the World Commission on Environment and Development (WCED) received little attention in Germany.[3] Preparatory drafts and the final Commission report were reviewed and heavily criticized by the environmental administration. Indeed, BMU gave the impression that this was an issue of minor importance for the federal government. The aim of sustainable development and the report as a whole were perceived to represent a step back from what had already been achieved through the introduction of the precautionary principle and subsequent regulatory enactments. Practical experience had already demonstrated the difficulty of integrating precaution into day-to-day politics—particularly in environmentally crucial sectors. Therefore, an agreement on 'integrating' economic, ecological, and social concerns in decision-making, rather than on 'precaution' as the major political guiding

---

[3] At that time, however, 'sustainability' was not new in Germany. Historically, comparable ideas have origins in German forestry management practices of earlier centuries.

principle, was judged to be a political 'fudge' resulting from international negotiations that might weaken the German domestic commitment to environmental protection (Müller 1997). Acceptance of sustainable development might undermine the legitimation of preventative action under uncertainty, which had been won with the precautionary principle.

Over the following years the Brundtland Report was not discussed intensively. Prior to the United Nations Conference on Environment and Development (UNCED) the term 'sustainable development' was sometimes invoked as a slogan in parliament, particularly in connection with tropical deforestation and climate change (Beuermann and Burdick 1997). 'Sustainable development' was sometimes cited in connection with a general criticism of the government's climate and development policy. Interpretations of sustainable development offered by the federal government in response to formal requests by the opposition remained rather vague and were often complemented by an endorsement of the precautionary principle (Deutscher Bundestag 1988, 1989, 1992a).

Climate change was the dominant issue during German preparation for UNCED. It appeared relatively congruent with the traditional media-specific approach to environmental policy, and with the corresponding organization of the environmental administration. Given this domestic political focus, the public perceived UNCED as the 'Climate Summit'. During preparations for UNCED, only very specific areas of Agenda 21 were pushed by the federal government, in particular chapters 7 and 28 addressing human settlements and local authorities. To stress the relevance of the local level for implementing the issues negotiated at UNCED, a conference on municipal environmental protection was held in Berlin in February 1992, which adopted a resolution on 'worldwide co-operation on the environmentally sound development of cities' (BMU 1992b). Another element of the pre-Rio activities was the establishment of the 'National Committee' in 1991 to ensure the participation of all major groups in the preparation phase.

Overall, the period leading from Brundtland to Rio was characterized by the concentration of attention on domestic politics due to the unexpected political developments in the GDR, unification in 1990, and the subsequent political, economic, and social challenges.

Basic Government Response to UNCED

The BMU and the Federal Ministry for Economic Co-operation and Development (*Bundesministerium für Wirtschaftliche Zusammenarbeit und*

Entwicklung, BMZ) were jointly charged with co-ordinating the Rio follow-up. Significant responses to sustainable development can also be found in the Federal Ministry for Regional Planning, Building and Urban Development (BMBau, *Bundesministerium für Raumordnung, Bauwesen und Städtebau*). In 1994 the former Environment Minister was placed in charge of BMBau, where he took up issues from his previous post and as a former CSD chairman. The German Report to the Habitat II conference in Istanbul in June 1996 was characterized by a consistent reflection on the implications of sustainable development for urban issues (BMBau 1996; Töpfer 1996).

The Rio documents, including the full text of Agenda 21, were translated and published by BMU. However, the publication of Agenda 21 was not complemented by a major public education campaign. A more open discussion on Agenda 21 and sustainability was initiated somewhat later when the two expert councils (SRU, WBGU) issued a number of reports. Publication of the book *Sustainable Germany* by prominent NGOs in 1995 (BUND and Misereor 1995) probably had the most significant impact in stimulating public debate on sustainable development.

An agreed German translation of the term sustainable development does not yet exist. For example, four different translations are applied in legal texts of the European Union (EU) (Haigh 1996). One of these translations, *dauerhaft* (durable; long-lasting), was also used in translating *Our Common Future* (Brundtland and Hauff 1987). Criticism of this rendition is that it is too closely associated with the preservation of what already exists. Two other translations (*nachhaltig, zukunftsfähig*) are increasingly found in almost every context of public life, for example advertising. *Nachhaltig* means 'lasting', 'to have a strong, deep effect'. The BMU uses this translation in most official documents—for example, in the German translation of Agenda 21. However, this usage is also disputed. According to the SRU, the environmental connotation is not obvious. Moreover, it has a sense of 'insistent' and 'intensive' development (SRU 1994: 46). *Zukunftsfähig*—invented in 1991 by Simonis (Simonis 1991), and promoted by BUND and Misereor (1995)—is a very broad term, also without an explicit environmental connotation—but it does stress the future-oriented dimensions of sustainable development. It appears that in many cases the term sustainable development is used for green or social labelling or as a non-committal slogan (SRU 1996). As both *nachhaltig* and *zukunftsfähig* have become fashionable, there is a danger of diluting the use of the term sustainability to a commonplace expression in public discussion.

Basic Understanding of 'Sustainability'

In August 1994 the federal government approved the report 'Environment 1994—Policy for a Sustainable Development' (BMU 1994*a*). It was submitted together with the National Report (a completed questionnaire) in advance of the third session of the CSD held in April 1995 in New York (BMU/BMZ 1994). The 1996 CSD Report also took the form of a completed questionnaire (BMU/BMZ 1995). These reports provide basic information on the co-ordination of sustainable development activities in Germany, the participation of major groups, and the implementation of measures specified in the sectoral chapters of A21.

The report 'Environment 1994' identifies four models for German environment policy that the German government considered complementary, of which sustainable development is one. There, it is defined as 'a concept that harmonizes the improvement of social and economic living conditions of people with the long-term safeguarding of the natural environment'. The other models are:

- the preservation of 'Creation', stressing Christian tradition and responsibility;
- the ecologically responsible social market economy, which emphasizes the implementation of the precautionary principle; and
- the idea of common responsibility, which stresses the need to alter societal norms and values, but also 'international solidarity'.

The 1994 report is almost exclusively a description of the successes of German environmental policy. In the government's opinion, the report presents Germany's environmental strategy, as shaped by the decisions of UNCED and the EU Fifth Environment Action Plan (5EAP) (BMU/BMZ 1994). The official position was that existing environmental and development policy was to a large extent compatible with the aims of Agenda 21 (BMU/BMZ 1994; BMU 1994a). Because of the early introduction of the precautionary principle, domestic successes in raising air and water quality standards, as well as Germany's perceived position as an international frontrunner in the environmental field, the conviction (post-UNCED) has been that a reorientation of German environmental policy to stimulate a sustainability transition is not necessary. Consequently no effort was put into developing a national environmental policy plan or a sustainable development plan. Moreover, the Environment Minister openly expressed opposition to the idea, because of the negative experiences with national planning in the former GDR.

In its progress report on the implementation of the 5EAP the EU Commission concluded that Germany did not have a national sustainable development strategy at all (European Commission 1995). Regarding the precautionary principle, a general implementation gap has been observed (Weidner 1995). Moreover, the SRU considers the government's confidence in the existing policy matrix to be little more than rhetoric (SRU 1996).

The government response did become more pro-active after the publication of the volume *Sustainable Germany* in 1995 by prominent German NGOs (BUND and Misereor 1995). This book discussed the transition towards sustainability in Germany, proposed policies and targets, and argued that progress could not be achieved by technological measures alone, but would also require broader societal shifts, institutional adjustments, and lifestyle changes. The editors launched an intensive campaign involving their regional and local offices to put sustainability on the public agenda. This first major campaign received an enormous response from the public, and appears to have marked a new trend in German engagement with Agenda 21. NGOs and others subsequently pushed continuously for the preparation of a national plan (e.g. Jänicke and Weidner 1997b; Hustedt 1999).

In February 1997 the federal government adopted the German report for the UN Special Assembly (UNGASS) entitled 'Transition Towards Sustainable Development in Germany' (BMU 1997a). The report contained three parts: an official interpretation of sustainable development; an assessment of environment protection across different environmental media; and a description of strategies to attain sustainable development. Sectors dealt with were the economy, energy supply, transport, agriculture, forestry, fisheries, urban and spatial planning, tourism, health, research and development, environmental education, international environmental co-operation, development co-operation, public administration, and the armed forces.

As in the 1994 report the government continued to stress that the core of the 'sustainability postulate' was the inseparable unity of ecology, economy and social security. It noted that since they are starting from very different circumstances, the sustainability transition in the industrialized countries will differ from that of developing countries. According to the report, common criteria for sustainable development are that:

- the use of renewable resources (forests, stock of fish, etc.) must not in the long run exceed their regenerative capacity;
- the use of non-renewable resources (fossil fuels, etc.) must not in the long run exceed possible substitution (e.g. replacement of fossil fuels by hydrogen from solar electrolysis); and
- the release of substances and energy must not in the long run exceed the adaptive capacity of the natural environment (BMU 1997a).

Though the importance of the integration of environmental considerations into all areas of policy and life is highlighted in the Minister's foreword, any major new strategic initiative to secure the integration of social, economic and ecological factors in decision-making is absent. Later in 1997 the

Environment Minister announced that a national policy programme would be carried out in close co-operation with the major groups represented in the National Committee.

In June 1997 a second study entitled *Sustainable Germany (Nachhaltiges Deutschland)* was published by the UBA (Storm 1997). 'Sustainable development' was interpreted as a combination of the integration of economic, social, and ecological concerns with the strict application of the precautionary principle—as laid down, for example, in the Rio Declaration. Recalling 25 years of successful environmental policy, and political leadership on climate policy in the run-up to Rio, the government was urged to follow a vigorous approach so as to maintain international credibility (Storm 1997: 15). In line with recommendations of the Enquete Commission 'Man and Environment' (see below), targets for environmental quality were developed on the basis of three scenarios ('status quo', 'efficiency gains', and 'structural change/awareness raising') for the following areas: energy, mobility, food production, management of material flows, consumption patterns, policy instruments, and indicators.

The extraordinary character of this study is illustrated by a—to some extent tendentious—'anonymous insider report' on its preparation published in the Greenpeace magazine (Greenpeace 1997). Normally the UBA does not carry out uncommissioned studies. But because of frustrating experiences with interministerial co-ordination and discontent with the role of the BMU, UBA staff started work on a sustainable development strategy without informing BMU. On learning of this development, BMU's reaction was astonishment at such 'audacity' from a subordinate level. Given the irritation in BMU, the study was completed only because of the strong commitment from high level UBA staff including its president. The final UBA report was submitted directly to the Environment Minister in May 1996 with a covering letter from the UBA president. In an unusual practice a single joint working group was set up to discuss the document, probably to avoid conflictual interactions between BMU and UBA departments. Positive feedback was combined with dire warnings over the troubles that publication would cause other ministries. UBA was therefore obliged to keep the report strictly confidential. Only with the approach of UNGASS was the Environment Minister convinced by some BMU staff (against the wishes of powerful departments within BMU) that a more far-reaching report was required to complement the status report (BMU 1997a) since some countries had prepared demanding national plans.

Activities during 1997–8 focused on the organization of a new 'dialogue process' with major groups. Finally, in 1998 a draft environmental policy priority programme was published (BMU 1998b). Its general theme was to build on the high level of environmental protection already achieved, and to develop this further towards sustainability. Proposing quantified targets for five priority areas (the atmosphere, ecosystems, resources, health, and mobility) and a simplified system of indicators for sustainable development—so that the public could monitor progress—it went beyond previous reports issued by BMU. Published in draft form, however, the priority programme has not passed through the complex process of interministerial co-ordination, and thus it is not an officially agreed policy of the government.

Pattern of Institutional Engagement

Reports to the Commission on Sustainable Development (CSD) and other documents are prepared by BMU and BMZ. They emerge through close consultations with the Chancellor's Office and other federal ministries. Interministerial co-ordination with working groups is the established procedure as regards cross-sectoral issues and is not a particularly new institutional development.

Due to the non-legally binding character of Agenda 21, a formal commitment to implement this document has not been institutionalized. An informal commitment, however, is expressed in official statements and reports. Reflecting the high priority of environment issues in Germany—rather than any specific commitment to sustainable development—the German Constitution (Grundgesetz, GG) was amended in 1994 to include the protection of the environment as a national goal (Art 20a GG). In its 1997 report, however, BMU explicitly argues that this amendment has successfully anchored sustainable development in the German Constitution. Therefore, it would appear that 'the protection of the environment' is not just a task for environmental policy-makers, but a general cross-cutting policy objective to be addressed by all tiers of government.

A national committee had already been founded in June 1991 by the Federal Chancellor to involve major groups in preparations for UNCED. Participants originally included thirty-five representatives from environment and development policy organizations, science and research institutes, industry and commerce, trade unions, churches, agriculture, women's and youth organizations, Bundesländer and local governments, the German Parliament, and the political parties. Meetings took place two or three times a year and were chaired by the Environment Minister. Yet the significance of the Committee was limited, and high-level representatives of the major groups did not attend its meetings. There have been several attempts to reorganize the committee (BMU 1996a) with the general aim of ensuring greater policy relevance, wider participation of relevant groups, and improved inputs from parliamentarians.

In 1996 the Environment Minister launched a new initiative to reanimate social participation in the sustainable development process. Six working groups were established on climate, the balance of nature, resources, human health, environmentally friendly mobility, and environmental ethics respectively. At regular meetings representatives of major groups with interests in the specific issues discussed their perceptions of sustainability and its implications for future policy. In June 1997 the results were published and discussed in a public workshop (BMU 1997b). The workshop was attended by high level officials from industrial associations, trade unions, and environmental NGOs. In a podium discussion these representatives expressed their assessment of the operation of the working groups. Surprisingly, several of the representatives had only a vague idea of what sustainable development was intended to imply.[4] Particularly controversial were discussions in the working groups on climate protection and environment-friendly mobility. The working group reports show open dissension on a number of issues, mainly between industry and other major groups. Follow-up work resulted in the preparation of the 1998 draft environmental policy priority programme described above.

Following the two 'successful' Climate Enquete Commissions, the parliamentary Enquete Commission 'Protection of Man and the Environment' was established in February 1992 (Deutscher Bundestag 1992b).[5] At the outset this Commission was not explicitly working on sustainable development. Concerning itself first with the ecological effects of material flows, the Commission later extended its perspective to include social and economic dimensions. At this point, the topic of 'sustainable development' entered the discussion and gradually became the dominant theme of the Commission's work. Although the final report dealt with issues on a rather abstract level, the Commission has contributed important work on the necessity of cross-party compromise to achieve a common interpretation of

---

[4] Personal observation at a BMU workshop on 'steps towards sustainable development' in Bonn, June 1997.

[5] Enquete Commissions are composed of politicians and scientific experts providing the opportunity for dialogue and transfer of information. The Commissions have the potential to be the most important platform for discussions about the transformation of science into political action.

sustainable development (SRU 1996). Dissolved as planned at the end of the 1994 legislative period, it was reinstated in 1995 with the mandate of working out approaches to make sustainable development operational (Deutscher Bundestag 1995). The Commission was given the task of preparing a national ecological action plan. Its interim report 'Concept Sustainability' (Enquete Kommission 1997) focused on how to apply the model of sustainability to policy in the areas of 'soil' and 'construction and housing'. The report also highlights the relevance of social innovation and technical advance, particularly emphasizing the importance of the latter for the sustainability transition.

The Council of Environmental Experts (*Rat von Sachverständigen für Umweltfragen*, SRU) was first established in 1971. SRU publishes reports every two years. It focused on the concept and implementation of sustainable development in its 1994, 1996, and 1998 reports. In 1992, the 'Scientific Advisory Council of the Federal Government on Global Environmental Changes' (*Wissenschaftlicher Beirat der Bundesregierung Globale Umweltänderungen*, WBGU) was established—in recognition both of the relevance of global issues for German society, and the need for specific advice. From the outset the Council focused on global change as a whole, systematically analysing the different types of global change (e.g. WBGU 1993). The Council publishes the results of its work annually. The activities of both these advisory councils has continued to add momentum to the sustainability discussion.

Measurement and Monitoring

Concerning the measurement and monitoring of progress towards sustainable development, the government points to the significance of the existing system of environmental reporting. Since 1984 the Federal Environmental Agency has published a biannual report—'Information on the environment'. Other sources of data are reports by the Federal Agency for Nature Conservation (*Bundesamt für Naturschutz*, BfN), the Federal Agency for Protection from Radiation, as well as the environment report of the BMU. The further development of environmental indicators follows the work and recommendations of the OECD. In mid-1997 UBA proposed the establishment of a system of indicators stressing the internationally agreed set of Driving Force–State-Response indicators for sustainable development (DSR) developed by the CSD. The German government has participated in testing this indicator set, and has called for a broad national discussion on sustainable development indicators (BMU 1997a).[6] In a book entitled *The Price of Survival* (Merkel 1997), the former Environment Minister Angela Merkel suggested four themes (ecosystems, energy use, economic life cycles, human health) around which indicators have been proposed, including a few 'headline' indicators for each theme. These have become the basis of the system proposed in the 1998 draft environmental policy priority programme. One of the suggestions of that programme is to identify a small number of lead indicators—the 'Environmental Barometer'—to present information in a form that is readily accessible to the general public (BMU 1998b). [7]

International Responses and Obligations

The German government acknowledges the particular responsibility of industrialized countries to decrease their resource consumption (BMU 1997a). Arguing that it is not just the environment but economic structures and practices around the world that are being affected by 'globalization', the government supports political strategies to further sustainable development.

Based on its past achievements Germany perceives its position in international environmental negotiations as a 'frontrunner', pushing for demanding policies and targets and providing a good example to others. With its 25 per cent CO_2-reduction target and its advocacy of strict targets and timetables for industrialized countries in the negotiations around the Kyoto Protocol in December 1997, Germany helped propel climate change negotiations forward (Fermann 1997b). There is much less momentum behind the themes of Agenda 21 and biodiversity.

BMZ officials present sustainable development as being compatible with recent efforts to 'modernize' German development co-operation—for example, with the introduction of obligatory environmental impact assessments. In a status report on German development policy five years after Rio (BMZ 1997a), BMZ proposes including sustainable development in its policy dialogues with partner countries. In addition, it has suggested including sustainable development as a basic principle for the internal phase of priority setting, for example to support specific projects on the

---

[6] Reports on the German testing phase are provided at http://www.un.org/esa/sustdev/indi4de.htm

[7] Since 1989, the Federal Statistical Office has been continuously working on the concept of an environmental accounting system aiming at the integration of the changes in natural capital into the economic accounting system. This accounting system will cover emissions, consumption of material and energy as well as the use of soil, etc.

protection of the environment and resources (tropical forests, combating desertification).

In quantitative terms, however, the acknowledged 'responsibility of the North' is still not being adequately addressed. While the international community has repeatedly endorsed the official development assistance (ODA) target of 0.7 per cent of the GNP, German ODA has steadily fallen since 1992, reaching 0.28 per cent of GNP in 1996—the lowest figure ever. Because of continuing budgetary difficulties (meeting the Maastricht criteria, reunification related financial transfers to East Germany, and so on) an increase of ODA is not to be expected in the near future. However, the downward trend was at least arrested in the 1999 budget (Eid 1999).

Relationships with Other Actors

The tasks of different governmental levels are clearly defined in the German Constitution according to the subsidiarity principle. The responsibility for specific aspects of sustainable development is therefore split between governmental levels. For example, the federal government is responsible for framework legislation and strategic policies, while more specific regulations have to be adopted and implemented by the *Bundesländer*. In principle municipalities enjoy rights to substantial autonomy. Within the federal government there is a formalized procedure stipulating how cross-cutting issues are to be treated. The competencies of the federal government and of the *Bundesländer* to initiate new legislation are also defined in the Constitution (Art. 70–72 GG). At the federal level, the *Bundesländer* are represented by the German *Bundesrat*. In specified classes of legislation the *Bundesrat* can block the government, by frustrating its legislative agenda—particularly if the majority of *Bundesländer* are governed by a party which is in opposition at the federal level. In that case a complex process of reworking the proposals starts (Article 77 GG) (Böhmer-Christiansen and Skea 1991). Strategies, policies, and measures to implement sustainable development have been discussed within the existing hierarchical structure. For example, the implementation of Agenda 21 at the local level (LA 21) has only been minimally supported by the federal government on the basis of the municipalities' right to autonomy.[8]

Government efforts to mobilize 'major stakeholders' has focused on the establishment of the National Committee and on the dialogue process

---

[8] LA 21 in Germany is discussed in detail in Beuermann (1998).

described above.[9] Apart from official participation in the National Committee, some NGO activities are funded by BMU. Prior to UNCED an umbrella organization of environment and development NGOs 'Forum Umwelt und Entwicklung' was established. It still plays a crucial role in assessing the government's follow-up to UNCED. The forum is networking with other internationally active NGOs and observes international negotiations. It has been suggested that both BMU and BMZ have an interest in securing a moderate and co-ordinated input from NGOs in order to back their own positions in inter-ministerial bargaining (Unmüßig 1995).

The federal government explicitly supports the position of the large industrial associations that—wherever possible—measures for sustainable development should be identified and implemented by the different actors themselves. Various industrial branches have, for example, offered to contribute to solving climate change and ozone depletion by making voluntary commitments. The government has accepted that this approach is likely to prove most effective—particularly with respect to CO_2 reductions. A widespread perception of fiscal solutions among non-governmental actors, particularly industry, is that the main objective is to generate additional non-earmarked revenue. And the primary motivation for the voluntary agreement to reduce CO_2 emissions was the consensus reached with the government not to introduce an energy or CO_2 tax. Critics argue that voluntary agreements are insufficient substitutes for instruments such as taxes because they are not legally binding (Kristof and Ramesohl 1997).

Sustainable Production and Consumption

Sustainable production and consumption has not been comprehensively addressed as an issue in its own right by the German government. In its report on the Rio conference (BMU 1992a), BMU devoted only a short section to 'changing consumption patterns'. It particularly emphasized the provision of consumer information, for example through eco-labelling, as a supplement to regulatory approaches because of Germany's positive experiences with the 'Blue Environment Angel' labelling scheme.

In 1994 a general statement on the importance of policies and measures to change production and consumption patterns in a number of different policy sectors was included in the above-mentioned report 'Environment

---

[9] Trade unions, churches, and other stakeholders also started discussions on sustainable development but these are not covered here.

1994'. Addressing this issue more explicitly was perceived as an important step for the continuation of German precautionary environmental policy. In this regard the reduction of waste, increased producer responsibility, the introduction of environmentally sound and efficient technologies, as well as changes in patterns of mobility, energy use, and leisure were seen as being particularly important.

Further information can be found in the 1997 report (BMU 1997a) under the specific sections on transportation, tourism, environmental education, and so on. However, this essentially focuses on existing approaches. New strategies and measures have not been developed. Indeed measures discussed earlier have not been implemented. This is most obvious in the transport sector, where policies to reduce traffic, encourage environment-friendly changes in modal split, increase the efficiency of motor vehicles, and improve public information are presented as essential to build a more sustainable transport system. In practice, however, little has been done to implement such changes.

The issues of waste and energy consumption are obviously of relevance to the transformation of production patterns. The first topic was addressed by the 1996 Closed Substance Cycle and Waste Management Act (*Kreislaufwirtschaftsgesetz*). By the end of 1998, CO_2 emissions from fossil combustion had fallen by approximately 13 per cent compared to 1990 levels. From a sectoral perspective, road transport emissions grew by 11 per cent. But this was eclipsed by a reduction of emissions from electricity generation, industrial energy generation, and light industry and services. Residential emissions have remained largely constant since 1990 (Schiffer 1999: 155). Significant strategic innovations such as an energy/CO_2 tax had not been implemented before the change of government in 1998. The implementation of an ecological tax reform has been agreed as a priority task by the Social Democratic and Green government, and was initiated on 1 April 1999. So far, Germany has not succeeded in its attempts to achieve an EU-wide consensus on the implementation of a CO_2 tax.

German Climate Change Policy

Public interest in climate change was initially spurred by a report of the German Physical Society (DPG) in 1986. The press covered the issue extensively—for example the cover of the political magazine *Der Spiegel* showed the cathedral in Cologne half submerged under water. Discussion in the Federal Cabinet, the German Bundestag and the German Bundesrat was followed by the establishment of the Enquete Commission *Vorsorge zum Schutz der Erdatmosphäre* (Preventive Measures to Protect the Earth's Atmosphere) in October 1987. Following the Enquete Commission's work, climate change policy emerged on the ministerial agenda in early 1990. The Chancellor requested BMU to prepare a Cabinet decision for a CO_2 reduction target. Armed with this mandate BMU worked for four months on a feasibility study which concluded that a reduction of CO_2 emissions of 30.5 per cent could be achieved. Thus a 25 per cent reduction seemed practical. In June 1990 the federal cabinet adopted the CO_2 reduction target of 25–30 per cent by the year 2005 based on 1987 levels. Prior to Rio, this target was reconfirmed several times (Beuermann and Jäger 1996).

Investigating the implementation of the target, an interministerial working group (*Interministerielle Arbeitsgruppe* (IMA)) under BMU supervision was established in June 1990. Members of several federal ministries were represented. The IMA initially developed a programme of thirty measures for the reduction of CO_2 emissions, and later extended this to a programme of 109 measures (BMU 1994c: 86–136). Moreover, potential reductions for greenhouse gases other than CO_2 were assessed for the first time. However, national targets for these gases were not adopted.

BMU commissioned two groups of scientific institutes to assess the effectiveness of these national measures. They concluded that the policies would lead to a CO_2 reduction of 15 to 17 per cent by the year 2005 (BMU 1997c: 2). Thus the domestic target would not be realized without additional measures. The IMA 'CO_2 reduction' was then mandated to consider further such measures in its fourth report. In contrast to the earlier rounds, this time the IMA went no further than to 'suggest' measures for consideration—a fact that reveals the inability of the group to achieve a consensus and the declining priority allocated to climate policy by the government (BMU 1997d). Though the Cabinet adopted the fourth report, little was to come of its recommendations. Domestically, however, climate change is not the main argument for changes to tax regimes. For example, discussion on the introduction of ecological tax reform focused more on the socio-economic effects (stimulation of employment) rather than primarily on the environmental benefits.

Because its policy initiatives are frequently at odds with the priorities of other ministries, BMU tries to compensate for its lack of clout by intense public relations activity (Müller 1990: 168). Moreover, international events and commitments are often invoked as arguments to push national policy forward. For example, both the Environment Minister and the Federal Chancellor played a leading role at UNCED (Loske 1996: 286). Therefore, Germany has been described as 'a leader in rendering climate change a top international political issue' (Fermann 1997b). This was apparent when Germany pushed for an early EU ratification of the FCCC—connecting its own ratification to the EU decision. Led by the Netherlands and Germany, six of the EU-12 countries attempted to link EU ratification to the introduction of a carbon/energy tax, a proposal which was heavily resisted by the UK (Bergesen et al. 1994: 20). In the end Germany ratified independently, as the forty-fifth party to the Convention, in order to speed up the entry into force of the FCCC (which required fifty ratifications). The EU ratified the treaty somewhat later, without any explicit connection to taxes, but 'minimizing the loss of face for proponents of the tax' (ibid.).

In the negotiations preparing the first COP, Germany again took a robust position—arguing that existing commitments under the FCCC were inadequate. Germany suggested they be strengthened at COP-1. The German position was that a protocol should be adopted or, at minimum, a mandate to negotiate such a protocol should be enacted—to establish binding limits for CO_2 emissions. Though the chances of adopting a protocol at COP-1 were small, Germany submitted a draft document, just before the deadline of 28 September 1994, in order to push the whole process forward.

COP-1 took place in Berlin from 28 March to 7 April 1995. The conference was followed intensively by the German media. The German government perceived COP-1 as a success, not least due to the negotiating tactics of the Environment Minister and the demanding address given by the German Chancellor Kohl. Kohl explicitly stressed the need for a protocol on greenhouse-gas emission reductions, and reiterated the German reduction goal (Oberthür and Ott 1995: 144). The main accomplishment of COP-1— the so-called Berlin Mandate—was negotiated in separate sub-groups representing different country interests. As the elected President of the Conference, the German Environment Minister moved from group to group to actively seek a compromise. On the whole, however, the public perceived the results as disappointing, considering the resources employed to organize such a big event.[10]

Following COP-1 climate policy has assumed a less prominent position. Yet Germany still took a vigorous position within the EU, urging more stringent national reductions and a 'single gas' approach. Despite the opposition of many countries, at the third meeting of the Ad Hoc Group on the Berlin Mandate (AGBM3), Germany (together with a group of other like-minded countries) proposed a 10 per cent reduction of CO_2 emissions by 2005, and a 15 to 20 per cent reduction by the year 2010. Finally, to achieve consensus,

[10] This reflects inexperience with hosting UN Conferences. COP-1 was not regarded as one in a series of annually held conferences but was put in line with bigger events such as the UNCED or, later, UNGASS.

the EU formally accepted the so-called 'EU bubble' proposed by Ecofis, a Dutch research institute, as the basis of its international climate policy (Blok, Phylipsen, and Bode 1997). While the EU would have had to achieve the proposed Protocol target of 15 per cent reductions in 2010 jointly, individual member states would have been allowed to reduce less, or even to increase emissions, if this was offset by other member-states. Thus Germany, Austria, and Denmark would have had to reduce their emissions of CO_2, CH_4, and N_2O by 25 per cent, while Portugal would have been allowed to increase emissions by 40 per cent, Greece by 30 per cent and Spain by 17 per cent (Ott 1997). From March 1997 Germany advocated the EU bubble, calling for a commitment by protocol signatories to reduce CO_2 emissions by 7.5 per cent by the year 2005, and 15 per cent by 2010 on 1990 levels (BMU 1997e). This was a far more demanding negotiating position than the proposals made by the USA and Japan (BMU 1997f).

Although the EU proposal was not fully accepted, the German government judged the Kyoto Protocol (KP) adopted at COP-3 in December 1997 to represent a 'milestone in the history of environmental protection' (BMU 1997g). By committing industrialized countries to reducing emissions of a basket of six greenhouse gases by an average of 5.2 per cent, one of the major goals was pushed through despite the opposition of a number of countries. However, the conditions under which the KP comes into force are complicated: fifty-five ratifications are required. Furthermore, of these fifty-five, industrialized countries must be represented that contribute at least 55 per cent of the total global emissions in 1990. Therefore, entry into force largely depends on US ratification (Ott 1998). German ratification has been linked to the further development of some specific issues, in particular emissions trading which was brought into the treaty at the insistence of the USA (BMU 1997g). With respect to the so-called flexibility mechanisms more generally, the German position is supportive, but agreement is linked to how these mechanisms will be made operational (limited utilization, monitoring, verification, etc.). Following COP-3, the EU bubble was renegotiated to accommodate the EU Kyoto reduction commitment of 8 per cent. Germany is now committed to a 21 per cent reduction under the EU bubble, whereas other EU member-states reduced their original commitments considerably (European Commission 1998).

German Biodiversity Policy

The German parliament and *Bundesländer* approved ratification of the Convention on Biological Diversity (CBD) in 1993. Responsibility for implementation is split between the federal government and the *Bundeslän-der*. BMU is charged with developing national strategies in order to implement obligations under the CBD, while the *Bundesländer* are responsible for specific regulations on nature conservation. It has been argued that split responsibility makes implementation of international agreements on issues of nature conservation more difficult (Knapp 1997: 28).

The CBD was the last of a series of international environmental agreements (Ramser, CITES, etc.). Germany attached a low priority to the negotiations as the government believed they were unlikely to result in any significant outcomes. Furthermore, potential domestic benefits of such an international convention were unclear (Müller 1998). In contrast to the FCCC, which was largely pushed in order to move domestic policy forward, the CBD was not thought to be an instrument that could help to get domestic policy goals accepted. Furthermore, in the law on its ratification, the government states that:

the implementation of the measures in the Convention will not impose any extra cost either on the federation, the *Bundesländer* or the local authorities given that these measures have already been implemented or are in any case being implemented within the framework of existing national policy on nature conservation and the specific regulations set out there. Nor will the implementation of the Convention give rise to any extra charges on the domestic economy, with the result that there should not be any direct effects on retail prices and the general price index, particularly consumer prices.

This has been taken as an indication that the CBD was given a low priority in Germany right from the signing of the Convention (Gettkant, Simonis, and Supplie 1997).

Indeed, for some time the interpretation of the CBD appeared to have been narrowed to conservation issues exclusively, although Article 1 of the CBD explicitly points to three objectives: conservation of biological diversity, the sustainable use of its components, and the fair and equitable sharing of the benefits arising out of the utilization of genetic resources. The Federal Nature Conservation Act (FNCA) of 1976, which has to be implemented by the *Bundesländer* through specific regulations, certainly does not cover the latter two objectives. Nevertheless, the official position is that the FNCA is the basic legal framework, and contains almost sufficient legal instruments, for implementing the CBD (BMU 1995). Any remaining inadequacies were to be addressed through a comprehensive amendment of the FNCA. Focusing on access and the right to use conservation areas, the proposed amendment was judged sceptically by nature conservation NGOs, as it gave sport and tourism associations the same status as conservation organizations.

Furthermore, the compensation scheme for farmers for refraining from using environmentally damaging agricultural processes caused much controversy. It demonstrates how difficult it is to co-ordinate federal legislative initiatives if responsibilities of the *Bundesländer* are involved. Ultimately the *Bundesrat* rejected the amendment in 1996 (BMU 1996*b*), and a consensus on how to solve the most conflictual issues was not achieved (BMU 1997*h*). A new proposal designed to avoid co-ordination difficulties with the *Bundesrat* was finally adopted by parliament in April 1998 (BMU 1998*c* and 1998*d*).

Following ratification of the CBD the Federal Agency for Nature Conservation (*Bundesamt für Naturschutz*, BfN), a subordinate agency of the BMU, carried out a very comprehensive status report on the 'situation of biodiversity in Germany' (Schäfer 1995). This work was only partially reflected in the first report on the implementation of the CBD prepared for COP-2 in Jakarta in 1995. Instead the report focused mainly on the 'positive German framework conditions'. For example, it explicitly stressed the high priority accorded to environmental protection in Germany, the high environmental awareness of German citizens, the existing legislative framework, and in-situ and ex-situ conservation programmes. Further measures to implement the CBD were presented only in a very general way.

Nevertheless, activities of other parts of the federal government are interesting. The Federal Ministry for Agriculture, Nutrition and Forestry (*Bundesministerium für Landwirtschaft, Ernährung und Forsten*, BML) is responsible for negotiations with the Food and Agriculture Organization (FAO). Discussing 'plant genetic resources for food and agriculture', the international process has been actively pushed and the existing legislative framework is assessed critically by BML. Here the need for more integrated and co-operative approaches is highlighted. Furthermore, BMZ stresses that biological diversity is an issue to be addressed in development co-operation (BMZ 1997*b*).

Since 1995 the issue of biodiversity has gradually been accorded more attention. According to Article 6 of the CBD, signatories had to prepare a National Report in time for the Fourth Conference of Parties in May 1998. This obligation included the description of national strategies, plans, and programmes—judged to be a difficult task for Germany (Websky 1997). In 1996, in a working paper prepared for the start of the dialogue process between BMU and the major groups mentioned above, the Environment Minister stated that in the past attention to the issue had been insufficient and that it had not then been recognized as urgent by the German public (BMU 1996*a*).

Since then, a number of key activities were initiated. Access to genetic resources, sustainable tourism, and the clearing house mechanism under Art. 18 of the CBD have been identified as priority issues internationally (BMU 1998e). For example, a mandate to establish a working group to develop international guidelines for sustainable tourism was proposed at the fourth COP of the CBD. Though such a mandate was not actually adopted, the initiative succeeded in so far as the COP agreed that parties should provide the Secretariat of the CBD with comprehensive information on biological diversity and sustainable tourism. Moreover, a link to the 1999 discussion of the CSD on sustainable tourism was to be established (BMU 1998f).

Domestically, biological diversity has now been recognized as being 'the most important issue of nature conservation' (BMU 1998g). Besides the amendment to the FNCA, a number of activities have been agreed upon with regard to the CBD, such as the amendment of the Federal Soil Protection Act (*Bundesbodenschutzgesetz*) to reduce the sealing-off (paving-over) of the land surface. The very comprehensive national report to the CBD (BMU 1998a) includes many activities and programmes. Furthermore the relevance of integrating issues of the CBD into German development policy has been stressed several times (Auer and Erdmann 1997: 113; BMU 1998a). An interesting feature of the National Report is that, for the first time, statements by NGOs regarding their activities to implement the CBD are included in an annex.

Conclusion

At the time of writing, at the turn of the millennium sustainable development in Germany has not yet become an organizing focus that sets domestic policy in a broader international context. A firm domestic commitment to its implementation, expressed for example in the preparations of a national policy plan, has not been adopted. Nevertheless, a shift in the priority given to several UNCED issues can be observed. Prior to and during UNCED, interest focused on negotiation of the FCCC. Though legally binding, the CBD was of only minor interest. Agenda 21, being 'soft law', was also neglected. Yet at present, the concept of sustainable development enjoys wide rhetorical acceptance. Interest in climate policy has fallen. Biodiversity remains an underdeveloped policy issue, although both activities and visibility have increased.

Indication of such a shift is provided by the reporting patterns of the BMU. Reports on climate policy and the national communications to the Secretariat of the FCCC dominated between 1987 and 1994 (BMU 1994*b*). At the same time, reflecting their different legal status, reports to the CSD were not published at all. Recently an increasing number of reports focus on the transition towards sustainable development. At the same time the concentration on the environment component of sustainability—as for example demonstrated in the title 'Environment 1994', which was supposed to represent the first sustainable development strategy—had become less apparent. The debate was then propelled forward by the dissemination of the book *Sustainable Germany* by two NGOs in 1995. Later the approach of UNGASS in 1997 focused the attention of parts of the government and resulted in a higher priority being accorded to Agenda 21.

However, the federal government still addresses sustainable development within established institutional parameters, particularly in the field of interministerial co-ordination. The existing mechanisms to seek expert advice (Enquete Commissions, scientific advisory councils) were used once the issue acquired political priority. The establishment, and later the reorganization, of the National Committee is the only (very weak) organizational innovation observed so far. At the moment, for example, a reorganization of BMU is unlikely—apart from the move to Berlin.

The political momentum for more far-reaching domestic policy reform appears to have slowed since Rio. Regarding climate policy, with the 1987 reduction target Germany set the pace internationally. The reduction of CO_2 emissions achieved by 1999, together with the commitment to further reductions under the burden-sharing agreement, is central to the implementation of the KP in the EU. The domestic reduction of CO_2 provides Germany with a good negotiating position within the EU, and internationally. Focusing on a co-ordinated EU negotiating position, however, lowers the public profile of climate policy. At the same time, discussions on innovative policy, e.g. the tax debate, had come to a dead-end before the change in government.

Within government, a common understanding of Agenda 21 and of the necessity of an integrated domestic policy approach was not developed: hence the perspective on future policies differed widely among ministries. Within the environmental administration, major controversies appeared as, for example, in the process of preparing the UBA study *Nachhaltiges Deutschland*. With the change of government, new momentum has developed with regard to a number of topics, most particularly the first phase of an ecological tax reform. Whether sustainable development will be set at the core of this reform effort, however, remains to be seen.

A number of factors appear to account for the comparatively modest German response to sustainable development and Agenda 21. The early and comprehensive focus on environmental issues in domestic policies, and the concentration on climate change prior to, and in the first years after UNCED have played an important role. Due to high population densities, the environmental impact of intense industrial activities were experienced directly by a majority of the population. Therefore, 'a healthy environment' was identified early as a scarce good. Competing uses of the environment were as a sink by industry or for fulfilling social needs such as mobility; competition in the use of space/soil by different economic sectors is another reflection of environmental scarcity. As a result, the environment was established early as a policy sector. The complex regulative framework led to considerable improvements in traditional pollution control. Hence, the environmental element of sustainable development was perceived to have been already well covered.

During the 1980s the environmental agenda was widened from local to transboundary and global concerns. Germany strove for leadership in environmental policy in particular at the EU level, pushing a number of EU directives (Huber 1997: 65). The issues of ozone depletion and climate change were quickly put on the political agenda. The early domestic focus on climate change was driven by at least three causes: first, an intense public debate following the report of the German Physical Society. Second, there was a direct connection to the preceding priority issue of ozone depletion, as CFCs deplete ozone and have a global-warming potential at the same time. Third, there was a direct connection to energy issues, and within BMU a strong energy group existed that was competing with the Ministries for Economics and for Transport. Given this BMU interest, climate change appeared an ideal 'umbrella' for entrepreneurial policy development. At the same time, climate change helped to legitimize the environmental political-administrative system to deal with energy-policy issues. The strong German (BMU) focus on international climate policy appears to have supported this strategy of preserving responsibility for domestic policy sectors related to climate change. Positive experiences with the Montreal Protocol showed that international legally binding agreements or environmental regimes could help BMU push through domestic environmental policy goals. Given that such an 'external' leverage effect could more probably be expected on the issue of climate change than for biodiversity, the lower attention accorded to the CBD becomes understandable. In fact, national and international German climate policy was mutually reinforcing: given the high priority of the issue, BMU was able to get the ambitious CO_2 reduction target of 25 per cent accepted and adopted prior to German reunification. Emission reductions achieved in the new federal states following reunification then helped to maintain political leadership in the EU and in international climate-policy negotiations, even though other (non-environmental) issues became predominant domestically.

From a conceptual point of view, the Brundtland Report and Agenda 21 were received critically as the 'integration principle' was judged to be inferior to the precautionary principle. Because it was feared that environmental policy might regress, the issue of 'sustainable development' was not taken up by the environmental administration. However, given the decline in priority accorded to environmental policy in response to the surge of economic and social problems that followed reunification, combined with a serious recession and a general structural crisis manifested in more than four million unemployed (and a steadily increasing number of long-term unemployed), sustainability gradually became more appealing to the environment-oriented sections of the political-administrative system: for they began to believe that the relevance of environmental concerns for policy and decision-making could be safeguarded through 'integration'. This shift towards integration was reinforced by two forces; the enormous public impact of studies like *Sustainable Germany* published by BUND and Misereor, and the international CSD process and the approach of UNGASS.

At present, sustainable development enjoys a wide acceptance rhetorically across the government. Consensus has been achieved, however, only on an abstract level. The main political obstacle to the implementation of sustainable development is that the traditional political priorities do not seem to have changed. So far UNCED and Agenda 21 have not been used as an opportunity to reorient German politics and policy-making, and no strategy to implement Agenda 21 has been elaborated by BMU. The Council of Environmental Experts came to the conclusion that the concept of sustainability has not yet become a leading driver of political practice within the federal government. It is still predominantly understood as a theme of relevance only for ecological or Third World development politics. This was demonstrated early in the coalition agreements after the federal election of 1994. For the federal states it is also true that ecological questions are not sufficiently connected with economic and social questions (SRU 1996). The impact of the change of government in 1998 on sustainable development policy is yet not clear.

So far an adjustment of institutional and organizational structures at the federal level has not taken place. As the case of climate policy demonstrates, environmental policy-making has reached a 'mature' stage with established forms of policy advice, administrative organization, interministerial coordination, preparation of legislation, and so on. Within the environmental administration a structure based on environmental media has been established, and there are no indications that a reorganization is considered necessary. Neither government nor the Ministries have created organizational units which are explicitly responsible for the realization of sustainable development or of Agenda 21.

Strategic decisions on recourse to new instruments (as recommended by the various expert councils, politicians, researchers, or NGOs), have still not been made. The proposed environmental policy priority programme has a draft status, and is not sufficient to refocus government attention, although it contains interesting proposals for quantified targets. Still, the priority programme is the only official assessment of where Germany stands in the sustainability transition so far. Again, the impact and further development of the first stage of the ecological tax reform remains to be seen.

More generally, the paradigm of stable and sustained economic growth as the precondition for raising social welfare is a major factor affecting the implementation of Agenda 21. The influence of environmental policy ends whenever a negative impact on economy and industry or on the locational advantage of the industrial base is feared. On the government's reading the concept of sustainable development implies no fundamental change of social, political or economic paradigms. In the last two elections to the *Bundestag* (October 1994 and September 1998) environmental policy and its further development towards sustainable development played hardly any role.

With the emergence of sustainable development as an international political priority issue, German policy-making is faced with a quandary. Although it successfully adapted to the new political issue of 'environmental protection' since the 1960s, sustainable development presents a double challenge: first, the new concept is unlikely to be implemented successfully through the existing organization of the political-administrative system. More is required than a shuffling of existing institutional portfolios between departments. The general decision-making procedures and existing forms of interministerial co-ordination must be reconsidered to increase the effectiveness in implementing cross-sectoral issues. Second, and more fundamentally, the traditional political, and more general societal, norms and models have to be scrutinized and re-discussed, adapted and further developed to the needs of a more sustainable society.

The latter will definitely take longer than the twelve years since Brundtland. But the establishment of various issues related to sustainable development at the top of the political agenda is a first step in the right direction—though at present a complete strategy cannot be presented and not all levels of government are equally convinced of the pertinence of the new concept. The further development of the environmental policy priority programme into a national plan for sustainable development would be a useful step in the right direction.

Moreover, there are several important issues on the German political agenda that have not so far been connected to the discussion of Agenda 21. At the turn of the millennium Germany is faced with a multitude of challenges, which have been increased by reunification. Most obviously, reforms to the fiscal and social system are needed as Germany experiences a decoupling of economic growth and employment, in combination with an erosion of the 'intergenerational treaty' which has formed the basis of the German social security system. The present crisis of German social and economic policy is accompanied by an increasingly wide public discussion about the future and the basic model of German society. In a political situation where far-reaching reforms cannot be implemented because of a lack of agreement between Government and Opposition, sustainable development could become a positive driving force, creating additional momentum for reforms—if an understanding was developed that this concept is not only environmentally motivated, and that it does seek to eclipse precautionary environmental protection.

5

Japan: Law, Technology, and Aid

MIRANDA SCHREURS

As the second largest economy in the world, Japan's economic activities have a major impact both on the domestic and the global environment. Japan is a resource-scarce nation that imports essentially all of its natural gas and petroleum and many raw materials for consumer products from overseas. It is also highly dependent upon agricultural imports to feed its own large population (Ohta 1998). There are 125 million Japanese, approximately half of the US population, living in an area that is not much larger than California. Because Japan is so heavily dependent on foreign countries for natural resources, energy, and food, sustainable development is a particularly complex goal. Even more than is true for most other advanced industrialized countries, sustainable development has little meaning for Japan if it does not address the international dimension of Japanese consumption.

Sustainable development (*jizoku kanô na hatten*) is a concept that was first discussed by Japanese policy-makers after the publication of the World Commission on Environment and Development's 1987 report, *Our Common Future*. Although the concept of sustainable development is relatively new in Japan, the question of how to achieve economic development in a resource poor nation has long faced the country. Yet sustainable development asks the Japanese public and policy-makers to go far beyond any of the policies previously introduced to enhance energy security or protect the domestic environment. Japan must take a new look at how its economic, agricultural, and social activities impact on the global environment and whether or not in the long-term these activities will remain environmentally, socially, and economically viable.

As a result of the growing awareness of the concept of sustainable development, in the 1990s there has been some public and political debate on what must be done to make it a reality in Japan. Areas that are receiving much attention are recycling and energy-efficiency gains. Considerable interest exists too in improving environmental management within industry and introducing 'environmentally-friendly' automobiles. Yet there is also a general feeling that Japan already has taken major steps to improve energy efficiency and reduce waste, and that there are limits to how much more it can do domestically in this regard without causing major problems for the nation's current socio-economic structures. Thus, there is much interest in working with developing states, and particularly those in Asia, to reduce pollution overseas as long as Japan is recognized for its efforts. The message Japan is starting to send to the countries of Asia is that they can learn from Japan's own bad experiences with severe environmental pollution resulting from unchecked economic growth. Japan is urging the developing world to follow a different path, and instead of ignoring pollution, to emulate its own relatively successful efforts in the 1970s to introduce pollution control regulations, develop environmentally friendly technologies, and improve energy efficiency (e.g. Chikyû Kankyô Kenkyûkai 1991; Government of Japan 1997).

The Political Context

Japan is a one-party dominant parliamentary democracy. From 1955 to 1993 and again from 1995 until the time of writing (1999), the Liberal Democratic Party (LDP) has been a ruling party. Under the LDP, a kind of corporatist politics emerged that placed heavy emphasis on economic development. There are strong ties among the LDP, the bureaucracy, industry, and agriculture. Civil society, as it is thought of in the West, is relatively weak. Today Japanese politics is in a period of transition. The policy-making process is undergoing change and shows signs of becoming somewhat more open (Richardson 1997). A new electoral system has been introduced and this has contributed to the decline of old parties and the formation of new ones. There is also growing acceptance of the role that non-profit organizations can play in society. This has the potential to change environmental policy-making in Japan in the future.

In Japan's quasi-corporatist political system, administrative guidance, rather than strict regulatory enforcement, is a preferred tool for policy implementation. Administrative guidance is a tool used by the powerful Japanese bureaucracy to influence the behaviour of industry (Johnson 1982). It is viewed as a flexible means for achieving policy goals. Thus, laws in Japan tend to be vague, allowing room for flexible implementation.

Typically, policy change in Japan is a slow process because of the importance accorded to consensus-building. Japan has difficulty taking on a leadership role internationally in introducing new policy ideas because of the

need first to build consensus among concerned parties. Given Japan's fragmented bureaucracy and the factionalization of Japan's political parties, this
is not always an easy task (Van Wolferen 1989). The prime minister, moreover, is typically not a strong figure (Hayao 1993). Implementation, on the
other hand, is typically relatively effective once policy goals have been
agreed. This is in part due to the unitary structure of the political system
which gives the central government a strong influence over local bureau-
cracies, but also to the close ties that exist among bureaucrats and
corporations.

Environmental Policy Actors

Japanese environmental policy-making in the post-war period can be divided
into four stages: a period prior to the 1960s when environmental protection
was extremely limited and largely left to local governments; a period of
active environmental policy-formation and bureaucratic capacity-building at
the national level during the 1960s and early 1970s; a period from the mid-
1970s to the late-1980s when environmental protection was a low-priority
issue and there were only incremental changes to existing environmental
policies; and the 1990s, when global environmental protection and sustainable development have become increasingly important areas of public policy
debate.

Beginning in the 1960s, there were many actors influencing the shape of
Japan's environmental programmes. They included the courts, the media,
environmental citizens' movements, local governments, and the Environment Agency (and prior to the Agency's formation, the Ministry of Health
and Welfare, MoHW). The Ministry of International Trade and Industry
(MITI) played a formidable role in shaping Japan's energy policies and industrial pollution-control policies (Gresser, Fujikura, and Morishima 1981;
McKean 1981; Ui 1991; Broadbent 1998).

By the end of the 1970s, the number of environmental citizens' groups
had declined and the level of attention to environmental issues was down
relative to its early 1970s peak. Environmental policy-making became
increasingly routinized within the bureaucracy. The main bureaucratic
actors in this process were the Environment Agency, MITI, the Ministry of
Construction, and the Ministry of Finance (MoF). Fierce struggles for influence over the direction of environmental policy often erupted among them.
Within these inter-ministerial battles, not all agencies and ministries had
equal influence. The Environment Agency did reasonably well in inter-
ministerial negotiations when it had strong public support. Once public

interest in environmental preservation dropped after the first oil shock of 1973, however, the Environment Agency no longer had enough strength to push through new policy initiatives over the powerful opposition of the economic ministries. Japan's environmental groups were too weak to lend much support to the Environment Agency and there were few politicians who were strong supporters of environmental protection issues (Miyamoto 1989; Schreurs 1997a).

Since the late 1980s, environmental policy-making has entered a new, more pluralistic, and more globally oriented phase. The key players determining the shape of Japan's sustainable development policies are the Environment Agency and MITI. Other ministries also play some role in the process, including the MoF, the Ministry of Foreign Affairs (MoFA), the Ministry of Transportation, and the Ministry of Agriculture, Forests, and Fisheries. Numerous politicians are also starting to play a more visible role in getting new legislation passed. Many of these politicians are members of the inter-parliamentary group Global Legislators' Organization for a Balanced Environment (GLOBE).

New types of environmental groups are also emerging. International environmental groups like Greenpeace Japan, World Resources Institute, and Friends of the Earth have opened offices in Japan. While still small and at times financed by overseas affiliates, these groups are starting to make themselves heard. In preparation for the 1997 Kyoto Conference of the Parties (COP) to the Framework Convention on Climate Change (FCCC), an umbrella organization of non-governmental organizations (NGOs) concerned with climate issues formed. Kikô Forum (literally, 'Climate Forum') prepared policy ideas for how Japanese society and industry could reduce greenhouse-gas emissions beyond the targets being considered by the government (Schreurs 1997b).

Still, Japanese NGOs remain small in comparison to those in Europe and North America. The internationally oriented NGOs that have started to form since the late 1980s have really only been able to react to the government's agenda. They are still marginal players in influencing Japanese approaches to environmental protection and sustainable development. Their role is likely to grow in the future, however, as the Japanese political system becomes more pluralistic and institutional barriers to their formation are dismantled. A positive development in this direction was the passage of new legislation governing the establishment of non-profit organizations in Japan in 1998. Under the new legislation, it has become easier for groups to obtain certification as non-profits although it is still not possible for individuals and corporations to write off contributions to non-profit organizations from their taxes. Another positive change was the introduction of a Freedom of Information Act in the spring of 1999.

Sustaining Economic Growth versus Sustainable Development

Throughout its modern history, Japan has been forced to struggle with the question of how economic growth can be sustained in a mountainous nation, with a large population, but few natural resources of its own. In the first half of this century it found an answer to this problem through colonization: thus Korea and Taiwan were forced to be its agricultural extensions. During the Pacific War, Japan marched into the South Pacific in part because of the country's need for energy to fuel its war efforts. Colonialism provided a way for Japan to live beyond its national carrying capacity (Ho 1984).

After its defeat in World War II, colonization was no longer an option for obtaining access to food, labour, energy, or other natural resources. For about a decade, Japan was forced to do what it could to feed its own population and fuel its own damaged economy; it received food aid from the Allied Occupation, and domestic coal production supplied a large portion of its fuel needs.

By the 1950s, Japan was back on its feet and the economy was showing signs of recovery. There was a general consensus in the country that rapid economic growth was essential for Japan to join the ranks of industrialized states. National agricultural production and energy production were insufficient to meet rapidly growing domestic demand. Growth could not be sustained without resources from abroad, and Japan began to trade consumer goods for oil, food, and other resources.

Things looked quite rosy in Japan in the 1960s. By 1967 it had become the third richest country in the world (after the United States and the former Soviet Union), and the material quality of life was relatively good. No consideration, however, had been given to what the impact of rapid industrialization might be on Japan's own natural environment or the health of the people. Industrialization and urbanization resulted in serious pollution of the air, soil, and water and in the production of masses of waste. Horrific pollution-related diseases broke out. These included instances of mercury poisoning, cadmium poisoning, poisoning from cooking oil, and severe respiratory ailments from polluted air (Huddle and Reich 1975; Kawana 1988).

Eventually the pollution crisis became so bad that it spawned an environmental movement. The public began to question the advisability of development policies that generated such serious pollution problems. After many years of battling government and industry with demonstrations and in the courts, the environmental movement succeeded in forcing the government into taking policy action. As a first major step, in 1967, the MoHW drafted one of the world's first framework laws for environmental preservation: the Basic Law on Environmental Pollution Control. A 1970 amendment to the Basic Law removed a controversial 'harmony clause' that required that enforcement of environmental laws be tempered with the 'natural harmonization of industries', essentially giving priority to industrial concerns (Gresser, Fujikura, and Morishima 1981: 18–26 and 417 n. 60). A new legal understanding of the relationship between the economy and the environment, particularly as it pertained to human health, started to take hold in Japan. After the Japanese courts ruled in several pollution-related health cases that government and industry had been negligent in their failure to take measures to protect human health from polluting activities, it became widely accepted within Japan that economic growth could not be pursued at the expense of environmental preservation or human health (Upham 1987).

Many new environmental laws were introduced in Japan in the early 1970s in an effort to improve the quality of the air and water and to address the sufferings of pollution victims. They included ambient air and water-quality standards, a law designed to compensate pollution victims, and a Nature Conservation Law. An Environment Agency was established in 1971 (Hashimoto 1988; Ninomiya 1989; Tsuru and Weidner 1989; Kankyôcho 1991).

The oil shocks of 1973 and 1979 resulted in more painful lessons for Japan, and focused political and industrial attention on the need for energy conservation and diversification of energy supplies. They led to major efforts to improve energy efficiency. MITI stepped up nationwide efforts to diversify energy sources and to improve energy efficiency through tax incentives and subsidies. In 1974, a 'Sunshine Project' was introduced to develop alternative energy technologies, including solar, wind, and geothermal power, and in 1978 a 'Moonlight Project' was initiated to improve energy efficiency and to promote nuclear energy (Agency of Industrial Science and Technology, MITI, n.d.). Between 1973 and 1988 GDP increased by 81 per cent in real terms, but growth in energy demand was held to about 16 per cent. While dependence on oil remained at a high 56 per cent as of 1994, reliance on alternative energies (nuclear, natural gas, and hydro) went from 3.3 per cent in 1973 to 12.7 per cent in 1979, 24.5 per cent in 1990, and 26.4 per cent in 1994 (International Energy Agency 1991 and 1994).

The oil shocks helped Japan to become one of the most energy-efficient nations in the world. At the same time, however, support for environmental regulations declined. Japan's fledgling environmental movement slowly faded from the political landscape. In sharp contrast with the situation in the other countries in this study, few environmental NGOs established themselves at the national level. With the economy in recession national attention shifted away from the environment and back to the economy. Industrial opposition to environmental regulations gained renewed support in the Japanese Diet because of concerns about Japanese competitiveness. Economic development and environmental preservation were still seen as somewhat competing objectives.

The laws that were introduced in the 1970s and the government's response to the oil embargo did much to stimulate more energy-efficient manufacturing processes and the development and introduction of less polluting technologies. Less progress was made in implementing measures to protect the natural environment from development. For example, a Cabinet ordinance regarding environmental impact assessments was introduced only in 1984 (Barrett and Therivel 1991), and an Environmental Impact Assessment law only in 1997. Japan was also criticized for exporting its most polluting industries to other nations in Asia as a result of the structural transformation of its own economy, and of exploiting the natural resources of other countries with little regard for the environmental implications of those activities.

Sustainable Development as a Policy Concept in Japan

Japan claims credit for the idea of establishing the World Commission on Environment and Development (WCED) within the United Nations. In 1980 a special advisory committee to US President Jimmy Carter prepared a report on the condition of the global environment known as the 'Global 2000' report. This report was read with much interest by the Japanese Environment Agency and resulted in the establishment of an Ad Hoc Committee of Global Environmental Problems. After studying the 'Global 2000' report as well as the work of the Club of Rome, the committee recommended international action on the problems of rapid deforestation, desertification, and global warming. In 1982 Environment Agency Director General Bunbei Hara proposed the establishment of the WCED to the United Nations Environment Programme (UNEP) (Kankyôcho Chikyûteki Kibo no Kankyô Mondai ni Kansuru Kondankai 1982; Hara 1982). UNEP accepted the proposal and in 1984 the WCED was established.

Perhaps because of the role Japan played in promoting the WCED, it was only six months after the publication of *Our Common Future* that the Japanese government issued an Environmental White Paper focused on global environmental issues and the concept of sustainable development (Japanese Environment Agency 1988: 1–86, esp. 37–40). Prior to 1988 most Environmental White Papers made only very brief mention of global environmental issues. The 1988 Environmental White Paper was one of the first documents published in Japan to address sustainable development with direct references to the WCED's report. The White Paper, which was drafted by the Environment Agency, defines sustainable development as development which 'is made without impairing the environment' and suggests several steps that Japan can take toward achieving this goal. They are: (1) making an active contribution to sustainable development in developing countries through 'effective co-operation' and 'appropriate aid'; (2) the accumulation of scientific knowledge about the global environment; (3) development of technology for the conservation of the global environment; (4) co-operation with international organizations; (5) the organization of a network of organizations for environmental co-operation; and (6) the raising of public awareness.

In the following years, many new institutions were created to determine how Japan should respond to the growing international enthusiasm for global environmental protection and the concept of sustainable development. In May 1989, two months before the G-7 Economic Summit meeting in Arche, France, the Japanese government created a new position for a Minister for Global Environmental Affairs to be filled by the Director General of the Environment Agency. A Ministerial Council for Global Environmental Conservation was also established. At the first meeting of the ministerial council, on 30 June 1989, the government announced Japan's Basic Policy Directions for Global Environmental Conservation. The report concluded that economic activities should be carried out in a manner which places less burden on the global environment, resource conservation and reductions in energy use should be encouraged, and environmental education should be supported (Japanese Environment Agency 1990).

UNCED received a tremendous amount of media attention in Japan. It helped to heighten further public awareness of global environmental issues and to fix the term sustainable development in the Japanese vocabulary. Since UNCED there have been numerous policy changes in Japan. Reacting to heightened criticism from abroad of its international environmental record and to growing popular interest in global environmental protection, in the late 1980s and early 1990s the Japanese government put a stop to drift-net fishing and the importation of products made from endangered species. At the international level Japan became a signatory to the Montreal Protocol, the Framework Convention on Climate Change, the Basel Convention on the Control of Transboundary Movements of Hazardous Wastes and their Disposal, and the Convention on Biological Diversity.

At the domestic level numerous new environmental laws with implications for Japan's approach to sustainable development were passed, including a new recycling promotion law, a law to reduce nitrogen-oxide emissions from transportation, and a law regulating the import and export of hazardous wastes. A new Basic Environment Law, with a more comprehensive understanding of the meaning of the environment, was also introduced. The old emphasis on control of pollution (*kôgai*) was replaced in the language of the law by a new emphasis on protection of the environment (*kankyô*), nationally, regionally, and globally. A National Action Plan for Agenda 21 was formulated and a Law Concerning the Promotion of Measures to Cope with Global Warming was passed.

Environmental budgets have increased substantially over the course of the 1990s, although some of this may simply be a redesignation of previous budget figures as part of the environment budget. In FY 1985 the government's environmental budget, as reported in the Government of Japan's Environmental White Paper, was ¥1.1 trillion, and in FY 1988, the budget still stood at only ¥1.28 trillion. By FY 1993, however, the figure had climbed to ¥1.71 trillion, and by FY 1997 it stood at ¥2.8 trillion.

There is growing concern in Japan about whether or not the current socio-economic system is sustainable. Still, as is true for all of the countries in this volume, the sustainable development policy measures that are being introduced really are only changing current economic activities at the margins. Policy change is occurring, but not to the degree indicated by *Our Common Future*.

Patterns of Institutional Engagement

National Action Plan for Agenda 21

At UNCED, each country committed to drawing up a national action plan implementing the forty areas of action designated in the Rio action plan 'Agenda 21'. In November 1993, the Japanese Environment Agency released a draft National Action Plan for Agenda 21 with a 7 December 1993 deadline for public comment. During this three-week interval, NGOs, including People's Forum 2001, demanded that the document be revised. The fact that NGOs had any voice in the process is noteworthy. In the past, NGOs had little, if any, say in policy formulation. Thus, even if the changes to the

National Action Plan that the NGOs were able to achieve were limited in substance, their participation in the process suggests that slowly the policy-making process is becoming somewhat more open to the voices of NGOs. This is a sign of the positive effects that international norm-building can have on national-level politics.

As a result of public comments on the draft plan, about one hundred modifications to the original draft were made (Shinobu 1994: 130–8). In its final form, Japan's National Action Plan for Agenda 21 states that:

Japan intends to restructure its own socio-economic system into one which will enable sustainable development with reduced environmental load in order to make future generations inherit favorable global environmental conditions. At the same time, Japan is determined to take advantage of its own capability to make positive contributions to the furtherance of preservation of the global environment through international co-operation, in a way which is commensurate with the position Japan occupies in the international community.   (Government of Japan 1993: 1)

The document further suggests that Japan can play a role as intermediary between the developed and developing world in establishing a consensus on action. No specific definition, however, is given for what is meant by 'sustainable development'. The document focuses attention, in particular, on what Japan can do to address environmental pollution overseas, including capacity building, surveys, and financial transfers (through the Global Environment Facility) (Government of Japan 1993: 1–2).

It also lists measures Japan needs to take to address global warming domestically. These include energy-conservation measures designed to reduce CO_2, methane, and other greenhouse-gas emissions; measures to enhance CO_2 sinks; the promotion of scientific research, observation, and monitoring; education; international co-operation; and the development and dissemination of technology.

Many local governments with support from the national government have also created Local Agenda 21s. In November 1995 Kanagawa Prefecture hosted an international conference on environment-friendly towns and lifestyles and adopted the Kanagawa Declaration, which supports the creation of a 20-per-cent-club for 'sustainable urban lifestyles'. To join the 20-per-cent-club, local government authorities must declare their intention to achieve 20 per cent reductions in greenhouse-gas emissions within approximately five years.

The Environment Basic Law

The UNCED process and Japan's self-proclaimed interest in becoming an international environmental leader has forced the country to reconsider the shape of its domestic environmental laws. At the basis of all environmental laws in Japan is the 1993 Environment Basic Law, which replaced the Nature Conservation Law of 1972 and the Basic Law for Pollution Control that was introduced in 1967, and then amended in 1970 when its infamous 'harmony clause' was removed. It is one of only a dozen basic laws in Japan. Basic laws are important because they spell out the fundamental concepts upon which laws in a given area like the environment are to be based. They do not include specific targets or measures. Both the Basic Law for Pollution Control and the Nature Conservation Law had a domestic focus and neither was well equipped for addressing global-scale environmental issues. The new basic law was based on these two earlier laws but also incorporated new ideas about regional and global environmental responsibilities. The three primary additions to the old laws were: principles calling for local and global environmental conservation for the enjoyment of present and future generations; development of a society based upon the notion of sustainable development; and international co-operation (Kankyôcho Kikaku Chôseikyoku Kikaku Chôseika (ed.) 1994).

Article 4 of the Environment Basic Law addresses the concept of sustainable development. The article reads:

Environmental conservation shall be promoted so that a society can be formulated where the healthy and productive environment is conserved and sustainable development is ensured by fostering sound economic development with reduced environmental load . . . (Kankyôcho Kikaku Chôseikyoku Kikaku Chôseika (ed.) 1994: 143)

This is to be achieved by having individuals and organizations voluntarily reduce 'as much as possible the environmental load generated by (their) socio-economic activities'. The process behind this law's formation speaks to the powers that different actors in Japan have had in defining the concept of sustainable development. Initial elements to be included in a bill were drawn up by a team established by the Environment Agency. This team submitted its proposals in the summer of 1992 to the Central Council for the Environment and the Nature Conservation Council (*Mainichi Shimbun*, 15 July 1993: 13). Initially the two councils adopted many of the Environment Agency's ideas, which included environmental impact assessment legislation and the introduction of an environmental tax. A draft proposal dated September 1992 stated that the existing Basic Law for Pollution Control and the Nature Conservation Law were inadequate to deal with the kinds of environmental issues facing society in the 1990s. The proposal called for the formulation of a new law that would be based on the principle of sustainable development. As part of this, the proposal suggested adoption of a new environment basic law requiring environmental impact assessments for new projects, and the introduction of economic measures, including taxes and surcharges, to spread the cost of environmental protection across society.

In January of the following year, the Environment Agency issued a proposal for an Environment Basic Law. The bill included a carbon tax and an environmental impact assessment clause. Due to opposition from MITI and the Japan Federation of Economic Organizations (*Keizai Dantai Rengôkai*, henceforth, *Keidanren*), however, the tax idea was watered down to a statement that the government would research and study the effects of economic disincentives on polluters. When the Cabinet approved the bill for a Basic Law on the Environment on 12 March 1993, the bill simply stated that the government will seek public understanding and co-operation in introducing economic sanctions as a way of preserving the environment. Reflecting the relative power balance of the main bureaucratic actors in this struggle, the legal obligation to conduct environmental impact assessment was also dropped. The cabinet-approved bill included no statement about mandatory environmental impact assessment, stating only that environmental impact assessments should be promoted (*Daily Yomiuri*, 29 March 1993: 2). It took until the spring of 1997 before an Environmental Impact Assessment Law was introduced in Japan.

Environment Basic Plan

Following passage of the Environment Basic Law, the Prime Minister asked the Central Council for the Environment in January 1994 to deliberate over the need for an Environment Basic Plan. The council's policy committee met fifteen times and another special sub-committee met an additional four times to consider the shape of the plan. The council included many academics and journalists, numerous representatives of industry, and a few representatives each from labour unions, women's groups, and research institutes. In drafting the plan, the council surveyed government ministries and agencies, local governments, industries, and twenty-six citizen groups on their thoughts regarding environmental preservation. The council also studied the environmental plans of the United Kingdom, Australia, the Netherlands, Canada, France, and the European Community.

An interim report was produced in July 1994. Public review of the plan was made in the following months. In December 1994, the Cabinet announced the Environment Basic Plan, a long-term comprehensive government plan for environmental protection into the twenty-first century. Its four long-term goals were: (1) the realization of a socio-economic system based on a looped (or closed) and efficient material cycle that will have only a limited burden on the environment; (2) the co-existence of man and nature; (3) participation in environmental conservation activities; and (4) the promotion of international efforts. Specific measures for meeting these goals were also listed in the plan along with the roles and responsibilities of the national and local governments, industry, and the people. The Central Council for the Environment is supposed to examine progress made toward realizing the Basic Environment Plan on a yearly basis. The plan is expected to be reviewed after five years based on the annual reviews.

Building upon this effort, in July 1995, the Cabinet decided on an Action Plan for Greening Government Operations, alternatively known as the 'Lead Action Program' (Government of Japan 1995). The idea behind this pro-gramme was that government agencies should take the lead in conserving the environment. The secretariat of the programme, for example, was tasked with determining the volume of paper and gasoline consumed and the volume of wastes generated by each ministry and agency. The goals of the action plan included the introduction of environmental considerations in the purchase and use of goods and services, in the construction and main-tenance of buildings, and in carrying out administrative affairs. Under the programme government ministries were to replace 10 per cent of the cars they used with low-polluting cars; to reduce gasoline use by 10 per cent; and to cut waste by 25 per cent and combustible waste by 30 per cent by the FY 2000 (all relative to 1995 figures). The Central Environmental Council was given the task of annually reviewing the progress of ministries and agencies in meeting the goals of the programme.

Progress remained slow. According to a December 1996 report conducted for the Lead Action Program, the use of recycled paper in the government had increased, but the 'number of low-polluting cars introduced was negli-gibly small, hardly meriting the claim as a pioneering action program' (Japanese Ministry of Foreign Affairs 1997: 3). Government ministries and agencies had only 12 low-emission cars in operation, or just 0.1 per cent of the vehicles used by the government.

Progress may be faster within society than within the government. According to a report in the *Washington Post* (12 July 1997: A 17), based on the work of the US Department of Energy's National Renewable Energy Laboratory, the National Alternative Fuels Hotline, and World Watch Insti-tute, Japan was second only to Brazil in the number of alternative-fuel vehi-cles on the road. Japan had 200,000 vehicles running on compressed natural gas, 1.5 million running on liquefied petroleum gas, and 1,300 running on electricity. (In comparison, Brazil had a total of 4 million alternative vehicles and the US 385,900. Considering its much smaller population, however, the

Netherlands' 560,800 alternative fuel vehicles may put it at the top of the rankings on a per capita basis).

Japan and the United Nations Commission on Sustainable Development

The importance accorded Japanese participation in the United Nations Commission on Sustainable Development (UNCSD) has increased over time. Japanese Environment Agency Director General Miyashita first attended the third meeting of UNCSD held in April 1995. In his speech to the Commission, he broadly discussed national level experiences, the need for changing consumption and production patterns, financing issues, and deforestation. Particular attention was focused on Japan's new Basic Law for Environmental Protection of 1993, the Environment Basic Plan of 1994, and Japanese ODA. Miyashita noted that in preparing the Basic Law public hearings were held in nine municipalities and citizens also expressed their opinions through the post. He also announced that Japan would co-host, with UNEP and the United Nations Development Programme (UNDP), an international conference on Environmentally Friendly Urban Living in November 1995 as an integral part of efforts to develop sustainable societies. He further discussed Japan's contributions to the revision of the International Tropical Timber Agreement, its expanded financing of the International Tropical Timber Organization, and its efforts to help build a framework for sustainable management of tropical forests (Shinobu 1995: 161–9). The following year Environment Agency Director General Sukio Iwatare presented a more detailed speech on Japanese initiatives, and at the June 1997 conference of the UNCSD in New York, Prime Minister Hashimoto presented Japan's 'Initiatives for Sustainable Development (ISD) Toward the 21st Century'. The document notes that as of FY 1996, Japan's environmental official development assistance (ODA) had grown to ¥1.44 trillion, exceeding the target set out five years earlier for environmental ODA by more than 40 per cent (Government of Japan 1997).

Japanese NGOs, including People's Forum 2001 and Citizens Alliance for Saving the Atmosphere and the Earth (CASA), also have attended meetings of the UNCSD. Their participation has been important since they could provide direct reports on developments to the grass-roots movements in Japan.

In June 1996, the Japan Council for Sustainable Development (JCSD) was established. It aims to promote common understanding and dialogue among government, industries, NGOs, and other major actors related to the promotion of sustainable development. The first project of the JSCD was to prepare the Japan Report for the Rio +5 Process announced in March 1997. The report found that:

New efforts have been initiated by a variety of actors aiming at sustainable development. The concept of sustainable development has gradually spread, opening a new age of environmental management. The performance of these efforts suggests, however, that the movement is still in the early stages of development. It is also not yet certain that the new movement will be established as a new norm in society, or that various measures will work to strengthen the overall effects of such efforts. Present socio-economic activities are still posing problems. (Japan Council for Sustainable Development 1997)

Economic Activities and the Concept of Sustainable Development

MITI is a primary actor in Japanese environmental technology research and development and has worked hard to influence how the concept of sustainable development is interpreted in Japanese policy. MITI sees the promotion of global environmental technology research and development as one of its major roles in the future. Knowledgeable observers suggest that one reason why MITI has taken on environmental issues with considerable intensity is that it found its power declining over the course of the 1980s as a result of deregulation. Global environmental technology development and research will require governmental involvement to help finance research and development.

A distinctly Japanese element to sustainable development programmes has been the formulation of very long-term policies. In preparation for UNCED, for example, MITI proposed 'New Earth 21,' a 100-year plan designed to help the planet recover from 200 years of greenhouse-gas emissions. The first fifty years are to be spent in developing and introducing environment-friendly technologies. The next fifty years are to be spent recreating a green planet (Tsûshô Sangyôshô 1993). This programme has been criticized by some as a way of diverting attention from the need for immediate action. Others, however, point to progress already underway under the plan.

As a major part of the plan, MITI and sixty companies established a Research Institute of Innovative Technology for the Environment (RITE). RITE's primary areas of research are in CO_2 fixation (biotechnology-based and chemical-based), new-generation refrigerants, bio-degradable plastics, and environmentally friendly bioreactors. 'New Earth 21' was incorporated as one of the 'Fourteen Proposals for a New Earth' announced by MITI in 1993. Other proposals included the introduction of measures to improve energy efficiency; revision of the Energy Conservation Law; the building of district energy systems; promotion of the supply of non-fossil-fuel energy sources, including nuclear energy and new and renewable energy sources; encouraging environment-friendly consumer and business behaviour; the promotion of recycling; and the promotion of technology development and international co-operation (Tsûshô Sangyôshô 1993).

The government has issued reports encouraging industry to green their activities. In October 1992, MITI made a request to eighty-seven industrial groups, including automobile and electric power industries, to formulate voluntary environmental plans and in 1994 issued an 'Environmental Vision of Industry' report, which reviewed the environmental impacts of corporate activities in fifteen industrial groups and proposed new directions to integrate environmental measures into corporate activities (Global Environmental Affairs Task Force of the Industrial Structure Council of MITI 1994). In February 1993, the Environment Agency issued a report entitled 'Guidance for an Environment-Friendly Firm'.

Because of the importance of administrative guidance as a tool for promoting implementation, it is not enough to look simply at governmental programmes to understand how the Japanese government is approaching sustainable development: specific policy measures are being left for industry to formulate. While this system of leaving guidelines and legislation vague is criticized by some as being too easy on industry and unlikely to lead to any substantial changes in behaviour, it is supported by others as promoting flexibility in meeting sustainable development policy goals and encouraging voluntary industrial compliance.

Until recently the idea of sustainable development was largely ignored by the Japanese business community. Japanese corporations lagged behind their business counterparts in the US and Europe in terms of corporate environmental reporting. Today, a growing number of corporations in Japan are moving beyond green corporate activities to incorporate eco-efficiency as a key component of their long-term business plans (Park 1997). *Keidanren* wants to improve Japan's corporate environmental image. In 1991 it publicized a 'Global Environment Charter', a list of environmental guidelines for industry to follow in operations domestically and overseas (Keizai Dantai Rengôkai 1991). The charter calls on each company to be a good global corporate citizen, recognizing that grappling with environmental problems is essential to its own existence and its activities.

Five years later, in July 1996, *Keidanren* announced its 'Environmental Appeal', a voluntary action plan aimed at environmental conservation in the twenty-first century. Four specific fields were mentioned: measures to cope with global warming; the establishment of a recycle-based society; restructuring of the environmental management system and environmental auditing; and introducing environmental considerations into overseas operations.

The Environmental Appeal was the product of a consensus-building effort within Japanese industry. Individual industries were asked by *Keidanren* to draw up action plans.

Keidanren's 'Global Environmental Charter' has been criticized as being mere rhetoric. There are some signs, however, of change. By December 1996, over 30 industries and 130 industrial organizations had drawn up plans to reduce their burden on the environment with yearly review plans (Japan Council for Sustainable Development 1997: 12–13). A June 1997 *Keidanren* report announced that these numbers had climbed to 37 industries and 137 industrial organizations (Keizai Dantai Rengôkai 1997). As another sign of change, according to the Agency of Industrial Science and Technology of MITI, a total of 248 Japanese applications for the International Standard Organization's (ISO) environmental management series had been accepted as of April 1997 (Bureau of National Affairs, Inc. 1997: 434).

Overseas Co-operation and Sustainable Development

Official Development Assistance

For Japan, ODA is a critical element of efforts to address sustainable development and environmental protection. Whereas ODA levels have declined in many Organization for Economic Co-operation and Development (OECD) countries, in Japan ODA was targeted as a growth area throughout the late 1980s and the first half of the 1990s. The ODA budget was cut, however, by 10 per cent between FY 1997 and FY 1998 as part of government-wide budgetary cuts designed to address a severe government deficit. Environmental protection has become a central component of ODA programmes. Whereas in 1986, the ratio of environmental aid to official development aid in Japan was 4.8 per cent, by 1990 it had climbed to 12.4 per cent and by 1996 to 20 per cent (OECD 1994a). While some of this has just been a relabelling of projects that in the past were not categorized as environmental, Japan now requires its aid recipients to include environmental projects in their aid requests.

Japan has heavily publicized its environmental ODA budget. At the G-7 meeting organized in the summer of 1989, Japan announced that it would spend ¥300 billion in foreign aid to be targeted specifically for environmental measures over the FY 1989–FY 1991 period (Murdo 1990). At UNCED, Japan further enhanced its commitment to global environmental protection initiatives through environmental ODA. The government pledged to spend

¥900 billion to ¥1 trillion on aid for the environment over a five-year period beginning in 1992.

Three ministries and one agency have primary jurisdiction over Japan's foreign assistance. These are MITI, MoFA, MoF, and the Economic Planning Agency. The main implementing arms for Japanese development aid are the Japan International Co-operation Agency (JICA), which is responsible for technical assistance, and the Japan Bank for International Co-operation (JBIC) formed in October 1999 for the extension of government yen loans. Each ministry attempts to put its own stamp on the aid process, and there is often considerable inter-ministerial rivalry in the process (Orr 1990). Although aid for the environment now accounts for over one-fifth of Japan's foreign assistance expenditures, the Environment Agency is only a minor player influencing Japanese ODA practices. It should be noted, however, that as part of its budget, the Agency is allocated funds for the promotion of international environmental co-operation outside of regular aid channels. Thus, the Environment Agency's 1993 budget for the first time included funds for the establishment of an environmental monitoring network in Asia.

In the past Japanese aid has been strongly criticized as being primarily a means to promote Japanese industry and highly detrimental to the environment overseas (Potter 1994). Richard Forrest (1989), formerly of the National Wildlife Federation, for example, produced a report criticizing Japan for aid programmes that were destructive of the environment, such as major dam projects and projects that financed logging road construction in the tropical forests of Southeast Asia. Richard Tobin (1996) criticized Japanese Grant Aid for Increased Food Production for donating fertilizer and pesticides without taking due consideration of the health implications of toxic pesticides.

Because of this kind of criticism of its aid programmes, since the late 1980s, Japan has taken steps to strengthen environmental considerations in determining aid disbursements. In June 1988, for example, JICA established a Council for Environmental Assistance and in 1990 they formulated Guidelines on Environmental Impact Surveys for Dam Construction Programs. In FY 1993, the Economic Cooperation Bureau of MoFA decided against further donation of pesticides that the World Health Organization deemed highly hazardous (Tobin 1996). In June 1997, Japan announced plans to enhance sustainable development funding to developing countries through its Initiatives for Sustainable Development toward the 21st century. The plan was announced at the Special Session of the United Nations General Assembly for the Overall Review and Appraisal of the Implementation of Agenda 21.

The importance of environmental protection, moreover, was acknowledged in Japan's 1992 ODA Charter, the first systematic official statement of Japan's aid philosophy. The ODA charter stipulated four principles: (1) the pursuit of development in conjunction with environmental conservation; (2) measures to prevent ODA from being used for military purposes; (3) monitoring against the development and manufacture of weapons of destruction; and, (4) the promotion of democratization, introduction of a market economy, the observation of basic human rights, and the guarantee of freedom in countries and areas where Japanese ODA is provided. The Charter specifically mentioned the importance of Japan's historic ties with Asian countries and its close political and economic links with them as reasons for offering greater ODA to these countries (Government of Japan 1992).

Green Aid Plan

In 1991 MITI announced that it was launching a new environmental ODA initiative: 'The Green Aid Plan'. As originally established, this plan was an effort by MITI to strengthen the link between aid disbursements and Japanese technological know-how in pollution control and energy efficiency. The Green Aid Plan stressed prevention of water and air pollution, treatment of waste, recycling, and energy conservation and alternative energy sources. Under the programme, MITI sends experts to recipient countries and trains developing country personnel in the use and maintenance of energy and environmental technologies. MITI also supports joint research between Japan and recipient countries in the development of appropriate environmental and energy technologies and has several demonstration projects. Centres for Energy and Environmental Technology have also been established to serve as liaison offices for co-ordination purposes. The Green Aid Plan is largely financed through special energy research and development accounts that are supported by producer taxes on oil and electricity. Host countries for the Green Aid Plan have expanded since Thailand and China became the first recipients in 1992. Since then Indonesia (1993), the Philippines and Malaysia (1994), and India (1995) have also become recipients of Green Aid. Between 1992 and 1998, twenty-eight projects were allocated funding in China and another seven in Thailand (Evans 1995; New Energy and Industrial Technology Development Organization, n.d.)

These institutional developments suggest that there are important changes occurring in Japanese ODA in an effort to make it a central part of Japan's approach to achieving sustainable development. Efforts to green ODA, however, are relatively recent. It will be years before the new philosophies underpinning Japanese ODA take firm root: organizational change is slow and the barriers to turning ODA green, particularly at the recipient country level, remain large. Moreover, ODA accounts for only a small part of the overall effort. In today's global economy, far larger financial and technological transfers occur outside of ODA channels.

Promoting Regional Co-operation for Sustainable Development

The Asia Pacific region is in a period of transition. For the first time in modern history, the region is beginning to co-operate on environmental problem-solving and regional approaches to sustainable development. Japan is taking a lead in promoting regional approaches to environmental monitoring, agenda-setting, and problem-solving. There are still very few regional institutions for promoting environmental co-operation of any kind in Asia, thus each and every new institution represents a major change with the past. Some of the new institutions that have been formed in the 1990s at Japan's initiative include the Asian Acid Rain Monitoring Network; the Environmental Congress for Asia and the Pacific (Eco Asia)—a forum for environment ministers from throughout Asia to discuss environmental issues and come to agreement on regional policy priorities; and the Institute for Global Environmental Strategies—an international research institute focusing on sustainable development issues in the Asia Pacific Region. All of these institutions were established on the initiative of the Environment Agency.

Climate Change

There has been considerable disagreement within Japan about how to respond to the climate change problem (Tanabe 1999; Kawashima 1997; Ohta 1995; Schreurs 1996; Schreurs 1997a). Japan first announced that it would address its CO_2 emissions at the World Climate Conference in Geneva in November 1989. At the time, Japan was the world's fourth largest emitter of CO_2. Its position moved to fifth with the reunification of Germany. After considerable inter-ministerial bargaining, the Council of Ministers for Global Environmental Conservation announced Japan's Action Program to Arrest Global Warming in October 1990 (Government of Japan 1990). The programme endorsed two different targets for carbon-dioxide emissions, one set by MITI and the other by the Environment Agency. MITI's target called for a freeze of CO_2 emissions on a per capita basis by the year 2000 while the Environment Agency's called for stabilization at 1990 levels. The difference between these plans was substantial since MITI's plan assumed there would be a 6 per cent growth in population and hence a 6 per cent increase in emissions. The Environment Agency's stabilization plan, in contrast, demanded a stabilization of emissions whether or not there was a change in population levels. In the end, the Action Program stated that per capita annual emissions should be stabilized at about 1990 levels in and after 2000, and then went on to say that efforts would also be made to stabilize total annual emissions if research and development into alternative energies and CO_2 fixation progressed more quickly than expected. That both targets were incorporated in the Action Program showed the widely different viewpoints that existed within the Japanese bureaucracy at this early stage of policy formation and the difficulty the bureaucracy had in achieving consensus on action. This situation has remained a defining characteristic of inter-ministerial negotiations within Japan on climate change since this time (Schreurs 1996).

At UNCED, Japan announced its Action Program and became a signatory to the FCCC. It reported to the Secretariat of the FCCC in September 1994 that CO_2 emissions in Japan in FY 2000 would be approximately 330 million tons (an increase of 10 million tons, or 3 per cent over FY 1990 levels) and that per capita emissions would be roughly equal to 1990 levels at 2.6 tons. In other words, Japan expected to meet the weaker of the two goals proposed in the Action Program.

Progress toward meeting the goals of the Action Program has been monitored by the Central Environment Council. In June 1996 the Council released its first report. In FY 1995 a total of 406 projects were in progress at a cost of approximately 11.6 trillion yen (US $96.6 billion at a rate of 120 yen to the dollar). The Council noted, however, that the sense of commitment to the programme is not adequate and that the public lacks awareness of the critical nature of global warming. The Council called for greater public education of the dangers of global warming.

There is good reason to believe that Japan will have difficulties in meeting the CO_2 reduction goal set out in the Action Program. Difficulties in meeting these goals stem from increased energy demand particularly in the household and transportation sectors. In FY 1994, total CO_2 emissions levels were up by 7.2 per cent over FY 1990 levels or 5.8 per cent when measured on a per capita basis. In FY 1994, close to 40 per cent of emissions were from the industrial sector with another 19 per cent from transportation, 12.5 per cent from the household sector, and 11.3 per cent from office buildings. CO_2 emissions in the industrial sector had continually, if only gradually, declined every year since the oil crisis of 1973, but this trend was broken in FY 1994 when emissions surpassed the previous year's levels (Schreurs 1996). Emissions from the transportation sector and the household sector have been steadily increasing as income levels have risen. There has been a substantial rise in the number of private automobiles and in the use of air conditioners, dryers, and large refrigerators. In addition, there has been a large growth in the number of trucks on the road.

In comparison with other OECD countries, Japan's per capita CO_2 emissions are in fact at the low end of the scale. This is a result of the energy-saving and diversification measures taken after the oil shocks of 1973 and 1979. Whether or not Japan can maintain its energy-efficiency lead over other countries, particularly in Europe, remains to be seen. The government of Japan appears reluctant to push for major additional reductions.

The first Conference of the Parties (COP) to the FCCC was held in Berlin in 1995. At this meeting the parties agreed to negotiate a 'protocol or other legal instrument'. This is now known as the Berlin Mandate. Negotiations were to be concluded by the third COP in December 1997. Japan offered to host the meeting, now commonly referred to as the Kyoto Conference.

At the second COP held in Geneva in July 1996, several proposals were put on the table by different states in an effort to influence the direction of international negotiations in the period leading up to the Kyoto Conference. Japan's stance at the Geneva meeting was indecisive. There was no mention of emission-reduction targets or timetables. Instead, the Japanese backed the idea that the advanced industrialized states as a whole should reduce emissions in an equitable way, with each country establishing its own target.

Differences among the Environment Agency and MITI over what the Japanese position in international negotiations should be made it difficult for Japan to take on a leadership role internationally prior to COP-3. It is important to realize that there was disagreement within Japan about even hosting COP-3. MITI was opposed to the idea because it would place pressure on Japan to take on a leadership role in proposing sharp reduction targets for a 'Kyoto Protocol.' Both the MoFA and the Environment Agency favored hosting the meeting. They successfully lobbied for it on the grounds that it would be bad for Japan's international image if it did not host a major international environmental conference. MITI in the end agreed, but no agreement was reached on what Japan's position in the negotiations should be.

In the following months, the Environment Agency and MITI were brought to a stalemate over Japan's position on climate change. The Environment Agency leaned more in the direction of the European Union (EU), which had proposed a 15 per cent 'bubble' reduction target for the EU as a whole. The bubble would allow some states in the EU to increase emissions while others substantially reduced theirs. The Environment Agency proposed, at a minimum, that Japan pursue a 5 per cent reduction in CO_2 emissions by 2010 although the Agency argued that further CO_2 emissions reductions were feasible. The Environment Agency insisted that by using energy conservation technologies such as co-generation, improving auto fuel efficiency, and home and building insulation, such a reduction would be possible. MITI wanted to wait for the US to first adopt a position and did not want to see anything more than a stabilization target for 2010. MITI sided with the cautious US position that even a stabilization of CO_2 emissions at 1990 levels would be difficult. MITI's position was that even if as many as 30 new nuclear power plants were commissioned, CO_2 emissions in 2010 would at least be at 1990 levels (Tanabe 1999; Kawashima 1997).

In the end, Prime Minister Ryutaro Hashimoto intervened after Japan was criticized internationally (particularly by Germany) for failing to take on a leadership position even though it was the host country to the international negotiations. Hashimoto urged the bureaucracy to come to a compromise. The advocacy of green politicians, such as Kazuo Aichi, helped to throw support behind a modest reduction plan. Thus, in the final months leading up to Kyoto, Japan proposed a flexible 5 per cent reduction target relative to 1990 levels for 2012 for Annex I countries. This left room for some Annex 1 countries to have lower reduction targets because of their specific national circumstances while falling short of the EU position, it nevertheless represented a more ambitious target than the US target of stabilization at 1990 levels by 2010.

During the contentious high-level international negotiations at Kyoto, the US and Europe struggled to reach some kind of agreement between their widely divergent positions. In the end, the US negotiators with what appears to have been the backing of the White House, agreed to make sharp reductions in greenhouse-gas emissions on the condition that both Japan and the EU did the same. The US agreed to a 7 per cent reduction in greenhouse-gas emissions between 2008 and 2012. The EU came out of the negotiations only having to agree to an 8 per cent reduction (down sharply from the position the EU had taken going into the negotiations). As host country to the meeting, Japan was desperate to see a successful outcome to the negotiations. Thus, the Japanese negotiators agreed to commit to a 6 per cent reduction in greenhouse-gas emissions relative to 1990 levels by 2008 to 2012, a target that went 1 per cent beyond the maximum amount they had originally said was possible. According to one source, this was done at the behest of US Vice-President Al Gore in a telephone call to Prime Minister Hashimoto (Warrick 1997). Japan joined the US in supporting the idea of joint implementation in the negotiations, which would allow developed countries to gain credit towards their own emissions reductions by reducing greenhouse-gas emissions in developing countries. Japan has already launched preliminary joint implementation projects with Russia.

A noteworthy development is the passage of a Law Concerning the Promotion of Measures to Cope with Global Warming in October 1998. The law outlines responsibilities of the central and local governments, businesses, and citizens in mitigating global warming. The central and local governments, for example, are to take measures to restrict their own greenhouse-gas emissions. Businesses are also to strive to adopt measures to limit greenhouse-gas emissions.

The Convention on Biological Diversity

Japan signed the Convention on Biological Diversity at UNCED in June 1992 and became the eighteenth country to ratify the convention on 28 May 1993. In line with Article 6 of the Convention, the Council of Ministers for Global Environmental Conservation established an inter-ministerial co-ordinating committee in January 1994, consisting of eleven ministries and agencies and headed by the Director General of the Nature Conservation Bureau of the Environment Agency. It was tasked with developing strategies for implementing the convention.

In August 1995 the Council of Ministers for Global Environmental Conservation released its draft report of the National Strategy of Japan on Biological Diversity. After a period for public comment and revisions, the Council of Ministers for Global Environmental Conservation released the National Strategy of Japan on Biological Diversity on 31 October 1995 (Council of Ministers for Global Environmental Conservation 1995). There are four main sections in the National Strategy report: the first describes the current state of biological diversity in Japan and the world; the second describes Japan's basic policies for the conservation and sustainable use of biological diversity and its long-term goals; parts three and four describe existing policies and future goals for implementation of the convention. Much of the initial work focused on improving data about the status of Japan's natural environment.

Biological Diversity in Japan

The Japanese archipelago consists of over 3,000 islands that extend from sub-tropical to sub-Arctic regions. Climatic diversity and a long history of relative isolation has given Japan a remarkably high level of biological diversity. Much of this diversity, however, has been threatened or destroyed by development or war (World War II). Forests cover 67.5 per cent of the country.

Of this figure, virgin forests only constitute 18.2 per cent, secondary forests 24.6 per cent, and planted forests an additional 24.7 per cent. Hokkaido, the northernmost of Japan's four main islands, accounts for more than half of Japan's natural vegetation. There are many unique tropical species in the Ryukyu and Ogasawara Islands of Japan. Many island ecosystems, however, have been damaged by development and the invasion of non-native species. Japan also has many rivers and lakes. A 1985 National Survey, however, found that, of 113 rivers that were surveyed, only thirteen had no river-crossing structures or river-crossing structures that permitted sufficient fish passage. This has led to a serious loss in migratory fish species. Of the 32,817 kilometres of coastline, only 55.2 per cent remains natural. The National Survey on the Natural Environment conducted between FY 1989 and FY 1992 found that there were about 34,000 hectares of coral reefs in the waters of the Southwestern Islands. Only 8.2 per cent of these coral communities were found to be healthy. There has also been an estimated loss of over 4,000 hectares of tidal flats in Japan. Heavy industrialization, in other words, has had a devastating impact on much of Japan's biota and wildlife.

Many plant and animal species are threatened by development. According to the Environment Agency's Red Data Book (February 1999), Japan has 7,087 vascular plant species, about 200 mammalian species, and sixty-four species of reptiles. As of 1999, four mammalian species had become extinct and forty-seven were endangered. Of the 700 bird species, thirteen bird species and subspecies were extinct and ninety were endangered. In the 1990s the Environment Agency employed new compilation and evaluation criteria for the Red Data Book. The new data suggested that there were a larger number of endangered species than had been previously thought. Japan's National Strategy on Biological Diversity states that this loss is due to a rapid decrease and deterioration in the quality of habitats caused by development projects and the introduction of alien species.

Many of Japan's NGOs focus on nature conservation and wildlife-protection issues. The Wild Bird Society is one of Japan's oldest and largest environmental groups. Keikichi Kihara, a leader of efforts to introduce a National Trust movement in Japan on the British model, has spent years promoting nature conservation. The younger son of the Emperor of Japan is honorary chairman of the World Wide Fund for Nature in Japan. While these groups have done much to protect some species from extinction (like the Japanese crane) and some areas from development, they have failed in their efforts to stop several major construction projects, including the damming of the Nagara River and of Isahaya Bay. In these cases, there were strong environmental reasons for abandoning the dam projects, but both projects were planned and approved long before environmental impact assessment was initiated. In Japan, once a project is planned it is very diffi-cult to stop it. Jurisdictional rivalry among Japan's ministries and agencies can make it difficult to implement sustainable development goals. This may be improved somewhat if Japan's ministries are reorganized as is planned and the Environment Agency is made into a ministry.

Basic Policies for Conservation and Sustainable Use of Biological Diversity

The Japanese government's National Strategy on Biological Diversity has two long-term goals. The first is the conservation and sustainable use of bio-logical diversity. The second is the management of comparatively large and connected protected areas. To meet these goals, the National Strategy calls for surveys and monitoring, enhanced information collection systems, research on evaluation and maintenance mechanisms, mitigation measures to address adverse effects, and technology development for sustainable use. The plan also calls for the strengthening of protective measures for plants and animals, expanding and properly managing protected areas, and intro-ducing educational programmes to increase public awareness. The Biodi-versity Centre of Japan was opened in 1998 to improve the collection and dissemination of information. The Centre will publish the results of its Green Census on the internet.

Japan's support for a sustainable-use paradigm deserves attention since it has had a mixed reception in negotiations related to the Convention on Inter-national Trade in Endangered Species (CITES). Japan, like Zimbabwe and Norway, has pushed for recognition of the concept of sustainable use as opposed to strict conservation within CITES (Mofson 1997: 174). The idea behind a sustainable use approach is that species are more likely to be pro-tected if human beings have a material interest in their survival. It is an idea that has been proposed, for example, in relationship to the hunting of some species of elephants and whales, species which are currently protected but for which there is some scientific evidence suggesting that they are no longer endangered.

In-Situ Conservation

In 1971 when the Environment Agency was established, it gained jurisdic-tion over Japan's national parks. Japan has twenty-eight national parks, fifty-five quasi-national parks, and 301 prefectural natural parks regulated by the Natural Parks Law. These total approximately 14.1 per cent of the total area of Japan. Regular surveys are conducted on the condition of Japan's national parks. In addition to the national parks, there are also lands designated as Wilderness Areas and Nature Conservation Areas. Similar systems exist at the prefectural and local levels. Eighteen per cent of Japan's national forests as of 1 April 1995 were designated as Nature Conservation Forests.

There have been some efforts to protect natural areas within Japan in relation to international treaties. Shirakami-sanchi and Yakushima are included as natural heritage areas under the Convention for the Protection of the World Cultural and Natural Heritage. As of 1999, eleven sites, totalling 83,725 hectares, are protected under the Convention on Wetlands of International Importance Especially as Waterfowl Habitats. Finally, Yakushima, Mt. Odaigahara, Mt. Omine, Mt. Hakusan, and Shiga Highland are recognized by the Programme on Man and Biosphere of the United Nations Educational, Scientific, and Cultural Organization.

In response to UNCED and the efforts of Japan's environmentalists, in 1992 the government passed the Law for the Conservation of Endangered Species of Wild Fauna and Flora. The Environment Agency is to draw up a plan for the Rehabilitation of Natural Habitats and Maintenance of Viable Populations for National Endangered Species.

The largest problem for Japan in terms of protection of natural areas is heavy use by tourists and the lack of adequate policing. There are too few rangers to patrol the national parks effectively. Thus, although these areas are conservation areas, illegal catching of endangered butterflies and birds has been a problem.

Ex-Situ Conservation

Japan has been widely criticized for the ecological shadow that its economic activities cast on other parts of the world. Domestically, Yôichi Kuroda, founder of the Japan Tropical Action Network has long criticized Japanese corporations and the Japanese government for the role they have played in tropical deforestation. Peter Dauvergne (1997) likewise paints a dark picture of Japan's responsibility for the deforestation of much of Southeast Asia. This type of criticism has not gone completely unnoticed in Japan. There are some signs of change in corporate and government policies as they pertain to biological conservation overseas.

One particularly important area to consider is the role Japan has played in tropical deforestation. Apart from the producing countries themselves, the main actors with influence over the fate of tropical forests are the importers. As the world's largest importer of tropical hardwoods Japan has played a major role in the deforestation of the Philippines, Indonesia, and Malaysia. Japanese corporations are now moving into Papua New Guinea.

The rising level of domestic and international scrutiny of Japanese involvement in the tropical timber trade in the 1980s proved embarrassing for the Japanese government and industry. Japan's new-found interest in the global environment and ODA put the country in a difficult position. If Japan planned to become a global environmental leader, then it would have to address the thorny question of its role in tropical deforestation in Asia. An active policy to address global warming could not easily be divorced from the tropical forestry issue. Nor could major Japanese corporations easily push a green image when they were threatened with overseas boycotts because of their role in tropical deforestation.

These pressures have been successful in making some changes in Japanese official and corporate behaviour. Thus, Japanese corporations have funded some reforestation projects and are moving away from clear cutting. ODA for tropical forest preservation and reforestation has also been initiated (Schreurs 1997c). The changes, however, are still small in scale and implementation is slow relative to the speed at which forests are disappearing.[1]

Evaluating Japan's Approach to Sustainable Development

Japan was certainly not among the first of the industrialized states to jump on the bandwagon calling for policy action to save the global environment or to promote sustainable development. Today the situation is quite different. Global climate change, stratospheric ozone depletion, acid rain, biological diversity, and the concept of sustainable development have attracted considerable policy attention. In the years leading up to and immediately following UNCED, numerous domestic environmental laws have been passed, new environmental philosophies have started to take root, and organizational changes are occurring to strengthen the position of environmental policy advocates.

There are several reasons for the new interest expressed by Japanese leaders in global environmental protection and sustainable development (the two terms are used almost interchangeably in policy documents) beginning in the late 1980s. They include Japan's concern with future energy security, the nation's search for areas in which it can play a larger global role, a recognition that there are major potential markets in environmental technologies, and changing environmental norms.

Because of Japan's heavy dependence on imported oil, energy security

---

[1] Discussion with Yoichi Kuroda, 5 Nov. 1997, Yokohama, Japan.

remains an important issue. China's expanding energy demand raises additional concerns about energy stability in the Asian region in the future. A June 1997 MITI document outlines three areas that will require future policy attention by the ministry: (1) increasing competition and the ageing of society; (2) the globalization of the economy and the hollowing-out of urban and village areas; and (3) the growing seriousness of energy and environmental problems. The document states that:

In the near future, the Japanese economy is in danger of being shocked by the Asian region's rapid industrialization and its impact on world energy demand. In addition, rising international demands to deal with the global-warming problem and the growing seriousness of waste management will seriously constrain our economy. These show the limitations of economic systems based on mass production, mass consumption, and mass waste.   (Tsûsho Sangyôshô 1997: 1, translation by the author)

Japan has had trouble playing the role of a 'normal state' in global politics because of constitutional restrictions on Japan's deployment of military forces overseas. With continued domestic opposition to changing Japan's peace constitution as well as considerable concern from Asian neighbours, Japan is instead pursuing other foreign policy areas in which it can play a larger global role. These include ODA and global environmental protection.

There are also clearly economic interests at stake. A June 1994 report by the Industrial Structure Council, a state advisory panel, noted that energy consumption by the nation's fifteen major manufacturing sectors (steel, aluminium, non-ferrous metals, materials, chemicals, synthetic fibres, paper-pulp, cement, autos, household electrical appliances, electronic equipment, electric power, gas, petroleum and, distribution) accounted for 84 per cent of the total energy use by all manufacturers. Efforts by the private sector, and in particular these industries, to develop energy-efficient, easy-to-recycle products, and pollution-free manufacturing processes could lead to a substantial environment-related business. The report estimated that Japan's environment-related business could grow to ¥23 trillion in 2000 and to ¥35 trillion in 2010 compared with ¥15 trillion at present (*Japan Times*, 28 June 1994: 10).

Finally, global environmental awareness is growing in Japan. This can be seen in the extensive newspaper reporting on global environmental issues and the efforts of *Seikatsu Kyôdô Kumiai* (co-operatives run largely by women that are to be found in virtually every city of Japan) to promote environmental protection within the household through recycling and the consumption of pesticide-free foods.

The concept of sustainable development is taking root, but it is still poorly defined. Japan's sustainable development policies have been shaped primarily by the Environment Agency and MITI with some input by other ministries and agencies. International opinion has also influenced changes in policy and practice. Despite dramatic changes to Japan's NGO community in the last decade, the community remains small and on the political margins. It is not yet well integrated into the policy-formation process although this could change in the future. Some politicians have started to speak up on environmental issues and to try to influence the shape of Japan's sustainable development policies. In the future, there may be more green campaigning.

Japan's sustainable development policies touch upon a wide range of policy areas, including environmental ODA, energy conservation and development, pollution control, recycling, and education. What sustainable development means in a resource-poor nation like Japan, however, remains ambiguous.

Japan is unlikely to become an international leader in forging new understandings of sustainable development. Policy formation remains largely dominated by bureaucrats. There are few think-tanks in Japan, and the NGO community does not have the resources to make effective policy recommendations. Bureaucratic fragmentation makes it difficult for Japan to formulate new policy proposals until they have already been introduced in some other country, and this can then be used to justify the need for policy change within Japan as well. Jurisdictional divisions also make it difficult to introduce sustainable development policies that are government-wide. The Environment Agency's authority is very limited.

Still, despite major hurdles, over the longer term, Japan may well outperform the US, and match or even outperform northern European countries, in implementing sustainable development programmes and policies. Once committed to action, Japan often performs well in implementation.

6

The Netherlands: Ambitious on Goals— Ambivalent on Action

MARIE-LOUISE VAN MUIJEN

Introduction

The Netherlands often regards itself as setting an example in the world of international environmental politics. With respect to sustainable development, extensive policies had already been put in place before UNCED. The intensity of governmental attention to environmental protection had been growing since the 1970s. Already by the 1980s the Dutch government began to recognize that environmental issues could not be considered as isolated phenomena, and that integrative planning policies would be needed to deal with these problems successfully.

A recognition of the seriousness of global environmental problems encouraged Dutch efforts at the national and international levels. The global character of environmental problems made it clear that effective policies abroad were essential if domestic environmental targets were to be obtained. This confirmed Dutch commitment to international negotiations and made the success of Dutch environmental policy explicitly dependent upon foreign policy measures and uncertain outcomes in the international arena.

While the Dutch obviously have a reputation to maintain, the question is whether the country really provides an example to be followed when it comes to sustainable development. In this chapter it will become clear that numerous White Papers have been written since UNCED, policies have been carried out with more or less rigour, and have provoked more or less discussion. However, although Dutch environmental policy is considered relatively successful, this does not mean that the Netherlands is necessarily developing in the direction of sustainable consumption and production. Indeed, while the Ministry of the Environment has been able to mobilize broad societal support for sustainable development and public co-operation in carrying through initiatives, its efforts appear to have lost momentum now that most of the cost-effective measures have been implemented. This creates the risk that pollution will again start to rise, even in those sectors where policies have been successful in recent years.

The Netherlands: Facts and Figures

The Netherlands is situated in the delta of the Rhine, IJssel and Meuse rivers. About 24 per cent of its territory is below sea level. The land surface covers 34,000 square kilometres. This area consists of 59 per cent agricultural land, 9 per cent forest, 5 per cent 'natural land', and 27 per cent land devoted to urban, infrastructural, and other uses (VROM et al. 1997a). The period 1980–95 saw a population increase of 9.5 per cent, from 14.1 million to 15.4 million inhabitants. This is the highest average population density in the OECD: 454 inhabitants per square kilometre (CBS 1996). The population concentration is highest in the Randstad, which includes Amsterdam, Rotterdam, The Hague, Utrecht, and the smaller cities in between (with densities between 600 and 1,200 inhabitants per square kilometre). The Randstad is located in the western part of the country. Rotterdam is important for its oil-refining capacity and its ports, which are the biggest in the world. Schiphol Airport, near Amsterdam, is a major transit point for the rest of Europe.

The Dutch economy is very open. GDP grew from NFL 516,000 million in 1990 to 568,000 (using 1990 prices) in 1995, an increase of 10 per cent (CBS 1996). The export of goods and services now constitutes almost half of GDP (VROM 1997a: 8). The country has a comparatively large amount of industry and intensive farming, leading to a considerable import and export of environmental pollution. In addition, an important part of the European transport network is to be found in the Netherlands. In economic terms the Netherlands is one of the most successful countries in Western Europe; therefore the 'Dutch model' is often praised.

As for the political system, it may be described as highly consensus-based with a strong tradition of planning in many areas of social life. The Dutch system is characterized by a long tradition of government consultation with various groups in society. In the Netherlands corporatism has been associated with 'pillarization' (Lijphart 1968). Pillarization denotes the simultaneous existence of a number of subcultures which organize social activities under separate ideological auspices. The image is one of separate pillars, jointly supporting a common state. During the past two and a half decades the pillars have disintegrated almost completely, but this has not erased the patterns of consultation. Yet today consultations are much less focused on consensus than in the past. Now involvement is primarily a reflection of the representation of conflicting interests, and the increasing interdependence of policy questions.

Current practice in the environmental field continues and strengthens this custom. Consistent with the central role of planning in the Dutch administrative system, the first impulse for a more integrated approach was elaborated in a series of Indicative Multi-year Programmes for the Environment, starting in 1984 for the period 1985–9. These were issued by the Ministry of Housing, Physical Planning and Environment (VROM), which was established in 1982. While the well-known National Environmental Policy Plans (NEPPs)—published since 1989—are the paramount environmental plans of the Netherlands, they must be regarded in the context of the overall administrative and planning culture. The NEPPs help to redirect environmental policies, to associate all levels of government and all relevant societal groups with these policies, and to better integrate environmental concerns into sectoral policies and practices (VROM 1994: 15–19).

The Road to National Environmental Policy Planning through *Our Common Future* and 'Concern for Tomorrow'

The late 1980s witnessed an upswing in public interest in environmental issues. Thus the publication of *Our Common Future* (WCED 1987) did not go unnoticed. In 1988 the Dutch National Institute of Public Health and the Environment (RIVM—a governmental institute, financed by national government) published a report titled 'Concern for Tomorrow', which assessed the deterioration of the Dutch environment by grouping the main environmental impacts (problems and pollutants) according to their economic drivers (RIVM 1988). On the basis of this analysis the RIVM recommended strict reductions in the use and emission of polluting substances, and stressed the need for radical changes to present patterns of production and consumption, since even with a consistent application of end-of-pipe technologies it would not be possible to prevent a further decline in environmental quality in the Netherlands. It was at this point that the influence of the Brundtland report was felt.

Our Common Future contributed to growing public environmental awareness and an acceptance of the need for urgent action. This was reflected in, and reinforced by, the Queen's 1988 Christmas Address, which along with her formal speech at the annual opening of the Parliament in September, was devoted to environmental themes.

The government responded by presenting an integrative National Environmental Policy Plan (NEPP) in 1989. NEPP I was written on the basis of the alarming situation sketched out by the RIVM, and reflected the central message of the Brundtland report (that concern for the economy and for the environment should not be seen as contradictory, rather protection of the environment is an essential condition of sustainable development). During this period worries about global environmental problems, such as the greenhouse effect and the depletion of the ozone layer, rapidly increased. Another factor that helped to push the environmental issue to the fore was the character of the politicians responsible for national environmental policy. During the 1980s two politicians from the Conservative party held the environmental portfolio. The first, Winsemius (1982–6) introduced the policy of 'verinnerlijking' (internalization of environmental values), the essence of which was to encourage environmentally friendly behaviour among citizens by appealing to their sense of responsibility. A firm believer in positive management theory, he applied his own ideas on strategic management to the reorganization of the environmental domain. He emphasized the importance of new partnerships with other authorities and with target-groups in society. According to Winsemius, the debate on pollution should not be regarded as a political struggle between polluters and polluted, but as a matter of innovation versus inefficiency (Hajer 1995: 186). His successor, Nijpels (1986–9), was particularly influential in securing co-operation with other ministries. Although VROM bears responsibility for the NEPP, the plan was endorsed by the ministries of Transport, Public Works and Water Management (V&W), Agriculture, Nature Management and Fisheries (LNV), Economic Affairs (EZ), Foreign Affairs (BuZa) and Development Co-operation (OS).

According to the Dutch government, national environmental policy planning has been considered the appropriate approach to introduce sustainable development policies in accordance with the recommendations of the Brundtland Report. NEPP I outlined the strategy that the Dutch authorities wished to follow in order to make the Netherlands—within the span of one generation—a sustainable society, by which they meant a society that does not exceed the limits of what the environment can bear. The NEPP strategy was introduced as the political response to the analysis presented in 'Concern for Tomorrow'. While the RIVM report attempted to define the conditions within which Dutch development could be considered sustainable, the focus of *Our Common Future* was global and not national. The perspectives of the two reports do not really coincide: the RIVM report focuses on the negative consequences of luxury and abundance (the critical factor being sustainability), whereas the Brundtland Report particularly emphasizes the vicious circle of poverty and exhaustion of natural resources (the critical factor being the lack of development). The link between 'Concern for 'Tomorrow' and the NEPP is therefore much more direct. As Jansen and Opschoor put it, 'Concern for Tomorrow' offers the scientific analysis upon which NEPP is based (Jansen and Opschoor 1989: 310).

The Impact of the Brundlandt Report

The debate in the Netherlands about the relationship between economy and environment was given a fresh impetus with the publication of the Brundtlandt Report. The provisional governmental response to the report endorsed the concept of sustainable development, but did not go into much detail (VROM 1987–8). During the parliamentary discussion it was decided that the government had to present a definitive response by the autumn of 1989 at the latest, which should include a presentation on how each ministry intended to translate the Brundtland recommendations into concrete policies (motion Boers-Wijnberg c.s.; VROM 1987–8). This motion was adopted by the government in NEPP I as Action Point A141, which specified a promise to evaluate the extent to which existing policy instruments contributed to sustainable development. The actual results of Action A141 were sent to Parliament in 1995 (VROM 1995–6). All ministries (except the Ministry of Education, Arts and Science) had carried out research on policy instruments, which led to the announcement of eighty measures. Yet this analysis offered few new insights, nor did the ministries make any changes in the process through which they formulate policies, or in the organization of policy making with respect to strengthening environmental integration.

NEPP I and Sustainable Development

The planning process for NEPP I was jointly co-ordinated by the Minister of the Environment and his Director General. Other key ministries were also involved (VROM 1994: 8), but given the fact that the political climate was strongly in favour of environmental issues, VROM was temporarily able to set the agenda. The process was guided by a strong steering committee, comprised of the directors general of all the ministries involved, and a representative from the RIVM.

The committee adopted the concept of sustainable development as a point of departure and sought to spell out the Brundtland recommendations in the Dutch context along several lines (VROM 1988–9: 105):

• Closing substance cycles, aimed at consciously managing the entire chain of production, consumption and disposal, to maximize reuse and recycling

and minimize emissions at each stage (Integrated Life Cycle Management);
- conserving energy and using cleaner energy sources;
- quality enhancement, i.e. promoting the highest quality of production processes and products;
- 'high quality' denotes minimized demand on the environment in terms of raw material and energy consumption, emissions and discharges and final disposal requirements.

The overall goal of NEPP I was sustainability by the year 2010. The definition of sustainability presented in the Brundtland report was endorsed by the Dutch government: satisfying the needs of the present generation without compromising the ability of future generations to meet their own needs. NEPP I elaborates on this definition, by identifying one generation as the equivalent of twenty-five years, and by suggesting that the maintenance of the earth's carrying-capacity requires precise reductions in emissions of pollutants to be achieved within this period. However, only a short time later it was recognized that it would not be possible to completely solve all existing environmental problems within a 20–25 year horizon. The goal was therefore modified and it became the 'aim of Dutch environmental policy to make these problems manageable within that period' (VROM 1997a: 10).

NEPP I integrated national and international priorities by identifying problems using a system of geographical scale, with categories such as local, continental and global, clearly indicating the international dimensions of environmental issues. The classification included climate change (global warming and depletion of the ozone layer), acidification (acid deposition on soil, surface water and buildings), eutrophication, dispersion, waste disposal, noise nuisance, water depletion, and resource management (sustainable use of renewable and non-renewable resources and energy). These areas became central to the policy development process: they helped to identify the physical sources of environmental degradation, the responsible economic sectors, and the levels at which impacts are felt.

Since many areas could only be addressed through international cooperation, environmental protection became an important concern of Dutch foreign policy, and environmental aid to developing countries was expanded. In this field NEPP I contained a number of suggestions, including the improvement of global management structures.

The overall objectives of NEPP I were further broken down into detailed reduction targets for specified substances and waste streams. The responsibility for achieving these emission-reduction targets was allocated to target-groups. 'Target-groups' represent the key groups of polluters in Dutch society. A continuing feature of environmental policy in the Netherlands has been an effort to arrive at agreement on the division of responsibility for achieving specific targets among different target-groups and between the members of each target-group. Target-groups established in NEPP I include agriculture, traffic and transport, industry and refineries, gas and electricity supply, construction, consumers, and retail trade.

NEPP I set out the national environmental agenda and created the momentum for many groups in society to develop their own plans. It can be considered as a plan to integrate environmental concerns into all areas of public policy. The function of subsequent plans has been to follow up these initiatives, and to ensure that the original objectives are realized. In fact, after the publication of the NEPP I eighty-eight organizations in the Netherlands published comments on this plan (Van der Straaten 1992: 48). The idea of sustainable development and its basic premises, however, were hardly disputed, a situation which is likely to have been a result of the growing consensus on the basic lines of environmental policy—from end-of-pipe to more fundamental changes, but without breaking with modern, industrial society. NEPP offered scope for continued economic growth, which dampened possible fears of more radical change.

The presentation of NEPP I can, however, be seen as an anticlimax. First, the Cabinet fell over one element of NEPP I, even before it had been presented officially. The issue was a simple one: for many years Dutch taxpayers had been allowed a tax deduction on their expenses for commuting to work. As part of its general strategy to discourage private car use, NEPP I proposed to abolish the tax deduction. The Conservative fraction in Parliament decided to oppose this provision of the plan and threatened to withdraw from the coalition. This placed minister Nijpels in the difficult position of having to oppose the provision as a member of the Conservative Party, while supporting it as a minister and member of Cabinet. In view of the Conservative withdrawal from the Christian Democrat/Conservative coalition Prime Minister Lubbers (Christian Democrat) had to request a dissolution of Parliament and a general election (Weale 1992: 144).

Second, rather than following all the recommendations of RIVM, NEPP I sought merely to intensify and elaborate on existing policies. Its chief purpose appeared to be the specification of environmental objectives in quantitative terms, with targets to be achieved by the year 2010. The policy instruments that were promoted for that purpose were essentially traditional measures (such as decreasing emissions and regulation). NEPP I represented

an extension, in a more comprehensive way, of the existing system of pollution control (Van Muijen 1995).

After the Lubbers-II Cabinet fell in 1989, the incoming minister of VROM
(Alders, Social Democrat) wanted to make additions to the NEPP, particularly with regard to CO_2 and NOx emissions. These were incorporated in a
revised version of the NEPP I, and published in 1990 as the NEPP+ (VROM
1990). This process took about five months.

The speed of developments on paper is also evident from the policy statement issued by the Lubbers-III government (Christian Democrats and Social
Democrats) upon taking office after the Lubbers-II government fell in 1989.
According to that statement (27 November 1989), environmental policy had
become the third mainstay of government policy. The need for a change of
direction, which could only be achieved by far-reaching measures was
acknowledged, but the character of these far-reaching measures remained
to be defined. In many respects, this can be considered a missed opportunity
(Waller-Hunter 1991: 719).

A World of Difference

Until 1990 Dutch development-aid policy lacked an integrated vision of the
relationship between the environment and development, and the manner
in which ecological and developmental problems should be reflected in
the implementation of policy. With the arrival of Jan Pronk, the Social
Democrat who became Minister of Development Co-operation (OS) in
1989, a major change occurred.

The governmental White Paper 'A world of difference' (OS 1990–1) paid
a great deal of attention to those aspects of the sustainable development
concept that concern the relationship between industrialized and developing countries. Three such aspects were identified: (1) growth in production
(economic development); (2) fairer distribution (the fight against poverty);
and (3) maintaining environmental reserves (ecological sustainability). This
analysis led to the announcement of a number of measures designed to overcome the negative ecological consequences of aid projects and programmes,
and to promote international co-operation in the field of environmental
conservation.

The White Paper's analytical section was praised widely and regarded as
a break with existing approaches. The process of translating this orientation
into policy, however, raised many questions. These questions related not so
much to the specific policy area of development co-operation, but to the
linkages with the internal policies of the Netherlands.

Preparing for UNCED

During the preparation of the Dutch position for UNCED, the government documents discussed above were of decisive importance. Thus the Netherlands entered the UNCED debate well prepared at the domestic level: it had accepted sustainable development as part of its policy. Yet it was also recognized that sustainable development could not be achieved worldwide merely by means of environmental measures and co-operation with developing countries. Rather, both these policies must be deployed in a broader context of redistribution. This had been mentioned explicitly in the letter on UNCED from ministers (VROM and OS) to Parliament, which regarded the challenge to be finding a balance to prevent irreversible damage to the global environmental reserve while improving the socio-economic position of the developing countries (VROM and OS 1990–1). The Cabinet defined its goals for UNCED as: strengthening international environmental co-operation, broadening national support for such an international approach, accepting an equal sharing of costs and burdens, and integrating environmental care into development policy. The Dutch government stressed particularly the interests and problems of developing countries, and their special position in both causing and solving global environmental problems.

The Dutch were actively involved in preparing recommendations on the interrelationship between environment and development (e.g. by organizing a conference on 'Sustainable Development From Concept to Action' in November 1991). Furthermore, they took several initiatives to break the often recurring impasses during the Prepcom meetings (VROM and OS 1991–2). The Netherlands also made a special point of enabling the developing countries to participate in UNCED, by providing the UNCED Secretariat with additional finances for this purpose, and by promoting Dutch NGO participation by subsidizing organizations taking initiatives towards developing countries.

The EU has been regarded as the primary framework for Dutch international environmental policy. Alders (who took office in 1989), devoted much of his time and attention to the EU. His active diplomacy paid off during the UNCED meetings, when he was elected as one of the vice-chairs of the Presidium. Moreover, he had a decisive influence on the adoption by the EU of a separate climate statement which contained more stringent CO_2 reductions, and which announced that a study was to be carried out on the feasibility of a carbon/energy eco-tax.

With regard to the other UNCED areas dealt with during the Prepcom meetings, the cabinet based its standpoint on existing White Papers like the ones on Nature Policy, Tropical Timber, Energy Saving, the Transport Structure Plan, and the Memorandum on Water Management (VROM and OS 1990–1). As a consequence, the Dutch National Report to UNCED did not contain new policies.

Broad governmental participation was guaranteed by the creation of interdepartmental working-groups engaged with the various UNCED areas. Co-ordination was provided by existing forums. The Dutch input in international environmental negotiations with relevance to foreign policy is co-ordinated by the Co-ordination Commission for International Environmental Affairs (CIM), chaired by the Minister of Foreign Affairs, and composed of civil servants from several ministries. Within VROM, the Directorate for International Environmental Affairs co-ordinates all international efforts.

Parliament was informed on the progress in the preparations for UNCED on a regular basis by ministers from both VROM and OS. Their reports often reflected disappointment with the lack of progress and the unwillingness to make decisions.

A number of advisory councils commented upon the position the government intended to take. The National Advisory Council for Development Co-operation (NAR 1991; NAR 1992) made a plea for strengthening the UN institutional framework for sustainable development (strengthening enforcement by involving the International Court of Justice or the Security Council) and the creation of an Environmental Ombudsman (an international bureau competent to investigate environmental complaints). The Social Economic Council's Commission on International Social Economic Affairs (SER 1992) stressed the importance of binding agreements on the sharing and effective use of the global environmental space. The Government Advisory Committee on the Environment focused on the concept of environmental space, drawing upon ideas presented by Friends of the Earth in their 'Action Plan: Sustainable Netherlands' (1992).[1]

In addition, much attention was paid to the organization of domestic societal support. Many of the organizations which are involved with the issues of environment, development, and security receive financial support from the government. The government is in fact paying for its own opposition, without posing any conditions with respect to the content or political

---

[1] 'Environmental space' is concerned with the space the Earth provides for humans (and other species) to exploit. A rough calculation of the global environmental space was made by Milieudefensie for the key resources energy, wood, water, raw materials, and arable land. Dividing the global environmental space by the number of world citizens produces the environmental space available per person. The key consequence of the equity principle is that the use of resources in the rich countries must be reduced significantly.

position of organizations. NGO participation had also been stimulated by the financial support given to the establishment of 'Platform Brazil 1992' in 1990. Its mission was threefold: to spread information; to stimulate 'sustainable awareness'; and to formulate ideas and plans (Platform Brazilië, 1992). The Platform consisted of representatives from environmental and consumer organizations, development-aid groups, business, youth and women's organizations, and scientists. The ministries of VROM and OS both participated as observers. The Platform managed to prepare an NGO–UNCED standpoint that inevitably—given the number and range of organizations involved—appeared to be a compromise. Some groups, united in the Alliance for Sustainable Development, therefore decided to write their own report (Alliantie voor Duurzae Ontwikkeling 1992). Eventually NGO representation to the official Dutch UNCED delegation came to be organized through the Platform, while participation in pure NGO affairs, like the Global Forum, was organized through the Alliance for Sustainable Development.

Post UNCED Reaction

In August 1992, a couple of months after UNCED, the government presented to Parliament its ideas and strategy on the implementation of the UNCED agreements. The short-term focus was on spreading information: thus the Dutch translations of the UNCED documents were in preparation immediately after the Rio meeting. Platform Brazil 1992 was willing to continue its activities under a new name and therefore continued to receive financial support.

The long-term focus was on implementing structural measures in national, EU, and international policy-arenas, based on an analysis of UNCED outcomes and a comparison with Dutch policies already in place (VROM and OS 1991–2). This analysis suggested that additional measures (new policies and strategies) were required with respect to the issues of forestry, environment and trade, environmental security, and individual environmental rights and duties. With regard to environmental space, sustainable production and consumption, technology co-operation, integrative planning, and bilateral agreements, Dutch ministers intended to propose concrete actions in the context of NEPP II.

The analysis of UNCED outcomes with respect to Agenda 21 and its relation to Dutch policy was presented to the Parliament by letter on 16 July 1993 (VROM 1992–3b). The official conclusion was that Dutch policy was already in line with the goals and actions formulated in Agenda 21 (VROM 1992–3b). NGOs on the other hand, were much more critical in their judgement of Dutch performance.

Incorporating UNCED in NEPP II

The ministries involved in developing environmental policy started work on preparing NEPP II in mid-1992. The document was published in September 1993, and approved by Parliament in 1994. NEPP II covered the planning period through to 1998.

Sustainable development within one generation was retained as the overall goal, and the environmental quality objectives established for the various areas and the targets set for target-groups were not changed either. However, NEPP II was a different sort of document. While NEPP I set out the government's environmental agenda, and created the momentum for many groups in society to develop plans, the aim of the second plan was to follow up these initiatives, and to ensure that their objectives were realized.

In several newspaper interviews it was argued by the then Minister for the Environment (in 1994 the office was taken over by De Boer, Social Democrat) that there had been no need for additional plans, because the government was satisfied with its integral, long-term approach and emphasis on responsibility. The Minister was quite optimistic about realizing the targets within the planning period. None the less, she argued that special attention should be paid to 'difficult target-groups', such as consumers and retail-businesses. New implementation strategies and measures should be directed at target-groups since they were ultimately responsible for making all government policy operational. The NEPP II approach therefore focused on providing clear targets, tasks, and information, improving the implementation infrastructure (technology, facilities, and markets), and tailoring measures more specifically to the needs of target-group members. Since NEPP II the central focus has been on: (1) the implementation of existing plans; (2) the introduction of additional measures where targets cannot be met with existing policy plans; and (3) working towards sustainable patterns of production and consumption (VROM 1994).

A shift towards a more collaborative relationship between public and private actors which corresponded well with basic ideas of UNCED had already been initiated in the mid-1980s. At first (during NEPP I), the policy process was organized rather top-down, but the project team became more of a co-ordinating body later in NEPP II, seeking to involve all interested parties. During NEPP II (and later NEPP III) the project team regularly consulted NGOs and target-groups. The NEPP II process was more of a consultative process aimed at persuading the target-groups to participate in discussing what changes they should make and in monitoring implementation.

In NEPP I a tension could be detected between unilaterally established norms and targets on the one hand, and policy implementation by co-operation with target-groups on the other. This created the impression that the role of target-groups was crucial in the process of implementing policies, but was neglected as far as the formulation of policies is concerned. As a result, target-groups might feel that they have been handed targets which they would have to meet anyway, instead of being engaged in a two-way dialogue on the overall strategy. With NEPP II the government intended to allow target-groups greater freedom in setting priorities for the implementation of policies. None the less, policies remain subject to certain conditions, and within a framework of targets to be achieved by the target-groups and the authorities.

Institutional Arrangements and Strategies

A formal national council for sustainable development does not exist in the Netherlands. This is because the Netherlands already had policy-planning procedures involving various actors before the term sustainable development became well-known internationally. These planning procedures are not just developed by the national government. It is a combined effort involving other authorities as well. Although policies are formulated mostly at the national level, they are implemented largely at the regional and local level, which involves twelve provinces, 600 municipalities, and 120 water boards. The implementation of environmental policies is in fact organized along the lines of the well-known motto 'think globally, act locally'. This is reflected by the way competencies have been distributed in the Environmental Management Act (1993). The different authorities are involved in negotiations on the joint implementation of goals, and the results of these talks are worked out in administrative agreements between VROM, VNG (Association of Municipalities), IPO (Association of Provinces), and the UvW (Association of Water Boards).

The majority of the policy instruments that were promoted in the context of NEPP I concentrated on measures like decreasing emissions and regulation. NEPP I merely extended, in a more comprehensive way, the existing system of pollution control. Environmental policy thus depended on a strong regulatory framework backed up by inspection and enforcement agencies. Over time, however, a general development can be observed from

imperative-and-generic to voluntary-and-specific instruments. This development is connected to the observation that instruments are applied in an institutional context in which there is a mutual dependency between governors
and governed, and in which target-groups are characterized by complexity.
These characteristics provided for a context in which a consensus method
based on the use of communicative instruments may succeed best. The key
role for the authorities then is to bring different agencies and individuals
together. NEPP II therefore offered—at least on paper—the foundation for
an incentive structure which encouraged (and required) all groups in society
to make decisions that will reduce adverse environmental impacts. Consultation and negotiation are central to mobilizing this co-operative effort
because it leads to a greater sense of involvement and commitment by all
parties. The chances of achieving policy objectives are further improved if
implementation procedures are shaped by those who are responsible for carrying them out. NEPP II thus established a number of implementation
strategies (VROM 1994):

- The integration of environmental policy considerations into other sectoral ministries was specifically targeted as a governmental aim (so-called
  'external integration'). The policy-planning phase involved extensive consultation and negotiation with all affected government departments.
- Strong links have been established between central and regional governments, and extra funding provided for developing environmental plans and
  action programs at the provincial and municipal levels. Negotiations are
  used to determine the most appropriate NEPP targets and actions for local
  implementation, given the linkage between NEPP targets and Agenda 21
  commitments.
- An open planning process has been used to develop environmental policy
  with target-groups and industry sectors, which has led to the development
  of implemention sector plans with all designated target-groups and the
  conclusion of a number of voluntary agreements with industry.
- The Netherlands explicitly aims to play the role of initiator and stimula-
  tor in international environmental policy, because in its perception the
  achievement of NEPP goals depends on action being taken by the international community. Active environmental diplomacy (VROM 1994: 57
  and 68), supported by institutional reinforcement at the international level,
  form the basis of this approach.
- NEPP II sets out a strategic framework, but was designed as an action plan
  as well: its main strategy lines were reinforced by over 200 specific actions
  to be carried out by government and target-groups in close co-operation.
  Specific actions relate both to environmental quality achievements and

process measures, such as research, production of policy papers, and development of implementation and enforcement structures.

Periodic evaluations are carried out on the basis of two types of environmental review. The first, environmental monitoring, measures data such as emissions or environmental quality. The second, performance monitoring, measures the effectiveness of environmental policy and reports on its economic aspects. Environmental monitoring is the responsibility of the RIVM, which publishes National Environmental Outlook at the midpoint of each four-year NEPP programme to evaluate the current policies and sketch optional choices and scenarios for the next period. For this purpose RIVM has developed environmental indicators. Indicators are weighted by their absolute importance to the environment and aggregated to show precisely how far the Netherlands is from achieving sustainability. Environmental policy is regularly adjusted, based on performance monitoring. VROM publishes a yearly Environmental Programme, which assesses the current NEPP and accompanies the ministerial budget.

In the most recent 'Environmental Balance' the RIVM (1997a) concluded that the emissions of a number of pollutants have been decreasing, possibly as a result of policy measures taken in the beginning of the decade (e.g. increasing duties on fuel and the introduction of the catalytic converter). However, these positive results have been partially neutralized by increasing environmental pressures caused by 'difficult' target-groups (increasing consumption of electricity and gas, agricultural waste, and mobility), a situation which makes the overall picture less promising.

In March 1998 NEPP III was presented. Whereas the earlier plans had contained specific objectives and measures for concrete action, NEPP III had more the character of a policy document which surveyed progress and outlined a range of options to be considered in order to progress toward the quality objectives already set. Political decisions on these alternatives was postponed until after the general elections and the formation of a new government.

The elections were held in May 1998. The new government—Kok-II—took office in August. In the Kok-II Cabinet the Social Democrat Pronk held the VROM office (this has been considered a remarkable appointment, because until that time his interests were in development co-operation). Despite earlier intentions to prepare a policy document setting out an integrated approach to provoke the external integration of environmental issues, Pronk started preparations for NEPP IV in the beginning of 1999.

In NEPP IV the Dutch long-term policy on sustainable development will be central. Environmental policy will be re-evaluated on the basis of a historical analysis of the last 30 years, and redesigned on the basis of expecta-tions for the next 30 years. Pronk aims at strengthening the international aspects of environmental policy-making and the international approach (his international orientation can easily be explained by his experience in the development co-operation field). In NEPP IV the creation of conditions for environmentally benign processes will be stressed. Some of them were men-tioned already in the Kok-II governmental statement, such as the use of market instruments (including taxes and subsidies of technologies and cost-effective solutions).

The preparation for NEPP IV will take place in four phases. The first agenda-setting phase (with the organization of public debates) will lead to government decision-making on the agenda in the Summer of 1999. In the second phase—until spring 2000—the issues included on the agenda will be elaborated. Further revision will dominate the third stage, and the decision-making stage starts from autumn 2000. The NEPP IV will be presented to Parliament in the beginning of 2001.

Sustainable Funding

At an early point the Dutch recognized that the UNCED initiatives could only be implemented with additional finances. In his speech to the plenary UNCED meeting in 1992 the Minister of the Environment, Alders, made it clear that the Netherlands would support the call for new and additional resources to assist developing countries in dealing with global environmen-tal issues. This funding should come on top of existing aid budgets, which should be increased to reach the target of 0.7 per cent of GNP by the year 2000, or as soon as possible thereafter:

My government is already committed to an annual amount of 1.5 per cent of Net National Income (more than 0.9 per cent GNP) for development assistance. Within that budget allocation, the financial resources available for the promotion of envir-onmentally sound development in developing countries will double in the next two year, to reach a total of almost 250 million dollars per annum. In addition to the current commitments for development assistance, my government will provide new and additional financial resources up to a maximum of 0.1 per cent GNP for imple-menting their activities related to global environmental agreements, provided that the substantive outcome of UNCED warrants such an increase and that other coun-tries will take a similar course.   (Staatscourant 9 June 1992)

The opening of the Earth Summit +5 meeting in 1997 was marked by a widespread recognition that the implementation of the UNCED goals so far had not been successful. The Global Environment Facility (GEF)—the only major institution whose formation was pledged at UNCED—remained far too small to make an impact on development in poor countries, and development aid from the rich countries had fallen sharply. According to Minister Pronk from OS the Netherlands did not really help to prevent this failure.

The Climate Convention presupposed that the developed countries would support the developing countries to prepare their own climate policies by means of the GEF. Over a period of three years, the Netherlands contributed more than US$ 70 million. The Dutch have been active in the field of Joint Implementation (JI) since the international climate meeting in Berlin in 1995. In February 1998 the Minister of the Environment signed the first post-Kyoto JI agreement, the reduction targets of which count for the national CO_2 target (Staatscourant 3 February 1998). For a period of four years the Dutch will make available 48 million guilders to be spend in developing countries, and 36 million guilders to be spend in former Eastern European countries. In addition the Dutch support developing countries financially in performing climate studies. Additional funds were made available in order to intensify the CO_2 reduction plan (Staatscourant 6 April 1998).

As far as the Biodiversity Convention is concerned, the Dutch (financial) decisions have been inspired mostly by the Tropical Rain Forest Agreement (1991), and the government decided to contribute 150 million guilders annually to protect (tropical) forests. That expenditure objective was realized in 1996 for the first time. In addition, actions have been undertaken with respect to trade; i.e. the introduction of an eco-label for sustainable wood. Bilateral talks have been started with Malaysia, Indonesia, Cameroon, and Gabon.

During the past few years a number of so-called Sustainable Development Treaties (DVOs) have also been concluded—between the Netherlands and Buthan, Costa Rica, and Benin—as an immediate consequence of UNCED. Co-operation in the context of these treaties is based on reciprocity, equivalence, and participation. The DVOs were supposed to provide an example for future development policy-making. The purpose of the treaties, for which 43.9 million guilders was made available in 1998, is that the convening countries address one another on economic and social-policy measures that relate to sustainable development. The DVOs, however, almost failed to pass Parliament. The Conservative and Christian Democratic parties opposed the plans (June 1995), because they feared that the developing countries involved would interfere with domestic issues, such as the expansion of Schiphol airport. At present, such reservations appear to be the main obstacles to the realization of the plans. An official evaluation will take place in 2001.

As far as the finances for domestic sustainable development initiatives are concerned, the focus should be on the local level, where most of the responsibilities for carrying out environmental tasks and sustainable development initiatives are located. Local authorities can make use of several financial sources: special earmarked funding for environmental goals from the national Municipality Fund; subsidies; taxes; levies, and so on.

The most important financial source for sustainable development implementation is the VOGM programme (Follow up Grants Scheme for the Development of Municipal Environmental Policy), which started in 1995 for a period of three years. Although VOGM payments are not Local Agenda 21 instruments, most of the municipalities started Agenda 21 activities subsidized by VOGM payments. The annual budget allocated to the VOGM scheme is 93.9 million guilders. Whether municipalities get funding depends upon the adequacy of their plans and the number of inhabitants. VOGM funding ended in January 1998. From that point onwards financial contributions are placed in the national Municipality Fund, which means that there is no guarantee at all that the money will be used for environmental goals.

Sustainable Production and Consumption

During the period 1950–95 the Dutch population grew from about 10 million to some 15.5 million. Since the average household size declined over the same period, from approximately 4 persons in 1950 to approximately 2.5 persons in 1994, this means that the number of households grew more rapidly than the population. Indeed, the number of households more than doubled over this period, from some 2.5 million in 1950, to some 6.5 million in 1994. The proportion of single-occupancy households grew from some 20 per cent in 1980 to 30 per cent in 1995. This has become an important factor in the discussion of sustainable consumption and its relationship to economic development in the Netherlands.

Until UNCED the Dutch assisted other countries, in the context of their development-aid programme, in the formulation and implementation of population policy, but they did not have one themselves. As a consequence of Agenda 21 the issue has been given attention in NEPP II (VROM 1992–3a). An analysis has been made of the environmental loads caused by consumption activities, which shows that transport, food, heating, and domestic electrical appliances are most relevant to environmental policy. The quantitative background data on consumer behaviour has been insufficient, and this appeared to be especially true with regard to trends in consumption patterns and related environmental pollution. Consequently, studies which seek to form a quantified picture of trends in consumption—both past and future—and of the implications of those trends for pressures on the environment, have been published (Slob *et al.* 1996).[2] So far, this conceptual thinking suggests that in addition to providing information, policy needs to focus more on creating the conditions which enable the consumer to consume in an environmentally friendly manner.

With NEPP II, the government announced that it intended to promote a debate within society on the social and economic implications of sustainable development. The concept of 'environmental space' (in terms of resources, energy and physical space) available at individual, national and global levels is to be developed for that purpose. This debate was supposed to promote the emergence of long-term perspectives for industry relating to sustainable production methods, and for consumers in relation to present consumption patterns and lifestyles. In fact, one of the three core elements underpinning the strategy of NEPP II concerned working towards sustainable patterns of production and consumption, which included: (1) integrated life-cycle management in industry; and (2) environmentally sound consumer behaviour.

It should be remembered that during the period immediately after UNCED, confidence in consumers was great. The government was convinced that consumers would be willing to make individual sacrifices in order to stimulate sustainable development. It has however been forced to change this perception over time, not least following the newspaper debates which followed in the wake of the publication of the Action Plan Sustainable Netherlands (Milieudefensie 1992). The plan's authors were accused of crypto-communism, presenting a plan which, if implemented, would make life a misery (less meat, no vacations involving air travel, no waterbeds, etc.). These strong reactions illustrated public and political resistance to the idea of imposing measures to achieve radical changes in consumption and production patterns. The consumer may be conscious of environmental burdens in theory, but this does not mean he or she is willing to act according to this awareness in daily practice! High prices and restrictions on car-use appear to be too much of a barrier.

With respect to the production sector the Dutch government has been encouraging business to implement environmental management systems. Since 1989 a specific policy has been developed to achieve this (VROM

[2] Private consumption increased in the Netherlands by 30 per cent in the period 1980–95. Since 1993 the annual growth has been between 1 and 3 per cent, peaking in 1994 at 4 per cent. In recent years households in the Netherlands have purchased a relatively high number of electrical appliances (VROM 1997a: 34). Combined with the growth in the number of households, this has led to a significant growth in residential consumption of electricity.

1990–1). This policy is based on the principle of voluntary implementation, which means that there is no statutory requirement to have a company environmental management system.[3] Government uses a mix of instruments to implement this policy, like the Environment and Industry target-group policy, certification, licensing, statutory environmental reporting regulation, and environmental auditing. Financial instruments are being used to encourage further research, development, and demonstration of new technologies, processes and management practices which promote cleaner and less wasteful patterns of production. In addition, clean technology policy is to be guided by the 'Long-term Programme for Sustainable Technology'.

While not a national-level scheme, the most innovative initiative with respect to the consumption sector has been the so called 'Ecoteams'. The idea of Ecoteams arose after the UNCED conference at a meeting of Global Action Plan for the Earth. The underlying principle is that behaviour can only be changed if consumers are aware of the resources they consume. In an Ecoteam, members measure and compare their individual environmental efforts. This generates an element of social control, and gives consumers a direct sense of responsibility. The main emphasis is on measuring, on knowing the facts. Each team member calculates exactly how much electricity, water, gas, etc. is used from the outset, and progress is charted at every meeting. The team's average is also calculated at each meeting and compared to other teams and to average consumption in the Netherlands. The idea became relatively popular in the Netherlands.

The policy document 'The Environment and the Economy', which outlined the prospects for a sustainable economic development, was released in July 1997. It proposed specific suggestions and practical solutions for the medium term (until 2010) for which the goals set by the NEPP II form the framework, aimed at producers, consumers and the authorities. The goals included product enhancement, the promotion of environmental management systems, the greening of the tax system, better regulations, taking a more market-oriented approach, and encouraging consumers to exhibit more environmentally friendly behaviour. For the long term (after 2010) the document outlined some of the considerations which are likely to feature

[3] A company environmental management system is a package of policy, administrative, and organizational measures that can enable business to manage and reduce its environmental impact. An effective environmental management system consists of the following eight elements: an environmental policy statement (which lays down the environmental goals that the company has set itself); an environmental programme (each year the company draws up an environmental programme containing the planned environmental measures for that year); integration of environmental management into business management; measurement and recording; internal checks; information and training; environmental reports; and evaluation (VROM 1997a: 14).

in the future. These considerations include policy in relation to the infrastructure, the use of means of transport, the structure of agricultural production and the use of natural resources including energy, and consumption patterns.

According to the Cabinet, most cost-effective environmental measures had already been taken. This creates the risk that the reduction of environmental load per unit-product will fall behind the growth in consumption, with the danger that pollution will again start to rise, even in those sectors where reductions had been achieved in recent years. The purpose of the above-mentioned White Paper, therefore, was to take the next step in the process of sustainable development by charting the economic dimension:

Within the intended objective of sustainable economic development, economic growth, increased competitiveness and job creation are combined with careful management of land-use, nature and biodiversity, a reduction in pollution and a substantial reduction in the consumption of fossil fuels and non-renewable resources. At the same time, goods and services become more attractive to consumers both at home and abroad. The aim is to achieve an *absolute decoupling* of environmental pressure and economic growth, in other words to generate economic *growth* combined with a *reduction* in the environmental pressure. Production, consumption and vehicle use will therefore have to be made far more efficient than they are at present. (VROM et al. 1997c: 3)[4]

The publication of this White Paper was accompanied by widespread criticism. Its central message (the aims of economic growth and decreasing environmental problems are not contradictory, but can be achieved successfully through changes in production, prices, taxation, and government policy) were thrown into doubt by figures and data presented by the RIVM less than a week after the document was published. Besides, the document included numerous success stories, but hardly offered any new policies, nor additional funding. For the coming five years only 250 million guilders extra is to be spent by the four ministries that endorsed the document (VROM,

---

[4] 'Decoupling' refers to improving living standards (economic growth) while at the same time reducing the environmental pressure. A distinction is made between relative and absolute decoupling. Relative decoupling occurs when the environmental pressure rises, albeit at a slower rate than the level of economic activity: i.e. environmental pressure grows more slowly than the economy. Absolute decoupling occurs when the environmental pressure reduces or at least remains constant while the level of economic activity is increasing. The term 'recoupling' is used when the initial reduction in the environmental pressure is reversed as the economy grows. Although the term decoupling may be new, the underlying idea is not. In fact it has always been the objective of Dutch environmental policy to sharply reduce the environmental pressure for a given level of economic growth. In other words, the NEPP I and NEPP II also aimed to achieve decoupling. The objective was to reduce emissions per unit GNP by a factor of between 2 and 10 (VROM 1998).

V&W, EZ, and LNV). Thus, it is not surprising that the environmental pressure groups reacted negatively. According to their perspective, the Cabinet had not made any significant progress in realizing sustainable development since NEPP I.

The White Paper once again represented an example of the continuing fixation on economic growth. The minister of EZ keeps stressing the importance of 3 per cent economic growth. No new visions and no fundamental measures have been suggested to radically increase the efficiency of the use of resources, to develop sustainable technologies, or to alter lifestyles (reducing commuting!), which might increase the end-use benefits of the consumption of environmental space. Instead of offering credible strategies to realize this, decisions are postponed and new paper promises are made.

Following the White Paper on The Environment and the Economy, the key point in NEPP III has been the decoupling of economic growth and environmental pressure (especially with regard to CO_2 emissions). Only a few new elements have been introduced—such as price mechanisms and greening of the tax system—but these are not enough to reach the environmental goals agreed in NEPP II, nor to fulfil the Koyoto targets. No difficult choices have been made in NEPP III, which sketches a series of measures on which the new Cabinet will have to decide. This, and the fact that NEPP IIII includes an evaluation of previous plans, makes it more of a political 'fudge' than an inspiring plan to bring sustainability nearer.

Climate Change

The high population density, the intensive use of land, the high level of industrialization, and the location of the Netherlands in a delta of three rivers with intensive traffic, are all factors that place great stress on the environment. For centuries the Netherlands has been threatened by floods. This, and the fact that the Dutch economy in the past was based on international trade by sea, has fostered a strong national interest in climatology and meteorology. It is, therefore, no surprise that Dutch climate change policy was already well established before the Framework Convention on Climate Change (FCCC) was signed.

Dutch global-warming policy is based on the provisions of the NEPPs and the Memoranda on Climate Change and rests on three main pillars: energy (under EZ), transport (under V&W), and waste (under VROM). Climate policy is basically the sum of these areas, each with its own set of policy instruments. Part of the national policy-process involves a periodic update of policies and measures on the basis of monitoring and evaluation.

Since NEPP I climate change has been dealt with as one of eight policy areas (VROM 1988–9: 130–2). In NEPP+ Minister Alders demanded the strengthening of a preventive policy on climate change (VROM 1990: 20–4), particularly with regard to CO_2 emission reduction. As an outcome of NEPP+ the Memorandum Climate Change was published in 1991 (VROM 1990–1). Points of departure for the Dutch climate policy, as formulated in the Memorandum Climate Change, are: sustainable development; the precautionary principle; and the containment of health risks and loss of environmental functions and nature values. The starting point for sustainable development is expressed along the lines of long-term environmental goals concerning closed substance cycles and the preservation of nature values. Emission goals should be carefully formulated and be consistent with other national and international sustainability measures (VROM 1990–1: 7). New targets for the reduction of CO_2 were formulated in NEPP II (VROM 1994).

In spite of intensified climate policies from NEPP II onward, the Dutch are still faced with increasing CO_2 emissions. For this reason, the government decided to allocate an additional 750 million guilders to realize improvements to the energy infrastructure (in line with the 1996 CO_2 Reduction Plan). The publication of the Supplementary Memorandum Climate Change in 1996 (VROM 1996c) had been announced in NEPP II. The ministerial letter that the Minister for Environmental Affairs sent to the Parliament (VROM 1994–5) about the (lack of) realization of NEPP II policy goals provoked the Second Chamber Commission on Environmental Affairs—inspired by German experiences—to set up a societal/parliamentary inquiry (VROM Commission 1995–6). For this purpose a Temporary Commission on Climate Change was established on 20 December 1995, chaired by MP Van Middelkoop. The Commission's primary purpose has been to make an inventory of research findings and other information of relevance to the climate issue in order to provide MP's with information to make optimal political choices. This information has been gathered by means of a dialogue with experts, and public hearings. The Commission presented its findings to the Second Chamber in September 1996 (VROM 1996a; VROM 1996b).

On the basis of Kyoto and the agreements that have been made within the EU about the new distribution of the environmental burden, the Netherlands has been committed to play its part, which requires additional finance and social pressure. The Dutch contribution to the European reduction target (of 8 per cent below the 1990 level) was settled in Luxembourg in June 1998: the Dutch will have to reduce their CO_2 emissions by 6 per cent. Before going to Kyoto, however, the Dutch Parliament resolved (motion Lansink) that the Netherlands should, no matter what Kyoto would bring, reduce CO_2 emissions by 10 per cent by 2010. The issue has been elaborated on in the so-called Kyoto letter (VROM 1997–8).

The Minister of VROM awarded additional funds for intensifying climate policies and signed the first post-Kyoto Joint Implementation agreement, where the reduction targets count towards the national CO_2 target in February 1998 (Staatscourant 3 February 1998). It is obvious that the Dutch desperately 'need' this kind of project co-operation to reach their CO_2 targets.

Outcomes and Effects

The Dutch did not manage to reach their own CO_2 reduction goals despite a number of covenants, energy taxes, public campaigns, and subsidies. Thus far little headway has been made towards achieving these objectives.[5] Internationally the Netherlands committed itself to stabilize CO_2 at 1990 levels by 2000. However, in practice the country had increased its CO_2 emissions on 1990 levels by 12 per cent by 1995. Ambitious goals, which provided the Netherlands with a starting point for active environmental diplomacy, have not been supported by adequate policies. This is hardly surprising since the Minister of EZ (Weijers, Liberal) has stated that Dutch exporting firms should not be forced to cease their activities because of Dutch climate policy (for their products would then be produced less efficiently elsewhere, which would on balance have an adverse impact on the climate (EZ 1996)). For this reason, no absolute volume limits are set, either for the economy as a whole, or for each industry. This grossly limits the effectiveness the CO_2 policy, because a growth in CO_2 emissions remains possible as a consequence of general increase in energy use.

Up to 1999 awareness-raising campaigns seem to have been the most important tool for involving the general public in issues concerning climate change. Since 1990 several campaigns have been conducted, including a

---

[5] Dutch emissions of greenhouse gases covered by the Climate Treaty were 14 per cent higher in 1995 than in 1990. Total carbon-dioxide emissions have increased, despite reductions resulting from the import of electricity and energy-conservation measures. The increase is mainly attributable to the growth of the economy, structural shifts, and changes in the fuel mix (shifts from gas to coal). Dutch use of CFCs and halons was discontinued completely in 1995 (VROM 1997b: 123–4).

campaign on climate change and energy, an energy-conservation campaign by the energy distribution sector, and awareness-raising campaigns in the areas of traffic and transport.

It is the Dutch municipalities that have made the most tangible contributions towards sustainable development, and the reduction of greenhouse gas emissions and energy conservation in particular. Success stories have been published to stimulate other municipalities towards new actions (VNG and VROM 1993). The Climate Alliance, an initiative sparked by an organization of Indians from the Amazon forests aimed at the reduction of emissions of greenhouse gases and the preservation of the tropical rain forests, is a growing movement in the Netherlands (VNG and VROM 1993: 48).

Biodiversity

The Biodiversity Convention was ratified by the Dutch in 1994. By ratifying the Convention, the Netherlands has committed itself to incorporate considerations for the conservation and sustainable use of biological diversity into a number of areas of social and economic policy. According to the government, key mechanisms for the protection of biodiversity are provided by the combination of the Nature Policy Plan (NBP 1990), the NEPP II (1993), the Third Water Management Policy Document (1990), the VINEX (1990), and memoranda dealing with development co-operation. One analysis of these various plans, however, indicated that although the Netherlands had complied with the letter of its obligations, the Convention's intention has not been adequately reflected in Dutch policy (VROM 1997b: 34). The NBP, for example, did not present an analysis of the societal and economic activities which cause the decrease of biodiversity. Moreover, the NBP is defensive in its search for solutions (Jansen and Opschoor 1989: 316).

The Strategic Action Plan for Biodiversity (the SAP) was drawn up in 1995, and set forth how existing initiatives could be strengthened so that the gaps in existing biodiversity policy could be plugged (LNV 1995–6). In the Netherlands biodiversity has been disappearing fast as a consequence of intense agricultural production, urbanization, fragmentation and disruption of the landscape, and industrial pollution. The purpose of the SAP, therefore, has been to operationalize the biodiversity objectives (into thirty concrete actions), broaden the concept of biodiversity, strengthen capacity in the Netherlands, address the constraints which apply, and focus political and administrative attention. A first report on the implementation of the SAP was sent to the Parliament when COP-3 was being prepared in October 1996.

On the fiftieth anniversary of the Ministry of the Environment (and its predecessors), Minister De Boer stressed the importance of the issue (De Boer 1995). According to her, attention should be paid to the interrelationships between three different key resources which determine whether a sustainable society can be attained in the long term: energy (how and when should society make the transition from fossil fuels to renewable energy sources?); biodiversity (how can biodiversity be conserved so as to safeguard the natural environment and the life-support functions?); and space (how should space be apportioned between the different functions, having regard to the quality of the space and taking account of indirect space usage?). Her speech can be understood as an implicit approval of the recommendations already presented by the NGO Platform Brazil 1992. These recommendations emphasize the importance of integrating biodiversity criteria in development policy in North and South, imposing levies on genetic resources, paying more attention to the interests and knowledge of indigenous peoples and women, education and information, and finally increasing financial resources for environmental policy.

There are three fields in which VROM is taking action in close co-operation with LNV and V&W. First, to create the conditions for implementing the Ecological Structure Plan as intended before 2020. The 'ecological structure' is defined as a closed network of the main natural areas connected by 'green strips'. These natural areas and green strips should encompass all varieties of habitat. Consisting of 7,000 hectares it should be enough to give most species of plants and animals a chance to survive. In that context national parks are to be developed. Second, to develop policy in order to protect the life-support system. The term biodiversity as defined in the Convention also included the life-support or regulatory functions of biodiversity. Lower organisms, for example, play an important role in the ability of the environment to support ecosystems and human activities. In their orientations the ministries have restored the emphasis on the life-support function. Third, to influence and participate in the global biodiversity discussion on the protection of tropical forests, sustainable forestry and the development of (safety) norms concerning biotechnology. There is no overall plan or strategy covering all the issues related to biotechnology. However, there is government policy covering aspects such as securing human health and the environment, workers' protection, ethics, animal welfare, and Third World issues. At least five ministries are involved in biotechnology-related issues.

The concept of area-specific policy-making is of particular importance in the context of biodiversity. Area-specific policy-making encourages provincial and local authorities to take an integrated approach to environmental problems in specific areas. This may be related to a large actual or expected concentration of pollution sources, or the special requirements of the environment in a nature conservation area, or an area where drinking water is extracted.

All in all the issue of biodiversity has not been much of a 'crowd-puller' in The Hague, although some interesting initiatives have been taken in the area of nature conservation by authorities and farmers at the provincial level, and by NGOs.

Tough on Goals, Easy on Actions?

The Netherlands considers itself top of the class in the world of international environmental politics, and enthusiastically completes its country profile to the CSD every year. The Dutch country profiles review at great length the benefits of sustainable development policy. Much is made of the greening of the tax system and the environmental tax on energy for small-scale users introduced in 1996. Another example of sustainable development policy described in the report is sustainable building. Over a hundred thousand new homes will have to meet the latest requirements for energy and water consumption, and when building houses, the construction industry is expected to consider factors such as increasing the life expectancy of buildings, reducing the amount of paving, ensuring a closed water management system and reducing vehicle use. Sustainable development policy has been considered a particular success at the municipal level. Around a third of local authorities are implementing their own Local Agenda 21. In most cases this comes down to supporting Ecoteams, initiating dialogue with the public, and co-operating with twin towns.

Although—compared with a number of other countries—Dutch environmental policy has been relatively successful, this does not mean that the Netherlands is developing in the direction of sustainable development.

The RIVM concluded that the state of the environment in the Netherlands can be described as reasonably good (emissions of a large number of pollutants have decreased in the period from 1985 to 1994). However, there is still a long way to go before the objectives of the NEPPs are met. Moreover, environmental issues which cannot be felt, noticed, heard, or smelled book much less progress! In addition, CO_2 emissions are still increasing dramatically, as the Cabinet acknowledges (BuZa and VROM 1997).

The environment did become an issue on the political and policy agenda, but all the information campaigns in the Netherlands could not prevent a decline in the attention to and care for the environment.[6] Prior to 1994, the environment was for some years considered as the most important problem. But in 1994 the issues of 'minorities' and 'unemployment' pushed the environment aside. The public's willingness to act in accordance with the motto 'a better environment starts with oneself' has been decreasing as well: in 1991 56 per cent of the Dutch population wanted to contribute to a better environment, but in 1996 this percentage had decreased to 31 per cent (both times women were more 'in favour of the environment' than men). Nevertheless, in 1997 40 per cent of the people are still prepared to pay more taxes for the sake of the environment, and if necessary they would settle for a lower standard of living (BuZa and VROM 1997: 71).

However, as the White Paper on the Environment and the Economy (1997) and NEPP III illustrate, the main concern of the Dutch authorities remains economic growth. As a consequence, CO_2 emissions are still rising, as though there had never been a Climate Convention. Thus, despite all the efforts, the Netherlands only just passes when it comes to the implementation of the UNCED agreements at home.

Understanding Strategies

The previous section focused on the Dutch performance on sustainable development. It did not say much, however, about the choices made with regard to the way sustainable development policies are implemented. The importance and relative success (compared to a number of other countries) of policy-making in this field should be understood in the context of what has been written above on the Dutch style of policy-making. The consensual style of policy making combined with a recognition of the limits to increasing the effectiveness of regulatory instruments, provoked a quest for the 'internalization' of environmental values; the essence of which was to encourage environmentally friendly behaviour among citizens by reminding them of their own responsibility. This policy fitted in well with the overall policy orientation of the government in the 1980s, which aimed at minimizing its involvement in social engineering and stimulating industry to take the lead. As ministers of the environment, both Winsemius and his successor Nijpels were very attracted to this line of thinking.

As a result of the discussions on the range and scope of governmental concern, public–private partnerships were introduced. Traditional

[6] Numerous communicative efforts have been undertaken by the government and a number of other organizations on the issue of sustainable development. The campaigns form part of a long-term general information programme designed to raise environmental awareness, with the motto: 'A better environment starts with oneself!'

hierarchical relations were replaced by horizontal relations, where government no longer found itself opposed to the private sector, but rather in an interdependent position. Direct regulation has been partly replaced by agreements, contracts, covenants, and individual citizens have been approached through information campaigns (on energy, water, and waste). The ultimate goal became to solve environmental problems by way of self-regulation.

In this vein the Dutch government engaged in negotiations with target-groups responsible for particular environmental problems. Essentially the government informed these groups about its intentions, and offered them two options: either traditional regulation or covenants—a voluntary agreement giving the target-group more control over the interim goals and measures undertaken to fulfil the governments' targets. Governmental steering has been directed at the contributions of relevant actors towards realizing governmental goals formulated at the national level. In other words, target-groups were approached in an instrumental way (self-regulation within a framework, VROM 1997b: 8). This—limited—instrumental perspective presupposes the existence of predefined goals. Consequently the roles of other parties (the target-groups) are judged in terms of their contribution to these given goals. As a consequence of the fact that target-groups have at least some discretion over implementation, they have a degree of bargaining power in their relationship with government. Such bargaining can, at a minimum, delay implementation, but may even undermine efforts by the government.

As a result, policy has slowly moved away from the assumption that effective protection of the environment could be achieved by the imposition upon target-groups of a politically and administratively determined set of norms. Instead, the preconditions for a successful realization of environmental objectives are to be found in the relation between the policy-maker and the target-group. Target-group consultation has thus become both the context within, and the process through which, goals of sustainable development are to be achieved.

As far as the private sector is concerned, target-group policy brought about two rather contradictory tendencies. On the one hand, regulatory reform has been designed to provide leeway for economic actors in order to improve their ability to respond to market signals and development (deregulation). On the other hand, they have had to take responsibility for the development of pollution prevention strategies within the parameters set by the governments' environmental policy objectives (re-regulation). A serious commitment to the strategy of sustainable development, with its premise of a mutually supportive integration of economic development and environmental quality, provoked the search for a new framework for market activity. Deregulation, as well as re-regulation, were meant to provide the appropriate kind of interventions intended to shape and steer economic activity. Thus far, the expansion of market-based regulation does not indicate a reduction of state activity. Policy instruments are instead employed pragmatically to allow politically bargained agreements to be implemented.

Conclusion

As we have seen, despite all its efforts, the Netherlands just 'passes' when it comes to the implementation of the UNCED agreements. Although Dutch environmental policy, when compared to that of other countries, is quite often considered successful, this does not automatically mean that the Netherlands is developing in the direction of sustainable development.

It is quite possible that, at the turn of the century, the Netherlands is already suffering from the 'law of diminishing environmental returns'. In the late 1970s and early 1980s the country was so polluted that measures had to be taken quickly. It was relatively easy to combat the side-effects of an increasing use of raw materials. Continued economic growth could be reconciled with a reduction in environmental pressures ('decoupling'). Yet the government is now facing the risk that the reduction of environmental load-per-unit product will again start to rise (recoupling). It has been the Cabinet's aim (VROM et al. 1997b; VROM 1998) to take the next step in the process of sustainable development by charting the economic dimension.

The question then is whether the new Minister of the Environment (Pronk, Social Democrat) will be able to exert influence on his colleagues to push sustainable development higher on the agenda again, and break through the win-win dogma—according to which the only measures that can be taken are those where environmental care and increasing economic development can be realized at the same time. The question is also whether the government ultimately is willing to steer policy towards focusing on inputs (the cause), rather than outputs (the effects of pollution).

Despite the fact that the Kok-I Cabinet in its governmental statement ('Choices for the Future', 13 August 1994), wrote that its challenge would be to strive for a transformation to a sustainable society and sustainable environmental growth, policy practice shows little success thus far.

The White Paper on the Environment and Economy, which was supposed to translate sustainable economic development into concrete policy actions, has been received with disappointment. The priorities made in this White

Paper reflect a strong faith in technology and in win-win policy measures. The suggestions presented do not pose any threat to continued economic growth. Apparently VROM did not manage to 'externalize the environment' by means of a consensus strategy.

On policy sub-areas the Ministry has applied this consensus strategy rather successfully. The greening of the Dutch tax system—a tool by which environmental costs can be internalized in the prices of goods and services is already underway.[7] A tax raise for small-scale energy users has been intro-duced and green saving has been made fiscally attractive. The Secretary of State for Housing has made progress in the area of sustainable building, where a variety of considerations are being integrated into the decision-making process.

In 1989, when NEPP I was introduced, environmental issues were enjoy-ing widespread attention: a sustainable development wave washed over society. During this period VROM set the agenda, negotiated with private interests and arrived at agreements. However, with the publication of the Third White Paper on Energy, EZ appeared to have taken the lead again. While maintaining co-operation, VROM was forced to accede to less strin-gent measures. VROM, for example, opted for an absolute decrease in CO_2 emissions, but EZ pleaded for a relative decrease and 'won' the political battle. This raises doubts as to whether the political advantages of involve-ment by bargaining outweigh the disadvantages of having to compromise on crucial issues of sustainable development.

Parallel to these developments, the societal support for sustainable devel-opment has been declining. Consumers are dutifully separating their waste, but as soon as it gets more expensive to act in an environmentally friendly way, support from the 'calculating citizen' will ebb away.

Dutch sustainable development goals and NEPP ambitions are far-reaching, but the government has failed to follow through on the imple-mentation challenge. The Netherlands is losing its position as a model for environmental policy-making, because—despite the NEPPs—it fails to become more oriented towards inputs rather than outputs.

It has become increasingly obvious that the organization of the economy should be restructured to make it more sustainable. This would provide a 'litmus test' for the Dutch model. The discussions in the wake of the publi-

---

[7] A 'Working party on the greening of the tax system' was set up by Secretary of State for Finance on 24 March 1995, charged with identifying the extent to which the tax system could be used to promote environmental protection and sustainable economic development. The members of this group included taxation experts and environmental economists, gov-ernment departments, employers organizations, and representatives of small and medium-sized enterprises.

cation of the Environment and the Economy White Paper gave grounds for pessimism: it focused from the outset on win-win situations, and the controversy over growth or decrease in economic sectors was carefully avoided (NCDO 1997). Recent decisions concerning infrastructural and spatial planning projects (e.g. Schiphol Airport) illustrate the fact that sustainability is still not used as a guiding principle when important decisions are made. Uncertainty about the future is taken for granted in economic policy-making. When it comes to sustainable development, however, uncertainty about the future effects of present decisions seems to remain a major obstacle to the implementation of the UNCED agenda.

7

Norway: Reluctantly Carrying the Torch

OLUF LANGHELLE

Introduction

Since the publication of *Our Common Future* in 1987, sustainable development has been a declared policy goal of the Norwegian government.[1] The dual position of Gro Harlem Brundtland as both leader of the World Commission on Environment and Development and Prime Minister of Norway (between 1986–9 and 1990–6),[2] makes the case of Norway special in the sense that there was a very strong connection between the World Commission and national politics. One might therefore expect that the understanding of sustainable development found in *Our Common Future* forms the basis of the Norwegian approach to sustainable development.

To a large degree this proves to be the case. The definitions, dimensions, and prescribed solutions in *Our Common Future* can be traced in several official documents and publications. None the less, discrepancies between the goals and strategies found in *Our Common Future*, and official documents and publications, can already be detected in the first White Paper outlining the Norwegian follow-up to the WCED (Norwegian Ministry of the Environment 1988–9). The changes are not so much in the understanding, but rather in the weight given to different aspects of sustainable develop-

The author would like to thank Gard Lindseth and Marit Reitan for their insightful comments on an earlier draft of this chapter.

[1] There was a debate in Norway on how to translate the term 'sustainable'. The term chosen, '*bærekraftig*', had been little used in the Norwegian language and lacked clear associations. The Ministry of the Environment and the Prime Minister's Office played an important role in choosing what was believed to be a suitable translation (Sverdrup 1995). The translation has gained broad acceptance, but Brundtland herself has later stated that she did not think the translation was adequate (1998: 70).

[2] Gro Harlem Brundtland was prime minister for the first time from February until October 1981. Prior to that, she was Minister of the Environment from 1974–9. Before being appointed to head the World Commission on Environment and Development in 1984, she was also a member of the Palme Commission.

ment, and in what sustainable development is believed to imply in a national context.

It is also evident that sustainable development has lost some of its political momentum. While interest in environmental issues and sustainable development was at its highest in the parliamentary elections of 1989, it fell dramatically between 1989 and 1993. In the 1989 election, 37 per cent rated 'energy and environmental policy' as the most important issue. Of all the issues in the election, energy and environmental policy ranked as the second most important. By contrast, in the 1993 election only 7 per cent considered energy and environmental policy as the most important (Aardal and Valen 1995: 183).

This shift in opinion is reflected in the priorities established by Parliament. Norway was hit hard by economic recession in 1991–2, when unemployment rates reached their highest levels since the inter-war period (8.5 per cent of the working force) (Benum 1998). Full employment, economic growth, and economic competitiveness again rose to the top of the political agenda. This reordering of priorities was acknowledged by the Minister of the Environment Thorbjørn Berntsen when, in his annual report to Parliament in 1994, he included employment in the concept of sustainable development: 'Social development is not sustainable if there are significant levels of unemployment' (Norwegian Ministry of the Environment 1994, translation by the author).

Despite fluctuations in priorities within the electorate and political system, sustainable development has been further developed and integrated into the Norwegian policy structure. Perhaps the most important aspect of the national follow-up process is that sustainable development has become an integral part of the language and justification of policy and politics. In a sense, the Norwegian follow-up to Our Common Future can be described as a deliberate attempt to 'institutionalize' sustainable development within the existing political structure.

This attempt to 'institutionalize' sustainable development has not been without problems. There are two underlying conflicts which have been especially important in the Norwegian case. First, it has been a declared goal to integrate sustainable development concerns in every sector of society, a goal which has proved difficult to achieve in practice. Moreover, sectoral integration has been the source of many conflicts and disputes between various ministries and branches of government.

Second, there is considerable underlying conflict relating to the global dimension of sustainable development, especially with regard to the problem of climate change. The conflict here has not been about whether sustainable development is an important goal, or whether climate change is

a serious environmental problem. Here there is general agreement. The conflict has rather focused on how the goal of sustainable development should
be converted into national policy, with a tension between a national and
an international orientation.) Should Norwegian climate change policy be
directed primarily towards reducing emissions nationally? Or should it aim
at reducing emissions at the lowest cost, regardless of the country where
such cuts are implemented, the principle of cost-efficiency?

The debates surrounding the 'institutionalization' of sustainable development, sectoral integration, and the 'conversion' of sustainable development
into national policy goals, have interacted, creating contradictions and
further problems for the national follow-up. These controversies can also be
seen as conflicts related to Norway's self-imposed role as a 'forerunner' for
sustainable development on the international scene.

Norway: Facts, Figures, and Context

With a population of 4,392 714, and an area of 385,639 square kilometres,
Norway is one of the most sparsely inhabited countries in Europe, with
approximately 14 persons per square kilometre. The largest urban area (Oslo
and its surroundings) has only 722,871 inhabitants. About one-third of
Norway is covered by forests, with cultivated areas accounting for between
3 and 4 per cent of the land (Statistics Norway 1997). Wilderness, mountains, the large number of fjords, lakes, and waterfalls, are also characteristics which form an important background for the development of
environmental politics in Norway (Reitan 1997).

Historically, nature conservation has primarily concerned the protection
of waterfalls and watercourses (Berntsen 1994). The industrialization of
Norway after independence from Sweden in 1905 was to a large extent based
upon the exploitation of hydro-electric power. After WWII, the development
of waterfalls and watercourses became a central part of the reconstruction
programme, and an overall goal of the growth-oriented strategy initiated
by the Labour government (Knutsen 1997). During the 1960s and 1970s,
however, this strategy became increasingly controversial, and there were
several major confrontations between 'developers' and 'conservationists'
concerning the exploitation of waterfalls and watercourses, the most important being the disputes over the Mardøla waterfalls in 1970, and the Alta
waterfalls in 1980 (Berntsen 1994).

The environmental movement which developed in this period was
strongly connected to a revitalization of populist ideas in Norway. Populism
was an ideology of local community, decentralization, political mobilization,

and anti-capitalism, which emerged as a fundamental critique of the social-democratic post-war reconstruction programme. The fusion of populist and environmental ideas lead to the emergence of a new political cleavage dimension in Norway: economic growth versus environmental concerns. The main antagonists on the left–right dimension, as well as the parties most firmly rooted in the industrial cleavages (Labour and the Conservatives), were the most growth-oriented parties, and those that most clearly opposed environmental interests and values (Knutsen 1997).

Energy policy—related to energy forms and consumption—became a dominant issue on the political agenda in the 1970s. Labour, the Conservatives, and the Christian Democratic party were the most growth oriented, while the Centre, Liberal, and Socialist Left parties spoke of a confrontation between 'growth ideology' and what they explicitly called an 'equilibrium society' (Knutsen 1997). During the 1980s, however, there seemed to be greater agreement between all parties on the issue of energy production and consumption. In 1986 a parliamentary committee unanimously agreed on a set of energy goals, which included a stabilization of energy consumption (Knutsen 1997).

The growth versus environmental-protection cleavage, however, re-emerged in the context of the petroleum sector. During the 1970s Norway became a major petroleum-producing country. While the question of state control over oil activities fell along the left–right dimension, the questions of the pace of construction and extraction, as well as the controversy over proposed drilling off the coast of the High North, grouped the parties along the same axis as growth versus protection issues of the 1970s (Knutsen 1997). The extraction rates proposed in the 1970s have been dramatically exceeded during the 1980s and 1990s (Willoch 1996), and Norway is now the second largest oil exporter in the world. Moreover, Norway has become an increasingly large exporter of natural gas to other countries in Europe. Gas production is expected to double by 2005, with a potential for further increases (United Nations 1996).

The problems of pollution played a less important role in the early days of environmental politics in Norway. This must be understood in light of the modest levels of urbanization, low population density, ready availability of water, and relatively late industrialization. However, the problem of pollution gradually evolved, and was given high priority after the establishment of the Ministry of the Environment in 1972. It became a major issue in the 1980s, with several new environmental NGOs focusing upon the problem of industrial pollution (Reitan 1997).

The Ministry of the Environment was organized as a sector ministry, without direct legal authority over other ministries (Jansen 1989: 145). Its present legal status is based on the responsibility to administer certain laws, primarily the Planning and Building Act and the Pollution Control Act (Jansen and Osland 1996: 204). Beyond this, the Ministry of the Environment can only advise the other ministries, and so disputes among the different ministries must ultimately be settled by the government as a collective body.

The establishment of the new ministry resulted in the imposition of new and more comprehensive regulations on industry (Reitan 1998a). Furthermore, an increased awareness of the international causes of national environmental degradation led Norway to play an active role in international environmental co-operation. Among OECD countries Norway remains among those most exposed to transboundary air pollution, with over 90 per cent of acid precipitation originating abroad. In addition, Norway is heavily exposed to marine pollution, being 'downstream' from the rest of Europe. Not surprisingly Norway has played an active role in establishing international agreements to reduce sulphur-dioxide emissions and control marine pollution (Skjærseth and Rosendal 1997).

The concept of sustainable development broadened the environmental agenda in the late 1980s. But as we have seen, many of the issues and problems addressed by the World Commission touched upon existing debates and conflicts within Norway. The World Commission's report was also to a large degree in accordance with traditional Norwegian views on the United Nations. Since the creation of the United Nations, Norway has viewed the organization as the primary tool for extending international peace and security, and for promoting political solutions to international conflicts (Fermann 1997a).

Norway has been a strong supporter of UN work on development problems, on attempts to create a new economic world order, and on human-rights issues. In addition to support for multilateral arrangements, Norway has maintained an active bilateral aid policy, which has been justified by reference to the values of freedom and independence, norms of social justice, and a humanitarian tradition. Other motives, such as trade and economic interests, are also clearly relevant, but they have, historically, been less prominent in the aid debate. The level of Norwegian ODA reached 1 per cent of GNP in 1982 (Stokke 1985; Fermann 1997a; Sørbø 1997).

Our Common Future and the Initial Response

The Norwegian follow-up of *Our Common Future* actually started a few weeks before the release of the report. In a letter from the Prime Minister all ministers and ministries were requested to examine the report and its recommendations, and to determine which of its numerous possible changes could be implemented (Dalal-Clayton 1996: 165). A State Secretary Committee for Environment and Development was established and it conducted broad soundings within the ministries for foreign aid and the environment, among local and regional authorities, as well as external hearings which included business and labour organizations, political parties, voluntary organizations, research communities, etc. The participants in this process were all requested to provide their opinion on *Our Common Future*, and the Ministry of the Environment collated the various statements.

In 1988 a Government Environmental Committee continued to consider the political implications of, and responses to, *Our Common Future*, proposing the presentation of a White Paper as a follow-up to the World Commission's report (Sverdrup 1995). White Paper 46, entitled 'Environment and Development: Norway's Follow Up of the Report of the World Commission', was presented to Parliament in April 1989, after conflicts between the Ministry of the Environment and other ministries had led to the compilation of several drafts (Norwegian Ministry of the Environment 1988–9; Sverdrup 1995). According to Dalal-Clayton (1996: 169), the conflicts between the ministries were so acute that the sector ministries made it clear that they would not wish to see another such report prepared. The level of conflict was high, with ministries disagreeing about what exactly the White Paper should be about, how each of their ministries would be affected, and, more generally, how the term 'sustainable development' was to be understood. None the less, the White Paper introduced principles and measures which shaped much of the Norwegian approach (Brundtland 1990).[3]

The Understanding of 'Sustainable Development'

White Paper 46 confirmed that 'the Government endorses the report's [*Our Common Future*'s] main viewpoints'. Sustainable development was declared the overriding objective for the government's future policy, even though the

[3] Gro Harlem Brundtland (1990) gives the following description of White Paper 46: 'The white paper is the Norwegian Government's major policy document on sustainable development. It presents a plan that involves all ministries, not only that of the environment, and implies a change in attitudes and policies, as well as tough challenges for ministries such as energy, industry, transportation, finance, foreign affairs, and trade. The Prime Minister's Office has been directly engaged in charting a course for the future that cuts across all these sectors' (Brundtland 1990: 155).

White Paper maintained economic development, full employment, and a good environment as the 'corner-stones' of the government's policy to further develop and improve the welfare society (Norwegian Ministry of the Environment 1988–9: 8).

In accordance with *Our Common Future* sustainable development was defined as 'development that meets the needs of the present without compromising the ability of future generations to meet their own needs' (Norwegian Ministry of the Environment 1988–9: 7). The White Paper continued: 'Sustainable development is a dynamic economic and social-growth term, and presupposes a process in the direction of a more even distribution of goods both between countries and within each country' (Norwegian Ministry of the Environment 1988–9: 15, translation by the author). The concept was interpreted to include democratic reforms and better access to participation in decision-making. Furthermore, both consumption patterns in the rich countries and population growth were to be brought within the global ecological carrying capacity.

According to White Paper 46 sustainable development would require:

profound changes in the ways energy and other resources are used before development in Norway is brought within the bounds of nature's carrying capacity. The seriousness of the situation demands strong environmental efforts. This will affect the whole population, have considerable costs, and challenge strong interests. (Norwegian Ministry of the Environment 1988–9: 8, translation by the author)[4]

Norway's prevailing development trajectory was presented as unsustainable. 'The present foundation of knowledge implies that if important aspects of development in energy use and economic growth are to continue as present, we risk unacceptable and maybe irreversible damage of the environment' (Norwegian Ministry of the Environment 1988–9: 67, translation by the author). Accordingly, it was regarded as necessary to redirect the economy in several areas for development to become sustainable (Norwegian Ministry of the Environment 1988–9: 68).

White Paper 46 addressed many different issues related to sustainable development. The Norwegian follow-up to *Our Common Future* will be discussed with reference to four distinct dimensions which arguably constitute the core of the initial national approach: (1) the international perspective; (2) Norway as a forerunner for sustainable development; (3) the sector-encompassing approach; and (4) national goals and targets.

---

[4] It is interesting to note that the exact opposite is stated by the Ministry of Foreign Affairs: 'The Government thinks that Norwegian oil and energy policy is broadly in accordance with the recommendations from the Commission' (Norwegian Ministry of Foreign Affairs 1988: 25).

The International Perspective

The international perspective of the initial response was directly related to the understanding of the concept of sustainable development. Sustainable development, it was argued, is meaningful first and foremost in an international perspective (Norwegian Ministry of the Environment 1988–9: 8). Already in 1988, the government decided that sustainable development should be integrated in all sectors of Norway's foreign policy (Norwegian Ministry of Foreign Affairs 1988). In the same vein, White Paper 46 contained chapters on international co-operation (ch. 3), and on Norway's relations with developing countries (ch. 17).

The emphasis on international co-operation was based on the perception that many of the threats to sustainable development are of a global nature. Climate change, ozone depletion, air-pollution, deforestation, and desertification are all classified as global problems which cannot be solved by individual countries (Norwegian Ministry of the Environment 1988–9: 6). Consequently, each country must co-ordinate its efforts on the basis of common goals and priorities. This diagnosis was firmly placed within particular national circumstances and experiences:

A substantial part of our environmental problems are due to pollution from other countries . . . this means that we have a clear interest in further developing international environmental co-operation . . . Our national efforts will, in a global context have meaning first and foremost if they contribute towards accelerating a broad process in which other countries participate.   (Norwegian Ministry of the Environment 1988–9: 8, translation by the author)

The White Paper, in accordance with *Our Common Future*, also addressed global developmental problems in general: the gap between North and South, and the relationship between poverty and ecological degradation. Poverty was seen as both a cause and a consequence of environmental degradation which also affected the industrialized countries. Thus, both developing and developed countries were seen as having a mutual interest in achieving economic growth and poverty reduction in the developing world.

Norway as a Forerunner in Sustainable Development

A second distinctive feature was the self-imposed goal that Norway should take the lead in implementing sustainable development in all its aspects, including ODA, international co-operation, and a domestic strategy for sustainable development (Norwegian Ministry of the Environment 1988–9: 7). The official ambition of being a forerunner in sustainable development was maintained throughout White Paper 46 (Norwegian Ministry of the Environment 1988–9: 8, 9, 42, 43, 44, 45, 57, 58), and is clearly expressed in the following passage: 'The Government believes that Norway should be in the forefront in the work to reduce emissions which result in ozone depletion, climate change, acid rain, and sea pollution' (Norwegian Ministry of the Environment 1988–9: 9, translation by the author).

National efforts were seen as part of the international perspective on sustainable development: they should first and foremost contribute to accelerating a broad international process (Reitan 1998a: 121); and in order to have credibility in the international domain, it was necessary also to be in the forefront nationally (Norwegian Ministry of the Environment 1988–9: 57). The adoption of an 'instigator' role internationally and a 'forerunner' role nationally, thus constitutes a central aspect of the formulation of the initial Norwegian response to *Our Common Future*.

The Sector-encompassing Approach

In the White Paper, the government declared that sustainable development considerations were to be built into all societal planning and sectoral policy. This was described as a 'sector-encompassing' policy, including all levels of Norwegian society. This gave the authorities in areas such as agriculture, fisheries, energy, transport, and so on, the responsibility to ensure that development and planning within their respective sectors were in accordance with sustainable development, and that budgetary and other measures were applied to ensure that 'existing environmental problems would be reduced and new ones prevented' (Norwegian Ministry of the Environment 1988–9: 71, translation by the author).

The sector-responsibility approach consequently made most ministries actors in the pursuit of sustainable development. The White Paper argued that environmental policy should be conducted through the establishment of targets. The vertical component of the sector-encompassing approach included the following steps: 'Target-setting—Implementation—Monitoring—Revision'. While implementation was to be the responsibility of the sector authorities, the actual goals within the different sectors were to be set by government. The role of the Ministry of the Environment was limited to co-ordinating this work, and to ensuring the development of suitable systems of surveillance (Norwegian Ministry of the Environment 1988–9: 72).

National Goals and Targets

Following from the above, another central aspect of the initial response was the further development of national goals and targets. The adoption of quantitative targets has been described as one of the most distinctive features of Norwegian environmental policy (OECD 1993a). White Paper 46 proposed general goals in the areas of energy, transport, industry, management of genetic resources, agriculture, fishing, education, health policies, consumer policy, and local administration. It also proposed several quantitative targets, including stabilization of Norway's CO_2 emissions, and a gradual levelling of total energy consumption, both by the year 2000.

During the parliamentary debate following the publication of White Paper 46 a more ambitious goal to stabilize CO_2 emissions at the 1989-level by the year 2000 emerged. This outcome has subsequently been described as the result of a 'green beauty contest', in which opposition parties sought to outbid the government with ambitious CO_2 goals (Bergesen, Roland, and Sydnes 1995; Sverdrup 1995). The more ambitious target was none the less approved by the government, despite Gro Harlem Brundtland's warnings that it would be difficult to reach, and the scepticism expressed by the Ministries of Finance, Industry, and Energy (Sydnes 1996).

The CO_2 target was, however, viewed from the very beginning as preliminary. It was to be reviewed in light of further deliberations, technological development, and international negotiations and agreements. Reitan (1998a: 121) argues it was the international strategy which first and foremost justified the national target. It was seen as necessary in order to get an international agreement (Norwegian Ministry of the Environment 1988–9: 57–8).

White Paper 46 also offered the following conclusion regarding Norway's energy policy, with explicit reference to the World Commission:

Norway should work for the large energy-consuming countries to reduce the growth of, and—if possible, the consumption of—environmentally polluting energy. A follow-up, however, must first and foremost concern measures which can reduce the global environmental consequences of the Norwegian consumption of energy. (Norwegian Ministry of the Environment 1988–9: 92, translation by the author)

This conclusion can be seen as a fusion of the international perspective and the self-imposed goal of being a forerunner in sustainable development. This, together with the sector-encompassing approach, and the national goals and targets, constitutes the core of the initial national approach, and forms the background for the Norwegian engagement in the UNCED process.

Preparing for Rio

As part of the preparations for the Earth Summit, Norway hosted the regional conference 'Action for a Common Future' for the UN Economic

Commission for Europe in Bergen in May 1990. This conference addressed the issues of awareness-raising and public participation, sustainable energy use, industrial activity, and the economics of sustainable development (Norwegian Ministry of the Environment 1990). For the first time, NGOs were granted full delegate status, and NGOs participated in both the preparations and the actual negotiations (Sverdrup 1995).

The conference was important in two respects. First, the precautionary principle was included in the Ministerial Declaration, and this was viewed as a major step forward by the Norwegian government. Second, on the basis of the experience of the Bergen conference, the Norwegian government established the Norwegian National Committee for UNCED. Led by the Minister of the Environment, it was composed of representatives from eight ministries and eight NGOs. The committee participated in both the preparation of the Norwegian negotiating positions, and in the drafting of the National Report to UNCED (Sverdrup 1995; 1997).

Assessment of the Earth Summit

The Earth Summit represented a climax in the Norwegian efforts to promote sustainable development internationally. After the Earth Summit, the achievements were assessed by the government in White Paper 13 'On the UN Conference on Environment and Development in Rio de Janeiro' (Norwegian Ministry of the Environment 1992–3). The aim of the White Paper was primarily to give Parliament an overview of the decisions made in Rio, and of the government's assessment of the results. In Rio Gro Harlem Brundtland had already offered the following judgement: 'We owe to the world to be frank about what we have achieved here in Rio: progress in many fields, too little progress in most fields, and no progress at all in some fields' (United Nations 1993: 191).

White Paper 13 presented a mixed assessment of the Rio accords. On the one hand, it concluded that the Earth Summit had not managed to create a new foundation upon which environment-and-development policies could be reoriented. This conclusion was drawn in view of the antagonistic conflicts between different groups of industrialized countries, and between industrialized countries and developing countries. On the other hand, the government seemed quite pleased with the two Conventions, although it was more critical of Agenda 21. Several shortcomings were identified in Agenda 21:

- the agenda did not establish clear priorities among its various goals;
- many of the chapters reflected compromises between strongly antagonistic interests, and the recommendations were often not concrete;

- some issues were not elaborated, among them environment and military security issues;
- the documents (and the UNCED process in general) did not express clearly enough that developing countries had also to take responsibility for global environmental problems;
- the chapter on financial resources and mechanisms (ch. 33) was seen as a key chapter, but a weak one. The proposal from the Nordic countries that industrialized countries should commit themselves to a schedule to reach the UN target of 0.7 per cent of GDP in ODA by the year 2000, was supported in principle, but a schedule for when the target was to be met was not agreed (Norwegian Ministry of the Environment 1992–3).

The Norwegian Follow-up of the Earth Summit

The Norwegian follow-up of UNCED continued within the framework of the initial response to *Our Common Future*. But the Earth Summit took much of the steam out of the national effort to implement sustainable development. Environmental interest fell dramatically, and the priorities changed towards fighting the economic recession and unemployment.

Other factors also contributed to slowing down the national effort: among them was the aforementioned disappointment with Agenda 21. While the White Paper assessing the Earth Summit argued that a precondition for the success of Agenda 21 was that every nation worked out national action plans with the Agenda as the starting point (Norwegian Ministry of the Environment 1992–3: 25), the government never produced any further documents based on Agenda 21. Not only did the bureaucracy feel more at home within the framework they already had developed as a response to *Our Common Future*, but Agenda 21 seemed somewhat irrelevant and 'directed towards countries which are at a different level of development than Norway' (Norwegian Ministry of the Environment 1992–3: 10, translation by the author).

Moreover, the White Paper argued that Norway had started its implementation early and was already out in front in several areas. According to Sverdrup (1995: 8; 1997: 74), the impression given that Norway's environmental policy was running ahead of other states actually contributed to slowing down the national process towards sustainable development. Another interpretation is that Norway was disappointed with the response from the large 'important' countries, and therefore decided to apply the brakes to its national processes. An increasing awareness of, and focus on, abatement costs within government and industry; concern for international competitiveness; and the failure of the EU to implement a CO_2 tax, all contributed to this.[5]

So while the global dimensions of sustainable development were important for initiating the whole process, they also proved crucial for slowing down national engagement. The Framework Conventions paradoxically reinforced this development. The Conventions had the effect that important dimensions of sustainable development politics were 'lifted out' of the national context. Thus national follow-up became more dependent upon international bargaining processes.

White Paper 46 (1988–9) had already concluded that climate change would be the major environmental issue of the 1990s. And, since Norway increasingly viewed itself as a land of 'milk and honey' with respect to energy resources, national authorities quickly realized that reducing greenhouse-gas emissions could have serious consequences for the oil-dependent Norwegian economy. The issue of climate change thus became a matter of 'high politics' in Norway, and possibly the single most important factor slowing down the national follow-up.

Norway's Climate Policy

Already in 1989, the government had established an Inter-ministerial Climate Group and an investigative commission[6] to develop a foundation for climate change policies, and to see how the Norwegian CO_2 target might be achieved. The report of the Inter-ministerial Climate Group was released in March 1991 and the report of the Environmental Tax Commission appeared in February 1992.

The Inter-ministerial Climate Group recommended several criteria for co-ordinating national and international climate policy, which became the foundation for the Norwegian position in negotiations within the International Negotiating Committee (INC). At the third INC meeting at Nairobi in September 1991, Norway tabled a proposal covering all the main elements of a climate agreement, something which no other nation was able to do at the

[5] These arguments are also used in White Paper 41 (Norwegian Ministry of the Environment 1994–5): 'Government expected international co-operation to make more progress during the 1990s than has been the case thus far. For instance, important, influential countries have not introduced taxes on emissions' (translation by the author).

[6] One year earlier, the Centre for International Climate and Environmental Research (CICERO) was established in order to strengthen the research by the social sciences on the issue of climate change (Norwegian Ministry of the Environment 1991: 206).

time (Sydnes 1996).[7] When the UN Framework Convention on Climate Change was agreed in its final form at the fifth meeting of the INC, and later opened for signature at the UN Conference in Rio de Janeiro 1992, many of the original Norwegian proposals had entered the Framework Convention (Ringius and Søfting 1997).

The strategy outlined in the report from the Inter-ministerial Climate Group was based on the following principles:

- Climate policy, both nationally and internationally, should be framed so that emission targets can be reached at the lowest societal cost. An effective international climate strategy should seek cost-efficient solutions across nations, sectors, and climate gases. That is:
- the strategy should be cost-efficient across climate gases, so that reductions occur where costs are lowest;
- the strategy should be cost-efficient across countries, so that countries or regions can work in partnership to limit emissions of climate gases. In addition, the use of measures in the different countries should be harmonized as far as possible;
- a climate agreement should be based on equitable burden-sharing between countries at the same level of development, and seek to avoid substantial distortion in competitiveness;
- the strategy should be cost-efficient across sectors. A harmonized use of measures across sectors would contribute to this;
- in addition, measures which are profitable for other reasons, and which also have positive impacts on climate-gas emissions, should be implemented before measures which are not profitable in themselves (Norwegian Ministry of the Environment 1991).

Other key elements in the Norwegian negotiating strategy, closely related to these criteria, were proposals for: a clearing-house mechanism; joint implementation of climate efforts; additional resource and technology transfers from the North to finance climate measures in the South.

The conclusions of the Interministerial Climate Group were restated by the first Environmental Tax Commission, with one important difference: the Environmental Tax Commission proposed a 'flexible' attitude towards the national CO_2 goal. This conclusion was interpreted by the representative from the Ministry of the Environment as a recommendation to 'lower the

---

[7] Already in 1991, however, Norway established an environmental fund, 'the Climate Fund', which was used to finance two pilot projects in Poland and Mexico respectively, for the purpose of reducing CO_2 emissions in these countries. Poland and Mexico have since become OECD members (in 1996 and 1994), and Norway has also established Joint Implementation efforts with developing countries.

ambitions' of climate policy and he refused to endorse this part of the Report.

The above principles were reaffirmed once again in White Paper 41, 'On Norwegian policy to mitigate climate change and reduce emissions of nitrogen oxides' (Norwegian Ministry of the Environment 1994–5).[8] This White Paper restated the Norwegian goal of stabilizing CO_2 emissions at the 1989 level by the year 2000, but in reality little remained of the original goal: 'In the government's opinion, it is not possible to prepare for a policy that will ensure a stabilization of our CO_2 emission by the year 2000' (Norwegian Ministry of the Environment 1994–5: 9, translation by the author).[9]

Due to severe conflicts between the ministries involved, the release of White Paper 41 had been delayed. When it finally was released, the controversial issues of the CO_2 tax structure and rates were not addressed. These were left instead to the second 'Green Tax Commission', established by the government on 9 December 1994.

Norway's carbon tax levied on gasoline, diesel, and mineral oil, was first introduced in 1991. An additional CO_2 tax on coal was introduced in 1992. Together, the taxes covered approximately 60 per cent of emission sources (Sydnes 1996). The exemptions from the CO_2 tax have remained at the same level, and they have been motivated by a concern for international competitiveness. The exemptions relate to mineral oil used in air transport, ships engaged in foreign trade, the North Sea supply fleet, the national fishing fleet, and non-fuel combustion process emissions from industries producing steel, aluminium, methane, cement, and concrete. Domestic pulp and paper industries, the fish-meal industries, and the coastal goods transport sector pay only 50 per cent of the tax.

However, the problem is that if the CO_2 tax is to function cost-efficiently across sectors nationally, these exemptions would have to be removed. So while Norway has argued strongly for the principle of cost efficiency internationally, the government has not carried out a cost-efficient policy at home. The issue of removing exemptions to the CO_2 tax in order to make it more cost-efficient nationally constitutes an important background to the

---

[8] The report from the review-panel of national communication with the Framework Convention on Climate Change, concluded that the 'so-called "White Paper" cannot be regarded as a national climate action plan. Rather, it highlights the importance for Norway of international co-operation and co-ordination in the pursuit of effective mitigation options . . .' (United Nations 1996: 11).

[9] In addition to the principles of cost-efficiency and equitable burden-sharing, the White Paper proposed measures for improving energy efficiency and promoting renewable energy sources, especially bio-mass energy. Further, the White Paper proposed the introduction of voluntary agreements with the industrial sectors exempted from the CO_2 tax.

controversies within the 'Green Tax Commission', and also to the controversy regarding the building of two gas-fired power plants on the west coast of Norway.

The Second 'Green Tax Commission'

The aim of the second 'Green Tax Commission' was to determine what role the tax policy could play to achieve both increased employment and environmental improvement in the long term, by switching taxation from manpower to activities that involve resources use and pollution. The Commission was also supposed to look at energy usage within the industrial structure, and at which activities and businesses tax policy actually stimulated. In addition, the practical consequences for some branches of industry were to be examined in order to detect transition problems with a tax-system reform (Rasmussen 1997).

In its final (1996) report the Green Tax Commission argued that the CO_2 tax should vary according to the carbon content of the fossil fuels; that exemptions from the CO_2 tax should be removed; and that, in the short term, the tax should be set at NOK 50/ton CO_2. The majority of the members in the Commission were of the opinion that the introduction of a low carbon-graded tax would be a more cost-efficient structure, that would minimize undesirable readjustments in the Norwegian economy (Rasmussen 1997; NOU 1996: 9, 83).

The majority based their recommendations on macro-economic calculations and business studies partly conducted by Statistics Norway. On the assumption that the income from the CO_2 tax would be used to reduce employers' social security contributions, the macro-economic model showed a reduction in unemployment. Thus removing existing exemptions from the tax would benefit the economy, employment rates, and the environment (Rasmussen 1997).

Moreover, the Commission found no support in any of its analyses that the opposite might be the case, i.e. that unemployment and/or emissions would increase after such a reform. Furthermore, calculations showed that unemployment (and CO_2 emissions) would be further reduced if a heavier tax was placed on CO_2 emissions (Rasmussen 1997). Calculations carried out by the Green Tax Commission showed that an increased CO_2 duty (and the removal of exemptions), combined with lower taxation on labour, would benefit the Norwegian economy, regardless of the environmental effects, and whether other countries enacted similar measures or not (Vennemo 1996).

Representatives from three departments; the Ministry of Finance and

Customs, the Ministry of the Environment, and the Ministry of Transport and Communication originally supported the proposals of the Green Tax Commission. The Ministry of Trade and Energy was against the proposals. At the last meeting of the Commission, however, all the ministerial representatives 'changed their minds' uniting on a footnote to the CO_2 question, which stated that issues regarding the CO_2 tax should be left to politicians to resolve (Rasmussen 1997). This rather odd development, was later explained by the Commission's Chairman as a result of political pressure from members in the Labour Government (Lund 1996).

The Controversy over Gas-fired Power Plants

Another important dispute relates to the domestic use of natural gas. Most of Norway's gas production is exported, with virtually no use of natural gas on the Norwegian mainland. White Paper 46 (Norwegian Ministry of the Environment 1988–9: 90), however, had already considered the use of gas for energy generation. The arguments presented here, are remarkably similar to those used later. The White Paper stressed that gas use in Norway should be seen in relation to possible positive effects in the other Scandinavian countries, and that the goal of reducing national CO_2 emissions could set limits on Norwegian gas consumption.

If built, the gas power plants would increase Norway's CO_2 emissions by approximately 6 per cent. While representatives from both government and industry have argued that this would reduce total emissions if the impact on other Scandinavian countries is included, environmental NGOs have been more or less united in their rejection of this proposal (Odegaard 1996). The environmental argument has not, however, been the most important for the government.

In the White Paper on gas-fired power plants, it is the anticipated increase in electricity demand which is most prominent: 'even with a strong effort towards bio energy and energy efficiency, it will be necessary to increase power production based on more traditional forms of energy to cover the increasing demand for electricity'. And further: 'even if we manage to halve the growth we have had since 1985, the consumption of electricity in Scandinavia will grow equivalent to one of the gas-fired power plants each year' (Ministry of Trade and Energy 1995–6: 1, 13, translation by the author).

But a major problem for the government has been that, if the exemptions from the CO_2 tax are removed, these power plants would most likely not be profitable at all. Thus, a precondition for building the plants is that the exemptions are maintained. This explains the resistance towards removing existing exemptions, and the political pressure imposed on the ministerial representatives on the Green Tax Commission.

Justifying Norway's Climate Policy

Norway's climate policy can be viewed from different perspectives, and it is not clear whether the principles which Norway has stressed in the international negotiations—cost-effectiveness, equitable burden sharing, and Joint Implementation—should be seen as constructive or not. Opinions are mixed.[10]

The main focus of Norwegian climate policy has been heavily influenced by what is seen as special national circumstances which, in the government's view, make abatement costs particularly high in Norway, and so justify an appeal to the principle of equitable burden-sharing. The arguments for this are based on the following:

1. *The energy structure*: virtually 100 per cent of electricity demand in Norway is met from hydroelectric power. This means that CO_2 reductions must be achieved in other sectors, while countries using coal-fired generation can switch to cleaner forms of energy at lower cost. Consequently, CO_2 taxes in Norway would have to be significantly higher than in other countries to obtain the same percentage reduction, and this in turn would cause problems for Norwegian industry and commerce in terms of competitiveness, resulting in reduced productivity and employment (Norwegian Ministry of the Environment 1994–5; Jansen and Osland 1996).

2. *Energy intensive industry*: because of the availability of clean and cheap energy, Norway has become a major producer of aluminium, steel, methane, cement, and concrete. These industries have been exempted from the CO_2 tax because of international competitiveness considerations. Compared with other countries, however, Norwegian operations are said to be among the cleanest in the world. Imposing heavy taxes on these facilities could push these firms off-shore, transferring pollution to other countries, or drive them out of business altogether, so leaving the market to more polluting companies based in other jurisdictions (Norwegian Ministry of the Environment 1994–5; ECON 1997).

3. *The transport sector*: due to Norwegian topography and a highly decentralized settlement pattern, the transport sector is politically a very difficult

---

[10] It is worth nothing, however, that even the Norwegian proposals for equitable burden-sharing within the Framework Convention imposed higher costs on Norway than most other countries (Alfsen and Holtsmark 1997).

area, with strong rural interests in Parliament being very sceptical towards new measures imposed on transport, as the Norwegian taxes on transport fuels already are among the highest in the world (Sydnes 1996).

4. *The oil and gas sector*: emissions from the petroleum sector, and especially the increasing production and transport of gas, has made it difficult to reach the national CO_2 goal. Still, this has been justified as an environmentally sound policy in the following sense: since the use of gas involves less emission of CO_2 per energy unit than coal and heavy oil (and no emission of sulphur dioxide), increased Norwegian gas exports contribute to improving *other nations* climate accounts, and to reducing the total emissions of CO_2 in Europe (Norwegian Ministry of the Environment 1994–5: 9).[11]

5. *Regional politics*: in the 1950s and 60s, regional politics focused upon establishing large-scale industry in small communities, first as a means to economic growth, and later as a means to equalize living conditions (Teigen 1995). Many of these plants are among the largest emitters of climate gases, but they also offer employment opportunities and provide important sources of tax revenue for many small communities (ECON 1997).

These special circumstances made the government reluctant to impose new measures to reduce emissions. As the Kyoto meeting drew closer, the overall CO_2 target was given less and less importance. Instead Norway invested its time and resources in achieving the best possible agreement for Norway. Ultimately, the Norwegian government was quite pleased with the Kyoto Protocol, although it is acknowledged that it is insufficient and only a first step (Norwegian Ministry of the Environment 1997–8).

In 1997 the Labour Government was replaced by a new Centre Party/Liberal Party/Christian Democratic government. The new government did not alter the basic orientation of Norway's climate policy, but White Paper 29 'Norway's follow-up of the Kyoto Protocol' (Norwegian Ministry of the Environment 1997–8), proposed some modifications to the energy taxes, a new tax on the end-treatment of waste, and (most controversially) the removal of exemptions from the CO_2 tax.

The process industry was to be taxed at NOK 100/ton CO_2. Industry was to be fully compensated for the tax, but the compensation was to be gradually reduced. Yet, the only proposal which received the necessary support in Parliament was the end-treatment tax on waste. Instead of removing the

---

[11] The precondition for this is, of course, that gas actually replaces existing, or planned, development of other energy sources like coal and heavy oil.

exemptions, Parliament asked the government to develop a national system of tradable quotas for climate gases, and an investigative commission on the issue was established on 23 October 1998.

The problem for Norway, however, is that even if all the proposed taxes (including the compensation for the CO_2 tax) were implemented, it would only reduce the estimated increase in emissions of climate gases from 23 per cent to 22 per cent. That is, from 22 per cent *above* the Norwegian Kyoto target to 21 per cent *above* the target. Other proposed measures, such as licensing of emissions, voluntary agreements, information, education, new voluntary agreements (one agreement has already been secured with the aluminium industry), pilot projects through joint implementation and the green development mechanism, are estimated to reduce emissions by between 5 and 8 per cent—which still leaves Norway 13 to 16 per cent *above* the Kyoto target. Thus, if no new measures are introduced, the only option for Norway would seem to be the buying of quotas internationally.

There are, however, other perspectives to be found in the national follow-up on sustainable development which are relevant for the climate change issue. These perspectives have played a less important role for the actual climate policy, but they have been more important for the general under-standing of sustainable development. In fact, one feature of Norway's climate policy has been the separation of climate change from the broader perspect-ives of sustainable development. This is the case both in relation to the under-standing of sustainable development expressed in the national follow-up; and in relation to the aspects of sustainable development given most attention in *Our Common Future* (the issues of energy and social justice).

The Lost Perspectives of Our Common Future—*Energy*

Seen in relation to the crucial role *Our Common Future* attached to the energy issue, this is one area to which the national follow-up clearly gives less weight than the World Commission's report (Hille 1992; 1997). It is also an area where actual developments in Norway are out of line with the recommen-dations in *Our Common Future*.

Since the start of implementation in Norway, there has been a steady increase in total energy consumption. The price of electricity has been relatively stable, and little has been done to stabilize or reduce total energy consumption. Furthermore, despite the often stated goal of supporting renewable sources of energy, state grants for research and development have varied considerably, but have in general remained low. In fact, renewable energies now constitute a lower share of total energy production than they did ten yeas ago (Langhelle 1997).[12]

The goal in White Paper 46 of a gradual levelling of total energy consumption has been given only marginal attention, and the goal itself was eventually changed in April 1997 when the Parliamentary Committee on Energy and the Environment reached a new consensus on Norway's energy policy. The new agreed goal was to moderate the growth in energy consumption, and to stipulate that in a normal year electricity consumption should be covered by renewable energy sources (Parliamentary Committee on Energy and the Environment 1997–8).[13] However, this consensus did not last long.

Social Justice as a Challenge for Sustainable Production and Consumption

Yet another area where the weight given to the different aspects of sustainable development in the national follow-up differs from the World Commission's report, is the way the climate change issue has been linked to the issue of global justice. Climate policy has focused primarily on the question of equitable burden-sharing, a principle which can also be viewed as a principle of social justice.

Following Henry Shue (1993), however, one can recognize other equity issues raised by climate change than that of a 'fair allocation of the costs of preventing the global warming that is still avoidable'. Thus far, this is the issue which has been negotiated within the Convention on Climate Change and which the Norwegian climate change strategy has focused upon through the principle of equitable burden-sharing.

Another equity issue raised by climate change is the following: 'what is a fair allocation of emissions of greenhouse gases (over the long-term, and during the transition to the long-term allocation)?' (Shue 1993: 39). This issue has not been raised in the national follow-up on climate change, but has been indirectly addressed by the more general approach to sustainable production and consumption.

Sustainable production and consumption has become one of the key

[12] This does not imply that there is no research on energy issues in Norway. Research programmes on energy include NYTEK (primarily bio-, sun-, wind-, wave energy and energy efficiency); EFFEKT (energy efficiency in the Norwegian hydropower and electricity production); SAMRAM (framework conditions for energy- and environmental policy); and KLIMATEK (technology for the reduction of climate gas emissions).

[13] The only dissenting member was the representative from the Progress Party (*Fremskrittspartiet*).

issues in the Norwegian understanding of sustainable development. First, it is assumed that even though the environmental problems linked to high production and consumption levels in industrialized nations primarily concern these societies, they 'will in time affect the developing world even more strongly and hinder their development' (Norwegian Ministry of the Environment 1992: 52).

Second, it is acknowledged that 'the poor people of the world have a legitimate right to increase their own level of welfare, but the carrying capacity of the Earth will break down if an increasing world population tries to adapt to the present consumption patterns and levels of the industrialized countries'.

Third, all people share a 'common ecological space': the atmosphere; the seas; and biological diversity. The main challenge is that economic resources, and shares of this ecological space, are so unevenly distributed. 'This is the reason why the world's consumption and production patterns have to be changed, and why the industrialized countries have a special obligation to lead the way in this process' (Norwegian Ministry of the Environment 1996–7b: 9–10, translation by the author).

Norway has pushed this issue internationally, and took an initiative at the first session of the CSD to facilitate further advances on sustainable production and consumption. Norway has hosted three conferences on the topic, which served as input to the CSD on its work on chapter 4 of Agenda 21 (Lafferty 1996). Nationally, however, the follow-up has mainly focused upon waste management and 'eco-efficiency'.

In 1995 the Ministry of the Environment established the GRIP Centre (the Norwegian Centre for Sustainable Production and Consumption). GRIP works to develop, field test, and promote methods that increase eco-efficiency (value added per environmental load), and aims to contribute towards sustainable development in private and public enterprises. The board includes a wide range of NGOs.

Another initiative to follow-up the Earth Summit was the establishment of 'The Environmental Home Guard' (*Miljøheimevernet*). It was set up by the NGO community, and is funded by the government (75 per cent of the total budget). The aim of this organization is to promote environmentally friendly choices by consumers and families. The organization does not have 'members', only 'participants', which reflects the fact that to join you have to commit yourself to certain types of action. Both the GRIP Centre and the Environmental Home Guard are seen by the government as important tools for changing production and consumption patterns (Norwegian Ministry of Foreign Affairs 1997: 4–5).

The issue of climate change and CO_2 emissions has not, however, been prominent within the general perspective of sustainable production and consumption. While the high production and consumption levels in industrialized nations are said to affect the developing world strongly and to hinder their development, within the perspective of Norway's climate strategy, increasing Norway's CO_2 emissions are said to have the opposite effect.

Thus there seem to be two parallel, but different, global perspectives in the national follow-up: (1) a global perspective on climate gas emissions related to the actual global effects and costs of Norwegian measures, expressed in and through the principle of cost-effectiveness and equitable burden-sharing; (2) a second global perspective which is more related to social justice, global distribution, and ecological limits, based on the assumption that the poor people of the world have a legitimate right to increase their level of welfare, and thus to occupy a larger share of the available 'ecological space'. The conclusions following from these different perspectives do not, however, necessarily go hand in hand.

The Convention on Biological Diversity

The problem of biological diversity has been less conflictual than the climate change issue. None the less, there have been tensions between the concern for conservation on the one hand, and for sustainable use on the other, particularly in two areas; the conservation of conifer forests, and the protection of mammal predators.

As with climate change policy, the issue of biological diversity was central to the Norwegian government's follow-up of *Our Common Future*. Norway, in close co-operation with the other Scandinavian countries, also played an active role in negotiations which led to the UN Convention on Biological Diversity (Rosendal 1995). Norway's position was that a Convention should include all biological diversity, address the issue of sustainable use, the equity issues related to biological diversity, and biotechnology. Norway has also been one of the driving forces for the development of a bio-safety protocol under the Convention, and Norway passed its own biotechnology law in 1993 (Schei 1997).

Norway ratified the UN Convention on Biological Diversity in July 1993. There was no need for any changes to national law to ratify the convention, but some areas were seen to be in need of legal improvement. The work on a national strategy to fulfil the other obligations of the convention started immediately after the ratification (Schei 1997).

Many conservation plans had, however, already been developed independently of the Convention. By 1998, fifty-six municipal plans had been completed, and fourteen more were to be finished by the year 2005. 415 square kilometres of productive conifer forest is to be conserved by 2001, and by 2008 thirty-six new conservation areas were to be added to the expansion of fourteen already protected. In addition, there are thematic conservation plans to be developed for bogs, marshlands, sea birds, and hardwood forests by 2005. When implemented, the share of protected areas will increase from about 6.4 per cent to about 13 per cent in 2010 (Norwegian Ministry of the Environment 1996–7b).

By summer 1994, seven ministries had completed sector plans for how the Convention on Biological Diversity was to be followed up. The integration of these sector plans into a national strategy and action plan for biological diversity has proved, however, to be more difficult than expected. The national strategy was not released before the summer of 1997. The work on the action plan has started, but the Ministry of the Environment is at present unable to set a date for when it will be completed. The intention, however, is to revise the different sector plans once again to further improve them (Schei 1997).

The national strategy was founded on three principles: (1) further loss of biological diversity should be curtailed by addressing the causes of loss; (2) the use of biological diversity should be ecologically sustainable; and (3) threatened and vulnerable biological diversity should be protected and if possible restored. These principles are further specified in a number of concrete goals. Programmes for mapping and value-classification, and for the surveillance of biological diversity, are scheduled to be in place and operative by the year 2002–3 (Norwegian Ministry of the Environment 1996–7b).

However, one major problem is that most of the forest resources in Norway have been exploited for centuries. Moreover, the building of roads, powerlines, and the development of watercourses has led to a dramatic reduction of virgin forests, the area of which now constitutes less than 0.5 per cent of the forests in Norway. Of the 1,839 species which are on the Norwegian 'red list' of threatened and rare species, half are connected to forests (Norwegian Ministry of the Environment 1996–7b: 123–4).

The aim of the first conservation plan for conifer forests (1990), was to protect a representative selection of conifer forest sites, and to conserve important aspects of biological diversity. The plan, which covered less than 1 per cent of conifer forests, was evaluated by the Norwegian Institute of Nature Research (NINA). It concluded that the plan was inadequate, and that

a total protected area of at least 5 per cent was needed to conserve biological diversity (Framstad, Bendiksen, and Korsmo 1995).[14]

Partly as a response to the evaluation report, Parliament decided in June
1996 to increase the protected area by 120 square kilometres, to a total of
415 square kilometres. Yet this still constitutes only 1.06 per cent of productive conifer forest in Norway. Friends of the Earth Norway (*Norges
Naturvernforbund*) have argued strongly for a further increase in the total protected area. The majority of the Energy and Environment Committee in
Parliament also acknowledged that the expansion was insufficient to secure
biological diversity (Parliamentary Committee on Energy and the Environment 1995–6).

Most likely, therefore, the issue of the overall framework for conservation
of conifer forests will be taken up again in Parliament. Two problems are,
however, connected to an expansion of conservation. The first problem is
that the estimated costs of enlargement are high. This is partly because most
of the areas are privately owned, and partly because they are concentrated
in highly productive conifer forests. It was the Ministry of Finance and
Customs rather than the Ministry of Agriculture which resisted a further
enlargement of the conservation plan for conifer forests. The second problem is that the pattern of settlements in Norway is heavily based on the
use of biological resources, including forestry and logging.[15] A 5 per cent
enlargement could therefore contradict the declared goal of upholding the
'main characteristics' of the existing settlement pattern (Norwegian Ministry of Local Government and Employment 1996–7: 7).

Another, but equally important, problem for biological diversity relates
to the regulation of forests *not* covered by the Nature Conservation Law.
Ninety per cent of forests in Norway are under the Forest Law. In 1995 the
government established a three-year project, 'Living Forests', with the aim
of developing criteria, indicators, standards, and measures for sustainable
forestry. The project had participants from all the major stakeholders, and
in 1998 reached consensus on the criteria and indicators for sustainable
forestry.

The processes outlined in the 'Living Forests' initiative will eventually
enable a voluntary forest certification system, which complies with the international standard ISO 14001, the Forest Stewardship Council (FSC) prin-

[14] In addition, for this to be enough, it assumes 'that the entire forest landscape is managed
in context, with strong multiple-use management on land under harvesting, including several
key areas exempt from logging' (Framstad, Bendiksen, and Korsmo 1995: 3).
[15] The export value of forest and forest-industry products constitutes approximately 9 per
cent of the total land-based exports, and forestry and forest-industry products are thus one
of the most important land-based industries in Norway (Solberg 1997).

ciples, and the Helsinki resolution following from the UNCED process in Rio. But before the certification system is in place, there is nothing which can guarantee consumers that the timber they actually buy has not contributed to loss of biodiversity in Norway. The Forest Law is due to be amended, but it is not yet clear how strict the environmental regulations on forestry will be.

As with the issue of conifer forests, there are strong conflicts of interests related to the protection of larger mammal predators. This conflict has primarily been between reindeer herders and sheep farmers on the one hand, and those groups which want a more rigorous protection of larger mammal predators on the other. The four large mammal predators in Norway are bear, lynx, wolverine, and wolf: as a consequence of extensive hunting, the stocks of these mammals had already been reduced to a minimum at the start of the twentieth century (Norwegian Ministry of the Environment 1996–7a: 5).

The decline of these predators contributed to the development of new and more extensive forms of rough grazing. At the same time there has been a significant transition from cattle to sheep farming, and a large increase in the number of sheep and domesticated reindeer. The practice depends on the fact that sheep and reindeer can graze in an environment more or less free of larger mammal predators. Norway still has the highest loss of domesticated animals per individual of lynx, wolf, and bear. In no other European country with substantial stocks of wolf and bear are small domesticated animals allowed to graze freely in forested areas (Norwegian Ministry of the Environment 1996–7a).

Changes in practice, combined with a moderate increase in the stock of mammal predators (an increase, however, which is disputed at least for bears), constitutes the background for growing tension between farming interests and the protectors of mammal predators. In the early 1990s Parliament established five administrative core areas for the protection of larger mammal predators. In these areas the reproduction and survival of predators are supposed to be given greater emphasis, although the killing of single animals can be approved if the animal has done 'sufficient damage' and the overall stock is not threatened by the killing (Norwegian Ministry of the Environment 1996–7a: 21).

White Paper 35 'On the Management of Wild Predators' (Norwegian Ministry of the Environment 1996–7a), was an attempt to resolve the growing conflict in parts of Norway. The proposed approach was to uphold the administrative core conservation areas, and to introduce new preventive measures to limit the contact between predators and sheep/reindeer through changes in the practice of rough grazing within the core areas, by the use of dogs, traditional herding, fences, and other measures.

The White Paper was approved by a majority in Parliament in June 1997. Opponents wanted to abandon the core areas, and to change the self-defence paragraph which regulates the conditions under which permission to kill a predator is given, so as to make it easier to issue permits for killing. Since then the conflicts have escalated, and will most likely increase in the years to come.

Sustainable Development Implementation: Sector, Cross-sector, or Sector-encompassing?

As we have seen, both climate change and biodiversity have touched upon conflicting interests within Norwegian society. One obvious reason for this is the cross-sector nature of the problems. Different sectors contribute to the problems in different ways, and solving the problems requires co-ordinated efforts in all of the sectors.

Norway's initial follow-up of *Our Common Future*, White Paper 46, introduced the 'sector-encompassing' approach as the organizing principle for Norway's implementation of sustainable development. This implied that sustainable development considerations were to be built into all societal planning and sector policies, at all levels and in all areas of Norwegian society.

Yet tensions within this approach remain. On the one hand, it is not clearly spelled out in the national strategy what a truly 'sector-encompassing' approach implies. At a minimum level, we could assume that it requires the following: (1) integration of sustainable development concerns in every sector and level of society; and (2) cross-sector integration linked to, and in accordance with, the specific national goals and targets. A system which includes both of these would be truly 'sector-encompassing'.

The sector-encompassing approach retained the Ministry of the Environment as a sector ministry, in the sense that its role was limited to the co-ordination of the sector plans. The actual targets, both the national targets and the targets *within* each sector, were to be set by the government. While White Paper 46 outlined the first sector plans, these plans were neither pulled together into one coherent plan, nor linked to the national goals and targets. Thus the effect was that sustainable development concerns were integrated into the different sectors, but the cross-sector integration and the link to national goals and targets were left out, leaving a system which in reality was not 'sector-encompassing'.

There has been no systematic follow-up of White Paper 46, not even within the Ministry of the Environment itself (Dalal-Clayton 1996). But there have been several attempts to strengthen the sector-encompassing approach through different mechanisms of horizontal integration. Sverdrup (1995: 13) points to four such integrative mechanisms: new planning and budget routines related to the national budget; the establishment of a state Secretary Committee for Environmental Issues; the use of inter-ministerial working groups; and a new routine for environmental impact assessments within ministries. These mechanisms have no doubt been of great importance for the government's ability to act as a co-ordinating body (OECD 1993a; Sverdrup 1995; Jansen and Osland 1996; Reitan 1997).

Moreover, the planning and budget routines have been further developed. Since 1989 an overview of the green profile of the State Budget and allocations attached to environment-related goals within each ministry were published separately as the 'Green Book'. From 1992 this reporting effort was split into three categories according to the degree to which expenditures had been motivated by environmental concerns. Expenditures were thus categorized as 'solely', 'substantially' or 'partly' motivated by environmental concerns.[16]

While this practice has continued, White Paper 58 'Environmental Policy for Sustainable Development. Joint Efforts for the Future' (Norwegian Ministry of the Environment 1996–7b), states that the 'Green Book' is to be replaced by a new publication: 'The Government's Environmental Profile and the Report on the State of the Environment in the Realm'. This is to be issued every year in relation to the annual budget, and is to be linked to two other new measures: (1) new sector plans for each ministry, to be prepared by the ministries themselves; and (2) a new National Achievement Monitoring System based on the individual ministerial plans and systems. This system is designed to lay the foundation for a better and more goal-oriented reporting system, as well as a more thorough use of environmental data and indicators. It is to serve as both a reporting tool to Parliament on the state of the environment, and for the preparation and revision of governmental environmental policy.

White Paper 58 stipulated, however, that the sector plans should not be prepared prior to the Kyoto meeting on the climate change convention. Thus far, two ministries have developed their sector plans, the Ministry of Defence and the Ministry of Transport and Communication (Norwegian Ministry of Defence 1998; Norwegian Ministry of Transport and Communication 1998).

---

[16] The 'Green Book' was also heavily criticized by the Investigative Commission on 'Instruments for Environmental Policy'. It was seen more as a passive collection and reporting of pro-environmental efforts than an instrument for evaluating and controlling processes in the direction of sustainable development (NOU 1995: 148).

There is nothing in these plans, however, which would appear to change the conclusion drawn by former Minister of the Environment, Thorbjørn Berntsen, that 'the national goals and targets have been more or less floating in the air'.[17] They are still floating in the air, in the sense that the overall national goals have not—except in a very general way—been translated into specific targets within the sectors in question, and an overall cross-sector integration plan is absent.

Thus, there are two different ways to assess the approach in White Paper 58.[18] On the one hand, if implemented, the new monitoring system could actually strengthen the Ministry of the Environment's co-ordinator function, and also speed up the implementation efforts in other sectors. On the other hand the approach could be seen as a further *segmentation* of the different sectors. It amounts to 'within-sector' integration without cross-sector integration, and is thus not truly sector-encompassing. That it should represent 'a quantum leap forward', as maintained by the former Minister of the Environment, Thorbjørn Berntsen, hardly seems justified.

The Vertical Structure and Local Agenda 21

The problem of institutionalizing a truly sector-encompassing approach at the state level creates problems also for the vertical administrative structure—the relationship between state, county and municipalities. As of January 1999, Norway was divided into eighteen county and 435 municipal units. Counties and municipalities both have separate elected councils. The counties, and particularly the municipalities vary considerably, however, with regard to both population and geographic extent (Aall 1997). Further, there is no general legislative or constitutional provision stipulating the division of authority between the state, county, and municipality. The Norwegian Parliament and government regulate the tasks which are, at any one time, delegated to the various levels.[19]

The municipal administration in Norway has for decades been responsible for policy areas crucial for environmental policy, such as land use, physical planning, waste disposal, and water treatment (Jansen and Osland

[17] Berntsen's statement was made at the conference '*Energi for et bærekraftig samfunn*', 18 March 1997, Oslo, Voksenåsen, arranged by the Research Council of Norway.

[18] I owe this point to Peter Johan Schei (Interview 26 Nov. 1998).

[19] In 1982, an Environmental Department was established within the County Governor's Offices. These environmental departments are regional administrative entities subordinate to the Ministry of the Environment, and thus part of the hierarchical structure of state author-

1996; Reitan 1997). There has also been a further decentralization of authority during the past decade, with the revision of the Local Government Act in 1993. The aim was to strengthen and further develop both municipal and county autonomy, and to create the conditions which would enable these sub-units to become more efficient suppliers of services to their inhabitants (Aall 1997; 1998).

After a period with initial pilot studies, a reform programme for 'Environmental Protection in the Municipalities' (the EPM programme), was established in 1992. The programme created political and administrative units with responsibility for the environmental issues within the municipalities (Hovik and Johnsen 1994; Sverdrup 1995; Reitan 1997; Aall 1997; 1998).[20] Though the government initially viewed the EPM programme as 'well in accordance with the recommendations of Agenda 21' (Norwegian Ministry of the Environment 1992–3: 8, translation by the author), it was criticized for not taking chapter 28 of the Agenda seriously (Armann, Hille, and Kasin 1995: 15). All this changed in 1996, however, when the Ministry of the Environment acknowledged that there were important differences between Local Agenda 21 and more traditional municipal environmental policies, and from that point forward the government has strongly encouraged municipalities to work out local Agenda 21 plans (Lafferty, Aall, and Seippel 1998).

Studies of how the EPM programme actually functioned showed that, with few exceptions, municipalities seemed to be most concerned with local environmental problems (Hovik 1994). White Paper 58 (1996–7) included guidelines for what a Local Agenda 21 should contain. Municipalities were asked to relate to global environmental problems, as well as national environmental goals, and to look for local solutions to these problems. This included biological diversity, reduced energy consumption, reduced greenhouse-gas emissions, improved public transport, renewable energy, waste treatment, the need to preserve cultural heritage, and arrangements for recreational activities in the municipalities (Norwegian Ministry of the Environment 1996–7b: ch. 8).

But the work of improving environmental quality at the municipal level

---

ity. The County Environmental Departments have the function of guiding and giving advice in the processes of municipal planning. Although the county has no legal authority in the process of municipal planning, municipal plans are submitted to the County Environmental Departments, and in the interchange the departments can have significant impacts on municipal plans (Jansen and Osland 1996: 213–15; Reitan 1997: 11–12).

[20] From 1997, the former earmarked allocations for environmental officers are included in the general framework grants from central government to the municipalities (Norwegian Ministry of the Environment 1996–7b: 29).

was also linked to the broader agenda of sustainable development including: social equalization; equal opportunities; preventing health problems and social problems; improving the conditions for youth, the elderly, and the disabled; improving democratization and popular participation; and finally improving the development of commerce (Norwegian Ministry of the Environment 1996–7b: ch. 8).

This linkage to the broader agenda of sustainable development was, however, out of line with what the Ministry of the Environment, as a sector ministry, had established for itself. White Paper 58 identified three dimensions of the concept of sustainable development: the welfare perspective; the generations perspective; and the ecological perspective. The goal of White Paper 58 was, however, limited to 'clarifying' and 'deepening' the ecological perspective, without going into detail on the other two aspects.

The municipalities have, therefore, been pretty much left to themselves to set the priorities, make the trade-offs, and integrate the different aspects of sustainable development (along with the other aspects of municipal policy), into a coherent municipal plan. As such, the difficulties and problems of sustainable development have been left to the municipalities to solve. As Naustdalslid (1994: 49) points out, the effect is that the lack of policy co-ordination at the national level is being transferred downwards by prescribing stronger co-ordination at the lower level.

Concluding Perspectives

In their earlier review of Norway's environmental performance, the OECD (1993a: 79) argued that the overall national goals needed to be translated into specific targets for sector ministries and local authorities. As has been shown here, the actual sector plans and the guidelines for local authorities developed to date are still far from achieving this. But efforts and investments made to 'institutionalize' sustainable development in Norway have no doubt led to substantial progress in selected areas such as waste management, pollution control, conservation, environmental law, and planning.

Waste management is a prime example. Since the Earth Summit, recycling of municipal waste has increased from 8 to 20 per cent in 1996, and to 25 per cent in 1997. Special arrangements for different types of waste have been introduced, and producer responsibility for waste treatment has been developed through changes in law and voluntary agreements. The latest agreement in 1998, on recycling of electric and electronic (EE) products, sets targets for the branch to secure the collection of 80 per cent of EE waste within a five-year period.

But waste management also illustrates the problems of sustainable development in a broader sense. Despite progress in the area, municipal waste has increased by 50 per cent over the last fifteen years, and the growth is estimated to be a further 44 per cent during the next fifteen years (Norwegian Ministry of the Environment 1996–7b: 188). Moreover, current projections anticipate a tripling of private consumption between 1995 and 2050 (Norwegian Ministry of Finance and Customs 1996–7). Thus, Norwegians are clearly becoming richer and richer; producing and consuming more and more.

Despite the fact that environmental goals and targets have been further developed by the Ministry of the Environment (their budget for 1996–7 contained no less than 114 goals and targets divided among nineteen different policy areas), many of the goals and targets in the different sectors, and even within specific sectors, are irreconcilable if not directly contradictory.

Implementing sustainable development necessarily implies adjusting contradictory goals and making trade-offs. But the lack of both sectoral and cross-sectoral integration implies that trade-offs are not being made. Sydnes (1996: 295) has argued, for example, that oil and transport policies 'are still on different tracks, largely unaffected by the climate debate, driven by domestic interests and powerful lobbies'.

Others have suggested that the Ministry of the Environment should be accorded status as a 'super ministry', responsible for the overall implementation of environmental policy (Jansen 1989). While this would improve the Ministry of the Environment's power in relation to other ministries, the real problem seems to be that most public goals and targets represent not only different interests, but also *legitimate* interests. To secure full employment, economic growth, economic competitiveness, individual freedom, and so on, are aims which cannot—and probably *should* not be easily overridden. Even a 'super' Ministry of the Environment would, therefore, have to weigh environmental interests against other (legitimate) interests.

Traditionally, the Norwegian answer to contradictory goals and increasing complexity, has been *planning*, and sustainable development has been integrated into the long-term planning conducted by the Ministry of Finance and Customs (Norwegian Ministry of Finance and Customs 1992–3; 1996–7). Pollution figures have been integrated into the macro-economic models, and the models are used to estimate projected emissions under varying conditions. Furthermore, regional planning, local planning, biodiversity planning, climate change planning, waste planning, and so on, have been further developed. Thus, planning for sustainable development is perhaps the most visible result of the 'institutionalization' of sustainable development in Norway.

At the local level, the Ministry of the Environment has stressed popular participation as one of the main elements in Local Agenda 21 planning and at the state level, NGO participation has continued after Rio in forums established to formalize the interaction between government and the NGO community. Two co-ordinating bodies were set up by government to follow up the implementation of Agenda 21; the 'National Committee for Sustainable Development', and the 'National Committee for International Environmental Matters' (NIM).

NIM has functioned relatively well as a consultative body for the Norwegian follow-up of Agenda 21, and for the ongoing work in the United Nations Commission on Sustainable Development (UNCSD). There are regular meetings and a broad spectrum of stakeholder representatives. None of the newly established commissions can, however, be said to play the central co-ordinating role which is claimed in the Norwegian National Reports to the CSD (Norwegian Ministry of Foreign Affairs 1995; 1997).[21]

Different forms of participation have, however, been institutionalized and formalized in most phases of the policy-making process in Norway. Even though environmental NGOs still participate to a lesser degree in the formally established corporate channels than do NGOs in the traditional policy fields (Jansen and Osland 1996), this has been partially offset by a decline in significance of traditional corporatist boards and committees, and a general increase in the power of the legislature which has led both business and environmental NGOs to invest more resources in the lobbying of Parliament (Rommetvedt and Melberg 1996; Opedal 1996).

Jansen and Osland (1996) argue, however, that adequate environmental policies are dependent on a radical break from a political system based on mere adjustments of socio-economic interests and bargaining. A transformation of some of the existing institutional characteristics of Norwegian state and society is seen as essential (Jansen and Osland 1996: 250). But does 'public awareness and citizen involvement in the dimensions of environmental problems' necessarily imply 'another type of interest representation and authority structures'? (Jansen and Osland 1996: 250). Clearly not in and of itself. There is nothing like a 'pure' system of politics freed from the introduction of (legitimate) socio-economic interests. Bargaining processes

---

[21] The National Committee for Sustainable Development has only met a few times, and has not functioned according to plan. This appears to have been due to an overall lack of political will, as well as internal differences of opinion as to the actual purpose and function of the committee.

between government, parliament, ministries, interest organizations, and political parties are inevitable within the broad agenda of sustainable development. This obviously creates problems for the implementation of sustainable development, and even for the possibility of creating truly 'sector-encompassing' policies.

But seen in this way, it becomes a problem of a different character. Implementing sustainable development becomes more complex, unpredictable, and uncertain, because the very notion of sustainable development and what it actually implies, and should imply, in a national context is highly contestable and in need of interpretation. Complexity, unpredictability, and uncertainty relates to all of the four distinctive dimensions of the Norwegian approach to sustainable development identified above: the global or international dimension; the implications of trying to maintain a stance as 'forerunner'; the problems of establishing a truly sector-encompassing approach; and the problem of establishing national goals and targets.

Because of the global dimension of sustainable development, the actual goals are extremely hard to specify. While the overall target for climate-gas emissions in Norway was set in Kyoto, it is still unclear how much of the reductions will have to be taken at home. It is also unclear what Norway's position actually is on the matter. The present government has stated that it wants to achieve the Kyoto target by the year 2005, and the current Minister of the Environment, Guro Fjellanger, has stated that in accordance with the Kyoto Protocol, Norway would achieve most of the reductions at home. It remains very doubtful, however, whether a majority in Parliament will support this.

Another problem with the goals and targets is that some of the 'consensual' goals turn out to be not that consensual after all. The environmental cleavage seems to reappear more or less regularly in relation to the energy issue. Both the Labour party and the Conservative party accept that the goal stating that electricity consumption, in a normal year should be covered by renewable energy sources, does not rule out the domestic use of gas in *exceptional* years. Thus, even a 'consensual' goal needs to be interpreted.

Technology and technological development further exemplify the unpredictability and uncertainty of what implementing sustainable development actually implies. The gas-fired power-plant controversy more or less dissolved when Norsk Hydro launched its new concept for hydrogen-fuelled power plants. This would reduce emissions by approximately 90 per cent compared with modern gas-fired plants, totally transforming the question of the domestic use of gas. With the new technology, natural gas (methane) would be used as a feed stock to produce hydrogen. The by-product is CO_2, which would be injected into oil reservoirs, which again increases oil recovery.

What appears to be a much more stable feature of the Norwegian situation, however, is the continuity in the basic positions of the political actors. It was this feature which struck Reitan (1998b) in her study of Norwegian environmental policy from the early 1970s. In her view, 'this stability can be observed despite the changes that have taken place during these years regarding both environmental problems on the agenda and choices of solutions to cope with these problems' (Reitan 1998b: 21). Knutsen's (1997) work also points in the same direction, so it would appear that, just as environmental policy was adapted by the political parties to their general ideologies (Aardal 1993), the same case applies to sustainable development.

But sustainable development implementation, and especially climate change policy, has also challenged strong interests. This can be illustrated by looking at the principle of cost-efficiency, which has long been a cornerstone of Norway's climate policy. While Sydnes (1996: 294) seems to argue that Norway's climate policy is the result of a learning process within and between ministries, Jansen and Osland (1996) claim that the principle of cost-efficiency is associated with—and its present ascendance is partly derived from—the most long-standing principle of Norwegian environmental policy: that is, the principle that Norwegian policy should not put Norwegian industry and commerce in a disadvantageous position compared with foreign competitors (Jansen and Osland 1996: 189).

This argument conceals, however, the fact that the principle of cost-efficiency has quite different implications for industry, depending on whether or not cost-efficiency is seen in a *national* or an *international* context. Thus, it seems more appropriate to conclude in accordance with Skjærseth and Rosendal (1997), that it is first and foremost in relation to Norway's self-imposed role as an 'instigator' in international forums, and Norway's own stated ambitions as a 'forerunner', that there has been a growing gap between rhetoric and action. And yet Norwegian authorities seem to be aware of the seriousness of the situation, recognizing that the problems require stronger environmental efforts. Such an awareness must also be tempered by the realization that Norway is a very small country with an open and oil-dependent economy. Reconciling these two positions is what the debate on sustainable development in Norway has been all about.

8

Sweden: Progression Despite Recession

KATARINA ECKERBERG

Introduction

Sweden is often regarded as a pioneer in the field of environmental policy and a champion of generous development assistance (Lundqvist 1996; Lafferty and Eckerberg 1998; Kronsell 1997). Indeed, since the 1960s Sweden has often been viewed as a 'model society', which has combined high and fairly evenly distributed social welfare with rather far-reaching environmental policy goals and solidarity with the Third World. With this record, one might expect that Sweden would also be among the pioneers in implementing sustainable development.

The Swedish government has, without doubt, taken the UNCED agreements seriously. In March 1996 the then newly appointed Prime Minister Göran Persson declared that Sweden should set an example to the Western world in building an environmentally sustainable society. And yet in this chapter it will be argued that the overall picture of Swedish national policy for sustainable development is inconsistent. In some respects the response to UNCED may seem overwhelming, and is probably unique by international comparison. This has occurred despite the economic crisis that Sweden faced in the 1990s, which has changed the context of welfare distribution, and created a new and difficult situation for energy and environmental policy as well as foreign assistance. But conflicting government messages are present within at least five areas that relate to sustainable development policy: connecting sustainability to the distribution of welfare within Sweden; maintaining a high level of Third World assistance; limiting emissions of greenhouse gases within transport and energy policy; protecting biological diversity; and supporting monitoring and research for a sustainable society.

Government policy currently relies on a revival of the traditional Social Democratic vision of the *Folkhemmet* (The People's Home) originally launched by its leader Per Albin Hansson back in 1928. This vision combines an emphasis on raising material prosperity with guaranteed social security for the entire population, both to be created through a broad political consensus on the conditions of production. Thus, a tension between continued economic growth on one hand and protection of the global environment (including aspects of global justice and equity) on the other appears to be embedded in the official vision of the new 'green welfare society'. It is also true that the current political objective of reducing public spending has particularly hit the above-mentioned areas, and stands in sharp contrast to the government commitment to a massive new investment programme in sustainable development.

I will begin by outlining the political, administrative, and economic background to environment and sustainable development policy and by briefly describing Swedish involvement in the run-up to UNCED. I will then move on to review the major changes in national policy that have occurred since 1992, and to discuss the general response to sustainable development in Sweden. Three policy areas will be analysed in greater depth: foreign assistance; climate change policy; and the preservation of biological diversity. Each of these represents an area of particular concern for high-consumption societies, and two of them resulted in conventions signed in Rio. The chapter will conclude with an attempt to evaluate the main trends in Swedish policy for sustainable development.

The Swedish Welfare State and Environmental Policy in Transition

The Swedish Model

Like the other Nordic countries, Sweden has been known for its strong welfare state during the post-war era. Although the private sector traditionally accounted for a very limited proportion of service provision (education, health care, social services, etc.), private business—but also labour unions and other interest groups—have influenced public policy formation ever since the earliest days of the long Social Democratic government's rule (1932–76; 1982–91; 1994–). An important strategy has been to co-opt actors in the labour market, the big companies, and different kinds of sectoral interests into the policy formulation process in a (weak) corporatist manner, and to build consensus 'behind closed doors'. Since the 1930s, the idea of *Folkhemmet* has symbolized the Social Democratic vision of creating a welfare state through social engineering. However, it also became a metaphor that legitimized rather paternalist and interventionist patterns of decision-making *vis-à-vis* the general public (Eduards 1991: 161–81).

The apparent success of the project of *Folkhemmet*, particularly during the 1950s and through to the 1970s, also affected the conduct of international politics. Sweden emphasized the establishment of solidarity with the Third World through foreign aid and by adopting the role of international critic (particularly during the Vietnam War), and the setting of a 'good example' in the international context. Environmental concerns fit quite neatly into this picture (Kronsell 1997: 55). As long as the economy was growing, and all interests could be paid off through increased material welfare and different social support systems, the model worked.

During the last ten years, however, the welfare state has weakened considerably. This process—to some extent explained by international economic developments, but also by the increasing fragmentation of Swedish society into separate interest groups—has been expressed in deregulation, privatization, and a growing emphasis on market solutions. Whereas until the early 1990s Sweden maintained one of the lowest unemployment levels within the Western world (1.9 per cent in 1990), this has now risen to the average EU level.[1] In the wake of the financial turbulence during most of the 1990 to 1995 period there have been substantial reductions in social welfare spending. Savings within local government budgets were made repeatedly during the 1990s, and state contributions towards municipal spending in the educational, cultural, and social sectors has been reduced. This has led to increased social cleavages within Swedish society, with reduced social benefits for less privileged groups, including many old people, single women, children, and unemployed youth. According to a recent survey of Swedish living conditions, a clear shift occurred in 1990 when the proportion of people living in poverty began to increase.[2] Working women in particular have experienced growing health problems, and psychological well-being[3] has also deteriorated during the 1990s (SCB 1997). Some of these social changes have

[1] Official unemployment has recently fluctuated from a high 9.8 per cent in August 1997, down to 6.9 per cent in January 1998 and 5.3 per cent in November 1998. In addition, 4.2 per cent are occupied in labour-policy measures—mainly education (Svenska Dagbladet 1998*b*).

[2] In the 1990s the living standard measured by household income and average housing area began to decrease after having increased ever since 1975. This especially affected young people, families with children, and low income groups. The share of poor people, which had decreased from 8 to 3 per cent between the years 1983 and 1990, increased again to 7 per cent in 1995. Until the beginning of the 1980s equality between social groups had increased, but since then the cleavage has grown. Compared to other EU countries, Sweden and the Nordic countries still show, however, the smallest differences in income between social groups, and the least share of poor people (SCB 1997).

[3] Psychological well-being is measured by sleeping problems, tiredness, worry, and anxiety.

environmental implications. For example, the number of single-person households has increased from 16 to 25 per cent since 1975, which implies increased per capita use of energy and other resources.

Traditional reliance on the state to provide for social welfare has changed and the share of services provided by the voluntary sector is increasing. Membership in 'organizations for help and charity' grew from 9 per cent of the population in 1990 to 22 per cent in 1996.[4] Similarly, voluntary donations to charity have almost tripled from 1989 to 1996, while the state's share of contributions to voluntary organizations has decreased from about two-thirds to less than half (Svenska Dagbladet 1998a). Reductions in public spending have also affected the environmental sector, reducing staffing and funds available for environmental protection. In the three-year period from 1997 to 2000, for example, the Swedish Environmental Protection Agency sustained a 25 per cent cut to its overall budget. Similarly, funding for international assistance has declined significantly.

Sweden became a member of the EU in January 1995, after a national referendum in which the possibilities of favourably influencing European environmental policy were emphasized. In the international arena Sweden has been among the countries that have been most active in raising environmental concerns. The first United Nation conference on environmental and development issues (The UN Conference on the Human Environment) was held in Stockholm in 1972. Since then Sweden has continued to play an important role, particularly in negotiations over long-range transboundary air pollution and emission of CFCs. Sweden also promotes intensified environmental action in Central and Eastern Europe, particularly in the Baltic states. Recently the project of creating an Agenda 21 for the Baltic region to encompass all the countries around the Baltic Sea was launched (Swedish Ministry of the Environment 1997g). A similar Agenda 21 initiative for the Barents region, including the northern parts of Scandinavia and Russia, is also getting underway.

Decentralized Environmental Policy

The Swedish Environmental Protection Agency (SEPA), established in 1967, has been the prime motor in developing and implementing environmental policy. Two years after its founding came the first Environmental Protection Act, regulating air, noise, and water pollution. The National Franchise Board for Environmental Protection was set up in 1969, under the jurisdiction of SEPA, with the task of issuing permits and directives on emission levels and

---

[4] This figure comes from the Swedish survey in World Value Studies and builds on about 980 interviews (Svenska Dagbladet 1998a).

regulating the location of new industrial plants. Yet at the beginning of the 'new' era of environmental policy, which emerged from the consciousness-raising of the late 1960s and early 1970s, a number of institutional peculiarities persisted. Issues of environmental policy remained the responsibility of the Ministry of Agriculture, and it was not until 1987 that a Ministry for Energy and the Environment was set up. The new ministry was charged with 'an offensive and co-ordinating role within the Cabinet', and it was to introduce and integrate environmental considerations into other policy sectors (Lundqvist 1996: 270). The current size of the Ministry of the Environment[5] (about 150 employees), in contrast to that of SEPA (about 470), reflects a characteristic feature of Swedish central government: the ministries are focused on strategic policy-making, while the central agencies are entrusted to make decisions on matters concerning implementation within their area of competence.

In the early years Swedish environmental policy was rather centralized around SEPA. Inspectors employed in the County Administration's environmental units, and as health and environment inspectors within municipalities, were closely connected to SEPA. During the 1980s, municipal environmental units were significantly strengthened. In the early 1990s, the personnel of Sweden's municipal environmental inspectorates numbered about 2,100, of whom 1,500 were directly engaged in the field (Swedish Ministry of the Environment 1993b: 73 ff.). From having played a role in both formulating and implementing environmental strategies, the main function of SEPA in the 1990s has shifted towards formulating and evaluating policy, and the various sector agencies, county administrations and municipalities have largely taken over implementation tasks. The guiding principles in current environmental policy are sector responsibility, integration, and decentralization (SEPA 1996). This is in line with the general administrative decentralization process that has taken place in Sweden over the last decade. It has implied a shift of responsibility from national institutions to municipal government in environmental policy. Swedish municipalities are required by law to include environmental concerns in all their activities (Government of Sweden 1990–1).

By tradition, the municipalities have a general power to 'govern their own affairs' (Gustafsson 1988). Municipal autonomy includes rights to levy taxes on the citizens and to develop local policies within most sector areas. Gradually, the autonomy of municipalities in environmental decision-making concerning their own territory has been strengthened. The 1991 Municipal Act permits municipalities greater autonomy to create boards and

[5] In 1990 the new Social Democratic government reorganized the Ministry of the Environment and Energy and returned energy issues to the Ministry for Industry.

inspectorates according to local priorities. As a result, the administrative organization of environmental affairs varies among municipalities (Swedish Ministry of the Environment 1993b: 43).

While early environmental policy relied mostly on regulation and administrative procedures, more recent policy initiatives have involved a greater use of information and economic instruments. A breakthrough in the area of environmental taxation occurred in the government's economic reform of 1990–1, when around SEK 18 billion (about £1.5 billion) was transferred from taxes on income and private wealth to taxes on energy and emissions. This tax reform was triggered by the need to maintain state revenues despite the general reduction of income tax levels that had occurred during the 1980s. By referring to environmental policy goals, it was easier to achieve political consensus in Parliament to maintain state income. At this time, environmental issues scored high in public opinion polls and it was therefore important to all political parties to show their willingness to act. A clear sign of the saliency of environmental issues was that during the 1988 election the Green party (formed in 1981) became the first totally new party in seventy years to break into the traditional Swedish party system (Bennulf 1990; Vedung 1988; 1989).

At the time of the 1987 Brundtland report the momentum for environmental policy was high, and all political parties accepted the new challenge. Their political programmes were revised accordingly. It became increasingly difficult to distinguish between parties regarding their concern for environmental issues. This may help explain why the Green party lost its seats in Parliament at the 1991 election. The new government that replaced the Social Democrats relied on the Centre party, which launched the idea of the 'recycling society' (Kretsloppssamhället) as a response to sustainable development. Reuse of waste products and recycling of resources became the number one issue on the environmental policy agenda. The business community and local governments also took up these ideas. A new wave of consciousness-raising emerged around 'life-cycle analysis' and the notion of managing industrial processes 'from-the-cradle-to-the-grave'. This laid the ground for active Swedish preparations in the run-up to UNCED.

Preparations for UNCED

The Environmental Advisory Council (EAC) had been created in 1968 to assist the then Social Democratic Cabinet on environmental issues. At first, its role was primarily one of investigating and providing information. At the time of UNCED it began to assume a more strategic advisory role under the new Cabinet consisting of non-socialist parties. Chaired by the Minister of the Environment Olof Johansson from the Centre party, its members included about twenty experts from varying disciplines and policy sectors. It introduced new organizational forms and issues to environmental work by bringing together scientists and policy-makers in two conferences examining the Swedish position prior to UNCED, including one on the perspective of the South. Several reports were published in collaboration with the UNCED secretariat and the NGO co-ordination group called Environment and Development 92, which contributed largely to wide dissemination around the UNCED issues. There was also a special information project for children and youth, and a newspaper about UNCED was directed towards this audience.

The official Swedish delegation to UNCED was led by the Prime Minister and included nine groups: ministers and state secretaries, representatives from political parties, from sector agencies, from veterans, business and labour organizations, NGOs, experts, public officers from various national ministries, and officials from Swedish offices in foreign countries. The Swedish delegation insisted that UNCED should aim to achieve concrete results, which would confirm the close relationship between environment and development. It urged UNCED to support preventative environmental policy, poverty alleviation, the reduction of pollution loading (especially from industrial countries), and the improvement of trade and economic relations for developing countries, while also encouraging democracy and public participation. The Swedish delegation strongly supported ideas such as 'sustainable development', 'recycling of resources', 'the precautionary principle', and 'the polluter-pays principle'. Among the more specific issues that this delegation wished UNCED to address were: the connection between military activities and the environment; renewable energy and energy efficiency; transport problems; financial resources (in particular meeting the 0.7 per cent of GNP target for development aid); technology transfer to developing countries; combating desertification; and supporting the availability of clean water and sanitation (Eduards 1996).

The basis of the Swedish position in the climate negotiations was established by a three-party agreement on energy policy between the Social Democrats, the Centre party and the Liberal party concluded in January 1991. Sweden was among the countries that pushed hardest for international co-operation in order to achieve binding targets for greenhouse-gas emissions, and which succeeded in uniting the OECD in a proposal to stabilize climate-gas emissions by the year 2000.

From a Swedish standpoint the results of UNCED were largely

satisfactory. Many of the core principles mentioned above were included in the Rio Declaration and in Agenda 21, and the conference was regarded as a major step towards integrating environmental issues with social and economic policy. It also recognized the need to support democracy and participatory decision-making. Some issues were, however, less successfully handled from a Swedish perspective—especially questions relating to climate change and finance. The Swedish delegation was disappointed with the negotiations regarding energy and transport issues, and would have liked to see a more vigorous strategy for mobilizing international financial assistance to support developing countries (Eduards 1996).

Implementing UNCED in National Policy Programmes

The Swedish government responded promptly to the UNCED agreements. In the late summer of 1992, a follow-up conference of experts was arranged to discuss issues such as energy, transport, development aid, international co-operation, trade, research and technical development, the military and the environment, education, and biological diversity and biotechnology. The result was a short guide 'Our task after Rio' (Swedish Ministry of the Environment 1992) that presented ideas on what should be done. It became a source of inspiration for many organizations, not least for the government itself in preparing new bills (EAC (Sweden) 1994). In the autumn of 1993 a newsletter was launched. As noted earlier, the momentum for environment and development policy was already high before UNCED. After UNCED, however, the flow of government commission reports and government bills on UNCED related issues increased dramatically. Of these, the bill on 'Targeting Sustainable Development: Implementation of the UNCED Decisions' (Government of Sweden 1993–4) stands out as one of the core documents. Overall it is clear that there has been a massive response to UNCED from a variety of national actors as well as at the local level.

A report on 'A Sustainable Society' was published in 1993 by the Swedish Environmental Protection Agency (SEPA 1993a). It was launched as a National Plan for Sustainable Development, and it identified thirteen major threats to the environment. This reflected a rather pure environmental view of sustainable development, rather than attempting any integration of social, economic, and environmental goals. More recently the government proposed a series a measures to attain 'Ecological Sustainability' (Swedish Ministry of the Environment 1997h), including ninety-three specific steps within the various ministries. The government declared in 1997 that ecologically sustainable development basically involves three objectives: protecting the environment (so that pollution does not exceed the environment's capacity to absorb wastes); developing efficient resource use (so that we employ more efficiently the energy and raw materials that we consume today); and ensuring sustainable future supplies of resources (by extending the use of renewables) (Swedish Ministry of the Environment 1997a: 3). Still, this plan of action should be regarded as a way to augment sector responsibility rather than as a co-ordinated strategy for sustainable development. Within its provisions twenty-four national authorities have been given special tasks (Government of Sweden 1997–8c).

Understanding 'Sustainable Development'

It took some time before a common Swedish translation was accepted for the concept of 'sustainable development'. Three different translations into the Swedish language have been used: *bärkraftig utveckling*, *uthållig utveckling*, and *hållbar utveckling*. These alternative words for 'sustainable' have somewhat different meanings. According to the dictionary, *bärkraftig* means 'capable to sustaining weight, strong'; *uthållig* means 'with [good] staying power', while *hållbar* means 'durable, lasting, hard-wearing' (Norstedts 1988). All three variants have been used in practice by various organizations, but the government and most others now seem to have agreed on the third (*hållbar*). However, the concept is seldom used without the prefix 'ecologically' sustainable development. This probably reflects the Swedish perspective on how 'sustainable development' should be understood: placing emphasis on the ecological dimension and on the limits of natural resources and the environment. As is pointed out in the final report of the government's National Committee for Agenda 21 'Five years after Rio':

Agenda 21 includes three dimensions of societal development that must work together for making development sustainable: the social dimension, the economic dimension and the environmental/nature resource dimension, or the ecological dimension. It is natural that these dimensions are emphasised differently at different times and by different parts of the world . . . in industrial countries with a high resource consumption and high pollution the ecological aspects should be stressed. Industrial countries have a special responsibility to be pioneers in the development of environmental technology and resource efficiency . . . In Sweden, the concept of 'sustainable development' is often equalled with environmental work. (Swedish Ministry of the Environment 1997g: 13–14)

Although the National Committee for Agenda 21 proposes to widen the concept of 'sustainable development' to embrace the social and economic

spheres, it is clear that so far the ecological dimension dominates in its interpretation of what should be done. According to its own statement 'this is
due to the need to limit the task in a reasonable way, and because the experiences from Swedish follow-up of Agenda 21 is concentrated within this
area' (Swedish Ministry of the Environment 1997g: 15). In Agenda 21 work
within Swedish local authorities, the environmental and ecological dimensions of sustainability have also been emphasized (SALA 1995; 1996). The
most recent Environmental Policy Bill concludes that the social, economic,
and ecological dimensions of sustainable development are mutually interdependent. It is, in the government's view, important to further the
ecological dimension with the aim of resolving the major environmental
challenges faced by Sweden within a generation (Government of Sweden
1997–8c: 19).

The Ecocycling Society

In 1993 the government presented a proposal to operationalize sustainable
management using an ecocycle approach to societal planning (Government
of Sweden 1992–3b: 'The Ecocycle Bill'). It introduced a cyclic rather than a
linear model of societal development, where traditional growth-scenarios
were questioned and recycling and the reuse of materials became essential.
An important accomplishment of this emphasis on ecocycling has been the
introduction of producer responsibility where the producer, and not the consumer or the municipality, is made responsible for the life cycle of a product
(Kronsell 1997: 61). In the words of the 1991–4 Centre party Environmental
Minister, the Ecocycle Bill represented a 'first major step towards an eco-
cyclic society', which would 'mean that our way of life does not give rise to
problems for future generations' (Swedish Ministry of the Environment
1993a: 3). The Bill specified governmental targets, but the producers (of
certain packaging materials and other products) were obliged to find ways
to achieve these targets (Lundqvist 1996). According to SEPA a total of
75,000 firms are covered by this legislation. Its 1997 assessment of how the
regulation has worked establishes that most producers were able to achieve
the required standards of re-use and recycling. For example, 72 per cent of
glass packaging is now recycled (original goal 70 per cent). For other categories the figures are: glass bottles for soda and light beer 96 per cent (goal
95 per cent); plastic packaging more than 30 per cent (goal 30 per cent); paper
and carton, more than 45 per cent (goal 30 per cent); and corrugated card-
board 81 per cent (goal 65 per cent). However, some producers have not
attained the objectives set: this is the case for glass for wine and liquor (only
80 per cent compliance with a goal of 90 per cent), and aluminium cans (19

per cent compliance with a goal of 50 per cent). Revised targets and a wider programme for producer responsibility are included in the new Environment Policy Bill (Government of Sweden 1997–8c).

Despite the new ecocycling approach, the understanding of the concept of sustainable development within Sweden seems largely to revolve around the idea of continued economic growth. In a survey conducted in June 1997, thirteen key policy-makers were asked how they interpreted sustainable development (Svenska Dagbladet 1997). The respondents included representatives from private business, environmental experts, political parties (including party leaders and ministers), and NGOs. None of them talk about the possibility of going back to a simpler life, using fewer resources, or regulating business. Overall, the answers are very modest in terms of the requirements for life-style change. All respondents put great faith in technological development, and most claim that economic growth can be successfully combined with a sustainable society. The only exceptions here were the representatives of Friends of the Earth and of the Green party.

Reforms towards a Sustainable Sweden

At the time of UNCED, the coalition government[6] which remained in power between 1991 and 1994, introduced a number of environmental policy reforms. Cross-sectoral thinking had already been introduced with the major 1987–8 Environmental Bill, but was further emphasized with the 1990–1 Bill which stated that 'responsibility and care for the environment should permeate all walks of life and society. The mission of the 1990s is to readjust all societal activities in an ecological direction' (Government of Sweden 1990–1: 11). The integration process continued in the proposal from a Commission set up in 1991 to develop a new Environmental Code that would combine fifteen environment-related acts into one single ordinance (Swedish Ministry of the Environment 1993c). The Commission recommended a shift from control of individual pollution sources to 'environmental quality standards'. It also introduced the principle of 'cyclical and producer liability'—the rule that had been adopted in the Ecocycle Bill (Government of Sweden 1992–3b). In 1996, following the receipt of supplementary terms of reference from the government, the commission proposed that the Environmental Code should be based on the principles adopted at UNCED. Its recommendations included an administrative reform to create five Regional Environmental Courts (to replace the existing Water Courts and the National Franchise Board for Environmental Protection). Stricter

---

[6] This government was composed of four parties: the Moderate party, the Centre party, the Christian Democrats, and the Liberal party.

rules concerning supervision, criminal liability, and penalties were also brought in early in 1999 (Government of Sweden 1994–5a; Swedish Ministry of the Environment 1996; 1997c; Government of Sweden 1997–8b). The purpose of the new Environmental Code is to fill gaps between existing laws, and to encourage the courts and the police to concentrate on severe crimes as compared with 'small offences', for which a special fee is now being levied by the country or municipal environmental administration. Still, the new legislation has been criticized by both environmental and judicial experts for being inadequate and inconsistent.

Local Agenda 21

The immediate response in Sweden to *implementing* sustainable development occurred at the level of local government, within the 288 Swedish municipalities. According to the Swedish report to UNGASS in June 1997, virtually all of these local governments had embarked on the process of initiating a Local Agenda 21 (LA21) process. Already by the end of 1995, more than half had employed LA21 co-ordinators, and were involved in organizing seminars, courses, and practical counselling for various groups, including the general public (SALA 1996). In practice, however, many of the local projects carried out in the name of Agenda 21 resemble traditional environmental policy rather than representing any radically new approach to sustainable development. Problems with approaches confined to specific sectors, an absence of integration and an unwillingness to spend resources on LA21 projects are still frequent. A group of about forty to sixty pioneer municipalities have initiated a wide range of activities, of which some projects and policy goals may be seen as early signs of more fundamental changes in local government policies concerning infrastructure, resource use, and individual lifestyles. Environmental education within schools and day-care centres is often included in such interpretations of LA21. In several cases, these municipalities have adopted policy goals and instruments which are much more far-reaching in their orientation towards achieving sustainable development than approaches endorsed at the national level. Many have also introduced new forms of participation and have included neighbourhood groups, schools, and local business in the process (Eckerberg *et al.* 1998). The general public's awareness of Agenda 21 is remarkable. Three per cent of the population claims to have participated in an LA21 project; 20 per cent acknowledge receiving written information; and some 40 per cent have heard about it (SEPA 1997a). This is the result of the impressive amount of information on Agenda 21 that has been distributed by SEPA, the Association of Local Authorities (SALA) and the Society for the Conservation of Nature (SSCN) together with q2000, a youth network created especially for implementing sustainable development. q2000 has developed new ways of disseminating information based largely on the Internet (q2000 1997). Compared to mass participation within political parties which has now fallen to only 3 per cent of the total population, the level of environmental organization among Swedes is very high[7] and their interest in political issues has grown (SCB 1997).

The work with Local Agenda 21 in Sweden clearly preceded similar efforts at the county and national levels. The 'bottom-up' approach was emphasized by the NGOs and supported by SALA. Moreover, it was a deliberate strategy from the Environment Advisory Council, which arranged regional seminars to which municipalities and county representatives were invited, but from which SEPA and the National Chemical Inspectorate were excluded.[8] Initially, the national government did not attempt to guide the Agenda 21 process other than by encouraging the exchange of information and experiences between municipalities. Later, financial incentives were created, and a National Committee for Agenda 21 was set up in 1995. Since 1994 there has been a special fund (administered by SEPA) of SEK 7 million annually for LA21 projects carried out by local authorities and NGOs. This amount increased dramatically with a new government investment programme of SEK 5.4 billion for three years for local sustainable development projects beginning in 1997. This became a politically contested issue in the election campaign of 1998, and was portrayed by its critics as a Social Democratic attempt to bribe the voters. Still, a further SEK 2 billion was added to the programme in 1998, and it was also extended until 2001. In June 1998, the National Committee for Agenda 21 was abolished and replaced by a National Co-ordinator for Local Agenda 21. A new Advisory Council on Ecological Adjustment, consisting of representatives from national and local authorities, was also formed. Its task was to maintain a dialogue with local Agenda 21 efforts, to disseminate experience on methods and approaches in Agenda 21 work, and to channel suggestions for change to national agencies. It was to report back to the government before the end of 1999.

Yet it remains unclear how many municipalities will be able to benefit from the new investment programme. The requirement for physical investment that provides both new jobs and direct environmental benefits will probably favour larger and urban municipalities. Moreover, there are recent

---

[7] According to the recent survey by the National Board of Statistics, 3.5 million of the almost 9 million Swedes are members of an NGO and 29 per cent of the population have a commission of trust within an NGO. However, political party membership has decreased by one-third to 10 per cent in the mid-1990s. Alienation from political parties is most pronounced among the young (SCB 1997).

[8] Interview with Gunnel Hedman, 15 Oct. 1997.

signs of stagnation within the Local Agenda processes. Perhaps the time for relatively 'easy' and 'cheap' projects[9] of the kind that have been most common during the early LA21 response has now passed, and the second round of initiatives will require much more effort and more consistent financing. Furthermore, many of the LA21 co-ordinators who were employed on short-term contracts are now being made redundant because of a shortage of funds.

Building Ecologically Sustainable Sweden

Possibly the understanding of sustainable development among key policy-makers—which focuses on efficiency and technological solutions in close partnership with industry—merely reflects the deeply embedded faith in the notion of *Folkhemmet* within Swedish politics. Indeed, the Social Democratic version of the new 'Ecologically Sustainable Sweden' that has been presented can be seen as a dusted-off version of the old building of the Swedish welfare state (Thalén (Social Democratic Party Secretary) 1997). According to the Social Democrat party leadership, the ecological changes that are required can be placed in the same category as the building of the *Folkhemmet*. This was carried out by establishing a broad consensus about the conditions for production, improved standards of living, and increased security for each citizen (Eriksson 1997). Hence, the Social Democratic mantra for the twenty-first century is to combine economic growth with ecological sustainability, thus creating new 'green' jobs.

The vision of a new Ecologically Sustainable Sweden combines tradition *and* innovation in the Social Democratic party programme. In the words of Prime Minister Göran Persson:

We will rebuild the country step by step. To build a Sustainable Sweden concerns our values, what we value in life. An existential dimension, which touches our view of what is holy and indispensable. The vision of a Sustainable Sweden has all requirements needed to combine the best of labour union traditions and the new challenges we are now facing: A comprehensive view and reforms in small steps; Justice and internationalism; Employment and the struggle for a living environment on planet Earth.   (quoted from Svensson 1997: 19)

The government's policy declaration of 17 September 1996 reiterated that 'Sweden shall be a leading force and an example to other countries in its efforts to create ecologically sustainable development. Prosperity shall be

---

[9] Waste treatment, green purchasing and water projects have dominated so far among LA21 activities, representing problems which are easy to grasp, and within the capacity of local government to influence (q2000 1997; SALA 1996).

built on more efficient use of natural resources—energy, water and raw materials.' Still, it took until the beginning of 1997 for the government to appoint a Commission for Sustainable Development, consisting of the Ministers for Environment, Schools, Equal Opportunities, Agriculture, and Taxation (Finance). These ministers were selected on the basis of their youth and gender (four of the five were female), which Göran Persson explained to be necessary personal features of a group that was to be innovative and to dare to challenge traditional structures.

In March 1997, this Commission presented the government's plan to implement sustainable development in Sweden. This involves an investment programme of SEK 27.6 billion (more than £2 billion) until the year 2001 directed towards various initiatives for (1) improved ecological sustainability, such as reduced environmental loading, (2) more efficient use of energy and natural resources, and (3) increased use of renewable resources and increased recycling. Finally, the purpose of this investment programme is (4) to increase employment, and this is likely in practice to become the overriding goal. The investment programme for sustainable development was endorsed by all the political parties except the Moderate and Liberal parties. Out of the total, SEK 1 billion goes directly to the building sector for eco-cycle adjustment.[10] Second, as mentioned earlier, SEK 7.4 billion will be paid to municipalities for collaborative projects with other local bodies, including NGOs and private enterprises. A committee appointed by the Cabinet selects which projects are to be financed.[11] That such a politically appointed panel of experts should establish the criteria according to which projects are to be assessed contrasts starkly with the Swedish tradition of policy implementation through national agencies. Third, SEK 9 billion over 7 years goes towards the transformation of non-renewable energy sources into renewable ones, and also towards energy-efficiency projects. Finally, SEK 12 billion is to be invested in agri-environmental measures under the framework of the Common Agriculture Policy (to which the EU will contribute matching funds). The Commission for Sustainable Development was wound up after the September 1998 election, when all of its ministers were reshuffled to new posts or lost their positions, although the Social Democrats kept power. Instead, the new Social Democratic wording of 'sustainable development' has changed into 'Ecologically Adjusted Economic Growth', and the role of

[10] Thirty per cent of the total investment cost may be state sponsored as long as it fulfils all of the following three goals: improving the environment; using new environmental technology; and creating new jobs.

[11] In the first round of applications to the local investment programme (1997–8), SEK 2.3 billion was allocated to forty-three municipalities: 40 per cent went to the building sector and about 25 per cent towards energy-saving measures.

the Minister of the Environment in co-ordinating the government efforts has decreased.

Consumption and Production Patterns

According to the government, further measures to change patterns of consumption and production are required. One of the stated objectives is to target the *level* of consumption. The Factor 10 approach, launched originally by the Wüppertal Institute in Germany, and discussed by the Business Council for Sustainable Development and the OECD, calls for a tenfold increase in resource and energy efficiency over a 30–50-year time-frame. In order to meet these requirements, only one-tenth of current resource and energy inputs must be used to fulfil the same needs as today. To achieve this, measures will be necessary in all sectors, and methods for monitoring consumption and production must be developed, including indicators for measuring progress towards sustainable development (Swedish Ministry of the Environment 1997g). The Factor 10 approach is regarded as a long-term political goal by the government, and will be targeted through a combination of measures, which include public procurement policy, economic instruments, and information and follow-up systems.

Public sector procurement in Sweden was estimated to be SEK 300 billion or more in 1994 and constitutes an important part of the national economy. The Public Procurement Act provides some scope for making procurement subject to environmental criteria. Many municipalities[12] have already begun to apply green purchasing within their Local Agenda 21 programmes. The government also appointed about twenty-five pilot agencies to take a lead in developing environmental management systems within the national administration. This has bolstered the demand for 'green' products. For example, the Road Agency decided in June 1997 to restrict the use of company cars to those that consume less than 0.86 litres of petrol per 10 km. This provoked an outcry from the powerful Swedish car industry, whose cars would no longer be eligible for official use. Despite an open split between the Minister of Industry and the Minister of the Environment on this issue, the Prime Minister publicly defended the decision made by the Road Agency. From 1998 sixty-six national ministries and agencies are required to use environmental criteria for procurement (Swedish Ministry of the Environment 1998), a figure which increased to ninety-nine in 1999. Hence, environmental audit systems can be expected to make a substantial impact on Swedish public administration in the near future. Coupled with

[12] According to the Swedish Association of Local Authorities, as many as 60 per cent of municipalities have adopted environmental procurement policies (SALA 1996).

the introduction of similar systems in the private sector, where ISO 14001, EMAS, and environmental labelling are growing rapidly, public environmental awareness is likely to increase even more. The government has recently appointed a new Commission for Ecologically Sustainable Procurement (the EKU-delegation) to stimulate the greening of procurement policy.

Safe handling of chemicals is one component of creating sustainable production and consumption patterns. A specialized national agency for this purpose was established in 1986, with the task of controlling and monitoring the use of chemical products. The so-called substitution principle, whereby producers and importers of chemical products are obliged to switch to less hazardous products as soon as alternatives become available, has been very important in effecting the replacement of hazardous chemicals by more environmentally-friendly products. In 1996 the government set up a commission to review chemicals policy and to recommend further changes, which were included in the Environmental Policy Bill (Swedish Ministry of the Environment 1997e; Government of Sweden 1997–8b).

Swedish industry has to some extent led this development of environmental work. Some of the larger Swedish firms took on the challenge of sustainable development already in 1987 by developing environmental strategies. To maintain international competitiveness, the large companies in particular have employed environmental experts, initiated applied environmental research, and introduced innovative audit schemes. About 160 Swedish firms currently employ ISO 14001,[13] which is the third 'best' performance in Europe (after the Netherlands and Switzerland) when considered in terms of sites per million population (Environmental Data Services 1997: 3). Much of this has been triggered by consumer pressure from Europe, where the forest industry and the chemicals industry were the first to respond.[14]

Representatives from industry were invited by the Swedish government to join the official delegation to UNCED only after pressure. Also at the request of industry, one representative was included at the last minute in the official delegation to the five-year follow-up of Agenda 21 in New York in 1997.[15] Probably, this treatment of industry has not helped to improve its relations with the government in the subsequent implementation process. It should be noted that the national Agenda 21 committee has not had a

[13] Interview with Inger Strömdahl, 21 Jan. 1998.
[14] Interview with Inger Strömdahl, Christina Molde Viklund, and Anita Ringström, 21 Jan. 1998.
[15] Inger Strömdahl, Industriförbundet, was invited to participate two weeks before UNGASS.

representative from industry either. However, the youth organization q2000—an NGO created at the time of UNCED—has regularly met with industry since 1994 to discuss issues of implementing sustainable development.[16] In late 1998, the Environmental Advisory Council was instructed to report to the government by the year 2000 on strategies for an ecologically sustainable industry (Swedish Ministry of the Environment 1998).

Dissemination of information to consumers is regarded as a key factor in changing consumption and production patterns. Since there is no major independent consumer organization in Sweden, such information is provided by an array of different public and private organizations, including state agencies, municipalities, NGOs, media, industry, and local consumer groups (Swedish Ministry of the Environment 1997g). To some extent, consumers have adopted new behavioural patterns, at least in areas where no fundamental changes are required, such as sorting waste and recycling packaging materials. Some of the more successful substitutions include washing detergents and chlorine bleach. It has been suggested that environmental labelling may be one of the most powerful instruments for changing consumer patterns (Magnusson 1997). Also, in the waste management sphere the government has recently introduced a general ban on the deposit of combustible and compostable materials, and this is expected to reduce the production of waste by 50 per cent by the year 2005 (Swedish Ministry of the Environment 1997g). An action plan for sustainable consumption has been developed, which contains measures to improve product information and testing, in order to enhance the demand for more ecologically sustainable products and services (Swedish Ministry of the Interior 1998). A database providing environmental information for households on the Internet is currently being produced by the National Consumers' Agency.

Monitoring and Research for Sustainable Development

The government's general (national) aims for achieving sustainable development were adopted in 1990, and formulated as four environmental goals: to protect (1) human health; (2) biological diversity; (3) natural and cultural landscapes; and (4) sustainable use of natural resources (Government of Sweden 1990–1). Further national goals have been generated in subsequent government bills. In total, 167 different environmental goals have been formally adopted. The National Committee for Agenda 21 has studied how these goals are used in policy practice (National Committee for Agenda 21 1996). Their conclusion is that a coherent picture of their implementation is lacking. Many

[16] Interview with Inger Strömdahl, 21 Jan. 1998.

of the goals are difficult to implement. When goals that are vague (time and measurability) are presented without designating a responsible agency, or when information about the initial situation is unavailable, it is not surprising that even those authorities which *should* know have problems defining which goals are relevant for their particular activities. SEPA has evaluated eighty-five of the above mentioned national goals. Less than half (thirty-nine) of these have been achieved, or will be achieved, within the designated time-frame. It should be noted that many of these are interim objectives, and that further measures will be required to reach the final goal. One-fourth of the goals have not been achieved. Perhaps even more problematic is that the remaining one-fourth are so formulated that it is impossible to say whether or not they have been, or ever will be, achieved (ibid. 10–11).

In Sweden most environmental control and supervision was established during the 1980s, and focused on industrial pollution. This was connected to the permits issued by the regional and local authorities, which required quantifiable data on the total emissions for each industry. Internal measurement of process emissions was not considered at the time. However, the new requirements for statistical follow-up from the EU, the Convention of Climate Change and other international agreements call for a new approach and different monitoring systems. European figures show production totals multiplied by standard emission factors, while the Swedish figures have been more precisely measured at source. One reason for the different standards is that the experts responsible for environmental reporting tend to be statisticians in the EU, but technicians in Sweden. This has led to considerable problems in adapting the Swedish system to international standards.[17]

A revision of the national goals has been proposed by SEPA, coupled with a study of the challenges and possibilities implied by future scenarios (SEPA 1997*b* and *c*). As a result, fifteen new national environmental goals were adopted by Parliament in 1999. Yet these reviews do not show any significant change in the understanding of sustainable development as something different from traditional environmental policy. They point out three areas of concern, (1) land and water, (2) non-renewable resources, and (3) pollution; while economic, cultural, and social aspects are not included among the goals to be defined and measured. Statistics on environmental change (*Naturmiljön i siffror*) have been published by the Official Statistics of Sweden since 1977 (SCB 1996).[18] The data is collected from a range of different

---

[17] Interview with Bernt Röndell, 14 Nov. 1997.

[18] *The Yearbook of Environmental Statistics* (Natural Environment) was published in 1977, 1979 and 1981, followed by the *National Environment in Figures* in 1984, 1987, 1990, and 1996. It is a popular collection of current information and statistics on the natural environment, drawing on data from many agencies, research institutions and sector organizations.

sources, including sector agencies, but it represents what is *available* rather than any co-ordinated effort to follow up the most urgent areas and variables.[19] Much of the information is not available for extended time-series, nor is it possible to compare it with other relevant data in any systematic way. Nevertheless, in many areas the statistics are probably unique by international comparison; for example, some of the forest statistics extend back to the beginning of the century.

According to a recent government commission, future environmental monitoring will require further adaptation to the new national environmental goals, to EU directives, to the environmental quality standards of the new Environmental Code, and to the provision of long-term financial resources. Those sector agencies that will need data for their own follow-up should contribute to the total costs of this system (Swedish Ministry of the Environment 1997*d*). The political interest in monitoring sustainable development, however, is mostly concentrated on the use of 'indicators'. Politicians and decision-makers want data that is as simple as possible. The Environmental Advisory Council has recently developed a set of eleven (only!) indicators that are meant to be easy to understand and follow up. They are intended to measure energy and resource efficiency, environmental protection, and sustainable production and consumption. Six additional indicators are proposed for the future, where current statistics are lacking (EAC (Sweden) 1998).

There is a clear difference between the provision of technical data on the state of the environment, and more actor-orientated indicators. While the EU reporting system supports the collection of technical data, the Agenda 21 movement is geared towards local needs and follow-up.[20] Since the Swedish government has decided to adapt to the EU system, this has led to a conflict between domestic requirements and international reporting. Moreover, the government's financial support for national statistics is now declining, thus creating additional tension between different monitoring goals.

Resources for environmental quality monitoring have also been cut back in the county administrations. Between the budget years 1993–4 and 1995–6 county support for environmental work decreased by 10.2 per cent (RRV 1997). This can be contrasted with the increased role for regional environmental monitoring that the government assigned to county administrations

[19] Even in areas where substantial monitoring of biological variables is running, such as bottom fauna and flora of freshwater and seas, the selection of variables and location of measurement sites was not made to indicate the development of biological diversity. In other areas, such as wetlands and mountains, monitoring is completely lacking (SEPA 1997*d*: 9–10).

[20] Interview with Bernt Röndell, 14 Oct. 1997.

in the beginning of the 1990s (Government of Sweden 1990–1). As a result of criticism from the regional level, national support for environmental quality monitoring will be increased by 25 per cent from 1999 (Swedish Ministry of the Environment 1998). In practice, national reporting has always been difficult to co-ordinate from the data collected at county level, due to varying regional and local systems. In particular municipal autonomy has hampered the development of coherent national monitoring systems based on local reporting. Instead, many municipalities have developed their own methods, adapted to local needs, resources, and conditions. The situation is similar within the private sector, where new environmental audit systems are emerging. As mentioned earlier, 'green auditing' has also made its way into ninety-nine national agencies. The government's financial plan was 'greened' for the first time in 1997.

The funding and organization of Swedish environmental research is currently undergoing major changes, which may affect the possibility of monitoring sustainable development. In 1995 the government launched a new Strategic Fund for Environmental Research (MISTRA), drawing on capital accumulated by the controversial wage-earner investment funds. MISTRA contributed an additional SEK 150 million to the national funds for environmental research that between 1990 and 1995 had totalled between an annual SEK 450 and 600 million. From 1995, however, other research funding was reduced by about 15 per cent.[21] In 1997 SEPA, which represented about a third of the total funding for environmental research in 1994, had to save 25 per cent of its total budget according to the government's financial plan. To minimize the direct damage to its policy functions SEPA chose to completely abolish all of its environmental research in 1998.[22] The hope was that MISTRA would be able to make up the gap. By 1998 the MISTRA capital had grown, and the annual contributions was raised to SEK 300 million. Thus, by 1998 MISTRA funded more than half of all environmental research in Sweden. MISTRA's contribution means that Swedish environmental research is still funded at an annual level of SEK 550–600 million.

Nevertheless, many researchers are critical of this new situation. MISTRA's research priorities are quite different from SEPA's, focusing on applied solutions to environmental problems, rather than on basic research. Moreover, MISTRA is charged with promoting Swedish competitiveness, and is governed by a range of representatives from different stakeholders

[21] The three most important environmental research funds—NFR, SJFR, and FRN—were all cut back about 15 per cent in 1995.

[22] Another programme that was affected by this budget cut was the SEPA subsidies to restoring and cleaning-up toxic waste sites that are not covered by the 'polluter-pays principle'.

(including industry). Also, large projects involving a range of research disciplines and many target-groups (and implying complex organizational arrangements) are prioritized by MISTRA, while many individual researchers within the natural and social sciences risk losing out (Lundqvist 1997). For example, it is estimated that support for projects within the field of the previous SEPA research committee for land and ground water was reduced by about 36 per cent from 1997 to 1998 (Esselin and Arvidsson 1998). Also, research on chemical (toxic) effects on the environment has been cut back by more than one-third over the same period, according to a leading researcher in environmental chemistry (Bergman 1997). In 1997, the government charged the Swedish Council for Planning and Co-ordination of Research (FRN) with developing proposals for future research in support of an ecologically sustainable society. This work has recently been completed (FRN 1998) and will lay the ground for a new Research Bill in 1999. At present, however, no new funding has been earmarked for this initiative.

Sustainable Development in Swedish Foreign Assistance

Sweden is one of the few countries in the world that lives up to the UN goal of allocating at least 0.7 per cent of GDP to foreign assistance. The decision to freeze current aid expenditure however, has meant that it has dropped from around 0.9–1.0 per cent during the 1980s and early 1990s to the present fixed level of 0.7 per cent in 1997. The share of tied aid (requiring purchases from Sweden) has increased, and now amounts to around 11 per cent of the total aid. According to the deputy Foreign Minister,[23] Swedish products and expertise are often preferred because of their environmental quality, and so around half of Swedish ODA is actually returned by voluntary purchasing. For Eastern European aid, this figure is even higher (about 90 per cent). The cuts in ODA were made in the context of general reductions in public spending that occurred in the 1990s. In 1996, when this decision was made in Parliament, the government faced a wave of protests from the NGO sector, and the Archbishop of the Swedish Church led protestors outside the Government Office. Four out of the seven political parties have joined the 'Percentage Campaign' (Sandberg 1996), whose stated objective is to revert to 1 per cent of GNP (Swedish Ministry of the Environment 1997g). According to current projections it will reach 0.72 per cent of GDP by the year 2000 (Government of Sweden 1997–8a).

---

[23] Radio interview with Pierre Schori, 4 Oct. 1997.

Since the early 1960s, Swedish development aid has been guided by four principles:

1. welfare growth—to contribute to increased production of goods and services;
2. economic and social equality—to decrease the gap between poor and rich and to provide basic living conditions for everyone;
3. economic and political independence—to assist developing countries in their struggles for independence; and
4. democratic societal development—to improve the possibilities for everyone to determine her/his own development needs.

In 1988, a fifth principle was added:

5. ecological balance—to contribute to the preservation of resources and to protect the environment.

And in 1996 a sixth principle was adopted:

6. gender equality—to focus on the different conditions for women and men in development work (Government of Sweden 1996–7b).

A content analysis[24] of government documents related to the implementation of sustainable development in Swedish foreign aid policy from 1987 to 1996 shows that UNCED had a substantial impact on how the Swedish International Development Agency (SIDA) formulated its Action Programme in January 1996. Many of the goals coincide with established principles for Swedish foreign assistance. Nevertheless, there are also numerous examples of policies formulated as a direct response to UNCED.

In 1996 the government further emphasized the need to prioritize poverty alleviation, sustainable development, and human rights in its foreign aid programmes as well as within UN work (Swedish Ministry of Foreign Affairs 1996). The government continues to support the United Nations as an instrument for international co-operation in the economic and social spheres, and to work to increase the efficiency and financing of multilateral aid. In 1997 negotiations were initiated on the second replenishment of the Global Environmental Facility (GEF), which is geared to funding developing countries' efforts towards protecting biological diversity and international waters, and preventing climate change and depletion of the ozone layer. The Swedish

---

[24] In this analysis we have compared the forty chapters (under the four section headings) of Agenda 21 to the content of nine major government reports, bills, and investigations that guide Swedish policy with respect to the support for sustainable development in Third World countries.

contribution to GEF is predicted to decrease somewhat in 1998 compared to previous years. The government argues that new donors should be recruited to this fund in order to spread the commitments (Government of Sweden 1997–8a). In general, Sweden has a good reputation for prompt payment of its contributions to the UN system.

Organizational Changes

Along with changes in policy formulation, a reorganization of development assistance within Sweden has taken place as a response to the UNCED challenge. In July 1995 four different development agencies (BITS, SAREC, SIDA, and SwedCorp)[25] were merged into one—'the new SIDA'. This new agency is now undertaking education in environmental issues for all its personnel, and its departments have been strengthened with additional environmental expertise. Within SIDA the department for environmental and natural resources is responsible for co-ordinating the agency's work on sustainable development, as well as for administering special funding allocated for environmental aid.

Moreover, the Ministry of Foreign Affairs was reorganized in July 1996. It now contains both geographical 'desks', and functional units for Global Co-operation, Global Security, and Human Rights. The new organization implies that work on sustainable development—which is co-ordinated in the Global Co-operation unit—now assumes a more significant place in foreign policy. The Ministry of the Environment is responsible for international negotiations related to environmental issues, in particular Sweden's contacts with UNEP and with the EU. It also allocates some environmental aid.

In recent years, collaboration and contacts between the different national agencies and institutions have increased considerably. This has been encouraged by a combination of factors including EU membership and UNCED. In particular, co-operation between SIDA and the Swedish Environmental Protection Agency has intensified. In December 1996, this co-operation was regularized through an agreement whereby SEPA is to assist SIDA, both by providing environmental expertise and by supporting the establishment of environmental offices in recipient countries. Contacts between the Ministries of the Environment and Foreign Affairs have also become more frequent as a direct result of UNCED.

The overall magnitude of environmental aid has been relatively stable

---

[25] BITS worked with technical aid, SAREC with research, and SwedCorp with business aid.

since the beginning of the 1990s. The great leap occurred in 1989–90, when it reached 0.1 per cent of the state budget. Over a period of two years— between 1987–8 and 1989–90—the total amount of environmental aid increased almost twentyfold. It has fallen back slightly during the last few years as a result of state savings on all kinds of public spending. However, the share of environmental aid channelled through various NGOs is steadily increasing. About 300 NGOs receive governmental support towards ODA with countries in the East and South, corresponding to about 15 per cent of the total aid (Swedish Ministry of the Environment 1997g).

There were great expectations in Sweden that EU membership would facilitate regional efforts to manage environmental issues. In practice, some of these expectations have not been met. The Common Agriculture Policy has been a particular disappointment (Swedish Ministry of Agriculture 1996; 1997). The government considers the following four issues as top priorities within the EU framework:

1. measures to combat acidification and climate change;
2. resource management and product recycling;
3. the conservation of biodiversity;
4. tougher and more stringent regulation of chemicals.

The government has declared that it will prioritize work towards creating an 'ecologically sustainable society' in the EU, especially during 2001 when Sweden will assume the European Presidency. There is a broad consensus among all Swedish political parties (except the Moderates) that EU environmental policy must be strengthened.[26]

Sweden also actively promotes environmental action in Central and Eastern Europe, particularly the Baltic states (Estonia, Latvia, Lithuania, and Poland). Since 1974 support has been channelled through the Baltic Sea agreements and HELCOM, but efforts were intensified from 1996 with the meeting of prime ministers at the Visby Summit. As a result, Sweden initiated the project of creating an Agenda 21 for the Baltic Sea region. The plan for 'Baltic 21' was adopted by the Foreign Ministers in 1998. Foreign aid for environmental investment in the Baltic countries increased during the 1990s through the Prime Minister's so-called 'Baltic Sea Billion' launched in 1996 (SEK 1 billion towards co-operation and development in the Baltic region). During the last decade, there has also been a major change in the role of the municipalities in relation to regional and international work. Today most municipalities have twin-town arrangements with cities in other countries, especially in the Baltic states and in Poland. Increasingly international

---

[26] Interview with Minister of the Environment Anna Lindh, 24 Sept. 1997.

assistance is being channelled through the local level as direct aid to the respective twin-towns.

Transport and Energy Challenging Climate Change Policy

The history of Swedish climate change policy is filled with contradictions (Lundberg 1997; Löfstedt 1997). At the international level, Sweden is one of the nations which has been most active, and which has not hesitated to criticize the United States for failing to living up to international agreements. Before UNCED the Swedish government had already taken action to encourage investment in energy-reduction technologies and the use of bioenergy fuels, and Sweden had the most stringent building standards in the OECD (Löfstedt 1997: 173–4). In contrast to most other countries, Sweden reduced its use of oil and coal significantly from the 1970s by investing in nuclear and hydroelectric power.[27] In 1988 a freeze on CO_2 emissions was adopted as a national goal. In fact, only a 9 per cent reduction was achieved over the fifteen-year period despite the introduction of a large number of energy-saving measures and new economic policy instruments (Swedish Ministry of the Environment 1993d). Since the signing of the Convention on Climate Change emissions have actually increased steadily.

In 1991 the Social Democrats abolished this policy commitment following negotiations with the Centre and Liberal parties. Instead, they decided that Sweden should 'work towards freezing the total emissions in Western Europe so that they will not exceed present levels in year 2000, and thereafter be reduced'. The change of government in the autumn of 1991 did not result in any major change to this orientation. The new Minister of the Environment (Olof Johansson, Centre party) issued authorizations for the construction of new power plants.[28] Furthermore, the government reduced carbon taxes on industrial emissions to 25 per cent of the amount levied on other sectors (Löfstedt 1997: 171). In 1993 the Swedish Parliament decided that by 1995 the CO_2 emissions should be reduced by 30 per cent from a 1980 baseline. After the next change of government in 1994, Anna Lindh (Social Democratic Minister of the Environment) renewed consents for several oil-based power plants. As a result, CO_2 emissions rose by 8 per cent from 1990 to 1996 (Swedish Ministry of the Environment 1997b). In March 1996 the CO_2 tax was altered once again. Henceforth industry was to pay

[27] Nuclear power was introduced in Sweden at the time of the oil crisis in the 1970s.
[28] For example, he accepted one plant in Stenungsund that adds 1.2–5 million tons of CO_2 per year.

SEK 135 per tonne of CO_2 and other users to pay SEK 370 per tonne (Löfstedt 1997: 171).

If Sweden were to achieve per capita CO_2 emissions equal to the global average a reduction of 50–80 per cent would be necessary (Swedish Ministry of the Environment 1997b). In 1999 the national policy goals on climate change were that:

1. Sweden should contribute to ensuring that total CO_2 emissions in Western Europe do not exceed 1990 levels by year 2000, and thereafter decline (Government of Sweden 1990–1: 18);
2. nationally CO_2 emissions from fossil fuels should be stabilized at 1990 levels by the year 2000 (Government of Sweden 1992–3a: 36);
3. emissions of methane from waste storage should be reduced by 30 per cent by 2000 (ibid.);
4. by 2000 emissions of HFC and FC compounds and similar gases should be reduced so that (measured as CO_2 equivalents) they account for no more than 2 per cent of the total CO_2 emissions (Government of Sweden 1994–5b: 29).

Of these, only the last two goals are likely to be achieved by the year 2000. Emissions of methane have already been reduced by 28 per cent as compared to 1990, and the other climate gases are estimated to represent only 1 per cent of total emissions. Both methane and HFC and FC compounds are produced as point sources of pollution, which make them relatively easier to tackle through changes in industrial processes.[29] CO_2, however, represents about 80 per cent of the total climate-gas emissions in Sweden. The dominant sources are from the transport and energy sectors. In comparison to point sources they require much broader and more thoroughgoing policy measures. Sweden's second national report to the IPCC predicted that Swedish climate gases will increase by 10 per cent by 2010 with 1995 as the base year (Swedish Ministry of the Environment 1997b: 47). SEPA has recently proposed new goals to be included in the upcoming Environmental Bill, which include a reduction of CO_2 discharge from fossil fuels by 20 per cent by 2020 and 60 per cent by 2050, taking 1995 as the base year (SEPA 1997b). A Parliamentary Committee on Climate Change (chaired by former Minister of the Environment Olof Johansson) has recently been set up to review targets on the basis of the Kyoto agreements and the climate

[29] HFC and FC compounds are produced within the aluminium industry, fire extinguishers, and refrigeration. There is a contradiction between climate change goals and ozone depletion, because HFC is used as a replacement for ozone-destroying CFC and HCFC. Hence, SEPA has issued several new prescriptions to make the refrigerator industry develop alternative cooling media and new refrigeration processes.

objectives previously adopted by Parliament. As the new Minister of the Environment Kjell Larsson has declared, the intent is to not make use of the possible 5 per cent increase in CO_2 emissions Sweden was permitted under the EU burden-sharing agreement.

Energy

The biggest problem for Sweden with respect to CO_2 emissions lies with the 1980 referendum commitment to close all nuclear plants by 2010. Between 1980 and 1997 the position of nuclear energy production in Sweden which in per capita terms is amongst the highest in the world has remained unchanged. However, in the spring of 1997 the government finally decided to close down the two reactors in Barsebäck—the nuclear site which has stirred up the most controversy because of its proximity to Copenhagen (Government of Sweden 1996–7d). The shut-down of the first one of the twelve reactors began in December 1999.

Over the past twenty years the Swedish government has invested SEK 21 billion in developing biomass, SEK 1.4 billion in solar power, and SEK 76 million in wind power. As a result, bioenergy increased from 43 TWh of Sweden's energy mix in 1970 to 65 TWh in 1990, and 78 TWh in 1994 (Sand 1995, quoted in Löfstedt 1997: 173). The largest producer and user of biomass for energy purposes is the pulp industry which accounted for 30 TWh in 1994. Due to a favourable tax regime (wood fuels are exempted from CO_2 and SO_2 taxes), the use of wood fuels in this sector almost doubled between 1992 and 1994 (ibid. 174). Still the share of renewable energy (with the exception of hydroelectric power which contributes 68 TWh per year) is rather small (about 92 TWh) compared to fossil fuels (about 240 TWh) and nuclear power (70 TWh) (Swedish Ministry of the Environment 1997b: 37, figures from 1995).

Transport

Transport emissions account for about 33 per cent of the CO_2 production in Sweden, and have steadily increased (Swedish Ministry of the Environment 1997b: 13). The Communications Committee (KomKom)[30] proposed an interim goal of reducing CO_2 emissions from transport by 15 per cent by the year 2005 (Swedish Ministry of Communications 1997). Five areas for action were identified: (1) reducing the need for transport; (2) developing the

---

[30] The KomKom committee consisted of representatives from the car industry, oil companies, industry, along with experts from the environmental movement and national agencies.

integration of the transport system; (3) reducing emissions within transport modes; (4) technical improvements to vehicles and fuels; and (5) changes in infrastructure (SEPA 1996). To reduce traffic emissions the government's main instrument is differentiated taxes on fuel. The environmental rating of cars was introduced in 1992. Both the Road Agency and the Railroad Agency are required to produce yearly environmental reports since 1992. Despite various attempts to reduce car emissions, energy use within the transport sector continues to increase. CO_2 emissions from transport were 8 per cent higher in 1995 as compared to 1990 (Swedish Ministry of the Environment 1997b: 121).

One of the main reasons is that people's movements are increasing: in Sweden road transport alone is predicted to increase by 30 per cent between 1993 and 2010 (Swedish Ministry of Communications 1997). Investment in infrastructure has not counteracted this dependency on road transport: the government's grants to road-building tripled between 1989 and 1995 (Swedish Ministry of Communications 1996: 35; Government of Sweden 1996–7a: 17). Today Swedes move about 45 kilometres on average per person per day, while in 1900 the corresponding figure was one kilometre per day. Men travel more than women. Every day on average Swedes spend 68 minutes travelling. At least half of this relates to leisure travel. One problem that is difficult to overcome is the long transport distances—with only eighteen inhabitants per square kilometre Sweden has one of the lowest population densities in the world.

A project has been initiated to increase co-operation between national agencies and private organizations in order to develop more environmentally friendly transport systems. The goal is to come up with joint solutions to achieve climate change goals by 2020. Apart from the national transport agencies and SEPA, the auto industry, Swedish Petroleum, and various research institutes are included in this project. This reflects the close relations between the government and economic interests within the transport and energy sectors. Co-operation with environmental organizations is, however, less frequent. Indeed, the government's climate policy has been developed without any significant participation from NGOs (Löfstedt 1997: 170). The chief negotiator explained why:

We have not had the energy to engage NGOs in this work. We are too few who work with these issues in order to hold regular meetings with them. The Swedish Society for Conservation of Nature, Greenpeace and others have not had these questions on the agenda either. Instead, they have prioritized [the abolition of] nuclear power.[31]

---

[31] Interview with Tomas Levander, 14 Oct. 1997.

Involving grassroots organizations and developing local climate change policy goals is generally time and resource consuming. This is the reason put forward by the chief of the Environmental Advisory Council for the absence of any real effort to increase the input of popular movements to decision-making.[32] According to a spokeswoman for SSCN, the government is afraid to grasp the most difficult questions, namely those related to lifestyle and the use of private cars. The many small emissions within the transport sector are probably the biggest obstacle to achieving CO_2 reduction goals.[33]

Instead of tackling these national issues, the Swedish standpoint is to work towards cost-efficient international agreements, which open up avenues for joint implementation, particularly with Eastern Europe. Sweden could reduce marginal costs of national CO_2 abatement if it could also count reductions achieved through technology investment in neighbouring countries on the eastern side of the Baltic. Here much could be achieved without costly investment. The problem, however, is that such cost-efficient measures are most likely to be picked up by international co-operation, thus leaving the more expensive and high-technology projects aside for no one to act upon (Baltscheffsky 1997).

Swedish membership in the European Union has probably pushed the government towards introducing more vigorous measures than it would otherwise have done.[34] Carbon taxes were introduced in 1991, but were reduced for industry from 1993. As a means of financing the EU membership fee, energy taxes were again increased from 1996. The government has recently announced its intention to further increase carbon taxes for industry, which the EU will permit for a three-year period (Swedish Ministry of the Environment 1997b: 61–2). Since Sweden was ahead of other European countries on energy-saving measures before 1992, pressure from the EU to act in concert with the other countries might be the only way for the government to justify more costly national CO_2 reduction measures in the near future.

Protecting Biological Diversity in Forestry and Agriculture

National implementation of the Convention on Biological Diversity began with ratification by Parliament in 1993 (Government of Sweden 1992–3c).

[32] Interview with Lars-Erik Liljelund, 5 Nov. 1997.
[33] Interview with Gunnel Hedman, 14 Oct. 1997.
[34] Interviews with Tomas Levander and Leif Bernegård, 14 Oct. 1997.

The adoption of a national strategy and the compilation of a 'country study' followed in 1994 (SEPA 1994); development of action plans by sector agencies in 1995; and finally a government bill on the protection of biological diversity in 1997 (Government of Sweden 1996–7c). From the late 1980s biological diversity became an issue of public debate. Five sector agencies have produced action plans to protect biological diversity: the Forestry Agency; the Fisheries Agency; the Agricultural Agency; the Housing, Building, and Planning Agency; and the Environmental Protection Agency.

Threats to biological diversity in Sweden come mostly from forestry and agriculture. The number of animal and plant species per unit area has decreased significantly due to 'modern' land-use management. In particular, areas of 'natural forests', meadows, pastures, and wetlands have diminished. Hydroelectric power plants and fish farming have reduced biodiversity in watercourses and lakes. Eutrophication and acidification of water systems have also contributed to a worsening situation, along with fragmentation of the landscape through infrastructure development. In total, about 3,500 plants and animals have been placed on the national 'red lists' of threatened species, representing 7 per cent of the known stock.

Thus the Swedish situation is similar to the global figures for threatened biodiversity (SEPA 1993b). Many of those species belong to forest ecosystems—among threatened plant species more than half of them (51 per cent). Since two-thirds of Sweden is covered by forests the situation for biological diversity in forestry is the most debated as well as the most challenging. Three strategies are used to protect biodiversity in forestry (Liljelund et al. 1992): (1) a network of large reserves; (2) many small reserves (biotopes); and (3) environmental standards in all commercial forestry. These strategies are endorsed by government policy as well as by the private forest companies (Swedish Ministry of the Environment 1997f).

Still, large reserves are scarce in Sweden. In 1997 only 3.7 per cent (830,000 hectares) of the forested area was protected. Most of the reserves are located in the montane region of the north. Only 0.8 per cent (173,000 hectares) lie below the limit for montane forests (Swedish Ministry of the Environment 1997f). According to the government's Environmental Advisory Council, another 900,000 hectares of forest land must be protected in the short-term (10–20 years) in order to secure the survival of threatened species. This implies a doubling of the present protected forest.

A new instrument to protect small areas of great value for endangered species (so called biotopes) was introduced in 1992. Since then the National Forestry Agency has made an inventory of key habitats. Some 70,000–80,000 areas covering around 1 per cent of the forest are included in this classification. It has been estimated that a total of SEK 2–4 billion would be required to preserve these areas of up to 5 hectares each. The annual budget for land purchases has been SEK 20 million, but will increase to about SEK 60 million from 1999. Still, it will take more than 100 years to protect those biotopes that have already been identified. To date only a few hundred areas have been protected through this instrument. According to reports from environmental organizations, many of the most valuable areas are now being exploited due to the lack of state funds.

Since 1974 the Swedish Forestry Act has required environmental values to be considered in all forest management. In 1979 special regulations were introduced that made it possible to punish forest-owners who did not live up to the recommendations. In practice, however, very few sanctions have been used. In the new Forestry Act of 1994 the environmental goal was for the first time placed at an equal footing with the production goal. Several studies have been carried out to evaluate how environmental considerations are implemented in forest clear-cutting. The situation has improved somewhat from 1981–4, when only 50 per cent of the measures required according to the Forestry Act were actually implemented (Eckerberg 1990). Subsequent follow-up by the Forestry Agency in 1992–3 and in 1997 showed satisfactory environmental protection measures on three-quarters of clear-cut sites.

Environmental organizations have been very active in bringing biological diversity onto the political agenda. The Swedish Society for the Conservation of Nature (SSCN) has organized several campaigns among its members, and has also managed to activate the research community. Compared to climate change, where involvement of NGOs in the making of public policy is less apparent, biodiversity has brought about considerably more co-operation between environmental organizations and forest-owners.[35] Moreover, the attention on biodiversity from environmentalists has also raised awareness about sustainable forestry among consumers of forest products, particularly in Europe. As a response to consumer demand, Swedish forestry has negotiated with NGOs to adopt environmental labelling. It uses environmental indicators related to biological diversity goals to ensure that forest products derived from a certified forest-owner have been extracted in an environmentally sustainable manner. Two parallel systems have been developed—the Forest Stewardship Council system, and a system applied by the Forest-Owners' Association. A consensus on the Forest Stewardship Council system was finally reached in June 1997, after the Swedish Association of Forest-Owners decided to quit and instead develop their own system. Most

---

[35] One indication of the earlier involvement of NGOs in biodiversity compared to climate change policy is the topic of the SSCN yearbook (SSCN 1990; 1997).

of the large forest companies have now adopted these systems within their territory, including international standards of ISO 14000 and EMAS. The Swedish forest industry considers itself to be in the forefront internationally. It remains to be seen, however, whether such voluntary instruments can succeed where national agencies have failed in their efforts to maintain (and improve) biological diversity in the forestry sector. Several conflicts between forest-owners and environmentalists over how the new standards are to be interpreted have already been reported.

Within agriculture, the Farmers Union has initiated a project to encourage farmers to carry out their own 'self-audit' with respect to environmental goals (so-called 'green housekeeping') on the farm. This includes biological diversity goals. The majority of measures promoting biodiversity in agriculture, however, come with EU support. The Swedish EU environmental programme for agriculture in 1997 amounted to SEK 1,050 million, of which SEK 420 million was targeted to improving biodiversity (mostly meadows and natural pastures). The new budget for 1998 adds a further SEK 700 million per year to the Swedish EU environmental programme.[36] This means that Sweden will be able to use all of the budget share initially negotiated with the EU (which was not previously taken up, partly due to administrative difficulties). Apart from direct support to farmers practising environmentally sound farming, the grant is also geared towards more effective follow-up systems in county administrations (Swedish Ministry of Agriculture 1998: 3).

At present, there is no system in place to monitor changes in biological diversity within Sweden (Swedish Ministry of the Environment 1997d). According to SEPA, criteria for the sustainable use of land and water resources are badly needed to supplement those that are beginning to emerge for forestry. Further clarification of the responsibilities of national sector agencies is also required, as well as better relations between public agencies and private organizations. Nevertheless, the draft report to the CBD made by SEPA claims that the Biodiversity Convention has become a catalyst for initiating further work in Sweden. First, more attention has been given to genetic variation, to the relation between in-situ and ex-situ conservation, and to the introduction of exotic species. Second, the role of biodiversity for the functioning of ecosystems has been given more weight. And third, a wider range of actors at national, regional, and local levels have been drawn into the work (SEPA 1997d: 11–12). There has been great pressure on

---

[36] Of the total SEK 13.7 billion towards agricultural support in 1998, two-thirds comes from the EU while the rest is provided by the Swedish government. SEK 2.8 billion (20 per cent) of this goes to environmental measures, in particular biological diversity and leaching of nutrients from agriculture.

the Ministry of the Environment to release funds to buy land from owners in order to protect it, and to encourage forest-owners not to clear-cut areas valuable for biodiversity in the near future. The government has recently approved an increase of state funds for forest protection from an annual SEK 190 million to about 360 million from 1999. In the short term, however, the few remaining virgin forest areas now being considered for commercial felling are probably the biggest threat to the government's legitimacy in defending biological diversity goals both within Sweden and among the international community.

Conclusions

As this analysis has indicated, the national policy strategies and initiatives to follow up the UNCED challenge are inconsistent. There is, on the one hand, an impressive array of new financial initiatives for building an 'environmentally sustainable society' from the national government. Also, the response at the municipal level is excellent by international comparison. Local Agenda 21 has been taken on, not only by local authorities, but also by a range of non-governmental organizations, schools, and other institutions representing a great majority of the Swedish population. More recently, however, it seems as if the bottom-up initiatives, which have characterized this movement, are at a stand-still, awaiting the result of the national programme of new investment. Probably most of the simple and low-cost measures have already been taken at the local level, and the remaining task is to alter priorities that require more substantial support from national level policies.

On the positive side of the coin, it is also clear that much has been done to encourage sectoral policy integration. Green accounting has been introduced in many sector agencies, and measurability has thus improved. New goals have been developed, and most organizations within society are heavily involved in implementing more environmentally friendly management practices. Within foreign aid policy, the concept of sustainable development has penetrated government documents and also generated new forms of organization in line with the UNCED recommendations. National expert agencies have increasingly diverted the responsibility for implementation, as well as the goal-setting, to the sector agencies.

Nevertheless, there are contradictions in this positive picture. The current political goal of the government concentrates on efficiency rather than on 'democracy'. Representation of stakeholders in the policy process is still rather rare. In particular, NGOs are still largely kept outside; but industrial representation in the development of national strategies for a sustainable society are also scarce. The links between the local and the national level are still surprisingly thin in the implementation of Agenda 21. Sustainable development in Swedish national policy is equated with 'green leadership', that is, essentially a top-down policy approach. The increasing role of the Cabinet in decision-making contradicts the Swedish constitutional tradition of leaving implementation to the agencies. Possibly, this reflects a harmonization with the prevailing institutional style within the EU and in line with many other countries' ministerial ruling.

In the new investment programme projects that create new jobs will be prioritized. The majority of municipalities will therefore not benefit from national support. The question is how long they will persist in extending local actions for sustainable development if they do not receive encouragement through national financial means. And at the same time well-established national systems for environmental monitoring, cleaning-up 'old sins' from toxic waste sites, SEPA environmental-research funds, and county administration environmental units, suffer from cutbacks or complete abolition.

With respect to the two conventions signed at UNCED, it could be said on the positive side that much had already been done in Sweden before 1992. Energy-saving measures had been introduced on a large scale as a result of the 1970 oil crisis, and CO_2 emissions decreased accordingly. In Swedish forestry, which accounts for a great part of the current threat to biological diversity, public as well as private forest-owners had already begun to apply environmental criteria in commercial forest management. Likewise, Swedish foreign assistance was generous by comparison with other countries in the industrialized world. In all of these areas, however, the situation since UNCED has worsened. Swedish assistance to Third World countries (and Eastern Europe) has been cut back since 1992 and is now down from 1 to 0.7 per cent of GDP. For climate gases, emissions have increased particularly in the transport sector, while the abolition of nuclear energy plants in accordance with the public referendum in 1980 has not been complemented with the development of alternative bio-energy sources. Thus, CO_2 emissions are likely to increase still further with the closing down of two nuclear reactors within the next few years.

It is difficult to say whether the situation of threatened plants and animal species in Sweden has worsened since 1992; no one really knows, although the 'red lists' developed by the 'Threatened Species Unit'[37] grow longer and longer. There is no functioning system yet in place to follow up and monitor

[37] The Threatened Species Unit at the Swedish University of Agricultural Sciences in Uppsala was established in 1991 and is responsible for the follow-up and research about biodiversity in Sweden together with national agencies.

biological diversity. However, the area of protected natural forests, old-growth and species-rich forests, particularly in the southern part of the country, is very low by international standards. Voluntary measures are increasing, but at the same time virgin forest areas and species-rich biotopes are disappearing at a rapid rate. Environmental organizations have mobilized great attention to the issue, pointing also to the risk of losing credibility for the Swedish policy in an international perspective.

The Social Democratic vision for the new 'green welfare society' embodies a conflict between continued economic growth and the protection of the global environment and social equity. Welfare reductions and increased social cleavages have occurred during the 1990s, showing up in high unemployment figures and growing numbers of poor people. This development has not yet been connected to the building of an ecologically sustainable society. The government has chosen to concentrate on more technical and purely environmental issues, rather than interpreting sustainable development in terms of social and economic welfare distribution, equity, and justice. Clearly, changing social and economic conditions will also have implications for the natural environment and public health. But gender, racial, and other social inequalities have rarely been acknowledged as a problem in the Agenda 21 movement. The Swedish focus has been purely on the *environmental* side of sustainable development. It is probably safe to conclude that it has also been focused on the most easy-to-grasp and easy-to-change issues of a technical and simple organizational nature, rather than on problematizing the more fundamental issues of economic growth and individual life-styles. The Swedish government has come up with a programme that intends to combine goals of economic growth, job creation, and environmental sustainability. The critical point is the extent to which the national government responds to local priorities and whether the new investment programme will be received as a centralized and politically contested initiative by those major groups who are active in the implementation of sustainable development in the Swedish context.

9

The United Kingdom: From Political Containment to Integrated Thinking?

STEPHEN C. YOUNG

In the United Kingdom (UK) the Agricultural and Industrial Revolutions trig-gered processes of land improvement and urbanization which produced a problematic legacy in the 1980s and 1990s.[1] Much nineteenth-century infra-structure—railways and water plants—remained in use in the post-war period, increasingly in a state of decay. There is now virtually no natural landscape left. About 20 per cent of the landscape of the United Kingdom has special protection status—as with the National Parks (Department of the Environment (DoE) 1994a). The UK's population increased from 55.1 million in 1971 to 55.7 million in 1981, reaching 57.6 million in 1992 (DoE 1994a; Fothergill and Vincent 1985). By 1992 the average population density of the UK was 235 people per square kilometre, but three-quarters lived on just 13 per cent of the 2,447,555 square kilometres of land (DoE 1994a; Countryside Agency 1999). With 746 people per square kilometre, the South-East had one of the highest densities in Europe. In contrast, Scotland had, at 66 people per square kilometre, one of the lowest densities in Europe—despite having more than two million in its central belt.

During the 1979–87 period, the first two Thatcher governments were dominated by industrial restructuring and the drive for economic growth. The 1970s' perception—of the choice being either environmental protection or jobs and growth—continued to hold sway in central government and Par-liament (Weale 1992; Hajer 1995). Those analysing 1980s environmental policy stress two aspects (Blowers 1987; Lowe and Flynn 1989; Bradbeer 1990). First there was the centrality of deregulation. The government had

---

[1] Most of this chapter discusses the United Kingdom. However, in a number of cases there are separate government documents for Scotland, Wales, and Northern Ireland, especially as Labour's devolution initiative got under way in 1998–9—e.g. Scottish Office (1999), 'Down To Earth: A Scottish Perspective on Sustainable Development'. However, there is no space to cover all these separate dimensions here.

'little sympathy for any regulatory controls if they are perceived to obstruct growth or development' (Lowe and Flynn 1989: 261). This especially applied to the land-use planning system (Thornley 1993; Rydin 1998). Second, the government continued the well-established, informal, negotiated consent approach to operating regulation. It was based on voluntary compliance, discussion, and codes of practice (Vogel 1986; Lowe and Flynn 1989; O'Riordan and Weale 1989). However, Thatcher adapted it to reduce the burden placed on industry by abolishing some advisory committees; appointing more industrialists to agency boards; and cutting the budgets of the regulatory agencies so fewer field staff were employed. Environmental controls were thus effectively weakened. The DoE had initially been set up by Prime Minister Heath in 1970 partly for political reasons, although this was during an earlier period of environmental awareness. In the 1980s the DoE marginalized its environmental functions, focusing mainly on limiting the role of local government (Stoker 1991).

The administration's emphasis on economic growth obscured growing environmental problems (Blowers 1987; Lowe and Flynn 1989; Rose 1990). In the 1980s Britain was the largest sulphur polluter in Western Europe; it pressed ahead with nuclear power while failing to find storage sites for low-level nuclear waste; cut energy efficiency budgets; had declining water quality in rivers; and starved its public transport system of investment (Whitelegg 1989). Moreover, Britain was increasingly out of step with the rest of Western Europe. Much of what the Royal Commission on Environmental Pollution (RCEP) was recommending on pollution control during the Thatcher era was ignored (Lowe and Flynn 1989; O'Riordan and Weale 1989). Britain frequently blocked international anti-pollution proposals, as over the North Sea (Skjærseth 1998: 357). This was all at the time of growing international concern about the ozone hole and the greenhouse effect (Rose 1990).

However, the international context was changing. From the mid-1980s, the European Union (EU) became steadily more interested in environmental dimensions (Hildebrand 1992). This led to a spate of directives. The ministerial response, as over the drinking and bathing water directives, was delay. In particular, government held out against EU pressures to cut power station sulphur-dioxide emissions that were linked to the acid rain falling in Scandinavia, and on the European mainland. Britain's style—variously described as procrastinating, obstructive, and self-satisfied—led to Britain being christened 'the dirty man of Europe' (Rose 1990). Against this background, Thatcher's two key speeches in the autumn of 1988 seemed to mark a turning point. In these she accepted the idea of 'sustainable development', and argued that each generation had a life tenancy—not a freehold—on the

Earth, and a duty to repair damage done to the planet (McCormick 1991: 60–2). In 1989 Patten was appointed as Secretary of State for the Environment—the sixth in ten years.

Meanwhile the Brundtland Report had been published (World Commission on Environment and Development (WCED) 1987). The resulting academic debates had more impact in some parts of the local government world (Stoker and Young 1993; Ward 1993), and amongst the NGOs and in the media (McCormick 1991), than in central ministries and Parliament. In the media and NGOs, interest in Brundtland connected with issues like Chernobyl, anti-roads campaigns, and green-belt battles.

Thatcher's U-turn came as a result of her government being caught in a pincer movement. The international pressures from Brussels and elsewhere combined with an emerging groundswell from below. Thatcher was concerned that the record memberships of environmental groups would be transformed into a significant anti-Conservative vote at the next election. The Liberals had already developed tough policies on many environmental issues. However, at the May 1989 European elections it was the Green Party that rode this growing wave of concern, and scored what was in British terms a spectacular success. Although they did not win any seats, they sent shock-waves through the main parties by attracting 14.9 per cent of the vote. It was possible for mainstream political leaders to dismiss this as a mid-term protest vote (Carter 1994; Rootes 1996). In fact competition between the parties had politicized the environment in a new way (Lowe and Flynn 1989: 276). By 1989, there was thus an even greater need than there had been a year earlier at the time of the Thatcher speeches, for the Conservative leadership to win back support ahead of the next election.

The White Paper on the environment that was published in the autumn of 1990 was essentially a pragmatic, political response designed to contain a problem that was alienating Conservative voters. 'This Common Inheritance' (DoE and Other Departments 1990) reviewed the range of government policies that impinged on the environment in a way that had not been attempted in Britain before. The document listed more than 350 measures already in place, and made various proposals. But it was essentially weak and limited, and was widely criticized as a missed opportunity.

Nevertheless, its production highlighted two important features of British policy-making across the range of environmental issues before Rio. First, the main focus was on a sector-by-sector approach, despite the document being subtitled 'Britain's Environmental Strategy'. This emphasized the way policy towards different sectors evolved in an incremental, piecemeal fashion (Lowe and Flynn 1989). Second, the weakness of the DoE within central government was not so much revealed as highlighted. The Ministry of Agriculture,

Fisheries and Food (MAFF), the Department of Trade and Industry (DTI), and particularly the Department of Transport (DTp) proved themselves able to repel incursions into their spheres of influence and their tightly closed policy communities. As Secretary of State, Patten found his position undermined as Thatcher sided in Cabinet with ministers defending their departmental interests. Their concern was containing the issue. Their aim was to reduce the scope and ambition of the White Paper's attempt to develop a cross-cutting strategy (McCormick 1991: 168–72).

The process of producing 'This Common Inheritance' had two important consequences for the post-Rio period. First, it extended the growing interest in central government in the potential of economic instruments. The 1989 budget had introduced a lower tax on unleaded petrol. Second, it strengthened the unit within the DoE working on the consequences of Brundtland. This became firmly established during the winter of 1990–1. It prepared the papers for Rio, and revised some of the Planning Policy Guidance Notes (PPGs) (Stoker and Young 1993). These provide guidance for the preparation of statutory land-use plans by local councils. Relating them to issues like health, climate change, and water shortages represented the very beginning of a more holistic and cross-sectoral approach that this chapter argues was slowly to become more widespread during the 1990s. The sustainable development policy network began to grow, drawing together people from the central administration, the local government world, and prominent NGOs. The Advisory Committee on Business and the Environment (ACBE) was set up at this time.

Government's Response to the UNCED Process

Rio gave the DoE's engagement with sustainable development new impetus. Major, then Prime Minister, was persuaded to put his authority behind Whitehall's response to Agenda 21 and the other documents he had signed in Rio. After Rio, what became the Environmental Protection Strategy and Europe Division within the DoE was able to carry the work forward quite quickly. Britain's national strategy document 'Sustainable Development: The UK Strategy', was published in January 1994 (DoE 1994a). This firmly established the annual White Paper review process. Three reports updating the 1990 White Paper had been published (DoE 1991; 1992; 1994b). In 1995, 1996, and 1997 these annual reports were widened to include analysis of progress with the 1994 Strategy, as well as the earlier White Paper (DoE 1995; 1996a; 1997a). This rolling process was significant. It pulled in civil servants from other departments, confronting them with the need to work out in more and more detail the consequences of what their departments had signed up to in agreeing to 'The UK Strategy' (Young 1994).

The May 1997 election brought Tony Blair to power as the new Labour Prime Minister. In opposition Labour had shown that parts of the party understood some of the complexities of sustainable development (Labour Party 1993). The party's 1997 manifesto did not bury sustainable development in an environment section (Labour Party 1997: 4, 28–9). The idea of putting the environment at the heart of government was one of the prominent themes running through the manifesto (Young, forthcoming). Within three months of assuming office ministers published consultation documents on transport, and within ten months on updating 'The UK Strategy'. The latter was entitled 'Sustainable Development: Opportunities for Change' (Department for the Environment, Transport and the Regions (DETR) 1998a). These led to two White Papers—'A New Deal for Transport: A Better Deal for Everyone' (DETR 1998b) in July 1998; and 'A Better Quality of Life: A Strategy for Sustainable Development in the UK' (DETR 1999a) in May 1999.

Differing Interpretations of Sustainable Development 1990–9

'This Common Inheritance' was widely criticized because of its lack of engagement with the concept of sustainable development. Its starting point was

the ethical imperative of stewardship . . . We have a moral duty to look after our planet and to hand it on in good order to future generations. That is what the experts mean when they talk of 'sustainable development': not sacrificing tomorrow's prospects for a largely illusory gain today. We must put a proper value on the natural world: it would be odd to cherish a Constable but not the landscape he depicted. (DoE and Other Departments 1990: para 1.14)

This conveys the way the focus was mainly an environmental one which largely ignored the social and economic dimensions.

Although more was written in 1994 at the start of 'The UK Strategy' about sustainable development, the emphasis was still mainly on the environmental aspects. The key passage went as follows:

Sustainable development does not mean having less economic development: on the contrary a healthy economy is better able to generate the resources to meet people's needs . . . Nor does it mean that every aspect of the present environment should be preserved at all costs. What it requires is that decisions throughout society are taken with proper regard to their environmental impact.   (DoE 1994a: para 12)

However, 'The UK Strategy' did highlight principles for policy-makers to follow. This marked a shift from the incremental UK tradition. These included the 'polluter-pays' principle, considering ecological impacts, the precautionary principle, and best possible scientific advice. 'The UK Strategy' had three main sections. Section 2 on the state of the environment had ten chapters covering the different media and resources. Section 3 focused on economic development with fourteen chapters dealing with how sectors like fishing and energy could relate to the sustainable development agenda. Section 4 dealt with the different actors and the instruments available to help promote sustainable development. The climate change document (DoE 1994c) analysed sources of emissions, forecasts of trends, and various measures designed to get emissions of the main greenhouse gases back to 1990 levels by 2000. The biodiversity report (DoE 1994d) listed a set of principles for action and a set of broad aims. A shorter, vaguer report on forestry was also published (DoE 1994e).

The limitations of the approach adopted in 1994, and in particular the neglect of the social dimensions became clear during the 1994–7 period. This was often revealed by the way politicians and commentators slipped between referring to environment and sustainable development as if they were interchangeable. Frequently an environmental gloss was added to a policy, with the implied claim that this took it into the realms of sustainable development. A typical example here was the way ministers at the DTp announced in the early 1990s that they were planting more trees along new roads than the Forestry Commission was in the rest of the country—quite regardless of the other effects of the road-building programme. Similarly politicians often referred to 'sustainable economic growth' or 'sustainable growth'.

Although it was unclear at the time, the next significant development came after the Environment Agency (EA) was set up in 1996. Its most important objective was the ministerial instruction to 'adopt, across all its functions, an integrated approach to environmental protection and enhancement which considers impacts of substances on all environmental media and on natural resources' (EA 1996: 5). Ministers had envisaged the EA largely as a streamlined, 'one-stop shop', permitting organization; however, it had been given extensive powers, and people within it were able to promote a broader interpretation of sustainable development than that adopted in central ministries during the Major years. In practice, the strategic-thinking people within the Agency and on its board were able to exploit the policy vacuum that emerged at the end of the Major administration. Much of this lateral thinking took place within the EA's Sustainable Development Unit. It began to emerge as the centre of new thinking about sustainable development in Britain. It was here that more ambitious and cross-cutting approaches went furthest, more quickly, than elsewhere in government. During the 1996–7 period for example, the Agency did not approach the issue of climate change simply as a sectoral issue about CO_2 emissions from industry. It analysed all the sources, and all the implications—higher sea levels, flood defence, water management, the land-use planning dimensions, and so on. These included such issues as identifying sites which were liable to coastal or river flooding and where it would be unwise to locate major new housing developments or landfill sites. The more comprehensive, cross-cutting approach also came out at the local level in the preparation of integrated Local Environment Agency Plans (EA 1997; 1998).

When Labour came to power the debates about the need to broaden out the government's interpretation of sustainable development emerged more into the open. Labour's 'Opportunities for Change' document included much the most detailed definition of sustainable development to emanate from government during the post-Brundtland period, based on four objectives:

- social progress that recognizes the needs of everyone;
- effective protection of the environment;
- prudent use of natural resources;
- maintenance of high and stable levels of economic growth and employment (DETR 1998a: para 9).

This approach was subsequently reproduced in other documents like the indicators discussion report (DETR 1998c). More significantly, it was given centre stage and repeated in the new sustainable development strategy 'A Better Quality of Life' (DETR 1999a: 9).

Here the interpretation of sustainable development was fleshed out by ten guiding principles (ch. 4). These are: putting people at the centre to give them a better quality of life; taking a long-term perspective; taking risks, costs, and benefits into account; creating conditions to encourage trade and competition; combating poverty and social exclusion; respecting environmental limits; operating the precautionary principle; using a wide-ranging set of scientific viewpoints; providing information to encourage participation and transparency; and making polluters pay. The strategy's approach to indicators (ch. 3); and to the decision-making institutions and policy instruments (ch. 5) are discussed below.

Five main features stand out from the new strategy. (1) The establishment of wide-ranging monitoring processes is the most prominent theme: this had been referred to before, but not endorsed so strongly. (2) The UK's global obligations are taken much more seriously than in previous documents (ch. 9). (3) A more holistic, cross-cutting approach is adopted in the three main policy chapters—chapter 6 on creating a sustainable economy; chapter 7 on creating sustainable communities; and chapter 8 on protecting environmental conditions and natural resources. Each of these deals with the economic, social, and environmental dimensions of sustainable development. The contrast with earlier documents, with their narrower, sector-by-sector approach, is quite stark. (4) About ninety actions and commitments are listed. Some had already been announced; some were new; and some were extensions of existing programmes. There were also lists of the next round of issues for government and other actors to tackle. (5) The strategy only provides a partial picture. On some significant issues—including waste, air quality, minerals, and construction aggregates—Labour had yet to show how its policies would be integrated into the wider strategy.

The Slowly Changing Institutional Framework

The advent of sustainable development has illustrated the long-established British approach of adapting existing institutions to cope with new demands. In 1992, the main government departments with an interest in the issues apart from the DoE, were MAFF, the DTp, and the DTI. The attempts under the Conservatives to inject sustainable development into policy-making within central ministries had very little impact. The DoE published two reports trying to set out ways in which departments could appraise policy proposals from a sustainability perspective (DoE 1991; 1994f). But answers to Parliamentary Questions revealed that no department—including the DoE itself—could show it had used these approaches. Similarly, the attempts before and after Rio to establish co-ordinating committees of officials and ministers were largely stillborn (O'Riordan and Jordan 1995; Council for the Protection of Rural England (CPRE) 1996). Sustainable development was *added onto, rather than integrated into*, programmes—as with the urban regeneration programme, the Single Regeneration Budget. Much of the government's response fell back on minor housekeeping issues, on steps to green institutions via purchasing policies, energy conservation, and the like (Environmental Audit Committee (EAC) 1998a: 287).

Outside the central ministries, government agencies are run by boards appointed by the sponsoring secretary of state, to whom they are accountable. The most important development was setting up the Environment Agency in 1996. This was created by merging the National Rivers Authority with Her Majesty's Inspectorate of Pollution, and drawing in the local waste regulation bodies to create one organization with wide-ranging regulatory responsibilities (Carter and Lowe 1995). This was more of a narrow, parochial, administrative response than a response to Rio. However, it did create the opportunity both to develop more comprehensive approaches and to move away from the Pollution Inspectorate's negotiated consent style towards the National Rivers Authority's more aggressive interventionist approach with its greater preparedness to go to court (Jordan 1993). The Conservatives did not create new executive agencies expressly to address sustainable development. Rather they tried to incorporate sustainable development into the programmes of some new and existing ones. In cases like the Office of Electricity Regulation this had little impact. The Rural Development Commission's positive approach was more of an exception.

Finally, the Conservatives announced the setting up of three new advisory and educational bodies in the 1994 'UK Strategy' to supplement the work of the Royal Commission on Environmental Pollution (RCEP): the British Government Panel on Sustainable Development (BGPSD); the UK Round Table on Sustainable Development (UKRTSD); and Going for Green (GfG). The Panel was established to advise the Prime Minister about significant strategic issues; it was chaired by Crispin Tickell, a scientist and former ambassador who had become an academic. He had been one of the key figures in persuading Thatcher to take the environment more seriously in the late 1980s. Its four members contributed experience from banking, industry, science, government bodies like the RCEP, and international environmental bodies. The Round Table began work in 1995. Its main function was to draw stakeholders together to help generate consensus. It was co-chaired by Gummer, the Secretary of State, and Professor Southwood. The latter was a zoologist with experience of industry, and of government and international advisory committees. The Round Table's initial membership of thirty-three was reduced after a review, by a third. It drew together people from academia, local government, industry, and the NGOs (UKRTSD 1996; 1997). It worked largely through subgroups studying specific issues (UKRTSD 1996; 1997).

The Round Table had more impact on policy as it focused on specific issues like freshwater (UKRTSD 1997). In dealing with strategic issues the Panel was more ambitious though. It made recommendations to the Major government on fourteen topics in the 1994–7 period (BGPSD 1995; 1996; 1997), and was openly critical of government responses to its reports—as on environmental education, forestry, and radioactive waste (BGPSD 1997).

The last of the three new organizations was Going for Green. During 1995–6 GfG commissioned research into peoples' attitudes towards, and awareness of, environmental issues. The research revealed extensive interest, but people were unsure how to 'do their bit'. GfG was officially launched in February 1996 on the basis of its five-point Green Code—cutting down waste; preventing pollution; saving energy and natural resources; looking after the local environment; and travelling sensibly (GfG 1997). GfG thus started with a clear message and a coherent strategy. One of its first acts was to print its logo and environmental tips on 1.7 billion sugar sachets for use in cafes.

After the 1997 election the DoE was merged with the DTp to create a new Department for the Environment, Transport and the Regions (DETR) with John Prescott, the new Deputy Prime Minister, as Secretary of State (DETR 1999b; 1999c). This was partly because Prescott wanted a 'super-ministry'; and partly because of Labour's determination to control the old DTp and move away from a demand-led, roads-centred transport policy. But it was also about implementing the manifesto pledge to put the environment at the heart of government. Labour's 'Greening Government Initiative' involved setting up a Cabinet Committee to focus on environmental issues; and a committee of departmental green ministers (EAC 1998a). The Conservatives' similar attempts to promote cross-departmental integration in the early 1990s had 'been allowed to wither on the vine' (O'Riordan and Jordan 1995: 240). Labour also created an Environmental Audit Committee (EAC) in the House of Commons to parallel the Public Accounts Committee and monitor the government's approach on sustainable development. The evidence from the DETR, and the government's positive response to the EAC's report (DETR 1998d) show that ministers at least aimed to take the institutional changes seriously.

The Sustainable Development Unit (SDU) was announced in July 1997 (EAC 1998a). It began with fourteen staff. This was increased to sixteen within a year. Despite continuing constraints on staff, its numbers grew significantly in the early months of 1999 as ministers came to understand its importance. In contrast, ten staff had been involved in equivalent work within the DoE in the mid-1990s.

The SDU's remit was to promote sustainable development across all government departments. Its main initial job was to revise the Conservatives' 1994 Sustainable Development strategy. This involved producing 'Opportunities for Change'; inputs into consultation documents on issues like construction and tourism (DETR 1999a: 10); organizing the consultation programme; the indicators work (DETR 1998c); and drafting and finalizing 'A Better Quality of Life'. The SDU's other responsibilities included the Greening Government Initiative; the government's involvement with Local Agenda 21; and the environmental dimensions of the proposed Freedom of Information legislation. SDU was also charged with advising departments how environmental appraisals of policy could be carried out. 'Policy Appraisal and the Environment' (DETR 1998e) set out stronger mechanisms and guidance for departments. This work was extended by input into 'Modernising Government' (Cabinet Office 1999). This committed ministers to working out and operating an integrated set of appraisal tools. The aim was to promote sustainable development by analysing the impacts of proposals on business, the environment, health, and different groups. These documents related to work in the Cabinet Office on equal treatment and better regulation (DETR 1999a: 25–7).

SDU's central aim and its potential are probably best summed up in an Environment Agency memorandum. This argues that the DETR's SDU provides a valuable focus on sustainable development within government, enabling it to move beyond being 'the only place where sustainable development issues are considered in detail' to become 'a catalyst for action by other departments' (EAC 1998a, vol. II: Appendix 5, para. 5.1).

Labour continued with the Round Table and the Panel, broadening their members' collective experience (UKRTSD 1998a; BGPSD 1999). The Table was 'encouraged by the . . . content and tone' of government responses. The government had 'accepted, or is giving serious consideration to, most of the recommendations made by the Round Table' (UKRTSD 1998a: para 3.2). Despite expressing support for some government initiatives, such as transport levies, the Panel remained more critical, as over Genetically Modified Organisms (GMOs) and fish stocks (BGPSD 1999). The new government also devoted more resources to environmental education (GfG 1998).

Together with the Environment Agency, the Panel and the Round Table provided an important element of continuity when Blair and Prescott replaced Major and Gummer (the Secretary of State for the Environment from 1993 through to the 1997 election). The reports of the Table and the Panel played an influential role in persuading civil servants—outside the individuals at the committed core of the DoE and the DETR, and some agencies—of the need to focus more explicitly on integrating the environmental, social, and economic dimensions of sustainable development. The Conservative government was repeatedly criticized for its narrow environmental perspective; its neglect of the economic and social aspects of sustainable development; and the need to develop holistic strategies across a broad front. The Panel and the Table were saying in public what the Environment Agency was arguing in greater detail on a wide range of issues behind the scenes. The Agency was probably in touch with more people in more government departments and agencies before and after the change in government, and having a more substantial impact that way. Significantly, senior people within the Agency had a strong hand in helping civil servants draft position papers for the Panel. Once the DETR's SDU became established it also started to have an impact on spreading understanding of more integrated and cross-sectoral approaches via interdepartmental committees.

The 'Better Quality of Life' strategy announced an important institutional initiative. The Panel and the Round Table will be subsumed into a new Sustainable Development Commission (SDC) from 2000. It will have two main functions—'to monitor progress on sustainable development; and to build consensus on action to be taken by all sectors to accelerate its achievement' (DETR 1999a: para. 5.25). While its precise remit remains to be determined, this could be a significant step—thirteen years after Brundtland and eight years after Rio.

Monitoring, Indicators, and Targets: Changing Perceptions

Initially the reporting process was quite weak. The annual review process established in 1990 and extended in 1994 led to reports with commitment tables setting out progress on undertakings by different departments and other actors. Thus the 1996 annual report listed 642 commitments (DoE 1996a). Each one is summarized from previous documents, with the action taken in 1995 and future commitments set out. The information varies from detailed progress, as on biodiversity, to banal generalizations, as on the roads programme.

Conservative ministers were suspicious of establishing targets—partly for fear of being held to them. In the context of economic planning in Western Europe in the 1960s and 1970s it was often observed that it was impossible to plan without targets (Kenny and Meadowcroft 1999). The RCEP for example argued that establishing targets made it possible to assess progress, identify weaknesses, and target resources at corrective action (RCEP 1994). A House of Lords inquiry was particularly critical of ministers' vague approach to monitoring, as on agriculture and transport (House of Lords Select Committee on Sustainable Development 1995). The 1996 annual report defended the use of generalized, indicative targets.

This tentative approach gradually gave way to a wider acceptance of the need to develop detailed targets and indicators. Experience with biodiversity (see below), the Local Government Management Board (LGMB)'s work on sustainability indicators with pilot authorities (1995), and the advice of the Environment Agency and the Round Table all encouraged the DoE to go further. In 1996 it published a national indicators report (1996b); and the annual report included a range of more detailed, quantifiable, binding targets (DoE 1996a). The debate emerging before the 1997 election carried over into the new administration. Labour was very clear about the importance of targets, monitoring, indicators, and time-scales. Almost immediately on coming to power ministers insisted that the water companies establish targets to reduce leakages (EAC 1998a). Meacher (a Minister at the

DETR) announced that it was Labour's intention 'to establish targets wherever we can and indeed, to ensure that they are monitored' (EAC 1998a, vol. II: para. 58). In November 1998 Labour published a discussion document (DETR 1998c) with thirteen suggested headline indicators, and responded positively to the Round Table's reports (DETR 1998f), and to the EAC's recommendations (EAC 1998a; DETR 1998d). The detailed work on developing national environmental accounts continued, but did not seem to influence mainstream policy (Office of National Statistics 1999).

As on the institutional front, the 1999 'Better Quality of Life' strategy moved on substantially with regard to indicators. Labour had responded positively to the debates about the need to monitor, and the role of indicators. One of the thirteen suggested headline indicators in the November 1998 document was widened from social capital to include investment in all public, business, and private assets. The other twelve were confirmed—total output of the economy; proportion of people of working age in work; qualifications at 19; expected years of healthy life; homes judged unfit to live in; emissions of greenhouse gases; days when air pollution is moderate or high; road traffic levels; rivers of good or fair quality; populations of wild birds; new homes built on previously developed land; and waste arisings and management (DETR 1999a: ch. 3). Crime levels was also added as a fourteenth indicator, and a 'satisfaction with quality of life' indicator is to be developed as a fifteenth. The importance of the need to monitor was stressed throughout chapters 5–8 where a second tier of about 120 further indicators was set out. The work on some of these remained to be finalized. There is more emphasis here on the social dimensions than in the Conservatives' 1996 report.

The 'Better Quality of Life' strategy announced that the government would publish (once a year starting in 2000) information about each of the headline indicators, and an account of the action taken. This re-established the annual reporting process which was suspended when Labour came to power. There were no annual reports for 1997, 1998, or 1999. The SDC will be centrally placed here, with responsibility to monitor progress on

the state of sustainable development in the UK as revealed by the indicators; whether the action being taken by each sector is, in its view, sufficient; and if not what needs to be done.   (DETR 1999a: para. 10.13)

Sustainable production and consumption was seriously addressed for the first time via the new emphasis on indicators. A fifth of the second-level indicators are set out in chapter 6 on creating a more sustainable economy. Some apply to individual sectors—energy and water consumption by sector, chemical releases to the environment, and primary aggregates per unit of construction value. Some are more waste specific—construction waste going to landfill, and hazardous waste. Some relate to consumers—energy efficiency of new appliances, and consumer information. Others relate to transport and distribution—energy efficiency of road passenger travel, mileage intensity of heavy goods vehicles, and freight transport by mode. Lastly, there are some which relate to the economy as a whole—environmental and sustainable development reporting, and an index of corporate environmental engagement. Up to the 1997 election, eco-efficiency and other aspects of sustainable production and consumption had been much discussed—as the DoE's and ACBE's annual reports show. But the attempts to move beyond rhetoric were confined to isolated initiatives like the Energy Savings Trust, best practice approaches, and voluntary codes of practice. The only real exception was the 1996 landfill tax.

Government's Links with Other Actors

Local Agenda 21 (LA21) was primarily a local government initiative in Britain (Young 1998). A small number of pioneering councils got involved with sustainable development initiatives before Rio. Afterwards the DoE passed the promotion of LA21 over to the LGMB. LGMB devoted its energies mainly to a series of publications highlighting emerging best practice approaches. LA21 was handicapped by not being a statutory duty in Britain. In effect, it was optional. It soon became clear that all LA21s were not going to be completed by 1996 (Morris and Hams 1997). LGMB fell back on trying to get every council started, but still had only a limited impact (EAC 1998a; CAG 1998; Young 1998). LA21 was never a core part of the Conservatives' response to the UNCED process. The DoE was supportive, but in a generally passive way. It spelt out the positive contribution that councils could make in promoting LA21 (DoE 1994a). It encouraged community involvement, but there was no systematic engagement with the nine chapter 28 groups. A little extra money was forthcoming for LA21, as with the DoE funds to help set up the Environmental Management Systems Helpdesk in 1994. However, councils were inhibited in a variety of ways by the Conservatives' regime of financial cuts and reduced powers (EAC 1998a).

Things appeared to change when Prime Minister Blair announced at UNGASS in June 1997 that he wanted all councils to complete their LA21s by the year 2000. DETR subsequently published a report explaining to the late starters how they should proceed (1998g), which drew substantially from an earlier LGMB document (1994). This led to an increase in the numbers of LA21s. Although the quality of some documents was certainly good, for the most part LA21s continued to be done in a tokenistic way and were usually given a low status within the authority. Under Labour, local government began to refocus the energies that had gone into LA21 in line with Labour's modernizing agenda. Attempts were made to get core sustainable development ideas into statutory land-use planning documents; into community development partnerships in the local social economy; and into two initiatives in Labour's Modernising Local Government White Paper (DETR 1998h)—the Best Value approach to service provision; and the community planning initiative. In retrospect it is clear that this process of LA21 fragmenting had begun well before the 1997 election.

The government's response to the UNCED process created opportunities for environmental groups to get involved in affecting the promotion of LA21 and the details of reports and proposals. For example NGO leaders were appointed to the Round Table (UKRTSD 1997; 1998a); and the committee advising the government on the transport White Paper (DETR 1998b). However, some—Greenpeace for example—avoided being drawn in for fear of becoming compromised. More broadly, NGOs were increasingly involved in consultation programmes on issues as varied as waste and indicators, especially after Labour came to power and adopted a more inclusive approach. The successful struggle to include sustainable development in the terms of reference of the new Regional Development Agencies showed how NGOs were exploiting their involvement in the more open policy networks. The biodiversity case below shows environmental NGOs at their most influential, involved not just in policy-making, but in implementation processes. Lastly, direct action focused on a widening range of issues.

Business interests were largely able to limit change during the early and mid-1990s to voluntary codes and the like. But industrialists on ACBE, the Panel, the Round Table, the boards of government agencies, and Task Forces like the Cleaner Vehicles one that Labour introduced, began to exert a practical influence not just on policy-makers, but on the wider links between government and the Confederation of British Industry, and attitudes within boardrooms. Trade associations mostly co-operated with the Environment Agency during the discussions to introduce the Integrated Pollution Prevention and Control Regulations (IPPC). Labour encouraged such co-operation by consulting widely, with long lead times, as in the climate change case discussed below.

The UK's Attitude to its International Obligations

The 1992–7 Major government was interested in the EU, but not in the North/South or global dimensions (Wilkinson 1999). The 50 per cent cut in overseas aid in real terms between 1979 and 1988 set the scene. Britain continued to languish at the foot of the table of eighteen Western aid donors (Rose 1990: 288). There were some contributions— as with biodiversity and forestry policies in former dependencies. Thus Britain allocated about £15m to the Darwin Project over five years to help developing countries implement the Biodiversity Convention (DoE 1997a: 50).

After 1997, Labour took these aspects more seriously in principle, but the rhetoric was still ahead of the action. It set out to 'provide strong leadership within a new environmental internationalism' (DETR 1998b: para. 93). The Department for International Development's White Paper (1997) spelt out the detail in terms of twelve strands, and 'Opportunities For Change' called for suggestions as to how the principles like ethical trading could be put into practice (DETR 1998b). A commitment was made to reverse the decline in development assistance, reaffirming Labour's adherence to the 0.7 per cent UN target. The 'Better Quality of Life' strategy reaffirmed the White Paper and emphasized the need to press international organiza- tions to take more account of sustainable development (DETR 1999a). Also, holding the EU Presidency in 1998 created opportunities for leadership— as over the Climate Change case and working out the shares within the EU bubble after Kyoto. In 1999 the Chancellor, Brown, issued a four- point plan to cut Third World debt, and £660,000 was committed to tech- nology transfer. However, the turmoil on the South-East Asian stock markets cast a long shadow. The issue of Multilateral Agreements on Investment posed difficult questions and highlighted the government's apparently largely neo-liberal approach to international trade and globaliza- tion (Environment Committee 1998). Britain is primarily a trading nation. The rhetoric about incorporating environmental concerns into inter- national trade policy continued. But the environmental and global justice dimensions seemed to remain add-on aspects of policy rather than core fea- tures (Wilkinson 1999).

Climate Change

The 1990 White Paper acknowledged that climate change presented an enor- mous challenge (DoE and Other Departments 1990: 5.1). Thatcher's scien- tific background meant that this was one part of the whole to which she could relate strongly and positively. Consequently Britain was involved in international initiatives before Rio. At Rio Major signed the Framework Convention on Climate Change (FCCC), committing the UK to reduce its greenhouse-gas emissions to 1990 levels by 2000. Under the Conservatives this remained a consistent commitment (DoE 1994c; DoE 1997b). In fact the UK looks set to achieve this objective—somewhat fortuitously—as a result of the closures in the coal industry, the privatization of energy supplies, and the expansion of gas-fired energy plants.

At UNGASS and Kyoto in 1997, and at Buenos Aires in 1998, the Labour Government committed itself to playing its part in the international efforts on climate change over the next decade. At Kyoto in particular, Prescott claimed some of the credit for brokering the eventual deal. The government committed itself to a target of a 12.5 per cent reduction in greenhouse-gas emissions by 2010, under the EU bubble; and to a further voluntary reduction of 20 per cent on CO_2 alone by 2012, in the 1997 Labour election manifesto. Late in 1998 the DETR published UK Climate Change Programme: A Consultation Paper (DETR 1998i). It specifically emphasizes the equity dimensions of sustainable development.

Under the Conservatives, the main focus was on regulatory approaches and especially on extending the range of advice (ACBE 1994; DoE 1997a). Regulatory measures included bus lanes, and the tightening of planning guidelines. But the main emphasis was on advice and persuasion. Examples include promoting energy efficient buildings, and research that would help policy-makers limit emissions—as in controlling methane emissions from sewage works; and assessing human influences on climate change. There were also voluntary recycling targets; attempts to get people out of cars and onto public transport; voluntary labelling explaining the energy efficiency of domestic white goods; promoting alternatives to CFCs via dialogue with industry; and companies joining the 'Making a Corporate Commitment Campaign' to review their energy management programmes. Taxes, prices, and markets were endlessly discussed by the Conservatives, from 1990 onwards (DoE and Other Departments 1990; DoE 1993). But ministers shied away from deploying economic instruments. The main exception was the 'fuel-price escalator'. In the November 1993 budget, the Chancellor announced that petrol prices would go up, year by year, by about 5 per cent above the rate of inflation. There was also a small renewables programme designed to generate up to 1,500 MW by the year 2000 through four rounds of the Non-Fossil Fuel Obligation scheme. Further, the Conservatives also used financial intervention and incentives to tackle climate change issues. These ranged from a DTp project to spend £116,000 converting 10 buses to compressed natural gas and 6 to liquid petroleum gas; up to £3 billion being invested in the railways; and £3 billion in the London underground during the 1994–7 period.

Labour continued with advice and persuasion approaches of the kind discussed above (ACBE 1998). ACBE held seminars and argued for voluntary agreements on a sector by sector basis. Labour also doubled energy-efficiency spending from £109m in 1998–9 to £223m in 2001–2; and continued the 'Foresight Programme'. This was designed to promote collaboration between business on the one hand, and the science base within government and universities on the other in order to identify projects beyond normal timescales. But the emphasis of Labour's strategy shifted to a tighter regulatory approach on the one hand, together with a wider deployment of economic instruments on the other. The main developments here were the use of IPPC mechanisms to promote energy savings at major installations; developing the landfill tax; and the Marshall Report (Marshall 1998) proposing an energy tax, as opposed to tradeable permits.

The March 1999 budget may represent something of a watershed (*UK Environment News*, April 1999: 12–13), announcing a set of measures that amounted a more serious attempt to get industry to reduce its carbon emissions. The Chancellor announced that, after consultation, a Climate Change Levy—or energy tax—would start from April 2001, collecting a forecast £1.75 billion in its first year. It would apply to gas, coal, and electricity used by business, agriculture, and public sector bodies for energy. A two-tier road tax was introduced, with owners of 1,100cc cars paying £100 rather than £155. A number of other economic instruments were deployed to encourage a switch to clean engines, and public transport. This budget came after the 1998 transport White Paper (DETR 1998b) which had set out a strategy to increase public transport and shift haulage to rail. This had important long-term implications for reducing the transport contribution to climate change. Measures included a Strategic Rail Authority, a cancellation of road schemes, and measures to promote travel by bus.

Yet it is clear that the government remains concerned about alienating car-users, and sensitive to industry complaints that the new Climate Change Levy will harm the UK's competitive position and cost jobs. By the close of 1999 the Chancellor was ready to scale back the proposed Levy and extend exemptions to numerous user-classes. The structure of the Levy made it unclear whether the primary objective was environmental or revenue-raising. The government also announced the suspension of the fuel-price escalator, the reinstalment of some road-building schemes, and a series of other 'car-friendly' initiatives.

Thus at the time of writing the picture remains mixed, with many critics arguing that the measures so far in place are inadequate to ensure UK compliance with the 2008–12 targets (EAC 1998b).

Biodiversity

A longstanding feature of British wildlife policy has been the strong links between NGOs and the wildlife agencies. Vigorous policy networks were thus widely established before Rio, involving NGOs like the Royal Society for the Protection of Birds (RSPB), the British Trust for Ornithology (BTO), World Wide Fund for Nature (WWF), smaller specialist groups as with bats and butterflies, and local county wildlife trusts. During the late 1980s and early 1990s, the whole basis of wildlife policy, enshrined in the 1981 Wildlife and Countryside Act, was changed. The focus shifted from regulation and sanctions, towards a process-oriented approach involving persuasion and specialist education; discussion and co-operation (Young 1995). Programmes were implemented flexibly through informal structures. The emphasis was on learning and using the implementation feedback loop to improve policy and programmes.

The publication of 'Biodiversity: The UK Action Plan' in January 1994 (DoE 1994d) had the effect of channelling a great deal of latent energy, imagination, and determination into positive outcomes. In a situation where policy had changed and was still being developed in a new direction, the 1994 plan created opportunities for NGOs which had been increasingly critical of government policy during the 1980s. It encouraged a vigorous pluralism. A UK Biodiversity Steering Group was established to draw up a detailed programme of action to implement the UK Action Plan's broad strategy. The UK Steering Group Report was published in two volumes in 1995 (UK Biodiversity Group 1995), and endorsed by the DoE in 1996 (DoE 1996c). There was so much activity that the government established a Biodiversity Secretariat to produce a newsletter, and facilitate implementation partnerships by drawing in industry, academic institutions, farmers, landowners, and other interests.

The strategy revolved round promoting Local Biodiversity Action Plans to implement the national plan; and developing costed targets for threatened species and habitats. A typical example is the Red Squirrel Action Plan. This involves public and private sector landowners on the West Lancashire coast—Sefton Council, the Forestry Commission, the National Trust, English Nature, the Territorial Army, the Mersey Forest, and a golf club. It is sponsored by a pensions company, and action involves rope ladders across main roads to prevent deaths; supplementary feeding; grey squirrel control; and the planting of Corsican pines—most of the existing pines are nearly a hundred years old and the cone crop is decreasing (*Lapwing*—the Journal of the Lancashire Wildlife Trust 1999). By the end of 1998 there were costed action plans for 400 species and thirty-nine habitat types (Biodiversity Secretariat 1998; UK Biodiversity Group 1998).

What had emerged was a rational planning approach, rather than an incremental one (Kenny and Meadowcroft 1999). Surveys identified threatened species. Targets were established. Systems for collecting and organizing the data at local and national levels were set up. Some of this was done within government agencies like the Environment Agency and English Nature; and some in the NGOs like the BTO. By then the UK Biodiversity Group had created subgroups on targets, information, research, and LA21 connections, together with four country subgroups. Species protection programmes were developed, often involving commercial sponsorship to inject extra resources—the Species Champions Scheme (UKRTSD 1998*b*). National programmes led to regional programmes—as in the case above. This then led down to the local level, where help ranged from ecologists employed by government agencies and councils to local groups organizing surveys and management work by volunteers. Comprehensive planning led to a process-oriented approach which initiated a cascade of initiatives involving a vast range of surveys and projects on the ground to implement Local Biodiversity Action Plans.

In this domain central government has developed a top-down empowering, partnership approach, drawing in groups at all levels, and exploiting the expert knowledge and inexpert energies of volunteers. Biodiversity has been well suited to the steady development of more and more detailed policies and programmes through the annual reporting process. The Labour government continued this approach, and was more open-minded in initiating reviews of the Sites of Special Scientific Interest (SSSIs) arrangements. The Conservatives had refused to do this—despite continuing damage to SSSIs. Progress was also the result of steady pressure from the EU. The Habitats Directive required the nomination of Special Areas of Conservation and Special Protection Areas.

Conclusions

The 1990s saw a substantial shift in Britain, from simply trying to contain the environmental issue, to the emergence of some serious cross-sectoral thinking within a stronger framework with greater potential for responding to the UNCED process. This represents a surprising amount of headway, given the in-built attitudes and the almost instinctive opposition to EU directives in the 1980s. The annual reporting process during the 1990s shows spurts of initiatives, most of which were sectorally-based. This fits in with Garner's assessment that the development of environmental policy reveals 'an incremental and cautious pattern with occasional periods of heightened activity' (1996: 108). There was an intermittent dimension to the progress—a kind of 'pause-Go! pause-Go!' approach. It was an environmental equivalent of the postwar stop-go approach to economic policy. The development of policy—and of the machinery—came mainly during the 1989–90, 1992–5, and 1998–9 periods.

This 'pause-Go!' approach to policy produced a ratchet effect, which then reinforced it. What often happened was that civil servants produced a report as a result of the annual reporting process, or of working out in detail the consequences of applying a principle to a policy sphere. Often it was watered down by opposition within government departments prior to publication. Once in the public domain groups took different sides. Government sought to resolve the different views in a package of proposals. Sometimes it was able to draw resisters into consensus-building arrangements—albeit at a less ambitious level. But the ratchet process kept movement going where before there had been none. Thus part of the point of the 'UK Environmental Health Action Plan' was to identify where to target resources and to develop measures that prevent illnesses—as through better air quality (DoE 1996a). This added sustainable development dimensions to health policies. Labour's enthusiasm on coming to office meant, as with waste (DETR 1998j) and the PPGs, that proposals were ratcheted further along towards an integration of sustainable development.

Three Stages

Britain's response to the Brundtland Report and the UNCED process can best be understood in terms of three stages. The first stage began before Rio but is important as it influenced the response to Rio. Thatcher's speeches in the autumn of 1988 marked the beginning of Stage 1. Its main event—and Britain's initial engagement with sustainable development—was the publication of 'This Common Inheritance'. Its core focus was the political containment of environmentalism. It did not satisfy environmentalists and it had restricted impact. But it took the steam out of the environment as a political issue; and it released forces that influenced subsequent events. In particular the non-environmental departments within central government were drawn into wider, developing processes. Examining the situation in terms of 'cogwheels', the parliamentary 'cog' engaged with the international 'cog' and responded to pressures from the NGO and civil society 'cogs'.

The focus of Stage 2 was on the bureaucratic engagement with sustainable development within central government. This began during the winter of 1990–1, and continued as the DoE team prepared the first two annual reports, and the papers for Rio. This involved them in promoting sustainable development ideas in other parts of the DoE and in other ministries and agencies. This process continued after Rio during the preparation and initial implementation of 'The UK Strategy'. The essence of Stage 2 was civil servants working out in detail the implications of sustainable development for their areas of responsibility. For the most part, Stage 2 was characterized by a sectoral approach, as with biodiversity. The central government 'cog' connected mainly with the international, business, and NGO 'cogs'.

Stage 3 can be dated from April 1996 when the new Environment Agency formally began to operate. In reality though, a lot of preparatory work had been done earlier. The distinguishing feature here was the shift from a narrow, sector-based approach to sustainable development towards a broader, cross-cutting, integrated strategy. This was symbolized by the Sustainable Development Unit within the Environment Agency. It began to emphasize thinking laterally, across the artificial boundaries between policy sectors in order to establish more ambitious and more focused policy frameworks. Whereas in Stage 2 government agencies tried to work out the implications of the principles of sustainable development for their policy sectors—as on industry—at Stage 3 the Environment Agency tried to focus on the consequences of a cross-cutting issue like climate change, for all policy sectors. The reports of the UK Round Table and of the Panel on Sustainable Development were also developing the theme of the need for more encompassing approaches.

In reality the start of Stage 3 and the end of Stage 2 overlapped. They are symbolized by the Environment Agency's corporate plan on the one hand (EA 1996), and the routine, sector-focused report on progress on Agenda 21 to UNGASS prepared within the DoE during the last months of the Conservative government on the other. Stage 3 thus began slowly during 1995–6 and picked up steam, becoming more widespread across government during the second half of 1997 as the new administration settled in. The pause for policy reviews when Labour first came to power encouraged policy entrepreneurs in the Environment Agency, inside the new DETR, and elsewhere, to question existing policies and develop more ambitious approaches. At the start of Stage 3 it was the central government 'cog' that was central. It interacted with the international 'cog', and increasingly after the 1997 election with the parliamentary and NGO 'cogs', and, as a result of the consultation programmes and the task forces, increasingly with business and civil society. Whether Labour's 1999 'Better Quality of Life' strategy and the planned creation of a Sustainable Development Commission in 2000 marks the start of a Stage 4, remains to be seen.

Explaining the Extent and Nature of the Changes

The 'pause-Go!' nature of Britain's response can be explained by the manner in which six factors combined in different ways during the three stages of the post-Rio period.

1. *International pressures.* Apart from the Brundtland report and the whole post-Rio process—as on climate issues, the EU was an important driver of change, forcing the pace of change (Jordan 1998). In cases like biodiversity and the Montreal Protocol, these international pressures directly influenced government because Britain had signed treaties committing it to action. But in cases where action on a treaty or directive had been delayed, the international pressures could still be influential as they dealt NGOs a stronger hand. Their lobbying became more effective as it was couched in terms of what other countries were already doing, and what Britain needed to do to fulfil its obligations—as on biodiversity.

2. *The strengthening of institutions.* A stronger focus on sustainable development was established within the DoE as it prepared 'The UK Strategy' during the 1992–4 period. Its publication led to the creation of the Panel, the Round Table, and GfG in 1994–5. Although they were advisory and slow to start, they became increasingly influential. The 1997 election then led to a further and stronger phase of institutional development, with the establishment of the DETR with its own Sustainable Development Unit, and Labour's Greening Government Initiative. Although ministers had not intended that the Environment Agency would be much more than a permits organization, it became increasingly influential from 1996–7 onwards because of the role of its Sustainable Development Unit both inside and outside the Agency.

However, crucial institutional weaknesses were also present under both the Conservatives and Labour. Much of the 1989–97 period can be explained in terms of the conflicts between DoE and DTp. The Treasury and the DTI consistently opposed the use of economic instruments under the Conservatives. The DoE also had trouble with Agriculture in the bilateral meetings leading up to 'The UK Strategy'. The DoE had hoped that just as the Treasury routinely made departments consider the capital and revenue implications of policies, so it could promote cumulative incremental change by forcing departments to relate their programmes to sustainable development (Young 1994). However, in contrast to the DTI over the competitiveness initiative, the DoE lacked the political authority to follow this through during the 1994–7 period, despite Cabinet support for the 'UK Strategy' (O'Riordan and Jordan 1995).

The establishment of DETR and Labour's Greening Government Initiative, from its Cabinet committee downwards, tried to address these issues. But other problems emerged. First, the new SDU went into the DETR, and not as originally proposed, into the Cabinet Office at the heart of government (Labour Party 1993). Although the DETR had more authority than the DoE, the SDU's influence did vary across departments. Second, conflicts emerged between DETR and its SDU on the one hand, and the enlarged Prime Minister's Policy Unit. The latter's role is to challenge and scrutinize departmental proposals. This delayed the implementation of the transport White Paper. So Labour did establish machinery, focused around the DETR, that was potentially stronger than the units within DoE had been. But, faced with pressure from industry and transport lobbies in 1998–9, and fears over the electoral impact of more radical policies, its strength proved more theoretical than practical.

When considering the role of institutions, it is important to draw in a wider feature of the Thatcher and Major years that continued to be influential under Blair. Rhodes has argued persuasively that a 'hollowing out' of the state took place: that, together, privatization, the promotion of executive agencies through the Next Steps Programme, and the removal of powers from local government, undermined the institutional capacity of government to implement programmes (1994).

Paradoxically though, the resulting fragmentation of government created opportunities. The shift toward 'governance' rather than government emphasized the need—as with biodiversity—to work through partnerships. In addition, policy entrepreneurs committed to the promotion of sustainable development ideas suddenly had increased room for manoeuvre. Fragmentation helped create a policy vacuum. During the last year of the Major administration sustainable development ceased to be a priority; and during the first year of the Blair government, reviews and task forces were active on all fronts. As a result a state of policy flux emerged, and genuine debates were breaking out. In a number of spheres positions were not being defended for eighteen months or two years. It was a Heaven-sent opportunity for policy entrepreneurs. It helps explain the expanding influence of the Environment Agency and especially its SDU.

3. *The use of a weak weak of policy instruments.* At the start of the 1990s, the emphasis was on using negotiated consent and other regulatory mechanisms, on the one hand, and voluntary advice and persuasion approaches on the other. This continued, with each being related more and more to sus-

tainable development issues. Thus the packaging regulations were strengthened, mandatory labelling was eventually enforced with regard to the energy efficiency of household appliances, and preparations were made for IPPC. The examples of using advice and persuasion are legion. The climate change experience was paralleled in many spheres. But the problem with the advice and persuasion approach is simply that companies, councils, and individuals can ignore every initiative. Industry's response in particular was very limited during the early 1990s beyond a relatively small number of pioneering companies (ACBE 1998), which saw commercial advantages in taking up European environmental management systems and the International Standards Organization's ISO 14001.

The other approach was to use economic instruments. The main examples—up to and including Labour's first budget in 1997—were the fuel-price escalator, the landfill tax, and reduced excise duty for buses and lorries with clean exhausts. However, as the climate change section above shows, Labour used the 1998 and 1999 budgets to extend the use of economic instruments. The 'Better Quality of Life' strategy picked up a constant ministerial theme and committed the government to continue exploring the potential of this approach (DETR 1999a). The greater use of economic instruments has also had a significant side-effect. It has broken down the Treasury's resistance to hypothecated taxes. The first real breach was the landfill tax. Part of the income is available to NGOs, working in partnerships, for environmental projects. Labour also intend to give councils powers to spend the income from workplace parking levies and road congestion charges on promoting integrated transport solutions to meet local needs (DETR 1998b). And the Chancellor has stated that should the fuel-price escalator be reintroduced the additional revenues will be allocated to transport.

It seems clear though that the use of predominantly voluntary approaches during the 1990s had a serious effect in limiting the impact of what governments could achieve. Labour's emerging approach was referred to as the 'market transformation approach'—a combination of better information for consumers; using research and best practice to encourage more sustainable production; and developing new frameworks to give industry a different combination of incentives, regulation and advice (DETR 1999a). It appeared stronger than that developed earlier by the Conservatives (O'Riordan and Jordan 1995). The potential for significant change was also undermined by the problem of bringing under control a number of policies that dated from the pre-Brundtland era. The road-building programme of the 1980s continued well into the 1990s. As a result new industrial estates, greenfield housing projects, and out-of-town retail centres were often built on sites where it was difficult to put in effective links to public transport. The Trafford Centre in South-West Manchester opened in 1998, in the midst of Labour's rethinking, with 10,000 free car parking spaces and very limited public transport links.

4. *Changes in the public mood towards the environment.* Through the 1990s, the public mood has, on the one hand, spurred governments on to action and supported change; while on the other, produced outbursts that led government to apply the brakes. It seems clear that Thatcher was responding to increased public concerns when making her 1988 environment speeches and initiating the 'This Common Inheritance' process. But this increased concern was slow to embrace changed lifestyles. The limited take-up of recycling facilities and the problems of pricing people out of their cars are prominent examples. However, polling evidence suggests that whereas levels of popular concern on salient issues move up and down, the underlying levels of latent concern and awareness about the significance of environmental issues continue to rise (Burke 1995; Worcester 1997). Public attitudes reflected greater awareness of environmental conditions, rather than a more positive understanding of the UNCED process.

It seems that Labour was able to take a stronger line on a number of issues during its first eighteen months in power because the public mood was more receptive to action. There seemed to be a slow but growing acceptance of environmental taxes. It was noticeable that in responding to various transport proposals in the mid-1990s, representatives of the motoring organizations began to accept that the sheer growth in traffic meant that some restraints on car use were needed; and that governments could not simply go on building motorways to meet demand—as in the 1980s. Instead the motoring organizations began to argue that viable public transport alternatives had to be put in place *before* governments could expect to get people out of their cars. However, during the winter of 1998–9 this mood began to evaporate. Criticisms of the government began to emerge across a whole range of issues—getting the ban on beef exports lifted; field trials of GMO crops; and new house-building on greenfield sites. The frustrations about traffic congestion, lack of investment in public transport, and rising fuel prices in particular burst into the media.

5. *The weight of economic interests.* This is the other side of the coin to sporadic but growing general opposition. Economic interests have greater access to decision-makers. The uneven implementation reflects strong economic interests supporting voluntary approaches, and vetoing other schemes. Where there were conflicts with environmentalists, the neopluralist state invariably sided with business. The Conservatives were reluctant to press the packaging industry too hard, for example. Economic interests largely retained the inside track, elbowing out the environmental

lobbyists when they felt seriously threatened. The heavy goods vehicle drivers' French-style opposition to increased diesel prices attracted a lot of media attention in 1999. Economic interests began to lobby against the proposed Climate Change levy. However the environmental NGOs were sometimes able to exploit the factors that were undermining the promotion of sustainable development. As the problems were revealed, groups were then able to argue well-informed cases about improving machinery, co-ordination, policies, and the use of targets and indicators. Many of their points were included as recommendations in Parliamentary committee reports. Here the shift from relatively closed policy communities to more open, fluid policy networks was important. This created more opportunities for groups to work with policy entrepreneurs within the system. The 1997–8 period, with the establishment of policy reviews and task forces as Labour went 'pause-Go!', became a classic political opportunity structure (Kitschelt 1996). In these circumstances the skills and contacts of ex-civil servants like Derek Osborn and ex-ministers like Gummer became further resources the NGOs could deploy. This tension between economic and environmental interests ran on through the 1990s, and remained unresolved.

6. *Political leadership, and the commitment to sustainable development principles.* Thatcher's role was critical during Stage 1. Major's support was important during the immediate post-Rio period while 'The UK Strategy' was being prepared. However, he became preoccupied with party unity over Europe, with lost by-elections and low poll ratings and subsequently lost interest. Conservative ministers were apprehensive about introducing road pricing and other economic instruments, fearing that they would further alienate voters. At this point the lack of leadership became a significant factor. Here though, Gummer played an important role. He became personally committed to sustainable development and deserves considerable credit for keeping the sustainable development effort alive in government; protecting the reduced numbers working on it in the mid-1990s; pushing the landfill tax; and maintaining the DoE's engagement with EU initiatives.

The Labour government did provide some political commitment at the end of Stage 3. Prime Minister Blair's UNGASS speech in New York in June 1997; Britain's role at Kyoto and Buenos Aires; the establishment of the Cabinet Committee; and the system of green ministers are examples. However, on some occasions Labour's courage has evaporated. The shifts back and forth over transport policy and climate change are cases in point. Labour had appeared to accept that the post-Rio experience had showed the need for a stronger combination of regulation, advisory approaches, and economic instruments. However, the extent to which the Labour leadership would stand up to the opposition that spread during 1999, was unclear.

Prospects

The 1999 'Better Quality of Life' strategy is not the ideal of a comprehensive, costed action programme with a challenging, wide-ranging set of targets developed from a clean slate. But it is considerably more ambitious than the 1994 strategy. Together with other initiatives from the 1997–9 period, it recognizes the importance of indicators and establishes clear monitoring processes; it provides a more focused, flexible and apparently robust institutional framework; and it brings into play a stronger set of tools and instruments. However, it must be stressed that it is only a potentially stronger approach. Its impact will depend on three factors. First, there is the issue of how ministers respond to what the annual indicator report reveals. Second, there is the question as to how Labour draws the balance between regulation, advice, and economic instruments; and the effect of this balance on the extent to which companies, councils, and individuals can ignore government programmes. Third, there is the issue of how decision-makers adapt the policies and instruments in the light not just of implementation problems, but of resistance from economic interests and the wider public. The clear commitment in chapter 10 to review the 1999 strategy after five years provides an important opportunity to adapt it to changing circumstances, and to develop further research.

10

The United States: 'Sorry—Not Our Problem'

GARY C. BRYNER

Introduction: US Environmental Law and Policy

The United States was a global leader in the early development of policies and regulatory programmes to protect environmental quality. Until 1970, environmental law in the US was largely a set of common law principles of nuisance, trespass, and negligence. A few states had passed environmental statutes but they were for the most part weak and non-binding. Nuisance law permitted property owners to seek damages through the courts against polluters who caused property damage. Trespass law could be used to remedy dumping of garbage onto the property owner's land. Negligence suits could be filed against parties that had a duty to not release dangerous substances, breached the duty, and caused harm to others (Stimson, Kimmel, and Thurin 1993: 1–16). In less than two decades, however, environmental law evolved from a local government responsibility into a complex system of national environmental regulation.

On 1 January 1970 President Nixon signed the National Environmental Policy Act, which required the federal government to assess the environmental consequences of every major action it undertook. Nixon's action initiated two decades of environmental activism. The Environmental Protection Agency (EPA) was created in the same year; subsequent years saw the passage of major environmental legislation including the Clean Air Act, the Resource Conservation and Recovery Act (RCRA), the Toxic Substances Control Act (TSCA), and the Comprehensive Environmental Response, Compensation, and Liability Act (CERCLA). Many of these acts were strengthened throughout the 1980s, culminating in the Clean Air Act amendments of 1990. These statutes include environmental standards, procedures for formulating rules and regulations, and deadlines for agency implementation and regulated industry compliance. Environmental regulation is built on a fragmented and complex statutory base of nearly a dozen major laws administered by the EPA, and dozens of additional statutes. An intricate infrastructure of agencies, legislation, regulations, and enforcement mechanisms are in place for protecting the environment. Federal, state, and local governments, regulated industry, the scientific community, and public interest groups all have invested significant resources in addressing the challenges of assessing environmental and health risks and enforcing laws and regulations.

US environmental law revolves around a complex system of shared authority and co-operative agreements between the federal government and the states, largely in response to the complexity of environmental programmes, the tremendous numbers of sources of pollution to be regulated, the desire to permit some tailoring of regulation to local conditions, and the inherent authority of states to regulate environmental conditions. The federal government's primary function is to establish policy, to develop national standards, to ensure that states enforce the laws and regulations in a way consonant with national standards, and to provide some funding of compliance costs. Most federal environmental statutes authorize states to issue permits and to enforce regulations if their programmes and standards are approved by the EPA. States have the primary responsibility to grant permits, to inspect facilities, and to initiate enforcement actions against violators. Environmental laws affect industrial and commercial activity in at least six ways: (1) they require information about the release of certain toxic chemicals into the environment; (2) they establish a system of pre-manufacturing approval for certain chemicals; (3) they require the treatment of emissions to air and water and the monitoring of the disposal of hazardous wastes; (4) they mandate the use of certain control technologies; (5) they create a special fund to clean up abandoned hazardous waste sites and provide standards to guide the remediation efforts; and (6) they prohibit some activities from taking place.

Public opinion polls and other measures of public sentiment show strong support for environmental regulation and most studies show that Americans favour even more protection than current efforts provide. For many years more than 70 per cent of respondents have replied in national polls that 'protecting the environment is so important that requirements and standards cannot be too high, and continuing environmental improvements must be made *regardless* of cost' (emphasis in original) (Dunlap 1991: 32). Environmental regulation has been a major issue in many congressional and state/local races, and has been a significant issue in presidential campaigns. Environmental law enjoyed strong bipartisan support in the 1970s, but in the 1980s it became a more divisive issue, as Republicans began responding to complaints of regulatory burdens by business interests and used the cost of regulation as an issue to expand their supporter base. The Reagan administration launched a major assault on environmental laws and regulations. The Democrat-dominated Congress resisted proposals to rewrite laws, but members were largely unable to block administrative changes that reduced enforcement of regulatory programmes and cut spending for research on environmental problems and other agency activities.

Criticism of environmental regulation and the costs of compliance continued to grow throughout the 1980s and early 1990s, and peaked in 1994 as the Democrats lost control of Congress and the Republican leadership identified the reform of environmental regulation as a high priority. The 1994 House Republican 'Contract with America' promised to 'roll back government regulations and create jobs' (Gillespie and Schellhas 1994: 125–41). Republicans sought to make major changes in the regulatory process; among their primary goals have been to ensure that more scientific and economic analyzes are performed before new regulations are proposed, increase opportunities for regulated industries to help shape the provisions, ensure that only relatively serious risks are regulated, require proof that benefits of regulation exceed the costs of compliance, and require federal agencies to compensate property owners for loss in property values resulting from environmental regulation. Opposition in Congress and from the Clinton administration blocked most of these proposals in 1995 and 1996; but they were reintroduced in various forms in 1997, 1998, and 1999, as Congress and the administration continued to clash over what changes should be made in environmental laws and regulatory decision-making. Congress made some inroads by attaching provisions to appropriations bills that cut spending for programmes it opposed, but most of those contentious riders prompted presidential veto threats and were deleted from the final bills (Environmental and Energy Study Institute 1997: 21–2). President Clinton vetoed several spending bills in 1995 because of their environmental provisions, and the impasse caused the federal government twice to shut down temporarily until the provisions were removed and the appropriations bills were enacted.

By 1999 Republican leaders had become wary of frontal attacks on environmental laws, but continued to use various ways to reduce the scope of environmental enactments, cut the costs of compliance, and slow down the regulatory process. For example, proponents of new procedural requirements sought to increase radically the analysis the EPA must perform in rule-making, while at the same time dramatically cutting the agency's budget. Although Congress was far from monolithic on these issues—different members had different views about what ails the regulatory system, about which industry groups needed to be accommodated, and what kinds of changes might raise the ire of voters—the predominant view among Republicans was that the cost, scope, and reach of regulation must be reduced.

However, the controversy surrounding environmental law extends well beyond political partisanship to more fundamental, structural problems. Congress has been overwhelmed by the complexity of environmental law. Most members have little understanding of these exceedingly detailed laws and how they work. The high turnover in congressional staffs produces little institutional memory and limited expertise in congressional committees. Congress is several years behind in the schedule it set for itself to reauthorize the major environmental laws; the authority for many environmental laws has expired, and the laws remain in effect only through provisions in annual appropriations. Congress cannot keep up with changes in technologies, environmental problems, and policy options, and its policy efforts are often mired in political gridlock (Vig and Kraft 1996: 119–42). Congress and the White House remain distrustful of each other and largely unable to move forward in dealing with new environmental problems and concerns. And the conflict and uncertainty surrounding environmental law has weakened US leadership in global environmental issues. The Clinton administration has been hesitant to support aggressive global positions because of its own domestic political problems arising from investigations and the President's impeachment, and its inability to compel Congress to accept any global commitments the administration might make.

The Basic Dimensions of Sustainable Development

The political conflict over environmental law and regulation has been so divisive and time consuming that it has precluded the nation from moving towards the next generation of environmental laws that might incorporate the idea of sustainable development. The Clinton administration has given some attention and resources to sustainable development, primarily through the President's Commission on Sustainable Development, and both the President and particularly the Vice-President have been involved in its activities. Much of the story of sustainable development in the United States lies in the work of the commission and the efforts by the Clinton administration to pursue its agenda. The US Environmental Protection Agency has launched numerous initiatives aimed at 'reinventing' government—making regulation more efficient and effective, engaging regulated interests in regulatory policy making, and integrating diverse regulatory programmes—that are consistent with many of the ideas underlying sustainable development.

The US Agency for International Development has endorsed sustainable development as one of the guiding principles for foreign aid. Moreover, many state and local governments have initiated sustainable community efforts.

However, sustainable development, like any other major policy commitment, ultimately requires the support of Congress and strong, effective legislation and the greatest failure to engage with the idea of sustainable development has been here. The Republican leaders in Congress have virtually ignored the idea of sustainable development and the United States' commitments made at the Rio Earth Summit. For them sustainable development is simply a problem for other countries to worry about, particularly developing countries. The hostility many congressional leaders have to international commitments, along with their opposition to environmental regulation, combine to create a major barrier to pursuing the idea of sustainable development in the United States. Congress continues to debate the question of whether there should be more or less environmental regulation. Rather than asking more fundamental questions about how to balance and integrate economic growth and ecological sustainability, policy-makers are mired in efforts to defend or attack the regulatory system that has been in place since the 1970s. As a result, there is no strong commitment to sustainable development, and the nation is far from having in place a comprehensive strategy that integrates sustainability into environmental, social, and economic activities (Dernbach 1997: 10507).

While Congress has resisted moving the debate over environmental regulation toward sustainable development, the Clinton administration has regularly argued that economic growth and environmental quality can be pursued together. The President, Vice-President, EPA administrator, and others rarely miss the opportunity to remind the public and regulated industries that environmental goals can be achieved without challenging the expectation of continual economic expansion. The administration has argued that it has developed a new paradigm of environmental policy, one that 'emphasizes goal setting, economic incentives, pollution prevention, a more holistic approach to environmental problems, simplification of regulations, more flexible problem-solving, and a more interactive approach with stakeholders and the community at large' (US Council on Environmental Quality 1995: 26). The Clinton administration has been quite engaged in discussing, writing about, reporting on, and urging sustainable development. It has been quite innovative in designing programmes to encourage voluntary efforts on the part of businesses to become more sustainable. It has tried to facilitate local efforts to build more sustainable communities. Nevertheless, it has largely been unsuccessful in fostering a commitment to sustainable development among the general public. The idea of sustainable development is still widely ignored or, at best, seen as something to guide developing countries as they grapple with population growth outstripping resources, uncontrolled pollution and the lack of resources to provide those controls, and the inability to meet basic needs. These countries, it is believed, must learn how to improve their material quality of life and consumption without undermining economic growth by degrading their environment. From the perspective of most policy-makers in the United States, sustainable development is simply someone else's problem, and the nation's massive economic clout insulates it from having to worry about sustainability.

The Clinton–Gore administration, given the Vice-President's past environmental record, is the logical leader for pressing the sustainability agenda, but it has for the most part been unwilling to go beyond voluntary programmes. Vice-President Gore quickly retreated from some of his more ambitious environmental views during the 1992 campaign after opponents charged him with extremism. Some of the most aggressive environmental actions taken by the administration, such as the new clean air standards, for example, were pushed by EPA officials, rather than by Clinton or Gore. The administration's positions on climate change and other global issues are much more modest than Gore argued in his book, *Earth in the Balance*, published before he was elected in 1992. But few political leaders have been willing to take on the broader questions of American values of economic growth, consumption, technology, land use, transportation, and individual freedom. Most Americans seem determined to view economic growth as limitless, constrained only by unwise policy or business choices. They resist strongly the idea that limits should be placed on material consumption, and exhibit tremendous faith in technological solutions to whatever problems confront them. Their strong commitment to private property rights places major limits on political decisions which seek to promote environmental ends but which involve limitations to established patterns of property usage. Their insistence on single occupancy vehicles and dislike for mass transit is intertwined with their fundamental commitment to individual freedom and ability to travel wherever and whenever they please. Jimmy Carter was the last major political leader to talk about limits and constraints, and he was widely derided for violating the American creed of limitless growth and opportunity.

The United States' participation in global sustainable development efforts has been quite modest, reflecting the lack of domestic political commitment to global environmental stewardship. It has played a dominant role in many negotiations, because of its economic power, but has not provided significant international leadership. The Bush administration was an unenthusiastic participant in the Rio Summit, and while it supported Agenda 21 and the Earth Charter, it opposed the climate change and biodiversity accords. Clinton administration officials have been careful to pursue an agenda that does not frighten US industries with radical change or suggest to citizens a major shift in their consumptive lifestyle. Congressional Republican leaders have been absolutely adamant in their opposition to US participation in any international agreements that will raise costs or increase regulatory burdens for US industries. Many congressional Democrats have been just as timid, supportive of organized labour's opposition to environmental or sustainable development related legislation that might result in job losses or industry relocations to developing countries.

Institutionalizing Sustainable Development: The President's Council on Sustainable Development

The idea of sustainable development has had some influence in the development of national policies and programmes, but that influence has largely been limited to the executive branch. The Clinton administration has pursued a number of initiatives it has described as part of its commitment to sustainable development, while Congress has largely failed even to address the idea. Central to the federal government's sustainable development agenda is the President's Council on Sustainable Development (PCSD), created by the Clinton administration in 1993. Its purpose was to bring together representatives from environmental groups, industry, and government to advise the President 'on matters involving sustainable development', defined as 'economic growth that will benefit present and future generations without detrimentally affecting the resources or biological systems of the planet' (PCSD 1993). The Council's 'vision statement' argues that a 'sustainable United States will have a growing economy that provides equitable opportunities for satisfying livelihoods and a safe, healthy, high quality of life for current and future generations' (PCSD 1996a: iv). The structure of the Council reflects one of its primary themes: 'Our most important finding is the potential power of and growing desire for decision processes that promote direct and meaningful interaction involving people in decisions that affect them' (ibid. 7). The role of government is to 'convene and facilitate, shifting gradually from prescribing behaviour to supporting responsibility by setting goals, creating incentives, monitoring performance, and providing information' (ibid.). The Council is co-chaired by the President of the World Resources Institute (a Washington, DC, environmental research centre) and a Vice-President of Dow Chemical Company. Members include the executives of several national environmental organizations, four US government Cabinet members, chairmen of the board/CEOs of several corporations, and representatives from state governments, labour unions, and civil rights groups (ibid. 177–84).

The Council proposed ten goals to guide public and private efforts in pursuit of the idea of sustainable development as shown in Table 10.1. The goals form an ambitious agenda that addresses environmental quality and natural-resource preservation, equity, economic growth, community and civic engagement, education, and international responsibility. The report then discusses in some detail needed changes in six areas: (1) making environmental regulation more effective and efficient; (2) increasing the amount of information available and access to it concerning sustainable development; (3) encouraging community planning, reducing urban sprawl, and creation of jobs and economic opportunities; (4) developing an ethic of stewardship to guide human interaction with natural systems; (5) expanding access to family planning and reproductive health services, increasing equity for women, and reducing illegal immigration; and (6) fostering US leadership in international efforts to promote democracy, scientific research, and sustainable development.

The Clinton administration created an Interagency Working Group on Sustainable Development in 1996 to oversee implementation of the Council's recommendations outlined in the *Sustainable America* report and to review federal programmes in light of sustainable development standards. The working group formed three Task Forces—local, state, and regional efforts; new national opportunities; and international leadership—and the work of these three Task Forces reach most of what is being pursued in the United States related to sustainable development.

Local, State, and Regional Efforts

The first Task Force, the Innovative Local, State, and Regional Approaches Task Force explored ways communities and regions could engage in strategic planning in managing economic development, community growth, protection of ecosystems, preservation of fisheries, and in creating incentives for environmental stewardship. The Task Force supports the following efforts:

• The Joint Center for Sustainable Communities, established by the National Association of Counties and the US Conference of Mayors, provides local elected officials with advice, technical assistance, information, and

Table 10.1. Goals and Indicators of Progress, Council on Sustainable Development

Goals	Indicators
Ensure that every person enjoys the benefits of clean air, clean water, and a healthy environment at home, at work, and at play.	Decreased numbers of persons living in areas that fail to meet air quality and drinking water standards, reduced releases of toxic chemicals, and decreased deaths and illnesses due to environment-related exposures.
Sustain a healthy US economy that grows sufficiently to create meaningful jobs, reduce poverty, and provide the opportunity for a high quality of life for all in an increasingly competitive world.	Increases in per capita GDP and NDP, wages, quality and number of jobs, higher per capita savings and investment rates, increased productivity, decreased number of people living below poverty level, development of new economic measures reflecting resource use and pollution.
Ensure that all Americans are afforded justice and have the opportunity to achieve economic, environmental, and social well-being.	Decrease in the income differences between top and bottom of population, development of measures of disproportional environmental burden on minorities and access to critical social services, and increased education.
Use, conserve, protect, and restore natural resources—land, air, water, and biodiversity—in ways that help ensure long-term social, economic, environmental benefits for ourselves and future generations.	Increase in the health of ecosystems such as forests, wetlands, surface waters, topsoil, grasslands, surface waters, and coastal lands; decreased number of threatened and endangered species; decreased release of toxins and excess nutrients that threaten ecosystems; reduced greenhouse and ozone-depleting gases.
Create a widely held ethic of stewardship that strongly encourages individuals, institutions, and corporations to take full responsibility for the economic, environmental, and social consequences of their actions.	Increased efficiency of material use; increased source reduction, reuse, recovery, and recycling; reduced energy use per unit of output; and decreased rate of use of fisheries, forests, soil, and groundwater.
Encourage people to work together to create healthy communities were natural and historic resources are preserved, jobs are available, sprawl is contained, neighbourhoods are secure, education is lifelong, transportation and health care are accessible, and all citizens have opportunities to improve the quality of their lives.	Increased per capita income and employment, decreased violent crime rates, increased urban green areas, increased investment in children, decreased traffic congestion and increased use of mass transit, increased library use and access to the internet and other sources of information, decreased number of homeless, and decreased infant mortality rate.
Create full opportunity for citizens, businesses, and communities to participate in and influence the natural resource, environmental, and and economic decisions that affect them.	Increased voting rates, citizen engagement and public trust, increased participation in professional and service organizations, and use of civic collaborations, partnerships, and planning.
Move toward stabilization of US population	Reduced population growth rate, increased educational opportunity and income equality for women, decreased number of teenage and unintended pregnancies, decreased illegal immigration.

Table 10.1. (*cont.*)

Goals	Indicators
Take a leadership role in the development and implementation of global sustainable development policies, standards of conduct, and trade and foreign policies, that further the achievement of sustainability.	Increased level of foreign aid for sustainable development, increased US exports or transfers of cost-effective and environmentally sound technologies to developing countries, increased research on global environmental problems.
Ensure that all Americans have equal access to education and lifelong learning opportunities that will prepare them for meaningful work, a high quality of life, and an understanding of the concepts involved in sustainable development.	Increased access to government information, public and private research, and right-to-know information; increased availability of teaching materials on sustainability; increased commitment to sustainable development curricula; improved skill performance on standardized tests; and increased high school graduation rates and college or vocational training.

Source: PCSD 1996b: 14–23.

financial support for sustainable communities. The Center provides leadership training, peer exchange programmes, information on policy tools, and an advertising and education campaign and conference workshops.
• The Metropolitan Approaches Working Group collects information on how cities, counties, business groups, citizens, and others can facilitate co-operative efforts that cross local government boundaries. The PCSD recommended that the group develop a pilot demonstration programme to facilitate metropolitan-scale sustainable development strategies, identify and seek to change policies that contribute to urban sprawl, and recommend legislative and administrative actions that would increase the flexibility of metropolitan areas to integrate economic, environmental, and equity concerns.
• The Pacific Northwest Regional Council, made up of twenty-eight regional leaders, promotes co-operation among regional non-profit and community groups, awareness of sustainable development concepts, and sharing of information about regional programmes. The PCSD is working to establish similar councils in other regions.

The PCSD's support of local government initiatives is particularly important, because it is at this level of government that the idea of sustainable development is helping to shape public policies. Communities in the Pacific Northwest, for example, have been actively pursuing sustainable development policies. The region has undergone dramatic economic growth over the past few decades and its economic base has been transformed. Metro-politan areas have aggressively developed policies to control urban sprawl and develop mass transit. Timber and ranching businesses in the region have emphasized stewardship and responsibility for sustainable use of resources (PCSD 1997a: 10–11). Other communities have also aggressively pursued sustainable development initiatives. The East–West/Gateway Co-ordinating Council in St Louis has developed a twenty-year transportation plan that integrates transportation decisions with economic, environmental, and community goals such as supporting mobility for low income residents and ensuring that development along rail lines is based on sustainability prin-ciples. Some communities have formed sustainable development forums to bring community members together to discuss issues and formulate plans. Non-profit organizations throughout the nation formed the Sustainable Communities Network to share information on demonstration projects and conduct outreach programmes (ibid. 13).

Many US cities have joined the International Council for Local Environ-mental Initiatives' (ICLEI) Cities for Climate Protection programme, have put in place action plans to protect the global climate and reduce local air pollution. Several major cities have embraced the goal of a 20 per cent reduc-tion in carbon-dioxide emissions, and a few have reduced emissions by as much as 15 per cent since 1995. Most of the progress is being made in retro-fitting municipal buildings, community energy efficiency programmes, and waste management initiatives (ICLEI 1998a; 1998b: 1–3). ICLEI has estab-lished a global programme to assist local governments in implementing Agenda 21 programmes. The first effort, Model Communities, focused on community planning. A second programme established Local Agenda 21 networks to report on the implementing, monitoring, and reporting of Agenda 21 programmes (ibid. 9). While it is too early to be able to assess the impact of these initiatives on local and global environments, they rep-resent important efforts to gain binding commitments for participation in the kinds of efforts envisioned in Agenda 21. A number of US communities have also developed their own greenhouse-gas reduction programmes, as discussed below.

National Environmental Policy

The second PCSD Task Force, New National Opportunities, examined options for improving the cost-effectiveness of the existing regulatory sys-tem and devising alternative approaches such as collaborative policy-making processes, extended product responsibility, and eco-industrial parks. The Task Force strongly endorsed collaboration as a way to improve environmental and social outcomes in collective decisions, give stakeholders more ownership of agreements, increase social learning about complex problems, and foster trust. It suggested that successful collaborative efforts have several characteristics: shared vision and objectives, measurable outcomes, equal management of the process by stakeholders, shared and defined decision-making processes, up-front planning, conflict-resolution mechanisms, and open communication among participants (PCSD 1997a: 21–2).

Extended Product Responsibility (EPR) is based on the idea that real progress in sustainable development requires an integrated assessment of all stages of economic activity and that all those involved in the life-cycle of a product—designers, suppliers, manufacturers, distributors, users, and disposers—share responsibility for the environmental effects of the products. EPR in the United States is much broader in scope than 'extended producer responsibility' programmes in other countries that emphasize the responsibility of manufacturers for ultimate disposal of their products. Government agencies establish performance standards and ensure accountability for achieving those standards, and businesses are then free to choose how to implement them. EPR is largely a voluntary programme in the United States; companies have pursued it in order to attract green consumers, make more efficient use of resources, avoid regulatory requirements, and achieve their own sustainability goals. Under EPR, companies find new ways to organize production and distribution to minimize wastes, treat wastes as assets, devise new ways of thinking about product delivery, and seek feedback from customers in redesigning products. A number of US companies, including DuPont, Ford Motor, and Georgia-Pacific, have used EPR principles to transform the way they produce their products (ibid. 24–5).

While this Task Force has focused on some important challenges in improving the current regulatory system, the EPA has undertaken a number of partnership efforts with industry to encourage efficiency and conservation and reduce emissions. While these initiatives are not expressly aimed at contributing to the shift toward sustainable development, they rest on many of the same underlying premises and values and provide a base on which more ambitious efforts could be built. In these voluntary programmes the EPA provides technical assistance and relief from some regulatory requirements for firms that make binding commitments. Among the most important EPA initiatives are:

- 'Green Lights', a programme that assists companies in installing energy-saving lighting.
- 'Waste Wise', which helps companies find ways to reduce the generation of solid wastes.

- 'Climate wise', a joint EPA–Department of Energy effort to help compan- ies reduce their emissions of greenhouse gases.
- 'Pesticide Environmental Stewardship Programme', an EPA–Agriculture Department–Food and Drug Administration programme to reduce pesti- cide use.
- 'Project XL', an effort by the EPA and state regulators to substitute company-devised plans for established regulations as long as results give more protection to the environment, involve local citizens in formulating and monitoring plans, and contribute to worker safety and environmen- tal justice (National Performance Review 1995: 43).
- The '33/50 Programme', where EPA officials worked with industries to reduce emissions of chemicals by 33 per cent by 1992 and 50 per cent by 1995 (both goals were achieved a year ahead of schedule for some 1,300 participating companies) (US EPA 1998).
- The 'National Environmental Goals Project', an effort to develop ten-year goals for achieving the environmental and public health improvements promised in US laws and international agreements by identifying the chal- lenges to be addressed, who is responsible for taking what actions, and targets to be achieved by the year 2005 (US EPA 1997).

The EPA has also established programmes expressly related to sustain- able development. Its Office of Sustainable Ecosystems and Communities, created in 1994, includes a Sustainable Ecosystems and Communities Clear- inghouse that provides information on ecology, economics, community planning and participation, and other topics, and seeks to encourage com- munities to plan for economic and ecological sustainability. The agency pro- vides technical expertise in developing indicators for sustainability, fostering public participation, assessing natural resources, and planning (US EPA 1996b).

The Clinton Administration's 'Creating Government that Works Better & Costs Less', initiative, chaired by Vice-President Al Gore, has issued hundreds of recommendations for improving the efficiency and effectiveness of government agencies and programmes, and for providing better service to citizens/clients that also approximate many of the goals of sustainable devel- opment (National Performance Review 1993). The emphasis of this major undertaking has been to reduce the costs of government and improve the quality of services, rather than environmental sustainability. Of the more than 250 recommendations the National Performance Review issued in 1993, few included an express reference to the term sustainable development, except those aimed at the EPA and Interior Department. Of the eleven re- commendations aimed at the EPA, eight appeared to have some impact on sustainability through improving agency policy-making, and three were aimed at internal management reform.

Two years after issuing its initial report and recommendations, the National Performance Review reported on progress in implementing its recommendations. It reported that the EPA had, by September 1995, implemented about 40 per cent of the recommendations, including a shift in emphasis from pollution control to prevention, and had also developed an agency action plan to encourage innovative technologies and develop partnerships to re-engineer common products and processes for pollution prevention. The Interior Department had successfully revamped the Bureau of Reclamation's mission and had proposed mining and national parks legislation (National Performance Review 1995: 98, 101–2). In 1995, 170 new recommendations were issued, including seven new recommendations for the EPA that primarily gave more power to states to intervene in Superfund clean-up decisions and to spend federal grants on state priorities rather than federal categoric mandates. One recommendation suggested the EPA create a US$60 million/year Sustainable Development Challenge Grant programme. Fourteen new recommendations were directed at the Interior Department, but those were largely administrative changes (ibid. 122–3, 129–30). The Energy Department recommendations included termination of the Clean Coal Technology Programme when ongoing projects were completed. The Transportation Department was to create a Unified Transportation Infrastructure Improvement Programme for highway, transit, rail, and airport projects (ibid. 122, 136).

International Policy

The final Task Force on International Leadership worked with councils from other nations and the UN Commission on Sustainable Development and other international bodies. It issued a number of recommendations to the federal government to encourage it to conduct research on global environmental trends, take the lead in implementing international treaties, increase support to institutions involved in sustainable development, protect domestic laws and regulations from being weakened by international trade accords, and facilitate export of products that are environmentally sustainable (National Performance Review 1995: 37–8).

For United States foreign policy, the goal of sustainable development is largely subservient to other global concerns such as economic growth and free trade. At Rio, the United States and other industrialized nations reaffirmed their commitment to contribute 0.7 per cent of their GDP to overseas development assistance as part of the funding proposed to implement Agenda 21. Like many other wealthy nations, the United States has fallen well short of that goal, contributing less than 0.2 per cent of its GDP to development assistance (Keating 1993: 52). There has been some shift in international assistance policy, however, that somewhat parallels the idea of sustainable development. Much of the spending for development during the past 40 years was driven by national security, Cold War concerns, rather than the needs of the recipient nations. Development programmes often emphasized large-scale, politically visible projects that imposed Western technologies, caused environmental damage, and were not viable in the long-term (Rich 1994; Bandow and Vasquez 1994). The US Agency for International Development (USAID) and many other national and international development agencies have begun to embrace an alternative view of development that is rooted in environmental preservation and sustainability. The USAID, for example, regularly uses the term sustainable development in its reports on activities and projects. Its primary objectives are 'achieving both sustainable development and advancing US foreign policy objectives' through six programmes: economic growth and agricultural development; population, health, and nutrition; environment; democracy and governance; education and training; and humanitarian assistance (USAID 1999).

The PCSD also established, in addition to the three broad Task Forces described above, three interagency working groups to ensure the implementation of sustainable development goals with the federal government: Education for Sustainability, Materials and Energy Flow, and Sustainable Development Indicators. The Education group is working on plans for regional and national business forums for sustainable development to help educate businesses and communities and develop new curricula in professional schools, and for a National Sustainable Development Extension Network that would build on existing federal extension services to assist communities, regions, and states in devising sustainable development programmes. The Materials and Energy Flows group seeks to identify and disseminate information on successful efforts to improve efficiency, reduce emissions, and increase recycling. The Sustainable Development Indicators group plans to devise a framework for indicators of sustainable development that will include three elements: endowments or assets and capacities such as natural resources, factories and infrastructure, and educational and legal systems; processes such as driving forces that increase productivity or deplete resources faster than they are replenished and the decisions that are made in response to the indicators themselves; and the goods and services that are produced (PCSD 1997a: 42–9).

In April 1997 the Council's charter was renewed through February 1999, to focus on four tasks: 'continue to forge consensus on policy, demonstrate implementation of policy, conduct outreach and constituency building, and evaluate and report on progress toward sustainable development.' These tasks included identifying and developing innovative policies and strategies in pursuit of sustainable development, publicizing successful projects, gathering and disseminating information on sustainable development, and identifying and reporting on indicators of progress (PCSD 1997b). The Council organized four new Task Forces: a Climate Task Force, to prepare policy options for reducing greenhouse-gas emissions; an Environmental Management Task Force, to explore options for improving the management of environmental programmes; the International Task Force, to propose ways to establish US global leadership in sustainable development; and the Metropolitan and Rural Strategies Task Force, to encourage co-operation in sustainable development efforts across political jurisdictions (PCSD 1997c).

PCSD officials have recognized that they have yet to foster a major commitment in the United States to the idea of sustainable development. The Commission sponsored a national summit in Detroit in May 1999. The purpose of the summit was to 'serve as a launching point to spark a national dialogue on sustainable development', recognizing that such a dialogue had not yet begun. Sustainable development was characterized as a way to 'demonstrate that environmental protection and economic progress really do go hand in hand', but the projects to be encouraged were primarily economic development ones, designed with increased sensitivity to environmental quality. The summit was characterized as a chance to 'showcase examples of successful initiatives that have brought together communities, businesses, all levels of government, and non-profit organizations across the country to implement sustainable development locally'; the summit was in Detroit, Michigan, in order to highlight the city's Roundtable on Sustainable Development that sought to 'redevelop brownfields and revitalize downtown by bringing business back to the inner city'. The mayor of Detroit highlighted the modest goals underlying urban redevelopment and the summit: 'the challenges faced by all Americans to continue to make progress economically without continuing to degrade our environment or increase the number of poor people are tremendous.' However, there is no discussion here of reorienting economic growth in ways that solve environmental and human problems, but only a promise to try and not make things worse (PCSD 1998). While it is too early to assess most of the initiatives of the Commission, it has clearly opted for voluntary, incremental efforts aimed at pursuing a modest vision of sustainable development.

Sectoral Responses

One factor that may account for the lack of progress in sustainable development in the United States may be that the 1992 UNCED conference mandate for sustainability was not articulated as an international agreement, but, rather, as part of the broad suggestions included in Agenda 21. The two conventions announced at UNCED, the climate change and biodiversity agreements, provide an alternative means of assessing national implementation of the idea of sustainable development, because those two accords focus on issues that are central to accomplishing the broad goals of sustainability.

Climate Change

President George Bush signed the United Nations Framework Convention on Climate Change (FCCC) at the Rio Earth Summit. The US Senate gave its advise and consent to the convention in May 1992, committing the nation to the non-binding target of limiting greenhouse-gas emissions by the year 2000 to 1990 levels. The Framework Convention obligates each country to publish an action plan, including an inventory of greenhouse-gas emissions and sinks and a 'general description of steps taken or envisaged by the Party to implement the Convention' (FCCC article 12, section 1 a–b). In October 1993, the Clinton administration released its Climate Change Action Plan, as required by the convention (United States of America 1992). The plan promised to reduce levels of greenhouse-gas emissions in the year 2000 to 1990 levels, about 1.5 billion tons, a reduction of some 110 million tons from 1993 emissions. The Climate Change Action Plan became the basis for the National Action Plan the United States submitted in 1994 to the secretariat of the FCCC.

Under the plan, US emissions for 2000 were to be about 100 million tons lower than if no plan were implemented. The plan called for a gradual shift from coal and oil to natural gas, and, since energy consumption is growing fastest in transportation and industrial uses, the plan proposed a modest effort at conservation of energy across the major sectors, with a smaller reduction in transportation than in other areas (US Department of Energy 1994a: 9–10). The plan included nearly fifty new and expanded initiatives: eighteen actions promised to promote energy efficiency among commercial, residential, and industrial users, including demonstration projects for emerging technologies, incentives for industrial equipment efficiency, upgrading energy efficiency standards, and funding for investments in energy efficiency

in government buildings. Four programmes would reduce energy consumption in transportation by reforming tax expenditures for employer-
provided parking, promoting telecommuting, reducing motor vehicles miles
travelled, and developing fuel economy labels for tyres. Nine programmes
were aimed at increasing the supply of energy, promoting use of cleaner
fuels, developing new technologies, and increasing the efficiency of energy
production. Eight initiatives would reduce methane production or increase
its recovery, primarily through research and development programmes and
regulation of landfills, coal mining, and livestock production. Four programmes promised to reduce use of CFCs, HCFCs, nitrogen oxide, and
other emissions from industries and fertilizer use. Four efforts called for
accelerated tree-planting and reduced loss of forests. Several policies were
aimed at increasing the use of natural gas through promoting the commer-
cialization of high-efficiency gas technologies and other policies sought to
improve the efficiency of hydroelectric generation at existing dams (US
Department of Energy 1994*b*: 37–70).

The US adopted the Berlin Mandate in March 1995, at the First Conference
of the Parties (COP-1), an agreement that structured future negotiations and
provided that developing countries would not be required to make binding
greenhouse-gas reduction commitments (Flavin 1995). The release of the
Intergovernmental Panel on Climate Change's Second Assessment Report, in
December 1995, prompted US officials to accept the idea of new, binding
commitments to reduce the threat of global climate change. Many scientists
had believed that there would be no definitive links found between human
activity and climate change until the twenty-first century, but the 1995 report,
involving some 2,500 scientists worldwide, concluded that the 'balance of
evidence suggests a discernible human influence on global climate' (Intergovernmental Panel on Climate Change 1996: 4–5). The US rejected as too
ambitious the proposal from the small island states to reduce greenhouse-gas
emissions by twenty per cent by the year 2005, but also conceded that voluntary commitments to reduce emissions were not working (Associated Press
1996: A5). In July, 1996, at the Geneva Climate Summit, the United States
announced a shift in policy and committed itself to negotiating legally
binding targets and timetables for reducing greenhouse-gas emissions in the
more developed world (Environmental Defence Fund 1996).

The Clinton Administration's Climate Change Action Plan was primarily
a set of voluntary actions the federal government suggested industries, commercial establishments, energy companies, and consumers take. However,
by 1994, carbon-dioxide emissions in the US exceeded the levels to be
achieved by 2000, and in that year Congress only approved half the funds
requested to comply with the convention (Flavin 1995). Within a few years

of issuing the plan, the Clinton administration acknowledged that the goal of reducing greenhouse-gas emissions to 1990 levels by the year 2000 would not be met. In late 1997, the US Department of Energy reported that emissions in 1996 were 7.4 per cent above 1990 levels, and the administration forecast that emissions would be 13 per cent higher in 2000 from 1990 levels. Strong economic growth, unusually severe weather, increased coal-use by electric utilities, growing popularity of less-efficient sport utility vehicles and light trucks all combined to increase carbon emissions. Energy efficiency actually declined by one measure in 1996, when energy use increased by 3.2 per cent while the economy only grew by 2.4 per cent (Cushman 1997a: 14).

Critics of the administration's 1993 plan argued that its refusal to pursue mandatory measures such as higher fuel efficiency standards or increased taxes doomed the plan from the outset. But congressional reductions in spending for energy conservation, Congress's opposition to new energy efficiency standards for household appliances, the failure of the Energy Department to issue new standards for electricity transformers on power lines, and lower than anticipated energy prices also contributed to the failure of the plan. Tax provisions for employer-provided parking were not revised by Congress, and new tree planting goals were not met. While 70 per cent of the projected reductions in emissions were achieved, those savings were simply overwhelmed by economic growth and the increased use of energy. The greatest progress in slowing the growth of emissions (but not actually decreasing them) occurred in the utility industry, mainly through shifts in fuel from coal to natural gas, that were likely to have occurred without a climate change plan, and through increased reliance on nuclear power. Only 7 per cent of the reductions in emissions came from investments in renewable energy. One of the most glaring shortcomings of the plan was its failure to offer any significant programme to reduce emissions from transportation sources, which are responsible for about one-third of emissions. Despite the overall failure of the plan to achieve its goals, the experience in voluntary efforts was not really ineffective; it was simply not balanced with some mandatory measures and more powerful incentives. In an area where traditional regulatory power was used, the EPA's regulation of methane releases from landfills produced 60 per cent more reductions than anticipated (Cushman 1997b: A9).

The United States Congress joined the debate in July 1997 when the Senate unanimously passed a resolution (Senate Resolution 98) aimed at ensuring that the US and other developed countries would not sign a climate change agreement that did not impose on developing countries at least some (if not a similar) commitment to reduce greenhouse-gas emissions (US Congress 1997). The resolution specified two key conditions the Senate expected to see in any climate treaty: it 'should include commitments for countries with developing economies (termed non-Annex I countries under the existing UN Framework Convention), and should not result in serious harm to the economy of the United States'. The resolution also requires the President to include in any submission to the Senate of a climate change agreement two documents: (1) a detailed explanation of legislation or regulations that would be required to implement the agreement; and (2) a detailed analysis of the financial and economic costs to the United States incurred by implementing the agreement submitted to the Senate. Senate Resolution 98 also included an unusual oversight provision, recommending that a bipartisan group of Senators be appointed 'to monitor the status of negotiations on climate change and report periodically to the Senate'.

In October 1997, during the preparations for the Kyoto meeting the Clinton administration announced it would support a requirement that developed countries commit to reduce greenhouse-gas emissions to 1990 levels between the years 2008 and 2012, and reduce emissions to an unspecified amount below those levels by 2017. The administration also stated that it would not 'assume binding obligations unless key developing nations meaningfully participate in this effort,' but offered no precise explanation of what that implied. Other industrialized countries have pushed for more ambitious reductions: Japan proposed a 5 per cent reduction below 1990 levels by 2012, and the European Union proposed a 15 per cent reduction (Franz 1997). In October 1997, the Clinton administration also issued another plan to combat climate change. It called for a five-year, US$5 billion programme of tax incentives and research and development aimed at reducing CO_2 emissions by the year 2008 to 1990 levels, and reduce emissions below that level in the future. The plan would eventually initiate an emissions trading scheme for greenhouse gases that would cut emissions by 30 per cent from projected levels in 2008. Sources that moved early to reduce emissions would get credits that they could use later when pollution permits are issued. The trading system would eventually expand internationally, so that US companies could buy and sell the allowances given them to emit greenhouse gases and encourage the most cost-effective ways of reducing emissions. Some industry officials welcomed the proposal because of its incentives for early reductions in emissions, while others warned that greenhouse-gas reduction efforts would be costly and disruptive to the economy (Fialka and Calmes 1997: 2). In order to achieve the plan's goal, the US will need to reduce emissions by an average of about 1 per cent a year for the next decade (Cushman 1997c: A1). The administration also announced that it would not accept binding reduction commitments unless the developing countries also agreed to take such actions. For the first time, the Clinton administration accepted the idea of binding targets for greenhouse-gas emissions, as long as countries have flexibility in implementing agreements, including the creation of an emissions budget that would allow participating nations to trade emissions in order to meet targets, and bank emissions for future years.

Strong lobbying by environmental groups and the intervention of Vice-President Gore resulted in the shift in policy, and the US agreed to reduce greenhouse-gas emissions by 7 per cent in the Kyoto Protocol it signed in December 1997 (Stevens 1997: A10). However, immediate prospects in the United States for ratification of this Protocol seem bleak because of the failure to gain binding commitments from the developing countries to reduce their emissions. Industry representatives charge that this failure will unfairly advantage developing country industries in global markets. In March 1998, the Clinton administration released its budget for the Climate Change Technology Initiative, which included US$2.7 billion for increased research and development spending and US$3.6 billion in tax credits to encourage energy efficiency. It also estimated that the cost of implementing the Kyoto agreement would be from US$7–12 billion a year between 2008 and 2012, in contrast to an industry estimate that the cost would be about US$50 billion a year. The Senate Budget Committee's FY 1999 budget resolution included no money for the climate change initiative, as Republican leaders promised to block any new spending on climate change until the treaty is submitted to the Senate; the House 1999 appropriations bill for the EPA and other agencies included a ban on spending for any effort to implement the Kyoto agreement, including meetings aimed at educating the public on climate change issues (Cohen 1998).

Members of Congress repeated their attacks on the Kyoto Protocol in late 1998. When the Clinton administration appeared to be ready to sign the agreement, a number of members of Congress quickly warned against it. Senate Foreign Relations chair Jesse Helms (Republican, North Carolina) wrote to the Secretary of State that the Protocol should not be signed, but if the administration did so, it should 'quickly submit the treaty for Senate advice and consent so that the Senate may reject [it] and scrap the Kyoto Protocol process altogether'. Opposition was bipartisan: Representative Ron Klink (Democrat, Pennsylvania) warned that the treaty 'would be the first major step toward the deindustrialization of this country' (Greenwire 1998a). When the administration announced it would indeed sign the Protocol, critics swiftly responded: 'It appears the President and Vice-President want to shove this protocol down the throats of the American people,' complained Sen. Larry Craig (Republican, Idaho) (Greenwire 1998b). Despite the weakened position of the Clinton administration resulting from the President's impeachment, the administration was surprisingly successful in warding off many of the more extreme congressional attacks aimed at its support for the Kyoto agreement, but was still sufficiently wounded that it could not provide much leadership on the issue even if it decided to do so. The treaty is unlikely to be submitted to the Senate for ratification until at least 2001, and that jeopardizes the entire ratification effort, since at least fifty-five countries, representing at least 55 per cent of total greenhouse-gas emissions, must ratify before the treaty takes effect. The only action Congress considered in 1999 and 2000 was legislation that would encourage companies to make reductions in greenhouse-gas emissions by giving them credit for those reductions in the event that an emissions trading programme for the gases is eventually created.

Biodiversity

The United States initially favoured a global convention on biodiversity as a way to bring the various global accords under one umbrella and to make international law more consistent with its own approach to protecting endangered species. But as negotiations proceeded and the agenda was broadened to include access to and control over genetic resources, US industries mobilized to challenge the idea of a global accord as a threat to American interests. The Framework Convention on Biodiversity, signed at the 1992 UNCED conference, engendered a great deal of controversy in the United States. The most controversial proposal dealt with the rights of states to control their own natural resources and their development by external powers. The United States has signed but the Senate has not ratified the treaty because of opposition by industry to the obligations it would impose on US industries.

The United States has a long history of policies aimed at preserving some forms of biodiversity. Until 1900, wildlife conservation was a state responsibility. Then Congress passed the Lacey Act, which prohibited interstate commerce of wildlife products that had been banned by states. In 1966 Congress responded to concerns raised in the Interior Department that native invertebrates were in danger of extinction by enacting the first federal endangered species law. The law suffered from a number of shortcomings: it only included native vertebrates, species were to be preserved only when it was considered 'practicable and consistent' with the 'primary purposes of the federal agencies;' wildlife refuge areas were narrowly defined; and Congress provided inadequate funding. Congress amended the law in 1969 by requiring invertebrates to be protected, but still required the protected species to be 'threatened with world-wide extinction', and made other changes in 1973.

The purpose of the Endangered Species Act is to protect species of fish, wildlife, and plants that are of aesthetic, ecological, educational, historical, recreational, and scientific value; and to ensure the US meets relevant international conservation commitments. Endangered species are defined as those in 'danger of extinction throughout all or a significant portion of its range'; threatened species are 'likely to become an endangered species within the foreseeable future throughout all or a significant portion of its range'. Interior and Commerce Department agencies are to determine which species should be listed; individuals may petition the agencies to have species designated. The Fish and Wildlife Service, in the Interior Department, deals with land species; the National Marine Fisheries Service, located in the Commerce department, has jurisdiction over marine species. Any 'interested person' may petition the Interior Secretary to list a species as either endangered or threatened. The 1978 amendments to the ESA created a Cabinet-level committee to resolve conflicts between species protection and federal projects—labelled the 'God Squad' or the 'Extinction Committee' (16 USC. 1536). The committee can authorize projects to proceed even if they jeopardize the continued existence of a species if five of seven members decide that protection interferes with 'human' needs. The specific criteria to be used in exempting actions from the act include: (1) there are no reasonable or prudent alternatives to the agency action; (2) the benefits of the agency action clearly outweigh the benefits of alternative courses of action which would preserve the critical habitat of the species; (3) the action is in the public interest and of regional or national significance; (4) neither the agency nor the exemption applicant has made irreversible or irretrievable commitments of resources; and (5) the agency establishes reasonable mitigation and enhancement measures, including habitat acquisition and improvement, to minimize the adverse effects of the action on the species' critical habitat.

In March 1993, Interior Department Secretary Bruce Babbitt launched the National Biological Survey, an attempt to map the animal and plant species in the country and 'produce a constantly evolving, computerized picture of the nation's biological diversity that adjusts to changes in land use, to ecological changes, and which must with the passage of time become more sophisticated and more detailed as knowledge of species and ecosystems grows'. When the Republicans gained control of Congress in the 1994 election, amending the Endangered Species Act was their top environmental policy goal. House leaders established an Endangered Species Task Force which held hearings throughout May 1995, and led to a bill which sought to eliminate species recovery as the primary goal of the act, give more opportunities for states and landowners to be involved in decisions related to endangered species, create biodiversity reserves, give more leeway to landowners, and reimburse private property owners for loss in land value resulting from endangered species regulation (104th Congress). The House Resources Committee approved the bill in October, but the House leadership subsequently refused to bring the bill to the floor for a vote in light of public perception that Republicans were attacking the environment. Senate proponents of a new Endangered Species Act worked throughout 1997 and 1998 to try and craft a bipartisan bill that would give more protection to critical habitats, create incentives for private landowners to protect endangered species, and provide more certainty in the law for developers and land owners, but Congress adjourned in 1998 without reauthorizing or amending the law, and as of the summer of 2000, has still not done so.

Assessing the US Commitment to Sustainable Development

The Council on Sustainable Development's agenda is a strong statement of the interrelatedness of economic, social, educational, and environmental issues. Sustainable development reaffirms the notion that everything is connected to everything else. Environmental regulations can be more cheaply achieved through pollution prevention and other incentives to change the way industries operate. Consensus-building groups and planning efforts are more likely to lead to technological innovations and natural-resource preservation than is litigation. It may have some impact on the development of new collaborative regulatory and planning approaches, the encouragement of voluntary efforts to reduce emissions and resource use, and the formulation of innovative policies. But it is not clear how the main report (and the reports of the Task Forces) will reshape industry and government policymaking. The report lacks a sense of strategic purpose, of identifying opportunities, key players, and timing, and specifying policies to pursue. There is little evidence that voluntarism is sufficient to produce the kinds of changes needed to ensure sustainable development. Specific policies that could have a major impact on environmental quality and on technological innovation, and are also relatively simple and administratively manageable, such as ending subsidies on harvesting natural resources or taxing energy, are not proposed. It is hard to imagine a policy that would be simpler and more likely to move the US toward sustainability than a major energy-tax increase such as a US$0.50 or $1.00/gallon tax hike, but there is little discussion of such an initiative, given the Clinton administration's ill-fated proposal in 1993 to raise energy taxes that collapsed in controversy. Collaborative and consensus-building efforts can take a great deal of time and may never produce agreements; pollution taxes, in contrast, are simple schemes that create clear incentives to make technological progress (US Congress Office of Technology Assessment 1995). Other studies have identified specific subsidies and tax expenditures that are environmentally damaging and should be eliminated, but it has been very difficult to challenge the political power of those who benefit from these policies (Roodman 1997).

The Council could also do more to make the case for US involvement in formulating and implementing global environmental accords. It is not at all clear that more US leadership is needed; perhaps it is more a problem of a lack of US support for and willingness to follow the proposals made by others to address critical concerns. The US failure to adopt the Convention on Biodoversity, the role of the US in producing a relatively weak and nonbinding climate change accord in 1992 (and the unlikelihood that the US Senate would ratify the 1997 Kyoto climate change agreement), and other actions have placed the US behind other industrialized nations. The US, at least as reflected by its lack of commitment to sustainable development, does not seem to see itself as part of the global community. It is, of course, not alone in such an isolationist posture, but its importance to a sustainable future for future generations is critical (Dernbach 1997: 10506). There is little discussion of the moral obligation the US has, as the major consumer of resources and producer of pollution, to reduce its contributions to global risks that threaten others who are much less responsible for them. The tremendous mismatch between the US contribution to greenhouse-gas emissions and the impact climate change is likely to have on developing countries who lack the resources to protect themselves against the consequences is a profound moral problem facing the United States. But there are also arguments to be made concerning the long-term self-interest of the US in a climate that is more stable, a developing world that produces more food, and oceans that are more productive (Daly and Cobb 1994).

The Council has also focused primarily on the intersection of economic and environmental issues, and has not taken on some of the broader social-equity issues raised in Agenda 21. One way of summarizing Agenda 21 is to divide its provisions into two categories. The first set of issues include specific environmental and development problems and challenges and actions to be taken. These can be further divided into two areas: improving the quality of life of the poor and fostering sustainable economic growth, and conserving natural resources and reducing pollution and the release of toxic chemicals. The PCSD agenda focuses primarily on the latter, with little effort to draw attention to the interaction of poverty and environmental degradation. The second category of Agenda 21's provisions focuses on increasing the capacity of governments, at all levels, to pursue sustainable development goals. The agreement calls for increasing participation by women in all decision-making forums at all levels; improving health and education for children, particularly girls; empowering indigenous peoples to participate in decisions affecting them; increasing the interaction between NGOs, governments, and international organizations; strengthening the role of public participation in development decisions; giving increased voice to workers and unions; and supporting new venture capital commitments for small businesses. The most ambitious and expensive undertaking is to make urban life more sustainable by helping the poor gain access to housing, land, and credit; increase clean water, waste collection, and sanitation services; develop mass transit, improve energy efficiency, and take other steps to reduce air pollution; reduce poverty through development of the informal economic sector; and improve rural conditions as a way of reducing urban migration (Keating 1993). The Council, in contrast, takes a much less comprehensive approach in defining the problems of sustainability and in suggesting solutions. It recognizes that ecological, economic, and social goals are interrelated. But it does not take on the hard questions of the impact of free trade on developing countries' social and environmental problems or the overwhelming power of multinational corporations in determining resource-use or the great disparity between the consumption of resources and production of pollution in the developed and the developing worlds.

The Council joins with many others in calling for a stronger, more vigorous civil society and participatory democracy. There is no question but that the kinds of changes required by sustainable development must involve changes in how people consume energy, pursue wealth, and live their lives. Education and public involvement are essential. But its reports are vague on what kinds of participation are most important and how they can be encouraged. Nor is it clear how increased participation in 'sporting leagues' will contribute to sustainable development (PCSD 1997a: 20). What is lacking is more thinking about what kinds of civic engagement build problem-solving capacity and engender support for collective goals. What is needed is more discussion of how civic engagement in local issues and fostering a sense of efficacy in local community efforts can help contribute to a global ethic and international citizenship, where people come to see that their future is inextricably linked with that of others throughout the world (Sandel 1996: 324–51).

Perhaps most problematic is the failure of the Council and other efforts to focus attention on improved environmental policy-making to engage Congress in their deliberations and encourage legislation to implement sustainable development, pollution prevention, and other goals (Report of the National Commission on the Environment 1993). While it is admirable to encourage industries to voluntarily improve their environmental stewardship, clear incentives, backed by governmental power, are essential. The relationship between Congress and industry in recent years has been strikingly different from the kind of co-operative ventures reflected in the Council's work. In Congress, industries have joined with congressional Republicans to seek regulatory relief—reduce regulatory costs—rather than to try and make regulation work better. Part of the problem may lie in the role of trade associations, lobbyists, and lawyers who have an economic incentive to exaggerate regulatory costs and delay regulations through litigation rather than to solve problems and find innovative solutions. Congress has lost most of its environmental regulatory battles with the Clinton administration as members have tried to cut back on regulations rather than explore the kinds of innovations that the Council and others have been discussing for years. Until Congress and its lobbyists and campaign contributors join the discussion over sustainable development, the US is not likely to make progress in national policy-making.

In contrast to the lack of interest in sustainability in Congress, there is growing interest at the local, state, and regional level in sustainable communities that is at the heart of the real debate over sustainability in the United States. Communities throughout the United States, for example, have devised innovative, collaborative means of reducing the use of agricultural pesticides, protecting watersheds, and conserving energy, that have created a great deal of experience and interest in how communities can become more sustainable (John 1994). A number of innovative programmes, often described as community-based environmental protection bring community members together to identify local problems and fashion broad, comprehensive solutions that include public health, environmental quality, and economic development (US EPA 1996a). Proponents of environmental planning, urban ecology, management of growth, bioregionalism, appropriate technology, and a number of other efforts are all contributing to the wellsprings of a vibrant, dynamic commitment to sustainability that is having a major impact in some communities and is likely to expand in the future. There is a growing literature that describes with optimism and enthusiasm the interest in sustainable communities, metropolitanism, regionalism, and other collaborative planning efforts that are aimed toward the goal of sustainability (See, for example, Milbraith 1991; Pirages 1996). Innovative industries are finding ways to contribute to the idea of sustainability, through changes in production and marketing that help conserve resources and reduce waste and pollution and also save money (Hawken 1993). Solutions to urban sprawl, including preserving undeveloped lands, creating parks, promoting 'smart growth,' cleaning up abandoned factory sites so that agricultural lands are not used for new construction, setting urban growth boundaries, and other programmes aimed at enhancing quality of life have become key elements of the idea of sustainability in communities throughout the United States (Kriz 1999).

Despite the energy and enthusiasm for sustainable communities, Congress remained determined, as the twentieth century closed, to resist the idea of sustainable development. Its recalcitrance is a puzzle, given the leadership the United States has played in environmental policy. Several theories of policy-making help explain congressional recalcitrance in facing head-on the global debate over sustainable development and related issues such as climate change. The other chapters in this book provide an opportunity to examine how important these kinds of institutional differences are for explaining national commitments to sustainable development.

First, as many scholars have argued, the separation of powers and the division of authority between the President and Congress for making foreign policy commitments, giving advice and consent, enacting implementing legislation, and establishing regulatory programmes poses tremendous barriers to effective policy making. The division of power between the President, who negotiates international treaties and accords, and the Congress, who must pass legislation to implement them, is a recipe for deadlock. The President, and the United States as a whole, cannot assume effective leadership in global environmental issues as long as Congress remains at home, willing to block commitment-making in response to narrow interests and constituencies (Thurber 1991; Sundquist 1992). Presidents must make policy in a kind of two-level chess game, where they must interact with Congress at one level, and with other nations at another, and that poses challenges for any administration, even a politically adept and popular one. Presidents and members of Congress represent different kinds of constituencies, and the broad, national scope of presidential elections aggregates national interests much differently than the decentralized system of congressional representation that gives great deference to those representing local interests. Congress and the White House remain distrustful of each other and largely unable to move forward in dealing with new environmental problems and concerns. That distrust has roots in the 1980s and the Reagan administration's assault on environmental laws and the conflicts between the two branches over what kind of environmental policy should be pursued (National Academy of Public Administration 1987; 1995).

The Clinton administration may have been so weakened by scandal and impeachment that nothing more from it should be expected. But it has been rather successful in achieving many of its economic policy goals, such as increased spending for education, and has received much of the credit for a robust economy in the late 1990s. In contrast, the administration has been willing to use little of its political popularity to make the case for sustainable development. It has capitalized on the national preoccupation with economic indicators and the political importance of protecting economic growth at all costs in ways that have diminished the discussion of competing policy concerns. Conversely, environmental groups in the United States have been less successful than their European counterparts in focusing attention on sustainability. There is no equivalent US effort, for example, to develop a 'Sustainable Europe' plan introduced by the Friends of the Earth. The lesson of the late 1990s is sobering: if the US cannot act in response to a major global environmental goal when its economy is unusually strong, how will it respond when its economy is in a recession?

Second, there is the decentralized and fragmented structure of Congress, and the challenges that poses for addressing issues like environmental policy and sustainability which cut across traditional jurisdictions and sectors. The EPA, for example, is subject to oversight hearings and investigations by dozens of congressional committees, and that places a heavy burden and time constraint on senior administrators as well as subjecting the agency to conflicting demands and instructions. Congress as an institution has not kept up with changes in technologies, environmental problems, and policy options, and its policy efforts are mired in political gridlock. The fragmentation of Congress is also manifest in environmental laws that are poorly integrated, that often result in pollution being transferred from one medium to another, rather than pollution prevention efforts that are, in the long run, more efficient and less costly (Davies and Mazurek 1998). Members of Congress are so jealous of their committee jurisdictions and so anxious to expand the number of subcommittee chairs and staffs available to members, that the institution regularly becomes bogged down in duplicative and conflicting legislative efforts (Kraft 1997). This fragmentation poses major problems in regulating effectively problems like air and water pollution, and the problems are orders of magnitude worse when Congress tries to deal with issues that cut across so many economic sectors and is affected by the vast scope of economic, commercial, and personal activity.

The third and most important explanation of the congressional response to sustainable development is rooted in the ideological differences among members of Congress that have shaped the debate over environmental and other policies, and that are part of broader debates over the role of government in regulating industry and individual behaviour. Sustainable development and climate change are part of the next generation of environmental challenges facing the United States and the world; yet while others are debating what kinds of actions are needed in designing a new generation of policies to promote sustainability, Congress is still mired in the debate over whether there should be more or less environmental regulation. The deadlock over how to amend existing environmental laws has diverted efforts that might have been directed towards designing the next generation of laws aimed at sustainability.

The conflict and uncertainty surrounding environmental law has weakened US leadership in global environmental issues. That weakness in US leadership is evident not just in climate change, as described above, but in the broader agenda of sustainable development. The US has fallen behind other nations in implementing Agenda 21 and the other commitments made in the 1992 Earth Summit to make the transition to sustainable economies. There is a remarkable level of hostility in Congress to the idea of international organizations and to global commitments, as evidenced by continual criticism of the United Nations in Congress and its unwillingness to fund the United States' financial obligations. Congress is the critical barrier to sustainable development in the United States and it would have to join the executive branch in taking sustainable development more seriously before major progress could be made. Congress's fragmented and decentralized structure and the access and influence industry enjoys, makes it a conservative, cautious institution, one ill-suited for taking the initiative to reconceptualize problems and integrate policies. Executive branch agencies and leaders are structurally better able to devise national strategies and co-ordinated efforts. But they need to be nudged forward by public opinion to take on the kind of rethinking required by sustainable development.

That is the paradox in which the United States finds itself in the beginning of the twenty-first century: sustainable development requires a comprehensive policy response, but its political system is so divided by federalism, the separation of powers, and other institutional devices, that coherent policy efforts seem impossible in the absence of a national crisis. A strong commitment to future generations and to the well-being of the global community must arise from a people and a political culture who see their future, and the future of their grandchildren, inextricably intertwined with those of their neighbours throughout the world. The way in which problems are defined is a critical step in the policy process. As long as sustainability is largely viewed as a problem for developing countries to solve, and is not understood as a challenge facing the United States and other high-consumption societies, little progress is likely. But the growing interest in sustainable communities may eventually contribute to the development of a national commitment to sustainability. If such a commitment springs from its people, the nation's policy-making institutions will find ways to devise effective, sustainable, economic, environmental, and social policies. There is no danger in the United States in dampening the commitment to development; the challenge is generating for the idea of sustainability the kind of power that other moral imperatives, such as freedom and equality, play in shaping public policy and personal behaviour.

11

The European Union: Integration, Competition, Growth—and Sustainability

SUSAN BAKER

This chapter examines the engagement of the European Union (EU)[1] with sustainable development. Its focuses on the EU's involvement in the processes set in motion following the Brundtland Report, including the Rio Earth Summit and the regulatory, reporting, and monitoring regimes established as a result of UNCED.

Complexities Shaping the Promotion of Sustainable Development by the EU

EU environmental policy has to provide an effective and common response to the diverse range of environmental challenges that arise across its fifteen member-states, with their varying climatic, topographical, and geological features, as well as differences in population density, degree of urbanization, and economic development. It also has to take account of, and complement, the separate responses of member-states to their own environmental problems, while guarding against member-state use of environmental regulations and standards as trade barriers—a use which has the potential to hinder the development of the Single European Market (SEM) and thus the overall European integration process. Despite more than two decades of common

---

[1] For the sake of simplicity, I use the term 'European Union' throughout this text. Since the Maastricht Treaty, the terminology which applies to the European Union/ European Community has become very complicated (See Nugent 1995: ch. 3), a complication I wish to avoid in this chapter. I have made the decision to use the term when referring to activities generated under 'Pillar One' of the Maastrict Treaty in cases where discussion involves consideration of the larger EU role as an international actors, even though technically speaking the term 'European Community' may be more correct here.

EU environmental policy, however, recent reports indicate a steady but inexorable deterioration of Europe's environment (EEA (European Environment Agency) 1995*a*, 1999).

While it faces considerable problems in making an effective response to its own environmental deterioration, the EU has nevertheless developed an important leadership role in global environmental politics and is an active participant in numerous international environmental regulatory regimes. To understand this role, and the limitations placed upon it, account must be taken of a number of features that arise as a result of the complex legal and political structures that have evolved within the EU. These features relate to (1) the capacity to act internationally; (2) the complex policy-making process; (3) the existence of different levels of socio-economic development across the Union; and (4) historical commitments to other policy priorities.

The Capacity to Act Internationally

The European integration process has resulted in a gradual shift from decision-making at the national, member-state, level, to collective decision-making at the Union level. Yet, while policies are increasingly adopted in common, member-states continue to retain their sovereignty, and intergovernmental decision-making prevails in many policy areas. This dichotomous character has led to the argument that the EU is a 'multi-level governance structure' (Marks *et al.* 1996), wherein different degrees of integration and levels of member-state intrusiveness coexist across various issue areas (Rhodes 1998: 2). Consequently, the EU cannot be characterized as either an international organization, or as a sovereign actor in its own right. Attempts to explain the EU's behaviour as an international actor must take this hybrid character into account (Rhodes 1998: 2).

The Community gained competence to act in international environmental arenas by both indirect and direct means. Indirect means include when areas of expressed competence have evolved to include an environmental component, such as aid and trade-related environmental measures. Direct means are from the series of Court of Justice rulings in the 1970s, as well as the Single European Act, which gave the Community express authority to conclude environmental agreements with third countries. Furthermore, following the Treaty on European Union (the 1993 Maastricht Treaty) the Community is able to make binding international agreements. In relation to environmental matters, the Treaty enables the EU to contribute to the pursuit of its environmental objectives by promoting measures at the international level to deal with regional or worldwide environmental problems.

However, while the Community has an explicit role on the international stage, member-states can act concurrently, and independently, in the international environmental arena (although the Commission,[2] on the grounds of incompatibility with international obligations, may refuse to authorize their actions). As a result of this multilevel engagement—with both Community and member-state involvement in international environmental management regimes—there is much ambiguity regarding the division of labour between the Community on the one hand, and the member-states, on the other. In practice, precise competencies and roles are often only decided as negotiations get under way. Such ad hoc procedures owe much to member-state reluctance to surrender competence in international affairs to the EU. The result is that the balance of power between member-states and the Union is in a constant state of flux, with a definite shift towards Brussels for a range of policy areas, and a sporadic reassertion of national sovereignty in others (Rhodes 1998: 5).

Institutional and Policy-Making Structures

EU policy is always an outcome of complex bargaining and shifting alliances among the member-states and between them and EU institutions. Differences can also emerge within institutions and in particular within the Com-

---

[2] The Commission of the European Communities, otherwise known as the Commission, is the main administrative organ of the EU. It is expected to rise above national interests and to represent and promote the general interests of the EU. It is the EU's principal policy initiator and carries certain responsibilities for policy implementation. Its key task is to ensure that EU policy accords with the Community's treaties and that, in turn, the principles of the treaties are turned into practical laws and policies. The Commission also acts as the EU's main external representation in dealings with international organization such as the United Nations. The Commission is divided into numerous directorates-general (DGs), which are the functional equivalent of national government ministries. The Commission is led by a group of Commissioners who jointly function as something like a European cabinet, headed by a President.

The European Council is the most powerful of the EU institutions, and is a collective term for the heads of governments of the member states, their foreign ministers and the president and vice-presidents of the Commission. This group meets for short summit meetings and provides strategic policy direction for the EU.

The Council of Ministers plays an important role in decision-making. It is the champion of national interests and consists of national government ministers and its make-up changes according to the topic under discussion.

The European Parliament (EP) is the only directly elected institution of the EU. Through treaty amendments it has gained some say over how Community laws and policies are made.

The Court of Justice rules on interpretations of the treaties and EU laws and ensures that national and European laws and international argreements meet the terms and spirit of the treaties. For further information see J. McCormick, Understanding the European Union: A Concise Introduction (Basingstoke, Macmillan 1999).

mission, which is composed of numerous Directorates General (DGs). The Commission as the highest administrative organ of the EU, acts to represent the supranational element of the Union and has the power to initiate policy. Commissioners are appointed to head the DGs, that is, the separate policy areas into which the Commission is divided, with one Commissioner being appointed as President. The Commission stands in contrast to the European Council and the Council of Ministers, which are the main decision-making authorities of the EU, representing the heads of state and government, and the national government ministers respectively.

Interest groups, especially those representing industry, also play a role in shaping EU policy through the influence they exercise on the negotiating position of member-states, the Commission, and on individual Commissioners. These complexities have their impact on environmental policy. The environmental policy-making process has been characterized as unpredictable, particularly at the agenda-setting stage (Mazey and Richardson 1994). This makes it difficult for the Commission, and in particular the Directorate General for the Environment (formally known as DGXI), to ensure that its commitment to sustainable development is maintained over the long-term.

Further, responsibility for the various stages of the policy process is fragmented: the Union plays a major role in policy formulation but has less direct control over the implementation stage, this being the job of the member-states. The task of monitoring is also difficult, as the EU is reliant upon member-states to provide it with information on policy achievements. As we will see below in relation to climate change policy, this information is not always forthcoming.

There is also a democratic deficit within the Union (Baker 1996a). The institutions that are central to the decision-making process are not directly elected by, nor are they accountable to, the citizens of the EU. The EU's democratic deficit diminishes its capacity to engage with the participatory strand of Agenda 21 in particular, but also with the promotion of sustainable development more generally.

Different Levels of Socio-Economic Development and of Commitment to Environmental Protection

The fact that the EU is composed of fifteen member-states is also relevant for our analysis in other ways. Member-states have different levels of economic development and there is a marked problem of regional disparity. This has resulted in different degrees of commitment to the promotion of sustainable development. In particular, the belief that environmental protection is at the expense of economic development is widespread in the less developed regions of the EU (Yearley *et al.* 1994).

However, the problem is not confined to the less-developed regions and some of the more economically developed states show the least commitment to environmental protection and are environmental laggards. In most member-states 'strategic assessments of the impact of policy initiatives on the environment have yet to take root' (CEC (Commission of the European Communities) 1994*a*) and targets and actions in relation to sustainable development are not well defined (European Environment 1996: 3).

Historical Commitment to Other Policy Priorities

Despite the passage of more than twenty-five years since the decision to expand its remit to include environmental policy, the Community still has difficulties reconciling its historical commitment to economic growth with its commitment to environmental protection (Baker 1993). In particular the creation of the SEM makes the promotion of sustainable development difficult. Since the late 1980s the completion of the SEM has been without doubt the overarching policy goal. It shapes policy priorities as well as the allocation of funding and resource across all policy fields. The initial decision to complete the SEM was taken without consideration of its environmental consequences, despite the fact that the completion of the internal market is expected to bring numerous negative environmental impacts. Retrospective attempts to take account of the environmental consequences of the SEM have proved highly unsuccessful (Baker 1997*a*).

The Shift to Sustainable Development

The beginning of the shift of policy focus from general environmental protection measures to the promotion of sustainable development can be dated from the 1988 Rhodes European Council Declaration which stated that sustainable development must be one of the overriding objectives of all Community policies (EC 1988). Commitment to the promotion of sustainable development was subsequently enshrined in the Maastricht Treaty (1993) and was reinforced by the Amsterdam Treaty (1997). In an EU context, such legal competence is important. This is because the Union has to justify its policy engagements in terms of the competencies it has been given under the Treaty of Rome and its subsequent amendments. If an area of policy falls outside the legal competence of the Union, then a great deal of energy can be spent defending such involvement against member-state opposition. The deepening of the commitment to sustainable development must be seen within the context of the commitments that have arisen as a result of EU involvement with the follow-up process set in motion after the Rio Earth Summit, which aims to make sustainable development a guiding principle in international environmental and economic management policies.

Participation in the UNCED Rio Earth Summit

Involvement in the UNCED Earth Summit and its subsequent regulatory, reporting, and monitoring processes has been motivated by the belief that it offers an ideal opportunity for the EU to develop a leadership role in international environmental management. This followed the 1990 European Council stipulation that the Community should 'exploit to the full its moral, economic and political authority' in order to accelerate international efforts to solve global problems, to promote sustainable development and respect for the global commons (EC 1990). There was a belief that the Community's own experience in managing environmental policy across the member-states gives it an edge in this task (CEC 1992a: 132).

Both the European Council and the Commission want to develop this leadership role for a number of reasons. It can confer legitimacy upon the Union, helping it to come of age politically and diplomatically. Further, by enlarging its field of competence, it offers the Commission in particular an opportunity to engage in institution building. But it is also of importance for economic reasons: if sustainable development is to become a norm of global politics then the Union has a vested interest in shaping how that norm is understood in policy terms, especially as the promotion of sustainable development is seen as having the potential to threaten the EU's economic competitiveness.

As the preparations for the 1992 UNCED meeting got underway, it seemed as if the Community might put this leadership role into practice, particularly as the USA did not appear to be giving much priority to environmental issues. But the results were to be disappointing. As the Earth Summit meeting drew nearer it became clear that the European Council was not prepared to play a vigorous role in advancing the negotiations. In the end, declarations of intent were scaled down to comply with political necessities (Johnson and Corcelle 1995: 25).

Despite the adoption of a more pragmatic and less inspirational role at the Rio Earth Summit, both the European Council and the Commission were pleased with the opportunity it provided to realize their leadership ambitions. The Commission sees its participation as having facilitated the

Union in developing a role as broker in the formulation of international environmental agreements, in particular in having served as 'the main interlocutor of the developing country group', so favouring 'the emergence of new alliances between industrialized and developing countries' (CEC 1996*d*: 110).

Satisfaction about its role within the UNCED process has not stopped the Commission expressing some criticisms. It has manifest considerable dissatisfaction with the institutional arrangements, in particular with the UNCSD, put in place after Rio to oversee the implementation of Agenda 21. The Commission has argued for the need to focus the work of the CSD and to ensure more co-ordinated implementation of its recommendations (CEC 1996*a*: 2; CEC 1996*d*). The Commission has also noted concern about the relative weakness of international environmental institutions, calling for another UN General Assembly Special Session (UNGASS) to deal with international sustainable development law.

These criticisms are best seen as part of the Commission's efforts to make the international regulatory and monitoring process put in place after the Rio Earth Summit more effective, rather than as an attempt to undermine either the process itself or the EU's engagement with it. The Commission has reasons for continuing its involvement. These were spelt out prior to the UNGASS held in June 1996 in New York: 'The EU has developed a domestic agenda for sustainable development, which is likely to be pursued irrespective of UNGASS. The main potential of UNGASS for the EU therefore lies in promoting sustainable development globally' (CEC 1996*a*: 1). Again we see how important it is for the Commission to ensure that the promotion of sustainable development is undertaken through multilateral agreements, which—by committing states to act together—pose less of a threat to EU economic competitiveness.

Participation in the UNCED process has conferred legitimacy on the EU as an international actor. However, the EU's ability to fulfil the promises of Rio and to promote sustainable development, both domestically and globally, is limited. Of particular importance is the fact that, relative to other participant states, the EU's status within the UNCED process and in relation to its international agreements and regulatory processes is rather complex. On the one hand, the Community was granted special status within UNCED, continues to enjoy special, full participant status in the CSD, and is a signatory to both the Climate Change and the Biodiversity Conventions. On the other hand, the EU is composed of fifteen member-states, each of which acts independently within UNCED and the CSD. However, while the Community shares competence with its member-states, there is no clear understanding of how the division of competencies between it and the member-states is to work in practice. In principle the EU has the role of ensuring that EU-wide policies reflect the commitments undertaken under UNCED—that is, a *strategic role*. Second, the EU is expected to monitor and evaluate member-states' own efforts to implement those commitments— that is, to play a *monitoring role*. The monitoring role is to ensure the member-states' actions do not hinder EU-wide efforts to promote sustainable development. International agreements and obligations are therefore supposed to lead to the introduction of common policies on the one hand, and to the co-ordination of national policies on the other. In the first case there is to be a transfer of responsibility to the Union. In the second, responsibility is supposed to remain with member-states (CEC 1992*a*: 1–2).

In practice, however, this delineation of responsibility has proven difficult to operationalize. It has been claimed, for example, that during the Preparatory Committee meetings leading up to the Rio Summit, except for areas of 'exclusive competence' such as trade, the Community's authority was rarely clear to anyone, including the Community participants themselves (Jupille and Caporaso 1998: 222). Similar difficulties surround the international environmental agreements reached after Rio. Thus, while the Community has gradually gained competence to act internationally, the manner in which that competence can be expressed in practice remains dependent upon the outcome of continuing negotiations between the EU and its member-states. The Community's capacity to act as a collective entity within UNCED has been constrained by the multi-level engagement of the EU and its member-states, as it has allowed member-states to limit the 'reach' of the EU's influence internationally. Multi-level engagement also makes it difficult to deliver on policy outcomes, as the member-states retain much of the responsibility for the implementation of agreements within their own borders. From an analytical perspective multi-level engagement in UNCED hinders attempts to isolate the Community's contribution from that of its member-states, and to evaluate how far EU action contributes to the promotion of sustainable development.

Strategic Response to the Promotion of Sustainable Development

How Sustainable Development is Understood

There is some linguistic confusion concerning the EU's commitment to the promotion of 'sustainable development'. The European Council has been the source of much of this confusion. To take an example, the 1988 Rhodes

European Council Declaration on the Environment declared that sustainable development must be an overriding aim of policy; it also spoke of the
need to confront environmental problems 'in the interest of sustained
growth' (EC 1988). At a subsequent meeting in Dublin in June 1990, the
European Council's 'The Environmental Imperative' stated that greater
efforts must be made to ensure that growth was sustainable and environmentally sound (EC 1990).

There is also confusion within legal documents. The Maastricht Treaty
speaks about promoting sustainable growth while respecting the environment. The Treaty, however, also refers to promoting economic and social
progress that is sustainable. To further complicate the matter, the Treaty's
section dealing with development co-operation requires Union policy to
foster 'the sustainable economic and social development of the developing
nations'. This appears to mean that the Union applies the concept of sustainable development to the developing countries while applying the more
unusual term 'sustainable growth' to the Union.

Thus we have a rather confusing situation, whereby the Maastricht Treaty
speaks about 'sustainable progress', 'sustainable growth', and 'sustainable
development'. The meaning of these formulations remains unclear. It could
be argued that the multiple terminology is accidental. However, for a
number of reasons this is not an entirely satisfactory answer. First, the Maastricht Treaty was the outcome of complex, protracted and politically sensitive bargaining among member-states. It is unlikely that in such negotiations
vagueness in wording or inconsistency in terminology would pass unnoticed. Second, when the formulation 'sustainable growth' appeared in the
first draft of the Treaty under the Luxembourg Presidency in April 1991
there was some (unsuccessful) pressure to revert to the original term 'sustainable development' (Verhoeve et al. 1992). The variety of terms used is
therefore far from arbitrary.

The use of different terminology is of significance for EU policy. First,
it increases the possibility of inconsistency in how sustainable development
is promoted. Second, it could allow the Union to adopt its old strategy of
economic development based on growth and onto which environmental
considerations can be grafted. However, the future of the developing world
must lie in a more integrated approach based on sustainable development,
which may involve foregoing growth in order to achieve environmental
harmony. This raises the worrying spectacle that the Maastricht Treaty
enshrines double standards with respect to operationalizing the Brundtland
and Rio imperatives. Third, it gives rise to uncertainty with respect to policy
objectives. Sustainable growth as a policy goal would seem to uncouple
environmental management from the more radical social, economic, and

political changes envisaged by the Brundtland Report and the UNCED process.

Recent amendments to the Treaty of Rome agreed under the Treaty of Amsterdam re-establish a commitment to sustainable development, stating that 'environmental protection requirements must be integrated into the definition and implementation of Community policies and activities . . . in particular with a view to promoting sustainable development'. However, the Amsterdam Treaty does not displace the Maastricht Treaty, thus leaving the issue of semantic confusion unresolved.

The Existence of a Plan

The main plan promoting sustainable development is the Fifth Environment Action Programme, 'Towards Sustainability: A European Programme of Policy and Action in relation to the Environment and Sustainable Development' (the 5EAP) (CEC 1992b). The Programme represents the Commissions efforts to translate the declaratory statements of the European Council, the legal commitments embedded in the Treaties, and the Community international obligations on sustainable development, into concrete policy proposals.

Although published three months before the Rio Earth Summit, the EU claims that the 5EAP was drawn up in parallel with preparations for Rio (European Community 1997: 7). As a result of their common origin, the Commission has argued that the 5EAP shares many of the same strategic objectives and principles as UNCED (CEC 1996d: 109). Since Rio, the 5EAP has come to form the main strategic response of the EU to the obligations incurred at the Earth Summit (CEC 1992a) and in particular, the response to Agenda 21 (CEC 1995a: 2).

According to the Commission, the 5EAP identifies six key elements in the promotion of sustainable development within the EU (CEC 1992b):

1. the integration of environmental considerations into other EU policies;
2. broadening the range of instruments used to bring about more environmentally friendly economic and social behaviour;
3. reliance upon *partnership*, involving the EU, the general public, the business world, and national administrations, and *shared responsibility* at the national and sub-national levels to effect change;
4. the elaboration of new policies designed to change attitudes to, and existing patterns of, consumption and production;
5. placing new emphasis on implementation and enforcement;
6. strengthening the international role of the Community.

It is worth noting the strong overlap between these elements and chapter 8 of Agenda 21, which outlines the steps necessary to integrate environmental considerations into development policy. There have been a number of reviews of the EU's efforts to promote sustainable development. These include the Commission's own reports, such as the 'Report of the Commission of the European Communities to the United Nations Conference on the Environment and Development—Rio de Janeiro, June 1992' (CEC 1992a), four annual reports to the CSD (CEC 1993a; 1994b; 1995b; 1996b), and a consolidated overview of progress, 'Agenda 21: The First Five Years: European Community Progress on the Implementation of Agenda 21 1992–1997' (European Community 1997). There were specific reviews of the 5EAP, including the 1994 interim review of the 5EAP (CEC 1994a), which was followed by the 1995 'Progress Report on the Implementation of the Fifth Environment Action Programme' (CEC 1995a). Furthermore, there are evaluations by other bodies, such as 'The Environment in the European Union 1995: Report for the Review of the Fifth Environmental Action Programme', prepared by the European Environment Agency for the Commission (EEA 1995a). The common message in these reports is that not enough is being done to deal with Europe's deteriorating physical environment let alone to put the commitment to sustainable development into practice. The EEA report, for example, stated that the EU 'is making progress in reducing certain pressures on the environment, though this is not enough to improve the general quality of the environment and even less to progress towards sustainability' (EEA 1995a: 1). We draw upon these reviews to examine, in turn, each of the six key elements in the EU's promotion of sustainable development.

The Integration of Environmental Considerations into Other Policy Areas   The 5EAP commits the Union and its member-states to integrating environmental considerations into other policy areas. Furthermore, under the Single European Act, member-states also have a legal obligation to undertake this policy integration, a commitment that was reinforced in the Maastricht Treaty and the Treaty of Amsterdam. In this context 'integration' means that environmental priorities are built into the planning and execution of policies in other, non-environmental spheres. Specifically, the 5EAP makes a commitment to achieving integration in five target sectors, namely tourism, (manufacturing) industry, energy, transport, and agriculture. The Commission has established a special co-ordinating unit to oversee this work (European Information Services 1993: 38).

The general consensus is that while some progress has been made in achieving policy integration, this progress is limited. The speed of integration differs across the five target sectors, with integration at a more advanced level in the manufacturing sector (although this excluded small and medium enterprises, SMEs) and less developed in agriculture and tourism (CEC 1995a: 3; Baker and Young 1996).

Integration is politically and administratively difficult and is inhibited by specific features of the EU policy-making process. First, there is the historical tendency for DGs to pursue sectoral objectives and to treat their impact on other sectors as side effects, taken into account only if compelled to do so. Indeed policy-makers within the other DGs resent what they see as the 'intrusion' of the Directorate-General for the Environment into their traditional areas of competence. In this context, relationships and vested interests within their policy communities can become unsettled when new sets of environmental considerations are introduced, especially when these are likely to be seen as having restrictive consequences for economic activity. Second, institutional rigidity within the EU makes the task of overcoming fragmentation difficult. Third, the fragmentation of responsibility for different stages of the policy process between the EU and the member-states adds to the difficulties.

The Directorate-General for the Environment has become acutely aware of its failure to achieve policy integration (CEC 1994a), but places the blame on other DGs, arguing that the main problem lies in 'a widespread belief that the promotion of sustainable development is the business of those who deal with the environment' (CEC 1994a).

Broadening the Range of Instruments   Broadening the range of instruments, to include fiscal, market, and voluntary policy tools, is an attempt to move from almost exclusive reliance upon a legislative approach (the use of Directives) in environmental policy to the development of a more consensus-based policy style of environmental management. The Commission hopes that the use of such tools will help to evolve an environmental policy that is more guided by the principle of partnership and shared responsibility and less by regulatory norms. These principles are seen as a key to the successful promotion of sustainable development in the EU. However, the move to broaden the range of policy tools is also closely linked to recent deregulation initiatives within the Union, and thus has much in keeping with the market-based ideology of the SEM.

Despite the strong ideological underpinning for such a move, progress in relation to broadening the range of policy instruments has been slow (CEC 1995a: 4). Some progress has been made in the use of voluntary (environmental) agreements with the industrial sector (European Community 1997: 9). However progress in the development of green tax instruments has been hampered by the failure to introduce a carbon/energy tax in 1992. This was the centrepiece of the Commission's initial response to the climate change issue. Despite strong backing from elements in the Commission and the support of some member-states, the proposal became embroiled in political controversy and technical difficulties. Vigorous opposition was put up by industrial lobbyists, and among member-states the UK in particular refused to countenance such an extension of the powers of the EU. In relation to problems of energy and taxation, issues of sovereignty and subsidiarity remain very much alive.

Partnership and Shared Responsibility   Agenda 21 states that 'critical to the implementation of Agenda 21 will be the commitment and genuine involvement of all social groups'. The commitment to partnership is seen as a backbone in the EU's approach towards the promotion of sustainable development and implementing the Rio accords (European Community 1997: 17). The then EU Commissioner for the Environment, Ritt Bjerregaard, echoed this sentiment when she argued that 'sound stewardship is not a task for government alone' (CEC 1997f: 10, 17).

The commitment to partnership and shared responsibility involves the EU, and in particular the Commission, in actions at five levels: at the institutional level, at the member-state level, at the sub-national levels of government, at the sectoral level, and at the level of interest groups. Beginning with the institutional level, civil society has specific institutional mechanisms for participating in EU policy-making. These include, for example, through the Economic and Social Committee and the recently established Committee of the Regions. These groups are not, however, directly connected with the Community's participation in UNCED. However, specific policy networks have been set up by the Commission to promote sustainable development, in particular, the General Consultative Forum on the Environment. This is discussed below.

The commitment to partnership and shared responsibility, in other words, to the principle of subsidiarity as understood in Maastricht, also means giving a greater role to member-states. This is important because it facilitates the growth of sustainable development from the bottom-up and allows policies to take account of differences in cultural, economic, and social conditions across the Union. However, it has also meant a great deal of unevenness in policy take-up, which 'varies considerably between and even within member states' (EEA 1995a: 17). Furthermore, the Directorate-General for the Environment believes that, despite the fact that 'many of the necessary mechanisms (e.g. interministerial and consultative groups) are now in place, there are signs that the necessary

political commitment to make shared responsibility a reality may be lacking'
(CEC 1995a: 13).

The use of the principles of partnership and shared responsibility has also
meant deepening the EU's relationship with sub-national government, for
example local authorities. This has led to financial support from the Commission to local authority networks dealing with issues such as traffic
planning, tourism management, and urban growth and to funding of
inter-regional environmental management co-operation (European Community 1997: 6; Baker 1996b). Emphasis is also placed on the principle of
shared responsibility at the sectoral level and in relation to the involvement of environmental NGOs in the policy process. The Commission, for
example, holds regular discussions with the largest environmental organizations and dialogue has also been facilitated by the establishment of an
NGO Development Liaison Committee in 1976.

NGOs were also represented on the Community's delegation to the Earth
Summit and to most sessions of the CSD. It has also opened up some
funding opportunities to NGOs, with DGXI providing support, for example,
to the Northern Alliance for Sustainability to launch a project aimed at promoting the involvement NGOs and other voluntary groups in Local Agenda
21 activities across Europe (ANPED 1997: 19; European Community 1997:
17).

Despite the fact that the adoption of the principle of partnership and
shared responsibility has, at least to some degree, opened-up the policy
process to environmental interests, some groups remain cautious. NGOs
still find that the EU's policy style is dominated by a culture of secrecy and
that business and commercial interests exercise a dominant influence upon
policy. Furthermore, some groups remain sceptical of the principle. The
European Environmental Bureau (EEB) has, for example, cautioned that 'the
implementation of the principle of shared responsibility should not lead to
the abandonment of responsibilities by public authorities' (EEB 1996: 6).

Changing Attitudes and Patterns of Consumption and Production   The Union
has claimed that it is following the two-pronged approach advocated in
Agenda 21 for dealing with this issue, namely, identifying unsustainable
patterns of production and consumption and then developing strategies to
change these patterns (European Community 1997: 20). Furthermore, the
Commission recognizes the strategic importance of this objective, in particular in helping it to meet other policy objectives (CEC 1997a: 3). However,
their efforts have in fact been very limited.

With respect to production, policies aimed at the ecological modernization of (manufacturing) industry, for example, have remained largely limited

to reducing resource wastage in the production process. There has been, for example, a voluntary Eco-Management and Audit Scheme, which came into effect in 1995. A European Integrated Pollution Prevention and Control Bureau has also been established and there have been new legislative moves in relation to integrated pollution control and waste management. Financial commitments were also made through the Fourth Research Framework Programme to develop clean technology. However, there is a great deal of pessimism with respect to meeting this objective, with the Commission arguing that industry continues to perceive the promotion of sustainable development as a stumbling bloc to economic progress (CEC 1994a: 4). With respect to the promotion of sustainable consumption, progress has been just as limited, with policies primarily focused on recycling and consumer information.

On its own admission, the Commission has agreed that little has been achieved with respect to changing attitudes towards and patterns of consumption and production within the EU (CEC 1995a). A report by the EEA has found that most production and consumption trends in the EU have remained unchanged compared with those operative when the 5EAP was first published (EEA 1995a: 2), although some attention has been now been given to this matter in the new environmental Action Plan (CEC 1997b: 20–2).

Implementation of Legislation and Enforcement Policy implementation is, as we have said above, the task of the member-states. Most member-states have issued sustainable development strategies or environmental policy plans. Furthermore, since 1992, the majority of member-states have either set up some form of national consultative forum on the environment or redefined the roles of existing bodies in order to provide a forum for dialogue and consultation (European Community 1997). Despite these efforts, the record for the implementation of EU environmental policy is poor. Implementation failure can partly be attributed to over-reliance upon the legislative approach, in particular, Directives, to regulate environmental behaviour (Baker 1996a). Here, subtle differences in drafting of legislation at the member-state level can contribute to the problem. In this context the terminological imprecision relating to 'sustainable development' in the Maastricht Treaty takes on increased significance. Recent institutional innovations, including the establishment of the EEA, the Environment Policy Review Group, and the Implementation Network may, however, help the Union to encourage member-states to achieve more effective implementation of policies aimed at the promotion of sustainable development.

The negative assessment of progress made under the 5EAP led to a new environmental Action Plan, proposed by DGXI and approved by both the EP and the Council (CEC 1997b). This Plan of action set new priorities for the 5EAP between the years 1997 and 2000, which, according to the Commission 'are aimed at steering the Union's implementation of Agenda 21 towards greater success' (CEC 1997b). Its central theme is the achievement of sectoral policy and it also contains proposals relating to the promotion of sustainable consumption and production patterns, with special focus on SMEs. The Action Plan forms, as it were, a stopgap measure between the 5EAP and the proposed new 6EAP. The Commission has argued that this was necessitated by significant new developments effecting EU environmental policy, in particular the setting of new objectives by UNCED and the adoption of Agenda 21 (CEC 1997b), none of which were envisaged when the 5EAP was formulated. However, it has also been necessitated by the delay in the production of the 6EAP, a delay caused by a number of factors, including preparations for Economic and Monetary Union, negotiations concerning the reform of the CAP and the Structural Funds, enlargement, including Eastern enlargement and German reunification, as well as uncertainty about the operationalization of the principle of subsidiarity in the environmental policy arena.

The International Role   For convenience the international role of the Union can be divided into: (1) participation in international environmental management forums; and (2) promoting sustainable development in third countries.

1. *Participation in international environmental management forums.* The 1988 Rhodes European Council Declaration committed the Community to engage in actions to protect the world's environment, including striving for an effective international response to the problem of climate change (EC 1988). This commitment is reflected in the 5EAP (CEC 1992a: 81). The new Environmental Action Plan argues that strengthening the international role of the EU requires four key steps: reinforcing the EU's role in international sustainable development issues; integrating environment and trade policies; strengthening co-operation with Eastern and Central Europe and the Mediterranean countries; and improving the environmental dimension of development co-operation (CEC 1997b: 9).

2. *Promotion of sustainable development in third countries.* The Commission has argued that promoting sustainable development in third countries involves linking economic issues with social considerations, particularly as they relate to the downward spiral of poverty, population, and poor health. This spiral can be a cause and a consequence of unsustainable use of resources (European Community 1997: 7). This had led to some limited

attempts to integrate environmental considerations into EU policies in relation to developing and transition countries.

Recent developments in Eastern and Central Europe have given the Union a new role in international environmental management, which was not envisaged when the 5EAP was adopted. The fact that membership of the Union has become a determining factor in shaping current environmental policy in a number of countries in Eastern and Central Europe (Baker and Jehlička 1998) has placed the Union in a powerful and influential position to promote sustainable development. However, the Union is failing in this role for a number of reasons. First, the concentration by the EU on enabling transition countries to develop functioning market systems has, by and large, been at the expense of the promotion of sustainable development (Baker and Jehlička 1998). Second, despite the existence of mechanisms for mutual consultation, the relationship between Eastern and Central European countries and the Union is an asymmetrical one, with power skewed heavily in favour of the Union (Caddy 1997: 328). Third, there has been little promotion of public discussion on the political and economic conditions that the European Union is establishing for 'association' and, ultimately, for membership of the EU, or about the elements of pluralist democracy that association is intended to encourage (Pinder 1991: 38). This lack of public discussion is hindering the development of civil society and thus democratic participation in the process of change.

The EU is also engaged with developing countries. Space does not permit a full analysis of EU efforts to integrate environmental considerations into its trade and development policies, instead we focus on the general framework of engagement and the underlying principles upon which EU policies rests.

Concerning trade, environmental provisions have been included in trade agreements between developing countries and the EU, and new trade instruments have been created to encourage sustainable production in developing countries (European Community 1997: 24). Similarly, the Union's Generalized System of Preferences includes an environmental clause, although this is limited to wood products from sustainably managed forests. The Union is also a member of the International Tropical Timber Agreement and the EU has been one of the major forces behind the establishment of the Inter-Governmental Panel on Forests (Sandbrook 1997).

Union initiatives are, however, limited by the Commission's belief that there is no inherent conflict between international trade and environmental protection. On the contrary, it argues that 'strong environmental and sustainable development strategies can ensure that trade ultimately contributes to increased economic efficiency and thereby conserves resources and protects environmental quality (European Community 1997: 24). The Commission also believes that trade liberalization can have a positive impact on the environment (CEC 1996d: 118).

Concerning aid, disbursement of EU development aid funds are made through the Lomé Convention and its programmes of support to Asian and Latin American states (ALA), its Mediterranean programme, and a number of sectoral programmes such as food aid. In 1989 the principle of sustainable development was integrated into the general principles of Lomé, and aid under this Convention has been subject to environmental assessment since 1990. In 1995 a revision to the Lomé Convention introduced a Protocol on sustainable management of forest resources. This, the Union has argued 'builds explicitly on the Rio Declaration, the Conventions linked to UNCED (climate change, biodiversity, and desertification) and the Rio Statement on Forest Principles' (European Community 1997: 139).

Besides these broad policy developments, there have also been initiatives aimed at integrating environmental considerations into aid programmes for specific regions. In 1992 ALA regulations specified that at least 10 per cent of aid should be spent on meeting environmental needs. Similarly, the strategy for co-operation with Asia adopted in 1994 included the stipulation that policy should contribute towards sustainable development. A Europe–Asia Strategy in the Field of the Environment is aimed at identifying areas where the EU has particular strengths to offer Asia in environmental co-operation. Similarly, Latin America has received EU support for biodiversity projects, and the environment is one of twenty areas of assistance to Mediterranean states. A small budget for Environment in Developing Countries was established in 1982 (at its highest this had a budget of ECU 26 million in 1993). Forest management also has a specific budget of around ECU 50 million a year. The EU also supports nature-protection policies in developing countries, including programmes for the protection of endangered species and the management of national parks. For example, it currently supports the World Bank/IMF efforts to lighten the debt burden on the heavily indebted poorest developing countries. Eleven of the thirteen countries involved are linked to the Union through the Lomé Convention. In 1996 the Commission began an evaluation of environmental performance of EU programmes in developing countries, with the objective of identifying opportunities to improve the integration of environmental considerations into Union policy.

While these initiatives may appear numerous, the limited financial resources granted to them by the member-states have weakened their impact. In 1998 the Directorate-General for the Environment has admitted that 'there has been a setback in terms of the flow of financial resources to assist developing countries in moving towards sustainable development' (CEC 1996d: 118). Furthermore, member-states have failed to reach agreement on how to meet the commitment made at Rio to allocate ECU 3,000 million to help implement Agenda 21 in developing countries. More fundamentally, however, the EU can be criticized for failing to deal with the causes of non-sustainable resource-use that are rooted in its trade policies and in inequality of access to and use of global resources.

Patterns of Institutional Engagement

Chapter 8 of Agenda 21 points to the need to strengthen institutional structures, capability, and capacity to integrate social, economic, and environmental issues. In this section we look at the impact of the promotion of sustainable development on EU institutions.

The Commission is the main institution charged with ensuring that the declaratory statements of principle made by the European Council and the Council of Ministers are reflected in actual concrete policy proposals. The European Council, which is the collective organ of the heads of government of the member-states, has gradually taken over responsibility for virtually all major advances in the European integration process and also for the framing of broad principles and directions of policy, which are then passed on to the Council of Ministers and the Commission for further consideration.

The Directorate-General for the Environment is, however, regarded as institutionally weak, with a small budget and limited staff, although both have increased over the last few years. Nevertheless, the EU's commitment to the promotion of sustainable development has led to a number of institutional and administrative changes within the Commission.

In 1993, for example, DGXI issued an internal Communication advising other Directorates General to each designate an official with specific responsibility for dealing with policy integration and for ensuring that legislative proposals take account of the commitment to sustainable development. These have now been established. A special co-ordination unit has been set up within DGXI to oversee this development (European Information Service 1993: 38). Furthermore, some services have created environmental units. However, uptake has been uneven, as has the response to the submission of annual reports on progress in integrating environmental considerations into other policies (European Community 1997: 35).

The establishment of three dialogue groups by the Commission also needs to be noted. The first of these, the General Consultative Forum on the Environment, was established in 1993 with the specific aim of opening up the

policy process to outside interests. Initially composed of thirty-two representatives of enterprise, consumers, trade unions, environmental groups,
and local and regional authorities, it has been used by the Commission to
consult on environmental policy, including on the White Paper on Growth,
Competitiveness and Employment (CEC 1993b). In 1995 the Forum agreed
twelve Principles of Sustainable Development (CEC 1997c). The Forum has
also produced 'Options for a Sustainable Europe: Policy Recommendations
for the General Consultative Forum on the Environment' (EC 1997d).

In 1997 the Commission expanded the Forum's mandate, its membership
and retitled the group the 'European Forum on Environment and Sustainable Development'. This Forum is considered as the Union level equivalent
of a national Sustainable Development Commission (European Community
1997: 114).

In addition, two governmental bodies have been established to promote
collaboration between countries and different levels of government: the
Environment Policy Review Group (EPRG) and the Implementation
Network. The EPRG is composed of members from Departments of the
Environment of the member-states and the Commission. To date, it has
focused on sectoral integration, in particular the five sectors targeted in the
5EAP. According to the Commission, the Group has 'played an important
role in improving dialogue between the Commission and Member States on
strategic issues affecting the environment and sustainable development'
(CEC 1994a: 48). The third group is an informal Network for the Implementation and Enforcement of Environmental Law and has a narrower
membership base. It is aimed at the exchange of information and expertise
on practical issues arising from member-states' tasks in implementing environmental legislation. The body facilitates closer contact between regulators
and policy-makes and those concerned with day-to-day implementation,
such as environmental enforcement agents.

The Commission has also established sector-specific policy networks.
These include the Consultative Committee on Energy, which has as one of
its aims to assess how the Energy dimension of the Community's climate
change strategy can be reinforced by economic actors (CEC 1997e: 13).
Other EU institutions have also played a role, albeit a more indirect one. The
European Parliament (EP) has a Committee on Environment, Public Health
and Consumer Protection, which was set up in 1973. The Committee is
responsible for reviewing and giving opinions on environmental initiatives
proposed by the Commission. The Environment Committee is important in
terms of EU policy as a whole because approximately one quarter of all
European legislation passes through the Committee. Given the increase in

the powers of the EP to shape policy following the Treaty of Amsterdam, the influence of the Committee is expected to rise. The Committee has also been active on several issues in relation to environmental legislation, including the adoption of a number of 'own-initiative' resolutions. It has also placed emphasis on the integration of environmental considerations into other policy fields, the 'greening' of the EU budget, and Union action to ensure better implementation at the member-state level of the 5EAP (Official Journal, OJC. 362/115 1996). The Committee has also focused on biodiversity and the protection of birds.

The European Court of Justice (ECJ) has, so far, played no direct role in relation to the promotion of sustainable development. The ECJ is another key institution of the EU, with responsibility for laws and ensuring that EU institutions and member-states conform with the provisions of the founding Treaty of Rome and its subsequent amendment Treaties. The Court does play an important role in relation to general environmental management. Since the SEA, the Court is charged with the interpretation of the provisions of the Treaties with respect to environmental legislation and also has the task of dealing with infringements of these laws.

Finally, of importance is the EEA, which was set up in 1993 as an independent agency with a mandate to provide information on the state of the European environment. This agency was not established directly as a result of the EU's involvement in international efforts to promote sustainable development, but rather as a consequence of the EU's increased involvement in environmental management, of which its engagement with the UNCED and the CSD is but one example. The EEA is also worth mentioning because the reports it produces on the state of the environment in Europe are expected to provide a major input into policy evaluation and subsequent changes in policy direction and emphasis put forward by the Commission (see, for example, EEA 1995b).

Sectoral Responses: Climate Change

The Community ratified the Convention on Climate Change in December 1993. In contrast to the USA the EU has long maintained that international agreements should include clear timetables and quantified targets for reduction of CO_2 emissions (CEC 1997f: 3), and believes that climate change policy can be technology forcing. The conflict between the USA and the EU over the most acceptable means of approach has dominated international efforts to deal with climate change. This led the Community, for example, to work hard at the first meeting of the Conference of the Parties in Berlin in 1995 to get agreement on the so-called Berlin Mandate, most of whose provisions were proposed by the Commission (CEC 1996d: 110).

The Community entered into international negotiations on climate change having worked out a common negotiation position with its member-states on emission targets and timetables: only with such unity could it hold its own in international negotiations. The Community, for example, arrived in Kyoto armed with a common proposal for a 15 per cent reduction in emission levels. This target did not meet with US approval, the USA believing that such targets were neither technically nor economically feasible (CEC 1997f). Despite the differences, however, the Commission was determined to reach a compromise at Kyoto because they believed that 'there can be no question of our European economy suffering the consequences of an unilateral global environmental protection policy while our trading partners could avoid measures influencing energy prices and hence the competitiveness of industry and employment' (CEC 1997g: 14).

Yet the Commission was dissatisfied with the Kyoto outcomes, as they were lower than the negotiating objectives (CEC 1996d: 110). The Directorate-General for the Environment was particularly dissatisfied (Guardian 12 Dec. 1997) and also expressed concern about the possibility of the USA trading emissions, thus avoiding positive policy initiatives at home (CEC 1997f). Yet the Commission was pleased about its own role in the negotiations (CEC 1997g), which is widely recognized to have been a positive one. John Gummer, former UK Secretary of State, reflected the positive assessment of the EU's role in the Kyoto negotiations:

The United States was full of fine words about what had to be done but wholly lacked the will to take the leadership role, which befitted the world's biggest polluter. The European Union was at last living up to its position as the world's greatest trading grouping and seeking to establish a world order capable of countering a global threat (Gummer 1997: 1628).

Pillars of EU Climate Change Policy

The task of translating the Climate Change Convention and its Protocol into policy proposals rests with the Commission. The Commission's task is guided by three explicit principles: first, that a successful climate strategy needs to be cost-effective, technically and politically feasible, and avoid negative social or regional side effects; second, that policy needs to initiate a process of technological and behavioural change; and third, that the right

mixture of instruments needs to be chosen in order to put policy into practice (CEC 1997a: 8).

Guided by these principles, the EU climate change strategy has, according to the Commission, come to rest on four pillars (CEC 1996b: iv):

1. the establishment of energy conservation and energy technology
   programmes;
2. the adoption of fiscal measures;
3. the establishment of a monitoring mechanism;
4. the achievement of complementary with national programmes;

However, two further pillars can be added:

5. integration with sectoral policies;
6. the use of voluntary schemes.

We examine each of these in turn.

1. *The establishment of energy conservation and energy technology programmes.*
There are a number of programmes of relevance here, including the JOULE-
THERMIE programme (1995–8), the ALTENER programme (1993–7), and
SAVE I and II. Yet these programmes are limited in nature and poorly funded
(EEA 1995a: 51; see also CEC 1997e), and the low level of funding approval
for these programmes has been criticized by the Commission (CEC 1997a:
5). The EU's energy conservation programmes remain limited because of
the failure to develop a more general and comprehensive EU energy policy.
As a result, a vital, strategic component of an effective response to the
Climate Change Convention remains absent. Consequently, EU climate
change policy has been the subject of considerable criticism from environmental NGOs, including Greenpeace (Greenpeace International 1995) and
the EEB (EEB 1997: 6).

The lacuna is acknowledged by the Directorate-General for the Environment (CEC 1997b: 9) resulting in recent efforts to develop a more strategic
and integrated approach (see e.g. CEC 1997e). However, despite these
actions, the Directorate-General for the Environment believes that the
proposals on the table and in the pipeline are not sufficient to meet EU
climate change targets (CEC 1997a: 9). Furthermore, it is unlikely that the
future will see much progress in relation to the development of a Union-
wide energy policy. Energy policy remains orientated towards deregulation,
is premised on a strong belief in market-based energy solutions, and
member-states are reluctant to concede further competence to the Union in
this area. Furthermore, the efforts of the Directorate-General for the Environment are hampered by its own relatively weak position within the

Commission, and by the lack of commitment to environmental protection by other DGs.

2. *The adoption of fiscal measures.* The adoption of fiscal measures is part of an overall Commission strategy of making greater use of a broad range of policy instruments in environmental policy (CEC 1997a). However, as a result of the failure to introduce a carbon tax, the fiscal component has proved to be the weakest element of the EU's climate change strategy. To date, the UK remains opposed to new taxes on energy and fuel; Ireland has said that it will not sanction any tax rises for industry or private individuals; Germany is opposed to any moves which would mean higher energy bills for industry; while Spain is calling for a voluntary approach (*European Voice*, 18 Dec.–7 Jan. 1998).

3. *The establishment of a monitoring mechanism.* In 1996 the Commission drew up a 'Greenhouse Gas Emissions Inventory', to be used to evaluate target attainment within the Union as a whole. A Monitoring Committee has also been established, composed of representative of the member-states and chaired by the Commission. Member-states are required to submit their national programmes for evaluation to this Committee, which in turn details measures that need to be taken by the member-states.

In March 1994 the Commission presented its first evaluation of national programmes (CEC 1994c: 67), a rather incomplete evaluation due to lack of information. The report found that member-states were at very different stages of development. A further report in 1996 indicated that the majority of member-states were expected to increase CO_2 emissions in 2000 compared to 1990 (CEC 1996c: x).

It is also the task of the Commission to evaluate the member-state submissions in order to assess progress in the Union *as a whole*. However, trying to get a clear picture of progress across the EU is complicated because of shortfalls in the information provided by member-states and by their use of incompatible modelling tools and different input assumptions, making aggregation impossible (CEC 1996c: 65).

4. *Complementary with national programmes.* Both the Community and the member-states are contracting parties to the Climate Convention and share competence in the area. Successful policy outcome requires that policy at *both* levels be complementary. However, putting this principle into practice has proved difficult. There are problems related to the so-called burden-sharing arrangements between member-states. The common negotiating position agreed with member-states in preparation for Kyoto included an agreement on what cuts individual member-states would make in order to achieve Union-wide targets. This allowed individual member-states to con-

tribute to overall EU targets according to their level of economic development and other national circumstances. This agreement actually allowed some EU member-states to increase their emissions levels. Ireland, for example, was allowed to increase its emissions to 15 per cent above 1990 levels. The Netherlands played a lead role in bringing these negotiations to conclusion. However, the burden-sharing agreements were initially contentious resulting in a period of deadlock prior to Kyoto. Moreover a few months after Kyoto the Netherlands expressed its dissatisfactions with the burden-sharing arrangement, seeking to reduce the cuts it was obliged to make in light of the agreement finally reached in Japan (*European Voice*, 2–8 April 1998). A Council conclusion in March 1998 resulted in some agreement on burden sharing, including Dutch agreement to reduce emissions by 6 per cent, Britain by 12.5 per cent and allowing Ireland to increase emissions by up to 13 per cent (EC 1998). However, the EU climate change strategy continues to face difficulties, especially in relation to emissions trading (*European Voice*, 5: 16, 22 April 1999).

5. *Sectoral integration*. Climate change policy is related to a wide range of diverse policy areas, including energy, transport, and agricultural policy. Here a major difficulty is that environmental objectives frequently stand in conflict with the other, more traditional, aims of sectoral policies. For example, despite the 1992 reforms of the CAP, the integration of environmental considerations into agriculture remains weak. Integration of environmental considerations into transport policy is also proving difficult (CEC 1997e: 9). The construction of the Trans European Transport Network, combined with the completion of the SEM, makes the transport sector one of the fastest growing and least environmentally sensitized sectors in the EU. Policy responses to this are limited.

Programmes also exist within the industrial sector, including the SPRINT programme, aimed at ecological modernization of industry. This programme is cited by the Commission in its evaluation of the progress that the Union has made in implementing Agenda 21 as being among the most important of several programmes that have been set up since the Rio Summit (European Community 1997: 22). However, like many of the programmes, policies, and projects cited by the Commission in this evaluation, it is not primarily concerned with the promotion of sustainable development.

6. *Voluntary schemes*. Following the failure of the proposed carbon tax, the Commission is increasingly placing emphasis on voluntary schemes and auto-regulation. These schemes are in keeping with the market-led ideology underlying the completion of the SEM.

Evaluation of EU Climate Change Policy

The EU has played an important role in shaping the international response to the problem of climate change. It has acted as a leading protagonist for a stringent international regime, frequently holding out in negotiations against the USA for higher targets for emission cuts. Coming to the negotiation table having reached a common position with its fifteen member-states has helped the Union develop its international standing.

However, the potential impact of the EU is limited by the fact that it is only prepared to put the negotiated agreements into effect if other countries follow suit. The Union is not prepared to put itself at a competitive disadvantage in an effort to deal with global environmental problems. This has made the EU particularly cautious in how it puts the terms of the Climate Convention into effect.

In contrast to its strong role in influencing international policy formulation, the EU has a poor record in implementing the obligations it incurred under the Climate Convention. Implementation is the weakest link in EU climate change policy. Implementation failure has been caused by a number of specific factors. First, it is hampered by the existence of inconsistencies between the goals embedded in the deepening of the integration process, especially the completion of the SEM, and those entered into as part of the climate change policies. Second, it is linked to the more general failure to integrate climate change policy into sectoral policy. Third, failure is linked to an over-reliance upon market-led solutions to the environmental problems arising within the energy and transport sectors and to lack of progress in developing a strategic EU-wide energy policy.

At the member-state level implementation failure is linked to the difficulties in reaching agreement on how the Union should achieve the reductions signed up to in Kyoto. Deadlock over the use of fiscal measures as an implementation tool still continues to hamper progress. Added to this is the fact that member-states are often reluctant to implement policy if it poses a competitive threat to their industry, in particular in relation to American and Japanese producers.

The Commission admits that reducing emissions of greenhouse gases remains one of the most intractable problem facing the Union today (European Community 1997: 10). This problem can only be overcome if the tension at the heart of the integration process is resolved, that is, the tension relating to where to draw the boundary line to demarcate the competence of the EU on the one hand and of the member-states on the other. Until this tension is resolved, the EU may continue to expand its international environmental management role, but domestically it is unlikely to make a real contribution to resolving the problem of global warming.

Sectoral Responses: Biodiversity

As is the case with general environmental policy, Union concern for the preservation of biodiversity is primarily grounded on economic motives (CEC 1998: 1). The Commission is also interested in biodiversity management because it is seen as helping its ambition of playing a leadership role in relation to international environmental management (CEC 1998: 2), while at the same time allowing the Commission to appear to be responding to the 'expectations and aspirations' of its citizens (CEC 1998: 2). This is linked to research from the EEA, which shows that biodiversity in the EU is under pressure from a broad range of human activities (EEA 1995b: 106).

The Community signed the Convention on Biological Diversity (CBD) in June 1992 and ratified it in 1993. Yet the EU has also made criticisms of the CBD, expressing regret at the insufficient environmental objectives and concern about the Convention not fully respecting existing rules in relation to intellectual property rights (Johnston and Corcelle 1995: 465). The Council has also expressed a wish to see major changes in the institutional arrangements put in place to monitor the implementation of the Convention. These include the establishment of a clearing house, the pooling of information, more transfer of technology and the designation of the Global Environment Facility as the main agency responsible for funding the implementation of the Convention. Immediately after signing the Convention the Commission published a declaration regretting the inadequacy of its environmental objectives (CEC 1992c). This sentiment was reflected in a speech four years later by the then Environment Commissioner, Ritt Bjerregaard, when she called for greater focus and selectivity in the tasks set by the parties. In particular the Commission is keen to see prioritization of tasks, a reduction in the size of the agenda, and more focus of resources for greater efficiency (CEC 1996c: 3).

Ad Hoc Policy

Measures in relation to the maintenance of biodiversity are dealt with in the 5EAP, and between 1993 and 1998 EU biodiversity policy relied on five initiatives:

1. habitat protection, under the 1992 Habitats Directive;
2. the Birds Directive;
3. the promotion of sustainable land management practices in and around habitats of importance;
4. the use of the LIFE programme;
5. a number of legal instruments, including CITES and the 1990 Directives on Genetically Modified Organisms.

Many of these initiatives were in existence prior to the Rio Earth Summit and have a history of controversy associated with them. The initial expansion of Union competence into habitat and bird protection, for example, met with member-state opposition. A number of member-states questioned the political and legal basis of Community action in this area, arguing that it was moving away from the economic activity on which the Treaty is based. A determining factor in the gaining of competence in this new policy arena was the support given to the Commission by the EP (Johnston and Corcelle 1995: 298). This led in 1979 to the Council adopting a Directive on the conservation of wild birds (Official Journal, L103, 25 April 1979). The Birds Directive has proved difficult to implement at the member-state level (CEC 1997a: 70). It was followed in 1992 by the Habitats Directive (Official Journal, L206, 22 July 1992).

The Habitats Directive is potentially the most important of the EU instruments for the maintenance of biodiversity, although it does not have its origins directly in the commitment to promote sustainable development. The Directive came into effect in June 1994 and provides for the establishment of the NATURA 2000 programme, aimed at the creation of a comprehensive, linked network of European habitats. However, the transposition of the Habitat Directive into national legislation has been considerably delayed in several member-states (CEC 1997a: 69). Both the EP and the Commission have expressed concern about this (CEC 1997a: 69; EEA 1995a: 114; CEC 1995a: 57). The reluctant response of member-states has weakened the EU's efforts to protect European biodiversity. The heavy reliance on the Habitats Directive in EU biodiversity policy has been severely criticized by the EEB (EEB 1997: 10).

Similar criticisms have been made of the use of the LIFE (Lending Instrument for the Environment) fund which was established in 1992. LIFE is connected with the Structural and Cohesion Funds which, taken together, are seen by the EU as the main mechanisms through which the Union finances the promotion of sustainable development (European Community 1997: ch. 33). However, historically the prime function of the Structural Funds has been to promote economic development, although they are increasingly also used to facilitate environmental improvement through, for example, physical infrastructure developments. This additional, environmental, function has been added without fundamental changes to either the nature of the Funds or their development priorities. The Commission has admitted that Structural Fund support during the period 1989–94 resulted in 'problems in reconciling the needs for economic growth and nature conservation' (European Community 1997: 74). Furthermore, despite the recent reforms of the Funds, the integration of environmental considerations into the Funds remains unsatisfactory. The Commission admits that 'the goals of protecting biodiversity and promoting development in poorer rural areas are often in potential conflict' (European Community 1997).

The Development of a Strategic Approach

Despite the incorporation of biodiversity preservation objectives into the 5EAP, the EU has made little progress in maintaining European biodiversity. During the period 1993–8 heavy reliance was placed, as we have seen, on a set of weak and controversial initiatives in existence prior to the Earth Summit and the CBD. During this period response to the obligations incurred under the Convention was essentially ad hoc. The Commission is aware of its failure to develop an adequate, coherent response to the CBD and this was mentioned in the Commissions 1997 Agenda 21 evaluation report (European Community 1997) and in the evaluation report of the 5EAP (CEC 1995a). However, it was not until 1998 that the Commission published a Biodiversity Strategy (CEC 1998).

The Commission is quite explicit about the relationship between the proposed new biodiversity strategy and its CBD obligations, stating that 'The Community Biodiversity Strategy . . . will provide the framework for developing Community policy and instruments *in order to comply with the CBD* (CEC 1998: 2, emphasis added). Indeed what strikes the reader is the number of times the document claims that policy proposals have their origins in the obligations incurred by the Community as a result of the Rio accords. It is highly likely that these appeals are being used by the Commission to try and force reluctant member-states to concede increased competence in the area of nature conservation to the Union.

The Role of the Member-States

Because both member-states and the Community are signatories to the CBD, the Strategy document had to deal with the sensitive issue of delineating the boundaries of competence of each. Here we see the implications of the principle of subsidiarity, as defined by Maastricht, taking effect. It explains why the Biodiversity Strategy document is quick to point out that action in relation to the maintenance of biodiversity is only proposed at the Union level in order to complement national efforts (CEC 1998). It is for this reason that the Commission has confined its role in relation to CBD obligations to matters that relate to Union-wide policies and instruments, and to strengthening the capacity of member-states to develop national strategies.

To date, Union activity in relation to member-states has been confined to monitoring their performance under the CBD. A first assessment of member-states' efforts was made by the EEA in 1996 (EEA 1996). This found that biodiversity conservation was not a high priority and that the emphasis placed on the various themes of CBD differed across the member-states. This difference may well be justified by different ecological conditions and conservation needs at the member-state level. However, when judged from the point of view of the Union as a whole, such fragmentation of responses may result in, at best, policy inconsistency and, at worst, policy incompatibility and failure. However, the development of a more interventionist approach by the Commission is politically sensitive, given the historical reluctance of member-states to concede competence over nature protection.

Evaluation of EU Biodiversity Policy

The reasons for the failure of the EU to act decisively in the area of biodiversity protection lies, in part, with dissatisfaction with the Biodiversity Convention itself. The Convention is weak and lacks clear focus and specified targets. However, there are issues specific to the EU that need to be taken into account in assessing the causes of implementation failure. First, there is the fact that the approach taken to date by the EU has been *ad hoc* and has relied on initiatives in existence prior to the CBD. Some of these initiatives, in particular, the Birds and Habitats Directives, have a long history of implementation failure. The Union has only recently responded to the task of providing a strategic framework within which a coherent response to its CBD obligations can be situated. Although the response was slow, becoming a signatory to the CDB has forced the hand of the Union, resulting in a shift from an *ad hoc* to a more coherent approach to the maintenance of biodiversity within the EU, at least at the level of policy formulation.

Second, the success of EU policy in relation to the maintenance of bio-diversity crucially depends on the extent to which its transport, agriculture, and tourism policies dovetail with its environmental policy. To date, this policy integration has not occurred (Baker 1997*a*). As a consequence, across the Union as a whole many important areas of biodiversity continue to be threatened. In its assessment of the extent of biodiversity loss, the EEA has found that all types of European ecosystems are facing severe stresses and loss of biodiversity is far more likely to increase in the future than to stabil-ize (EEA 1995*b*).

Third, problems arise in relation to fragmentation of responsibility between the EU and the member-states. Here, member-states have been very slow to respond to their obligation to implement the Convention through the formulation of national strategies. The principle of shared responsibility appears to have broken down as is evident by member-states' reluctance to play their part in helping the EU as a whole meet the obliga-tions incurred under the Convention. At the same time, they remain reluct-ant to allow the Union to expand its competence in this area, seeing nature protection as by and large outside the scope of the Treaties. The recent attempt by the Commission to make a strategic response to the Biodiversity Convention may well force the Union as a whole to move beyond this impasse, resulting in a significant shift of competence in relation to nature protection away from the member-state level upwards to the European Union level.

Conclusion

There is little doubt that participation in the UNCED Earth Summit and its subsequent regulatory, reporting, and monitoring processes has strength-ened the EU's role in the promotion of sustainable development. First, it has locked the Community into a framework of international commit-ments and co-operation procedures. These commitments are beginning to be reflected in EU environmental policy, albeit in a slow and somewhat limited way.

Second, participation in international efforts to promote sustainable devel-opment has allowed the EU to realize its aim of playing a dominant role in global environmental management. This role confers legitimacy upon the Union, helping it to come of age politically. The development of an inter-national role in environmental management is taken very seriously both by the Commission and the Council. In acting out this role, the EU has often fought for, and won, more stringent international policy regimes than those sought by other industrialized nations such as the USA and Japan. This was shown to be the case in climate change policy.

Third, it has given the European Community specific obligations which are generally understood as aiding the promotion of sustainable development. These include meeting emission standards for greenhouse gases within a particular time period and protecting biodiversity. The promotion of sustainable development is beginning to have an impact, albeit it limited, on internal EU policies, especially at the sectoral level.

Fourth, within the EU, but more particularly within the organizational setting of the Commission and within the Directorate-General for the Environment, the engagement in the promotion of sustainable development has resulted in a shift in policy focus. The attention of Commission Eurocrats has now shifted and sustainable development is increasingly becoming an organizing theme for policy. Even if policy outcomes fall short of this goal, or indeed the EU's own declaratory intent, the fact remains that the promotion of sustainable development has now entered into the discourse of the Commission. Thus we can expect to see more and more policy proposals from the Commission, including in relation to sectoral, regional and trade policies, reflecting the goal of promoting sustainable development.

Having said this, however, we must be aware that some of the policy initiatives discussed in this chapter have their origins in developments that lie outside the Community's involvement in UNCED and have not arisen directly as a consequence of the EU commitment to promote sustainable development. This is despite the fact that these policies have often been relied upon by the Commission to provide evidence of an EU engagement with sustainable development or as a response to the obligations incurred through its involvement in UNCED. This is the case, for example, in the energy field, where policy was as much a response to the rising energy costs as they are a response to environmental needs. This makes it difficult to evaluate the impact of the EU's commitment to promote sustainable development: often it is other obligations, priorities, and engagements that are stimulating response. Nevertheless, while it is not always easy to isolate examples of direct influence, there can be little doubt that, at a minimum, the EU's involvement in international efforts to promote sustainable development has strengthened the Commission's and in particular the Directorate-General for the Environment's resolve to steer Europe towards a path of sustainable development.

Furthermore, we must also take into account that the Union continues to encounter difficulties in implementing its commitment to the promotion of sustainable development. This is due to Union concern that measures aimed at environmental protection and the promotion of sustainable development may reduce its competitiveness. Thus whether or not the EU takes action in an area is highly dependent upon other industrialized countries taking similar moves. There are also institutional problems within the Union, including the democratic deficit that hinder performance. Closely related to this is the complex nature of the EU's policy-making process. This makes for an over-reliance upon legislation as a policy tool. Yet the Union continues to experience difficulty in its attempts to expand the range of policy tools. Issues of sovereignty and subsidiarity are of relevance here, particularly with respect to member-state reluctance to hand over competence in the field of taxation. This was highlighted by the failure of the carbon/energy tax proposal. There is also a lack of overall policy coherence within the EU. Despite the commitments made under UNCED and reflected in the 5EAP, environmental considerations remain marginal to the central project of deepening the integration process through the completion of the SEM. This, for example, is giving rise to worrying trends in the transport sector, particularly in peripheral regions. In addition, there is the politically important need to facilitate the spill-over of economic development into less prosperous regions, in an effort to attain social and economic cohesion across the Union as a whole, particularly in the face of Eastern enlargement. In this context it becomes all the more difficult to reduce the negative environmental impact of EU policies, in particular those funded through the Structural and Cohesion Funds. Thus, despite its engagement with UNCED, the existence of other policy priorities, particularly those rooted in the historical commitment of the Union to achieve economic growth, continues to slow down and at times even counteract efforts to promote sustainable development.

Problems also arise at the member-state level. In essence, there is the politically sensitive issue of achieving co-ordination horizontally between the multiple sectors of activity (*principle of integration*) and vertically between the levels of territorial competence (*principle of subsidiarity*). As the EU and the member-states struggle to come to terms with this division of responsibility, member-state action, or at times inaction, can undermine the basic principles upon which the EU commitment to the promotion of sustainable development is built, such as the principle of shared responsibility. Furthermore, the reluctant response at the member-state level can serve to undermine the ability of the Community to act effectively in the international arena and to deliver on its international agreements. This points to the ongoing tension between the Community's potential for international influence and its weak institutional capacity to ensure the translation of its obligations into actual policies and practices at the member-state level. The ability of the EU to promote sustainable development, both domestically and internationally, remains limited by its institutional shortcomings as well as the complex relationship that exists between the EU and its member-states.

12

Patterns of Governmental Engagement

WILLIAM M. LAFFERTY AND JAMES MEADOWCROFT

The preceding chapters have examined how central government in nine of the wealthiest countries of the world, along with the European Union, have responded to the task of promoting sustainable development. In this chapter we aim to bring the material together in a comparative context. The intent is to cast light on governmental engagement with sustainable development across jurisdictions, to identify similarities and contrasts, and to offer a preliminary typology of national responses. The discussion proceeds by first examining particular features of the governmental reactions, and then pulling back to present a more general assessment. In the concluding chapter to the volume we will continue to explore issues raised here and to reflect on their broader significance.

Some Initial Comparisons

As a point of departure we want to look at the question of *initial interpretation*, that is, the extent to which the *language* of sustainable development has been adopted in government circles. As observed in the first chapter, national 'implementation' of sustainable development implies integration of the norm in question into processes of domestic political decision-making. A precondition for such integration, however, is that sustainable development be taken seriously as a symbol and idea; that it be given explicit reference in official documents, plans, policies and programmes. An estimate of the idiomatic integration of sustainable development into the language of governance across the target jurisdictions, based upon the term's appearance in various official contexts up until mid-1998, is provided in Table 12.1.

In eight of the ten cases sustainable development has gained fairly widespread acceptance into the official vocabulary. It seems particularly well established in the Netherlands, Norway, Sweden, and Canada. It is perhaps

Table 12.1. Integration of 'sustainable development' into the discursive practices of central governments by 1998

Discursive context	A	C	G	J	Ne	No	S	UK	USA	EU
1. Agreed translation	na	na	no	yes	yes	yes	yes	na	na	na
2. Employed by official agencies, institutes and commissions	++	++	+	+	++	++	++	++	+	+
3. Employed in styles and titles of agencies and committees	+	+	+	+	−	+	+	+	+	+
4. Included in official remits of ministries or regulatory agencies	+	++	−	+	++	++	++	++	−	+
5. Invoked in prominent statements of government policy	+	+	−	+	++	++	++	+	−	+
6. Cited in significant legislative or administrative enactments	+	++	+	+	++	++	++	+	−	+
7. Cited in documents of potential constitutional significance	+	−	−	−	−	−	−	−	−	+
8. Presence in party political debate, party manifestos, etc.	+	++	+	−	++	++	++	+	−	−
9. Tally of items 2–7	7	8	3	5	8	9	9	7	2	6

Symbols: − = no
+ = yes
++ = yes, significant and widespread
na = not applicable

Notes: Item 1 considers whether governments in non-English speaking countries have settled upon a specific official translation of 'sustainable development', or whether confusion persists over how the expression should be rendered in the national language. The item is not applicable to the four English language jurisdictions, and to the EU (where many languages are spoken, and in some cases there is a single agreed translation while in others there is not). With respect to items 2–8, one + was awarded if sustainable development was invoked in a substantive way within the appropriate discursive context. A second + was awarded if usage was particularly significant and widespread. Strictly speaking, item 8 relates not to the official (state) discourse, but rather to the broader context of party-political debate, yet it provides an oblique indicator of the idiomatic integration of sustainable development into the governmental sphere. The tally of items 2–7 provides a crude indication of the depth of idiomatic integration in each jurisdiction. For item 7, a + was accorded to Australia because of the Inter Governmental Agreement on the Environment (IGAE); a + was accorded to the EU because of the references to sustainable development in the Maastricht and Amsterdam Treaties.

less firmly embedded in governmental idiom in Australia, Japan, the United Kingdom, and the European Union. On the other hand, in the United States, sustainable development retains a distinctly marginal status. The situation in Germany is somewhat equivocal. The German government was slow to engage with the idea of sustainable development, and its usage in official contexts has remained restricted. Indeed Germany was the only non-English speaking country in this study where substantial ambiguity as to the appropriate translation of the term persisted past the mid-1990s. Yet the increased interest in sustainable development displayed by the Federal Environmental Ministry (BMA) and the Federal Environment Agency (UBA) since 1996, and the change of government after the autumn 1998 election, suggest that the term will achieve a higher profile in coming years—perhaps not an entirely unexpected occurrence considering Germany's highly active and interdependent relationship with the European Union which, as we have seen, has gradually incorporated the idiom of sustainable development into its overall environmental policy.

Interpreting the Concept

Granted that the term has been accorded varying degrees of visibility across the different domains, how has the term been 'anchored' semantically? The first thing to be said is that, with the exception of the United States, all governments have regularly emphasized the significance of the report of the WCED in formulating the notion of sustainable development. Further, there is a strong general tendency to further relate the idea to the Rio Earth Summit when arguing for its global relevance and legitimacy. The standard reference from the Brundtland Report as to development that 'meets the needs of the present without compromising the ability of future generations to meet their own needs' (WCED 1987: 43), is cited regularly, but reference is frequently also made to the variety of ways sustainable development can be interpreted, and to the complexity of translating it into policy orientations and operational goals.

That sustainable development is not just about environmental protection, but also about quality of life, and that it, further, requires a balancing of economic, social and environmental goals, are also recurring themes. In *A Guide to Green Government*, for example, the Canadian government emphasizes the 'many factors—income, the state of people's health, their level of education, cultural diversity, vibrant communities, environmental quality and the beauty of nature—that are all part of the sustainable development equation' (Canada 1995a: 4). In *Sustainable Development in Germany*, the German Ministry of the Environment refers to 'ecology, economy and social affairs' as 'the three dimensions of sustainable development', and speaks of the 'challenge to every area of policy to formulate strategies for sustainable development, while taking account of ecological, economic and social targets' (BMU 1998b: 6).

Yet while such a broad purview of sustainable development is frequently acknowledged, in practice it has been most commonly invoked as an 'environmental' concept. The contexts where sustainable development has been used are those where environmental burdens are at issue, and where the official agencies and organizations sponsoring the concept have, in general, been those with particular responsibilities for environmental protection. This 'environmental' focus is so obvious and pervasive as to appear hardly worth comment, yet it is interesting to note that it was exactly this type of bias that the Brundtland Report warned against (WCED 1987: xi). It was a major purpose of the WCED to shift the focus away from 'narrow' environmental concerns to the broader issues of resource management, poverty and developmental imbalance, and generational equity.

It could be argued, of course, that, to the extent that developed countries already possess institutions which have proven reasonably successful in managing economic advance and providing social welfare benefits to their populations, the distinct contribution which 'sustainable development' can bring to the table is to encourage the integration of *environmental* considerations into established spheres of societal decision-making. Such a primary focus on the environmental rather than the developmental 'side' of sustainable development is evident in the national reporting process for the 1997 UNGASS meeting, where most of the governments with which this study has been concerned passed rather cursorily over the 'developmental' chapters of Agenda 21—suggesting that they believed their 'development' tasks to have been largely accomplished. Precisely in order to make explicit a primary concern with the environmental dimension, some governments have chosen to refer specifically to *'ecologically'* or *'environmentally'* sustainable development. Australia with its 'National Strategy for Ecologically Sustainable Development' is notable in this regard, but towards the end of the 1990s such formulations also gained popularity (at least in certain contexts) in Sweden, Norway, and Germany.

A number of qualifications must, however, be made concerning the primacy of this 'environmental' understanding of sustainable development. In the first place, when referring to conditions in less-developed countries the governments usually placed a more 'developmental' gloss on sustainable development. Thus international assistance for sustainable development was understood to imply not just environmental aid, but also aid to achieve more traditional (although perhaps environmentally audited) development objectives.

A second qualification is that in countries where government has insisted that *all* central departments and agencies must relate their operations to sustainable development, there has been a tendency to place more emphasis on the social and economic dimensions of the idea. Certainly this is the case in Canada, where the departmental audit process organized by the Office of the Commissioner for the Environment and Sustainable Development operates with an explicitly multidimensional understanding which highlights economic, social and environmental dimensions of sustainable development goals. It is also evident in Norway and Sweden, and perhaps to a somewhat lesser extent in the Netherlands.

Third, in contexts where 'development' policy is under consideration—say with respect to the regeneration of depressed regions, or in relation to the land-use planning system in the United Kingdom—sustainable development can be construed within the broader connotation.

Fourth, efforts to develop sustainable development 'indicators'—encouraged mainly by the OECD and UNCSD, and which relate explicitly to economic, social, and environmental dimensions of the concept—have also tended to broaden its application.

And, finally, specific mention must be made of the rather peculiar situation in the United States. Here the President's Council has interpreted sustainable development widely, formulating 'National Goals' which relate to economy, society and environment, and which deal with issues as diverse as nature conservation, social capital, teenage pregnancy, crime, and high-school graduation rates. Yet the Council has had virtually no meaningful impact on the work of the government as a whole. To the extent that sustainable development has been invoked by US officials or politicians at the national level, this has almost exclusively been in relation to the problems of the developing world. The concept appears, in other words, as something which *others* must pursue, mainly with respect to the promotion of traditional socio-economic development, but occasionally with an emphasis on environment and development. Despite these qualifications and differences, however, it remains broadly true that, for the governments surveyed in the present study, the environmental element of sustainable development has received dominant emphasis.[1]

An additional aspect of the varying interpretations and semantic applications of sustainable development lies in differences as to the understanding of the normative principles underlying the concept. Official strategy documents and plans typically include reference to the range of ethical ideas with which the concept has been vested as it has passed down through the UNCED process. The theme of protecting the global environment is prevalent, as is the idea of integrating environment and economy in decision-making at all levels of society. Other relevant ethical dimensions—domestic equity, international equity, concern for futurity, and social participation—are less consistently present. Considering the governments as a group, the themes of international equity and social participation received comparatively more emphasis in strategic policy documents, while those of concern for futurity and domestic equity were less consistently brought to the fore.

[1] To suggest that the environmental dimension of the concept has been set to the fore is not to argue that sustainable development has led to any substantive privileging of environmental over economic or social objectives. It is merely to observe that when the concept is invoked it is generally because environmental problems are at issue.

Yet significant national differentiation is also evident. International equity issues—fairness between North and South and global poverty reduction—have been especially prominent in official presentations of sustainable development by governments in the Netherlands, Norway and Sweden, but were clearly more weakly represented in Germany, the United States,[2] and the UK. The participatory strand of sustainable development (again, as part of national strategy) has been particularly evident in Canada, and more recently in the Netherlands, and least evident in Germany and Japan. Concern for futurity, on the other hand (intergenerational equity), is emphasized in Norway, Japan, and Germany, and received unique embodiment in the Netherlands' (NEPP) commitment to reduce the net environmental burden transferred to futurity to zero within one generation.[3] National equity, or burden-sharing within one country, received somewhat more emphasis in the Netherlands, Sweden, and Norway than it did in other jurisdictions. But such representations also have varied over time. Equity dimensions, for example, which were almost absent in the 1994 UK sustainable development strategy, were considerably strengthened in the 1999 strategy document. Similar variations in the participatory aspect could also be teased out, as these are more susceptible to the electoral cycle and day-to-day politics.

Principles of Management

Sustainable development has also routinely been linked with a series of 'socio-ecological management principles'—maxims to be applied to give the call for sustainable development greater operational substance (Fig. 12.1). Of sixteen such principles often encountered in national strategies, plans and policy statements, 'international co-operation', 'intergovernmental co-operation', 'environmental impact assessment', 'technological development', 'societal participation', and 'integrating economic and environmental decision-making' were most consistently presented as essential for the promotion of sustainable development. 'Factor- or eco-efficiency' approaches, 'the precautionary principle', 'materials cycles/ecocycle perspectives', 'integrated pollution control', employing 'the best scientific

---

[2] It might appear paradoxical that sustainable development has largely been invoked in the United States in a foreign-policy/foreign-aid context, but that the international equity dimensions of sustainable development are none the less not particularly prominent in American representations of sustainable development. An explanation lies in the fact that foreign aid is not conceptualized as an equity issue in the American context.

[3] As the ambitious character of this objective became clear, the commitment has been somewhat qualified in later versions of the NEPP.

very prominent	develop international co-operation
	develop intergovernmental co-operation
	conduct environmental impact assessments
	promote technological development
	encourage societal participation
	integrate economy and environment in decision-making
prominent	employ factor- or eco-efficiency approaches
	respect precautionary principle
	employ material cycles/ecocycle perspectives
	extend integrated pollution control
	employ best scientific knowledge
	take cost effective measures
less prominent	respect ecosystem carrying capacity
	conduct risk assessment
	respect polluter pays principle
	transform consumption patterns

Note: Analysis based on a qualitative assessment of national plans and strategy documents and major policy statements related to sustainable development across ten selected jurisdictions.

FIGURE 12.1. Emphasis on socio-ecological management principles in government policy pronouncements on sustainable development 1987–98

knowledge', and taking 'cost effective measures' were also cited regularly. In contrast, 'respecting ecosystem carrying capacity', 'conducting risk assessments', applying 'the polluter-pays principle', and 'transforming consumption patterns' were mentioned less frequently.

There was also clear variation across the jurisdictions. Technological development was strongly stressed by Japan, Germany, Sweden, and the European Union; material cycle/ecocycle perspectives received particular support in Germany, Japan, the Netherlands, and Sweden; the precautionary principle was frequently endorsed in Australia, Germany, Norway, and the European Union; and the polluter-pays principle was highlighted by government in Germany and the European Union. Norway appears to be the only state in the study which has given specific strategic focus to the carrying capacity of nature and the issue of modifying patterns of consumption and production. In Canada remedial technological development, and in the United States international co-operation, each received somewhat less attention than they did in the mix of management principles endorsed by the

very prominent	environment
	energy
	natural resources
	industry
prominent	agriculture
	transport
	urban policy
less prominent	aboriginal peoples
	education
	employment
	finance
	health
	immigration
	military
	regional policy
	social policy

Note: Analysis based on a qualitative assessment of national plans and strategy documents and major policy statements related to sustainable development across ten selected jurisdictions.

FIGURE 12.2. Emphasis on sectoral domains in government policy pronouncements on sustainable development 1987–98

other states. Variations over time were, however, also apparent here, with references in particular to 'Factor-4/Factor-10' and 'eco-efficiency' strengthening over time.

Policy Perspectives

Sustainable development can also be approached from the perspective of the domestic policy domains with which it is most commonly associated (Fig. 12.2). Considering the governments as a group, the policy areas of environment, energy, industry, and natural resources were most consistently cited in major policy statements, plans, and programmes related to the attainment of sustainable development. Agriculture, transport, and urban policy also received substantial attention. In contrast, the fields of education, employment, finance, health, military affairs, regional policy, social policy, immigration and aboriginal affairs have been much less systematically

very prominent	climate change
	nature conservation
	resource use
	waste management
prominent	air pollution
	biodiversity / species loss
	fresh water
	forests
	land use patterns
	oceans / seas
	ozone depletion
	soil conservation
less prominent	biotechnology
	consumption patterns
	population growth

Note: Analysis based on a qualitative assessment of national plans and strategy documents and major policy statements related to sustainable development across ten selected jurisdictions.

FIGURE 12.3. Emphasis on selected environmental themes in government pronouncements on sustainable development 1987–98

identified with the concept. Interesting elements of cross-national variation include the relative emphasis on agriculture in Australia and the Netherlands; on employment and economic recovery in Sweden; on military affairs in Sweden, and to a lesser extent in Canada; on population growth and immigration in Australia and the United States; and on aboriginal affairs in Australia and Canada. An indication of the environmental themes with which sustainable development is most closely associated is provided in Fig. 12.3.

Fluctuations over Time

Another important issue concerns the timing of governmental engagement with, and the fluctuations in intensity of initiatives related to, sustainable development. Table 12.2*a* offers a perspective on these temporal dimensions. It appears that Canada, the Netherlands, Norway, and Sweden moved early with a broad range of initiatives. Australia, Japan, the UK, and the European

Table 12.2a. The intensity of major new sustainable development related initiatives launched by central governments

period	A	C	G	J	Ne	No	S	UK	USA	EU
1987–1988	–	++	–	–	++	+++	++	+	–	–
1989–1990	++	++	–	++	+++	+++	++	++	–	+
1991–1992	+++	+++	–	+++	+++	+++	+	++	–	+
1993–1994	++	+	–	++	++	+	++	+	+	++
1995–1996	+	+	+	++	++	+	++	+	+	++
1997–1998	+	++	++	+	++	++	+++	++	+	++

Symbols: +   = some activity
       ++ = more widespread activity
       +++ = intense and widespread activity

Notes: This table tracks variation in the intensity of major new sustainable development related initiatives launched by central governments between 1987 and 1998. It is based on a review of relevant policy statements and legislative and administrative enactments.

Table 12.2b. The intensity of new environmental initiatives launched by central governments

period	A	C	G	J	Ne	No	S	UK	USA	EU
1987–1988	+	++	++	+	++	+++	++	+	+	+
1989–1990	++	+++	+++	++	+++	+++	++	++	+	+
1991–1992	+++	+++	++	+++	+++	+++	+	++	+	++
1993–1994	+	+	+	++	++	+	++	+	++	++
1995–1996	+	+	+	++	++	+	++	+	+	++
1997–1998	+	++	+	+	++	++	+++	++	+	++

Symbols: +   = some activity
       ++ = more widespread activity
       +++ = intense and widespread activity

Notes: This chart tracks variation in the intensity of major new environment-related initiatives launched by central governments between 1987 and 1998. It is based on a review of relevant policy statements and legislative and administrative enactments.

Union also took up the issue at the end of the 1980s, although the build-up of activity appears to have been more gradual. In Germany and the United States the response was delayed until the mid-1990s, although in the German case there is evidence that as the decade drew to a close sustainable development was moving up the policy agenda.

Considering the group as a whole, an intense phase of headline initiatives occurred during the 1989–92 period. After the Earth Summit many countries shifted attention to other (particularly economic) issues, and governments which had been most active in the earlier period appear to have decided that in comparative terms they were well ahead of the game, and could, therefore, slack off on the initiative. Nevertheless one should be cautious in interpreting this decline in the rate of major new initiatives as evidence of a substantive weakening of the sustainable development effort. Over the five years between 1993 and 1997 orientations and structures established during the late 1980s and early 1990s began to have significant impacts on policy formulation and implementation 'on the ground', and by end of the decade all of the governments covered by our study had far more elaborate patterns of engagement with the concept than they had at the beginning. Moreover, it appears that during the second half of the 1990s the pace of major initiatives again picked up as some states experienced (for very different reasons) a 'second wind'. Canada, for example, after a period of drift, comes back 'on line' with the Commissioner for Environment and Sustainable Development. Similar reorientations—largely connected to the electoral cycle—are also visible in the United Kingdom and Germany. In general, to the extent that sustainable development is largely identified with *environmental* policy, it is apparent that it becomes linked to cycles of issue attention characterizing this policy domain. Table 12.2*b* provides an assessment of the varying intensity of environmental policy initiatives undertaken by these governments over the same period. The principal difference between the two charts relates to the failure of sustainable development to make an early impact in Germany (while environmental initiatives were nevertheless highly significant in the early 1990s), and in the United States (where the pace of federal environmental innovation remained comparatively low throughout the period with which we are concerned).

Agenda 21

Attitudes towards the conventions on climate change and biodiversity will be examined later in this chapter, but it is worth pausing briefly to consider how governments have reacted to the other major international agreement signed at the 1992 Rio Summit—Agenda 21. Table 12.3 provides some indication of the relative importance governments have attached to Agenda 21 in terms of domestic political life. While six of the ten governments have regularly referred to Agenda 21 in prominent policy statements, only one has prepared an official Agenda 21 'action plan', and three have established national Agenda 21 committees. With respect to the local level—where Agenda 21 has been most visible—seven governments gave some encouragement to Local Agenda 21 activities, but apparently only three have provided central funding to facilitate the process.

In the United States, Agenda 21 has virtually no domestic political salience. It does not, for example, even rate a mention in the PCSD

Table 12.3. Central government responses to Agenda 21, 1992–1997

activity	A	C	G	J	Ne	No	S	UK	USA	EU
1. Agenda 21 translated into relevant language(s)	na	na	+	+	+	–	+	na	na	–
2. mentioned in prominent domestic policy statements	–	–	–	+	+	+	+	+	–	+
3. national action plan prepared	–	–	–	+	–	–	–	–	–	–
4. national Agenda 21 committee established	–	–	+	+	–	–	+	–	–	–
5. national information campaign organized	–	–	–	–	+	–	+	–	–	–
6. central encouragement of Local Agenda 21 activity (including indirect funding)	+	–	–	+	+	+	+	+	–	+
7. direct central funding of Local Agenda 21 activities	–	–	–	–	+	+	+	–	–	–
8. Tally of items 2–7	1	0	1	4	4	3	5	2	0	2

Symbols: – = no
  + = yes
  na = not applicable

Notes: This table charts Agenda 21-focused activity of central governments. 'National action plan' and 'national committee' refer to plans and committees *explicitly* established to promote Agenda 21 as a national programme (as opposed, for example, to less-focused national sustainable development strategies). Support for Local Agenda 21 activities has been included since this is one of the few areas where Agenda 21 has been actively taken up. Item 8 provides a tally which gives an approximation of the relative extent to which national governments have taken up activities under the banner of Agenda 21.

document *Sustainable America*. It is also very rarely invoked in Canada, despite the much higher profile which the government there accords to sustainable development. Agenda 21 has not been a significant focus for federal activity in Australia or until recently in Germany, although in the latter case action by environmental organizations has given the document a higher public profile. Governments in the EU, UK, and Norway have given Agenda 21 somewhat more attention—particularly in terms of supporting local initiatives—although it should be noted that the Norwegians have yet to translate the full document. Greater enthusiasm for the Rio action plan has been shown in Japan, and in Sweden and the Netherlands the governments have shown considerable interest, particularly in the areas of public education and support for local and regional initiatives.

Nonetheless it appears that none of the central governments monitored have taken the document seriously in a programmatic sense. To the extent that it features in public pronouncements it is essentially as a symbol of the international commitment to 'do something' about environment and development problems. This does not mean that the issues, ideas, and policy recommendations contained in Agenda 21 have been absent from domestic policy debates. What it does signify is that the plan *as a plan*, or even as a general set of guidelines for problematizing and working towards sustainable development, has not been carried through. True, periodic reporting obligations to the relevant bodies of the United Nations have encouraged officials in *most* countries to examine issues within a holistic context which they otherwise might not have applied, but the perfunctory nature of much of this reporting suggests that this has been of limited significance. Whatever may be argued about specific issue areas, it is clear that Agenda 21 has not been viewed by governments as a document for structuring the domestic policy agenda, or framing issues for national debate.

Organizational Engagement

In the countries with which we have been concerned the reception of sustainable development has not been primarily marked by the establishment of new executive agencies. No government has, for example, created a 'ministry for sustainable development implementation'. Considering that one of the key messages associated with sustainable development relates to the importance of *integrating* environmental concerns into existing decisional structures, this is hardly surprising. Where new central agencies have been created the impetus largely predates the new paradigm. Although discussions of sustainable development lent weight to the move to establish the UK Environment Agency—where sustainable development implementation is explicitly mentioned in the organization's official remit—the roots of the new body lie in debates about integrated pollution control and water privatization in the mid-1980s. Similarly, while a concern for sustainable development has provided a focus for the work of the European Environment Agency, the organization owes its existence to an agreement on the need to monitor environmental developments across the Union in the context of the project of creating the single European market.[4]

Institutional engagement with sustainable development has above all meant the taking up of sustainable development by pre-existing bodies—by

---

[4] The European Environment Agency (EEA) does not have executive powers. Its functions are essentially to gather data (via the efforts of member states—it has no independent collection network or inspection powers), to analyse this data, and to report its findings.

ministries, regulatory agencies, advisory groups, and research institutes. In the first instance this has been by organizations with established responsibilities for environmental governance. But in most jurisdictions this has also, and increasingly, involved other branches of the administration—particularly those in charge of foreign relations, international development assistance, resource management, and, in several cases, research and development. A number of governments—notably those of Norway, Sweden, and Canada (but also officially that of Australia)—have pursued a 'whole of government' approach to sustainable development, based on the principle of integrating responsibility for sustainable development implementation into the operation of every branch of public administration. Differences clearly remain, however, as to the extent to which the idea has actually been assimilated into the plans and operations of the various departments.

Ministries and Agencies

In almost every state environmental ministries and/or agencies have taken the most active role in promoting reflection and policy innovation related to sustainable development (see Table 12.4). Efforts have been particularly successful when they have been encouraged at Cabinet level and backed by the Prime Minister, as they have been for limited periods in Australia, Britain, and Canada, and with somewhat more consistency in Norway, Sweden, and the Netherlands. The clear exception to the trend for established environmental departments to take the lead is the United States, where the President's Council has been the most dynamic body. The functions of the US Environmental Protection Agency are circumscribed by a fairly rigid legislative framework, and the Agency has demonstrated little inclination to engage with the broader policy agenda raised by sustainable development.

An active role with regard to the externally oriented strands of sustainable development policy has been played by foreign ministries and international development agencies across the jurisdictions with which we have been concerned. The 'mission statements', thematic priorities, and project-vetting procedures of international development agencies have been revised to accommodate sustainable development. Environmental diplomacy has been a key concern for the foreign ministries of all the units in this study—although it is clear that in the smaller states the ministries have devoted considerably more attention to integrating sustainable development initiatives into their international priorities. Of the governments surveyed, the Netherlands has made the most intensive effort to reconcile domestic and foreign

Table 12.4. Central government organizations and the response to sustainable development (1987–1998)

	Most active pre-existing government bodies	New (post 1987) structures and organizations particularly concerned with sustainable development
Australia	Department of Environment, Sports and Territories (m) Department of Primary Industry and Energy (m) Department of Foreign Affairs and Trade (m) Australian Agency for International Development (ag)	Ecologically sustainable development working groups (1990–2) (c) Intergovernmental Ecologically Sustainable Development Steering Committee (1991–4) (ig) Intergovernmental Committee on Ecologically Sustainable Development (1994–8) (ig) National Environmental Protection Council (1994–) (ag) National Heritage Trust (1997–) (o)
Canada	Environment Canada (m) Natural Resources Canada (m) Agriculture and Agri-food Industry (m) Canadian International Development Agency (ag)	National Roundtable on Environment and Economy (1989–) (c) Parliamentary Standing Committee on Environment and Sustainable Development (1994) (p) Commissioner of the Environment and Sustainable Development (1995–) (p) International Institute for Sustainable Development (1990–) (r)
Germany	Federal Environment Agency (UBA) (ag) Federal Environment Ministry (BMU) (m) Ministry for Development Co-operation (BMZ) (m) Council of Environmental Advisors (RSU) (ad)	National Committee for Sustainable Development (reorganized in 1994). (1991–) (c) Enquete Commission 'Man and the Environment' (1994–8) (p) Scientific Advisory Council to the Federal Government on the Global Environment (1992–) (ad)
Japan	Environment Agency (ag) Ministry of International Trade and Industry (MITI) (m) Ministry of Foreign Affairs (m) Central Council for the Environment (ad) Nature Conservation Council (ad)	Japan Council for Sustainable Development (1996) Ministerial Council for Global Environmental Co-operation (1989–) (ig)
Netherlands	Ministry of Housing, Physical Planning, and Environment (VROM) (m) Ministry of Transport, Public Works, and Water Management (m) Agriculture, Nature Management, and Fisheries (m) Economic Affairs (m) Foreign Affairs (m) Development Co-operation (m) Dutch National Institute of Public Health and the Environment (RIVM) (r)	Temporary Commission on Climate Change (1995) (p) Platform Brazil (reorganized in 1992) (1990–) (o)
Norway	Ministry of Environment (m) Ministry of Industry and Energy (m) Ministry of Finance (m) Ministry of Foreign Affairs (m) Ministry of Agriculture (m) State Pollution Authority (ag)	State Secretary Committee for Environmental Matters (1989–) (ig) Parliamentary Committee on Energy and Environment (1993–) (p) Committee for Sustainable Development (1993–) (ad)

Table 12.4. (*Cont.*)

	Most active pre-existing government bodies	New (post 1987) structures and organizations particularly concerned with sustainable development
	Directorate of Nature Management (ag)	National Committee for International Environmental Matters (1993–) (ad) Centre for Sustainable Production and Consumption (GRIP) (1991–) (o)
Sweden	Environmental Advisory Council (EAC) (ad) Ministry of Environment (m) Swedish Environment Protection Agency (SEPA) (a) Swedish International Development Agency (SIDA) (a)	'Rio Group' Environment and Development 92 (1990–2) (o) National Committee for Agenda 21 (1995–8) (c) Commission for Sustainable Development (1997–8) (ig) Commission for Ecologically Sustainable Procurement (1998–) (ig)
United Kingdom	Department of the Environment (from 1997, of the Environment, Transport, and the Regions) (m) Ministry of Agriculture, Fisheries and Food (m) Department of Trade and Industry (m) English Nature (ag) Royal Commission on Environmental Pollution (ad)	Environment Agencies (1996–) (ag) Government Panel on Sustainable Development (1994–) (ad) Roundtable on Sustainable Development (1994–) (c) Going for Green (1994–) (o)
United States	Environmental Protection Agency (EPA) (a) US Agency for International Development (USAID) (a) State Department (m) Interior Department (m) Council on Environmental Quality (ad)	President's Council on Sustainable Development (1993–) (ad) Interagency Working Group on Sustainable Development (1996–) (ig)
European Union	DGXI (Environment and Nuclear Safety) (m)	European Environment Agency (1990–) (ag) General Consultative Forum on the Environment (1994–7) (c) European Forum on Environment and Sustainable Development (1997–) (c) Environment Policy Review Group (1993) (ig) Implementation Network (1993–) (ig)

Symbols: ad = specialist advisory body
ag = administrative agency
c = cross-sectoral forum
ig = intergovernmental body
m = ministry
o = other
p = parliamentary body
r = research institute

Notes: This list includes central ministries and agencies, as well as other types of organization created, supported and financed by the state (scientific advisory groups, cross-sectoral forums, research institutes, and so on) which have played an important role in central government responses to sustainable development. Because many bodies have been active, only the most significant are included here. The first column deals with established organizations—those created before 1987—which have been *most active* in engaging with sustainable development. The second column deals with organizations created since 1987, after sustainable development had emerged as an explicit focus for concern. Many of the newer bodies have been subject to frequent reorganizations (as indeed have the pre-established ministries and agencies) which cannot be fully captured here.

policy dimensions of environmental policy. But in Norway, Sweden, and Canada foreign ministries have also engaged actively with the politics of sustainable development. Also in Japan the foreign ministry has been particularly active in comparison with the rest of government, a profile which reflects both the weakness of the Japan Environment Agency (which had not yet achieved ministerial status), and the official understanding by the early 1990s that sustainable development was to be an area where the country could demonstrate international leadership (as an aspect of development policy). It is similarly interesting to note that in the United States, the State Department and the Agency for International Development (USAID) have been the most active cabinet-rank department and line agency, respectively, in adjusting their idiom (at least in their externally directed statements) to the notion of sustainable development.

In many countries energy and natural-resource-focused ministries have also become closely implicated in debates about sustainable development. Consider, for example, the Department of Primary Industry and Energy in Australia or Natural Resources Canada. While the programmes and priorities of these ministries may not always please environmentalists, their initiatives have been increasingly presented within the frame of sustainable development. The Norwegian Ministry of Industry and Energy also provides an interesting example of the use of the idiom. The ministry has formulated its argument for a vigorous expansion of North Sea gas extraction in terms of the potentially positive impact on sustainable development implementation in Europe (i.e. the benefits of replacing coal with gas as a source of power and heating). The situation with agriculture ministries is much more uneven, with the heavy engagement in the Netherlands standing in marked contrast to the slower uptake in the UK, Germany, and especially the European Union.

As for other governmental sectors, sustainable development does not appear to have made much of a policy impact on welfare, employment, health, or education ministries. Yet there are exceptions here also, notably in Sweden where sustainable development has been explicitly linked to employment generation. In the Netherlands and the UK some environmental health issues have been addressed in terms of sustainable development, and in Germany and Norway the education ministries have also shown some interest. Overall, the most significant 'absentee' has been the finance ministries, which in many states remain sceptical of major environmental policy initiatives as costly/low-return activities. In the UK, for example, the Treasury has been notably slow to relate to sustainable development, and traditional practices and routines—such as entrenched opposition to hypothecated taxation—have clearly slowed a 'greening' of the fiscal system. In Canada the first review by the Commissioner for Sustainable Development of departmental strategies cited Finance and also Revenue Canada as among the poorest performers (Minister of Public Works and Government Services, Canada 1998). Also here the Netherlands, Norway, and Sweden emerge as partial exceptions to the trend, with the finance ministries in all three countries showing evidence of a growing engagement with the concept, particularly with respect to long-term goals, planning and alternative tax-and-employment schemes.

Advisory Bodies and Sector Integration

In addition to operational departments, governments maintain an array of established advisory bodies and research institutes. Those with responsibility for the natural and built environments in particular have rapidly been drawn into the discussion of sustainable development. Sometimes such organizations have played an important role in bringing problems before the public and galvanizing political intention to act. In the Netherlands the highly respected Dutch National Institute of Public Health and the Environment (RIVM) has played a unique role in presenting expert advice on the state of the environment which has been accepted as a basis from which the discussion of official plans and policies has proceeded.

In most countries engagement of government with sustainable development has been accompanied by an array of organizational changes. These have included measures relating to departmental structure, relationships among ministries, interaction among different layers of public administration, and contacts with wider sectors of society. Within environment ministries reorganization has focused on improving capacities to interact with other ministries, to deal with the transnational dimensions of environmental issues, and to engage in strategic planning. The first two of these factors clearly motivated the 1989 reorganization of the Norwegian environment ministry, but they also hold true to varying degrees in other jurisdictions. With respect to non-environmental departments changes have been introduced to ensure that environmental or sustainable development related concerns are introduced at an early stage of decision-making. This was the justification for the British system of 'Green Ministers', where each major department had a junior minister particularly responsible for the environmental dimensions of its activity.

Structures to facilitate interdepartmental collaboration on environmental issues have also proliferated in most jurisdictions, although these are often of an 'ad hoc working group' or 'project-focused' nature. Institutionalization of national environmental policy and sustainable development planning processes has favoured closer interdepartmental contact. The first Dutch NEPP was signed by six departments, and the 1992 UK sustainable development strategy involved substantial cross-government consultation. Efforts to improve policy co-ordination from the top have led to the creation of high level committees on the environment: in Norway the State Secretary Committee for Environmental Issues, in Japan the Council of Ministers for the International Environment, in the UK the Cabinet Committee on the Environment.

Collaboration between different layers of government has been another recurrent theme. In Australia governmental engagement with sustainable development was closely linked with the conclusion of the Inter Governmental Agreement on the Environment and the establishment of an institutional framework for collective environmental policy-making among state and federal governments. In the Netherlands the environmental policy planning process has involved increasingly close contact between central government and provincial and local authorities including the water boards, and in Sweden emphasis has also been placed on national/local co-operation, here within the context of a conscious effort to delegate implementation to the localities and to concentrate the attention of national bodies on strategic issues.

Perhaps the most obvious organizational innovation associated with the coming of sustainable development has been the creation of an array of consultative and advisory bodies intended to draw social actors into dialogue with government over the orientation of sustainable development implementation. The best-known such bodies are the broad-based 'national committees' established in the wake of the publication of the Report of the WCED and during the run-up or follow-up to the Rio Earth Summit. These included the 'National Roundtable on Environment and Economy' in Canada, the 'National Committee for Sustainable Development' in Germany, the 'President's Council on Sustainable Development' in the USA, and the 'European Forum on Environment and Sustainable Development' in the EU.

Some of these bodies started with an explicit brief to co-ordinate the national input to the UNCED process or to popularize the Summit's achievements. Others had from the outset a more general remit. Typically the justification for their existence has focused on the need to involve all sectors of society in making development sustainable, to build consensus among social partners—government, business, environment-and-development NGOs, trade unions, and so on—over possible solutions, and to advance the education of the general public. Some have been more in the mould of advisory committees (such as the UK Roundtable), while others have engaged in widespread public consultation and popular education campaigns (such as the Swedish National Committee for Agenda 21). There has been considerable variation in the degree to which the committees have actually functioned, as well as in the significance they have been accorded by political leaders. The German National Committee for Sustainable Development met regularly, but it has been perceived as a 'second-tier' body, lacking dynamism and effective political potential. The Norwegian Committee for Sustainable Development has been essentially moribund—not even managing annual meetings. The Canadian Roundtable has had ups and downs, while the Swedish National Committee for Agenda 21 has been particularly active and effective. In the US, the President's Council consulted with business and community leaders and produced some impressive reports—but its work has had virtually no effect on the main lines of political or administrative life.

In addition to the national committees many other advisory and consultative forums have been established, often focused around specific themes or sectors. Indeed the trend to link government with non-governmental organizations of all kinds—to build 'partnerships', solicit interest from private and professional bodies, and to explore negotiated solutions, has been one of the constants of sustainable development implementation. This is an issue we will return to in the context of considering government/non government ment linkages later in this chapter.

Strategic Planning Processes

One significant institutional change associated with sustainable development over the past decade has been the emergence of strategic planning initiatives in which governments attempt to map out systematically how they intend to tackle issues related to the environment and sustainable development.

The governments of Australia, Canada, Japan, the Netherlands, Norway, Sweden, the United Kingdom, and the European Union have all experimented with such strategic planning processes. Australia produced its National Strategy for Ecologically Sustainable Development in 1992. The Canadian Green Plan was adopted in 1990, and in 1995 the federal government introduced a system under which departments periodically produce sustainable development strategies. In 1993 Japan issued a National Action Plan for Agenda 21, and a year later the first Environment Basic Plan appeared. Since 1989 the Netherlands has prepared three (and a half) National Environmental Policy Plans. In Norway the strategic orientation for sustainable development was established in a series of government 'white papers', and particular measures have been taken to integrate environment and sustainable development related issues into the established budget-cycle planning process. Sweden has adopted legislation which set out priorities for sustainable development implementation and the Swedish Environmental Protection Agency has prepared a National Plan for Sustainable Development. In the United Kingdom the strategy process revolved around the 'white papers' 'Our Common Inheritance' (1990), and 'Sustainable Development: The UK Strategy' (1994), and associated follow-up reports. In the European Union, the Fifth Environmental Action Programme fixed the orientation for action around the environment and sustainable development until the year 2000.

Equivalent strategy documents and processes have not been adopted in either Germany or the United States. In the United States the closest approaches have been the report of the PCSD and the EPA's 'Environmental Goals for America' project. However, the first is an advisory report rather than a commitment by government, while the second did not progress beyond draft stage and has now been abandoned. In Germany the Federal Environment Ministry issued a 'Draft Programme for Priority Areas in Environmental Policy' in 1998. Although this was only a proposal by the ministry, it appears that Germany may enact a formal plan in the near future. Further details on strategic planning initiatives in the ten jurisdictions are presented in Table 12.5.

In comparison to earlier efforts at environmental management, these new plans and strategies deploy a more comprehensive vision, attempting to describe the policy response to some significant proportion of the total national environmental burden. They adopt a longer term approach, focusing directly on the next three, four, or five years, but considering possible scenarios twenty, thirty or even fifty years into the future. National issues are discussed within the context of global problems and emphasis is placed upon the obligation to contribute to an international quest for solutions. Moreover, the idea of 'sustainable development' provides a key conceptual reference-point for these plans and strategies.

Yet despite points of substantive similarity these strategic planning initiatives are different in many respects. Important dimensions of variation include *thematic scope* (that part of the terrain of sustainable development which the plan includes); *politico/legal character* (the form of approach, the agencies that stand behind it, and how it is given legal force); intra- and intergovernmental *consultation* and social *participation* (the range of departments, governments, and social sectors which have had a role in its genesis); *goals and targets* (the objectives of the strategy, whether quantitative as well as qualitative targets are formulated); *review and iteration* (whether provision is

Table 12.5. Strategic planning for the environment and sustainable development (1987–1999)

	Australia	Canada	[Germany]*	Japan	Netherlands
Title of strategy document	National Strategy for Ecologically Sustainable Development	(1) Canada's Green Plan [(2) *Projet de Société* (Canadian Choices for Transitions to Sustainability)]* (3) Departmental Sustainable Development Strategies	[Sustainable Development in Germany: Draft programme for Priority Areas in Environmental Policy]*	(1) National Action Plan for Agenda 21 (2) Environment Basic Plan	National Environmental Policy Plans. NEPP; NEPP+; NEPP2; NEPP3.
Date of enactment	1992	(1) 1990 [(2) process, 1992–95] (3) 1995: individual strategies issued by the end of 1997	[Published April 1998]	(1) 1993 (2) 1994	1989; 1990; 1994; 1998
Legal basis	Policy document endorsed by the Council of Australian Governments. No further legal foundation.	(1) Tabled in parliament, but not voted on as a whole. Specific programme elements included in legislation where necessary. [(2) No legal foundation] (3) Amendment to Auditor General Act (1995)	[No legal enactment: draft document only.]	(1) and (2) Documents of government. Preparation of the Environment Basic Plan is required by article 15 of the Environment Basic Law.	Plans adopted by Parliament
Sponsoring agencies	Federal Cabinet	(1) Environment Canada. Ratified by the whole of the government [(2) National Roundtable on the Environment and Economy led the	[Published by Federal Environment Ministry.]	(1) Environment Agency (2) Central Council for the Environment. Both adopted by the Government.	VROM. Signed by other ministries.

		process, with political and financial backing from Environment Canada, and the Canadian Council of Ministers of the Environment.] (3) System endorsed by full cabinet; individual strategies submitted by each department.			
Cross departmental co-ordination during preparation	Yes, consultation across federal government	(1) Yes: intensive negotiations between Environment Canada, Finance and other departments with spending programmes under the Green Plan. [(2) no] (3) no: department specific	[No. But to be object of further consultations]	(1) Ministries and agencies commented on Environment Agency draft in the Council of Ministers for Global Environmental Conservation (2) Ministries and agencies made presentations to CCE during plan preparation.	Extensive negotiations among ministries during preparation of plans
Intergovernmental participation during preparation	Produced through an intergovernmental process, involving federal, state and local government inputs.	(1) no: programme of Federal Government. [(2) participation from provincial and municipal representatives] (3) no: programme of federal Government	[Federal government document]	(1) local governments given opportunity to comment (2) local government reports to CCE during plan preparation.	Provinces, municipalities and water boards consulted in planning process and detailed negotiations with VROM conducted over implementation.
Social participation during preparation	At many levels: through Ecological Sustainable Development Working Groups, community	(1) Opportunity for public commentary when Cabinet released initial draft.	[Based in part on recommendations of six working groups (established in 1996)	(1) Limited period for public comment on draft, and many criticisms resulted in	Limited during preparation of initial NEPP, but more extensive during

Table 12.5. (Cont.)

	Australia	Canada	[Germany]*	Japan	Netherlands
	consultation at beginning of process, and a period for public comment on draft NSESD	[(2) Inclusive multi-stakeholder process involving participants from more than 100 social groups] (3) Departments obliged by statute to consult with stakeholders in preparing strategies	with representatives from 130 major groups which delivered their reports in June 1997. To be object of further consultations.]	some substantive changes. (2) Representation to CCE and public hearings during plan preparation	subsequent plans. Emphasis is on particularly close co-operation during implementation phases rather than on objective setting phases.
Forward horizon	vague, open ended	(1) 1995 [(2) open] (3) variable	[Not explicitly mentioned, varies with issues addressed—from 2005 to 2050]	(1) and (2) vague	20 years
Iterative cycle	no	(1) no [(2) no] (3) yes, every three years	[unclear]	(1) perhaps (2) probably	4 years rolling
financing	no specific provisions	(1) Initially $3 billion over 5 years; later reduced to $2.5 billion over 6 years [(2) no] (3) no	[no specific provisions]	(1) primarily lists past commitments, for example on environment ODA. (2) no specific provisions	Budgeting of items of expenditure and assessments of impact on macro economic position.
targets	Mainly qualitative, with some quantitative objectives across 8 economic sectors and 22 intersectoral themes	(1) Mainly qualitative objectives across programme areas included [(2) yes, but main emphasis on 'choices'] (3) Yes, but nature	[Qualitative and quantitative targets presented for 5 priority themes (atmosphere, nature conservation, resource conservation, human health and	(1) primarily qualitative goals (2) Qualitative and quantitative targets—mainly taken from existing policy commitments. Stated	Strategic objectives; and detailed quantitative targets, disaggregated to sectors, with clearly defined time scales for the full range of elements

Review and monitoring	Every 2 years, co-ordinated by Australian Intergovernmental Committee on Ecologically Sustainable Development (1992–8). Later by a variety of agencies.	(1) no [(2) no] (3) Commissioner of the Environment and Sustainable Development reviews strategies and reports to Parliament. First such report completed in 1998. varies from department to department. Commissioner's 1998 Report recommends more clear goal setting and identification of measurable targets for future iterations.	early objective is the development of a comprehensive indicator set to monitor long term performance. [...environmentally sound mobility) and presentation of 'Environment-Barometer for Germany' with indicators for climate, air, soil, nature, water and resources.]	(1) to be reviewed 'as necessity arises' (2) Every year CCE will examine progress and hear public representations on progress, making recommendations to government if necessary. Full scale review by government in 'about 5 years'. [unclear, as this is only a draft for discussion with other branches of government and the public.]	Reviewed every year by VROM; environmental balances assessed every 2 years by RIVM. Progress for each target evaluated when preparing subsequent iteration and policies and/or goals for next period adjusted accordingly.
Basic character of strategy documents	A policy statement on sustainable development related objectives issued by the Australian governments. 'Implementation' is largely left to state and local administrations.	(1) Largely an omnibus environmental spending programme, with actions organized around 6 environmental themes. But also included measures to improve a) environment/economic decision-making and b) governmental environmental practice.	[Draft of an action plan for priority areas in environmental policy. It locates environmental policy as one aspect of sustainable development. It deals with many issues outside the formal competence of the Federal Environment Ministry in order to	(1) Action plan to meet Agenda 21 commitments. (2) Statement of environmental objectives. More specific environmental plans are to harmonise with its orientation; other sorts of public plans must in their environmental aspects not contradict	Fully integrated, target oriented environmental plan with detailed objectives, interim targets, and monitoring and review procedures. Sustainable development constituted fundamental objective of NEPP process.

Table 12.5. (Cont.)

	Australia	Canada	[Germany]*	Japan	Netherlands
		[(2) A 'visioning' document drawn up on the basis of multi-stakeholder consultation.] (3) Statements of departmental 'objectives and plans of action to further sustainable development'.	promote discussion and a co-operative response with other agencies, the Lander, local authorities and other stakeholders.]	the perspectives of this plan.	
current political status (autumn 1999)	Of declining public concern and political relevance. Now largely an internal and intergovernmental process with little public interest. Attention of environmental groups and industry has largely shifted to specific issues and/or forums such as climate change.	(1) The Green Plan is no longer operative, but many specific elements have been integrated into continuing programmes. [(2) Government withdrew support after 1993 election, business leaders lost interest and the process gradually succumbed to 'stakeholder fatigue'. After the mid-1990s it was essentially dead.] (3) Continuing cycle	[Draft for discussion]	(1) Remains relevant government document. (2) Remains relevant environmental policy orientation.	Remains at core Dutch of efforts to manage environmental burdens and implement sustainable development. First NEPP set core objectives, later NEPPs have focused on implementation and operationalising the target group approach.
Significance	Reflected development of Federal government influence in environmental domain;	(1) Ambitious combination of environmental 'clean up', and 'greening	[Suggests the Environment Ministry is now engaging more seriously with sustainable	(1) Signals Japanese intention to attempt to play important role in international	Most integrated and established environmental policy planning system in any

the extension of co-operation among all Australian governments on environment and sustainable development issues; and widespread public participation in formulating approach to environmental problems. While the NSESD document and process has influenced the behaviour of governments at all levels, it is now largely of symbolic importance.

government' programme. At the time a step towards approaching environmental issues in a more comprehensive fashion. But reveals difficulty of aggregating major reforms into a single package, and the resistance of established ministries to ambitions of a junior department (Environment Canada).
[(2) Ambitious participatory effort to envision a sustainable Canada. Drew many groups into dialogue, popularised sustainability issues and produced an innovative report. But shows difficulties of managing open ended, multi-stakeholder processes.]
(3) Innovative mechanism to integrate sustainable development issues into work all government departments.

development. Possible movement towards the preparation of national environmental policy plan or sustainable development strategy.]

environment and development related issues. Acceptance of Public comments suggests some (slight) opening of political system to NGO inputs.
(2) Indicates more comprehensive approach to environment management issues and adjustment to a) the idea that pollution must be handled in an 'all round' manner; and b) the 'globalisation' of environmental problems and related political debate.

OECD country. Identification of clear objectives and targets, and elaborate monitoring mechanisms makes policy failures evident. Questions remain about how future NEPPs will relate to the physical planning system and to broader sustainable development issues such as international assistance.

Table 12.5. (Cont.)

	Norway	Sweden	United Kingdom	[USA]*	EU
Title of strategy document or approach	(1) Report to Parliament (RTP) 46: 'Environment and development: Norway's follow-up of the Report of the World Commission'. RTP 13: 'On the UN conference on environment and development in Rio de Janeiro'; and RTP 58: 'Environmental policy for a sustainable development: joint efforts for the future'. (2) Integration of environmental planning into annual budget planning cycle with publication of 'Green Book' detailing environment-related goals and expenditure for each ministry. (3) Sectoral Environmental Action Plans for all ministries.	(1) National Plan for Sustainable Development (2) Government Bill (GB) 1993/4:111: 'Targeting sustainable development: implementation of the UNCED decisions'; and GB 1997/8:145: 'Environmental policy for a sustainable Sweden'.	'This common inheritance' (TCI); 'Sustainable development: the UK strategy' (SDS); and 'A better quality of life: a strategy for sustainable development in the UK' (BQL).	[(1) Sustainable America] [(2) Environmental Goals for America]	Fifth Environment Action Programme. Towards Sustainability: A European Community Programme of Policy and Action in Relation to the Environment and Sustainable Development.
Date of enactment	(1) RTP 46: 1989; RTP 13: 1992; RTP 58: 1997. (2) annually since 1989 (3) 1997	(1) 1993 (2) 1994; 1998	TCI 1990; SDS 1994; BQL 1999.	[(1) Published 1996] [(2) Published 1996]	1992

Legal basis	(1) Government policy statements (2) Endorsed by parliament (3) Endorsed by parliament	(1) SEPA policy statement (2) Parliamentary decisions	Government policy statements.	[(1) No legal enactment. A Report of the President's Commission.] [(2) No legal enactment. Draft published for review by government agencies]	Adopted by the Council of Ministers
Sponsoring agencies	(1) Cabinet; Ministry of Environment (2) Ministry of Environment; relevant spending department; Ministry of Finance. (3) Each ministry, in consultation with Ministry of Environment.	(1) Swedish Environmental Protection Agency (SEPA) (2) Ministry of Environment, the Government	Department of the Environment	[(1) President's Commission on Sustainable Development] [(2) Environment Protection Agency]	Initially prepared by DGXI, and presented by the Commission to the Council of Ministers.
Cross departmental co-ordination	(1) extensive discussions among ministries (2) discussions between Ministry of Environment, other departments, and Finance. (3) discussion between Department and Ministry of Environment.	(1) inputs from responsible ministries and agencies (2) extensive discussions among ministries	Extensive discussion among ministries.	[(1) Inputs from government agencies] [(2) Consultations across Federal administration]	Consultation with other DGs.
Intergovernmental participation	(1) RTP 46 and RTP 58: some consultation with other tiers of government; RTP 13: no (2) and (3) some	(1) inputs from municipal experts (2) comments from municipalities	TCI: no; SDS and BQL: yes.	[(1) Inputs from state and local government] [(2) extensive consultation with state and local officials]	Consultation with member states during drafting

Table 12.5. (*Cont.*)

	Norway	Sweden	United Kingdom	[USA]*	EU
	consultation with other tiers of government				
Social participation	(1) RTP 46: broad process of consultation; (2), and (3): no formal input	(1) no (2) GB 111: results of public discussion of UNCED collated.	SDS: broad public consultation during preparation. Opportunities for public inputs enhanced during drafting of BQL.	[(1) Commission meetings open to public and many groups and individuals invited to make presentations.] [(2) public consultation, including nine regional roundtable meetings, and circulation of drafts of goals in 1995.]	Limited consultations during preparation of initial draft, but wider participation encouraged during reviews of performance.
forward time horizon	(1) vague (2) one year, varies for different goals (3) varies for different goals	(1) 5–10 years (2) GB 111: vague. GB 145: 2020/5.	vague	[(1) vague] [(2) 2005]	8 years, rolling
Iterative cycle	(1) no (2) annual budgets (3) every four years	(1) and (2): no	TCI: SDS: no. BQL: yes, review in five years.	[(1) and (2) no]	yes
financing	(1) no precise budgets (2) yes (3) yes	(1) and (2): no precise budgets	no	[(1) and (2) no]	
targets	(1) qualitative and quantitative goals included in various white papers (2) specified in budget	(1) and (2): qualitative objectives, with some quantitative targets. Quantitative targets have been further	TCI and SDS: qualitative objectives, some 'indicative targets' and few quantitative targets. BQL: 15 headline	[(1) General qualitative goals around economic, social and environmental themes.] [(2) Clear and quantified	General objectives and many specific targets and time scales.

proposals for each ministry (3) some qualitative and quantitative objectives specified in each plan	developed and synthesized in GB 145	indicators and a comprehensive indicator set covering social, economic and environmental dimensions. Few quantitative targets.	targets organized around 12 key themes relating to environmental quality]	
reviews and monitoring	(1) no systematic follow up mechanisms (2) annual reviews of expenditure (3) new 'National Goal Achievement Monitoring System' to be used for reporting to Parliament on state of the environment and policy performance.	(1) no (2) Procedures becoming increasingly clearly defined with SEPA playing a central role.	Mechanisms unclear in TCI, but annual reports on TCI and then TCI/SDS emerged. BQL commits government to assess progress in relation to headline indicators annually, and to take account of ongoing assessments from new Sustainable Development Commission.	[(1) No] [(2) in principle supported, but mechanisms not established]	Mid term review conducted in 1995/6 by Commission with extensive consultation. The result was a new Action Plan to carry forward fifth EAP objectives.
Basic character of strategy document	(1) Authoritative statements of government policy on sustainable development in the wake of major international developments (2) 'Greening' of traditional budgetary and financial planning processes through inclusion of environmental goals and expenditure of all	(1) Environmental policy plan for areas of responsibility administered by SEPA (2) GB 111: Basic orientation for implementing sustainable development in follow up to UNCED; GB 145: further elaboration of challenges of achieving the environmental dimension of	TCI, SDS: statements of government policy on the environmental policy implications of sustainable development. BQL: statement of government policy on sustainable development more broadly interpreted.	[(1) Report by an advisory commission to the President. Proposes 10 general goals related to sustainable development and discusses changes in US society needed to achieve sustainability.] [(2) Draft of a comprehensive statement of environmental objectives (in areas for which EPA has	General plan for environmental action across areas for which EU has competence. Emphasises integration of environmental issues into sectoral decision-making.

Table 12.5. (Cont.)

	Norway	Sweden	United Kingdom	[USA]*	EU
	departments. From 1992 expenditure was classed into three categories according to the significance of the environmental factor. (3) Departmental environmental action plans including priorities, targets, and expenditures. Issued in order to strengthen both sectoral and cross-sectoral integration.	sustainable development.		responsibility) with clear goals, measurable targets and strategies for attainment.]	
current political status (autumn 1999)	(1) RTP 58 is currently the operative strategic document. (2) 'Green Book' abandoned in 1997. Replaced by an annual report on 'The Government's Environmental Profile and the Kingdom's Environmental State', first issued in 1999. (3) During 1998 the first sets of plans have been prepared.	(1) continues as active plan of SEPA (2) GB 111: remains as a statement of intent; GB 145 currently being implemented.	Process is ongoing, with BQL now the operative statement.	[(1) Largely irrelevant to current political concerns. Little interest by Congress or even the executive branch in its recommendations.] [(2) Dead. EPA currently uninterested in continuing this approach.]	Remains in force. Preparations for next EAP underway.

Significance	(1) Expressed government commitment to the WCED Report and the UNCED process, outlining how sustainable development is to be implemented in Norway. Follow up of RTP 46 was inconsistent, and RTP 58 revisits themes from the earlier document. (2) Initial attempt to integrate environmental issues into routine of budgetary planning. Much criticised, it was abandoned in 1997. (3) Renewed attempt to carry through sectoral integration along lines first elaborated in RTP 46. Greater obligation on departments and more robust monitoring suggest a step forward in institutionalising sustainable development.	(1) establishes general priorities and objectives for SEPA, and serves as benchmark for development of sectoral plans, and possibly more participatory approaches to envisioning future developments. (2) GB 111: Expressed national commitment to carry forward UNCED agenda in Sweden. This objective has subsequently been concretised in specific legislation such as the 1993 Eco-cycle Bill, and 1998 Environmental Code. GB 145: proposes further initiatives on the environmental dimension of sustainable development including a systematisation of goals and targets.	TCI: first comprehensive statement on managing environmental burdens, initiated system of follow up reporting. SDS: put sustainable development firmly on government agenda, carried forward theme of sectoral integration. BQL: increased emphasis on social and economic dimensions, strengthened commitment to monitoring progress, but unclear whether it will feature prominently in government priorities.	[(1) Core of US response to sustainable development] [(2) First attempt by EPA to quantify environmental goals. Shows difficulty of enacting such approaches in context of fragmented US political system.]	Represents step forward in EU environmental policy and planning. More extensive than earlier EAPs and adopts sustainable development as a framing conception. Borrows target group approach from the Dutch NEPPs. But it is not 'target focused', but rather centred around agents and economic activities, allowing countries with different environmental approaches to collaborate.

Notes: *Entries for initiatives in Germany and in the USA, and for the Canadian Projet de Société, have been included for completeness, but they are enclosed in square brackets ([ ]) to indicate that these plans have not been adopted by the respective governments as official documents. Additional material derived from Dalal-Clayton (1996) and Jänicke and Jörgens (1999).

made for monitoring progress and if it is part of an ongoing process); and *political and administrative salience* (the significance of the strategy for officials, politicians and the general public, and whether this grows or declines over time).

In terms of thematic scope, the strategy prepared by the Swedish Environmental Protection Agency is concerned with the particular subset of environmental policy issues for which SEPA has statutory responsibility. In the Netherlands, the NEPPs and, in the UK, the early strategy documents deal principally with environmental policy, while in Norway, and later in the UK (1999), the white papers and strategy documents attempt to engage with the overall problem of sustainable development. In some ways the most comprehensive thematic coverage is achieved in the Canadian process of preparing and reviewing departmental sustainable development strategies— although this is realised at the cost of abandoning any formal attempt to reconcile the separate plans into a single strategy document.

With respect to political/legal character, the Australian NSESD was essentially an intergovernmental agreement to pursue certain environmental objectives; the early UK and Norwegian strategy documents are authoritative presentations of central government policy (although in the UK case the government was more concerned to restate existing commitments than to launch new initiatives); and the Japanese Environment Basic Plan rests on the provisions of the Environment Basic Law, one of the country's fundamental framework laws.

In terms of consultation and participation, Canada's Green Plan involved substantial interdepartmental negotiations, but no consultation with provincial and municipal governments, and only limited opportunities for public inputs. In contrast, preparation of the Australian strategy involved contributions from all levels of government and provided significant opportunities for public participation, particularly in its initial phases.

With respect to objectives, the Dutch NEPPs are goal-oriented, with detailed targets and timetables. The early UK strategy documents, on the other hand, contained mainly qualitative targets. Quantitative targets are the result of commitments under international treaty regimes, or are included for 'indicative' purposes only—that is to say they are non-binding.

With respect to review and assessment, Canada's Green Plan included no formal procedures for monitoring performance, as the initiative was not conceived as launching an iterative planning process. The early UK strategy documents also lacked specific provisions for periodic review, but over time a system of reporting and reappraisal has become established. In the Netherlands the first NEPP included explicit assessment procedures and the plan has already passed through three iterative cycles.

As to political and administrative salience, the level of 'visibility' varies considerably both across the different domains and over time within each domain. The Australian plan was greeted initially with considerable public enthusiasm, yet with time its relevance has faded. The Canadian Green Plan absorbed for a time the attention of national leaders and was a focus of acute interdepartmental rivalry, yet as the environment declined as a headline issue, the government lost interest and the programme was eventually abandoned. On the other hand the Dutch NEPPs have proven considerably more resilient and remain at the centre of the country's environmental policy process and debate.

Reviewing the more salient aspects of these initiatives it is apparent not only that they are diverse, but also that they are characterized by considerable instability. Many countries have experimented with more than one process, not hesitating to discard early experiments in favour of later initiatives. Canada launched and then abandoned the Green Plan; Norway has now abandoned the Green Book approach to budgetary management; and the UK has redrafted its sustainable development strategy. Even in the Netherlands, where national environmental policy planning has appeared most solidly established, there have been recent debates over whether NEPP-3 should be the last of its type.

It is not just that as circumstances and governments change, plans need updating; but rather that governments remain unclear as to which sorts of strategic planning mechanisms are most appropriate. In particular there are issues about the range of sustainable development related themes that can be integrated successfully within a single planning processes; the relationship between strategic planning for the environment and sustainable development and pre-existing governmental structures and planning modalities (particularly budget cycles and financial planning processes on the one hand, and land use planning on the other); and the most appropriate mechanisms to secure societal inputs.

Yet to the extent that specific strategic planning initiatives do survive and become anchored in the institutional complex of government operations, two trends are clear. First, there is a tendency for goals to become more carefully defined, and measurable targets to be identified. In Sweden and the UK such a process is clearly at work, and the Report of the Canadian Commissioner is propelling departmental strategies in this direction. In Japan too there is a growing interest in establishing appropriate targets and indicators. Pressure to make objectives clear and verifiable comes from forces advocating more stringent environmental controls, but also from business organizations that wish to reduce uncertainty over government intentions. International agreements establishing environmental standards, and work by organizations such as UNCSD and OECD on measuring environmental performance and developing indicators of sustainable development, also feed back into national processes. And, of course, over the past decade there has also been a general movement to emphasize goal-setting and performance-monitoring to improve efficiency in public-sector management.

A second tendency is for the collaborative and participatory dimensions of these strategic planning process to be extended. This has been particularly evident in the Netherlands, but also in the UK, Sweden, Canada, and the European Union. Formal and informal mechanisms through which diverse social sectors can influence the planning process have gradually been expanded. This movement is rooted in the growing appreciation on the part of government of the complexity of underlying issues, and of the need for consultation to legitimize outcomes and programmes. Pressure to open these strategic processes comes also from society more generally—for, as their potential significance is appreciated, a broader range of groups and interests seeks to ensure that their perspectives are given due consideration.

While the discussion here has concentrated on strategy processes at the broadest possible level, much could be said about sectoral and thematic plans. The focus for some of these—particularly those mandated by the international processes related to biodiversity and climate change—are common across the jurisdictions. For the most part, however, they vary across the units according to political priorities and the division of administrative responsibilities. For example, in conjunction with the NSESD, the Australian government prepared a series of strategies including many related to the protection of rural environments such as the National Soil Conservation Strategy and the National Strategy for Rangeland Management. An Arctic Protection Strategy has been an important component of Canada's engagement with sustainable development. In the UK a white paper on transportation was an early contribution by the Labour Government elected in 1997.

The extent to which specific plans are integrated with overall strategy processes varies, however. In the Netherlands component initiatives are closely integrated with the NEPP process; in Norway sectoral ministries have freer reign within the general framework of government priorities; in Canada sectoral plans are only assessed *post hoc*. Often these sectoral and thematic plans are of greater operational significance than the national 'master-strategies' to which they are formally subordinate. This is partly because they can be focused more clearly on particular problems, target-groups, and objectives. It is also the case, however, that they tend to be generated by more manageable processes, involving a smaller number of administrative units, with an ability to tap into established policy networks.

Approaches to Domestic Actors

That sustainable development should not merely preoccupy central authorities, but must be taken up actively by society at large, is a theme which runs throughout the international discussion of the issue. As we have already seen, this is one of the principles governments most consistently repeat in national plans and policy statements about sustainable development. Agenda 21 specifically refers to the importance of participation by nine 'Major Groups' ('women', 'children and youth', 'indigenous people', 'non-governmental organizations', 'local authorities', 'workers and trade unions', 'business and industry', the 'scientific and technological community', and 'farmers'); but in the interests of simplicity the discussion here will be organized in terms of two more general categories: (1) other tiers of government and (2) societal groups and organizations.

Intergovernmental Contacts

Central authorities have taken steps to encourage the involvement of other levels of government with sustainable development. In Australia, for example, the NSESD was a product of intergovernmental agreement; in the Netherlands provincial and municipal authorities were extensively consulted in the preparation of the NEPPs; in Sweden Local Agenda 21 activities have been actively supported by the central government; in the United Kingdom local councils have been instructed to use the development planning system to assure development becomes sustainable; and in the European Union the Commission provided financial resources to encourage the sustainable-cities initiative.

Since the 1960s the growth of mechanisms for environmental governance in developed countries has seen the emergence of complex patterns of interaction among various governmental tiers. Everywhere local and regional government has become heavily involved in environmental management, but the powers and responsibilities of authorities at different levels differ from political system to political system. Practice in the environmental domain has been shaped by the basic character of intergovernmental linkages established by constitutions and broader political settlements, but the particular way in which environmental problems have emerged onto the policy agenda and experiences of specific attempts to deal with them have also left their legacy. Within the European Union during the 1980s, for example, the Commission clearly perceived the environment as an emergent domain within which it could expand its competence, while in Japan early involvement by local government in the environmental field and the comparative weakness of the central environmental agency meant that in some matters local administrations preserve considerable leverage. The question that interests us here, however, is not the particular configurations of centre/region/local arrangements that have evolved in each country, but whether engagement with sustainable development has prompted national governments to reconsider and/or practically reconfigure interactions with other tiers of government.

In some jurisdictions there have been changes that relate to the adoption of the idea of sustainable development. In Australia, for example, the government integrated the preparation of the NSESD with negotiations for the IGAE, in an attempt both to normalize the extension of federal authority into the environmental domain and to establish a more co-operative framework for intergovernmental decision-making. In Sweden reforms to the environmental administration in 1988/9 increased the responsibility of counties and municipalities for environmental certification procedures and inspection. In 1991 municipal autonomy was extended, and further r-eforms strengthened SEPA's capacity to focus on long-term strategic issues. Norway also experienced decentralization of its environmental administration. Reforms in the late 1980s delegated some management functions to the county and municipal levels, mandating the preparation of local environmental plans, supporting the establishment of local environmental officers, and encouraging regional and local input to central policy-making. A trend towards delegation of responsibilities to the local level is also discernible in the otherwise fairly centralized Dutch system.[5] However, in the European Union, the tendency seems to be moving in the opposite direction, with the period of the 5th EAP coinciding with a considerable strengthening of Union directives and legislation on environmental issues, and a conscious effort to harmonize environmental regulation across EU member-states.

In each of these cases the exigencies of sustainable development were invoked to justify shifts in the duties of central, regional, and local government. But the changes proceeded very much *with* the grain of prevailing policy sentiment. In Sweden, shifting the burden of environmental administration downward and focusing central resources on policy development was consistent with the challenging character of the environmental themes raised by sustainable development. But by the late 1980s the enhancement of municipal autonomy had become an accepted general objective of policy.

---

[5] In Germany reforms of nature-conservation legislation have enhanced the role of the *länder*—although explicit linkages to sustainable development are less clear at this level.

Similarly, the devolution of responsibility for environmental supervision to lower administrative units heralded in the Norwegian government response to 'Our Common Future', was entirely consistent with the broader governmental programme for administrative reform. Moreover, the move to harmonize Union-wide regulation and to improve central monitoring on environmental issues in the EU flowed as much from concern about the implications of varied standards for competition within the single European market, as from an autonomous interest in sustainable development and environmental quality.

Looking across the ten jurisdictions it is clear that sustainable development has not prompted central governments to embark on major changes to established patterns of territorial governance. A coherent strategy based on encouraging the emergence of regional approaches to sustainable development—a strategy which involved devolving significant powers to subnational units, or providing major stimulative funding where such powers exist already—could be imagined, but this has not been taken up by the governments with which we have been concerned. More generally, it is possible to suggest three broad tendencies.

1. In unitary states sustainable development has been linked with modest administrative devolution with respect to the more routine functions of environmental administration, and rather vague or sporadic injunctions to local or regional administrations to integrate sustainable development into all aspects of their work. Few new resources, however, have followed these general injunctions, and in this context the expectations placed on subnational governments—for example in Norway to achieve integration of sectorally-oriented central policies *at the local level*, or in the UK to employ existing land-use planning law to improve settlement patterns—are probably unrealistic. In some contexts calling on other levels of government to take up sustainable development is probably seen as an easy option for central governments: it costs little, and can even serve as a dumping ground for problems that defy ready solution.

2. In large federal systems, sustainable development has brought to the fore the difficulty of reconciling regional and national priorities, and of establishing a single 'national' orientation towards sustainable development in an extensive and diverse political unit. In Australia and Canada environmental issues—particularly those involving international treaty negotiations and which relate to climate change, energy and natural resources—remain an important focus of tension between central authorities and the states/provinces. In the US the comparative success of state and regionally based sustainable development initiatives in contrast to developments at the national level is also suggestive, as is the continuing paralysis over climate

change. The German system, however, has proven less vulnerable to such influences. But in the EU it is clear that the different levels of economic development characteristic of member-states—especially the split between northern and southern Europe—has obliged the Commission to formulate an approach which can be interpreted quite differently (or indeed virtually ignored) in different national contexts.

3. In both types of state (unitary and confederated) sustainable development has been accompanied by a growth in intergovernmental approaches—an extension of multi-agency, multilevel interactions in order to attempt to deal with the more complex, long-term, and structurally rooted problems associated with sustainable development. The focus here has been less on formal reassignments of responsibility, and more on the recognition that as far as sustainable development is concerned one needs to 'talk to the other guy' if the entire interdependent programme is to be made to work.

Major Societal Groups

With respect to relationships with societal groups, we shall confine our remarks to two sectors: non-governmental organizations and business.[6]

Over the past decade central governments have made serious efforts to involve environment-and-development NGOs in official sustainable development processes. NGO participation has taken numerous forms, including: membership of high-profile national committees, investigative commissions, and advisory panels; participation in national delegations to international activities such as the UNCED PrepComs, the Rio Earth Summit, UNCSD, and COPs to the climate change and biodiversity conventions; consultation in policy-making processes in environment-related domains; joint organization of public-education campaigns; and the practical administration (or co-management) of government-financed programmes (nature conservation, recycling activities and so on). This does not mean that NGOs have been welcomed into the inner sanctum of governments, or that decision-making has been devolved away from politicians and officials to NGO functionaries. What has happened is that there has been a tendency for previously closed policy communities to be opened outward to include a greater range of par-

---

[6] For the purposes of this discussion 'non-governmental organization' (NGO) is taken to designate groups which are neither government nor business—they are 'civil-society' organizations of the 'not-for-profit' sector. This usage differs from practice within the United Nations system, where the tendency is to view any actor which is literally not a government (including business corporations, producers' associations, and even individuals) as an NGO.

ticipants; that formal consultation with NGOs has become accepted increasingly as the norm; and that NGO perspectives have come to influence policy. This more intimate relationship between government and the NGO sector represents a shift away from the confrontational stance typical of the 1970s and 1980s.[7]

The country studies indicate that government departments expect to secure a variety of benefits through closer working relationships with NGOs. In some cases—particularly where issues are just emerging onto the agenda—NGOs can provide expertise not readily available within government. NGO involvement in official processes can also generally be counted on to enhance the legitimacy of resultant policies. Their presence can be used as a counterweight to other organized interests, and they may also provide a constituency for environment ministries and agencies involved in wrangles with other departments. There is an old adage that it is better to have critics on the inside than on the outside, and keeping (at least certain) NGOs inside the policy loop increases the information available to government, thereby reducing the possibility of radical 'surprises' farther down the line.

This trend towards a more collaborative relationship has not advanced smoothly or evenly, and the form and extent of state/NGO interaction differs among countries and across issue domains. In Australia environmental NGOs were particularly active in the Ecologically Sustainable Development Working Groups of the early 1990s. Yet over time the movement became disillusioned with the NSESD process, and dissatisfied with government priorities for supply-side reform. Still, today environmental organizations are regularly consulted about policy, even if they are wary about co-optation. NGOs in Canada decried restricted opportunities for input during the drafting of the 1990 Green Plan, and over the next few years government was careful to cultivate a more open approach. In some ways Rio marked a high point of enthusiasm on both sides, but during the UNCED follow-up multi-stakeholder encounters proliferated. By the mid-1990s all parties to such experiences had become more cautious about what they could be expected to produce. Nevertheless NGO participation in Canada is firmly institutionalized in federal government sustainable development activities—for example, in the requirement that departments consult with stakeholders during the preparation of sustainable development strategies.

---

[7] Comprehensive overviews of the role of NGOs and the emergence of a 'global civil society' can be found in Princen and Finger (1994).

In the Netherlands, Norway, and Sweden NGOs have been closely involved with the sustainable development processes, having achieved high-level consultation and input with respect to the preparation of international interventions and the development of official national positions. The Netherlands is well known for consultative decision-making, and over the past decade environmental NGOs have been increasingly accepted as legitimate interlocutors in the sustainable development debate. This is particularly true in the area of nature protection, but also in managing urban environments and in developing an agenda for sustainable production and consumption. On the other hand, however, it is also interesting to note that the covenanting processes—so central to Dutch policy implementation in the industrial field—has involved bilateral (government/business) rather than trilateral (government/business/NGO) interactions.

A rather different case is presented by Germany where, because of the delay in Federal government engagement with sustainable development and resentment over moves to restrict legal opportunities for citizen challenges to administrative decisions, NGOs often felt themselves outside the official process. Yet NGOs were involved with the German response to climate change, and once the government started to take up sustainable development, groups were drawn into the process. As compared to the other industrialized countries, Japanese NGOs have apparently been relatively passive. Yet the government is sensitive to this, and as the UNCED process advanced, politicians took some steps to assure an NGO presence at international forums and to set up consultation procedures that paralleled forms found in other high-consumption states. NGO criticisms do seem to have been taken on board during the revision of the National Action Plan for Agenda 21, but it is easy to remain sceptical about how far this opening of the political-administrative process extends.

During the period of the 5th EAP the European Commission has tried to facilitate the organization of pan-European NGO networks, and to draw these into a closer working relationship. NGOs now have access to decision-makers in Brussels, and are regularly consulted on environmental issues. But to date NGOs have had more success in placing issues on the policy agenda than in influencing outputs generated by a complex and somewhat unpredictable Union decision-making structure (Lévêque 1996). While DGXI seems intent on continuing to build bridges with the NGO community, there are institutional obstacles to the process which are rooted in the bureaucratic character of Commission activities and the obsessive secrecy in which they are shrouded—a secrecy which (to be fair) has been encouraged deliberately by specific national governments. It is not coincidental that in the recent negotiations of the UNECE treaty on citizen access to environmental information, the EU was among those political units which experienced the most difficulty adjusting to the notion of open government.

Finally, since the US government has not really taken up sustainable development, it is difficult to speak of any particular approach to NGO participation. Some groups have been involved with the President's Commission, and it is also true that EPA has tried a number of initiatives to involve environmental groups in negotiated regulation. Yet the overall pattern of government/NGO/business interaction around the environment (at least at the national level) remains essentially confined to well-established patterns of regulation, lobbying, confrontation, and litigation.

In terms of business, governments have taken steps to involve the corporate world in discussions and processes related to sustainable development. Business has had a prominent place in the broad consultative bodies on sustainable development set up in most countries. Business representatives have sometimes been included in official delegations attending UNCED-process meetings, and national and sectoral organizations (and individual firms) have been routinely involved in consultations around policy initiatives related to sustainable development. Most governments (regardless of ideological persuasion) seem to have acknowledged that relationships with business are crucial to the realization of innovative practices, so that it is hardly surprising that officials have gone out of their way to explain that sustainable development is compatible with economic growth and successful businesses. This approach—which is remarkably similar from country to country—has focused around three central themes: *opportunity*, *responsibility*, and *partnership*.

The 'opportunities' are for businesses to innovate, to develop clean products and processes, to pioneer new markets; 'responsibility' relates to the social obligation for business to be 'environment-friendly', and to be aware of the wider context within which it operates; and 'partnership' involves government and business working together to solve problems so as to guarantee a vibrant economy and a healthy environment. A basic premise of these arrangements is that government declines to act unilaterally without consulting business. Moreover all governments have pledged to avoid imposing sudden or onerous costs on particular commercial sectors; to eschew action that erodes the competitive position of national businesses *vis-à-vis* producers in other countries; and to give priority to voluntary and negotiated solutions over regulations imposed from above. Thus sustainable development is presented as relatively non-threatening, despite clear indications that change will require significant efforts from all sectors of society.

Several other general features of government approaches to business are also apparent. One is that governments have deliberately drawn business organizations into public interaction around sustainable development, encouraging the commercial sector to get involved with a wider range of social actors and social problems than has traditionally been the case. Another has been a conscious attempt to engage business on a sectoral level—a corollary of the shift from framing environmental problems in media-based terms to focusing on the overall burden placed on the environment by a set of enterprises in a branch of the economy. This is most famously evident in the Netherlands, but is also strongly developed in Norway, Sweden, and Germany. Even in the United States, which has proven most resistant to sustainable development, the EPA has attempted to move things in this direction (Fiorino 1996).

There has also been a more general tendency during the period to rely on self-binding commitments to secure environmental gains. Again this process has been most developed in the Netherlands with the 'covenants' in which industrial branches pledge to achieve explicit targets and objectives. While other countries have clearly not subscribed to the relatively formal Dutch approach to the same degree, environmental agreements of various sorts are becoming increasingly common. A recent study suggests that more than 300 such agreements exisited within the EU by the end of 1998 (European Environment Agency 1999). Particularly in the highly contentious and uncertain domain of climate change, governments have relied heavily on voluntary pledges from industrial sectors to control carbon emissions. These 'voluntary' agreements have often been secured with the implicit threat that if industry does not act 'responsibly' by announcing appropriate initiatives, the regulatory or tax route will have to be employed. Finally, it is worth noting that government efforts have focused on major corporations and business organizations, and only in the most enthusiastic jurisdictions (such as the Netherlands) has much been done to bring the sustainable development message to small and medium-size enterprises.

Viewing government approaches to involving other actors in a wider context, one is led to wonder whether interactions around sustainable development may reflect a partial convergence across many of the political systems with which we are here concerned; a shift with implications for both modes of interest articulation and policy styles. In systems which have in the past been described as 'corporatist' (Norway, Sweden, Germany, the Netherlands), there has been a weakening of the exclusivity of the state/business/labour triangle; while for those traditionally dubbed 'pluralist' (Canada, UK, Australia), there has been some movement in the direction of formalizing multi-partite structures for societal inputs.

Policy Instruments

With respect to more specific policy instruments, government discussion has focused mainly on instruments for environmental policy, or on instruments for better integrating economic and environmental concerns (EEA 1999), rather than on 'instruments for sustainable development' more broadly conceived. There is recognition that a varied portfolio of instruments must be deployed to manage environmental burdens, particularly with respect to problematic issues involving diffuse sources, long-term effects, and international ramifications. In practice the mainstay of environmental governance in all of the states studied remains regulation—instruments based on systems of prohibition, licensing and inspection, now often described as techniques of 'command and control'. This core has long been supplemented (to varying degrees in different jurisdictions) by other measures including pollution charges, subsidies, information campaigns and normative appeals. Over recent years there has been considerable interest in developing 'market-oriented' (particularly tax-based), as well as negotiated or 'voluntary', approaches to environmental management. Both sorts of instrument appeal to policy-makers because of technical and political difficulties with traditional regulatory approaches; and both figure prominently in discussions of sustainable development, as means by which environmental impacts can be 'internalized' into the sphere of economic decision-making. Negotiated instruments also resonate with the participatory dimension of sustainable development.

With respect to tax-based instruments, cautious steps to extend the range of environmental taxes and charges have been made in most jurisdictions— although the scale of change has fallen well short of the rhetoric. Energy provides the vast bulk of environment-related tax revenue, but the origin of excise taxes on fuel predates recent environmental concern. During the period of the study carbon taxes had been introduced in the Netherlands, Sweden, and Norway. These three states have also led the way on other forms of environmental taxation. The Netherlands has a manure charge, long-standing water-effluent and groundwater extraction charges, and a landfill tax. Norway has introduced fertilizer, pesticide, and hazardous-waste fees, and a sulphur-emissions tax. Sweden has brought in taxes or charges on fertilizers, pesticides, sulphur and NO_x emissions, and batteries.

Of the European states examined, Germany has been most reticent about environmental taxation. Although the UK has only a small number of charges, the landfill tax and fuel-price escalator were significant innovations, and road-pricing is under active discussion. Despite the failure of the carbon/energy tax proposal, the European Commission continues to float ideas for new Union-wide taxes, for example, in the areas of pesticide and fertilizer use. Another 'market-based' instrument—tradable emissions quotas—has also attracted wide interest, particularly in relation to climate change. But except for a recent German initiative on volatile organic compounds, other states have not introduced such systems, and experience remains largely confined to US air-pollution control measures, which have not explicitly been linked to sustainable development.

The broader idea of 'ecological tax reform'—that is of consciously shifting the weighting of the tax structure from labour and income towards environmental loadings—has been seriously discussed in the Netherlands, Norway, Sweden, and Germany. Of the countries examined here, Sweden has taken the most significant steps in this direction. The 1990/1 tax reform and subsequent amendments realized a tax shift in Sweden from labour to energy of about 4 per cent of GDP (EEA 1999), and environmental taxation accounted for 12 per cent of state tax revenue by 1993/4 (Lundqvist 1997). Similar changes have occurred in the Netherlands and, to a lesser extent, in Norway.

Negotiated or 'voluntary' agreements have become an increasingly important feature of environmental policy in most jurisdictions surveyed here. As we have seen, the Netherlands—with centrally determined environmental objectives, the target-group approach, and formal covenanting—has gone furthest down this route. A huge array of agreements involving varied industrial partners and goals, and different forms of legal commitment are now found in the Netherlands. Among the most important are the NEPP-related covenants with major sectors (including basic metals, chemicals, paper and printing, metal products, electronics, and dairy products) establishing the framework for continuous environmental improvement (which includes branch targets, implementation plans, annual reporting mechanisms, and consultative structures to steer each process), along with energy-efficiency agreements (Glasbergen 1998).

Germany also has a large number of environmental accords, but their bearing is quite different: they are not so closely integrated into an overall goal-oriented vision, and ententes typically take the form of a pledge by the industrial partners to behave according to certain norms (the German legal tradition does not favour contracts between the state and private parties). Sweden, Norway, and the UK have also concluded a number of environmental accords, and the EU is now actively encouraging this approach (CEC 1996e), having itself negotiated some Europe-wide agreements—for example, with car manufacturers mandating a 25 per cent average reduction (between 1996 and 2008) in CO_2 emissions from automobiles. Agreements have been invoked in the widest range of countries in emergent policy areas such as climate change and energy, and ozone protection. Yet the largest numbers of individual accords relate to industrial emissions and waste management.

Informational, process-oriented and normative instruments have also been deployed in forms such as eco-labelling; the legal recognition of citizens' rights to environmental information and participation; the promotion of corporate environmental management and audit schemes; and consumption-focused initiatives such as the Dutch eco-teams. While subsidies play some role in environmental policy (for example, in Germany), most governments have remained cautious in extending 'green subsidy' schemes—though there is considerable assistance to public transportation in northern Europe and some encouragement for alternative energy production (for example in the UK). Research and development with potential environmental benefits has attracted government assistance, but sums are usually derisory within the overall context of research expenditure. Some steps have been taken to dismantle energy and other resource subsidies (which generate significant environmental problems), for example, by liberalizing energy markets in Australia and the UK, or by reforming water-management systems in Australia. Yet extensive sectoral subsidies remain—particularly in energy and agriculture (e.g. the German coal industry and the Common Agricultural Policy in the EU).

With respect to legislation, much of what has been enacted in the area focuses less on establishing new 'command and control' mechanisms for environmental administration, and more on codifying existing sets of regulations; facilitating the use of other policy instruments; and promoting multi-stranded approaches to environmental governance. Examples of the more significant classes of initiatives include laws to: formalize planning mechanisms (Japan's 1993 Environment Basic Law or the Netherlands 1993 Environmental Management Act which placed the NEPP on a legal basis); harmonize and frame existing approaches (the EU's 1996 Air Quality Framework Directive or Sweden's 1997/8 Environmental Code); extend the use of environmental impact assessment procedures (Canada's 1995 Environmental Assessment Act or Japan's 1997 Environment Impact Assessment Law); encourage the adoption of environmental management and accounting systems (the 1993 EU Eco-Management and Audit Scheme); promote more comprehensive approaches to waste management (the Swedish 1993 Guidelines for an Ecocycle Society and the German 1994 Closed Substance Cycle and Waste Management Act); encourage the 'greening of government' operations (Japan's 1995 Lead Action Programme); and authorize domestic action in response to international developments such as UNCED, and the climate change and biodiversity Conventions (Australia's 1992 National Greenhouse Response Strategy or Sweden's 1993/4 'Towards Sustainable Development: Strategies to Follow up UNCED'). A stream of directives emanating from the EU from the mid-1980s has been followed in the 1990s by enabling legislation at the member-state level; but over time the EU has changed from an orientation focused on regulatory compliance (mandating specific technologies or emissions standards), towards a more process-centred approach (relying on framework directives, encouraging negotiated solutions, and the mobilization of societal actors) (Pehle 1997).

As sustainable development has come to the fore, the portfolio of environmental policy instruments has, therefore, become more complex, and discussion about how to combine different instruments for different goals and tasks has become more sophisticated. Traditional regulatory approaches are recognised as inadequate to the complexity of the issues which sustainable development attempts to address. Yet many analysts remain sceptical about the effectiveness of the new tax-based or negotiated approaches (Harrison 1999; Jansen, Osland, and Hanf 1998), and officials admit that methods of accessing certain key 'target groups', or of approaching certain types of problem, remain unclear.

Measurement and Monitoring

Efforts to set in place systematic procedures for monitoring the environment and tracking interactions between environment and economy have been closely associated with government engagement with sustainable development. Moves to operationalize sustainable development in terms of measurable targets, and to create mechanisms to review policy performance, have also been in evidence.

In the first place there has been an overall advance in 'state-of-the-environment' reporting. While some countries have a fairly long tradition of national-level reports on environmental trends and problems (the German Council of Environmental Advisers, for example, issued its first comprehensive report in 1974), the scope and sophistication of the work which has appeared since the late-1980s has greatly increased. A wider range of burdens has been assessed, national trends have been set in an international context, and more elaborate methodologies have been employed to track causal links among social and environmental processes. In the Netherlands, RIVM issued its first comprehensive state-of-the-environment study in

1988 during the preparation of the first NEPP. Important reports were released in Canada in 1991 and 1996, in Japan in 1994 and 1996, and in Australia in 1996. The first attempt to examine the overall condition of the European environment was published by the European Environment Agency in 1995, and in 1999 the Agency released *Environment in the European Union at the Turn of the Century*—an impressive study which employs a Driving Forces-Pressures-State-Impacts-Responses (D-P-S-I-R) framework to assess economic and social trends and environmental developments within the 15 EU member states and in the wider European context.

Since 1992 particular advances have been made in collecting and analysing data related to climate change and biodiversity. Reporting requirements under the two conventions have led to more reliable estimates for greenhouse-gas sources and sinks; improved understanding of sectoral contributions to national inventories; and more systematic mapping of domestic biological diversity and threatened habitats. In both areas information available to decision-makers has expanded dramatically, and significant scientific and technical resources have been mobilised to build an infrastructure to monitor developments and to further perfect measurement methodologies.

Work has also been carried out on integrating environmental impacts into the system of national accounts, and on including environmental expenditure in national budget cycles. Norway initiated a pioneering materials-based approach to environmental accounting even before the Brundtland Report, and work on 'satellite accounts' (which complement established national accounting procedures, and map detailed interactions between economy and environment) is relatively advanced in Canada, the Netherlands, Norway, and the UK. Tracking atmospheric emissions, oil and gas depletion, and waste generation across economic sectors, served as starting points for constituting such accounts, which have subsequently been extended to include a more comprehensive basket of resource inputs and environmental effects. With respect to integrating environmental effects into national budgetary processes, the Netherlands NEPP process stands out for its detailed attempt to track macro-economic impacts of environmental policy. Norway has also experimented with various ways of integrating environmental objectives into departmental spending plans, and most jurisdictions are now reporting overall annual environmental expenditure as well as revenue from environment-based taxation.

Sustainable-development indicators which track policy-relevant variables over time have been another area of interest. In the UK, for example, the government issued a preliminary set of 120 indicators of sustainable development in 1996, and these were revised and extended (to about 150) in 1999, primarily aimed at including a greater range of social issues. The Labour government also formulated a subset of fourteen 'headline indicators' to capture representative dimensions of sustainable development: total economic output; investment in public, business, and private assets; proportion of people of working age who are in work; qualifications at age 19; expected years of a healthy life; homes judged unfit to live in; level of crime; emissions of greenhouse gases; days when air pollution is moderate or high; measures of road traffic volume; rivers of good or fair quality; populations of wild birds; new homes built on previously developed land; and waste generation and management. A fifteenth indicator—'satisfaction with quality of life'—is still being developed (DETR 1999a).

The UK government has pledged to work for a positive evolution of each item of this indicator set over time. A rather different approach—focusing attention on a more narrow portfolio of indicators which capture the 'environmental-protection' component of sustainable development—has been preferred by the German government.

The 'Environment-Barometer for Germany' proposed by the German Environment Ministry in 1998 as part of its more substantive engagement with sustainable development, included indicators (and associated targets) for six environmental policy fields: air quality, soil conservation, nature protection, water quality, and energy and materials efficiencies (Federal Ministry of the Environment 1998). Detailed indicator work, involving collaboration between central statistical services, environmental ministries and agencies, and sectoral ministries, is particularly advanced in the Netherlands, Sweden, Norway, and Canada.

Finally, governments have set up monitoring and audit processes to track the effectiveness of sustainable development policy. Review and assessment functions have in the first instance been assumed by environmental ministries and agencies. This has been supplemented by inputs from expert review bodies and research organizations; broadly-based UNCED-related consultative committees; and parliament-centred audit mechanisms. Both SEPA and the National Committee for Agenda 21 have reviewed the formulation of environmental policy objectives in Sweden, and drawn attention to the problem of poorly defined goals. The tension between ministerial (VROM) and expert scientific (RIVM) assessments in the Netherlands has focused attention on whether current policies are adequate to achieve agreed environmental objectives, and in Australia the Productivity Commission report highlighted significant weakness in implementation of NSESD. A parliamentary Environmental Audit Committee has recently been established in the UK, but it is Canada which has taken the idea of parliamentary supervision farthest by establishing the independent Commissioner for the Environment and Sustainable Development.

Sustainable Production and Consumption

The fourth chapter of Agenda 21, entitled 'Changing Consumption Patterns', identifies the 'unsustainable pattern of consumption and production, particularly in the industrialized countries' as 'the major cause of the continued deterioration of the global environment'. The document urges the industrialized countries to take the lead in developing national strategies and policies to encourage the emergence of more sustainable patterns of consumption. Because recognition of the disparities in consumption between North and South and of the impossibility of universalizing Northern resource profligacy without subjecting the global ecosphere to intolerable stresses are key postulates of the argument for sustainable development, efforts to transform existing (unsustainable) patterns of production and consumption must be viewed as crucial to the sustainable development enterprise. But what have governments actually done in this area? Our studies indicate—not that much. Also here, however, we find interesting variation.

As part of its follow-up to the Earth Summit the Norwegian government, for example, organized two international conferences, the 1994 Oslo Symposium on Sustainable Consumption, and the 1995 Oslo Ministerial Roundtable Conference on Sustainable Production and Consumption. These meetings were specifically designed to draw attention to the importance of shifting consumption patterns and to provide stimulus to the international work programmes on sustainable production and consumption launched by the OECD and the UN Commission on Sustainable Development (UNCSD). Yet despite this very specific effort—and the unanimous adoption of the work programme by the UNCSD—national governments have hesitated to initiate domestic activities under this rubric.

This reticence is no doubt in part due to continued confusion over just what is to be included under this heading. The discussion in Agenda 21 throws together various issues including intermediate and final consumption, factor efficiency, the use of fiscal instruments and consumer education. It emphasizes materials and energy efficiency, waste reduction, the provision of information for consumers (especially through eco-labelling), greening government purchasing, and environmentally sound pricing. These are significant issues, but the relationship among them is unclear. The confusion was clearly evident in Rio, with some governments (such as the United States) hesitant to do more than emphasize consumer information, while others were willing to go further in directly problematizing Northern consumption.

Despite the follow-up by Norway, further clarification of the theme has proven difficult. If the focus is directed at 'consumers' as individual agents and/or as a target group, linkages between consumption and wider social processes can be obscured. There is a limit to what green consumer activists or consumer affairs ministries can be expected to accomplish in transforming deeply embedded consumption practices, and governments (for example, in the Netherlands) have not had notable success in approaching consumers as an environmental policy 'target group'. If, on the other had, one tries to avoid an overly individualistic orientation by bringing 'production' into the equation (as was specifically done at the second Oslo conference), the terrain then appears to expand to include environmental impacts from almost any conceivable economic activity. Thus the theme looses distinctiveness and risks becoming unmanageable.

More fundamentally, all the governments we have examined appear wary of engaging too directly with the issue of consumption. Talk of restraining consumption or of limiting growth for the sake of the environment makes both business and labour leaders nervous, and is certainly not seen as a vote-winner by mainstream politicians. An explicit intent to shift consumption away from certain goods and services rapidly calls forth opposition from the economic interests involved in these areas. Moreover large-scale efforts to alter consumption habits can revive critical discourses on the unfeasibility of social engineering and spectre of the 'paternalist state'. Of course, this is not how UNCED, UNCSD, and the OECD have conceptualized or presented the prospect of making consumption and production sustainable. Their emphasis is on, for example, educated consumer choice, expanding markets for environment-friendly goods and services, full environmental cost pricing, and corporate environmental responsibility. Yet it is obvious that the discussion of consumption brings to the fore difficult issues such as those associated with individual and collective choice, private and collective provision of goods and services, the social construction of desires, jobs contra environmental protection, and 'consumer sovereignty'.

Thus while governments have gone along with international activities organized under the sustainable-production-and-consumption rubric, most have preferred to deal with problems in a piecemeal fashion, declining to make a major domestic effort to integrate the diverse set of issues involved into any comprehensive, consumption-focused, orientation. This is not to say that attention has not been directed at specific issues. Energy and materials efficiency have been actively taken up in Germany, Japan, the Netherlands, Norway, and Sweden. In the Netherlands, for example, energy efficiency has been a major focus for covenants with industry. Waste reduction—rather than simply management of a waste stream that is accepted as a given—is now on the agenda in most countries. Those which had particularly high reliance on land fill, and low-materials recycling or energy-from-waste recovery rates—such as Canada and Australia—have set targets for landfill reduction and made progress in meeting them. In the UK ocean dumping has ceased, and the new landfill tax represents a step towards the use of fiscal instruments to manage environmental burdens.

In the European Union the packaging-waste ordinance has focused business attention on the issue, and in Sweden and Germany more innovative measures have been taken, whereby each has introduced framework legislation establishing producer responsibility for disposal and recycling, gradually extending regulations to cover new product types. The German legislation on packaging—with its 'take-back' clause, transferring packaging disposal obligations back up the supply chain—has clearly reduced packaging waste volumes. And yet the complex system provides few incentives for continuous innovation: early gains have not been followed by further reductions, and, given the prospect of significant transport externalities, doubts remain about the overall environmental benefit of the approach.

Governments have also formally accepted the importance of green procurement, although measures often are more cosmetic than substantive. Serious efforts do seem to have been made in this direction in Sweden and Germany, and to a lesser extent Japan. Yet tensions between different procurement objectives—including the cost-versus-the-environment trade-off—continue to bedevil such schemes. With respect to consumer empowerment, eco-labelling schemes have remained the mainstay. Costs of such initiatives can generally be transferred to producers (and ultimately consumers) and their implementation causes little disruption to established economic modalities and paradigms. Today attention is shifting from the establishment of the schemes to harmonization and mutual recognition among different national/regional programmes (the Nordic Swan, German Blue Angel, EC and so on).

In terms of the broader problematization of consumption, Sweden and the Netherlands probably have made the most headway, with Norway lagging some distance behind. At least these governments have encouraged public debate about resource consumption, social needs and future generations. One intriguing innovation has been support for community-based action directed at monitoring household consumption and improving environmental performance in the domestic setting. In Norway the government has supported the 'Environmental Home Guard' movement, while in Sweden the focus has been on 'eco-teams'.

At the time of writing it remains unclear how engagement with wider consumption issues will evolve. It is possible a clearer delimitation of the policy area will emerge through continued dialogue and expert meetings, such as the 'Kabelvaag Workshop' on indicators for sustainable production and consumption held in Norway in June of 1998, and the follow-up International Symposium on Policy Instruments held in Oslo in November of the same year. These efforts aim to move the debate in a more pragmatic direction, shifting attention more to the demand side of the equation by defining sustainable consumption in terms of 'choosing, using and disposing [of] goods and services', and by emphasizing 'private, intermediate and public consumption' and the use of the demand side to 'lever social and environmental benefits' (Robins and Roberts 1998). It remains to be seen, however, whether these efforts and shifts in problem definition prove more appealing to national governments.

The Global Dimension

Most foreign policy issues could in principle be linked to the sustainable development agenda. In practice, however, the governments with which we are concerned have viewed the global dimension of sustainable development implementation to be related to two main areas: (1) the development of institutions and procedures for transnational environmental governance and (2) the provision of assistance to developing countries. Other issues—ranging from the management of armed conflicts and the prevention of nuclear proliferation to the reform of international financial institutions and the reconstruction of the world trade system—have less frequently been brought into the frame.

The further internationalization of environmental policy-making has been one of the most significant developments of the past decade, and—with the exception of the United States—all the governments studied have repeatedly and explicitly justified their participation in an ever more elaborate web of institutions for global environmental governance in terms of the challenge of sustainable development. The two international conventions signed at Rio are usually given pride of place in this context, and we shall return to them in more detail later in the chapter. But governments also draw attention to numerous other accords and programmes which enhance institutional capacity to deal with global environmental problems. Agreements often cited in this context include the amended Montreal Protocol on Substances that Deplete the Ozone Layer (1987, 1990, 1992), the Basel Convention on the Control of Transboundary Movement of Hazardous Wastes and their Disposal (1989), the revised International Tropical Timber Agreement (1994), and the UN Convention to Combat Desertification (1995). All the governments with which we are concerned have signed these accords, although by the end of 1997 the United States had only ratified the ozone agreements, and Australia, Japan, and the European Union had yet to ratify the Desertification Convention.

Regional environmental co-operation has intensified over the past decade, and here the extension of EU competence into the field of environmental policy-making is of particular note. Until the early 1980s the EU was a relatively small player in the environmental domain, but by the end of the 1990s EU legislation had come increasingly to shape the environmental policy regimes of member-states. The governments of Germany, the Netherlands, Sweden, and the UK all emphasize the importance of the Union for achieving their sustainable development objectives—with the Fifth Environmental Action Programme, the packaging and hazardous waste directives, the eco-management and audit scheme, and the framework directives on air, integrated pollution control, and water, all cited as important.

In a broader European context conventions for the conservation of the Baltic and for the protection and sustainable use of the Danube were adopted in 1992 and 1994 respectively. Reduction protocols for NO_x (1991) and sulphur (1994) have been adopted under the UNECE Convention on Long-Range Transboundary Pollution (LRTP). And negotiations for a UNECE Convention on Access to Information, Public Participation in Decision-Making and Access to Justice in Environmental Matters were concluded in Denmark in 1998. The Netherlands, Sweden, and Germany were particularly active in securing protocols to LRTP, while Sweden has displayed particular interest in Baltic-protection initiatives.

On the other side of the Atlantic regional co-operation has been strengthened through the 1993 North American Agreement on Environmental Co-operation, which was linked to adoption of the NAFTA accord between Canada, Mexico, and the United States. NAAEC is developing state-of-the-environment reporting and procedures which allow individuals and organizations to make submissions alleging that parties to the accord have failed to uphold environmental obligations. Canada and the United States are also both participants in UNECE and signatories to its environmental conventions. Compared to Europe and North America, Asia has lagged in the development of regional environmental collaboration, but over the past decade

Japan and Australia have tried to raise environmental issues within APEC, and worked towards developing new bodies to monitor the environment in Asia. The Australia and New Zealand Environment and Conservation Council is a case in point.

While sustainable development has provided a context for these efforts to strengthen international co-operation in the environmental field, it is important to appreciate that sustainable development—as a distinct concept—has *not* always figured in the detailed negotiations or specific legal outcomes. Many of the conventions, protocols, or international arrangements concluded over the past decade result from processes that extend back before sustainable development emerged as an international objective. And yet it is clear that the national governments that have taken up sustainable development now interpret these international processes as essential to their efforts to implement sustainable development.

In addition to formal agreements governments have sponsored a great variety of favoured international programmes and projects, and supported gatherings related to managing environmental burdens. Australia hosted the International Conference on Certification and Labelling of Products from Sustainably Managed Forests in 1996, and Japan has supported the activities of the International Tropical Timber Association. The city of Bonn bid successfully to become the seat of the Climate Change Convention; Montreal has acquired the secretariat of the Biodiversity Convention; and Sweden has been the prime mover behind the Baltic Agenda 21 initiative.

Efforts to integrate the domestic and global dimensions of environmental policy at a strategic level are particularly evident in the Netherlands, Norway, Sweden, and Canada. The Netherlands NEPP3, for example, relates priorities for strengthening international co-operation to domestic problems and objectives. Policy goals are set in a context of economic globalization and the continued eastward expansion of the EU. Eight core themes for environmental foreign policy are identified, and a great number of detailed objectives are included: such as seeking an integrated policy on product labelling within the EU; negotiating an international framework for 'greening risk analysis for export credit and investment underwriting'; and initiating discussions for a worldwide ban on the production of certain substances including persistent organic pollutants (POPs).

Furthermore, these goals are set explicitly in the context of achieving sustainable development, implementing Agenda 21 and contributing to the work programme of UNCSD. Canada also has publicised priorities for international negotiations which point towards an 'International Forests Convention', a 'Global Convention on POPs', and a liability and compensation protocol under the Basel Convention. Again these objectives are explicitly understood in terms of contributing to sustainable development. Yet the degree of co-ordination between the domestic and foreign-policy dimensions of environmental policy in Canada is less advanced than in the Netherlands. Indeed the Canadian Commissioner's 1998 report on departmental strategies observed that the government as a whole had only a very confused idea of the range and complexity of commitments to which Canada was already bound by international accords. And there is nothing in our country reports to indicate that Canada is alone in this regard.

With respect to the other main strand of externally directed policy—international assistance—each of the governments has repeated official commitments to support the efforts of developing states, and to contribute to the eradication of global poverty. All remain formally committed to the United Nations target of devoting at least 0.7 per cent of GNP to official development aid. Government documents on sustainable development routinely cite examples of multilateral and bilateral assistance as evidence of compliance with their UNCED commitments.

We can identify several trends in the evolution of assistance which are of obvious significance for sustainable development.

In the first place, a great deal of attention has been devoted to the 'greening' of aid. This has taken two essential forms: (1) an increase in the proportion of assistance that is explicitly targeted for environmental purposes; and (2) the introduction of procedures to monitor the environmental impacts of aid programmes and projects. All the governments we have examined have made some moves in these directions. The governments of the Netherlands and Sweden are committed to devoting 0.1 per cent of GNP to environmental projects in the developing world, and in both countries all aid is now assessed for environmental impacts. In Australia the environmental component of aid rose from A$120 million in 1992 to $A160 million in 1995; and since 1991 the Australian Agency for International Development has conducted systematic environmental audits of its programmes. In Japan environmental aid rose from 4.8 per cent of development assistance in 1986 to 20 per cent in 1996, and the country's ODA charter was amended in 1992 to include environmental conservation as an explicit objective. By 1994 a quarter of German bilateral aid was for projects dealing with the environment and resource protection, and environmental impact assessments had become a mandatory part of ODA procedures. USAID also reported that 10 per cent of bilateral assistance could be classed as environmental aid in 1994, and noted further that all its aid must meet environmental criteria. It appears that this trend towards a 'greening' of aid has been somewhat slower to emerge at the EU level, perhaps because of the time-lag involved in reorienting priorities established on the basis of multilateral negotiations, and the general lack of transparency in EU aid programmes and procedures.

While figures for the general increase in environmental aid are impressive, it is nonetheless important to keep them in perspective. First, they do not reflect an increase in overall aid levels: rather a reorientation of priorities toward the environment. Second, the figures probably overstate the true extent of the change, since it is comparatively easy to reclassify traditional development projects (such as the provision of drinking water, construction of sewage facilities or energy projects) as 'environmental' in order to meet shifts in official priorities.

A second major observable trend has been an adjustment in aid priorities: away from the funding of general infrastructure development and prestige industrial projects, towards programmes that are explicitly focused on poverty reduction. This reorientation is broadly consistent with the needs and equity-oriented dimensions of the Brundtland report and the UNCED process. It is particularly evident in the Netherlands, Norway, and Sweden, but it is also manifest in reforms of aid programmes in Australia, Canada, and the UK. Evidence for such a shift in Japan, the United States, and the EU is weaker, and—across the range of all of our domains—rhetoric is once again well ahead of practice.

Both these trends must however be set against the background of the third and most problematic development: a general and significant fall in the overall level of direct aid (calculated as a proportion of GNP) provided by each of the governments we have monitored. In 1998 only three states—the Netherlands, Norway, and Sweden—remained above the 0.7 per cent target (see Table 12.6). While this was more than double the proportion of national resource levels allocated to development assistance by Australia, Canada, Germany, and the UK, it nonetheless represents a significant fall from rates common from the mid-1980s to the early 1990s. Despite the decline, the fact that these three states remain above the UN target level is of considerable political significance. Note also that it is in these three countries—especially in Sweden and the Netherlands—that the greatest efforts have been made to link together the domestic and the 'international-solidarity' elements of sustainable development, primarily through public-education campaigns. Canada stands out slightly from the remaining states, both in its recent attempts to reverse the slide in aid and in the relative attention placed on the 'global' dimensions of sustainable development.

Development assistance is a complex issue, and debate continues over the extent to which recipients actually benefit, the distorting effects of tied aid, and the appropriate relations between aid donors and recipients. Nevertheless, in political terms the dramatic slide in development assistance budgets

Table 12.6. Net official development assistance to developing countries and multilateral organizations as a proportion of GNP (1987–1998)

	A	C	G	J	Ne	No	S	UK	USA	total DAC[a]	average country effort[b]	UN target
1987	0.34	0.47	0.39	0.31	0.98	1.09	0.88	0.28	0.20	0.34	0.43	
1988	0.46	0.50	0.39	0.32	0.98	1.13	0.86	0.32	0.21	0.34	0.45	
1989	0.38	0.44	0.41	0.31	0.94	1.05	0.96	0.31	0.15	0.32	0.45	
1990	0.34	0.44	0.42	0.31	0.92	1.17	0.91	0.27	0.21	0.33	0.46	
1991	0.38	0.45	0.40	0.32	0.88	1.13	0.90	0.32	0.20	0.33	0.48	
1992	0.37	0.46	0.38	0.30	0.86	1.16	1.03	0.31	0.20	0.33	0.48	0.70
1993	0.35	0.45	0.36	0.27	0.82	1.01	0.99	0.31	0.15	0.30	0.45	0.70
1994	0.34	0.43	0.34	0.29	0.76	1.05	0.96	0.31	0.14	0.30	0.45	0.70
1995	0.36	0.38	0.31	0.28	0.81	0.87	0.77	0.29	0.10	0.27	0.41	0.70
1996	0.30	0.32	0.33	0.20	0.81	0.85	0.84	0.27	0.12	0.25	0.40	0.70
1997	0.28	0.34	0.28	0.22	0.81	0.86	0.79	0.26	0.09	0.22	0.40	0.70
1998[c]	0.28	0.29	0.26	0.28	0.80	0.91	0.71	0.27	0.10	0.23	0.40	0.70

Sources: Development Co-operation: 1992 Report; 1994 Report; 1997 Report (OECD: Paris), and Preliminary 1998 DAC esimates from OECD website.

Notes:

[a] Total contributions of the 21 country members of the OECD Development Assistance Committee (DAC) as a proportion of combined GNP.

[b] Average country effort of the 21 DAC members.

[c] 1998 figures based on preliminary estimates.

Table 12.7. Contributions to international environmental funds

	A	C	G	J	Ne	No	S	UK	USA
GEF contribution									
1994–7 (million Special		61.78	171.30	295.95	50.97	22.29	41.60	96.04	306.92
Drawing Rights)		2.15	2.05	2.36	3.27	5.07	4.67	1.76	1.15
per capita									
proportion of GDP									
(thousandth of a per cent)		9.5	9.2	8.8	15	15	17	8.7	4.6
UNEP contributions									
1996–7 (million US$)	0.81	0.66	5.69	5.00	2.06	2.30	2.68	6.75	5.60
per capitaz	0.05	0.02	0.07	0.04	0.13	0.52	0.30	0.12	0.02
proportion of GDP									
(thousandth of a per cent)	0.2	0.1	0.3	0.1	0.6	2	1	0.6	0.08

Sources: Communication with GEF Secretariat, Washington (May 1998) and OECD population and GDP data.

during the 1990s, and the continued failure of major industrialized states to make any serious efforts to achieve the 0.7 per cent of GNP commitment can only be interpreted by developing countries as reneging on one of the basic pillars of the Rio accords. Indeed, the OECD has expressed dismay at the continuing drop in ODA, commenting in 1998 that a 'disproportionate share' of the burden of reducing the public deficit of the industrialized countries from an average of 4.3 per cent of GDP in 1993 to 1.3 per cent in 1997, has been born by reductions in ODA (OECD 1998c).

Financial contributions to international environmental programmes and initiatives have often been flagged by national governments as evidence of both their support for developing countries and their commitment to building institutions to manage global environmental challenges. Table 12.7 presents data on recent contributions to the Global Environment Facility (GEF) and to the United Nations Environment Programme (UNEP). The most generous support for the GEF—assessed as a proportion of GDP—has come from the Netherlands, Norway, and Sweden. Contributions from Canada, Germany, Japan, and the United Kingdom have run at about half this level. Donations from the United States, although largest in absolute terms, have been half again the proportion of GDP provided by the other four G7 members. A similar story emerges from the figures for UNEP contributions.

Technology transfer is another key UNCED issue which draws together environment and development policy. Each of the governments with which we are concerned has initiated programmes intended to raise the technical capacity of developing states to meet environmental challenges. Germany established a Centre for the Transfer of Environmental Technology in Leipzig, with both commercial and non-profit operations, to encourage the export of German technology to Central and Eastern Europe, Asia, and Latin America. The Netherlands has many initiatives including MILIEV, a programme of grant aid to Dutch companies for investment in environmentally friendly technology in the developing world. The European Union established the Indian Technology Information Centre which spreads information on environmental technologies related to polluting industries such as chemicals, pulp and paper, leather tanning, cement production, and dye works. Finally, the issue of technology transfer plays a particularly important role in Japan's approach to sustainable development, where the government has defined the national role in terms of helping developing countries avoid the pitfalls Japan itself experienced during its own rapid industrialization. The best-known programme is MITI's 'Green Aid Plan', which emphasizes energy efficiency and environmental technology especially in China and South-East Asia. For most industrialized countries technology transfer has been closely tied to the expansion of markets for their own environmental technologies, and much more detailed work would be required to establish the extent to which recipients actually gain from these programmes.

Climate Change

Climate change emerged as a major international issue towards the end of the 1980s. Although intense negotiations preceded the completion of the Framework Convention in 1992, this was followed by a relative lull as the treaty awaited sufficient ratifications to trigger its entry into force. By 1995 momentum was regained with the publication of the second IPCC report, and the adoption by the first Conference of the Parties to the Convention (COP1) of the Berlin Mandate, opening negotiations for an enforceable instrument to regulate greenhouse emission by developed (Annex I) countries. Two years later the Kyoto Protocol was adopted at COP3, establishing binding reductions from 1990 levels for the budget period 2008–12. By the end of the 1990s climate change negotiations had become increasingly institutionalized, with the annual 'COP' representing a diplomatic, political, and media event of the first order.

All the governments with which we are here concerned were drawn into the international process at the end of the 1980s. Canada, Germany, the

Netherlands, Norway, and Sweden played important roles in the initial round
of negotiations which gave birth to the Convention. Germany pushed the
pace to secure adoption of the Berlin Mandate, while Japan assumed the
host's responsibility for mediating between EU and US concerns in the final
endgame to conclude the Kyoto Protocol. At the time of writing this Protocol had not been ratified by any major developed state. Of particular
concern was the situation in the United States, where the Senate remained
overwhelmingly negative, insisting on a significant commitment from developing countries to join the abatement effort before US ratification, and refusing funding for US climate-gas reduction initiatives in the interim.

In terms of domestic policy all of the governments monitored responded
to the climate change issue, although with varying degrees of enthusiasm.
Germany, the Netherlands, and Sweden introduced the most comprehensive
programmes, picking up the issue comparatively early and formulating
emission-reduction measures well before negotiations for the Convention
were completed. In Germany public interest followed on from worries about
acid rain and forest die-back in the 1980s. In the Netherlands the wave of
environmental concern in the late 1980s and the country's historic preoccupation with the sea assured that climate change became a central theme of
the first NEPP. Sweden too was a pioneer on this issue, announcing its initial
intention to stabilise emissions as far back as 1988. The Norwegian government also engaged with climate change promptly, although domestic
reduction measures were more narrowly focused. Like Sweden and the
Netherlands, but in contrast to Germany, Norway introduced a carbon tax
in the early 1990s. Australia, Canada, and the United Kingdom were somewhat slower off the mark, launching programmes in the wake of UNCED
which relied heavily on voluntary commitments from industry, and on
improving energy efficiency in government operations.

Liberalization of energy markets—while primarily motivated by competition benefits—was also cited for its positive effects on energy efficiency in
the UK, and particularly in Australia. The Japanese response was distinguished by its strong encouragement for technological development, particularly in the energy sector. Voluntary reduction commitments were
sought from industry, but as in Germany and the Netherlands—and in contrast to Canada, Australia, and the UK—here the government took action to
ensure that suitable volunteers were forthcoming. Although the EU advocated stringent targets internationally, its own implementation effort has been
weakened by the reluctance of many member-states to cede authority over
energy issues to the Union, or to accelerate liberalization of energy markets,
as well as by the defeat of the carbon / energy tax proposal which the Commission had first heralded as the centrepiece of its ambitious 'European'

approach to emissions abatement. Finally, the United States must be set in a class of its own. While the President's Climate Change Action Plan contained many useful measures, the administration proved unable to build the political consensus necessary to make serious headway in addressing US emissions. Key facts and figures related to climate change policy are presented in Table 12.8.

Analysis of the trajectory of actual emissions through the mid-1990s suggests that only two of the nine countries were likely to meet their UNCED commitment to stabilize CO_2 generation by the year 2000—Germany and the United Kingdom.[8] In 1997 German emissions were at 88 per cent, and UK emissions at 93 per cent, of 1990 levels (see Table 12.9). In each case the achievement was largely the result of factors not directly related to climate change policy—in the UK the virtual abolition of the coal industry and the substitution of gas-fired generating capacity for coal-fired plants, and in Germany the industrial collapse and clean up in the East which followed reunification. The other seven states have seen CO_2 emissions climb steadily. By 1997 they were higher than 1990 levels by between 2 and 18 per cent. Stabilization by 2000 is, therefore, extremely improbable. Indeed increases on 1990 levels of 10 per cent or more may be the norm.

The figures for aggregate emissions of greenhouse gases expressed in CO_2 equivalents tell a broadly similar story, although the increase experienced in some countries (Australia, the Netherlands, and Norway) is somewhat less due to reductions in the emission of other gasses. Inclusion of the estimated impact of land-use change and forestry in the calculations further improves the apparent situation for some countries considered here; nevertheless, only Norway then joins Germany and the UK as having 1997 emissions below 1990 levels (see Table 12.10). Furthermore, because of the uncertainty surrounding emissions and removals related to land-use change and forestry, some analysts remain cautious about using the aggregate figure.

All this is not to say that policy measures introduced so far have been unable to secure any emissions reductions. Rather it is that even countries which have applied relatively comprehensive programmes have seen their reductions eroded by new emissions stemming from increased economic activity and from the transportation sector. The failure of the policy measures deployed to date to achieve overall stabilization in these countries sets the Kyoto reduction targets in perspective. In particular it suggests that in the absence of exogenous factors—such as a protracted economic

[8] Carbon dioxide is only one of the greenhouse gasses covered by the Climate Change Convention. For the sake of simplicity in comparison, we focus here primarily on CO_2, which is the key predictor, since it makes up 80 per cent of weighted emissions over the next decades.

Table 12.8. Facts and figures on climate policy (1987–1999)

	Ratified FCCC	Original commitment	Kyoto target	EU burden sharing	National action plan	Policy approach
Australia	1992	In 1990: to reduce green house gas emissions by 20% based on 1988 levels by 2000. Later diluted	no more than +8% on 1990 levels between 2008 and 2012		National Greenhouse Response Strategy was endorsed by COAG in 1992. Revised NGRS was issued in 1997.	Government introduced a 'Greenhouse Challenge' of co-operative agreements with companies in various industrial sectors. A white paper on sustainable energy has been prepared. Some encouragement for energy efficiency and alternative energy supplies, as well as measures to reduce agricultural emissions.
Canada	1992	In 1992: to stabilize by 2000 at 1990 levels. Admitted by 1996 that this target was unlikely to be met.	-6% on 1990 levels between 2008 and 2012		National Action Programme on Climate Change agreed with the provinces and territories.	Voluntary Challenge and Registry programme (VCR) involving major companies from important industrial sectors. Educational programmes for municipalities and the public, and efforts to raise standards for electrical products. Purchasing of 'green power' is to be encouraged in government departments.
Germany	1993	In 1990: committed to 25% reduction of CO_2 compared to 1987 levels. Strengthened in 1995 to 25% reduction of CO_2 on 1990 levels (1990 was already down 5% from 1987).	-8% on 1990 levels between 2008 and 2012	-21%	After extensive national discussion which included reporting by two Enquete Commissions and an interministerial working group, a national Programme for Climate Protection was published in 1993/1994.	Largely programmes of grants and encouragement for positive action and investment. Voluntary agreements with industry in 1995 (19 industrial and trade federations) to reduce 'specific CO_2 emissions' by 20% on 1990 levels by 2005. In return government agreed not unilaterally to impose a carbon tax and also to urge exceptions for industry in the case of an EU tax. Local authorities have taken many initiatives. Proposals for carbon tax are now on hold; few transport related measures have yet been taken; divisions over nuclear power and the future of coal remain.
Japan	1993	In 1990: two objectives: MITI target: freeze per capital emissions at 1990 levels by 2000; EA objective: stabilise total emissions at 1990 levels by 2000. A firm commitment was made only for the per capita figure	-6% on 1990 levels between 2008 and 2012.		Action programme to Arrest Global Warming issued by Council of Ministers for Global Environmental Conservation in 1990. Global Warming Prevention law adopted in 1998.	Subsidy programmes to encourage energy efficiency, new energy technology, and reduced transport emissions. Voluntary commitments made by industry to reduce greenhouse-gas emissions.

Country	Year	Commitment	Target 2008–2012	%	National objectives	Policies and measures
Netherlands	1993	1990: 3–5% reduction in CO₂ by the year 2000 relative to 1989 base line.	-8% on 1990 levels between 2008 and 2012	-6%	National objectives are included in the NEPPs and also in Memorandums on Climate Change.	Budgetary allocations have been made to improve the energy infrastructure, and to encourage alternative energy and energy efficiency. Voluntary agreements have been secured with industry to reduce emissions. A 'small users tax' on energy was introduced in 1996 when it became clear that the EU carbon tax was stalled indefinitely. Tax relief for car commuting has been abolished and incentives to use public transport introduced. Measures to reduce agricultural emissions have been developed.
Norway	1993	1989: Stabilize at 1989 levels by the year 2000; this remained a formal objective but commitment was weakened by government acknowledgement (1995) that it could not be attained.	no more than $+1\%$ on 1990 levels between 2008 and 2012		Report to Parliament RTP 41 (1995) 'Policy to Mitigate Climate Change and Reduce Emissions from Nitrogen Oxides' presented outlines of a national strategy. It was replaced by RTP 29 (1998) 'On Norwegian Implementation of The Kyoto Protocol', which outlines short-, medium-, and long-term strategies to fulfil Norway's commitment under The Kyoto Protocol.	Focus has primarily been on a CO₂ tax with some attention also to education, research into energy efficiency, and support for the adoption of new technology. CO₂ tax was introduced in 1991. Rates for specific fuels and uses have varied. Exemptions are in place for the fishing fleet, North sea supply vessels, international trade, and non combustion emissions from industries such as steel, aluminium, cement. Pulp and paper, fishmeal and coastal transport pay at a reduced rate. About 60% of Norwegian CO₂ emissions fall under the tax. Voluntary agreements have been secured with some industrial sectors. Pilot joint implementation schemes have been developed with Poland, Mexico.
Sweden	1993	1988: objective to stabilize CO₂ at 1988 levels; subsequently revised (weakened) in 1991 to EU/FCCC objective of 1990 levels by the year 2000.	-8% on 1990 levels between 2008 and 2012	$+4\%$	After UNCED the government introduced a climate change bill (1993) which included provisions to reduce methane emissions, encourage investment in renewable resources. It has a joint implementation pilot programme with Baltic States.	Policies include: a CO₂ tax (first introduced in 1990, the rate has been adjusted on several occasions: there are exemptions for fuel used for power generation and for peat, and in 1996 industry paid 50% the rate of other users); energy conservation activities; and continuing investment in renewables, including biomass, solar and wind. Considerable action has also been undertaken at the local level. Enthusiasm exists for joint implementation, especially with Eastern Europe, because of difficulties securing further domestic reductions.
United Kingdom	1993	1990: stabilize CO₂ emissions by 2005. In 1992 accepted EU/FCCC goal of stabilisation by 2000.	-8% on 1990 levels between 2008 and 2012	-12.5%	After consultation a Climate Change Programme was published in 1994. This has been updated by succeeding governments.	Early measures revolved around imposition of VAT on fuel and energy efficiency efforts. In 1993 the government announced a 'fuel price escalator', which was suspended in 1999. Voluntary schemes have been introduced to encourage environmentally friendly behaviour. A 'Climate Change Levy' on energy use was announced in 1999.

Table 12.8. (*Cont.*)

	Ratified FCCC	Original commitment	Kyoto target	EU burden sharing	National action plan	Policy approach
United States	1992	Accepted stabilization at 1990 levels by 2000 as formulated in FCCC	−7% on 1990 levels between 2008 and 2012		President's Climate Change Action Plan in 1993. Included 50 new or expanded programme items to increase energy efficiency, reduce landfill emissions, encourage tree planting, and so on. Further plan in 1997 which emphasizes emissions trading.	Mainly encouragement for industry and consumers to undertake voluntary measures to reduce greenhouse gas emission. In some limited sectors administrative measures have been employed: e.g. EPA methane emission reduction from land fill. Some state and local government initiatives, particularly with respect to energy efficiency and electricity demand reduction.
European Union	1993	1990 commitment: to stabilize CO_2 by 2000 at 1990 levels.	−8% on 1990 levels between 2008 and 2012		In 1992 the Commission prepared the 'Community strategy to limit carbon dioxide emissions and improve energy efficiency'. This relied on programmes to enhance energy efficiency (SAVE); introduce a carbon/energy tax; develop alternative energy sources (ALTENER); and provisions for monitoring of emissions and reduction efforts of member states.	Framework directive instructing national states to prepare plans to improve energy efficiency; subsidies for some renewables; support for energy technology research; complementarity with other programmes on waste management, forestry, etc.; injunctions to national governments. Focus has been on the energy sector; transport has received only limited attention. Proposals for an EU carbon/energy tax were opposed by some member states and not adopted.

Table 12.9. Total anthropogenic CO_2 emissions, excluding land-use changes and forestry, 1990–1997

	A	C	G	J	Ne	No	S	UK	USA	EU
emissions 1990[a]	275,344	461,250	1,014,500	1,124,532	161,360	35,202	55,443	584,171	4,928,900	3,328,510[b]
emissions 1997[a]	308,413[c]	519,280	894,000	1,230,831	184,870[c]	41,430	56,428	540,643	5,455,553	3,337,872[d]
percentage relative to 1990										
1991	101	98	96	102	103	95	100	101	99	
1992	102	101	91	103	102	97	101	98	100	
1993	103	101	90	102	104	102	101	96	103	
1994	104	104	89	108	104	108	106	95	104	96[d]
1995	108	107	89	108	110	109	105	94	106	98[d]
1996	112	110	91	110	115	117	114	97	109	100[d]
1997		113	88	109		118	102	93	111	
per capita emissions[e]										
1990	16.1	16.6	12.8	9.1	10.8	8.3	6.5	10.1	19.7	9.1
1997	16.9[c]	17.1	10.9	9.8	11.9[c]	9.4	6.4	9.2	20.4	8.9[c]
emissions per unit GDP[f]										
1990	931	805	619	379	569	305	241	599	887	494
1997	870[c]	802	488	362	570[c]	274	233	491	805	443

Sources: Calculated from FCCC/SBI/1999/12, 29 September 1999, Tables B3, C1, C2, C3 and C4; and *OECD online national statistics (August 1999).*

Notes:
[a] Emissions in gigagrams.
[b] EU data are not entirely consistent with data provided for individual EU countries.
[c] 1996 data.
[d] 1996 EU figures include 1994 data for Portugal and 1995 data for Italy and Spain. 1995 EU figures include 1994 data for Portugal.
[e] Per capita emissions in tonnes.
[f] Emissions per unit GDP in grams per US dollar at 1990 prices and exchange rates.

Table 12.10. Estimated changes in emissions of greenhouse gases 1990–1997 (Index 1990 = 100)

	A[a]	C	G	J	Ne[a]	No	S	UK	USA	EU
CO_2[b]	112	113	88	109	115	118	102	93	111	100
CH_4[b]	99	123	64	90	91	110	92	75	106	87
N_2O[b]	105	117	96	113	113	94	92	90	114	97
Hydrofluorocarbons, perfluorocarbons and sulphur hexafluoride[c]	31	89	116	131[d]	126	43	[c]	177[d]	145	
aggregate emissions of all greenhouse gases excluding land-use change and forestry[c]	107	114	86	106	112	108	104	91	111	
aggregate emissions and removals of all greenhouse gases including land-use change and forestry[c]	102	119	86	113	112	93	116	90	121	

Sources: Calculated from FCCC/SBI/1999/12, 29 September 1999, Tables A1, A2, A11, B3, B8, B12, C1, and C4 and FCCC/SBI/1998/INF.9, 31 October 1998.

Notes:
[a] Figures for Australia and Netherlands are based on 1996 data.
[b] Based on emissions in gigagrams.
[c] Based on emissions stated as gigagrams CO_2 equivalent using IPCC 1995 GWP values with a time horizon of 100 years.
[d] Breakdown of exact chemical species not always provided by party, so calculation of CO_2 equivalent incomplete.
[c] 1990 figures not provided so change not calculated.

downturn—most of these states are unlikely to meet the objectives without either a considerably more vigorous domestic policy response, or significant reliance upon extra-territorial reductions secured through collaboration with other parties.

With respect to greenhouse-gas emissions and energy supply, the nine countries of the study present quite different profiles. Gross CO_2 emissions vary by a factor of more than a hundred—with the United States at nearly 5,500 million tonnes a year in 1997, contributing about a fifth of the global total; while Norway, at 41 million tonnes, adds only about 0.2 per cent. Annual per capita emissions vary by a factor of three across the sample, ranging from 20 tons in the USA to 6.5 tons in Sweden. Fossil fuel provides at least 70 per cent of the energy supply in all the countries except Sweden, where nuclear energy, hydro-power, and biomass make significant contributions, and Norway, which relies heavily on hydro-electricity. Australia emerges as particularly dependent on fossil fuels. Sweden, on the other hand, is the only state where non-nuclear and non-fossil fuels make up more than 10 per cent of the energy supply. Canada, Norway, the United States, and the United Kingdom are all major oil and gas producers. Norway is now the second largest oil-exporting country in the world, while Australia remains a major exporter of coal.

Population trends, the character of economic activity and the history of energy policy also shape the way the problem is structured in the different states. In contrast to northern Europe and Japan, relatively strong population growth continues in Canada, the United States, and Australia, largely as a result of immigration. Resource sectors remain the focus for a high proportion of economic activity in Canada, Australia, Sweden, and Norway, and Norway has both developed and attracted energy-intensive industries because of extensive sources of relatively cheap hydro-power. Japan and Sweden have managed to maintain energy-efficiency gains made in the wake of the 1970s oil shocks.

One of the paradoxes of climate change is that developed countries which burn the 'dirtiest' fuels and have lower energy efficiency than their neighbours have a greater potential for quick and cheap reductions than those already reliant on no- or low-emission fuels, and/or with more energy-efficient economies. In other words, carbon dioxide emission reduction does not become easier with success. With energy efficiency already high in Japan and Sweden, both countries find it very costly to secure further gains. Sweden in particular faces a dilemma over the planned phase-out of nuclear power, as any replacement by fossil-fuel fired plants would have a negative impact on carbon abatement. Norway's successful hydro development means CO_2 savings must come from elsewhere, such as energy-intensive industries which are vulnerable to foreign competitive pressures, or the transport sector. It is hardly surprising that these governments—especially the Norwegian and Japanese governments—are actively exploring the possibilities of securing a proportion of their abatement off-shore, primarily through flexibility provisions envisaged under the Kyoto Protocol: 'joint implementation', the so-called 'Clean Development Mechanism', and emissions trading.

The German government remains wedded to the most ambitious CO_2 reduction target in the European Union, but difficult decisions about the future of the coal industry and nuclear power will have to be made. The Netherlands is unlikely to meet its target domestically without further and more costly measures, and in the United Kingdom the 'dash for gas' has reduced the carbon intensity of the UK fuel mix, but the country could still achieve significant gains through improved building codes, expanded district heating schemes, and so on. States with the highest per capita emissions— Australia, Canada, and the USA—have enormous potential savings associated with increased energy efficiency by applying known technologies, but political obstacles remain significant: low-energy prices are habit-forming, and in each country powerful producer lobbies, which are convinced that carbon abatement strategies will damage their interests, are exploiting political leverage in these federal states to resist further measures.

Biodiversity

Compared to the high-profile initiatives associated with climate change, activity related to the Convention on Biological Diversity (BDC) has been distinctly low key. All the governments which concern us here had ratified the Convention by the close of 1994, with the exception of the United States which had yet to make a move in this direction by the end of 1999. All participated in ongoing convention processes (the US as an unratified signatory), including negotiations on the Bio-safety Protocol. In addition to domestic consultations related to these negotiations, the response of these governments to the BDC typically focused on: (1) conducting initial surveys of the state of biodiversity within their jurisdictions, and assessing the pressures leading to biodiversity loss; (2) preparing general and sector-specific biodiversity strategies; and (3) adopting modest additional measures intended to protect endangered species and habitats and to encourage the sustainable management of biological resource systems. Governments have also engaged in an externally directed strand of biodiversity policy by contributing to conservation and environmental remedial schemes in developing countries. (Information on the state of biodiversity policy, wildlife, and protected areas is presented in Tables 12.11, 12.12, and 12.13).

Once again the United States was the relative laggard, with biodiversity remaining a virtual non-issue in terms of domestic political priorities. Although the US signed the BDC early in the Clinton presidency, it soon became clear that there was little possibility of Senate ratification in the foreseeable future. Cutting its losses, the administration set the issue aside, resulting in widespread neglect of biodiversity issues by federal institutions throughout the 1990s. This is not to say that nature conservation and resource policy were not the object of continued political controversy. Indeed proposals to amend the Endangered Species Act provoked bitter exchanges throughout the decade. Rather it is that these conflicts were not set within the context of biodiversity politics, or related to compliance with international priorities established by the BDC.

Among the remaining countries Germany was slowest to engage with biodiversity, with the government initially insisting that the 1976 Federal Nature Conservation Act (FNCA) provided an adequate legislative

Table 12.11. Facts and figures on biodiversity policy (1987–1998)

	Signed BDC	Ratified BDC	National action plan	Policy initiatives
Australia	1992	1993	National Strategy for Biodiversity ratified by all tiers of government. It emphasises regional responsibility for biodiversity protection and management.	Aim by year 2000 to identify biogeographical regions and conservation priorities and establish system of protected areas for major ecosystems; to develop conservation plans and limit clearance of native habitats; and assure compliance with all international treaties. Biodiversity Advisory council has been established.
Canada	1992	1992	Canadian Biodiversity Strategy (1995). Agreement among governments to develop legislation and incentives to encourage conservation and sustainable use.	Creation of new national parks. Tax incentives for private landowners to participate in habitat protection. Agreements with provinces and territories. Initiatives with aboriginal communities. National Ecological Monitoring and Assessment Network will monitor developments across the country.
Germany	1992	1993	Strategy not yet adopted.	Amendments to the FNCA introduced in 1997, but not adopted. Work is proceeding on a national strategy.
Japan	1992	1993	National Strategy of Japan on Biological Diversity (1995).	Passage of Law for the Conservation of Endangered Species of Wild Fauna and Flora (1992).
Netherlands	1992	1994	A strategic Biodiversity Action Plan was drawn up in 1995: this links policy initiatives in NEPPs, Nature Policy Plan (1990) and other plans, and details how to fill gaps between them.	Develop area-specific policies and plans with provincial and local authorities. Develop network of 'ecological corridors' to preserve natural plants and animals. Continue detailed monitoring of the state of nature which was instituted at the national level in 1988.
Norway	1992	1993	National Strategy released in 1997, after research and preparation of sectoral plans. Detailed action plan under preparation.	Modest extension of system of reserves, particularly in forested areas. Development of biodiversity assessment programme with biological inventories of municipalities and monitoring of changes. Encouragement of sustainable forest management through 'Living Forests' initiative.
Sweden	1992	1993	National Strategy adopted 1994, action plans for sector agencies 1995, and a government bill on biological diversity in 1997.	Three-level approach to set aside major reserves, smaller connected reserves and to encourage sustainable forestry. Changes to forestry law to raise priority of environmental considerations. Encouragement of more environmentally sensitive agricultural practices.
United Kingdom	1992	1994	*Biodiversity: The UK Action Plan* published in 1994. The UK Biodiversity Steering Group Report was issued in 1995 and subsequently endorsed by government.	A large range of governmental and social partners have been drawn into collaborative partnerships to promote biodiversity action. Initiatives include a central Biodiversity Secretariat, Local Biodiversity Action Plans, and costed conservation targets for threatened species and habitats. By the end of 1998 plans for protecting 400 species and 39 habitat types had been drafted.

Table 12.11. *(Cont.)*

	signed BDC	Ratified BDC	National action plan	Policy initiatives
United States	1993	Not ratified	No Strategy prepared.	The US has long had domestic endangered species legislation, but in the 1990s it was subjected to attacks from affected economic interests. Since 1994 Republicans have tried to amend the Endangered Species Act and impede its implementation. In 1993 the US established the National Biological Service to develop methods to survey and assess biodiversity.
European Union	1992	1993	Strategy issued by Commission in 1998	The Directive on Habitats, Flora and Fauna (92/43) is the main instrument in the biodiversity field. It establishes a common framework for conservation of habitats in the EU through the creation of Nature 2000 network of protected areas and corridors. Sustainable land management practices to be encouraged around these areas. Preservation and restoration of these areas are key elements of 5th EAP. Other EU programmes such as environmental impact assessment directive, Birds directive, and introduction of environmental assessment in structural funds, are also of relevance.

framework to meet obligations under the Convention. However, by the late 1990s the issue was being taken more seriously with amendments to the FNCA and a draft national biodiversity strategy under discussion. While at the international level the EU has been an enthusiastic player on biodiversity, its domestic policy response has been hampered by member-state reluctance to cede authority over nature conservation. Failure to make significant headway in integrating environmental protection into sectors such as transport, agriculture, and tourism has further restricted the effectiveness of EU biodiversity measures. Still a draft biodiversity strategy was issued in 1998, and the Commission remains committed to extending its presence in this area.

Australia, Canada, Japan, and the United Kingdom issued national biodiversity strategies in 1996, 1995, 1995, and 1994 respectively. The Canadian and Australian strategies took the form of intergovernmental agreements, while the Japanese and UK plans were promulgated directly by the central authorities. Awareness of Australia's unique biological heritage and of the vulnerability of its ecosystems prompted the Commonwealth government to devote considerable attention to biodiversity in the NSESD and in related

Table 12.12. State of wildlife in selected OECD countries (1993)

	A	C	G	J	Ne	No	S	UK[a]	USA
Mammals									
known species	348	193	93	183	64	50	66	63	466
% threatened	14	24	40	8	16	8	18	22	11
Birds									
known species	850	514	273	652	170	222	245	517	1,090
% threatened	6	9	40	8	27	10	9	23	7
Fish									
known species	3,600	276	66	198	28	191	150	54	2,640
% threatened	0.4	22	68	11	82		5	11	2
Reptiles									
known species	700	43	12	87	7	5	7	7	368
% threatened	3	28	75	3	86	20		43	7
Amphibians									
known species	180	42	19	59	16	5	7	7	222
% threatened	5	10	58	10	56	40	54	29	4
Invertibrates									
known species	92,000	34,880		35,205	27,700	15,120	23,400	22,770	
% threatened				0.4			3	4	
Vascular plants									
known species	22,000	3,300	2,954	7,266	1,392	1,310	1,900	2,297	22,200
% threatened	4	3	26	11	35	7	11	9	0.5

Source: Adapted from *OECD Environmental Data Compendium 1997* (OECD: Paris, 1997).

Notes: 'Threatened' species include those classed as 'endangered' and 'vulnerable'. Data from this table must be interpreted with caution because: entries are inconsistent (some include and others exclude non-indigenous species); countries are more or less rigorous in applying 'endangered' and 'vunerable' catagories; species-counts are often approximations and 'known species' may not reflect range of species actually present; and information on the status of many species is incomplete. Data problems are especially acute for invertibrates and vascular plants (but extend to other classes for the continent-sized countries of Australia and the United States).
[a] Figures include Great Britain only.

Table 12.13. National Parks and protected areas in selected OECD countries (1996)

	A	C	G	J	Ne	No	S	UK	USA	EU
Major protected areas										
number of sites	1,068	807	525	65	78	128	182	153	1,701	1,969
total size (1,000 km^2)	670	945	94	26	5	94	21	49	1,772	373
% of national territory	8.7	9.5	26.4	6.8	11.5	24.2	4.7	19.8	18.9	12.3
National parks										
number of sites	376	319	3	15	9	20	19	0[a]	171	100
total size (1,000 km^2)	209	399	0.4	13	0.3	31	5.3	0	254	973
% of national territory	2.7	4.0	0.1	3.4	0.6	8.0	1.2	0	2.7	0.5

Source: Adapted from *OECD Environmental Data: Compendium 1997* (OECD: Paris, 1997).

Notes: [a] Areas designated 'national parks' in the UK do not correspond to OECD criteria.

environmental plans. Extensions have been made to Australia's reserve system and an inventory of ecosystem types has been undertaken. The 1998 Environmental Protection and Biodiversity Conservation Bill is the centrepiece of the current government's efforts around biodiversity, although critics charge that provisions aimed at avoiding duplication of state efforts represent an unfortunate retreat from Commonwealth involvement with conservation.

Federal/provincial relations have also complicated the Canadian response, for while the central government made much of the National Accord for the Protection of Species at Risk signed in 1996, only half the provinces had adopted endangered species legislation by the end of 1998. The system of national parks has been extended; fiscal incentives to encourage conservation introduced; and a variety of arctic preservation measures adopted. But the bitter controversies surrounding the Canadian Endangered Species Protection Act—which had not yet passed into law by the end of 1999—is reminiscent of the conservation-versus-resource-lobby battles so familiar in Canada's neighbour to the south. Japan introduced a law for the Conservation of Endangered Species of Wild Fauna and Flora in 1992, and recent conservation initiatives have focused on the preservation of forests and coastal and mountain regions. In the wake of the Rio conference the UK government launched a relatively open policy process around biodiversity, and the Report of the UK Steering Group helped establish urgent priorities and quantifiable targets for biodiversity conservation. A survey of Norway's biological resources was completed by 1992, and the preparation of sectoral biodiversity plans was then given official priority. The national biodiversity strategy based on these sectoral plans was released in 1997. As in Japan, the idea of 'sustainable use' has been a recurrent theme of Norwegian biodiversity policy.

Of the states considered here the Netherlands, and then Sweden, have displayed the most vigorous domestic responses to biodiversity. The Netherlands 1995 biodiversity strategy built on the 1989 Nature Policy Plan, supplementing existing programmes and initiatives across the range of government activity. Particularly ambitious is the scheme to complete an integrated system of national reserves envisaged in an 'ecological structure plan' by 2020. Sweden's national strategy was adopted in 1994, and issues of conservation and sustainability also figured prominently in the revised Forestry Act adopted the same year. Detailed sectoral plans for biodiversity appeared in subsequent years, and in 1997 the Swedish parliament adopted a bill on biodiversity. A summary of facts on biodiversity policy is presented in Table 12.11.

These initiatives suggest that many governments have begun to alter the way they approach conservation or nature protection. The emphasis is now somewhat less on individual species and more on safeguarding habitats and ecosystems. The multidimensional value of 'biodiversity' is more often stressed: the prospect that it may generate environmental life-support functions, resources for future development, treasured national assets, amenity and ethical values, and so on. Moreover the idea of sustainable use and management of biological resource systems has also been introduced into policy debates about forestry, fisheries, and agriculture. Preparation of national biodiversity inventories and strategies, and the establishment of targets and monitoring regimes have raised institutional capacity and are likely to lead to pressure for further action in the future. Yet the significance of these changes can easily be overstated. In public debate issues are often still framed in terms of prosperity *or* nature protection, jobs *or* conservation—and this is particularly true in the United States, Australia, and Canada. In none of the countries examined here is there any indication that measures governments have taken over the past decade have actually contributed to slowing the pace of biodiversity loss. Nor does there appear to be any real enthusiasm to engage with the hard issues of how to blunt the underlying development pressures which are destroying habitats and 'crowding out' other species.

Overall Patterns

Up to this point the discussion has been concerned with specific dimensions of the governmental response to sustainable development. We have considered the extent to which the term has been integrated into the idiom of governance; the way it has been understood; the timing and pace of engagement; organizational changes and strategic planning processes; governmental attitudes to other actors and to international obligations; and initiatives related to measurement and monitoring, sustainable production and consumption, climate change and biodiversity. We will now attempt to draw these strands together to offer a more synthetic account.

Assessing the overall behaviour of the ten governments across the decade following the publication of the Brundtland report, it seems that there have been three types of reaction to the introduction of sustainable development. The first response could be described as 'enthusiastic', 'extensive', and 'pioneering'. These governments responded warmly to the idea of sustainable development from the start; actively addressed issues associated with the sustainable development agenda; and have self-consciously

Enthusiastic	Cautiously Supportive	Disinterested
Netherlands	Australia	USA
Norway	Canada	
Sweden	Germany	
	EU	
	Japan	
	UK	

FIGURE 12.4. Government responses to sustainable development in selected OECD countries 1987–98

identified themselves as 'lead states' in the effort to implement the concept and its values.

At the other extreme is a response which can be characterized as 'disinterested', 'sceptical', and 'disengaged'. This profile reflects virtually no interest in sustainable development *per se*, manifesting only a minimal effort to integrate the idea into domestic political priorities.

Between these two poles lie a variety of reactions which can be described as generally 'supportive'—but also as 'hesitant' and 'uneven'. We refer to these governments as 'cautiously supportive'. They have responded positively to sustainable development, but the depth of their commitment has varied across issue-domains and across time. They are less determined than those in the first group to present themselves as embodying 'international best-practice' on sustainable development (see Fig. 12.4), but are clearly more involved than the 'disinterested'.

The 'Enthusiasts'

Governments of three of the countries we have examined displayed an 'enthusiastic' response: the Netherlands, Sweden, and Norway. This is a group that has consistently surfaced as relatively 'leading-edge' throughout the preceding evaluation. In each country government endorsed the conclusions of the Brundtland report, and linked the international call for sustainable development to a significant review of domestic and foreign-policy objectives. On the home front there have been relatively consistent efforts to deploy a new paradigm for environmental governance—one which emphasizes environment/economic integration, an expanded responsibility for sectoral ministries, an integration of sustainable development themes and concepts into long-term planning, and specific attempts to better integrate national and international environment-and-development processes. Some steps have also been taken in the direction of ecological tax reform, and each country has developed an active mode of 'environmental diplomacy' internationally, providing particular support for UNCED and the Commission for Sustainable Development. All three countries have also maintained levels of development assistance above the UN target, and have broadly advocated solidarity with the needs of developing countries. Each of these governments considers its nation to be in the vanguard of sustainable development implementation, and has, in various ways and consistently over time, emphasized the importance of trying to remain at the forefront of the international effort (see Fig. 12.5).

As the chapters on these states have shown, this does not imply, however, that their responses have been free from contradiction or ambivalence. It is in comparison with the other countries studied (and, in our opinion, with nearly all other OECD countries), that they have gone further in translating sustainable development into identifiable policy initiatives.

The Netherlands integrated themes from the Brundtland report with the preparation of the first NEPP, which had been initiated to tackle acute pollution burdens from intensive industrial and agricultural activity in this small and densely populated country. The comprehensive reach of the NEPPs, the development of a complex system of covenants binding target groups to national objectives, and the particular emphasis placed on integrating the domestic and foreign-policy dimensions of environmental policy, are all distinctive features of the Dutch approach.

Sweden has an established reputation as an environmental policy innovator, and this has been carried forward over the past decade into the policy realm of sustainable development. The initiatives on eco-cycles (which shift responsibility for product life-cycle management onto the producer), and the enthusiastic national programme for Local Agenda 21 are of particular note. So too are the attempts to fuse the environmental and internationalist objectives of sustainable development to established traditions of the Swedish welfare state. The more muted enthusiasm for the climate change issue is perhaps understandable in light of Sweden's relatively low per capita CO_2 emissions and the delicacy of the nuclear power issue. What is perhaps most remarkable here is that, despite the acute economic downturn in the early 1990s, and the subsequent economic restructuring and state retrenchment, sustainable development issues have not been obscured.

In Norway, following the release of the report of the Brundtland Commission, the government reformed the nation's environmental administration, integrating environmental responsibilities into the tasks of sectoral ministries, and developing capacity in the municipalities and counties to *common features*

- domestic and foreign policy stance is adjusted in conjunction with reception of Brundtland report
- strong support for UNCED and UNCSD
- 'pushers' on climate change and biodiversity
- consistent efforts to develop new paradigm for environmental policy
- emphasis on international environmental diplomacy and solidarity with developing countries
- UN aid target met
- modest ecological tax reform
- self-perception as leading states in sustainable development implementation

national particularities

Netherlands
- initial objective of reducing transferred environmental loads to zero within a generation
- focus on decoupling economic growth from environmental loadings
- system of National Environmental Policy Plans, endorsed by multiple ministries
- developed system of performance covenants with target groups
- success in meeting objectives of traditional environmental policy through late 1990s; but difficulties with targets for climate change, biodiversity, NOx and noise; relative recoupling

Norway
- emphasis on integration of environmental objectives into responsibilities of sector ministries, with supervisory role for environment ministry
- no single national plan, but integration and/or reconciliation of objectives in Cabinet, and at regional and local levels
- expanding oil and gas industry generates wealth, but makes domestic attainment of Kyoto target difficult
- launched international initiatives on sustainable production and consumption

Sweden
- ecocycle society: emphasizes recycling, environmental limits and producer responsibility
- 'ecological homeland' links sustainable development to welfare state
- strong national initiatives on Local Agenda 21
- difficulties with climate change targets because of low per capita emissions
- continued commitment to sustainable development despite serious economic problems in the early 1990s

FIGURE 12.5. Enthusiastic response to sustainable development

manage environmental problems. Somewhat disappointed with the achievements of UNCED, and confident in the orientation of its original response
to the Brundtland report, the Norwegian government has been reluctant to
pick up on Agenda 21. Once it grasped the broader implications of Local
Agenda 21, however, it quickly moved to promote the idea as a key aspect
of a renewed national strategy. Norway has also been a strong advocate of
a robust but flexible climate change regime, but the rapid expansion of oil
and gas production and an almost exclusive reliance on hydro-powered electricity has posed serious barriers for meeting the Kyoto targets on the basis
of domestic action alone. Norway has taken the lead in developing international activities around the theme of sustainable production and consumption, at the same time that the Norwegian oil-and-gas-driven economy has
paradoxically elevated the country into the 'wealthiest in the world' (per
capita) category.

The 'Disinterested'

Among the ten political units, only the United States government can be
described as having adopted the second—'disinterested'—approach. Sustainable development has gone largely unnoticed and non-supported. Even
allowing for the admirable efforts of the President's Council on Sustainable
Development, it is none the less true that sustainable development has
had virtually *no* significant impact on the operations of the US federal
government. It is not just that the term itself has failed to catch on, but also
that core values associated with the idea—particularly the global equity
dimension—have failed to gain even formal political acceptance. At a
national level, US environmental policy remains largely frozen in the conservationist, regulation/compliance, industry-versus-environmentalists, and
pollution-clean-up patterns that took shape either prior to or during the
1970s. Both UNCED treaties continue to face acute problems in the American context, and Agenda 21 is virtually non-existent at the federal level.
True, US agencies have experimented with negotiated and multi-partite
approaches to environmental management—modalities which in other
countries have been associated with sustainable development. But these
remain marginal to the overall pattern of environmental politics and regulation (see Fig. 12.6).

The 'Cautiously Supportive'

The most common reaction uncovered—displayed by governments in Australia, Canada, Germany, Japan, the United Kingdom, and the European

USA   • sustainable development largely understood as a problem for the developing world
• sustainable development not taken up by key government agencies
• limited influence of President's Council on Sustainable Development
• political difficulties ratifying Biodiversity convention and Kyoto protocol
• no acceptance of international solidarity dimension of sustainable development; foreign direct assistance only 10% of UN target
• environmental policy-making remains dominated by conservation/pollution control paradigm
• state and local initiatives on sustainability relatively independent of central support

FIGURE 12.6. Disinterested response to sustainable development

Union—has been a mixed response, often involving public support for the symbol of sustainable development—but with an uneven pattern of follow-up and implementation. In some cases substantive engagement was delayed; in others early enthusiasm faded; while elsewhere interest has ebbed and flowed according to wider political events. Initiatives have been more select-ive with respect to sectors, and, where applied, aspects of the sustainable development agenda have been much more diffuse. In each of these coun-tries the 'internationalist' and 'equity' dimensions of the concept have been accorded considerably less weight than for the group of 'enthusiasts', and none of the units have approached the level of development assistance re-commended by the UN (see Fig. 12.7).

Yet, while the responses of these governments can be described as 'mixed' and 'ambivalent', there is also considerable variation across the group. Over the time-frame covered here the Canadian government deployed the most systematic response, and would appear to lie closest to the group of 'enthu-siasts'. Canada's innovative Roundtables on the environment and economy were stimulated by the Brundtland report, and the Green Plan represented an early ambitious attempt to tackle environmental issues in a more com-prehensive manner. Canada also played a pusher role in the UNCED process, helping for example to secure US acceptance of the climate change conven-tion at Rio. Relatively inclusive forms of participation have also been asso-ciated with the Canadian profile, and the establishment of the Parliamentary Commissioner for the Environment and Sustainable Development and the *common features*

- official support for sustainable development as a national and international goal
- uneven pattern of initiatives, varying across time and between issue domains
- some attempt to apply new paradigm for environmental policy
- support for UNCED conventions, but cautious about pace and direction of their evolution
- failure to meet level of development assistance recommended by the UN

national particularities

Australia	• early support for *ecologically* sustainable development • participatory process around ESD working groups contributes to NSESD, which involves state and Federal agreement • shift in government priorities leads to downgrading of emphasis on sustainable development and multi-lateral negotiations • insistance on particular responsibilities as custodian of an island continent
Canada	• early emphasis on multi-stakeholder negotiations and wide participation • Green plan developed and subsequently abandoned • establishment of Parliamentary Commissioner for Environment and Sustainable Development, and review process for departmental sustainable development strategies • disappointments over CESPA and CEIA
Germany	• initial reluctance to accept sustainable development; presentation of sustainable development as the 'precautionary principle' writ large • early and vigorous response to climate change issue • first considers biodiversity sufficiently protected by existing conservation legislation • growth in concern for sustainable development and for national environmental planning in later stages of 1990s
Japan	• strong external focus—how Japan can assist other countries to make their development sustainable • particular emphasis on technological development and energy efficiency • limited opening of closed governmental processes to wider social participation
United Kingdom	• preparation of national strategy document and annual reviews of environmental objectives, with work continuing on indicators of sustainable development • sustainable development defined as objective of Environment Agencies and land use planning system • shift in approaches on transport and waste management • cautious response to climate change, but more collaborative policy launched around biodiversity • recent indications of greater willingness to use tax system for environmental objectives
European Union	• early confusion over whether goal is sustainable development or sustainable growth • attempt at co-ordination through 5th EAP which places sustainable development at its core • harmonisation through directives on EIA, packaging, water, air, and eco-audit • difficulty integrating environment into major sectoral programmes and CAP • difficulty assuring sustainable development issues taken up across all member states

FIGURE 12.7. Cautiously supportive response to sustainable development

process of preparing and reviewing departmental strategies represents a unique attempt to integrate sustainable development into the work of government as a whole.

Yet there has also been much inconsistency in the Canadian experience. Both the Green Plan and the Projet de Société were, for example, seriously compromised and (in the case of the Projet) abruptly terminated. After Rio, Canada adopted a 'wait and see' attitude on climate change, and there has been little movement on ecological tax reform. Legislation on environmental impact assessment and species protection has remained stalled or ineffectual, and budget trimming in the mid-1990s weakened environmental monitoring. Finally, despite recent efforts to improve the situation, the country remains well down from the UN target for foreign assistance.

Australia was characterized by an enthusiastic start on sustainable development, with the ESD working groups drawing in many sectors of the community, and the IGAE and the NSESD opening a new era in Federal/State co-operation. Yet over time the centrality of the NSESD to government preoccupations waned, and the enthusiasm of environmental organizations for the process declined. Other priorities—particularly economic deregulation, the trimming of budget deficits, and the opening of the Australian economy to world markets occupied the national government for much of the 1990s. Fears about the economic consequences for Australia of a strict climate change regime led to a cautious attitude to the development of the FCCC. At the end of the 1990s renewed tensions with the states also prompted the federal government to withdraw from some areas of environmental policy.

On the positive side, economic liberalization and subsidy reduction have eroded distortions in domestic energy markets and improved water management. A host of focused strategies have been put in place to improve land management, conservation, and the preservation of fragile habitats. Progress has also been made in the development of a biodiversity inventory, and in initiating environmental co-operation with Asia. Perhaps most promising is the linking of sustainable development to the idea of safeguarding what is unique about the Australian national heritage.

During the 1970s and 1980s the United Kingdom acquired a reputation as an environmental laggard because of its cavalier attitude towards transboundary issues in Europe, including emissions of SO_x and NO_x, radioactive discharges from nuclear facilities and sewage dumping at sea, as well as lax domestic standards on air and water-quality levels. Yet during the 1990s the British governments focused more specifically on the idea of sustainable development; made positive contributions to international processes around climate change and biodiversity; and began to modernize institutions and processes of environmental policy-making. The preparation of national strategy documents, the emergence of a system of annual reviews of environmental objectives, and the integration of sustainable development into the land-use planning system have given sustainable development a significant profile. There has also been movement on waste management and transport, and cautious experiments with environmental taxation. On the other hand, the domestic policy response to climate change has been minimal; assistance to developing countries has remained well below the UN target; and the gap in environmental standards *vis-à-vis* other North-European countries is still considerable.

As we have seen, the German government was initially hesitant about incorporating sustainable development as a conceptual foundation for domestic environmental policy. And, while the government had developed an early and vigorous response to problems of pollution and climate change, other elements of the UNCED agenda received less attention. Innovative environmental measures of the early 1990s (on packaging waste, for example) were not followed up; and other priorities—such as integrating the East German *länder* and advancing European integration—preoccupied the federal government. Despite having one of the more developed environmental policy regimes in the mid-1980s, ten years later German efforts lagged behind those of more pro-active European governments on cutting-edge issues such as negotiated and multi-partite approaches, comprehensive approaches to environmental planning, ecological tax reform, and biodiversity initiatives. After the mid-point of the decade however, the government's interest in sustainable development picked up, and even before the formation of the SDP/Green coalition government in the Fall of 1998, it was clear that sustainable development related initiatives were to be given a higher priority.

As for Japan, it assumed a relatively high profile in international environmental diplomacy during the 1990s, in particular by helping to broker the Kyoto accord on climate change. The government introduced substantial reforms to the environmental administration, including revising the Environment Basic Law and introducing the Environment Basic Plan. Particularities of the Japanese approach to sustainable development include a strong focus on transferring Japanese experience in coping with the environmental effects of crash industrialization to the developing world (which can be interpreted as either consonant with the internationalist dimension of sustainable development, or as constituting a distraction from reforms to Japanese domestic environmental practices); and an overwhelming emphasis on technological solutions to environmental burdens—increasing energy efficiency and cleaning up production processes. It is particularly unclear in the

Japanese case (although this is also true elsewhere) how far environment and sustainable development related priorities have been integrated into the operation of other ministries and agencies.

Finally, the unique character of the European Union as a hybrid political entity makes comparison of its performance with established states difficult. On one hand the EU has clearly taken on the symbol of sustainable development, engaging with international dimensions of the process, and attempting to adopt new approaches to managing environmental issues within the Union. Internationally it has also played an important role in the climate change negotiations. Over the last decade institutions of environmental governance have been strengthened (through action on packaging and on water and air quality, the establishment of the European Environment Agency, and so on), and somewhat opened to public scrutiny. Central EU institutions have also helped stimulate greater environmental awareness in lagging member states.

Yet the Commission has also had some spectacular setbacks, of which the ill-fated carbon energy tax is perhaps the best known. More significantly, much of the response to sustainable development takes the form of general ordinances, with member states retaining considerable latitude as to interpretation and implementation. To date sectoral integration remains little more than a well-promulgated ambition, with dominant segments of the Commission proceeding with established agendas as if sustainable development did not exist. At a time when the Common Agricultural Policy—to which environmental considerations are almost entirely marginal—still makes up nearly half the EU budget, it is hard to argue that the Commission really takes sustainable development seriously.

Concluding Comments

In drawing this chapter to a close it is as well to emphasize what is *not* being said. We are not suggesting that the assessment offered here should be interpreted as a simple 'scorecard' of sustainable development. We make no claim that the trajectories of the three 'enthusiastic' states are decisively more sustainable in outcomes than those adopted by the rest; that their environmental quality is unambiguously superior to that of the other high-consumption societies; or that the ranking we have found reasonable at this juncture will necessarily remain stable over the longer term. What we are saying is that, after a decade of working with the concept and goal of sustainable development, these three governments have gone further;

made the idea more central and visible to their activities; worked more con-scientiously with policy implications; and experimented with more inno-vative approaches—than their governmental counterparts in the other countries. The differences documented clearly illustrate that certain national governments take the international discourse on sustainable development—as well as the attempts by international bodies to give the concept pro-grammatic form—seriously. In the concluding chapter we will try to expand on the implications of these differences in a broader explanatory and pre-dictive framework.

13

Concluding Perspectives

WILLIAM M. LAFFERTY AND JAMES MEADOWCROFT

In the preceding chapter we focused on patterns of contrast and similarity in the approaches of the central governments of high-consumption societies with respect to sustainable development. Here we wish to consider what we believe to be certain key issues emerging from the study; and to offer some interim judgements on the character and significance of the processes we have examined. The discussion will be directed at answering four broad questions:

1. Given the distinct 'story-lines' presented in the earlier chapters, what general factors can help explain the differences revealed?
2. Considering the governments as a group, what can be said about the 'quality' of implementation efforts thus far?
3. (And in light of the previous assessment) what does this suggest about the evolution of environmental policy in the advanced industrialized countries, and how does this relate to the debate over 'ecological modernization'?
4. What perspectives emerge from the analysis with respect to the staying power and long-term viability of the sustainable development agenda?

Understanding Governmental Responses

We concluded in the previous chapter that the governments monitored can be grouped into three broad categories reflecting their reactions to sustainable development: 'enthusiastic' (the Netherlands, Norway, and Sweden), 'disinterested' (the United States), and 'cautiously supportive' (Australia, Canada, Germany, Japan, the United Kingdom, and the European Union).

As the individual country studies clearly have illustrated, many different factors have helped to shape the timing, scale and orientation of particular governments' reactions. The fact that the Chairman of the WCED went on to become her country's next prime minister no doubt encouraged early Norwegian engagement with the sustainable development agenda. That the final drafting and release of *Our Common Future* coincided with a period when Dutch public opinion was heavily focused on environmental issues, and during which the first NEPP was being prepared, clearly increased the receptivity of Dutch policy-makers to sustainable development. Similarly, but in an opposite direction, the substantial economic and social dislocation associated with German reunification, and the acute and continued economic stagnation in Japan over much of the 1990s, help to explain why these governments devoted relatively less attention to the concept at the time. We have also noted that economic conditions appear to have played an important role in moving the Canadian government from a clear 'pro-active' position towards a more cautious approach.

It should not be forgotten, however, that Sweden also experienced a serious political–economic crisis in the early 1990s, without significantly diminishing governmental support for the idea. Indeed, since 1996 the social-democratic government of Sweden has placed sustainable development at the centre of its efforts for job-creation and economic regeneration. It would appear, therefore, that while economic conditions clearly affect the general willingness (and actual economic potential) for pursuing the sustainable development agenda, these trends can also be modified, and even apparently reversed, by the vagaries of personal leadership and political cycles. Still, there would appear to be some underlying factors which, as nearly as we can determine on the basis of our case studies, appear to correspond with the evaluative categories.

History and Political Culture

Despite significant differences in cyclical economic and political trends among the enthusiastic countries—the Netherlands, Sweden, and Norway—they also display a cluster of similar characteristics. Each of these northern European states has a relatively small population; is heavily dependent on economic interaction with surrounding countries; and is significantly exposed to trans-border pollution from its neighbours. Each has a compact political elite, but an exceptionally open and highly mobilized civil society, including particularly strong and broad-based environmental movements— movements which had already acquired substantial political influence by the close of the 1970s (Jansen, Osland, and Hanf 1998). Further, all three of these countries have, throughout the post-war period, consistently ranked at the top of world listings for *both* economic development and welfare-state provision.

These perspectives can be systematized in terms of three general factors of recent history and political culture: factors which seem to bias the countries in question in a more supportive direction for sustainable development.

First, each assumes an open and supportive orientation towards international organizations, multilateral co-operation, and structures of world governance. All three are strongly committed to the United Nations system, readily provide finance and personnel for UN initiatives, and have played an active role in peacekeeping activities. Sweden and Norway have frequently operated as international mediators, while the Hague provides the seat for the International Court of Justice. The three states have also been disproportionately active in many other international and regional initiatives; the Netherlands as a key actor in the development of the European Union; Sweden as an active bridge-builder between East and West, and sponsor of numerous high-profile international conferences; and Norway as a leading peace mediator and driving force with the OSCE. Such profiles can largely be understood as part of a foreign-policy strategy through which small states seek to promote stable international surroundings and to maximize diplomatic influence (Andersen and Liefferlink 1997). A concomitant of such emphasis on multilateral processes, is an active promotion in domestic politics of the overall legitimacy and binding nature of international organizations and their decisions. It is in this light highly understandable that these states take the sustainable development agenda seriously, and do what they can to promote both the practical and ethical aspects of the UNCED process.

Second, these countries share a relatively dominant social-democratic and/or consensual political culture, which places significant emphasis upon equity, social planning, state intervention in the pursuit of common ends, and which involves neo-corporatist or negotiated modes of decision-making. In Norway and Sweden this takes the form of the classic social-democratic welfare state, with substantial social provision, relatively low wage differentials, and established 'corporate-pluralist' intermediation structures. In the Netherlands forms of consensual accommodation evolved from the 1960s, with the gradual dissolution of the traditional 'pillarized' political and cultural structures. Despite significant differences between these traditions, they share an apparent affinity with the social-equity and inclusive decision-making dimensions which form such an integral part of the idea of the UNCED sustainable development political culture.

Third, each country has established traditions of solidarity with the poorer countries of the world, manifest most clearly in disproportionately large development-assistance budgets, but also visible in the diplomatic role indicated above; as staunch supporters of international multilateral agreements and organizations, as well as a penchant for serving as intermediaries in various types of conflicts between East and West, North and South. In this perspective the sustainable development agenda appears as not only logically consistent with traditional international roles, but as a particularly holistic and synthetic expression of national self-perceptions, and international ambitions.

Looking at the other countries with respect to these three features, we find clear—and in several cases significant—differences. The strongest contrast is in relation to the sole country in the study which qualifies as 'disinterested' and 'disengaged'—the United States. By the early 1990s the US was enjoying unrivalled economic, political, and military ascendancy on the world scene. It stood at the core of the existing international order, and could, in effect, bask in the glow of its perceived 'triumph' in the cold war. The United States is accustomed to being an international policy 'maker' rather than a policy 'taker', and US domestic politics have traditionally been insulated from international developments to a far greater extent than all other OECD states. It is well known that the United States has long maintained a sceptical attitude towards transnational governance—refusing, for example, to place US troops under United Nations command, or to accept the jurisdiction of the International Court.

Moreover UN organizations have in recent years come in for sustained criticism from individual American politicians, and benign neglect from the Presidency and Congress. Indeed, it is hardly an exaggeration to say that in a US domestic context one could think of few more certain ways of killing a policy orientation than by emphasizing its UN credentials. Thus not only are US political leaders less likely to be receptive to a political idea if it has received a UN imprimatur, but the overall vision of international relations embedded in sustainable development is clearly out of focus for the American foreign-policy establishment. The United States, with its individualist, polarized, and highly litigious society, is far removed from a 'social-democratic' or 'consensual' political culture. Suspicion of the federal government and regulatory intervention runs deep in the US. Moreover, since the 1950s, foreign aid has been strongly constrained by perceived national-security requirements. Countries with a key strategic role (such as South Korea, South Vietnam, Israel, and Egypt) have traditionally absorbed the lion's share of US development assistance.

All in all, the articulation of a positive resonance between the normative principles of sustainable development and dominant values of American political life is problematic. Categorizing the United States as 'disinterested' in this context—recalling our empirical focus on central government activities—is a logical extension of what has come to be termed 'American exceptionalism'.[1]

If there is one case which points up the 'exceptional' character of the United States in this regard, it is Canada. While sharing large portions of both geography and history with the United States, Canada has shown an attitude towards sustainable development which is decidedly different. Canada has traditionally had a positive attitude towards international organizations, international co-operation, and the United Nations—partly as a direct foreign-policy counterweight to its close dependence on the United States. While its prevalent political culture cannot be described as either social-democratic or corporate-pluralist, elements of these strains are none the less present. Social and regional equity are recurrent themes in Canadian politics, and more recently ideas of 'negotiative federalism' and 'stakeholder representation' have come to the fore. Canadians are also more willing to accept interventionist government, as differences vis-à-vis the USA on welfare-state provisions, health care, and the environment clearly illustrate. Moreover, in relation to the developing world, Canada has often deliberately distanced itself from US policy, attempting in the process to cultivate an alternative image of pro-South, pro-development-assistance.

Looking at the other 'supportive' jurisdictions along the same general dimensions, we note that the most populous states—Germany, Japan, and the United Kingdom—have quite different relationships with the international system. The UK has a recent heritage as a world power, having retained its permanent seat on the Security Council, and continued to finance a disproportionately large military apparatus. Germany, divided for a generation, has been more recently preoccupied with the consequences of reunification, while Japan is still in the process of defining an international role commensurate with its economic status. As for the European Union, it is an emergent actor with the potential to became a major international player, but where the ambitions of the Commission in this regard appear to be running ahead of the willingness of the member states to surrender foreign-policy influence.

Yet the prospect of a 'natural' political affinity for sustainable development should not be overstated. After all, the fact that—with the exception of the United States—each of the countries examined has incorporated sustainable development into its policy idiom, suggests that the idea is sufficiently

---

[1] The 'father' of the concept of 'American exceptionalism' is apparently Seymour Martin Lipset. See his major overview (Lipset 1996) with subsequent texts by Halperin and Morris (1997) and Madsen (1998).

general to appeal across major politico-cultural divides; and sufficiently flexible to allow adjustments of emphasis that resonate with national pre-occupations and traditions. Thus in the United Kingdom it was possible to integrate sustainable development into a 'development-control' process which lies at the core of the local planning system. In Japan it could be inter-preted in the light of the country's own recent experience with acute envi-ronmental contamination attendant upon crash modernization, and defined in terms of the lessons Japan could pass on to developing countries. And in Australia a link could be made to the particular responsibility for securing for posterity the natural heritage of a unique island continent.

Indeed, as the individual case studies have illustrated, each of the gov-ernments has succeeded in identifying distinctive and established national 'markers' with which sustainable development could be identified. In other words, a significant aspect of the 'implementation' of sustainable develop-ment, has been to link the concept to established ideas, icons, and priorities. Needless to say, sustainable development is not the first concept to have strong roots in one particular political tradition—in this case European social democracy—but nonetheless prove capable of winning more general accep-tance across a broader political spectrum. Historically speaking, notions of representative democracy and human rights were first identified with liber-alism, and welfare rights with socialism, but all have gradually gained access and favour across a broad spectrum of ideological, cultural, and religious traditions.

Constitutional Structure and Cyclical Politics

Another underlying factor which is significant in determining the overall character of the governmental response to sustainable development relates to constitutional structure. Countries with federal structures appear to have had particular problems in developing a coherent response to the concept. In Germany the difficulty of making policy in areas where jurisdiction is divided between the *länder* and the federal government is particularly evident with respect to biodiversity. In the United States, Canada and Australia, conflicts have clearly emerged with respect to the commercial exploitation of natural resources. The economies of sub-national political units may be more directly based on the exploitation of particular resource-systems (oil and gas, minerals, forests, sea life, etc.) than is true of the country as a whole; and alliances between local political elites and powerful economic interests can combine to oppose 'meddlesome' regulatory intervention from the centre. In Canada for example the resource-rich western provinces (such as Alberta) have been markedly unenthusiastic about more vigorous climate change policies and species-protection initiatives. In Australia the states have acted as a brake on climate change initiatives, and within the European Union (which, in this context, can be considered as a proto-federal state), the North-Europe/South-Europe split has clearly diminished EU policy cohesion on sustainabile development issues. This is manifest in the general lack of priority accorded to environmental issues in several of the member states, but also in the dominant position of the EU on the Single European Market and the Common Agricultural Policy.[2]

With respect to party politics, the picture is much more complex and diverse. While the deeper traditions and value of equity and consensus seem to play an important supportive role (as indicated above), the specific 'colour' of party governance does not seem to have been as immediately important as one might have assumed. In Australia the election of a conservative government did mark a shift away from a positive stance on multilateral solutions as adopted by the outgoing Labour party, but in the United Kingdom and Canada reasonably energetic responses to sustainable development occurred under conservative administrations. On the whole governments of the right, with a pro-business orientation and a more complacent attitude towards existing institutions, could be thought less likely to embrace such an innovative concept. In retrospect, however, social democrats have focused strongly on reducing unemployment by promoting growth, leading them often to protracted foot-dragging on environmental issues. It may be that governments with a strong anti-regulatory bent (neo-liberal or neo-conservative, depending on the terminology one prefers) have been slower to press issues forward than governments of either the left or the right which are more sympathetic to macro-level governmental steering. But measures to cut back government intervention can also have favourable environmental impacts, and can appear as congruent with sustainable development. This applies, for example, to the abolition of water subsidies in Australia; the liberalization of energy markets in a number of the countries studied; and the introduction of new regulatory frameworks accompanying utility privatization in the United Kingdom.

---

[2] This should not be taken to support the idea that sustainable development is necessarily more compatible with centralized rather than decentralized political structures. Starting from the formal obligations placed on national governments by the international process, this study has focused on central governmental initiatives. It is certainly conceivable that elements of the sustainable development agenda could be more effectively pursued by highly autonomous regional or local governments, and in some contexts *the absence* of a requirement that a whole state follow a particular course could permit a more dynamic regional administration greater opportunities for innovation.

It is probably too soon to say how the party-political factor will work out in the longer run (given the current appeal of the sustainable development idea across the political spectrum), but traditional political cleavages can be translated into varied emphasis with respect to different dimensions of the concept. Consider, for example, the contrasting treatment of equity issues in the strategy papers prepared under Conservative and Labour governments in the UK. In the Conservative-sponsored policy document (*Sustainable Development: The UK Strategy*) equity issues hardly get a look in, while in the Labour party update (*A Better Quality of Life: A Strategy for Sustainable Development in the UK*) equity and the fight against social exclusion are central themes. Whether or not these difference convert into markedly different policies and outcomes is, of course, another matter.

Experience with Environmental Policy

Another important dimension is the impact of the pre-Brundtland/pre-UNCED environmental policy base-line: that is, the prevailing policy stance, regulatory culture, and set of environmental institutions in place prior to the 'arrival' of sustainable development. One might suspect that countries with a tradition of acting as environmental policy innovators, with well-established environmental ministries and reasonably flexible administrative practices, would be better placed to take up the idea of sustainable development. Certainly this seems to hold true for the Netherlands, Norway and Sweden.

But the relationship between existing environmental policy achievements and enthusiasm for sustainable development is somewhat equivocal. Consider the cases of Germany and the UK. By the end of the 1980s Germany was an acknowledged environmental policy leader—a proponent of tighter regulation within the European Union, particularly with respect to transborder air pollution, stratospheric ozone depletion, and climate change—while the UK was considered a relative laggard. A decade later, however, Germany was trying to shake off a perception of stagnation in the environmental policy realm, while the UK had undertaken a stream of environmental initiatives. During the 1990s the UK demonstrated an active interest in promoting the symbolism of sustainable development, while the German government retained a demonstrably low profile.

In the light of this comparison we can also now see that several features of the earlier German environmental administration were seemingly at odds with the cross-sectoral and participatory elements of the sustainable development agenda. This is particularly true for what appears to have been a relatively rigid administrative framework; a clear sectoral division of responsibilities; and elaborate legal strictures. The idea of 'covenants' nego-tiated between public authorities and private actors that became so popular in the Netherlands, for example, fits poorly with the 'authoritative state' tradition. Oddly enough, parallel mechanisms may also have been at play in the United States, where the very detailed legislative enactments on pollution control (which were extended during the period of Congres-sional resistance to the deregulatory initiatives of the Reagan presidency), and the routine reliance on litigation, also hampered experiments with multi-partite environmental governance. In contrast, it appears as though both the UK and Sweden, with their respectively informal and formal net-works linking regulators and industry, could be more easily opened to new actors in line with the inclusive and co-operative prescriptions of sustainable development.

An additional aspect of this perspective is the unique (and rather anom-alous) role of the 'precautionary principle' in Germany. By 1976 'precaution' had already emerged as a defining principle of German environmental policy (Jänicke and Weidner 1997a). It constituted a significant contribution to the international environmental debate, giving expression to an ethic of care and prudence with respect to human interventions in the natural world. Yet in practice the idea has proved difficult to operationalize. Without a clear understanding of the potential risks in any given case (not to mention the difficulties in measuring such risks), legal interpretation of the principle is likely to collide with other enforceable rights (Pehle 1997). There is little evi-dence that the 'precautionary' orientation has in fact worked to strengthen German environmental protection. The hope that an active application of prior concern would provide an effective rationale for avoiding the obvious 'trade-offs' implicit in sustainable development, was thus illusory. By focus-ing on only one aspect of the sustainable development steering logic—that aspect which was apparently most compatible with indigenous techno-administrative proclivities—the German environmental policy complex was seemingly distracted from a renewal of policy in a more dynamic, negotia-tive, and cross-sectoral mode.

Clearly a domestic perception that Germany was already ahead of the game on environmental issues came into play here. Why invest a lot of effort in new ideas and international political programmes when it is the 'others' who have to catch up? Key actors in the environmental administration appar-ently saw things this way, and considering Germany's record in the 1980s on air pollution, waste and recycling, and climate change, the perception was not without foundation.

Interestingly a similar effect can be observed in Norway after the initial enthusiastic response to the Brundtland Report and first white paper. The period between 1987 and 1992 was a particularly intense one, with ongoing preparations and widespread public debate leading up the Earth Summit. With the results of Rio on the table, however, the Norwegian civil-servant activists in UNCED felt let-down and disappointed: the achievements of the conference did not live up to expectations. The result was a very selective follow-up to Rio—with strong focus on the emerging climate change agenda and sustainable production and consumption within the CSD—but with a corresponding *lack* of interest in biodiversity and Agenda 21. In contrast, in the UK at the end of the 1980s there was a widespread perception—within the environmental sector, but also among politicians and officials more generally—that the country was lagging behind its European partners in terms of environmental reform. Environmental organizations were tireless in vaunting the merits of policies being implemented *elsewhere* in Europe, and with the impressive show made by 'green' parties in the EU parliamentary elections of 1989, the stage was set for a political discourse designed to modernise environmental policy through a rhetorical appeal to 'sustainability'.

Finally we can draw attention along this dimension to recent cross-national assessments of international environmental policy performance. Andersen and Liefferlink (1997), for example, classify the Netherlands, Norway, and Sweden among the European environmental policy 'pioneers'—a privilege they also accord to Germany.[3] With reference to the European Union, they distinguish between 'fore-runner' and 'pusher' strategies, with the former referring to leading by example, and the latter to efforts aimed at securing integrated environmental measures across the Union. Writing in the mid-1990s, they suggest that Sweden will continue its 'fore-runner' strategy; that the Netherlands will persist in a 'pusher' role; but that Germany will be an unlikely proponent of further environmental measures. The German hesitancy to take up the broader concept of sustainable development thus appears to be symptomatic of more general difficulties hindering a shift towards a more 'process-oriented' approach to a new generation of environmental problems.

The comparative analyses of Janicke and Weidner (1997b) add to this understanding by pointing out that the role of innovation with respect to environmental governance has passed 'periodically from one country to another'. The first industrial state, the United Kingdom, was also an early environmental policy leader. Likewise, in the late 1960s, the United States assumed a particularly dynamic status, exporting policy concepts (environmental impact statements, expert advisory groups, etc.), and directly

[3] Their full list includes also Austria, Finland, and Denmark.

influencing the establishment of environmental administrations in countries such as Germany and Japan. Japan took a more active role during the 1970s, and Germany during the 1980s, with each country becoming a world leader in the export of environmental technology. The Netherlands and Sweden, on the other hand, have maintained an innovative policy role for more than two decades, indicating that, while the larger states make more of an impact when 'out in front' (particularly with respect to technology), they also seem to have more difficulty than the smaller states in maintaining the effort over the longer term.

In sum, the comparative perspective indicates that the most important explanatory factors for the variation in implementation lie in well-established patterns of national political culture and international orientation. At the opposite ends of the evaluation spectrum we find countries well known for demonstrating opposite tendencies along two dimensions: (1) active versus cautious state-steering, and (2) enthusiastic versus sceptical international involvement. The positive patterns of sustainable development engagement in Sweden, Norway, and the Netherlands are clearly understandable in light of long-standing commitments to active state steering and enthusiastic international involvement; while the negative pattern of the United States is equally understandable in the light of opposite valencies on both dimensions.

The fact that the United States is much the largest, most powerful, and most independent of the established countries in the study, while Sweden, Norway, and the Netherlands are among the smallest, least powerful and most interdependent, is of note. But these are facts of national life which 'over-determine' both institutional and cultural patterns, and promise little in the way of more detailed understanding as to how the variations in implementation actually 'play out' over time.

Having said this, however, it is interesting to note that, among the 'cautiously supportive', the size dimension also has a certain degree of relevance. The implementation patterns of the European Union, Japan, Germany and the United Kingdom are somewhat less 'impressive' than that of Canada. While Canada can hardly be considered a small country, it is heavily dependent on its vastly more powerful neighbour to the south. This points towards an interpretation whereby (among developed countries) the underlying factor of *dependency within the international system* fosters a bias towards the UNCED-process and sustainable development agenda; while *self-perceptions of power and competitive economic advantage on the international scene* work against a more positive and serious engagement with the concept and the UN programme.

This is, at any rate, about as far as we feel we can push the explanatory mode of the analysis. In our view, given the moderately structured case-study approach of the project, the most important lessons to be learned at this stage of analysis are from the outstanding features of the implementation documentation. We turn, therefore, to a more focused look at the quality of implementation with respect to the meaning and goals of sustainable development.

Assessing the Effort as a Whole: How Far Have We Come?

In this section, we alter our frame of reference from considering differences among countries, to examining the process overall—how the governments taken as a group have reacted to sustainable development. We shall begin the discussion with six key themes which link the normative and policy dimensions of sustainable development. Four of these themes capture significant—and from the perspective of sustainable development, largely positive—changes that have occurred since 1987. The other two, while reflecting issues which governments acknowledge as important for the sustainable development agenda, remain more obviously problematic.

The first four themes are: (1) the *integration of environment and economy* in decision making; (2) the development of modalities for *environmental planning, measurement, and monitoring*; (3) the expansion of *societal participation* in environment-and-development decision-making; and (4) the *internationalization* of environmental governance. We identify the two more problematic themes as: (5) *support for environment and development in the South*; and (6) *sustainable production and consumption*.

Integration of Economy and Environment

The integration of economy and environment in decision-making is an essential postulate of sustainable development. On one level 'integration' has been pursued by assigning all ministries responsibilities for ensuring that their activities are environmentally sound. This can be referred to as 'intra-ministerial integration'. The Brundtland Commission (WCED 1987: 311–12) explicitly called for environmental concerns to be merged into the work of all government agencies. The idea has since been taken up in one form or another in most OECD states, including (as we have seen in earlier chapters) the countries of our study.

But the idea of 'integration' can also be invoked in a much wider sense to denote the various ways in which the environmental dimension can be 'factored into' societal decision-making—for example, by the widened deployment of environmental impact assessment methodologies, and by using educational or financial measures to ensure that social agents 'internalize' the environmental consequences of their behaviour. This can be referred to as 'sectoral integration', with 'sector' referring to the functional domains which fall under the purview of government. Sectoral integration involves an extension of the logic of intra-ministerial integration, whereby efforts are made to infuse sectoral activity as a whole with a deeper understanding of the interdependency between sector-specific dispositions and the norms of sustainable development. The significance of this form of integration has been explicitly acknowledged by governments which have engaged with sustainable development, and many of the environmental policy initiatives detailed in the preceding chapters can be understood as paths to carry this process forward.

Clearly there are limits to the extent to which either of these integrative projects has been achieved. With respect to intra-ministerial integration there is evidence that the processes have been more formal than substantive, and that environmental concerns routinely continue to be overridden by development interests. In some jurisdictions 'integration' has been almost entirely at the level of rhetoric—in Japan, for example, production-oriented ministries and plans operate in parallel with organizations and plans centred on environmental sensitivity; and in the European Union the environment has remained essentially marginal to key spending programmes such as the Common Agricultural Policy and the Structural Funds. Even where the intra-ministerial integrative ideal has been more thoroughly pursued—as in Norway or Canada—the quality of the departmental engagement with environmental concerns or the broader sustainable development agenda is typically weak. With respect to the more complex issue of sectoral integration, similar sorts of criticisms could be made. In most areas of social decision-making the environment remains an 'additional' consideration. True, it is now often understood as a necessary consideration (rather than as merely an optional one); but it cannot be said that environmental impacts are being factored in to sectoral processes from the outset.

Strategic Plans and Monitoring

As we saw in the last chapter, some of the most significant changes relate to the emergence of more comprehensive plans and strategy statements, and measurement and monitoring procedures. Most countries have developed general strategy documents or planning processes related to the environment and sustainable development. Although modalities differ significantly, all present a more integrated and comprehensive view; are based explicitly on sustainable development; and emphasize prevention and long-term environmental/economic management. Moreover, as compared to the early 1980s, there has been a considerable increase in the capacity for measurement of environmental conditions, and monitoring of policy initiatives. The pressure/state/response framework has been widely adopted. Also there has been movement to elaborate sustainable development indicators, linking economic, social welfare and environmental dimensions. Increased capacity relating to climate change and biodiversity are especially important in this regard. Legislative surveillance functions over government activities have also been expanded in the environmental domain in many jurisdictions.

Yet these reforms remain unconsolidated. We have already noted the instability of experiments with strategic visioning and planning, and difficulties in defining the appropriate range of planning exercises and the relationship to existing planning processes. Most 'plans' have no single agency responsible for overall implementation, and (with the partial exception of the Dutch NEPPs) objectives and targets are not disaggregated and assigned to particular ministries and agencies. More generally, there is a difficulty in establishing overall priorities for sustainable development *throughout government* as a whole. Emphasis on intra-ministerial integration, does not necessarily imply successful 'integration' of sustainable development policy across ministries—and implementation of a coherent overall strategy—as the Norwegian case illustrates. With respect to measurement and monitoring, new reporting procedures and indicators are but recent innovations, and the extent to which they will survive changes of government and cyclical reviews of public sector spending is unclear. Certainly the new measures do not rival the political salience of established headline indicators such as GNP and unemployment or inflation rates. On the other hand, they are increasingly being taken seriously by environmental decision-makers and sectoral actors. Clearly the collection of such data remains a prerequisite for future long-term and comprehensive approaches to managing environmental burdens.

Participation and Stakeholder Involvement

The participatory strand has been a constant in governmental commentaries on sustainable development. That sustainable development cannot simply be 'delivered' by politicians and officials, but demands an active and creative input from all sectors of society has been broadly acknowledged. Emphasis has been placed upon 'partnerships' between public and private actors as society attempts to derive novel solutions to the challenges raised by sustainable development. In every jurisdiction with which we have been concerned there has been some opening of closed policy networks. More social actors are involved in contestation, consultation, and implementation. Businesses have been drawn into more public activities, and environmental action groups into more collaborative ventures. This is not to say political decision-makers have surrendered their authority, but rather that an increased number of societal forces have been drawn into the policy circuit.

To date this 'opening' remains partial, and varies considerably among states and across sectors. In many of the countries we examined it would be possible to dismiss the large national committees as little more than 'talking-shops' or window dressing. Alternatively, the complaint could be made that all this dialogue and negotiation has complicated decision-making in the environmental realm, while permitting major economic actors to slow the pace of reform. Such a criticism would carry more weight were it not evident that the structural interdependence of various actors and processes underpins the increasing complexity of environmental decision-making, and that more state-centred implementation strategies have often not been a practical option. Above all, it misses the significance of drawing a greater range of social actors into social debate in a domain such as sustainable development, where the character and scale of future change remains to be determined.

Internationalization

The *internationalization* of environmental policy has in many respects been remarkable. The WCED report suggested states required environmental 'foreign policies', and this they now have. Governments have been drawn steadily into an ever more complex mesh of international accords established to monitor and manage global environmental problems. Regional and global regimes and negotiating processes have increasingly informed domestic environmental policy debates, and there has been a continuing diffusion of approaches and innovations from one jurisdiction to another.

Needless to say, this 'internationalization' of environmental policy is replete with difficulties. Setting aside problems with particular conventions and agreements, the most important issue to come to the fore in recent years relates to trade and the environment. The UNCED treatment of trade was hardly satisfactory, representing little more than a general call for further trade liberalization. More recently, the WTO has attracted criticism for resisting 'integration' of environment into its procedures. Trade now serves as a locus for disputes over environment and development priorities, and for conflicts among powerful commercial and national interests. There is also a worry that 'internationalization' of environmental governance has led to creeping domestic paralysis. On climate change, for instance, national governments express unwillingness to act more vigorously, as they await further clarification of the international regime.

Despite the partial nature of the accomplishments that we have rapidly sketched out under these four headings (and in relation to which further examples can be found in earlier chapters in this study), it is clear that by the end of the 1990s considerable progress had been made as compared with the situation a decade and a half earlier. To put this another way, with respect to the integration of environment and economy in decision making, strategic plans and monitoring, stakeholder involvement, and the extension of international environmental governance, some forward momentum has been in evidence. The same claim cannot be made with respect to the two remaining themes.

Support for Environment and Development in the South

While all the governments we have examined recognize support for developing countries as a component of their national obligations *vis-à-vis* sustainable development, the scale of initiatives in this direction has been modest. In the last chapter we noted the trends towards 'greening' aid, and targeting poverty relief—both in themselves laudable. But these must be set against a background of the falling proportion of GNP devoted to development assistance. Even among the sustainable development 'enthusiasts' there has been a decline in aid levels from the early 1980s. Only modest efforts have been made on the issue of technology transfer, on which governments routinely note their hands are tied because the relevant technology is owned by the private sector. Debt relief, too, has been slow to move forward, although at the very end of the 1990s some remission had been accorded to the very poorest countries. Nor has much progress been made in opening markets in the developed countries to goods from poorer states.

This is not to suggest that all problems are concentrated on one side of the North/South relationship. Over the past decade developing countries have sometimes acted as if the UNCED process and international environmental negotiations were of relevance only as a lever with which to extract better treatment from the North. Some states have even made a point of emphasizing that shifts in their domestic trajectories are not up for discussion. Nor is it to suggest that the key to successful environment and development in the South lies simply with increasing official aid flows from the

North. Yet as a global project sustainable development implies active efforts by the industrialized states to assist the developing world. To date, however, the governments of the major developed countries remain unwilling to confront domestic opposition or to commit the financial resources required to make debt relief, increased aid flows, technology transfer, or market-opening serious propositions.

Sustainable Production and Consumption

As we have seen in earlier chapters, with respect to movement towards sustainable production and consumption, progress has also been limited. Under the aegis of sustainable development governments have taken cautious steps to improve energy efficiencies and to encourage reductions in conventional pollutant loadings. By and large, however, they have hesitated to address broader issues. And yet movement not just towards process and efficiency gains, but also towards the adoption of new consumption and production regimes appears essential if the total environmental burden imposed by the developed countries is to be reduced. Overall, efforts to address the key challenge of the Brundtland Report—*to change the quality of growth*—have been modest. As we have seen, the Netherlands (followed by Sweden and Norway) have at least begun to *discuss* the issue; but even here practical initiatives and spending remain marginal.

Perhaps this should not surprise us. The international political and economic context is highly dynamic, and the pace of technical innovation rapid. Governments face great uncertainty concerning the scale of environmental risks. The financial and political costs of ambitious programmes to alter established socio-ecological production and consumption complexes are high, and the results uncertain. Even in situations where there is a clear net short-term social gain (and many issues related to sustainable development do not work out so conveniently) powerful groups may be opposed to change. And yet movement in this direction is essential if the wider agenda of sustainable development is in the long run to be addressed.

This brief consideration of progress in relation to these six themes gives some indication of how seriously we consider the governments—taken as a group—to have taken up sustainable development. The relative failure of governments in the most powerful industrialised countries to engage with the last two themes is significant. Note that both relate to responsibilities which rich countries are expected to assume *above and beyond their own internal challenges*. According to the WCED and UNCED, Northern states have an obligation not only to assist environment and development in the South, but also to reduce dramatically their resource consumption, in order to make environmental 'room' for Southern development. At the centre of UN-sponsored efforts in this area has been the belief that—with respect to environment and development—the fate, problems, and responsibilities of the wealthiest and of the poorest nations *are linked*. Yet, it is precisely here that the performance of high-consumption societies seems most problematic. On the other hand, the relative failure to move beyond rhetorical acceptance of this principle does *not* in our view vitiate the partial achievements recorded in other areas.

Throughout the above discussion we have been concerned primarily with the orientation of the governmental policy response. But there is another question one might raise with respect to these initiatives, and this is the extent to which they are adequate to secure practical outcomes that will actually contribute to achieving sustainable development. To address this issue systematically would take us well beyond the parameters of the present volume. Yet the material presented here is certainly suggestive, and on the whole points to the rather limited scale of what has been achieved so far.

Consider the issues of climate change and biodiversity which are so central to the sustainable development agenda. To date the policy response in the countries we have examined has had a scarcely discernible impact on the overall burden these societies impose upon the environment. Scientific evidence of human-induced climate effects continues to accumulate, and progress has been made in agreeing the detailed modalities of a climate change regime; but to what extent has this led to the modification of the actual profile of greenhouse gas emissions? Most of the countries with which we have been concerned failed to meet the original UNCED objective of stabilising emissions at 1990 levels by the year 2000. At the time of writing, the entry into force of the Kyoto Protocol is far from a foregone conclusion, and most countries covered by this study will have serious difficulties meeting their Kyoto targets without reliance on extra-territorial reductions secured under the Convention's 'flexibility mechanisms'. Despite the conclusion of the Biosafety Protocol, progress with respect to the Biodiversity Convention remains tenuous (McGraw 1998). Although biodiversity loss has made it on to the policy agenda in developed states, policies implemented so far will have had no more than a marginal impact on the rate of species loss. Climate change looms as an impending threat to biodiversity, but so too does the ever increasing space absorbed for human purposes.

One way to think about sustainable development is in terms of the requirement for a 'decoupling' of economic growth from increases in the environmental burden. Sustainable development is premised upon the idea that it is possible for the rich countries to go on developing while dramatically reducing environmental impacts. If this 'development' is to include improved material welfare and traditional economic growth, then such growth must be purchased by decreasing the environmental impacts of economic activity. The Dutch have spoken of a 'relative decoupling' (where environmental pressures rise, but at a lower rate per additional unit of output), and an 'absolute decoupling' (where environmental pressures fall, or at least hold steady, as economic activity increases) (Ministry of Housing, Spatial Planning, and the Environment 1998). Over the past decade governments in the developed world have been able to secure an absolute decoupling for a range of conventional pollutants emitted within their national territories (Jänicke and Weidner 1997b).[4] That is to say, water and air quality have improved (in some cases dramatically) even as economic growth has continued (OECD 1998b).[5] On the other hand, there have also been bouts of 'recoupling', where emissions have begun to rise again (RIVM 1997b). More significantly, environmental loadings have continued to increase on a number of fronts crucially related to sustainable development, including CO_2 emissions and habitat loss. In other words, increases in welfare in the industrialized countries are still being purchased at the cost of continued environmental loss.

Taken as a whole, the performance of the governments we have examined in this study is both impressive and disappointing. In some ways much more has been done than a sceptic might have anticipated. On the other hand, far less has been achieved than that minimum for which a committed proponent of sustainable development might have hoped.

Sustainable Development, Environmental Policy and Ecological Modernization

In the previous section we offered a general assessment of how the governments—taken as a group—have responded to the challenge of sustainable development. Considering performance in relation to six themes linking the normative content of the idea with the orientation of policy, this discussion proceeded from 'within' the logic of the sustainable development

---

[4] Whether global resource and pollutant burdens associated with domestic consumption in these countries have decoupled from growth is another question. To ascertain whether that was the case one would have to take account also of the displacement of certain productive sectors (for example, shipbuilding) towards the developing world.

[5] For an informed discussion of the environmental performance of industrialized states see Janicke and Weidner 1997b.

discourse. It started from what sustainable development implementation could be supposed to entail, and asked—'just how much has actually been done?'. In this section we intend to step outside the parameters of the implementation process, to consider the broader significance of governmental engagement with sustainable development.

As a distinct sphere of state action, the environmental policy domain is barely three decades old. This is not to deny that governments have long been preoccupied with issues we today classify as 'environmental'. Legislation, regulation, and agencies dealing with conservation of natural resources, protection of wildlife and heritage sites, control of noxious substances emitted to air and water, exposure to hazardous substances in the workplace, and so on, go back to the nineteenth century and earlier. Yet it was only towards the end of the 1960s and particularly during the 1970s that the structures and legislative framework of modern environmental policy were established. Major environmental laws were enacted in the pioneer countries from the late 1960s; environmental ministries in most of the leading industrialized states date from the early 1970s; and expert advisory bodies were set up at about the same time. This was a period of rapid diffusion of initiatives across frontiers, propelled by bilateral contacts and international forums such as the 1972 Stockholm Conference (Jänicke and Weidner 1997b).

Over the past few decades environmental policy has experienced repeated bursts of change. It has also undergone a continuous expansion of its horizons—spatially and temporally; in relation to the range of relevant impacts, actors, and sectors; and in terms of the variety of social practices where reform is deemed necessary. In a pioneering study, Albert Weale pointed out that in the early 1970s environmental policy 'relied primarily upon the techniques of administrative regulation', was based on legislation 'specific to the receiving medium', and assumed 'that environmental policy could be treated as a discrete policy area' (1992: 22–3). By the late 1980s implementation failures were manifest and public concern with the environment was at a high. It had become clear that government action in other sectors (farm subsidies or road building, for example) could often have a greater effect on environmental quality than policies of the ministry officially dedicated to the environment. Moreover the perception had become widespread that toleration of pollution was actually 'a device by which costs' could be 'shifted across space' or 'across time' onto others—a fact of both economic and ethical significance. The assumptions on which the older politics of pollution had been based rapidly unravelled. The belief 'that environmental policy stood in a simple trade-off relation with economic growth and development' (1992: 27), was supplanted by a perspective which emphasized that environmental protection was a precondition for long-term economic development. And the idea that environmental problems could be successfully handled by attention to legal and administrative issues, was replaced by a belief in the importance of social norms and the transformation of prevailing attitudes.[6]

Another perceptive commentator has argued that in the early 1970s environmental problems were seen largely in terms of threats to human health produced by industrial development, which could best be tackled 'by assigning responsibility' to 'one sector of the government', by tackling 'problems compartementally', and by emphasizing 'prohibitive regulation' (Glasbergen 1996: 179). This contrasted with the approach which emerged in the 1990s where environmental problems were 'considered as disruptions of worldwide eco-systems', associated not only with industrial development but also with underdevelopment. Solutions to such problems required an integrated and systematic approach, major adjustments in domains 'not previously covered by environmental policy', and great changes 'in the moral sphere', which could 'only be realised if the policy's target groups internalise the need to adapt their behaviour' (Glasbergen 1996: 181).

A central feature of Glasbergen's account is the emphasis on 'learning' processes. Attempts at policy implementation led first to 'technical learning': an increased appreciation of the interdependency of environmental burdens, of the difficulties with cross-media transference, of the implications of regulatory complexity, and so on. Gradually the inadequacy of the overall framework became apparent, leading to 'conceptual learning' and the emergence of a new paradigm. 'Cognitive learning' has been involved when governments collect data on emissions, industrial processes, the state of the environment, and policy impacts, in order to elaborate causal models to enable central steering. But part of the newer approach is the emphasis on 'social learning', which depends upon enhanced communication among actors, sectoral involvement in developing and implementing policy, and ample 'room for negotiations on problem perception, interest, uncertainties and alternative solutions' (1996: 189).

The changing constellation of actors involved in the environmental policy domain also plays a key role in the story told by Martin Jänicke and Helmut Weidner in their recent comparative study. They characterize the earlier period as one based on a 'strategy of dilution' and the deployment of 'add-on clean up technologies'. Here policy was 'preoccupied with mobilizing financial resources and formulating standards relating to particular environ-

---

[6] Weale invokes Matthew Arnold's distinction between 'mechanical' and 'moral' reform to capture this shift.

mental media such as water or air' (1997*b*: 307). Twenty-five years later, in the most developed countries, 'the debate has started to switch to the overall resource input to industrial production' (307). In the German case these authors provide a more detailed periodization including phases of 'dilution' (1969–74), 'dilution plus end of pipe treatment' (1974–82), 'intense end of pipe treatment' (1983–7), and 'ecological modernisation' (1988–94). These represent steps in a transition; but 'ecologically sustainable development' requires 'more than end-of-pipe treatment or even ecological modernisation', for it implies 'structural change' in the 'societal role and importance' of key sectors such as the 'construction complex', 'the road traffic complex', 'the energy complex' and the 'agro-industrial complex' (1997*b*: 19). Central to this vision of the evolution of the policy paradigm has been the changing involvement of societal actors. At first environmental policy was essentially a matter for the state and industry; then environmental organizations became active demanding more vigorous government intervention; later the environmental movement began to interact directly with industry, and the media became more influential. In the most recent phase a green business sector has began to effect other actors.

Drawing on these and other sources it is possible to summarize some of the key characteristics of the transformation undergone by the environmental policy domain in the (historically speaking, rather brief) span of three decades:

- over time the complexity, interconnectedness, and uncertainty surrounding environmental issues has become better appreciated, as has the intimate contact between environmental policy and other spheres of government and social activity;
- early optimism that difficulties could be resolved in a fairly straightforward manner has given way to a realization that the environment constitutes a long term problem that will require continuous policy intervention and adjustment far into the future;
- the idea of a necessary contradiction between environmental protection and economic growth has been replaced by an emphasis on environmental preconditions for long-term development, and on potential synergies between economic prosperity and environmental protection;
- emphasis has shifted from media specific measures towards integrated emissions control, and has begun to pass from managing 'pollution' towards a concern with the total load imposed by society on the environment;
- discussion has begun to move on from remedial measures (the treatment of waste, clean-up of contaminated land, and so on), towards prevention—

shifting production processes toward less polluting and more resource efficient alternatives, and (more tentatively) altering patterns of consumption;
- the notion that environmental management could be the (almost exclusive) responsibility of a single ministry (or super ministry) has given way to attempts to integrate environment into the work of all government departments;
- the idea that environmental protection was a task for government alone has given way to an emphasis on the mobilization of other social actors and interests;
- the preoccupation with traditional regulatory approaches has been partially displaced by interest in market-based control measures (such as environmental taxation and tradable emissions permits); and negotiated agreements and voluntary initiatives;
- the belief that national initiatives could form the mainstay of the environmental management system has been eclipsed by the focus on regional and global accords; and
- the linkage between international environment-and-development issues, and the differentiated needs and responsibilities of developed and developing countries has been formally recognized.

As this volume has illustrated, the idea of sustainable development and the international process with which it has been associated have been central to the transformation of environmental policy discourse in the industrialized countries. On the one hand, national experience of difficulties managing environmental burdens, and lessons drawn (particularly in the more innovative jurisdictions) through processes of technical and conceptual learning, constituted crucial inputs to the international processes (particularly the Brundtland Report, but also UNCED and UNCSD) which elaborated the sustainable development agenda. Thus sustainable development embodied accumulated insights from national policy-making. Such lessons were transmitted directly through personnel seconded to the international bodies and through official national contributions, but also indirectly via other international organizations (OECD, World Bank, UNEP), and inputs from specialist groups, from business and environmental organizations. On the other hand, sustainable development was launched from the international platform back into diverse national contexts. Here it provided coherence to changes in the approach to environmental policy-making which were already getting underway; it accelerated the transfer of policies and ideas from more advanced jurisdictions; it symbolized the official commitment to engage with a global environment-and-development process; and it provided international legitimacy to bureaucratic and environmental actors intent on strengthening mechanisms of environmental governance.

But sustainable development potentially signifies something more. As we have emphasized throughout this volume, sustainable development was never intended to be just another environmental policy concept. Rather its focus was on the global development trajectory. With sustainable development, environmental policy was supposed to be drawn beyond itself—broadened outward (sectorally) to merge with general societal decision processes; linked downwards and upwards (jurisdictionally) to local, regional, and international domains; and generalized (developmentally) by bringing it into contact with the urgent needs of the countries of the South. This transcendence was not intended to dissolve environmental policy as a distinct domain, for specialized institutions dedicated to environmental governance remain important. But neither were the changes to be confined to the 'environmental sphere'. Instead, they were to alter the way national 'development' decisions were considered, and to encourage a more equitable approach to the problems of the developing world.

As we have seen, the diverse dimensions of sustainable development have been taken up with varying degrees of enthusiasm in the states with which we have been concerned. Thus official adoption of sustainable development marks out not only what has been achieved, but also presents an ideal of what policy should imply, were the policy-makers to be faithful to their own declared ideas. As yet, however, the disjunction between the two remains deep. And so engagement with sustainable development has been simultaneously both profound and shallow. Change with respect to the pre-1987 base-line has been remarkable. On the other hand, compared with the scale of the socio-economic transformation and reforms to the international order implied by a consistent interpretation of sustainable development, they are very modest indeed. Rhetorically, most governments acknowledge the challenges, but fall short of understanding what they really imply. When hard choices about budgets, jobs, and economic competitiveness are to be made, the new paradigm is as often as not pushed into the background. This does not mean that the idiom of sustainable development counts for nothing— that it is all hypocrisy and capitulation to dominant economic interests (although there is plenty of that too). But rather that governments have been led to accept a framework whose implications they are not yet ready to follow through. And because many of the sorts of change sustainable development implies cannot be carried through without significant risks, and significant costs to particular economic sectors and actors, governments proceed cautiously.

To clarify this interpretation of events, it is helpful to contrast it with the influential account provided in the work of Hajer (1995), and Jansen, Osland, and Hanf (1998). These analysts interpret the shift in the approach to environmental policy manifest from the mid-1980s in terms of the triumph of an efficiency-oriented, technicist, and market-focused paradigm which they describe as 'ecological-modernization'.[7] Central to this perspective is the idea that environmental protection can be seen as an opportunity to modernize production techniques and develop new products, to improve efficiency and competitiveness, and to capture new markets for environmentally friendly goods and services. In short, environmental concern can be good for business.

These authors make a series of key claims about this new approach. Eco-modernization is said to posit 'a positive sum game' between economic growth and environmental protection. It is conceptualized as an efficiency-oriented, technicist, and managerialist approach to handling environmental burdens, which avoids a substantive critique of modern society, and assumes existing institutions can successfully internalize care for environment. The policy instruments it champions—economic instruments and negotiated or voluntary approaches—are held to be in tune with the neo-liberal assault on the state which gathered pace in the 1980s, and to threaten regulatory modes of environmental governance built up since the 1960s. This anti-regulatory bias, combined with the emphasis on efficiency, measurement, and economic calculus indicates that eco-modernization is part of a broader project to extend the logic of the market to new areas of social life.[8] It is argued that the new paradigm has become the hegemonic discourse or dominant strategy within the environmental policy domain. Moreover, this form of ecological modernization has successfully co-opted the bulk of the environmental movement, encouraging it to abandon a more fundamental critique of the market-based growth economy. Finally, the Brundland Report is taken as the paradigmatic statement of this new perspective, and the

[7] Like other concepts employed in the social sciences, 'ecological modernization' has rapidly acquired a range of usages. On the one hand, it has been invoked by social theorists to refer to broad processes of macro-level societal transformation—to characterize a profound shift in the way economy, ecology, and society interact in late modernity (Mol and Spaargaren 1993; Spaargaren 1997). On the other, it has been used by those pre-occupied with policy to describe shifts in the prevailing environmental management paradigm (Weale 1992, Hayer 1995, Neale 1997). It is this latter sense—where ecological modernization is associated with a particular ideology, pattern of discourse, or policy strategy—which concerns us here.

[8] It is ironic that in its social-theory guise 'ecological modernization' has served to make almost the opposite claim. A number of theorists argue the ecological modernist transition is a process whereby the environmental 'sphere' of interest is being separated out (or emancipated) from the political and socio-ideological sphere, but most importantly from the 'economic sphere' and the tyrany of economic rationality (Mol 1996).

appeal to sustainable development and adoption of the eco-modernist approach are assumed to be largely synonymous.[9]

There are two major points we would like to make in relation to these claims. The first is to contest the assimilation of the Brundtland Report and sustainable development with the eco-modernist variant outlined above; the second is to suggest that the triumph of this sort of eco-modernist perspective cannot be taken to provide a satisfactory account of the development of environmental policy in the industrialized countries over the past decade and a half.

The discussion throughout this volume should have gone some way towards convincing the reader that the content of the idea of sustainable development presented in the Brundtland Report and elaborated through the UNCED process differs significantly from the account of the ecological modernist outlook provided by Hajer and by Jansen, Osland, and Hanf. The two ideas do share a number of features. Proposals for moving beyond a remedial 'end of pipe' posture, to 'green' government operations, to increase the measurability of environmental performance, and to raise material and energy efficiencies, are associated with both perspectives. So, too, is insistence that long term economic progress depends on protecting the environment, and that environmental considerations should be integrated into decision-making across government and society. But the contrasts between them are also significant (Langhelle 2000).[10]

In the first place, sustainable development is explicitly international in focus: it was formulated to address global problems, and predicated upon an international effort to resolve dilemmas of environment and development. On the environmental terrain, it is closely linked to global issues such as climate change and biodiversity. On the other hand, despite some reference to the role of international organizations in popularizing eco-modernist ideas, and to the internationalization of environmental policy as a trend to

---

[9] Hajer describes 'the 1987 Brundtland report' as 'one of the paradigm statements of ecological modernisation' (1995: 26); while Jansen, Osland, and Hanf argue 'the report had the role of midwife for a new approach towards environmental problems' (1998: 291) and expresses 'a new general strategy to solve the environmental problems' which scholars have characterized as ecological modernization (292).

[10] In fact, these are really two different types of concept. Sustainable development has an overtly political character—it was formulated to reorient political behaviour and to draw together diverse constituencies. Ecological modernization has a somewhat more 'analytical' pedigree, having been deployed by social scientists to characterize a particular (emergent) construal of the environmental problematic. Sustainable development has been legitimated through an international process and is frequently invoked by public actors to explain their conduct, but ecological modernization features more rarely in the self-reflexive conceptualizations of contemporary societal actors.

which eco-modernist decision-makers have had to adjust, ecological modernization is presented as relating essentially to improvement in *national* environmental performance and competitiveness (Christoff 1996). Above all, the international equity dimension and the preoccupation with North/South tensions—which are essential to the idea of sustainable development—are virtually absent from the description of ecological modernization. Nor do domestic equity considerations—the idea that distributional concerns are necessarily related to environment-and-development policy—have a determinate place in this perspective. Indeed, in ecological modernization even the inter-generational component is attenuated.

What of the 'positive sum' relationship between economic growth and environmental protection? It is clear that the Brundtland Report postulates that both are necessary. But the 'positive versus zero sum' imagery does not adequately capture the core argument in the Report, which takes as its fulcrum neither 'growth' nor 'environment' but sustainable development. The point is that both economic growth and environmental protection are essential for sustainable development, but that sustainable development also implies that *not all of the environment* should be conserved, and that *not all patterns of growth* are desirable. In other words, the claims of growth and environment are reconciled because *both are subordinated* to the meta-objective of sustainable development. Practically, this reconciliation demands that much of the environment be transformed (with species and habitats lost and eco-systems altered for human purposes), while growth is reoriented to (1) privilege the needs of the poor and (2) avoid damage to environmental elements essential to long term prosperity. Together these points imply engagement with the North/South agenda. It is simply *not* true (as is so often implied) that the Brundtland Report and the UNCED process referred only to 'win-win' scenarios, to growth and environment walking hand in hand. On the contrary, there is talk about 'difficult choices', and such choices are necessary because all of the environment cannot be preserved and every form of economic growth cannot be tolerated if sustainable development is to proceed.

Nor can sustainable development be reduced to the sort of narrowly economistic and technocratic approach these writers have characterized as 'ecological modernization'. Consider Hajer's observation that 'although some supporters may individually start from moral premises, ecological modernisation basically follows a utilitarian logic: at the core of the idea of ecological modernisation is the idea that pollution prevention pays' (Hajer 1995: 26). Elsewhere he sums up his argument by explaining that 'ecological modernisation is essentially an efficiency-oriented approach to the environment. This is what made it possible for ecological modernization to become the dominant discourse within the environmental domain' (Hajer 1995: 101).

In contrast, moral concerns and arguments are absolutely central to sustainable development, and the language of Brundtland (and of the UNCED process more generally) is a language of moral injunction, as well as of prudential calculation. We are urged to turn to sustainable development not only because the alternative will prove unpleasant, but also because it is ethically right to do so. Of course pollution prevention 'pays'—but the rewards are supposed to accrue to the global community, to future generations, and to the world's poor, not just to 'lean and clean' businesses.[11]

Ideas of reducing waste and promoting energy and materials efficiency do play a significant part in the Brundtland Report and the UNCED proceedings, but it is a mistake to understand such notions in a narrow economistic vein. Certainly this is an idiom calculated to appeal to business leaders and to politicians concerned with economic performance. But since the mid-nineteenth century 'efficiency' and the reduction of 'waste' have consistently been invoked by social critics to build support for movements for reform.[12] Both terms can have substantial moral resonance, and in a world where millions remain in poverty and where societies face a risk of serious ecological disruption, 'waste' can be presented as not just bad for business, but as morally reprehensible; and 'efficiency' as not just good for the 'bottom line', but as a moral (ecological and humanitarian) virtue. Such dimensions are manifest in the way these ideas have been linked to sustainable development, and contrast to the narrower, economistic connotations of 'efficiency' and 'waste' which many analysts have associated with ecological modernization.[13]

---

[11] Hajer juxtaposes 'utilitarian logic' and 'moral premises'—but if the welfare that is to be promoted is that of the collectivity, of the poor, and of unborn generations, then utility is being invoked as a moral principle. Perhaps Hajer means to contrast 'self-interested' and 'disinterested motives' for action—but the relationship in political argument between prudential and disinterested reason is always complex. Even the radical environmentalists of the 1960s and 1970s (whom Hajer sees as the more authentic voice of the environmental movement), couched their arguments as much in terms of a warning of immanent catastrophe (save yourselves!) as they did in terms of a disinterested appeal to protect the biosphere.

[12] Nineteenth-century socialists and liberal reformers decried the lives 'wasted' in poverty; and 'waste' and 'efficiency' have long had stong religious resonances with ideas of pious thrift and the profligate 'waste' of divine gifts.

[13] Elsewhere Hajer acknowledges the social-democratic and equity-conscious dimensions of the Brundtland Report (Hajer 1995: 99). But that does not prevent him from simultaneously asserting the report's paradigmatic status for an 'ecological modernization', which uses 'the language of business' to conceptualize 'environmental pollution as a matter of inefficiency, while operating within the boundaries of cost-effectiveness and administrative efficiency' (Hajer 1995: 31).

In a related vein, the assimilation of features deemed typical of the neo-liberal and anti-regulatory dimensions of 'ecological modernization' with sustainable development, the Brundtland Report, and the UNCED process is unfortunate. The Report clearly advocates an active role for government in promoting the transition towards sustainable development. And while the UNCED outputs are sympathetic to the extension of free trade and the protection of intellectual property rights, they also call for more determined government action to protect the environment and ensure sustainable development. Indeed the call for Agenda 21 implementation and engagement with sustainable development can be interpreted as legitimating a significantly increased role for public power in mediating the social burdens of the environment (Meadowcroft 1997). As we argued in the first section of this chapter, to the extent that the intellectual genesis of sustainable development can be identified with a recognizable ideological tradition, this lies more in the direction of social democracy than market-liberalism.

Finally there is the charge that—like eco-modernization—sustainable development refuses to contemplate profound structural change to contemporary societies, believing that the environmental dimension can be successfully internalized by existing institutions. Now if 'structural change' in this context signifies the abolition of private property, the dismantling of the global economy, and the dissolution of the existing state system, then the claim is well founded. It is also trivial, as there are few serious political actors in the industrialized countries (to say nothing of governments) advocating 'structural change' of that sort.[14] But this does not mean that the changes sustainable development implies may not be radical and 'structural'. The call to shift production and consumption patterns and to alter *the quality of growth*, implies significant modifications to institutional practices, the structure of economic activity, and the nature of international economic relationships. Moreover, sustainable development leaves somewhat 'open' the scope of institutional reform that will ultimately be required. To secure 'internalisation', participation, international justice, and so on, far reaching reforms may been needed. Unsurprisingly, governments have started with rather modest (and not too costly) efforts; but the process may open the door to more significant change in the future.

So far we have suggested that there are significant differences between 'sustainable development' (as defined through the international process) and

---

[14] Hajer indicates just how radical change would have to be to count as 'structural' on his reading. He explains that ecological modernization 'does not address the systemic features of capitalism that make the system inherently wasteful and unmanageable' (32).

'ecological-modernization' (as often invoked in the academic literature).[15] Yet there remains the central issue of whether 'eco-modernization' of the sort envisaged by Hayer and by Jansen, Osland, and Hanf nevertheless captures the character of the shift in the approach to environmental policy which emerged from the mid-1980s. Of course, if one accepts that the content of these ideas really is different, the evidence presented in this volume—that governments have engaged with the notion of sustainable development, and with the Brundtland Report and the UNCED agenda— already provides an obvious reason to doubt the adequacy of a story-line centred on the triumph of a relatively narrowly conceived (efficiency-oriented, anti-regulatory) 'eco-modernist' discourse or policy strategy. Nevertheless, it could be argued that 'sustainable development'—with its grand normative agenda—has served simply as a rhetorical cover for a policy stance that in practice looks much more like 'ecological modernization'. Yet the difficulties of such an argument for any approach which takes discursive or idiomatic dimensions of policy formulation seriously are obvious. For the fact that governments *are* talking about sustainable development and its implications (rather than simply about national competitiveness, economic efficiency, and so on) matters. Still, it is worth examining more closely the implications of the claim that this 'eco-modernist' paradigm has achieved practical dominance.

The triumph of such an approach would imply that environmental policy has become increasingly dominated by an 'efficiency-oriented' logic, that prioritized economic rationality and technocratic inputs while marginalizing normative debate and diminishing the scope for collective (political) decision-making. Has this been the case? As far as we can see, the opposite trend is more in evidence. Since the mid-1980s environmental policy has been set in a broader intellectual frame, the normative implications of policy have been more systematically brought to the fore, and a wider range of perspectives and groups have had access to the policy process. Engagement with sustainable development has formed an important part of this process. Moreover, government officials and mainstream politicians have come to contemplate publicly the idea that profound social and economic changes

[15] It is certainly possible to recast the relationship between these two concepts to respect the distinctions made above. The thematic content of ecological modernization can be broadened to embrace elements manifest in the post-1987 international process, and the existence of a plurality of overlapping (and perhaps partially contradictory) perspectives within the ecological modernist current can be emphasized (Weale 1992: 78; Christoff 1996). Alternatively, if ecological modernization is to be reserved for a more economistic, business-efficiency oriented, and perhaps nationally focused reconstruction of environmental policy, then it need no longer be assimilated with the perspective of the Brundtland Report (Jänicke and Weidner 1997).

will be required in order to address the environment-and-development dilemmas that currently confront the world. Of course, economic considerations bulk large in political decision-making; the fate of governments is bound up with successful economic strategies; political leaders cannot afford to ignore the perceptions of domestic and international financial elites; and the environment is often subordinated to traditional economic objectives. Yet overall, the movement has not been towards an increasing economistic and technocratic domination of the environmental field, but rather (as we argued above) towards a widening of its conceptual and social basis.

Then there is the suggestion that the turn towards economic instruments and negotiated and voluntary approaches has eroded established regulatory mechanisms and represents an intrusion of 'market rationality' into the environmental domain. Again, this does not ring true. Existing regulatory structures and capacities in the environmental domain remain essentially intact and, if anything, established ministries and agencies have extended their reach. As we have seen, experiments with environmental taxation have been limited; but it is in any case a misconception to understand such mechanisms as extensions of 'market' rather than 'state'. Economic instruments involve government intervention (through decisions over what and who to tax, and at what rates) just as surely as more traditional regulatory approaches—and this helps explain the resistance which many businesses (as opposed to economists) have mounted to such extensions of government authority. The newer negotiative or 'voluntary' approaches have in most countries been focused on emergent issues—particularly climate change and biodiversity. If anything, they appear to herald *a dramatic extension* of the role of the state, rather than a withdrawal. Even though this intervention is achieved through negotiations rather than by legal enactment—it nevertheless draws new areas of social life under state purview.

Consider the issue of CO_2 emissions. For generations, businesses and consumers have been free to engage in CO_2 generating activities as they saw fit. Now these activities are to be scrutinized; emitters are to be cajoled into changing their practices; and the possibility of formal regulative action remains on the horizon. So, it seems odd to interpret such innovations in policy instruments as 'part of the overriding project of the ruling policy elites to expand the logic of the institutional order of the market' (Jansen, Osland, and Hanf 1998: 318).

Nor has the increased attention to measuring and monitoring resulted in a consolidation of economistic dominance. Economic valuation of the environment is one of a number of decision techniques to have attracted attention. While economic valuation has been more widely deployed, it has nowhere served as more than a useful adjunct to established decision procedures. Politicians and officials are (with good reason) unwilling to surrender important decisions to experts wielding the contested assumptions of these valuation techniques. Over the last decade and a half, much of the advance on the measurement front has actually focused on 'state of the environment reporting', indicators, and monitoring policy implementation. And these are essential for any reasoned and systematic approach to handling environmental burdens.

Then there is the idea that environmental movements have been seduced by the discursive wiles of 'eco-modernization'. According to Hajer, the 'new discursive order imposed new limits on what could be said meaningfully' (1995: 102), and so environmental movements 'effectively restricted their own possibilities of arguing their moral cause' (103). Yet there seems little evidence that over the past fifteen years environmentalists have grown more hesitant to invoke moral premises to advance their cause. Indeed, many have appealed to sustainable development as an internationally legitimated norm to press home their normative claims. As compared to the early 1980s, environmental organizations have greater access to policy-makers, understand more about the workings of industry and government, and are more often consulted in official decision processes. 'Mainstream' groups like Greenpeace and Friends of the Earth do not hesitate to resort to radical tactics when they feel politicians are not taking matters seriously—witness the recent confrontations over genetically modified foods in the UK. And there are plenty of radical groups even more eager to resort to direct action to push the social debate further. In short, there is little evidence that the environmental movement has surrendered much beyond a certain naivety.

For all these reasons the claim that 'eco-modernism' of the type described above has triumphed is implausible. Yet we would not seek to advance the counter-claim that paramount status should be accorded to the discourse or paradigm of 'sustainable development' (or to eco-modernization conceptualized in some alternative manner). The truth is that when assessing the current state of the environmental policy domain, the language of 'hegemonic discourse' and 'dominant policy strategy' appears unhelpful. The research we have done suggests that the situation is *much more fluid, contradictory, chaotic, and fragmented that the idiom of 'hegemony' suggests*. Many complex and contradictory social forces, and groups, of quite varied ideological complexions have had a hand in shaping events and in determining what the character of the engagement with sustainable development has actually been. True sustainable development has been broadly accepted as a legitimate goal—and this has a determinate normative and policy content. But there are very many legitimate interpretations of what this can in practice imply. Techno-optimists and eco-doomsters, regulatory enthusiasts and fans of market-mechanisms can (within bounds) accept sustainable development, yet disagree profoundly over the appropriate policy response in a given context. Moreover, there are societal elements which have not embraced sustainable development, or have explicitly repudiated it, and they too are part of the debate. Precisely because so many different perspectives and priorities can be articulated within the idiom of sustainable development, it makes little sense to refer to it in 'hegemonic' terms. Many orientations, priorities, and visions of the future (including the economistic variant of 'ecological modernization') are jostling for influence, and it remains to be determined which version will actually unfold.

A Future for Sustainable Development?

In concluding this study we would like briefly to consider the issue of the longer-term viability of the 'politics of sustainable development'. A comprehensive approach to this question would require analysis of a range of issues, including experience in developed societies more generally (especially in relation to the array of non-governmental social actors), in international organizations (across the UN system, the OECD, and so on), and in the countries which lie on the other side of the North/South divide. Obviously, this would lead us far beyond the more modest, central government-focused, remit of the current volume. Nevertheless, the study presented here does allow us to make some tentative suggestions.

In the first place, it is important again to underline the relatively rapid integration of the notion of sustainable development into political life in the developed states. It is not common for a new normative idea to gain widespread cross national acceptance—not just as a device employed by particular specialist constituencies—but as a concept that passes over into mainstream political usage in a great variety of national contexts. Yet sustainable development has achieved just such recognition in little more than a decade.

We have seen that the concept has been met with differing degrees of enthusiasm in different jurisdictions; that specific dimensions have been largely ignored by particular governments; that actual policy change has lagged behind rhetoric; and that as a group, governments have neglected significant elements of the sustainable development agenda. And yet, despite all these weaknesses, in almost all of the developed states with which we have been concerned, sustainable development remains as a high-profile, officially sanctioned, standard, against which environment and development initiatives can be weighed. It continues to be associated with innovation in the environmental policy domain, and governments remain formally committed to carrying forward and deepening the quest for 'sustainability'. In short, so far sustainable development has proven to be significant, and remarkably robust.

Holding to the evidence produced by the current study, there is enough variation across the individual case studies to warrant a balanced assessment. We find indications among the high-consumption societies which by turns provide grounds both for a mild optimism and for a (perhaps somewhat less) mild pessimism. For there are signs that over time the international political context has become less favourable to a substantive engagement with sustainable development and the UNCED agenda. The decade from roughly 1983 to 1993 was a period of strong environmental concern in Northern countries, and increased awareness of the dependency between environment and development in Southern countries. The mood of the Earth Summit in 1992 was one of optimism and apparent commitment. The fact that many Northern delegations returned to their countries feeling that the Summit had not achieved *enough*, speaks clearly to the prevailing atmosphere. Virtually no delegation questioned the need for UNCED and its agreements; nor where there any serious attempts to replace the concept of sustainable development as the foundational principle for the environment-and-development agenda.

By the time of the first five-year assessment in 1997, however, the mood had already altered. Despite the high profile given to the post-Rio review, through a special session of the General Assembly, the debate was guarded, critical and polarized. Representatives from Southern countries not only rebuked Northern 'back-tracking' from UNCED commitments (especially in relation to aid, technology transfer, debt relief and market-opening), but also sometimes appeared willing to ditch the idea of sustainable development entirely—for having been irrevocably co-opted by Northern (environmental) concerns. Even developed states which had previously distinguished themselves as sustainable development forerunners were reserved and hesitant as to where the programme might be headed. Ultimately the UNGASS meeting closed ranks to support the language of sustainable development, and adopted a new, and relatively ambitious, five-year programme for the CSD. But doubts had been sown, and in the corridors of the UN headquarters in New York there was open speculation as to whether the programme for environment and development had been overtaken by other preoccupations, or undermined by the rush to liberalize the international trade regime.

During the second half of the 1990s governments were preoccupied with a series of testing developments—including regional military conflicts; concern over the stability of the international financial system and a crisis in Asian emerging economies; continuing repercussions from the collapse of the Eastern bloc; preparation and launch of the single currency in Europe, and the opening of discussions on the possible expansion of the EU to twenty-five members and beyond; turmoil in the World Trade Organization; pressure to reform welfare provision and work regimes; an accelerated pace of international economic integration, and dramatic innovation in the communications and bio-technology spheres. Since sustainable development is a programme for change, it is unsurprising that without conscious and constant pressure, stagnation is possible. Certainly by the end of the 1990s many observers felt that momentum had been lost, and environment-and-development themes were slipping from the public mind. Whether this represents more than typical issue-cycling remains to be seen.

Any assessment of the future of sustainable development must take into consideration three dominant features of the idea: that it involves (1) goals and values which are at once *normative* and *relatively vague* with respect to specific policy proscriptions; (2) a 'programme' which has arisen *external* to normal national policy arenas; and (3) a political commitment which—largely due to the first two characteristics—is relatively 'soft' as a mandate for change. The combined effect of these features is to make predictions on the future of sustainable development difficult. Normative standards change; vagueness gives way to immediate needs and interests; international programmes come and go; and the ties that bind governments to national commitments made in international forums are tenuous.

We can note that despite the international 'wobble' described above, the normative status of the concept of sustainable development has not been seriously challenged within the high-consumption countries. The case studies provide no evidence of open political conflict as to the term itself—nor for that matter as to the basic elements associated with the idea from the Brundtland report. Conflicts abound as to the *realization* of the goals and values, but not (the United States excepted) with respect to the fundamental moral status of the core principles. Overall, we find no evidence of attacks on a need for moving from conservational and environmental concerns to ecological thinking; nor on the need for connecting economic decisions and dispositions with ecological consequences; nor on the importance of encouraging greater societal participation in environment and development decision-making; nor on the posited dependency between environment and development on a global basis; nor on a need for greater global and generational equity with respect to the use of resources and sinks. While academics seem to enjoy nothing more than arguing over *all* of these elements, national politicians seem broadly content to allow them their rhetorical due both domestically and internationally.

However, the fact noted above—that this is apparently *not* always the case with political representatives of the less-developed countries—indicates that the normative symbolic function of 'sustainable development' cannot be taken for granted within the UN system. The extent to which a move away from the rhetoric of sustainable development at the international level would alter the way high-consumption societies relate to the substance of the idea is an open question. Given the 'external' nature of the idea and its programme, a significant impact could be anticipated. It was an external UN commission which sponsored the term's passage into international parlance and programmes—largely to the presumed advantage of the poorer countries—and a reduction in its normative rhetorical status might be welcomed in some quarters in the North.

Yet the results of our case studies point in another direction. We have seen that the expanded normative conceptual scope of sustainable development has not only been taken seriously within high-consumption societies, but that it has also given rise to new constellations of political forces *within* the individual countries, as well as to new lines of cleavage *between* Northern governments (especially in terms of the tension between the 'disinterested' United States and a 'cautiously supportive' European Union). The 'external' has, in other words, been 'internalized', resulting in political conflicts over the *means* of achieving sustainable development which doubtfully would have arisen in the same form without the UNCED impetus. Issues of sustainable production and consumption, climate change, biodiversity, trade, developmental assistance and technology transfer, have all been taken up differently by different state groupings. In short, the footprints from Rio have already left a significant imprint on national and regional politics.

This brings us then to the third characteristic: the degree of commitment inherent in the Rio agreements and their follow-up. The problem for predicting the future for sustainable development here is that national politicians and their parties have (with one major exception—the United States) seldom to date registered serious differences of opinion over the endorsement of international agreements for sustainable development. Much of this has to do with a normal tendency towards non-partisanship in international affairs, but this is particularly strengthened when it comes to agreements designed to secure global peace, prosperity, and 'sustainable development'. The degree to which such commitments can be taken seriously as a predictor of the staying power of the idea is, therefore, highly contingent.

Two observations that emerge from the case studies here are: first, that the nature of competitive party politics indicates that there exists in *nearly* all of the countries studied a tendency for parties to align themselves with different elements of the sustainable development 'package'; and, second, that the 'consensual' nature of the national commitments to UNCED has provided both the mass media and concerned NGOs with moral leverage to push for more consequential action. The result is a new dimension of politics, whereby national commitments of a relatively non-reflective 'consensual' nature at the international level provide potential moral 'sticks' for party competition and political pressure from civil society.

Taking all these factors into consideration, it seems safe to conclude that the 'politics of sustainable development' are—for the foreseeable future— here to stay in high-consumption societies. While there may be further efforts within the UN system to play down the concept as an overriding developmental goal, there is no reason to believe that either the UN bureaucracy, the leading-edge countries of the North, or environment-and-development NGOs are willing to let this happen. If 'sustainable development' is to be dropped as a normative symbol, other ideas and symbols will have to take its place. In the meantime preparations for the ten-year review of Rio will proceed apace; the politics of climate change and the Kyoto Protocol will come to a head; implementing the Framework Convention on Biodiversity will become an increasing challenge; the trade-offs between free trade, the environment, and rising differentials in wealth and poverty will require continuous adjudication; and the 'social partners'—locally, nationally, regionally and globally—will be increasingly forced to confront their responsibilities for the interdependency between economy and welfare on the one hand, and ecology and the carrying capacity of nature on the other.

Given the indications we have seen in the country reports—all of these problems will impinge more or less directly on regional, national and local politics. The issues raised by the Brundtland Report; the politics leading up to and including the Rio Earth Summit; the more routine work of the Commission for Sustainable Development; plus the numerous innovative initiatives, policies and instruments documented in the present case studies—all indicate substantive processes of change which reflect a broader and 'deeper' understanding of the dependency between developmental priorities and environmental exigencies. Whether progress on altering this dependency is sufficient; whether the changes involved are more self-serving for established economic interests than for ecological balance and global/generational equity; whether sustainable development will ultimately prove to be a critically regressive ploy or a crucially transformative idea—these are questions whose answers lie beyond the purview of the present study.

Contributors to this volume have attempted to document the degree to which sustainable development is being taken seriously by governments in industrialized states as a *different* idea, goal, and agenda for change: different from conservation; different from environmental clean-up and protection; different from ecological modernization, narrowly conceived. We believe that the results indicate that this has been the case. To different degrees in different countries, and with differing intensity and different results within the same country, pragmatic efforts at implementation are being made to match the ambitious and often ambiguous language of the UNCED programme. We are convinced that these efforts are qualitatively different from environmental efforts prior to the WCED and Rio, and we hope to have illustrated in what this difference consists. If we have in our analyses and conclusions appeared more positive towards the state of sustainable development than is the academic norm—and perhaps even more positive than several of the individual contributors to the volume—that is an appearance we can live with. We have tried to keep a balance between critical and constructive perspectives, paying heed to a necessity for both—but at the same time feeling that the former is both easier and more prevalent than the latter. Evaluative research is always a matter of balance—and the relevance and use of evaluative research, usually a matter of intent. We have tried to get the balance right, and hope for a constructive application of the results.

Consolidated Bibliography

Aall, C. (1997), 'Norske kommuners oppfølging av Agenda 21', in W. M. Lafferty, O. Langhelle, P. Mugaas, and M. H. Ruge (eds.), *Rio +5. Norges oppfølging av FN-konferansen om miljø og utvikling*, Oslo: Tano Ascheloug.

——(1998), 'Norway: Confronting the Inertia of Existing Reforms', in W. M. Lafferty and K. Eckerberg (eds.), *From the Earth Summit to Local Agenda 21: Working Towards Sustainable Development*, London: Earthscan.

Aardal, B. (1993), *Energi og miljø. Nye stridsspørsmål i møte med gamle strukturer*, Rapport nr. 15, Oslo: Institutt for samfunnsforskning.

——and H. Valen (1995), *Konflikt og Opinion*, Oslo: NKS Forlaget.

ACBE (Advisory Committee on Business and the Environment) (1994), *Fourth Progress Report*, London: DTI/DoE.

——(1998), *Eighth Progress Report*, London: DTI/DETR.

Adams, W. (1990), *Green Development: Environment and Sustainability in the Third World*, London: Routledge.

Agency of Industrial Science and Technology, MITI (n.d.), 'New Sunshine Program'.

Alfsen, K. H., and B. Holtsmark (1997), 'Klimaforhandlingene: Status og norske posisjoner', *ProSus: tidsskrift for et bærekraftig samfunn*, 3: 5–27.

Alliantie voor Duurzame Ontwikkeling (1992), *Nederlands Nationaal NGO-Rapport in he kader van UNCED*, Utrecht: Het Kan Ook Anders.

Andersen, M. (1994), *Governance by Green Taxes*, Manchester: Manchester University Press.

——and D. Liefferink (1997) (eds.), *European Environmental Policy: the Pioneers*, Manchester: Manchester University Press.

ANOP Research Services (1991), *The Environment and the ESD Process: An Attitude Research Analysis*, vol. 1, Sydney: ANOP.

——(1993), *Community Attitudes to Environmental Issues*, Prepared for the Department of the Environment, Sport and Territories.

ANPED (1997), 'The Northern Alliance for Sustainability', *Northern Lights: Newsletter of ANPED*, autumn.

Armann, K. A., J. Hille, and O. Kasin (1995), 'Lokal Agenda 21. Norske Kommuners miljøarbeid etter Rio', *Prosjekt Alternativ Framtid Rapport*, 5.

Associated Press (1996), 'Nations Urged to Pass Laws on Emissions', *The New York Times*, 19 July: A5.

Auer, M., and K.-H. Erdmann (1997), 'Schutz und Nutzung der natürlichen Ressourcen. Das Übereinkommen über die biologische Vielfalt', in K.-H. Erdmann (ed.), *Internationaler Naturschutz*, Berlin u.a.: Springer, 97–116.

Australian Conservation Foundation (1997a), *The Australian Proposal for Differentiated Greenhouse gas emission Targets: Contradictory and Illogical*, Greenhouse Briefing Paper, Melbourne: Australian Conservation Foundation.

——(1997b), *Fifteen Ways the Commonwealth Can Reduce Australia's Greenhouse gas emissions*, Melbourne: Australian Conservation Foundation.

Australian Labor Party (1991), *Australian Labor Party Platform*.

Bäckstrand, K., A. Kronsell, and P. Söderholm (1997), 'Organisational Challenges to Sustainable Development', *Environmental Politics*, 5: 209–30.

Badaracco, J. L. (1985), *Loading the Dice: A Five Country Study of Vinvl Chloride Regulation*, London: MIT Press.

Baker, S. (1993), 'The Environmental Policies of the European Community: A Critical Review', *Kent Journal of International Relations*, 7/1: 8–29.

——(1996a), 'Environmental Policy in the European Union: Institutional Dilemmas and Democratic Practice', in W. Lafferty and J. Meadowcroft (eds.), *Democracy and the Environment*, Cheltenham: Edward Edgar, 213–33.

——(1996b), 'Punctured Sovereignty, Border Regions and the Environment within the EU', in L. O'Dowd and T. M. Wilson (eds.), *Borders, Nations and States*, Aldershot: Avebury, 19–50.

——(1997), 'The Evolution of Environmental Policy in the European Union: From Growth to Sustainable Development?', in S. Baker, M. Kousis, D. Richardson, and S. C. Young (eds.), *The Politics of Sustainable Development: Theory, Policy and Practice within the European Union*, London: Routledge, 91–106.

——and S. C. Young (1996), *The Implementation of Sustainable Development Policy in Member-States: An Appraisal of EU Policy to Date*, Paper presented at the ECPR Joint Sessions of Workshops, Oslo, April 1996.

——and M. Kousis, D. Richardson, and S. Young (1997) (eds.), *The Politics of Sustainable Development*, London: Routledge.

——and P. Jehlička (1998), 'Dilemmas of Transition: The Environment, Democracy and Economic Reform in East Central Europe—an Introduction', *Environmental Politics*, 7/1: 1–28.

Baltscheffsky, S. (1997), 'Världen samlas för att kyla klotet', *Svenska Dagbladet*, Stockholm, 29 November.

Bandow, D., and I. Vasquez (1994), *Perpetuating Poverty: The World Bank, the IMF, and the Developing World*, Washington, DC: Cato Institute.

Barrett, B., and R. Therivel (1991), *Environmental Policy and Impact Assessment in Japan*, New York: Routledge.

Beckerman, W. (1994), ' "Sustainable Development": Is it a useful Concept?', *Environmental Values*, 3: 191–209.

Bell, S., and B. Head (1994), 'Australia's Political Economy: Critical Themes and Issues', in S. Bell and B. Head (eds.), *State, Economy and Public Policy*, Melbourne: Oxford University Press.

Bennulf, M. (1990), *Grönt ljus. Väljarna och miljöpartiets valframgång 1988*,

Gothenburg: Gothenburg University, Department of Political Science.

Benum, E. (1998), 'Overflod og fremtidsfrykt 1970-', in *Aschehougs Norges Historie*, bind 12, Oslo: Aschehoug.

Bergesen, H. O., M. Grubb, J.-C. Hourcade, J. Jäger, A. Lanza, R. Loske, L. A. Sverdrup, and A. Tudini (1994), *Implementing the European CO₂ Commitment: A joint policy proposal*, London: Royal Institute of International Affairs.

——K. Roland, and A. K. Sydnes (1995), *Norge i det globale drivhuset*, Oslo: Universitetsforlaget.

Bergh, J. van den, and J. van der Straaten (1994), *Toward Sustainable Development*, Washington: Island Press.

Bergman, Å. (1997), 'Regeringen nedrustar miljögiftsforskningen', *Svenska Dagbladet*, 20 October: 10.

Berntsen, B. (1994), *Grønne linjer. Natur- og miljøvernets historie i Norge*, Oslo: Grøndahl Dreyer.

Beuermann, C. (1998), 'Local Agenda 21 in Germany. Five years after Rio and its still uphill all the way?', in W. M. Lafferty and K. Eckerberg (eds.), *From the Earth Summit to Local Agenda 21: Working Towards Sustainable Development*, London: Earthscan, 106–39.

——and J. Jäger (1996), 'Climate Change Politics in Germany: How Long will Any Double Dividend Last?', in T. O'Riordan and J. Jäger (eds.), *Politics of Climate Change*, London: Routledge, 186–227.

——and B. Burdick (1997), 'The Sustainability Transition in Germany', *Environmental Politics*, 6/1: 83–107.

BGPSD (British Government Panel on Sustainable Development) (1995), *Annual Report*, London: DoE.

——(1996), *Annual Report*, London: DoE.

——(1997), *Annual Report*, London: DETR.

——(1999), *Annual Report*, London: DETR.

Biodiversity Secretariat (1998), *Biodiversity Factsheet*, Bristol: Biodiversity Secretariat.

Blok, K., G. J. M. Phylipsen, and J. W. Bode (1997), *The Triptique Approach Burden Differentiation of CO₂ Emission Reduction Among European Union Member States*, Discussion paper for the informal workshop for the European Union Ad Hoc Group on Climate Change, Zeist, the Netherlands, 16–17 January.

Blowers, A. (1987), 'Transition or Transformation? Environmental Policy under Thatcher', *Public Administration*, 65: 277–94.

BMBau (Federal Ministry for Regional Development, Housing and Urban Development) (1996) (ed.), *Siedlungsentwicklung und Siedlungspolitik. Nationalbericht Deutschland (Habitat II)*, Bonn: BMBau.

BMU (Federal Ministry for the Environment, Nature Conservation and Nuclear Safety) (1992a) (ed.), *Bericht der Bundesregierung über die Konferenz der Vereinten Nationen für Umwelt und Entwicklung im Juni 1992 in Rio de Janeiro*, Bonn: BMU.

——(1992b), *Internationale Expertenkonferenz 'Förderung des kommunalen Umweltschutzes—Strategien und Handlungsansätze' zur Vorbereitung der UN-Konferenz für Umwelt und Entwicklung (UNCED)*, Bonn: BMU.

——(1994a), *Environment 1994. German Strategy for Sustainable Development—Summary*, Bonn: BMU.

——(1994b), *Klimaschutz in Deutschland. Erster Bericht der Regierung der Bundesrepublik Deutschland nach dem Rahmenübereinkommen der Vereinten Nationen über Klimaänderungen*, Bonn: BMU.

——(1994c), *Beschluß der Bundesregierung vom 29. September 1994 zur Verminderung der CO_2-Emissionen und anderer Treinhausgasemissionen in der Bundesrepublik Deutschland*, Bonn: BMU.

——(1995), *Schutz und nachhaltige Nutzung der Natur in Deutschland. Bericht der Bundesregierung zur Umsetzung des Übereinkommens über die Biologische Vielfalt in der Bundesrepublik Deutschland*, Bonn: BMU.

——(1996a), *Protokoll der Sitzung des nationalen Komitees für nachhaltige Entwicklung am 7. Februar 1996*, unpublished.

——(1996b), 'Bundesregierung hält an ihrer Konzeption für ein neues Bundesnaturschutzgesetz fest', *BMU-Pressemitteilung*, 144/96, 4 December, Bonn: BMU.

——(1997a), *Auf dem Weg zu einer nachhaltigen Entwicklung in Deutschland. Bericht der Bundesregierung anläßlich der VN-Sondergeneralversammlung über Umwelt und Entwicklung 1997 in New York*, Bonn: BMU.

——(1997b), *Schritte zu einer nachhaltigen, umweltgerechten Entwicklung*, Bonn: BMU.

——(1997c), 'Deutschland verstärkt Klimavorsorge. Vierter Bericht der Interministeriellen Arbeitsgruppe "CO_2-Reduktion" vom Kabinett beschlossen', *BMU-Pressemitteilung*, 61/97, 6 November, Bonn: BMU.

——(1997d), *Beschluß der Bundesregierung zum Klimaschutzprogramm der Bundesrepublik Deutschland auf der Basis des Vierten Berichts der Interministeriellen Arbeitsgruppe 'CO₂-Reduktion' (IMA CO₂-Reduktion)*, Bonn: BMU.

——(1997e), 'UN-Sondergeneralversammlung "Fünf Jahre nach Rio" vom 23.–27. Juni in New York', *BMU-Pressemitteilung*, 51/97, 22 June, Bonn: BMU.

——(1997f), '8. Sitzung der Ad-hoc-Gruppe Berliner Mandat geht heute in Bonn zu Ende', *BMU-Pressemitteilung*, 60/97, 31 October, Bonn: BMU.

——(1997g), 'Klimaschutzprotokoll in Kyoto verabschiedet', *BMU-Pressemitteilung*, 11 December, Bonn: BMU.

——(1997h), 'SPD verhindert Fortschritte im Naturschutz. Novelle des Bundesnaturschutzgesetzes im Vermittlungsausschuß gescheitert', *BMU-Pressemitteilung*, 88/97, 26 November, Bonn: BMU.

——(1998a), 'Bericht der Bundesregierung nah dem Übereinkommen über die biologische Vielfalt. Nationalbericht 1998', *http://www.dainet.de/bmu-cbd/new/nationb98_1.htm*.

——(1998b), *Nachhaltige Entwicklung in Deutschland. Entwurf eines umweltpolitischen Schwerpunktprogramms*, Bonn: BMU.

BMU (1998c), 'Bundestag beschließt Drittes Gesetz zur Änderung des Bundesnaturschutzgesetzes mit Ausgleichsregelungen für Land- und Forstwirtschaft', *BMU-Pressemitteilung*, 45/98, 24 April, Bonn: BMU.

——(1998d), 'Drittes Gesetz zur Anderung des Bundesnaturschutzgesetzes vom Bundespräsidenten ausgefertigt', *BMU-Pressemitteilung*, 126/98, 27 August, Bonn: BMU.

——(1998e), 'Kabinett stimmt Nationalbericht zum Übereinkommen über die Biologische Vielfalt zu', *BMU-Pressemitteilung*, 37/98, 1 April, Bonn: BMU.

——(1998f), '4. Vertragsstaatenkonferenz zum Übereinkommen über Biologische Vielfalt in Bratislava, Slowakische Republik beendet', *BMU-Pressemitteilung*, 55/98, 16 May, Bonn: BMU.

——(1998g), 'Bundesregierung hält an ihrer Konzeption für ein neues Bundesnaturschutzgesetz fest', *BMU-Pressemitteilung*, 20/98, 24 March, Bonn: BMU.

——(1998h), 'Sustainable Development in Germany. Draft Programme for Priority Areas in Environment Policy. Summary', Bonn: BMU.

BMU/BMZ (Federal Ministry for Economic Co-operation and Development) (1994) (eds.), *German Report to the 3rd CSD-Session 1995*, unpublished.

BMU/BMZ (1995), *CSD 96 Guidelines for National Information*, Part 1: *Cross Sectoral Issues*, unpublished.

BMZ (Federal Ministry for Economic Co-operation and Development) (1997a) (ed.), 'RIO-KONFERENZ Umwelt und Entwicklung—5 Jahre danach', *BMZ aktuell*, 97/080, Bonn: BMZ.

——(1997b), 'Erhaltung biologischer Vielfalt durch Naturschutz', *BMZ aktuell*, 97/087, Bonn: BMZ.

Böhmer-Christiansen, S., and J. Skea (1991), *Acid Politics: Environmental and Energy Politics in Britain and Germany*, London: Belhaven Press.

Boer, M. de (1995), *Milieu, ruimte en wonen; tijd voor duurzaamheid*, Den Haag, 26 juni.

Bosma, M. (1995), 'Gemeenten omarmen Agenda 21', *Binnenlands Bestuur*, 10, 10 March.

Bradbeer, J. (1990), 'Environmental Policy', in S. P. Savage and L. Robins (eds.), *Public Policy Under Thatcher*, Basingstoke: Macmillan, 75–88.

Broadbent, J. (1998), *Environmental Politics in Japan: Networks of Power and Protest*, Cambridge: Cambridge University Press.

Brown, L. (1981), *Building a Sustainable Society*, New York: W. W. Norton.

Brundtland, G. H. (1990), 'Global Change and Our Common Future', in C. S. Silver and R. S. DeFries (eds.), *One Earth One Future: Our Changing Global Environment*, Washington, DC: National Academy Press.

——(1998), *Dramatiske år: 1986—96*, Oslo: Gyldendal Norsk Forlag.

——and V. Hauff (1987), *Unsere Gemeinsame Zukunft: Der Brundtland-Bericht der Weltkommission für Umwelt und Entwicklung*, Greven: Eggenkamp.

BUND (Bund für Umwelt und Naturschutz Deutschland, and Misereor) (1995) (eds.), *Zukunftsfähiges Deutschland. Ein Beitrag zu einer Global Nachhaltigen Entwicklung*, Basel, Boston, and Berlin: Birkhäuser.

Bureau of National Affairs, Inc. (1997), *International Environment Reporter*, 30 April: 434, Washington, DC.

Burke, T. (1995), 'View From the Inside: UK Environmental Policy Seen from a Practitioner's Perspective', in T. Gray (ed.), *UK Environmental Policy in the 1990s*, Basingstoke: Macmillan, 11–17.

BuZA and VROM (1997), *Ontwikkelingen in Duurzaamheid 1992–1997*, Den Haag, June.

Cabinet Office (1999), *Modernising Government*, Cm 4310, London: TSO.

Caddy, J. (1997), 'Harmonisation and Asymmetry: Environmental Policy Co-ordination Between the European Union and Central Europe', *Journal of European Public Policy*, 4/3.

CAG Consultants (1998), *Perceptions of National Barriers to Local Sustainability: A Report for Friends of the Earth*, London: CAG.

Calgary Sun (1999), *Sustainable Energy and the Environment: A Special Supplement to the Calgary Sun, Edmonton Sun and The Globe and Mail*, July.

Canada (1990), *Canada's Green Plan—for a Healthy Environment*, Ottawa: Supply and Services Canada.

——(1991a), *Canada's National Report to UNCED*, Ottawa: Environment Canada.

——(1991b), *The State of Canada's Environment*, Ottawa: Supply and Services Canada.

——(1992), *Canada's Green Plan and the Earth Summit*, Ottawa: Supply and Services Canada.

——(1995a), *A Guide to Green Government*, Ottawa: Supply and Services Canada.

——(1995b), *Keeping a Promise: Toward a Sustainable Budget*, Ottawa: House of Commons Standing Committee on Environment and Sustainable Development.

——(1995c), *Canada in the World*, Ottawa: Foreign Affairs and International Trade.

——(1995d), *Canadian Biodiversity Strategy: Canada's Response to the Convention on Biological Diversity*, Ottawa: Supply and Services Canada.

——(1996a), *The State of Canada's Environment—1996*, Ottawa: Supply and Services Canada.

——(1996b), *Report of Canada to the United Nations Commission on Sustainable Development*, Ottawa: Foreign Affairs and International Trade.

——(1997a), *Building Momentum: Sustainable Development in Canada*, Ottawa: Environment Canada.

——(1997b), *Canada Year Book 1997*, Ottawa: Statistics Canada.

——(1997c), *The Canada Country Study: Climate Impacts and Adaptation*, Ottawa: Environment Canada.

—— (1997d), *Harmonization and Environmental Protection: An Analysis of the Harmonization Initiative of the Canadian Council of Ministers of the Environment*, Ottawa: House of Commons Standing Committee on Environment and Sustainable Development.

Canada (1997e), *Our Commitment to Sustainable Development: The Strategy of the Canadian International Development Agency*, Ottawa: Public Works and Government Services.

—— (1997f), *Securing Our Heritage: The Sustainable Development Strategy of the Department of Canadian Heritage*, Ottawa: Public Works and Government Services.

—— (1997g), *Sustaining Our Health: Health Canada's Sustainable Development Strategy*, Ottawa: Public Works and Government Services.

—— (1997h), *Sustainable Development Strategy: Human Resources Development Canada*, Ottawa: Public Works and Government Services.

—— (1998), *Caring For Canada's Biodiversity: Canada's First National Report to the Conference of the Parties to the Convention on Biological Diversity*, Ottawa: Environment Canada.

—— (2000), *The Budget Plan 2000*, Ottawa: Department of Finance.

Canadian Institute for Environmental Law and Policy (1998), *Ontario's Environment and the 'Common Sense Revolution': A Third Year Report*, Toronto: Canadian Institute for Environmental Law and Policy.

Carter, N. (1994), 'The Greens in the 1994 European Parliament Elections', *Environmental Politics*, 3/3: 495–502.

—— and P. Lowe (1995), 'The Establishment of a Cross-Sector Environment Agency', in T. Gray (ed.), *UK Environmental Policy in the 1990s*, Basingstoke: Macmillan, 38–56.

Cavender Bares, J. (1993), *Germany's Policy towards Global Environmental Risk Management*, Cambridge, Mass.: Center for Science and International Affairs, Harvard University.

CBS (Central Bureau for Statistics) (1996), *Statistical yearbook*, The Hague: SDU.

CEC (Commission of the European Communities) (1992a), *Report from the Commission of the European Communities to the United Nations Conference on the Environment and Development—Rio de Janeiro, June 1992*, Brussels: March, SEC (91) 2448 final.

—— (1992b), *Towards Sustainability: A European Community Programme of Policy and Action in Relation to the Environment and Sustainable Development*, Brussels: COM (92) 23 Final, 11.

—— (1992c), 'Convention on the Conservation of Biological Diversity', *Bulletin of the European Communities*, 25/6, pt.1.3.129.

—— (1993a), *European Commission Report to the CSD I*, Brussels: CEC.

—— (1993b), 'White Paper on Growth, Competitiveness, Employment: The Challenge and Ways Forward into the 21st Century', *Bulletin of the European Communities*, Supplement, 6/93.

—— (1994a), *Interim Review of Implementation of the European Community Programme of Policy and Action in Relation to the Environment and Sustainable Development* 'Towards Sustainability, Brussels: COM (94) 453 final.

—— (1994b), *European Commission Report to the CSD II*, Brussels: CEC.

—— (1994c), *Report from the Commission under Council Decision 93/389/EEC. First evaluation of existing national programmes under the monitoring mechanism of Community CO₂ and other greenhouse gas emissions*, Brussels: COM (94) 67 final.

—— (1995a), *Progress Report from the Commission on the Implementation of the European Community Programme of Policy and Action in Relation to the Environment and Sustainable Development 'Towards Sustainability'*, Brussels: COM (95) 624 final.

—— (1995b), *European Commission Report to the CSD III*, Brussels: CEC.

—— (1996a), *Commission communication to Parliament and the Council, A common platform: guidelines for the European preparation for the United Nations General Assembly Special Session to be held in New York in 1997 to review Agenda 21 and related outcomes of the United Nations Conference on Environment and Development held in Rio de Janeiro in June 1992*, Brussels: COM (96) 569 final.

—— (1996b), *European Commission Report to the CSD IV*, Brussels: CEC.

—— (1996c), *Speech by Mrs. Ritt Bjerregaard at the Third Conference of the Parties on Biological Diversity*, Buenos Aires, 14 November, 1996, EU Spokesman Services: Speech 96/294.

—— (1996d), *Progress Report from the Commission on the Implementation of the European Community Programme of Policy and Action in relation to the Environment and Sustainable Development 'Towards Sustainability'*, Brussels: COM (95) 624 final.

—— (1996e), Communication from the European Commission on Environmental Agreements, COM (96) 561.

—— (1997a), *The EU Approach for Kyoto*, DGXI Communication from the Commission to the Council, The European Parliament, The Economic and Social Committee and the Committee of the Regions, Climate Change: The EU Approach for Kyoto.

—— (1997b), *Towards Sustainability. The European Commission's progress report and action plan on the fifth programme of policy and action in relation to the environment and sustainable development*, Luxembourg: Office for Official Publications of the European Communities.

—— (1997c), *European Forum on Environment and Sustainable Development, Principles of Sustainable Development*, Luxembourg: Office for Official Publications of the European Communities.

—— (1997d), *European Forum on Environment and Sustainable Development, Options for a Sustainable Europe*, Luxembourg: Office for Official Publications of the European Communities.

—— (1997e), *Commission Communication to the European Parliament, the Council, the Economic and Social Committee and the Committee of the Regions on the Energy Dimensions of Climate Change*, Brussels, May: COM (97) 196.

—— (1997f), *Ritt Bjerregaard Speech No 275*, 8 December, Brussels: Commission Spokesman Service.

—— (1997g), *Press Release*, IP/97/1106, 11 December, Brussels: Commission Spokesman Services.

—— (1998), *Communication from the Commission to the Council and the European Parliament on a European Community Biodiversity Strategy*, Brussels: COM (1998) 42 final.

CESD (Commissioner of the Environment and Sustainable Development) (1997), *Report of the Commissioner of Environment and Sustainable Development to the House of Commons*, Ottawa: Public Works and Government Services.

—— (1998), *Report of the Commissioner of Environment and Sustainable Development to the House of Commons*, Ottawa: Public Works and Government Services.

—— (1999a), *Report of the Commissioner of Environment and Sustainable Development to the House of Commons*, Ottawa: Public Works and Government Services.

—— (1999b), *Moving up the Learning Curve: The Second Generation of Sustainable Development Strategies*, Ottawa: Department of Finance.

Chikyû Kankyô Kenkyûkai (1991), *Nihon no kôgai keiken*, October.

Chretien, J. (1997), *Notes for an Address by Prime Minister Jean Chretien on the Subject of Global Warming*, 3 November, Ottawa.

Christiansen, P. M. (1996) (ed.), *Governing the Environment: Politics, Policy and Organisation in the Nordic Countries*, Copenhagen: Nord.

Christoff, P. (1995), 'Market-based Instruments: The Australian Experience', in R. Eckersley (ed.), *Markets, The State and The Environment: Towards Integration*, Melbourne: Macmillan.

—— (1996), 'Ecological Modernisation, Ecological Modernities', *Environmental Politics*, 5: 476–500.

Clark, W. C., and R. E. Munn (1986) (eds.), *Sustainable Development of the Biosphere*, Cambridge: Cambridge University Press.

Climate Action Network (1997), *Rational Energy Program: Analysis of the Impact of National Measures to the Year 2010*, Ottawa.

Cohen, B. R. (1998), 'US environmental agency accused of being too hasty on climate change', *The Earth Times*, 20 July.

Collier, U. (1997), 'Sustainability, Subsidiarity and Deregulation: New Directions in EU Environmental Policy', *Environmental Politics*, 6: 1–23.

—— and R. Löfstedt (1997) (eds.), *Cases in Climate Change Policy*, London: Earthscan.

Commonwealth of Australia (1984), *A National Conservation Strategy for Australia*, Proposed by a conference held in Canberra in June 1983, Canberra: AGPS.

—— (1989), *Our Country, Our Future, Statement on the Environment*, Canberra: AGPS.

—— (1990), *Ecologically Sustainable Development. A Commonwealth Discussion Paper*, Canberra: AGPS.

—— (1992a), *National Strategy for Ecologically Sustainable Development*, Canberra: AGPS.

—— (1992b), *National Greenhouse Response Strategy*, Canberra: AGPS.

—— (1992c), *National Strategy for Ecologically Sustainable Development*, http://www.environment.gov.au/portfolio/esd/nsesd/intro.html (version: 31 July 1996).

——(1994), *Australian and New Zealand Environment and Conservation Council. Guide to Environmental Legislation in Australia and New Zealand*, 4th edn., Report No. 29, Canberra: Department of the Environment, Sport, and Territories.

——(1995a), *Australia's National Report for the United Nations Commission on Sustainable Development*, Canberra: AGPS.

——(1995b), *Progress in Implementing the National Greenhouse Response Strategy. Report by the Intergovernmental Committee for Ecologically Sustainable Development*, Canberra: Department of the Environment, Sport, and Territories.

——(1996a), *Report on the Implementation of the National Strategy for Ecologically Sustainable Development, 1993–1995*, Canberra: AGPS.

——(1996b), *Australia's National Report for the United Nations Commission on Sustainable Development*, Canberra: AGPS.

——(1996c), *The National Strategy for the Conservation of Australia's Biological Diversity*, Canberra: AGPS.

——(1996d), *Summary of the InterGovernmental Agreement on the Environment*, http://www.environment.gov.au/portfolio/esd/nsesd/appndxa.html (version: 31 July 1996).

——(1996e), *Monitoring and Review of the Strategy for Ecologically Sustainable Development*, http://www.environment.gov.au/portfolio/esd/nsesd/monitor.html (version: 31 July 1996).

——(1997a), *Australia and Climate Change Negotiations. An Issues Paper*, Canberra: Department of Foreign Affairs and Trade Development.

——(1997b), *Investing in Our Natural Heritage. The Commonwealth's Environment Expenditure, 1997–98*, Canberra: AGPS.

——(1997c), *Future Directions for Australia's National Greenhouse Strategy*, Canberra: Department of the Environment, Sport, and Territories, for the Intergovernmental Committee for Ecologically Sustainable Development.

Connolly, W. (1983), *The Terms of Political Discourse*, Princeton: Princeton University Press.

Costanza, R. (1991) (ed.), *Ecological Economics*, New York: Columbia University Press.

Council of Ministers for Global Environment Conservation (1995), *National Strategy of Japan on Biological Diversity*, 31 October.

Countryside Agency (1999), *The State of the Countryside 1999*, Cheltenham: Countryside Agency.

CPRE (Council for the Protection of Rural England) (1996), *Greening Government: From Rhetoric to Reality*, London: CPRE, unpublished paper.

Cushman, J. H., Jr. (1997a), 'U.S. Emits Greenhouse Gases at the Highest Rate in Years', *The New York Times*, 21 October: 14.

——(1997b), 'Why the U.S. Fell Short of Ambitious Goals for Reducing Greenhouse Gases', *The New York Times*, 20 October: A9.

——(1997c), 'Clinton Alters His Approach Over Warming', *The New York Times*, 21 October: Al.

Daily Yomiuri (1993), 29 March: 2.

Dalal-Clayton, B. (1996), *Getting to Grips with Green Plans. National-Level Experience in Industrial Countries*, London: Earthscan.

Daly, H. (1994), 'Operationalizing Sustainable Development by Investing in Natural Capital', in A. Janson, M. Hammer, C. Folke, and R. Costanza (eds.), *Investing in Natural Capital*, Washington, DC: Island Press.

——and J. B. Cobb (1994), *For the Common Good*, Boston: Beacon Press.

Dauvergne, P. (1997), *Shadows in the Forest: Japan and the Politics of Timber in Southeast Asia*, Cambridge, Mass.: MIT Press.

Davies, J. C., and J. Mazurek (1998), *Pollution Control in the United States: Evaluating the System*, Washington, DC: Resources for the Future.

Dente, Bruno (1995) (ed.), *Environmental Policy in Search of New Instruments*, Dordrecht: Kluwer Academic Publishers.

Department for International Development (1997), *Eliminating World Poverty: A Challenge for the 21st Century*, London: TSO.

Dernbach, J. (1997), 'U.S. Adherence to Its Agenda 21 Commitments: A Five-Year Review', *Environmental Law Reporter*, vol. 27 (October): 10504–25.

DETR (Department for the Environment, Transport, and the Regions— UK) (1998a), *Sustainable Development: Opportunities for Change*, London: DETR.

——(1998b), *A New Deal for Transport: A Better Deal for Everyone*, Cm 3950, London: TSO.

——(1998c), *Sustainability Counts*, London: DETR.

——(1998d), *The Government's Response to Environmental Audit Committee Report on the Greening Government Initiative*, Cm 4108, London: TSO.

——(1998e), *Policy Appraisal*, London: DETR.

——(1998f), *Government Response to UK Round Table Report 'Getting The Best out of Indicators'*, London: DETR.

——(1998g), *Sustainable Local Communities for the 21st Century: Why and How to Prepare a Local Agenda 21 Strategy*, London: DETR.

——(1998h), *Modern Local Government: In Touch with the People*, Cm 4014, London: TSO.

——(1998i), *UK Climate Change Programme: Consultation Paper*, London: DETR.

——(1998j), *Less Waste, More Value*, London: DETR.

——(1999a), *A Better Quality of Life: A Strategy for Sustainable Development for the UK*, Cm 4345, London: TSO.

——(1999b), *DETR Framework for the Future: The Three Year Strategy*, London: DETR.

——(1999c), *This is the DETR*, London: DETR.

Deutscher Bundestag (1988) (ed.), *Bundestags-Drucksache 11/3740, Erhaltung der Tropischen Regenwälder zum Schutz der Einheimischen Bevölkerung, des Klimas und der Genetischen Vielfalt durch Entwicklungspolitische Maßnahmen*, Bonn: Deutscher Bundestag.

——(1989), *Bundestags-Drucksache 11/4863, Erfolgskontrolle in der Entwicklungspolitik*, Bonn: Deutscher Bundestag.

——(1992a), *Bundestags-Drucksache 12/1951*, Bonn: Deutscher Bundestag.

——(1992b), *Bundestags-Drucksache 12/2286, Umwelt und Entwicklung. Politik für eine Nachhaltige Entwicklung*, Bonn: Deutscher Bundestag.

——(1995), *Bundestags-Drucksache 13/1533, Antrag auf Einsetzung einer Enquete-Kommission: Schutz des Menschen und der Umwelt—Ziele und Rahmenbedingungen einer Nachhaltig Zukunftsverträglichen Entwicklung*, Bonn: Deutscher Bundestag.

Dobson, A. (1996), 'Environmental Sustainablilities: An Analysis and a Typology', *Environmental Politics*, 5: 401–28.

DoE (Department of the Environment—UK) (1991), *This Common Inheritance: The First Year Report*, Cm 1655, London: HMSO.

——(1992), *This Common Inheritance: The Second Year Report*, Cm 2068, London: HMSO.

——(1993), *Making Markets Work For The Environment*, London: HMSO.

——(1994a), *Sustainable Development: The UK Strategy*, Cm 2426, London: HMSO.

——(1994b), *This Common Inheritance: The Third Year Report*, Cm 2549, London: HMSO.

——(1994c), *Climate Change: The UK Programme*, Cm 2427, London: HMSO.

——(1994d), *Biodiversity: The UK Action Programme*, Cm 2428, London: HMSO.

——(1994e), *Sustainable Forestry: The UK Programme*, Cm 2429, London: HMSO.

——(1994f), *Environmental Appraisal in Government Departments*, London: HMSO.

——(1995), *This Common Inheritance: UK Annual Report 1995*, Cm 2822, London: HMSO.

——(1996a), *This Common Inheritance: UK Annual Report 1996*, Cm 3188, London: HMSO.

——(1996b), *Indicators Of Sustainable Development For The United Kingdom*, London: HMSO.

——(1996c), *Government Response to the UK Steering Group Report on Biodiversity*, London: DoE.

——(1997a), *This Common Inheritance: UK Annual Report*, CM 3556, London: TSO.

——(1997b), *Climate Change: The UK Programme*, Cm 3558, London: TSO.

——and Other Departments (1990), *This Common Inheritance: Britain's Environmental Strategy*, Cm 1200, London: HMSO.

Doern, G. B., and T. Conway (1994), *The Greening of Canada: Federal Institutions and Decisions*, Toronto: University of Toronto Press.

Dotto, L. (1999), *Storm Warning: Gambling With the Climate of Our Planet*, Toronto: Doubleday Canada.

Downing, P., and K. Hanf (1983) (eds.), *International Comparisons in Implementing Pollution Laws*, Dordrecht: Kluwer-Nijhoff.

Downs, A. (1972), 'Up and Down with Ecology—the 'Issue-Attention Cycle', *Public Interest*, 28: 38–50.

Dryzek, J. (1997), *The Politics of the Earth: Environmental Discourses*, Oxford: Oxford University Press.

Dunlap, R. E. (1991), 'Public Opinion in the 1980s: Clear Consensus, Ambiguous Commitment', *Environment 33*, October: 32.

Dyson, K. (1982), 'West Germany: The Search for a Rationalist Consensus', in J. Richardson (ed.), *Policy Styles in Western Europe*, London: George Allen and Unwin, 120–41.

EA (Environment Agency—UK) (1996), *Corporate Plan Summary 1997/8*, Bristol: EA.

——(1997), *Environment Agency Annual Report 1996/7*, Bristol: EA.

——(1998), *Environment Agency Annual Report 1997/8*, Bristol: EA.

EAC (Environmental Audit Committee—UK) (1998a), *The Greening Government Initiative*, 2nd report, HC 517, Session 1997–8, 2 vols., London: TSO.

——(1998b), *Climate Change*, 4th report, HC 899, Session 1997–8, London: TSO.

——(Environmental Advisory Council—Sweden) (1994), *'I tid se och inse': Miljövårdsberedningens verksamhetsberättelse 1991–1994*, Report of the Environmental Advisory Council 1991–4, Stockholm: Ministry of Environment and Natural Resources.

——(1998), *Gröna nyckeltal för en ekologiskt hållbar utveckling*, Stockholm: The Swedish Cabinet Office and the Ministries.

EC (European Council) (1988), *European Council Declaration on the Environment*, Rhodes, December, Luxembourg: Office for Official Publications of the European Communities.

——(1990), *European Council Declaration, Dublin, The Environmental Imperative*, Luxembourg: Office for Official Publications of the European Communities.

——(1998), *Council Conclusion of Community Strategy on Climate Change*, 16 June, Brussels.

Eckerberg, K. (1990), *Environmental Protection in Swedish Forestry*, Aldershot: Avebury.

——B. Forsberg, and P. Wickenberg (1998), 'Setting the Pace with Pioneer Municipalities and Schools', in W. M. Lafferty and K. Eckerberg (eds.), *From the Earth Summit to Local Agenda 21: Working Towards Sustainable Development*, London: Earthscan.

ECON (1997), 'Symboler eller resultater? Norges bidrag til global klimapolitikk', *ECON Rapport*, 55/97.

Eduards, H. (1996), *FN:s Världskonferenser 1990–1996*, Stockholm: Ministry of Foreign Affairs.

Eduards, M. (1991), 'The Swedish gender model: productivity, pragmatism and paternalism', *West European Politics*, 14/3.

EEA (European Environment Agency) (1995a), *Environment in the European Union 1995: Report for the Review of the Fifth Environmental Action Programme*, Copenhagen: EEA.

——(1995b), *Europe's Environment: The Dobris Assessment*, Copenhagen: EEA.

——(1996), *The UN Convention on Biological Diversity: Follow-up in EEA Member-Countries*, Copenhagen: EEA.

——(1999), *Environment in the European Union at the turn of the Century*, Copenhagen: EEA.

EEB (European Environmental Bureau) (1996), *Memorandum to the Irish Presidency and the EU Member-States*, Brussels: EEB.

——(1997), *Memorandum to the Dutch Presidency and the EU Member-States*, Brussels: EEB.

Eid, U. (1999), *Statement at the NGO consultation meeting on January 29, 1999 in Bonn*, Bonn: BMZ.

Enloe, Cynthia H. (1975), *The Politics of Pollution in Comparative Perspective*, New York: David McKay.

Enquete Kommission (1997) (ed.), 'Konzept Nachhaltigkeit. Fundamente für die Gesellschaft von morgen', *Zur Sache*, 97/1, Bonn: Deutscher Bundestag.

Environment Committee (1998), *The Multilateral Agreement on Investment*, HC, Session 1997/8, London: TSO.

Environmental Data Services (1997), *ENDS*, no. 273, October, London: The Environmental Data Services Ltd.

Environmental and Energy Study Institute (1997), *Environment & Energy Briefing Book 1997*, Washington, DC: EESI.

Environmental Defender's Office (1998), *Submission in response to 'Reform of Commonwealth Environment Legislation'*, Consultation Paper, Sydney: Environmental Defender's Office.

Environmental Defense Fund (1996), 'U.S. Acts on Global Warming at Geneva', *EDF Letter*, September: 1.

Eriksson, G. (1997), 'Ekologi viktig fråga för s i EU', *Dagens Nyheter*, 27 July, Stockholm.

Esselin, A., and F. Andersson (1998), *Miljöforskning i förändring*, SEPA, Research Committee on Land, Water and Air, 14 January, unpublished memo.

European Commission (1995), *Progress Report on Implementation of the European Community Programme of Policy and Action in Relation to the Environment and Sustainable Development 'Towards Sustainability'*, Draft, 1 August, Brussels: EU Commission.

——(1998), *Community strategy on climate change—Council conclusions of the Council of Environmental Ministers*, 18 June, Brussels: European Commission.

European Community (1997), *Agenda 21—The First Five Years: European Community Progress on the Implementation of Agenda 21 1992–1997*, Luxembourg: Office for Official Publications of the European Communities.

European Environment (1996), 'European Commission: Progress Report on the Vth Environment Action Programme', *European Environment*, No. 469, 23 January, supplement.

European Information Services (1993), 'Greening the Commission: Integrating the Environment into Policy', *European Information Service*, Issue 141, July, 37–8.

Evans, P. (1995), 'Japan and the United States Diverge on Assistance to China', *Japan Economic Institute Report*, 19a, 19 May: 7–8, Washington, DC.

EZ (1996), *CO₂ Reduction Plan or '750 million letter'*, sent by the Government to Parliament (in Dutch), September.

Fermann, G. (1997a), 'Norge og FN', in T. L. Knutsen, G. Sørbø, and S. Gjerdåker (eds.), *Norges utenrikspolitikk*, Chr. Michelsens Institutt/Oslo: Cappelen Akademisk Forlag.

——(1997b) (ed.), *International Politics of Climate Change: Key Issues and Critical Actors*, Oslo, Stockholm, Copenhagen, Oxford, Boston: Scandinavian University Press.

Ferrera, P. J. (1994) (ed.), *Issues '94: The Candidate's Briefing Book*, Washington, DC: The Heritage Foundation, 71–87.

Fialka, J. J., and J. Calmes (1997), 'Clinton Proposes Global-Warming Plan', *The Wall Street Journal*, 23 October: 2.

Fiorino, D. (1996), 'Towards a New System of Environmental Regulation: The Case for an Industry Sector Approach', *Environmental Law* 26: 457–88.

Fischer, F., and J. Forester (1993), *The Argumentative Turn in Policy Analysis and Planning*, Durham: Duke University Press.

Flavin, C. (1995), 'Climate Policy: Showdown in Berlin', *World-Watch* 8, July/August: 8–9.

Forrest, R. (1989), *Japanese Economic Assistance and the Environment: The Need for Reform*, Washington, DC: Wildlife Federation, November.

Fothergill, S., and J. Vincent (1985), *The State of the Nation*, London: Pan Books.

Framstad, A., E. Bendiksen, and H. Korsmo (1995), 'Evaluering av verneplan for barskog', *NINA Scientific report*, 008: 1–36, Oslo: NINA.

Franz, N. (1997), 'Congress Prepares for Debate over Global Warming Treaty', *Environment and Energy Update*, 20 November.

FRN (1998), *Research to support Sustainable Development*, Reports 1–7, Stockholm: Swedish Council for Planning and Co-ordination of Research.

Gallie, W. (1956), 'Essentially Contested Concepts', *Proceedings of the Aristotelian Society*, 56: 167–98.

Garner, R. (1996), *Environmental Politics*, Hemel Hempstead: Prentice Hall/Harvester.

Gettkant, A., U. E. Simonis, and J. Supplie (1997), *Biopolicy for the Future: Cooperation or Confrontation between North and South*, Bonn and Bad Godesberg: Stiftung Entwicklung und Frieden.

GfG (Going for Green) (1997), *1997 Annual Report*, Manchester: GfG.

——(1998), *1997/98 Annual Report*, Wigan: GfG.

Gibson, R. B. (1999) (ed.), *Voluntary Initiatives: The New Politics of Corporate Greening*, Peterborough: Broadview.

Gillespie, E., and R. Schellhas (1994) (eds.), *Contract with America*, New York: Times Books.

Glasbergen, P. (1996), 'Learning to Manage the Environment', in W. Lafferty and J. Meadowcroft (eds.), *Democracy and the Environment*, Cheltenham: Edward Elgar.

——(1998) (ed.), *Co-operative Environmental Governance*, Dordrecht: Kluwer Academic.

Global Environmental Affairs Task Force of the Industrial Structure Council of MITI (1994), *Environmental Vision of Industry*.

Goggin, M., A. O. Bowman, J. Lester, and L. O'Toole (1990), *Implementation Theory and Practice: Towards a Third Generation Approach*, Glenville: Scott, Foreman / Little Brown.

Government of Japan (1990), *Action Program to Arrest Global Warming*.

——(1992), *ODA Charter*.

——(1993), *National Action Plan for Agenda 21*, 24 December.

——(1995), *The Action Plan for Greening Government Operations*.

——(1997), *Initiatives for Sustainable Development Toward the 21 Century*, June.

Government of Norway (1995), *Virkemidler i miljøpolitikken*, NOU 1995/4, Oslo: Statens Forvaltningstjeneste / Statens trykning.

——(1996), *Grønne skatter—en politikk for bedre miljø og høy sysselsetting*, NOU 1996/9, Oslo: Statens Forvaltningstjeneste / Statens trykning.

Government of Sweden (1990–1), *En god livsmiljö*, 1990–1/90, Swedish Parliamentary Record, Stockholm: The Swedish Cabinet Office and the Ministries.

——(1992–3a), *Om åtgärder mot klimatpåverkan m.m*, 1992–3/179, Swedish Parliamentary Record, Stockholm: The Swedish Cabinet Office and the Ministries.

——(1992–3b), *Riktlinjer för en kretsloppsanpassad samhällsutveckling*, 1992–3/180, Swedish Parliamentary Record, Stockholm: The Swedish Cabinet Office and the Ministries.

——(1992–3c), *Godkännande av konventionen om biologisk mångfald*, 1992–3/227, Swedish Parliamentary Record, Stockholm: The Swedish Cabinet Office and the Ministries.

——(1993–4), *Med sikte på hållbar utveckling: genomförandet av besluten vid UNCED*, 1993–4/111, Swedish Parliamentary Record, Stockholm: The Swedish Cabinet Office and the Ministries.

——(1994–5a), *Miljöbalk*, 1994–5/10, Swedish Parliamentary Record, Stockholm: The Swedish Cabinet Office and the Ministries.

——(1994–5b), *Vissa åtgärder mot utsläpp av försurande ämnen och andra luftföroreningar*, 1994–5/119, Swedish Parliamentary Record, Stockholm: The Swedish Cabinet Office and the Ministries.

——(1996–7a), *Budgetpropositionen för 1997*, 1996–7/1, Swedish Parliamentary Record, Stockholm: The Swedish Cabinet Office and the Ministries.

——(1996–7b), *Svenskt internationellt samarbete för en hållbar utveckling*, 1996–7/2, Swedish Parliamentary Record, Stockholm: The Swedish Cabinet Office and the Ministries.

Government of Sweden (1996–7c), *Skydd mot hotade arter samt aktionsplaner för biologisk mångfald*, 1996–7/75, Swedish Parliamentary Record, Stockholm: The Swedish Cabinet Office and the Ministries.

——(1996–7d), *Lag om kärnkraftens avvecklande*, 1996–7/176, Swedish Parliamentary Record, Stockholm: The Swedish Cabinet Office and the Ministries.

——(1997–8a), *Budgetpropositionen för 1998*, 1997–8/1, Swedish Parliamentary Record, Stockholm: The Swedish Cabinet Office and the Ministries.

——(1997–8b), *The Environmental Code. A summary of the Government Bill on the Environmental Code*, 1997–7/45, Swedish Parliamentary Record, Stockholm: Ministry of the Environment.

——(1997–8c), *Swedish Environmental Quality Objectives. A summary of the Swedish Government's Bill. Environmental Policy for a Sustainable Sweden*, 1997–8/145, Swedish Parliamentary Record, Stockholm: Ministry of the Environment.

Greenpeace (1997) (ed.), 'Bonns Blockade Ministerium', *Greenpeace Magazin*, 1997/5: 9–11.

Greenpeace International (1995), *Press Release*, archive number 9512/1067.

Greenwire (1998a), 'Climate Change: Talks Enter Key Phase: US to Sign Pact?', *Greenwire*, Washington, DC: hppt://www.nationaljournal.com/aboutgreenwire.htm.,11 November.

——(1998b), 'Climate Change II: Signature Sparks Strong Reactions?', *Greenwire*, Washington, DC: hppt://www.nationaljournal.com/aboutgreenwire.htm., 13 November.

Gresser, J., K. Fujikura, and A. Morishima (1981), *Environmental Law in Japan*, Cambridge: MIT Press.

Grubb, M., M. Koch, A. Munson, F. Sullivan, and K. Tompson (1993), *The Earth Summit Agreements: A Guide and Assessment*, London: Earthscan.

Gummer, J. (1997), 'Moment of Truth for the Human Family', *The Tablet*, 20–27 December: 1626–8.

Gustafsson, A. (1988), *Kommunal självstyrelse*, Stockholm: Liber.

Haigh, N. (1996), '"Sustainable" Development in the European Union Treaties', *International Environmental Affairs*, 8/1: 87–91.

——and F. Irwin. (1990) (eds.), *Integrated Pollution Control in Europe and North America*, Washington, DC: The Conservation Foundation.

Hajer, M. A. (1995), *The Politics Of Environmental Discourse: Ecological Modernisation and the Policy Process*, Oxford: Clarendon Press.

Halperin, R., and J. Morris (1998), *American Exceptionalism?*, New York: St Martin's Press.

Hamilton, C. (1994), 'A Comparison of Emission Sources and Emission Trends among OECD Countries', *Background Paper No. 1*, December, The Australia Institute.

——(1998), 'A Poisoned Chalice. Australia and the Kyoto Protocol', *Background Paper No. 13*, June, The Australia Institute.

——and J. Quiggin (1997), 'Economic Analysis of Greenhouse Policy. A layperson's guide to the perils of economic modelling', *Discussion Paper No. 15*, December, The Australia Institute.

——T. Hundloe, and J. Quiggin (1997), 'Ecological Tax Reform in Australia: Using taxes, charges and public spending to protect the environment without hurting the economy', *Discussion Paper No. 10*, April, The Australia Institute.

Hanf, K., and Jansen, A. (1998) (eds.), *Governance and Environment in Western Europe: Politics, Policy and Administration*, Harlow: Longman.

Hara, B. (1982), *Statement to the Session of a Special Character of the Governing Council of the United Nations Environment Programme*, Nairobi, 11 May.

Harrison, K. (1996), *Passing the Buck: Federalism and Canadian Environmental Policy*, Vancouver: UBC Press.

——(1999), 'Retreat from Regulation: Evolution of the Canadian Environmental Regulatory Regime', in G. B. Doern, M. Hill, M. Prince, and R. Schultz (eds.), *Changing the Rules: Canadian Regulatory Regimes and Institutions*, Toronto: University of Toronto Press, 122–42.

Hashimoto, M. (1988), *Shishi Kankyô Gyôsei*, Tokyo: Asahi Shimbunsha.

Hawken, P. (1993), *The Ecology of Commerce*, New York: Harper Business.

Hayao, K. (1993), *The Japanese Prime Minister and Public Policy*, Pittsburgh: University of Pittsburgh Press.

Hazell, S. (1999), *Canada v. The Environment: Federal Environmental Assessment 1984–1998*, Toronto: Canadian Environmental Defence Fund.

Hessing, M., and M. Howlett (1997), *Canadian Natural Resource and Environmental Policy: Political Economy and Public Policy*, Vancouver: UBC Press.

Hildebrand, P. (1992), 'The European Community's Environmental Policy 1957–1992', *Environmental Politics*, 1/4: 13–44.

Hill, R. (1996a), *The Greenhouse Challenge. Signing of Industry Cooperative Agreements*, Speech by the Hon Robert Hill, Leader of the Government in the Senate, Minister for the Environment, Hotel Intercontinental, Sydney, September.

——(1996b), *Tracking Progress: Linking Environment and Economy Through Indicators and Accounting Systems*, Speech by Senator Robert Hill, Commonwealth Minister for the Environment, Fenner Conference on the Environment, 30 September.

Hille, J. (1992), 'Norges oppfølging av Brundtland-kommisjonen', *Rapport 5/92*, Oslo: Famtiden i våre hender/Informasjonssenteret.

——(1997), 'Den alternative Nasjonalrapporten om Norges oppfølging av Brundtlandkommisjonen og Agenda 21', *Rapport 2/97*, Oslo: Framtiden i våre hender/Informasjonssenteret.

Ho, S. Pao-San (1984), 'Colonialism and Development: Korea, Taiwan, and Kwantung', in R. Myers and M. Peattie (eds.), *The Japanese Colonial Empire, 1895–1945*, Princeton: Princeton University Press, 347–98.

Hoberg, G. (1993), 'Environmental Policy: Alternative Styles', in M. Atkinson (ed.),

Governing Canada: Institutions and Public Policy, Toronto: Harcourt, Brace, Jovanovich, 307–42.

Hoberg, G., and K. Harrison (1994), 'It Is Not Easy Being Green: The Politics of Canada's Green Plan', *Canadian Public Policy*, 20/2: 119–37.

Hodge, T., S. Holtz, C. Smith, and K. Hawke Baxter (1995) (eds.), *Pathways to Sustainability: Assessing Our Progress*, Ottawa: NRTEE.

Hornung, R. (1999), 'The VCR Doesn't Work', in R. B. Gibson (ed.), *Voluntary Initiatives: The New Politics of Corporate Greening*, Peterborough: Broadview, 134–40.

House of Lords Select Committee on Sustainable Development (1995), *Report from the Select Committee on Sustainable Development*, House of Lords Paper 72, Session 1994–5, London: HMSO.

Hovik, S. (1994), 'Prioriteringer i kommunalt miljøvern', in J. Naustdalslid and S. Hovik (eds.), *Lokalt miljøvern*, Oslo: Tano/Norsk institutt for by- og regionsforskning.

——and V. Johnsen (1994), 'Kommunal organisering og lokalt miljøvern', in J. Naustdalslid and S. Hovik (eds.), *Lokalt miljøvern*, Oslo: Tano/Norsk institutt for by- og regionsforskning.

Huber, M. (1997), 'Leadership and Unification: Climate Change Policies in Germany', in U. Collier and R. E. Löstedt (eds.), *Cases in Climate Change Policy: Political Reality in the European Union*, London: Earthscan, 65–86.

Huddle, N., and M. Reich (1975), *Island of Dreams*, New York: Autumn Press.

Hustedt, M. (1999), 'Lokale Agenden und die Bundespolitik: Stärkung einer nachhaltigen Entwicklung durch einen nationalen Umweltplan', in IFOK/ZKE (eds.), *Was heißt hier Agenda?*, Dettelbach: Röll, 79–86.

ICLEI (International Council for Local Environmental Initiatives) (1998*a*), 'Local Agenda 21', *Initiatives*, no. 17, July: 9.

——(1998*b*), 'Cities to Report Success to COP3', *Initiatives*, no. 17, November: 1, 3.

IISD (International Institute for Sustainable Development) (1996), *The Bellagio Principles*, Winnipeg: IISD.

Intergovernmental Panel on Climate Change (1996), *Climate Change 1995: The Science of Climate Change*, Cambridge: Cambridge University Press.

International Development Research and Policy Task Force (1996), *Connecting With The World: Priorities for Canadian Internationalism in the 21st Century*, Ottawa.

International Energy Agency (1991), *Energy Policies of IEA Countries*, Paris: OECD.

——(1994), *Energy Policies of IEA Countries*, Paris: OECD.

IUCN/WWF/UNEP (1980), *The World Conservation Strategy*, International Union for the Conservation of Nature, United Nations Environment Programme, World Wildlife Fund: Geneva.

Jahn, D. (1998), 'Environmental Performance and Policy Regimes: Explaining Variations in 18 OECD Countries', *Policy Sciences*, 31: 107–31.

Jänicke, M. (1992), 'Conditions for Environmental Policy Success', *The Environmentalist*, 12: 47–58.

——A. Carius, and H. Jörgens (1997), *Nationale Umweltpläne in ausgewählten Industrieländern*, Berlin: Springer.

——and H. Weidner (1997*a*), 'Germany', in Jänicke and Weidner (1997*b*: 133–55).

——and H. Weidner (1997*b*) (eds.), *National Environmental Policies: a Comparative Study of Capacity Building*, Berlin: Springer.

——and H. Jörgens (1999), 'National environmental policy planning in the face of uncertainty', in M. Kenny and J. Meadowcroft (eds.), *Planning Sustainability*, London: Routledge.

Jansen, A. I. (1989), *Makt og miljø. Om utformingen av natur- og miljøvernpolitikken i Norge*, Oslo: Universitetsforlaget.

——and O. Osland (1996), 'Norway', in P. M. Christiansen (ed.), *Governing the Environment: Politics, Policy, and Organization in the Nordic Countries*, Århus: Nord, 5.

——————and K. Hanf (1998), 'Environmental Challenges and Institutional Changes', in K. Hanf and A. I. Jansen (eds.), *Governance and Environment in Western Europe*, Harlow: Longman.

Jansen, H. M. A., and J. B. Opschoor (1989), 'Voorrang voor duurzaamheid, Achtergronden van het voorgenomen natuur- en milieubeleid', *Milieu en Recht*, nr. 7–8, 308–19.

Japan Council for Sustainable Development (1997), *Japan Report for Rio +5 Process*, March. *Japan Times* (1994), 28 June: 10.

Japanese Environment Agency (1988), *Quality of the Environment in Japan*.

——(1990), *Quality of the Environment in Japan*.

Japanese Ministry of Foreign Affairs (1997), *Japanese Approaches to the Suppression of Greenhouse Gas Generation*.

John, D. (1994), *Civic Environmentalism*, Washington, DC: CQ Press.

Johnson, C. (1982), *MITI and the Japanese Miracle: The Growth of Industrial Policy, 1925–1975*, Stanford: Stanford University Press.

Johnson, H. D. (1995), *Green Plans: Greenprint for Sustainability*, Lincoln: University of Nebraska Press.

Johnson, S. P., and G. Corcelle (1995), *The Environmental Policy of the European Communities*, Den Haag: Kluwer.

Jordan, A. J. (1993), 'Integrated Pollution Control and the Evolving Style and Structure of Environmental Regulation in the UK', *Environmental Politics*, 2/3: 405–27.

——(1998), 'The Impact on UK Environmental Administration', in P. Lowe and S. Ward (eds.), *British Environmental Policy and Europe: Politics and Policy in Transition*, London: Routledge, 173–94.

Juillet, L., and G. Toner (1997), 'From Great Leaps to Baby Steps: Environment and Sustainable Development Policy Under the Liberals', in G. Swimmer (ed.), *How Ottawa Spends 1997–98: Seeing Red—A Liberal Report Card*, Ottawa: Carleton University Press.

Jupille, J., and J. A. Caporaso (1998), 'States, Agency, and Rules: The European Union in Global Environmental Politics', in C. Rhodes (ed.), *The European Union in the World Community*, London: Lynne Rienner, 213–30.

Kankyôcho (1991), *Kankyôcho niju nen shi*, Tokyo: Gyôsei.

Kankyôcho Chikyûteki Kibo no Kankyô Mondai ni Kansuru Kondankai (1982), *Chikyûteki kibo no kankyô mondai he no kokusaiteki torikumi ni tsuite: kokuren ningen kankyô kaigi 10 shunen ni atatte.*

Kankyôcho Kikaku Chôseikyoku Kikaku Chôseika (1994) (ed.), *Kankyô kihonho no kaisetsu*, Tokyo: Gyosei.

Katzenstein, P. (1987), *Policy and Politics in West Germany: The Growth of a Semisovereign State*, Philadelphia: Temple University Press.

Kawana, H. (1988), *Dokyumento nihon no kôgai*, Tokyo: Ryokufu.

Kawashima, Y. (1997), 'Comparative Analysis of Decision-making Processes of the Developed Countries towards CO_2 Emissions Reduction Target', *International Environmental Affairs*, 9/2: 95–126.

Keating, M. (1993), *The Earth Summit's Agenda for Change*, Geneva: Centre for Our Common Future.

Keizai Dantai Rengôkai (1991), *Chikyû Kankyô Kenshô*, 23 April.

——(1997), *Keidanren Kankyô Jishu Kôdô Keikaku*, 17 June.

Kenny, M., and J. Meadowcroft (1999) (eds.), *Planning Sustainability*, London: Routledge.

Kidd, C. (1992), 'The Evolution of Sustainability', *Journal of Agricultural and Environmental Ethics*, 5: 1–26.

Kitschelt, H. (1988), 'Organisation and Strategy of Belgian and West German Ecology Parties: A New Dynamic of Party Politics in Western Europe?', *Comparative Politics*, 20: 127–54.

——(1996), 'Political Opportunity Structures and Political Protest', *British Journal of Political Science*, 16: 74–84.

Knapp, H. D. (1997), 'Internationaler Naturschutz. Phantom oder Notwendigkeit?', in K. H. Erdmann (ed.), *Internationaler Naturschutz*, Berlin u.a.: Springer, 11–46.

Knoepfel, P., L. Lindqvist, R. Prud'homme, and P. Wagner (1987), in M. Dierkes (ed.), *Comparative Policy Research*, Aldershot: Gower.

——and H. Weidner. (1990) 'Implementing Air Quality Programs in Europe', *Policy Studies Journal*, 11: 103–15.

Knutsen, O. (1997), 'From Old Politics to New Politics: Environmentalism as a Party Cleavage', in K. Strøm and L. Svåsand (eds.), *Challenges to Political Parties: The Case of Norway*, Ann Arbor: The University of Michigan Press.

Kraft, M. E. (1997), 'Environmental Policy in Congress: Revolution, Reform, or Gridlock?', in N. J. Vig and M. E. Kraft (eds.), *Environmental Policy in the 1990s*, 3rd edn., Washington, DC: CQ Press.

Kristof, K., and S. Ramesohl (1997), 'Can Industry do better Alone? A Critical Discussion of the Voluntary Agreements on Climate Protection of the German Industry', in *Sustainable energy opportunities for a greater Europe—The energy efficiency challenge*, Proceedings ECEEE Summer Study 1997, Part 2, Prague, Copenhagen: The European Council for an energy-efficient economy.

Kriz, M. (1999), 'The Politics of Sprawl', *National Journal*, 6 February: 332–6.

Kronsell, A. (1997), 'Sweden: Setting a Good Example', in M. Skou Andersen and D. Liefferinck (eds.), *European Environmental Policy: The Pioneers*, Manchester: Manchester University Press, 40–80.

Labour Party (1993), *In Trust for Tomorrow*, London: Labour Party.

——(1997), *New Labour Because Britain Deserves Better*, London: Labour Party.

Lafferty, W. M. (1996), 'The Politics of Sustainable Development: Global Norms for National Implementation', *Environmental Politics*, 5/2: 185–208.

——(1999), *Implementing LA21 in Europe: New Initiatives for Sustainable Communities*, Oslo: ProSus.

——and J. Meadowcroft (1996), 'Democracy and the environment: prospects for greater congruence', in W. Lafferty and J. Meadowcroft (eds.), *Democracy and the Environment: Problems and Prospects*, Cheltenham: Edward Elgar, 256–72.

——and K. Eckerberg (1998), *From the Earth Summit to Local Agenda 21: Working Towards Sustainable Development*, London: Earthscan.

——C. Aall, and Ø. Seippel (1998), 'Fra miljøvern til bærekraftig utvikling i norske kommuner', *ProSus Rapport*, nr 2/98.

——and Langhelle, O. (1999) (eds.), *Towards Sustainable Development: On the Goals of Development and the Conditions of Sustainability*, London: Macmillan.

Langhelle, O. (1997), 'Nasjonal oppfølging og implementering', in W. M. Lafferty, O. Langhelle, P. Mugaas, and M. H. Ruge (eds.), *Rio + 5. Norges oppfølging av FN-konferansen om miljø og utvikling*, Oslo: Tano Aschehoug.

——(2000), 'Sustainable Development and Ecological Modernisation', *Journal of Environmental Management*, 12.

Lélé, S. (1991), 'Sustainable Development: A Critical Review', *World Development*, 19: 607–21.

Lévêque, F. (1996), *Environmental Policy In Europe*, Cheltenham: Edward Elgar.

LGMB (Local Government Management Board-UK) (1994), *Local Agenda 21: Principles and Process: A Step by Step Guide*, Luton: LGMB.

——(1995), *Sustainability Indicators Research Project*, Luton: LGMB.

Liberal Party of Canada (1993), *Creating Opportunity: The Liberal Plan for Canada*, Ottawa.

Lijphart, A. (1968), *Verzuiling, pacificatie en kentering in de Nederlandse politiek*, Amsterdam: De Bussy.

Liljelund, L.-E., B. Pettersson, and O. Zachrisson (1992), 'Skogsbruk och biologisk mångfald', *Svensk Botanisk Tidskrift*, 86/3, 227–32.

Lipset, S. M. (1996), *American Exceptionalism: A Double-Edged Sword*, New York: W. W. Norton.

LNV (1995–6), *Vaststelling van de begroting van de uitgaven en de ontvangsten van het*

Ministerie van Landbouw, Natuurbeheer en Visserij voor het jaar 1996, HTK 1995–6, 24400 XIV, nr. 4.

Löfstedt, R. (1997), 'Sweden: The Dilemma of a Proposed Nuclear Phase Out', in U. Collier and R. Löfstedt (eds.), *Cases in Climate Change Policy: Political Reality in the European Union*, London: Earthscan, 165–83.

Loske, R. (1996), *Klimapolitik. Im Spannungsfeld von Kurzzeitinteressen und Langzeiterfordernissen*, Marburg: Metropolis.

Lowe, P., and A. Flynn (1989), 'Environmental Policy and Politics in the 1980s', in J. Mohan (ed.), *The Political Geography of Contemporary Britain*, Basingstoke: Macmillan, 255–79.

Lund, B. H. (1996), 'Grønne hår i suppa', *N&M Bulletin*, no. 14.

Lundberg, F. (1997), *En het frågas väg mot lösning. Jorden vi värmde—människan, klimatet och framtiden*, Yearbook, Stockholm: Swedish Society for the Conservation of Nature.

Lundqvist, L. (1973), 'Crisis, Change, and Public Policy: Considerations for a Comparative Analysis of Environmental Policies', *European Journal of Political Research*, 1: 133–62.

——(1980), *The Hare and the Tortoise: Clean Air Policies in the United States and Sweden*, University of Michigan Press.

Lundqvist, L. J. (1996), 'Sweden', in P. Munk Christiansen (ed.), *Governing the Environment: Politics, Policy and Organization in the Nordic Countries*, Nord 1996/5, Copenhagen: Nordic Council of Ministers, 257–336.

——(1997), 'Tham stryper forskningen om miljö och samhälle', *Svenska Dagbladet*, 30 September, Stockholm.

McCormick, J. (1991), *British Politics and the Environment*, London: Earthscan.

McGraw, D. (1998), 'The Convention on Biological Diversity at the Cross-roads', paper presented to the workshop on 'Implementing policies of sustainable development examining actor relationships and negotiating processes', 25–26 May 1998, Geneva.

McKean, M. (1981), *Environmental Protest and Citizen Politics in Japan*, Berkeley: University of California Press.

McManus, P. (1996), 'Contested Terrains: Politics, Stories and Discourses of Sustainability', *Environmental Politics*, 5: 48–73.

MacNeill, J., P. Winsemius, and T. Yakushiji (1991), *Beyond Interdependence: The Meshing of the World's Economy and Ecology*, New York: Oxford University Press.

Magnusson, S. (1997), 'Sverige efter Rio—från Naturskyddsföreningens perspektiv', *Report*, 96/9357, Stockholm: Swedish Society for Conservation of Nature.

Mainichi Shimbun (1993), 15 July: 13.

Mangun, W. (1979), 'West European Institutional Arrangements for Environmental Policy Implementation—Especially Air and Water Pollution Control', *Environmental Conservation* 6: 201–11.

Marks, G., L. Hooghe, and K. Blank (1996), 'European Integration from the 1980s:

State-Centric v. Multi-Level Governance', *Journal of Common Market Studies*, 34/3: 341–78.

Marshall, Lord (1998), *Economic Instruments and the Business use of Energy*, London: Treasury.

Madsen, D. L. (1998), *American Exceptionalism*, Jackson, Miss.: University Press of Mississippi.

Mazey, S., and J. Richardson (1994), 'Policy Co-ordination in Brussels: Environment and Regional Policy', in S. Baker *et al.* (eds.), *Protecting the Periphery: Environmental Policy in Peripheral Regions of the EU*, London: Frank Cass, 22–44.

Mazmanian D. and P. Sabatier (1983), *Implementation and Public Policy*, Glenville: Scott Foresman and Company.

Meadowcroft, J. (1997), 'Planning, Democracy and the Challenge of Sustainable Development', *International Political Science Review*, 18: 167–90.

——(1999), 'The Politics of Sustainable Development: Emergent Arenas and Challenges for Political Science', *International Political Science Review*, 20: 219–37.

Meadows, D. H., D. L. Meadows, J. Randers, and W. Behrens (1972), *The Limits to Growth*, London: Pan.

Merkel, A. (1997), *Der Preis des Überlebens: Gedanken und Gespräche über zukünftige Aufgaben der Umweltpolitik*, Stuttgart: Dt. Verlags Anst.

Milbraith, L. (1991), *Envisioning a Sustainable Society*, Albany: State University of New York Press.

Milieudefensie (1992), *Actieplan: Nederland Duurzaam*, Amsterdam, April.

Ministry of Housing, Spatial Planning and the Environment (1998), *Third National Environmental Policy Plan: The Summary'*, The Hague.

Mitlin, D. (1992), 'Sustainable development: a guide to the literature', *Environment and Urbanisation*, 4 (1): 111–24.

Miyamoto, K. (1989), *Nihon no kankyô gyôsei*, Tokyo: Ohtsuki Shobô.

Mofson, P. (1997), 'Zimbabwe and CITES: Illustrating the Reciprocal Relationship between the State and the International Regime', in M. Schreurs and E. Economy (eds.), *The Internationalization of Environmental Protection*, Cambridge: Cambridge University Press, 162–87.

Mol, A., and Spaargaren, G. (1993), Environment, Modernity and the Risk Society: the Apocalyptic Horizon of Environmental Reform, *International Sociology*, 8: 432–59.

Morris, J., and J. Hams (1997), *Local Agenda 21 in the UK: The First Five Years*, London: LGMB.

Muijen, M. van (1995), 'Van "vrijblijvend" naar "algemeen verbindend" doelgroepenbeleid', *Milieu*, 2: 79–85.

Müller, E. (1986), *Innenwelt der Umweltpolitik: Sozial-liberale Umweltpolitik—(Ohn)macht durch Organisation?*, Opladen: Westdeutscher Verlag.

——(1990), 'Umweltreparatur oder Umweltvorsorge? Bewältigung von

Querschnittsaufgaben der Verwaltung am Beispiel des Umweltschutzes', *Zeitschrift für Beamtenrecht*, vol. 6.

Müller, E. (1998), 'Differences in Climate Change Policy in Germany and the U.S. from a Political Science Perspective', *Energy & Environment*, 9/4: 463–77.

Muller Rommel, F. (1982), 'Ecology Parties in Western Europe'. *West European Politics*, 5: 68–74.

Murdo, P. (1990), 'Japan's Environmental Policies: The International Dimension', *Japan Economic Institute Report*, 9 March.

Naess, P. (1994), 'Normative Planning Theory and Sustainable Development', *Scandinavian Housing and Planning Research*, 11: 145–67.

NAR (Nationale Adviesraad voor Ontwikkelingssamenwerking) (1991), *Advies UNCED*, Den Haag, 16 December, A277/91.

——(1992), *Nader Advies UNCED*, Den Haag, 26 February, A52/92.

National Academy of Public Administration (1987), *Congressional Oversight of Regulatory Agencies*, Washington, DC: NAPA.

——(1995), *Setting Priorities, Getting Results: A New Direction for EPA*, Washington, DC: NAPA.

National Committee for Agenda 21 (1996), 'Mål för miljön', *Report*, 1996/4, Stockholm: Ministry of the Environment.

National Performance Review (1993), *Creating a Government That Works Better & Costs Less*, Washington, DC: US Government Printing Office.

——(1995), *Common Sense Government: Third Report of the National Performance Review*, Washington, DC: US Government Printing Office.

Naustdalslid, J. (1994), 'Miljøproblema, staten og kommunane', in J. Naustdalslid and S. Hovik (eds.), *Lokalt miljøvern*, Oslo: Tano/Norsk institutt for by- og regionsforskning.

NCDO (Nationale Commissie voor internationale samenwerking en duurzame ontwikkeling) (1997), *Houdbare economie; kroniek van duurzaam Nederland*, Amsterdam: Kok/Agora.

New Directions Group (1997), *Criteria and Principles for the Use of Voluntary and Non-Regulatory Initiatives (VNRIS) to Achieve Environmental Protection Objectives*, Mimeo.

New Energy and Industrial Technology Development Organization (n.d.), *Green Aid Plan*.

Ninomiya, S. (1989), 'The Protection of Nature', in Tsuru and Weidner (1989).

Norstedts (1988), *Stora svensk-engelska ordboken*, Stockholm: Norstedts Förlag.

Norwegian Ministry of Defence (1998), *Forsvaret og miljøvern—utfordringer framover*, Oslo: Forsvarsdepartementet.

Norwegian Ministry of Finance and Customs (1992–3), *White Paper 4 (1992–93)*, Oslo: Finans- og tolldepartementet.

——(1996–7), *White Paper 4 (1996–97): Langtidsprogrammet 1998- -2001*, Oslo: Finans- og tolldepartementet.

Norwegian Ministry of Foreign Affairs (1988), *Miljø og utvikling. Norges bidrag til det internasjonale arbeid for en bærekraftig utvikling*, Oslo: Utenriksdepartementet.

——(1995), *The National Report of Norway to the United Nations' Commission on Sustainable Development 1995*, Oslo: Ministry of Foreign Affairs.

——(1997), *The National Report of Norway to the United Nations Commission on Sustainable Development 1997. Country Profile. Review of Progress made since UNCED—June 1992*, Oslo: Ministry of Foreign Affairs.

Norwegian Ministry of Local Government and Employment (1996–7), *White Paper 31 (1996–97): Om distrikts- og regionalpolitikken*, Oslo: Kommunal- og arbeidsdepartementet.

Norwegian Ministry of the Environment (1988–9), *White Paper 46 (1988–89): Miljø og utvikling. Norges oppfølging av Verdenskommisjonenes rapport*, Oslo: Miljøverndepartementet.

——(1990), *Action For a Common Future*, Report on the Regional Conference at Ministerial Level on the follow-up to the report of the World Commission on Environment and Development in the ECE region, 8–16 May 1990, Bergen, Norway, Oslo: Miljøverndepartementet.

——(1991), *Drivhuseffekten, virkninger og tiltak*, Rapport fra Den Interdepartementale Klimagruppen, Oslo: Miljøverndepartementet.

——(1992), *Norway's National Report to the United Nations Conference on Environment and Development, Brazil 1992*, Oslo: Ministry of the Environment.

——(1992–3), *White Paper 13 (1992–93): Om FN-konferansen om miljø og utvikling i Rio De Janeiro*, Oslo: Miljøverndepartementet.

——(1994), *Miljøvernpolitisk redegjørelse*, Oslo: Miljøverndepartementet.

——(1994–5), *White Paper 41 (1994–95): Om norsk politikk mot klimaendringer og utslipp av nitrogenoksider (NO$_x$)*, Oslo: Miljøverndepartementet.

——(1996–7a), *White Paper 35 (1996–97): Om rovdyrforvaltningen*, Oslo: Miljøverndepartementet.

——(1996–7b), *White Paper 58 (1996–97): Miljøvernpolitikk for en bærekraftig utvikling. Dugnad for framtida*, Oslo: Miljøverndepartementet.

——(1997–8), *White Paper 29 (1997–98): Norges oppfølging av Kyotoprotokollen*, Oslo: Miljøverndepartementet.

Norwegian Ministry of Trade and Energy (1995–6), *White Paper 38 (1995–96): Om gasskraftverk i Norge*, Oslo: Nærings- og energidepartementet.

Norwegian Ministry of Transport and Communications (1998), *Miljøhandlingsplan for samferdselssektoren*, Oslo: Samferdselsdepartementet.

NRTEE (National Round Table on the Environment and the Economy) (1993), *Toward Reporting Progress on Sustainable Development in Canada*, Ottawa: NRTEE.

Nugent, N. (1995), *The Government and Politics of the European Union*, London: Macmillan.

Oberthür, S., and H. E. Ott (1995), 'The First Conference of the Parties', *Environmental Policy and Law*, 25: 144.

Odegaard, J. T. (1996), 'Er gasskraft bærekraftig?', *ProSus tidsskrift for et bærekraftig samfunn*, 3: 8–27.

OECD (Organization for Economic Co-operation and Development) (1993a), *Environmental Performance Reviews: Norway*, Paris: OECD.

——(1993b), *Environmental Performance Reviews: Germany*, Paris: OECD.

——(1994a), *Environmental Performance Reviews: Japan*, Paris: OECD.

——(1994b), *Managing the Environment: The Role of Economic Instruments*, Paris: OECD.

——(1995), *Environmental Performance Reviews: Canada*, Paris: OECD.

——(1998a), *Environmental Performance Reviews: Australia. Conclusions and Recommendations*, Paris: OECD.

——(1998b), *OECD Environmental Data: Compendium 1997*, Paris: OECD.

——(1998c), 'Aid and private Flows fell in 1997', OECD News Release of 18 June 1998, Paris: OECD.

Office of National Statistics (1999), *UK Environmental Accounts*, London: TSO.

Ohta, H. (1995), *Japan's Politics and Diplomacy of Climate Change*, Ph.D. Dissertation, Columbia University.

——(1998), 'Japan's Environmental Foreign Policy and the Concept of Comprehensive National Security', in M. Schreurs and D. Pirages (eds.), *Ecological Security in Northeast Asia*, Seoul: Yonsei University Press, 151–70.

O'Mahony, P. (1996), 'Introduction'—'Environmental Sustainability and Institutional Innovation: Final Report', Cork: Centre for European Social Research, University College, Cork.

Opedal, S. (1996), 'Organisasjonenes påvirkningsmuligheter og dilemmaer i miljøpolitikken', in J. E. Klausen and H. Rommetvedt (eds.), *Miljøpolitikk. Organisasjonene, Stortinget og forvaltningen*, Oslo: Tano Aschehoug.

Opschoor, H., and J. van der Straaten. (1993), 'Sustainable Development: An Institutional Approach', *Ecological Economics*, 7: 203–22.

O'Riordan, T., and A. Weale (1989), 'Administrative Reorganisation and Policy Change: The Case of Her Majesty's Inspectorate of Pollution', *Public Administration*, 67/3: 277–95.

——and A. Jordan (1995), 'British Environmental Politics in the 1990s', *Environmental Politics*, 4/4: 237–46.

——and J. Jager (1996), *Politics of Climate Change: A European Perspective*, London: Routledge.

——and H. Voisey (1997), *Sustainable Development in Western Europe: Coming to Terms with Agenda 21*, London: Frank Cass.

Orr, R., Jr. (1990), *The Emergence of Japan's Foreign Aid Power*, New York: Columbia University Press.

OS (Ministry of Development Co-operation) (1990–1), *Een wereld van verschil: nieuwe kaders voor ontwikkelingssamenwerking in de jaren 90*, HTK 1990–1, 21813, nr. 1–2.

Ott, H. E. (1997), *Outline of EU Climate Policy in the FCCC—explaining the 'EU-bubble'*,

Climate Change and the Future of Mankind. Pre-COP3 International Symposium on Legal Strategies to Prevent Climate Change, September 13–14, 1997, Japan Center of International and Comparative Environmental Law (UNFCCC Protocol Working Group), 1–7.

——(1998), 'The Kyoto Protocol: Unfinished business', *Environment*, 40/6: 16–20, 41–5.

Owens, S. (1994), 'Land, Limits and Sustainability: A Conceptual Framework and Some Dilemmas for the Planning System', *Transactions of the Institute of British Geographers*, NS 9: 439–56.

——(1997), 'Interpreting Sustainable Development: The Case of Land Use Planning', in Michael Jacobs (ed.), *Greening the Millennium*, Oxford: The Political Quarterly, 87–97.

Pal, L. (1997), *Beyond Policy Analysis: Public Issue Management in Turbulent Times*, Toronto: Nelson.

Palumbo, D., and Calista, D. (1990), *Implementation and the Policy Process*, New York: Greenwood Press.

Papadakis, E. (1996), *Environmental Politics and Institutional Change*, Cambridge: Cambridge University Press.

Park, J. (1997), 'Companies Try to Reconcile Environmental Protection, Profit', *Nikkei Weekly*, 14 July, Opinion Section.

Parliamentary Committee on Energy and the Environment (1995–6), *Innstilling fra energi- og miljøvernkomiteen om opptrapping av barskogvernet fram mot år 2000* (Barskogvernmeldingen), Innst. S. nr. 220 (1995–6), Oslo.

——(1997–8), *Innstilling fra energi- og miljøvernkomiteen om miljøvernpolitikk for en bærekraftig utvikling, dugnad for framtida*, Innst. S. nr. 150 (1997–8), Oslo, http://www.stortinget.no/inns/199798-150-001.html.

PCSD (The President's Council on Sustainable Development) (1993), *Executive Order 12852*, 29 June, amended on 19 July 1993, 42 U.S.C. 4321, Washington, DC: The White House, Office of the Press Secretary.

——(1996a), *Sustainable Development: A New Consensus*, Washington, DC: US Government Printing Office.

——(1996b), *Sustainable America*, Washington, DC: US Government Printing Office.

——(1997a), *Revised Charter*, Washington, DC: PCSD.

——(1997b), *Building on Consensus: A Progress Report on Sustainable America*, Washington, DC: PCSD.

——(1997c), *Information Packet: Overview*, Washington, DC: PCSD.

——(1998), *President Clinton's Advisory Committee on Sustainable Development Announces Detroit as Site of 1999 National Summit*, 12 January.

Pearce, D., A. Markandya, and E. B. Barbier (1989), *Blueprint for a Green Economy*, London: Earthscan.

——and Jeremy Warford (1993), *World Without End*, Oxford: Oxford University Press.

Pehle, H. (1997), 'Germany: Domestic Obstacles to an International Forerunner', in M. Andersen and D. Liefferink (eds.), *European Environmental Policy: The Pioneers*, Manchester: Manchester University Press.

Pezzy, J. (1992*a*). 'Sustainability: An Interdisciplinary Guide', *Environmental Values*, 1: 321–62.

——(1992*b*), *Sustainable Development Concepts: An Economic Analysis*, World Bank Environment Paper 2, Washington: the World Bank.

Pinder, J. (1991), *The European Community and Eastern Europe*, London: Royal Institute of International Affairs.

Pirages, D. (1977), *The Sustainable Society*, New York: Praeger.

——(1996), *Building Sustainable Societies: A Blueprint for a Post-Industrial World*, New York: M. E. Sharpe.

Plaform Brazilië 1992 (1992), *Voorzet voor UNCED. Bijdragen van het Platform Brazilië aan de Verenigde Naties Conferentie over Milieu en Ontwikkeling*, Utrecht.

Potter, D. (1994), 'Assessing Japan's Environmental Aid Policy', *Pacific Affairs*, 67/2: 200–15.

Princen, T., and M. Finger (1994), *Environmental NGOs in World Politics: Linking the Local and the Global*, London: Routledge.

Productivity Commission (1999), *Implementation of Ecologically Sustainable Development by Commonwealth Departments and Agencies*, Draft Report, Canberra.

Projet de Société (1995), *Planning for a Sustainable Future: Canadian Choices for Transitions to Sustainability*, Ottawa: Supply and Services Canada.

q2000 (1997), *Ord eller handling?*, Stockholm: The Youth Campaign for a Sustainable Sweden.

Rasmussen, I. (1997), 'Bærekraftig produksjon og forbruk', in W. M. Lafferty, O. Langhelle, P. Mugaas, and M. H. Ruge (eds.), *Rio + 5. Norges oppfølging av FN-konferansen om miljø og utvikling*, Oslo: Tano Aschehoug.

RCEP (Royal Commission on Environmental Pollution) (1994), *18th Report: Transport and the Environment*, Cm 2674, London: HMSO.

Redclift, M. (1987), *Sustainable Development: Exploring the Contradictions*, London: Routledge.

Reed, M., and O. Slaymaker (1993), 'Ethics and Sustainability: A Preliminary Perspective', *Environment and Planning A*, 25: 723–39.

Rees, W. (1995), 'Achieving Sustainability: Reform or Transformation?', *Journal of Planning Literature*, 9: 343–61.

Reid, D. (1995), *Sustainable Development: an Introductory Guide*, London: Earthscan Publications.

Reitan, M. (1997), 'Norway: A Case of "Splendid Isolation"', in M. S Andersen and D. Liefferink (eds.), *Forerunners in European Environmental Policy*, Manchester: Manchester University Press.

——(1998*a*), *Interesser og institusjoner i miljøpolitikken*, Oslo: Institutt for statsvitenskap, Universitetet i Oslo.

——(1998b), 'Ecological Modernisation and "Realpolitik"', *Environmental Politics*, 7/2: 1–26.

Rhodes, C. (1998) (ed.), *The European Union in the World Community*, London: Lynne Rienner.

Rhodes, R. A. W. (1994), 'The Hollowing Out of the State: The Changing Nature of the Public Service in Britain', *Political Quarterly*, 65/2: 138–51.

Rich, B. (1994), *Mortgating the Earth*, Boston: Beacon Press.

Richardson, B. (1997), *Japanese Democracy: Power, Coordination, and Performance*, New Haven: Yale University Press.

Ringius, L., and G. B. Søfting (1997), 'Norsk gjennomføring av klimakonvensjonen', in W. M. Lafferty, O. Langhelle, P. Mugaas, and M. H. Ruge (eds.), *Rio + 5. Norges oppfølging av FN-konferansen om miljø og utvikling*, Oslo: Tano Aschehoug.

RIVM (National Institute for Public Health and the Environment-Netherlands) (1988), *Zorgen voor Morgen*, Alphen aan den Rijn: Samson H. D. Tjeenk Willink.

——(1997a), *Milieubalans 1997*, Alphen aan den Rijn: Samson H. D. Tjeenk Willink.

——(1997b), *Development in Sustainability 1992–1997*, Dutch National Institute for Public Health and the Environment, the Ministry of Foreign Affairs, and the Ministry of Housing Spacial Planning and Environment: the Hague.

Robins, N., and S. Roberts (1998), *Consumption in a Sustainable World*, London: International Institute for Environment and Development.

Rohrschneider, R. (1988), 'Citizens' Attitudes Toward Environmental Issues: Selfish or Selfless?', *Comparative Political Studies*, 21: 347–67.

Rommetvedt, H., and K. Melberg (1996), 'Miljø- og Næringsorganisasjonenes politiske påvirkning. Strategi, handling og innflytelse', in J. E. Klausen and H. Rommetvedt (eds.), *Miljøpolitikk. Organisasjonene, Stortinget og forvaltningen*, Oslo: Tano Aschehoug.

Roodman, D. M. (1997), *Worldwatch Paper 134, Getting the Signals Right: Tax Reform to Protect the Environment and the Economy*, Washington, DC: Worldwatch Institute.

Rootes, C. (1996), 'Britain: Greens in a Cold Climate', in R. Richardson and C. Rootes (eds.), *The Green Challenge*, London: Routledge, 60–90.

Rose, C. (1990), *The Dirty Man of Europe*, London: Simon & Schuster.

Rosendal, K. G. (1995), 'The Convention on Biological Diversity: A Viable Instrument for Conservation and Sustainable Use?', in H. O. Bergesen and G. Parmann (eds.), *Green Globe Yearbook 1995*, Oxford: Oxford University Press.

RRV (National Audit Office-Sweden) (1997), *Länsstyrelsernas miljövårdsarbete i förändring*, Report 1997:47, Stockholm: Riksrevisionsverket.

Russell, D. (1997), *Keeping Canada Competitive: Comparing Canada's Climate Change Performance to Other Countries*, Vancouver: David Suzuki Foundation.

Rydin, Y. (1998), *Urban and Environmental Planning in the UK*, 2nd edn., Basingstoke: Macmillan.

Sabatier, Paul A., and D. A. Mazmanian (1980), 'The Implementation of Public Policy: A Framework of Analysis', *Policy Studies Journal*, 8 (Special issue 2): 538–60.

Sadler, B. (1996), 'Sustainability Strategies and Green Planning: Recent Canadian and International Experience', in A. Dale and J. B. Robinson (eds.), *Achieving Sustainable Development*, Vancouver: UBC Press, 23–72.

SALA (Swedish Association of Local Authorities) (1995), *Villkor för en uthållig utveckling*, Stockholm: Swedish Association of Local Authorities in co-operation with the Ministry of the Environment.

——(1996), *Agenda 21 i Sveriges kommuner*, Stockholm: Swedish Association of Local Authorities.

Sandberg, S. (1996), 'Sweden' in J. Randel and T. German (eds.), *The Reality of Aid: An Independent Review of International Aid*, London: Earthscan, 177–80.

Sandbrook, R. (1997), 'Watered-down Dream', *The Guardian*, 18 June.

Sandel, M. (1996), *Democracy's Discontent*, Cambridge, Mass.: Harvard University Press.

SCB (Statistics Sweden) (1996), *Naturmiljön i siffror*, Stockholm: Official Statistics of Sweden.

——(1997), *Välfärd och ojämlikhet i 20 års perspektiv*, Stockholm: Official Statistics of Sweden.

Schäfer, H.-J. (1995), *Materialien zur Situation der biologischen Vielfalt in Deutschland*, Bonn: Bundesamt für Naturschutz.

Schei, P. J. (1997), 'Konvensjonen om biologisk mangfold', in W. M. Lafferty, O. Langhelle, P. Mugaas, and M. H. Ruge (eds.), *Rio + 5. Norges oppfølging av FN-konferansen om miljø og utvikling*, Oslo: Tano Aschehoug.

Schiffer, H.-W. (1999), 'Deutscher Energiemarkt "98" ', *Energiewirtschaftliche Tagesfragen*, 49/3: 154–69.

Schreurs, M. (1996), *Domestic Institutions, International Agendas, and Global Environmental Protection in Japan and Germany*, Ph.D. Dissertation, University of Michigan at Ann Arbor.

——(1997a), 'Domestic Institutions and International Environmental Agendas in Japan and Germany', in M. Schreurs and E. Economy (eds.), *The Internationalization of Environmental Protection*, Cambridge: Cambridge University Press, 134–61.

——(1997b), 'Japan's Changing Approach to Environmental Issues,' *Environmental Politics*, 6/2: 150–6.

——(1997c), 'Conservation, Development, and State Sovereignty: Japan and the Tropical Forests of Southeast Asia', in S. Hashmi (ed.), *State Sovereignty*, University Park, Pa: The Pennsylvania State University Press, 181–204.

SEPA (Swedish Environmental Protection Agency) (1993a), *Ett miljöanpassat samhälle*, Report 4234, Stockholm: SEPA.

——(1993b), *Biologisk Mångfald*, Report 4138, Stockholm: SEPA.

——(1994), *Biological Diversity in Sweden: A Country Study*, Monitor 14, Stockholm: SEPA.

——(1996), *Att miljöanpassa transportsystemen: Lägesrapport från MaTs-samarbetet*, Report 4636, Stockholm: SEPA.

——(1997a), *Agenda 21 i den offentliga sektorn*, Report 4679, Stockholm: SEPA.

——(1997b), *Ren luft och gröna skogar: Förslag till nationella miljömål 1997*, Report 4756, Stockholm: SEPA.

——(1997c), *Sverige år 2021*, Report 4747, Stockholm: SEPA.

——(1997d), *Underlag till Sveriges nationalrapport till konventionen om biologisk mångfald*, 3 November, Stockholm: SEPA.

SER (National Social Economic Council-Netherlands) (1992), *Commissie Internationale Sociaal-Economische Aangelegenheden: Interimadvies over UNCED 1992*, Den Haag.

Shinobu, T. (1994), 'Jizoku kanô na kaihatsu iinkai (CSD) dai 2 kai kaigô hokoku', *Kankyô Kenkyû*, 95: 130–8.

——(1995), 'Jizoku kanô na kaihatsu iinkai (CSD) dai 3 kai kaigô hokoku', *Kankyô Kenkyû*, 99: 161–9.

Shue, H. (1993), 'Subsistence Emissions and Luxury Emissions', *Law and Policy*, 15/1: 39–59.

Sierra Club of Canada (1996), *1996 Rio Report Card: Report on Commitments Made by Federal and Provincial Governments at the United Nations Conference on Environment and Development*, Ottawa: Sierra Club of Canada.

——(1997), *Canada Five Years After Rio: The Sierra Club of Canada's Rio Report Card 1997*, Ottawa: Sierra Club of Canada.

——(1998), *Rio + 6: The Sixth Annual Rio Report, 1998*, Ottawa: Sierra Club of Canada.

——(1999), *1999 Rio Report*, Ottawa: Sierra Club of Canada.

Simonis, E. U. (1991), 'Globale Umweltprobleme und zukunftsfaehige Entwicklung', *Aus Politik und Zeitgeschichte, Beilage zur Wochenzeitschrift 'Das Parlament'*, 41/10: 3–12.

Skjærseth, J. B. (1998), 'The Making and Implementing of North Sea Commitments: The Politics of Environmental Participation', in D. G. Victor, K. Raustiala, and F. B. Skolnikoff (eds.), *The Implementation and Effectiveness of International Environmental Commitments: Theory and Practice*, Cambridge, Mass: MIT Press, 327–80.

——and K. G. Rosendal (1997), 'Norges miljø—utenrikspolitikk', in T. L. Knutsen, G. Sørbø, and S. Gjerdåker (eds.), *Norges utenrikspolitikk*, Chr. Michelsens Institutt/Oslo: Cappelen Akademisk Forlag.

Slob, A. F. L. *et al.* (1996), *Consumption and the Environment: Analysis of Trends; Study Commissioned by the Ministry of Housing, Spatial Planning and the Environment*, May.

Solberg, B. (1997), 'Skogprinsippene og norsk oppfølging', in W. M. Lafferty, O. Langhelle, P. Mugaas, and M. H. Ruge (eds.), *Rio + 5. Norges oppfølging av FN-konferansen om miljø og utvikling*, Oslo: Tano Aschehoug.

Solesbury, W. (1976), 'Issues and Innovation in Environment Policy in Britain, West Germany, and California', *Policy Analysis*, 2: 1–38.

Sørbø, G. M. (1997), 'Norsk bistandspolitikk', in T. L. Knutsen, G. M. Sørbø, and S. Gjerdåker, S. (eds.), *Norges utenrikspolitikk*, Chr. Michelsens Institutt/Oslo: Cappelen Akademisk Forlag.

Spaargaren, G. (1997), *The Ecological Modernisation of Production and Consumption*, Wageningen.

SRU (Rat von Sachverständigen für Umweltfragen) (1994), *Umwelt-Gutachten 1994: Für eine Dauerhaft-Umweltgerechte Entwicklung*, Stuttgart: Metzler-Poeschel.

—— (1996), *Umweltgutachten 1996: Zur Umsetzung einer Dauerhaft-Umweltgerechten Entwicklung*, Stuttgart: Metzler-Poeschel.

—— (1998), *Umweltgutachten 1998. Umweltschutz: Erreichtes Sichern—Neue Wege Gehen*, Stuttgart: Metzler-Poeschel.

SSCN (Swedish Society for the Conservation of Nature) (1990), *Biologisk mångfald*, 1990 Yearbook, Stockholm: Swedish Society for Conservation of Nature.

—— (1997), *Jorden vi värmde—människan, klimatet och framtiden*, 1997 Yearbook, Stockholm: Swedish Society for Conservation of Nature.

State of the Environment Advisory Council (1996a), *Australia: State of the Environment 1996*, Canberra: AGPS.

—— (1996b), *Australia: State of the Environment 1996. Executive Summary*, Canberra: AGPS.

Statistics Norway (1997), *Statistisk årbok 1997*, Oslo: Statistisk sentralbyrå.

Statistisches Bundesamt (1996) (ed.), *Statistisches Jahrbuch 1997 für die Bundesrepublik Deutschland*, Stuttgart: Metzler-Poeschel.

Stevens, W. K. (1997), 'Despite Pact, Gases Will Keep Rising', *New York Times*, December: A10.

Stimson, J. A., J. J. Kimmel, and S. Thurin (1993), *Guide to Environmental Laws: From Premanufacture to Disposal*, Washington, DC: Bureau of National Affairs.

Stoker, G. (1991), *The Politics of Local Government*, 2nd edn., Basingstoke: Macmillan.

—— and S. C. Young (1993), *Cities in the 1990s: Local Choice for a Balanced Strategy*, Harlow: Longman.

Stokke, O. (1985), 'Samarbeidet med utviklingslandene: Idealer og interesser i brytning', in J. J. Holst and D. Heradstveit (eds.), Norsk Utenrikspolitikk, Oslo: Tano.

Storm, P.-C. (1997) (ed.), *Nachhaltiges Deutschland. Wege zu einer dauerhaft umwelt-gerechten Entwicklung*, Berlin: E. Schmidt Verlag.

Straaten, J. van der (1992), 'The Dutch National Environmental Policy Plan: To Choose or to Lose', *Environmental Politics*, vol.1, Spring; 45–71.

Sundquist, J. L. (1992), *Congressional Reform and Effective Government*, rev. edn., Washington, DC: Brookings Institution.

Svenska Dagbladet (1997), *Olika vägar till hållbar utveckling*, Stockholm, 23 June.

—— (1998a), *Fler frivilliga vill värna välfärden*, Stockholm, 27 January: 16.

—— (1998b), *Svart månad för industrin*, Stockholm, 6 November: 29.

Svensson, P. (1997), 'Rätt Pers(s)on?', *Moderna Tider*, 8/77: 14–19, Stockholm.

Serdrup, L. A. (1995), *Norway's Institutional Response to the Challenge of Sustainable Development*, Fridtjof Nansens Institutt Note: 002-1995, Oslo: Fridtjof Nansens Institutt.

——(1997), 'Norway's Institutional Response to Sustainable Development', *Environmental Politics*, 6/1: 54–82.

Swedish Ministry of Agriculture (1996), *Effekter av EU:s jordbrukspolitik*, SOU 1996/136, Stockholm: Ministry of Agriculture.

——(1997), *EUs jordbrukspolitik, miljön och regional utveckling*, SOU 1997/74, Stockholm: Ministry of Agriculture.

——(1998), 'God ny budget', *Ordbruk*, 7/1:3, Jönköping: Ministry of Agriculture.

Swedish Ministry of Communications (1996), *Ny kurs i trafikpolitiken: Delbetänkande*, SOU 1996/26, Stockholm: Ministry of Communications.

——(1997), *Ny kurs i trafikpolitiken*, SOU 1997/35, Stockholm: Ministry of Communications.

Swedish Ministry of Foreign Affairs (1996), *Sveriges utvecklingssamarbete för hållbar utveckling*, Rskr. 1996/97/2, Stockholm: Ministry of Foreign Affairs.

Swedish Ministry of the Environment (1992), *Vår uppgift efter Rio . . .* , SOU 1992/104, Stockholm: Ministry of the Environment.

——(1993a), *A Greener Sweden: The Environmental Strategy of the Swedish Government*, Stockholm: Ministry of the Environment.

——(1993b), *Kommunerna och miljöarbetet*, SOU 1993/19, Stockholm: Ministry of the Environment.

——(1993c), *Miljöbalk*, SOU 1993/27, Stockholm: Ministry of the Environment.

——(1993d), *Morot och piska för bättre miljö: förslag om utvidgad användning av ekonomiska styrmedel mot koldioxidutsläpp*, SOU 1993/118, Stockholm: Ministry of the Environment.

——(1996), *Miljöbalken. En skärpt och samordnad utveckling*, SOU 1996/103, Stockholm: Ministry of the Environment.

——(1997a), *Agenda 21 in Sweden. National Report. From Environmental Protection to Sustainable Development*, Stockholm: Ministry of the Environment.

——(1997b), *Sveriges andra nationalrapport om klimatförändringar*, Ds 1997:26, Stockholm: Ministry of the Environment.

——(1997c), *Följdlagstiftning till Miljöbalken*, SOU 1997/32, Stockholm: Ministry of the Environment.

——(1997d), *Övervakning av miljön*, SOU 1997/34, Stockholm: Ministry of the Environment.

——(1997e), *En hållbar kemikaliepolitik*, SOU 1997/84, Stockholm: Ministry of the Environment.

——(1997f), *Skydd av skogsmark*, SOU 1997/97 and 98, Stockholm: Ministry of the Environment.

——(1997g), *Agenda 21 i Sverige: Fem år efter Rio, resultat och framtid*, SOU 1997/105, Final report from the National Agenda 21 Committee, Stockholm: Ministry of the Environment.

——(1997h), *Ekologisk hållbarhet*, Rskr. 1997/98/13, Stockholm: Ministry of the Environment.

Swedish Ministry of the Environment (1998), *Hållbara Sverige—uppföljning och fort-satta åtgärder för en ekologiskt hållbar utveckling*, Rskr. 1998/99/5, Stockholm: Ministry of the Environment.

Swedish Ministry of the Interior (1998), *Konsumenterna och miljön—en handlingsplan för hållbar utveckling*, Rskr. 1997/98/67, Stockholm: Ministry of the Interior.

Sydnes, A. K. (1996), 'Norwegian Climate Policy: Environmental Idealism and Economic Realism', in T. O'Riordan, and J. Jäger (eds.), *Politics of Climate Change: A European Perspective*, London: Routledge.

Tanabe, T. (1999), *Chikyû Ondanka to Kankyô Gaikô Kyoto Kaigi no Kôbô to Sono Ato no Tenkai*.

Teigen, H. (1995), 'Langtidsliner i norsk distriktspolitikk og tiltaksarbeid', in H. Teigen, R. Nordgreen, and O. Spilling (eds.), *Langtidsliner i norsk distriktspolitikk og tiltaksarbeid*, Stabekk: Vett & Viten as.

Thalén, I. (1997), 'Vi kan återuppta folkhemsbygget', *Svenska Dagbladet*, Stockholm, 8 September.

Thornley, A. (1993), *Urban Planning Under Thatcherism*, 2nd edn., London: Routledge.

Thurber, J. A. (1991), *Divided Democracy: Cooperation and Conflict Between the President and Congress*, Washington, DC: CQ Press.

Tobin, R. (1996), 'Pest Management, the Environment, and Japanese Foreign Assistance', *Food Policy*, 21/2: 211–28.

Toner, G. (1994), 'The Green Plan: From Great Expectations to Eco-Backtracking . . . to Revitalization?', in S. D. Phillips (ed.), *How Ottawa Spends 1994–95: Making Change*, Ottawa: Carleton University Press, 229–60.

——(1996), 'Environment Canada's Continuing Roller Coaster Ride', in G. Swimmer (ed.), *How Ottawa Spends 1996–97: Life Under the Knife*, Ottawa: Carleton University Press, 99–132.

——and T. Conway (1996), 'Environmental Policy', in G. B. Doern, L. Pal, and B. Tomlin (eds.), *Border Crossings: The Internationalization of Canadian Public Policy*, Toronto: Oxford University Press, 108–44.

Töpfer, K. (1996), 'Städte sind die Zukunft der Menschheit. Ohne nachhaltige Stadtentwicklung wird es keine global nachhaltige Entwicklung geben', in BMBau (ed.), *Verstädterungsprozeß und Nachhaltigkeit*, Bonn: BMBau, 7–10.

Tsuru, S., and H. Weidner (1989), *Environmental Policy in Japan*, Berlin: Edition Sigma.

Tsûshô Sangyôsho (1993), *Chikyû saisei 14 no teigen; kongo no enerugii kankyô taisaku no arikata*, Tokyo: Tsûsho Sangyô Chôsakai.

——(1997), *Kongo no tsûsho sangyô seisaku no kento kadai*, June.

Ui, J. (1990), *Kôgai genron*, 3rd edn., Tokyo: Aki Shobô.

UK Biodiversity Group (1995), *The UK Steering Group Report*, 2 vols., London: HMSO.

——(1998), *Tranche 2 Action Plans*, 2 vols., Peterborough: English Nature.

UKRTSD (UK Round Table on Sustainable Development) (1996), *Annual Report*, London: DoE.

——(1997), *Annual Report*, London: DETR.

——(1998a), *Annual Report*, London: DETR.

——(1998b), *Integrating Biodiversity in Environmental Management Systems*, London: DETR.

UNCED (United Nations Conference on Environment and Development) (1992), *Agenda 21*, New York: United Nations Organization.

UNGA (United Nations General Assembly) (1983), *Resolution 38/161*.

——(1989), *Resolution 44/228*.

United Nations (1993), *Report of the United Nations Conference on Environment and Development, Rio de Janeiro, 3–14 June 1992 vol. 3: Statements Made by Heads of State or Government at the Summit Segment of the Conference*, New York: United Nations.

——(1996), *Norway. Report on the in-depth review of the national communication of Norway*, UNFCCC, http://www.unfccc.de/resource/docs/idr/nor01.pdf.

United States of America (1992), *National Action Plan for Global Climate Change*, Washington, DC: US Department of State.

Unmüßig, B. (1995), *Vortrag zur Entstehung und Arbeit des Forums Umwelt & Entwicklung anläßlich des Strategieseminars des Forums Umwelt & Entwicklung am 10./11. Februar 1995 in Mülheim/Ruhr*, unpublished.

UNSG (United Nations Secretary General) (1997), *Report on Overall Progress Achieved Since the United Nations Conference on Environment and Development*, E/CN.17/1997/Z.

Upham, F. (1987), *Law and Social Change in Postwar Japan*, Cambridge, Mass.: Harvard University Press.

USAID (Agency for International Development) (1999), *This is USAID*, http:\\www.info.usaid.gov/about, accessed January 2000.

US Congress (1997), *Expressing the sense of the Senate regarding the conditions for the United States becoming a signatory to any international agreement on greenhouse gas emissions under the United Nations Framework Convention on Climate Change*, S. RES. 98, 105th Congress, 1st sess., 25 July, http://thomas.loc.gov/cgi-bin/query/D?c105:3:./temp/~c105fUavyS, accessed 18 January 2000.

US Congress Office of Technology Assessment (1995), *Environmental Policy Tools*, Washington, DC: US Government Printing Office.

US Council on Environmental Quality (1995), *Environmental Quality*, Washington, DC: US Government Printing Office.

US Department of Energy (1994a), *The Climate Change Action Plan: Technical Supplement*, Springfield, Va.: National Technical Information Service.

——(1994b), *The Climate Change Action Plan: Technical Supplement*, Washington, DC: US DoE, March.

US EPA (Environmental Protection Agency) (1996a), *Community Partnerships for Environmental Action: A New Approach to Environmental Protection*, Washington, DC: US EPA, Office of Pollution Protection and Toxics.

——(1996b), *Community Based Environmental Protection*, Office of Sustainable Eco systems and Communities, ⟨http://www.epa.gov/ecocommunity⟩.

US EPA (Environmental Protection Agency) (1997), *National Environmental Goals Project*, ⟨http://www.epa.gov/ooaujeng/notebook/negphtm⟩.

——(1998), *33/50 [sic] Success Stories*, Office of Pollution Prevention and Toxics, ⟨http://www.epa.gov/opptintr/3350/⟩.

Van Wolferen, K. (1989), *The Enigma of Japanese Power: People and Politics in Stateless Union*, New York: A. A. Knopf.

Vedung, E. (1988), 'The Swedish Five-Party Syndrome and the Environmentalists', in K. Lawson and P. Merkl (eds.), *When parties Fail: Emerging Alternative Organisations*, Princeton: Princeton University Press.

——(1989), 'Sweden: The Miljöpartiet de Gröna', in F. Müller-Rommel (ed.), *New Politics in Western Europe: The Rise and Success of Green Parties and Alternative Lists*, Boulder, Colo.: Westview Press.

Vennemo, H. (1996), 'Håpet er lysegrønt, for såvidt', *Sosialøkonomen*, 7/8: 20–6.

Verhoeve, B., G. Bennett, and D. Wilkinson (1992), *Maastricht and the Environment*, London: Institute for European Environmental Affairs.

Vig, N. J., and M. E. Kraft (1996) (eds.), *Environmental Policy in the 1990's*, 3rd edn., Washington DC: CQ Press.

VNG (Association of the Netherlands Municipalities) and VROM (1993), *Preventing Climate Change: Urban Actions in the Netherlands*, The Hague.

Vogel, David (1986), *National Styles of Regulation: Environmental Policy in Great Britain and the United States*, Ithoca, NY: Cornell University Press.

——and V. Kun (1987). 'The Comparative Study of Environmental Policy: A Review of the Literature', in M. Dierkes (ed.), *Comparative Policy Research*, Aldershot: Gower.

Voisey, H., C. Beuermann, L. Sverdrup, and T. O'Riordan (1996), 'The Political Significance of Local Agenda 21: The Early Stages of Some European Experience', *Local Environment*, 1: 333–50.

VROM (Minister of Housing, Physical Planning and Environment) (1987–8), *Brief van de minister*, d. d. 2-11-1987, en Regeringsstandpunt op Brundtland rapport, HTK 1987–8, 20298, nrs. 1 and 2.

——(1988–9), *National Environmental Policy Plan: To choose or lose*, HTK 1988–9, 21137/1, Den Haag: SDU.

——(1990), *Climate change policy in the Netherlands and supporting measures*, November.

——(1990–1), *Nota Klimaatverandering*, HTK 1990–1, 22232, nrs. 1–2.

——(1992–3a), *Brief van de minister*, d.d. 13-5-92, HTK 1992–3, 22031, no. 4.

——(1992–3b), *Brief van de minister*, d.d. 16-7-93, HTK 1992–3, 22031, no. 16.

——(1994), *Environmental policy of the Netherlands*, The Hague, March.

——(1994–5), *Brief van de Minister omtrent de vorderingen bij het Nederlandse Klimaatbeleid*, HTK 1994–5, 22232, 7.

——(1995–6), *Brief van de minster over actiepunt A141*, d.d. 25-6-95, HTK 1995–6, 20298, no. 20.

——(1996a), *Kameronderzoek Klimaatverandering*, HTK 1995–6, 24695, no. 2–3.

——(1996b), *Kameronderzoek Klimaatverandering Gesprekken*, HTK 1995–6, 24695, no. 4.

——(1996c), *Notitie Hoofdlijnen Vervolgnota Klimaatverandering*, HTK 1995–6, 22232, no. 14.

——(1997a), *Environmental management; a general view*, The Hague, April.

——(1997b), *Towards a sustainable Netherlands; Environmental policy development and implementation*, The Hague, January.

——(1997–8), *Brief van de minister over de inzet en vewachtingen ten aanzien van Kyoto*, d.d. 17-10-1997, HTK 1997–8, 24785, no. 4.

——(1998), *National Environmental Policy Plan III, the summary*, February.

——and OS (1990–1), *Brief van de ministers*, d.d. 8-3-91, VN conferentie milieu en ontwikkeling 1992, HTK 1990–1, 22031, no. 1.

————(1991–2), *Brief van de ministers*, d.d. 28-11-91, VN conferentie milieu en ontwikkeling 1992, HTK 1991–2, 22031, no. 2.

——Commission (1995–6), *Brief aan de Tweede Kamer*, HTK 1995–6, 22232, 10.

——et al. (1997a), *Second Netherlands' National Communication on Climate Change Policies; prepared for the Conference of Parties under the Framework Convention on Climate Change*, The Hague, April.

————(1997b), *Summary Policy document on Environment and Economy: towards a sustainable economy*, The Hague, June.

————(1997c), *Environmental Program 1997–2000*, The Hague: English translation, February.

Wallace, D. (1995), *Environment Policy and Industrial Innovation. Strategies in Europe, the US and Japan*, London: Earthscan.

Waller-Hunter, J. H. (1991), 'The Netherlands en route for UNCED, a Highly Industrialized Country's Position on Environment and Development', *International Spectator*, 45/11: 718–22.

Ward, S. (1993), 'Thinking Global, Acting Local? British Local Authorities and their Environmental Plans', *Environmental Politics*, 2/3: 453–78.

Warrick, J. (1997), 'Climate Pact Rescued in Final Hours,' *Washington Post*, 13 December: A 1 and A 20.

Washington Post (1997), 12 July: A 17.

WBGU (1993), *Welt im Wandel: Grundstruktur Globaler Mensch-Umwelt Beziehungen. Jahresgutachten 1993*, Bonn: Economica.

WCED (World Commission on Environment and Development) (1987), *Our Common Future: Report of the World Commission on Environment and Development*, Oxford: Oxford University Press.

Weale, A. (1992), *The New Politics of Pollution*, Manchester: Manchester University Press.

Websky, M. von (1997), 'Die Biodiversitätskonvention und ihre Rolle für den Arten- und Biotopschutz in Deutschland', in NABU (ed.), *Biologische Vielfalt in Deutschland. Dokumentation der NABU-Fachtagung in Potsdam vom 24. bis 26.1.1997*, Bonn: NABU, 30–3.

Weidner, H. (1995), '25 Years of Modern Environmental Policy in Germany: Treading a Well Worn Path to the Top of the International Field', *WZB report FS II 95–301*, Berlin: WZB.

Weiss, L. (1998), *The Myth of the Powerless State*, Cambridge: Polity Press.

Wey, K. G. (1982), *Umweltpolitik in Deutschland. Kurze Geschichte des Umweltschutzes in Deutschland seit 1900*, Opladen: Westdeutscher Verlag.

Whitelegg, J. (1989), 'Transport Policy: Off the Rails?', in J. Mohan (ed.), *The Political Geography of Contemporary Britain*, Basingstoke: Macmillan, 187–207.

Wilkinson, R. (1999), 'Footloose and Fancy Free? The Multilateral Agreement on Investment', *Environmental Politics*, 8/4: 180–5.

Willoch, K. (1996), *En ny miljøpolitikk*, Oslo: Gyldendal Norsk Forlag.

Woodhead, W. R. (1990), 'Shortcomings in Decision-Making Frameworks: Past and Present Problems', *Canberra Bulletin of Public Administration*, 62: 57–9.

Worcester, R. (1997), 'Public Opinion and the Environment', in M. Jacobs (ed.), *Greening the Millenium? The New Politics of the Environment*, Oxford: Blackwell, 160–73.

World Bank (1994), *Making Development Sustainable: The World Bank Group and the Environment*, Washington, DC.

Yearley, S., S. Baker, and K. Milton (1994), 'Environmental Policy and Peripheral Regions of the European Union', in S. Baker *et al.* (eds.), *Protecting the Periphery: Environmental Policy in Peripheral Regions of the EU*, London: Frank Cass, 1–21.

Young, S. C. (1994), 'An Agenda 21 Strategy for the UK?', *Environmental Politics*, 3/3: 325–34.

——(1995), 'Wildlife Conservation Policies 1988–94: Running Up the Down Escalator', in T. Gray (ed.), *British Environmental Policy in the 1990s*, Basingstoke: Macmillan, 237–62.

——(1996), 'Stepping Stones to Empowerment? Participation in the Context of Local Agenda 21', *Local Government Policy Making*, 22: 25–31.

——(1998), 'The UK: A Mirage beyond the Participation Hurdle?', in W. M. Lafferty and K. Eckerberg (eds.), *From the Earth Summit to Local Agenda 21*, London: Earthscan, 179–203.

——(forthcoming), 'Labour and the Environment', in D. Coates and P. Lawler (eds.), *New Labour into Power*, Manchester: Manchester University Press.

Index

Printed in the United Kingdom
by Lightning Source UK Ltd.
118386UK00001B/11